AF673275

Interpreting Ramakrishna

Kālī's Child Revisited

INTERPRETING RAMAKRISHNA

Kālī's Child Revisited

Swami Tyagananda
Pravrajika Vrajaprana

With a Foreword by
Huston Smith

MOTILAL BANARSIDASS PUBLISHERS
PRIVATE LIMITED • DELHI

2nd Reprint: Delhi, 2014
First Edition: Delhi, 2010

© MOTILAL BANARSIDASS PUBLISHERS PRIVATE LIMITED
All Rights Reserved

ISBN: 978-81-208-3499-6 (Cloth)
ISBN: 978-81-208-3532-0 (Paper)

MOTILAL BANARSIDASS
41 U.A. Bungalow Road, Jawahar Nagar, Delhi 110 007
8 Mahalaxmi Chamber, 22 Bhulabhai Desai Road, Mumbai 400 026
203 Royapettah High Road, Mylapore, Chennai 600 004
236, 9th Main III Block, Jayanagar, Bangalore 560 011
Sanas Plaza, 1302 Baji Rao Road, Pune 411 002
8 Camac Street, Kolkata 700 017
Ashok Rajpath, Patna 800 004
Chowk, Varanasi 221 001

Printed in India

by RP Jain at NAB Printing Unit,
A-44, Naraina Industrial Area, Phase I, New Delhi–110028
and published by JP Jain for Motilal Banarsidass Publishers (P) Ltd,
41 U.A. Bungalow Road, Jawahar Nagar, Delhi-110007

CONTENTS

FOREWORD

When I was approached to write this Foreword, my initial reaction was that I was not an appropriate choice. I do not know Bengali and though my indebtedness to the Hindu tradition is inestimable, it is not my primary tradition. On further reflection, however, I found myself warming to the invitation. My field is comparative philosophy and religion, and I have grown restive with what seems to be a growing trend in religious studies—using religion for political ends. *Kālī's Child*, I realized, would give me a tangible target on which to focus my thoughts on this topic.

The hijacking I am thinking of takes place both within and between religions. Within Christianity, "politically correct" has emerged to designate the political orthodoxy that reigns on campuses, which is the liberal stance on issues of race, gender and lifestyles. My concern here, however, is with the way this orthodoxy moves across religious boundaries, *Kālī's Child* being the case at hand. In devoting this Foreword to arguing that charge, I admit that I am crossing a field charged with landmines, but the matter is important so I persevere.

With his 1978 book titled *Orientalism*, Edward Said was the first visible non-Westerner to blow the whistle on this foul play—two hundred years in which scholars laid down in Western mind a view of the non-Western world that purports to be accurate but actually is sharply skewed by Western assumptions. However much that book was needed, it is not a responsible book, for Said was victimized by his academic discipline, comparative literature, which in his generation was dominated by Michel Foucault's contention that truth is simply a cover for power plays, so in *Orientalism* Said plays his cards to put down the West and triumph over it.

The responsible treatment of this subject had actually been in place for over a decade when Said wrote *Orientalism*, but having been written by a less publicly visible figure, Seyyed Hossein Nasr, it did not receive the attention it deserved. In Nasr's book, the 1964 Gifford Lectures *Knowledge and the Sacred*, he uses his invitation to deliver those lectures to turn the tables responsibly on the West. What he says in effect is: "For two hundred years we Orientals have been listening to what you Occidentals think of us. This is my opportunity to let you hear what we think of you." And without raising his voice, he proceeds to tell us.

All he and I ask for, really, is what everyone wants, the author of *Kālī's Child,* Jeffrey Kripal, included: fair play. The problem is how to achieve it, and in cross-cultural dealings the difficulties compound, for stepping beyond one's own culture is a little like trying to step out of the shoes one is walking in. The requirement for those of us who work at this problem and who are at the top of the multicultural heap is how to steer clear of imperialism, for there is cultural as well as national imperialism. I may be unusually sensitive to this requirement for I grew up in the China that European imperialists had carved up among themselves, and Shanghai American High School was located in the French Concession where on walks off our residential campus I would pass parks marked "No dogs and Chinamen allowed." Be that as it may, when I decided to make comparative philosophy and religion my academic home, I vowed to do everything I could to try to deal fairly with the cultures I crossed over into.

How was I to overcome the gravitational pull of ethnocentrism and do this? Early on I settled on three guidelines. First, target the profoundest texts in the tradition in question and do my homework by steeping myself in them. Second, to test my comprehension I would then seek out the greatest living exponents of the tradition, pilgrimage to them, and apprentice myself to them for as long as sabbaticals and vacations allowed. (In the case of Hinduism, the scholars were T. R. V. Murty and T. M. P. Mahadevan, while at home my local swami in St. Louis, Swami Satprakashananda of the Ramakrishna Order, stood in for them admirably.) My final step would be to run everything I wrote about the tradition past these mentors to check it for accuracy. Kripal—with whom I have had a brief exchange in *The Harvard Divinity Bulletin*—thinks this last step would preclude criticizing other traditions, but not at all. I am a staunch believer in interfaith dialogue as a way religions can learn from one another, but only when critics withhold their criticisms until they have made sure that the targets at which they are aimed are rightly positioned.

Right positioning here begins with accurate translations of the documents the critic cites, as well as the cultural sensitivity to present that study in a contextually authentic way. The book in hand is devoted to a scrupulous report on places where Kripal's conveniently adapted "dictionary Bengali" fails to meet these requirements.

Fair play requires that people who enter other cultures do so tactfully, and here the shortcoming of *Kālī's Child* becomes glaring. In arguing that Ṣri Ramakrishna's ecstatic mystical experiences were powered by his homoerotic libido, the book has offended Hindu sensibilities more even than did the tracts of early bigoted, poorly informed and polemical Christian missionaries.

It is hard to believe that this took Kripal by surprise. With his admirable empathy for the plight of homosexuals, Kripal must have known that it is a sensitive issue to address publicly even at home; if a candidate in an election campaign were to refer to his opponent's lifestyle, it could cost him the election for being seen by the electorate as a low blow, foul play. Or put it this way: would Kripal have chosen to write his doctoral dissertation on the way the lifestyle of a beloved mentor powered the virtues that Kripal so respects? How, then, could he have thought that such discretion doesn't apply when one ventures onto foreign soil, especially since the meaning of sex is highly culture specific and almost incomprehensible to outsiders. Kripal doesn't even mention this decisive point, which raises the question of whether he was even aware of it.

Much more could be said, but it is not the mission of forewords to argue the case of their books, which in this case its authors do admirably. To put the best face I can on Kripal's unfortunate book, perhaps it can serve as an object lesson on the way cross-cultural discussions should not proceed. I sincerely commend the authors of this book for their self-respect in standing up to *Kālī's Child* wisely and with dignity.

—*Huston Smith*

Preface

> Problematizing the way in which Indian religion has been represented within Western scholarship ... is an exercise in calling into question the paradigms of knowledge and constellations of power that have continued to divide the world up into "us" and "them"—maintaining an asymmetrical relationship between the relatively powerful and the relatively disempowered.
>
> —Richard King, *Orientalism and Religion*

The question which greets the publication of any book is, why was it written? There are several reasons for writing this book: First, despite the controversy which has accompanied *Kālī's Child* since its publication over a decade ago, little has been written to contextualize it within the body of Ramakrishna literature.

Second, while a great deal has been written about the furor which has dogged *Kālī's Child*, the discussion has moved increasingly away from the text itself. Illustrative of the controversy it continues to provoke, political philosopher Martha Nussbaum has recently weighed in on the subject in *The Clash Within: Democracy, Religious Violence and India's Future.*[1] Significantly, Nussbaum places the *Kālī's Child* imbroglio within the context of Hindu right-wing extremism and the threat this holds to India's history of democracy, tolerance, and religious pluralism. This raises the question of how a book on Ramakrishna, of all the unlikely people, could have ended up in a book on Hindu extremism. A decade ago it is unlikely that anyone could have predicted this scenario. But *Kālī's Child* has taken on a life of its own, quite independent of the original text. To make sense of the reaction the book provoked and continues to provoke to this day, it is necessary to step back and examine the original text as well as the scholarship which preceded and followed it.

Third, it is important to examine the ways in which the *Kālī's Child* debate has changed over time. How and in what ways the controversy became transformed is an important study in itself.

Finally, in many ways the *Kālī's Child* debate embodies the tensions which exist between the believing community and the academic community, though these groups are not mutually exclusive. This tension is hardly unique to Ramakrishna studies or even Asian studies—the same tension exists between the believing Judeo-Christian communities and the academics who study their religious figures and leaders. Yet when dealing with religious figures from the South Asian traditions, other factors figure into the equation, such as the power differential between "the West and the rest" along with the scuff marks of colonialism and residues of Orientalism.

It all began quietly enough. Published in 1995, Jeffrey J. Kripal's *Kālī's Child: The Mystical and the Erotic in the Life and Teachings of Ramakrishna* was given the American Academy of Religion's History of Religions Prize for the Best First Book of 1995, an honor which, when discovered, deeply rankled the insider community (by "insider" we refer to both ethnic Indian Ramakrishna devotees as well as a much smaller group of non-Indian Ramakrishna devotees). *Kālī's Child* was greeted with nearly universal praise by those within the academic (largely "outsider") community. Later, the book would be buffeted by nearly universal condemnation from the insider community. Similarly, the author received both kudos—by and large from the academic community in the West—and denunciation, which again came largely from the insider community. So heated did the controversy become that the author became the recipient of hate mail and even death threats. One cannot doubt that the truly frightening outpouring of venom the author received played a part in the consequent outpouring of support which he received from the academic community.

Yet in a sense, the hostile outcry and the protective response only served to muddy the waters about what the text actually had to say. This condemnation/support motif prefigured a trend that would replay in the years to come: after the *Kālī's Child* controversy simmered down, the Paul Courtright/Gaṇeśa controversy arose, followed by the James Laine/Shivaji controversy.[2] This has presented no small difficulty for the present authors, who have found themselves unwillingly lashed to the mast of "Hindu fundamentalism," "right-wing Hindu extremism" and Hindutva polemic. Indeed, more than a decade after *Kālī's Child*'s initial publication, it is difficult to re-imagine the original circumstances into which the book fell.

Since that time, *Kālī's Child* has been effectively yoked to the Paul Courtright/James Laine controversies, which, like *Kālī's Child*, elicited a fevered response from the Hindu community. It should be noted that Ramakrishna devotees were to a great extent either ignorant of or not interested in either controversy; in fact, most Ramakrishna devotees remain unaware of the *Kālī's Child* controversy since most of them have little interest in what Western academics have to say about Hindu religious figures. Unfortunately, the polemic which has attended the Kripal/Courtright/Laine controversies has resulted in an "us" versus "them" paradigm, with core issues being obscured—opponents being branded as either aligned with Hindutva or armed with Western hegemonic motivations. Yet the issues at stake were never so simple as to be reducible to questions of Hindutva agendas or Western hegemony.

The interpretative waters surrounding *Kālī's Child* became further muddied by the work's being drawn into a discussion of the cultural acceptance of homosexuality, by the accompanying charges of homophobia leveled at those who contested Kripal's theses, and by the discussion of the question whether the academy should be the locus for human liberation movements. Yet lost in the ascending din was the fact that the focus of the debate had shifted away from the text itself. Lost in the furor were the primary issues of whether the theses presented in *Kālī's Child* were sustainable and whether the book presented material that could withstand critical scrutiny. These nuts and bolts of scholarship became almost extraneous to the debate, as issues of Hindutva and Indian democratic values, academic freedom, homophobia, and human sexual rights, and Hindu religious sentiments and religious orthodoxy took center stage. In such a highly polarized environment, created by years of controversy which was associated with multiple issues and multiple—often belligerent—respondents, contesting *Kālī's Child*'s theses became in itself prima facie evidence of Hindu extremism and homophobia.[3]

Indeed, one must think long and hard before walking into this controversy at all. First, since the author of *Kālī's Child* has already been the recipient of a concerted hate campaign, it seems particularly graceless to question his scholarship. If nothing else, one risks the impression of being considered a bad sport. *Hasn't he been put through enough?* Further, by questioning the theses in *Kālī's Child*, we are well aware that we risk being branded yet again with the stamp of Hindutva, guilt by association having already been used to discredit arguments against *Kālī's Child*. For the sake of transparency we need to clarify that we both self-identify as socially and politically liberal, sharing no agenda and having no truck with the Hindutva crowd except for a deep love for India (which most South Asia scholars share as well). While this kind of avowal seems unnecessary, because we have already been labeled with a "Hindu right-wing agenda" tag, the declaration must be made in bold large print.

Yet—certainly as far as the present authors are concerned—the issue was never one of right-wing (or left-wing) agendas, nor was it ever a matter of Ramakrishna's (or anyone else's) sexual preference. The issue was whether *Kālī's Child* withstood critical scrutiny: Were the theses presented in the book tenable? Did the texts quoted in *Kālī's Child* say what they purported to say? For all scholars, whether identifying themselves as outsiders or insiders, Hindus or non-Hindus, the real question at stake should be whether *Kālī's Child* withstands critical scrutiny. If it does, then—insider or outsider—let the chips fall where they may. If the book does *not* withstand critical scrutiny, then issues of Hindutva, India's democracy, academic freedom, human sexual rights, etc.—although deeply important—remain nevertheless peripheral to *Kālī's Child.*

Because *Kālī's Child* became so much more than a book in the intervening years between its publication and the present book's publication, it has been extremely difficult to unglue the text of *Kālī's Child* from later controversies involving Western academics and the Hindu community. However, in order to understand either the book or the ensuing controversy, we must first pull out the text from its subsequent accretions. In this book we unravel Kripal's work from the controversy by returning to *Kālī's Child* as text, in addition to closely studying the scholarship which provided its backdrop. From this vantage point we can see where the controversy began, how and in which ways the debate changed course, and in which direction we are headed.

Why did the debate surrounding *Kālī's Child* become so heated and why was there so little neutral ground? Certainly much of the antagonism surrounding the controversy was due to the fact that the academic and insider communities each viewed themselves as the appropriate location for the most authentic interpretation of Ramakrishna. Both the academic community as well as the insider community viewed themselves as the sole possessors of the credentials necessary for assessing Ramakrishna. As a result, it was not only the criteria and the methods by which to assess a Hindu religious figure that became contentious issues but also who was deemed a valid authority.

Ramakrishna literature has historically been dominated by two models, that of the insider community—the emic approach which exclusively employs insider literature—and that of the academic community, the outsider or etic approach. Each of these models has produced its own literature. The academic community has often written off insider literature as hagiography, thus dismissing serious studies by insiders on their own tradition. On the other hand, academic literature on Ramakrishna has generally failed to attract the attention of the insider community—*Kālī's Child* being the singular, notable exception. The publication of *Kālī's Child* and its reception by the academic community dramatically pitted the insider community (which we must remember included only those who were aware of the controversy) against not only the book's author but also a significant group of South Asia scholars. In contrast, those within the insider community who were aware of *Kālī's Child* greeted the book with near universal outrage and condemnation. In very short order the two independent and self-sustaining communities of Ramakrishna devotees and academics—generally complacent and isolated in their respective non-intersecting worlds—experienced a head-on collision.

Yet whether Ramakrishna is seen from the vantage point of Western academia or from the viewpoint of the insider community, the view of any religious figure when taken exclusively from any one side of the outsider/insider divide will only provide a partial glimpse of the subject in question. While Ramakrishna devotees will see Ramakrishna in one way, Ramakrishna scholars will very likely see him through a different lens. Yet both sides of the divide can benefit if they adjust their respective lenses to perceive what the other side has to offer. Only then can they locate a larger picture of not only the religious figure in question but also of those scholars and members of the insider community who inhabit the opposite sides of the divide. Both sides can gain from this endeavor since neither community can claim complete knowledge of their subject.

While this book critiques *Kālī's Child*, it was also written with the hope of creating a bridge between the two sides of the insider/outsider divide. We hope that this book will be one among many which will eventually create porous borders between the academic and insider communities. We see *Kālī's Child* as an opportunity for serious, constructive dialogue between academics and Hindu insiders.

This book is an attempt by two academically inclined monastics of the Ramakrishna Order to initiate a serious, constructive conversation between the academic world and the Hindu community. While most scholars of religion in the West are generally deeply respectful of the tradition they study, they often work from the stance of critical distance, willed or otherwise, and this is particularly true of the Hindu traditions. There is not a great deal of genuine close contact between scholars of religion and the Hindu believing community, and open-minded conversations between those associated with the two groups are infrequent. This is a loss for both sides of the divide. In order to share our respective visions and perspectives, a healthy dialogue needs to take place. In order for healthy dialogue to occur, forthright and respectful critiques also need to take place, particularly when it is perceived that some correctives are necessary to open and creative dialogue. As part of the project of creating space for dialogue, this book critiques *Kālī's Child*, honestly and respectfully and, just as importantly, it addresses a number of fundamental assumptions which not only supported *Kālī's Child*'s major theses and fueled its positive reception in the academy but also undergirded earlier academic studies of Ramakrishna.

We have written this book neither to assign blame nor to demonize anyone on either side of the insider/outsider divide. While there has long been a hermeneutic of suspicion within academia, a similar hermeneutic has recently been created within the Hindu community as a perceived means of self-defense. These mutual suspicions have only added more mortar to the existing walls between the two communities. It is easy to demonize those who write books about Ramakrishna in ways found offensive by the Hindu believing community. It is equally easy to demonize those who would wish to ban those books and demonize their authors. Rather than adding to the invective, it is much more productive, and much more interesting, to ask: Why do we see what we see? Why do we interpret the way we interpret?

If nothing else, *Kālī's Child* and the controversy surrounding it have amply demonstrated that Ramakrishna and Ramakrishna studies remain significant and relevant issues today. While Ramakrishna died well over a century ago, both Ramakrishna and Ramakrishna studies continue to provoke interest, debate and vigorous discussion. Academic exploration, continuing historical research and increasing levels of cultural awareness have augmented both the allure and the debate surrounding Ramakrishna, a process that will certainly continue in coming years.

Interpreting Ramakrishna examines Ramakrishna scholarship from its inception over a century ago and contextualizes *Kālī's Child* within that framework in the first chapter. Utilizing original source texts and historical findings, we examine both past and current Ramakrishna scholarship within its cultural and historical perspective. We closely study *Kālī's Child* as text in the second chapter and, in the next chapter, we analyze the history and the many-sided implications of the controversy surrounding the book. We examine the factors involved in the debate surrounding *Kālī's Child*, which in turn serves to demonstrate what elements are at play when religious figures from the Hindu traditions are placed in the context of modern Euro-American scholarship. In the fourth and the fifth chapters, we take a closer look at the issues of interpretation and translation within the context of *Kālī's Child*. The final chapter gives us the opportunity to share our vision of the future of Ramakrishna studies.

Throughout the course of this book we have found it difficult to avoid cultural/geographic generalizations such as "West" and "East" as well as "Western" and "Eastern." Edward Said famously condemned the exoticization of the "mystic East" as unreconstructed colonialism. Obviously, the "East" can be considered "East" only in relation to the West. It goes without saying that the "West" can only be "West" to the extent that there is an "East" as an antipodal geographic/cultural location. While we are aware that the use of these artificial dichotomies presents a minefield, we nevertheless have chosen to employ these generalizations because they still retain some usefulness. What is important is that we acknowledge their inherently problematical status.

On a similar note, we employ the terms "insider" and "outsider," sometimes in the context of the Hindu traditions but more often in the context of the Ramakrishna movement. These terms point to a dichotomy that does not always exist. There are a large number of Westerners, academics among them, who are "insiders." There are also a large number of Indian academics who are "outsiders," as their methods of assessing Hindu religious figures reflect their adherence to the methods of their Western academic training rather than their Hindu religious upbringing.

As to why we persevere in the use of these problematic generalizations, we state in our defense that our study begins with Ramakrishna scholarship in the 1880s, when polarized thinking about East and West as well as about insider and outsider was, by and large, firmly in place. With the passage of time, the traffic across these cultural and geographical borders has greatly accelerated in both directions, making these boundaries increasingly fluid, but the categories, although increasingly difficult to define, nevertheless continue to exist. Thus, the generalizations that we employ are just that—generalizations. We are well aware that they are hopelessly vague when used for mapping out categories that often have no hard and fast borders.

This book is an outgrowth of many years of involvement in the *Kālī's Child* debate. Pravrajika Vrajaprana's book review of *Kālī's Child*, published in the *Bulletin of Hindu Christian Studies* in 1997, was an early foray into the controversy. Swami Tyagananda came upon the issue only upon his arrival in the United States in 1999, when he began his work at Harvard.[4] When questioned by a faculty member about *Kālī's Child*, Swami Tyagananda read the book and immediately began thinking about writing a response to the issues raised in the book. At this point it seemed advantageous to join forces. As a result, Pravrajika Vrajaprana was actively involved in preparing the manuscript of "*Kali's Child* Revisited, or Didn't Anyone Check the Documentation?"—which was a four-month, breakneck effort to create a response to *Kālī's Child*, photocopies of which were informally distributed at the 2000 Annual Meeting of the American Academy of Religion. While we had anticipated there might be some interest in our rebuttal, we were astonished by how much interest there actually was.

"*Kali's Child* Revisited" soon morphed into a David-and-Goliath encounter when our Kinko's-photocopied response was refuted in a lengthy essay by Jeffrey Kripal in the *Harvard Divinity Bulletin* (Kripal, 2000/2001) and was rebutted in an even longer piece by him on the Harvard Divinity School's website (which was later revised and reprinted in *Evam* [Kripal, 2002]). While a response in kind was not permitted by the *Bulletin*, Swami Tyagananda was given an opportunity to write a 600-word letter to the editor of the *Bulletin*. Huston Smith and Indian psychotherapist Somnath Bhattacharyya also wrote letters to the editor to contest Kripal's article. While we had long been encouraged to write a book-length response to *Kālī's Child*, by this time it had become clear that we needed to do so. Moreover, as *Kālī's Child* garnered praise from other scholars, it began to be looked upon as an axial work for future Ramakrishna scholarship and has already been used as such.[5] For this reason, we felt compelled to contest *Kālī's Child* in order to provide current and future readers a necessary textual corrective.

There was yet another reason for embarking on this project—apart from the nuts-and-bolts issues of translation, documentation and interpretation. Interpreting across cultural, religious, and historical distances is always vexed, requiring great sensitivity and an openness to an enormous range of cultural issues and contexts. *Kālī's Child* thus merits wider discussion if only as a stellar example of a poor cultural translation. Richard King said it well when he wrote:

> When a western academic translates ... Indian texts into western cultural idioms and languages, the text is transformed not only linguistically but also in terms of the interests, rules and modes of life of the translator and her audience. . . . The claim to be able to discern the "real intentions" or meanings of a foreign text, person or event, is an

> attempt to privilege the academic discourse above all others. Often, however, the "insights" which the expert puts forward do not sit easily with the explanations given by the people he or she is claiming to examine. (King 1999a, 238)

True enough. The "insights" proposed by *Kālī's Child* and the issues they represent are significant enough to merit an examination of an enormous corpus of literature in order to address the debate in depth.

One might presume that, because we are members of the Ramakrishna Order, we are writing this book to present the "official" viewpoint of the Ramakrishna Order. That is not the case simply because there *is* no "official" view of Ramakrishna. Lest there be any misunderstanding about the genesis of this book, the creation of *Interpreting Ramakrishna* was entirely and absolutely our own idea. This book is not in any way a project of the Ramakrishna Order. We have not been asked by anyone in the Ramakrishna Order to write this book. We have not been asked to represent any viewpoint. Both of us have been writers for many years, and we have always been given full freedom in expressing our respective viewpoints. This is hardly exceptional, as it is also the case with every other monastic of the Ramakrishna Order. In writing this book, we are representing no one's views but our own, though we certainly have benefited from the assistance of some members of the Ramakrishna Order—notably Swami Prabhananda, the Order's leading scholar and historian, who helped us tremendously by providing material which was difficult to obtain in the United States. In short, our book is not an apologia for Ramakrishna or for the Ramakrishna Order. The work is our own and was done, as every worthy work is done, with the help and encouragement of many people, to all of whom we are enormously indebted.

Both of us, from different points on the planet, became immersed in Ramakrishna literature at a very young age. Both of us, again from different points on the planet, had extensive academic training and, finally, both of us decided in adulthood to become monastics of the Ramakrishna Order. Both of us have been monastics for more than thirty years, and both of us now—from different points within the United States—have found ourselves in frequent contact with the Western academy. This has been a happy and productive experience, and we are grateful for the enlarged perspective which this has provided. It has greatly enriched our lives.

Our experience has given us extensive contact with a world and body of literature that is infrequently seen by those in the Ramakrishna

Order. Being part of the insider community while frequently dipping into the academic world has allowed us a breadth of perspective that few have been able to enjoy. Because of our own positive experience, we strongly believe that the walls that separate insiders and outsiders need to be porous in order for both sides of the great divide to learn and experience as much of each other's worlds as possible.

This work could not have been done without the great number of people who made this project as meaningful and enjoyable as it became for both of us. The book owes much to the support and encouragement of the late Swami Ranganathananda and, as already mentioned, Swami Prabhananda. Our thanks are also owed to a number of monastics of the Ramakrishna Order who freely gave of their time and energy in tracking down materials for us. Swami Swahananda was extremely generous with his time and expertise, and we are very grateful for his assistance. On the same note, thanks are also due to Swamis Atmajnanananda, Baneshananda, Chetanananda and Gitatmananda. We are particularly grateful to our spiritual communities in both Boston and Santa Barbara for their unstinting support and encouragement.

Jayanta and Ilu Sircar did what few would have the patience to do: read through the entire *Śrī-Śrī-Rāmakṛṣṇa-Kathāmṛta* line by line and compare it with Nikhilananda's *Gospel of Sri Ramakrishna*, also line by line, in order to catalogue the untranslated portions. These portions have been meticulously translated and can be accessed at http://interpretingramakrishna.com.

Heartfelt thanks to Katherine Bucknell, editor of Isherwood's diaries, who has been enormously kind, helpful and extraordinarily generous with her time. Thanks are due as well to Don Bachardy, Christopher Isherwood's longtime partner, for his input and help. Narasingha Sil was also extremely generous in sharing his material with us as was Malcolm McLean in granting us permission to quote from his unpublished Ph.D. thesis, "A Translation of the *Śrī-Śrī-Rāmakṛṣṇa-Kathāmṛta* with Explanatory Notes and Critical Introduction."

Our deepest gratitude goes to Huston Smith for writing the book's Foreword. A large number of scholars and friends have been extraordinarily supportive and generous with their time and expertise. Our profound gratitude to every one who has helped us in this endeavor; we wish it were possible to acknowledge them all. Among those we wish to extend our particular thanks are: Debasis Bagchi, Ann Louise Bardach, Luisa Bird-Robinson, Francis X. Clooney, S.J., Srinivas Gandhi, Luis

Giron-Negron, Gerald James Larson, Jeffery Long, Lance Nelson, Anantanand Rambachan, Amiya Sen, Janet Walker and Steven Walker. Our deep gratitude to Mariana Masin and the late Francis Masin who steadfastly encouraged, coaxed and supported this project from the very beginning; their love and friendship have been invaluable. To Doug and Mikele Rauch, unending thanks. We have truly depended upon them for their indefatigable encouragement, support, good humor and warm friendship. Sometimes "thanks" just does not go far enough. Some of the greatest support came from Hilda Densmore (Shanta-Ma), whose daily readings from the *Caṇḍī* and endless prayers for the success of this project accompanied this work from conception to delivery. To Sister Gargi (Marie Louise Burke), departed and deeply missed, heartfelt gratitude for spirited encouragement, friendship and boundless inspiration. Our thanks to the University of Chicago Press for granting us permission to quote from *Kālī's Child*. Thanks also to Jim Aeby for his elegant work in formatting this book. Last but hardly least, we would like to thank Jeffrey Kripal for his unfailing courtesy and willingness to engage in dialogue. In many unexpected and unforeseen ways, we owe him thanks.

There are a number of other scholars whose work on Ramakrishna we examine and often critique. This critique should not be interpreted as a lack of respect for their scholarship or a lack of respect for them as talented, sincere, and generally quite admirable human beings. We simply disagree with them, that's all. While this obvious fact should not have to be so blatantly spelled out, recent experience has shown that insider critiques do not receive either the respect or the attention they deserve, largely because their motives are often pre-judged as Hindutva hatchet jobs. In general, insiders' critiques are often instinctively not placed under the rubric of "scholarship." Perhaps in some small measure, this book can help change this unfortunate prejudice.

We have drawn inspiration from both the wisdom of the religious tradition we have embraced as well as the integrity and intelligence of scholars with whom we have worked. Our debt to all of them is enormous. To them this book is dedicated, as well as to our respective parents, to whom our debt is unpayable.

A Note on Translation and Transliteration

Sprinkled throughout *Interpreting Ramakrishna* are quotations from Bengali, Sanskrit, and French as well. All translations that appear in this text are our own, except those that are included in quoted material. This part of the "Note" is the easiest. Transliterations are another matter altogether, for there are few tasks more maddening or seemingly capricious than that of transliteration. While we have used the standard international system for transliterating Indic words into the Roman alphabet, there is no standardized method for deciding which Sanskrit and Bengali words are to be transliterated and which are not. The author(s) must therefore create their own rule book and stick to it, informing the reader their reasons for having the text appear the way it does. Authors and publishers have their own peculiarities; ours belong to us alone. It is the scheme that we found worked best for the material presented here.

We have arbitrarily chosen the year 1800 C.E. as our line in the sand: there are no diacritical marks used in names of individuals who lived after 1800. Mythological figures such as Kālī, Viṣṇu, etc., are placed in diacritical marks as well as the names of ancient personalities such as Rāma and Kṛṣṇa (who may or may not be historical, depending on whom one asks) as well as Śaṅkara, Caitanya, etc. Thus we have the devotee Ramchandra Datta who revered Rāma, and Kali, Ramakrishna's disciple, who bowed before the goddess Kālī, and Narayan who reminded Ramakrishna of Nārāyāṇa himself. On the other hand, we have not used diacritical marks for Sanskrit words that have entered the general English vocabulary such as avatar, chakra, kundalini, etc.

Diacritical marks have not been used for any geographical names. However, the spelling of geographical locations, particularly cities, has become a truly vexing problem due to recent changes in the accepted spelling of their names. While we would have liked to have kept one standard spelling for "Kolkata/Calcutta," this has proved impossible. If, for consistency's sake, we had used a uniform spelling of "Calcutta" throughout this book, then the book would be dated before its publication, since the city officially changed its name in December of 2000. On the other hand, we cannot change quoted material. Thus we will state that the early years of Ramakrishna's life were spent in Kamarpukur, a village geographically near yet culturally distant from Kolkata, while

Partha Chatterjee will remind us that Ramakrishna "was a frequently discussed personality in the schools, colleges and newspapers of Calcutta." For this mildly schizophrenic usage, we can only apologize in advance in the hopes that forewarned is forearmed, and the reader will understand why such usage was necessary.

As for transliterated lines of Bengali script, we have tried to approximate the standard spoken language as much as possible. Hence we will indicate *bhāb*, *jogi* and *koro* rather than *bhāva*, *yogi* and *kara*. Again, to approximate the spoken language, the "a" sound generally (but not always) is transliterated as "o", whereas the "long a" sound has been transliterated with the standard "ā." For the sake of consistency, we have kept the spelling of proper names uniform and have used the most common form of spelling. We have used diacritical marks with Sanskrit religio-philosophical terms such as Vedānta, Vaiṣṇava, sannyāsa, bhāva, etc., though some of our decisions may appear arbitrary as well: we use "Tantric" to refer to the word's adjectival form (as in a Tantric form of worship) and when used as a proper noun we use "Tāntriks" to refer to the person who is a practitioner of Tantra. Diacritical marks have also been used when we refer to Sanskrit or Bengali texts, such as the *Rāmāyaṇa*, *Kathāmṛta*, *Līlāprasaṅga*, etc.

Abbreviations

CW	*The Complete Works of Swami Vivekananda*
GSR	*The Gospel of Sri Ramakrishna*
JB	*Śrī-Śrī-Rāmakṛṣṇa Paramahaṁsadeber Jībanabṛttānta*
KA	*Śrī-Śrī-Rāmakṛṣṇa-Kathāmṛta*
KC	*Kālī's Child* (2nd edition, 1998)
KC 1995	*Kālī's Child* (1st edition, 1995)
Life	*The Life of Sri Ramakrishna* (Advaita Ashrama)
LP	*Śrī-Śrī-Rāmakṛṣṇa-Līlāprasaṅga*
LR	*Life of Ramakrishna* (Romain Rolland)
LSV	*The Life of Swami Vivekananda*
MK	*Śrī-Śrī-Māyer Kathā*
RLS	*Ramakrishna: His Life and Sayings* (Max Müller)
RSV	*The Reminiscences of Swami Vivekananda*

1

RAMAKRISHNA SCHOLARSHIP: A BRIEF HISTORY

Both Ramakrishna and then Vivekananda have been constantly reinvented and represented in the light of the interests and concerns of those who have written about them.

—Gwyllem Beckerlegge, *The Ramakrishna Mission*

Ramakrishna, Vivekananda once remarked, "was contented simply to live that great life and to leave it to others to find the explanation" (CW 8.261). Finding the explanation is what scholars, psychoanalysts, spiritual seekers, politicians, historians, writers and an inexhaustible array of others have attempted to do for over a century. The process of finding the explanation, however, did not occur within a historical or cultural vacuum. The process itself has been complex and circuitous, mediated by a host of various forces, among them colonialism, Orientalism, European and Indian nationalism, and the catastrophic effects of two world wars, along with the ascendancy of the Western scientific model and the embracing of psychoanalysis. Ramakrishna scholarship has closely mirrored this complex movement of intertwining forces, for few Indian historical figures have calibrated European and North American attitudes toward each other as definitively as Ramakrishna.

It is for this reason that we begin this book with a brief survey of Ramakrishna scholarship from the 1880s to the present day. In order to contextualize *Kālī's Child*, its claims, and the controversy which surrounds it, we first need to locate the book within its historical framework. In this chapter we examine the various historical and cultural processes at play in interpreting not only a nineteenth-century Bengali mystic but also those who evaluated him. Only then can we identify the distance that often seems to disappear between the interpreter and the interpreted, between the Ramakrishna scholar and Ramakrishna himself.

In this brief survey, we will see interpreters of Ramakrishna who have employed Western intellectual paradigms to critique Ramakrishna and/or Hindu culture; we will see other interpreters who have used Ramakrishna for an anti-Western critique. What will remain more or less consistent in these interpretations is the privileging of a Western paradigm, along with a universalism which presupposes the wholesale applicability of European and/or North American norms to other cultures and eras. Moreover, until recent years these assumptions of universality were reinforced by the European and/or North American stranglehold upon political and economic power as well as knowledge production.

In characterizing attitudes as particularly "Western" as opposed to "Eastern," we realize that we are opening ourselves up to the charge of essentialism—the presumption that the "West" has a certain fixed essence which makes it utterly distinctive from the "East," another fixed essence antipodal to that of the West.[1] We use these categories consciously but sparingly, knowing (as does the reader) that there is no one vision or version of the "East" any more than there is one of the "West."

As we shall see in the course of this chapter, there has been a distinct change of direction and emphasis in Ramakrishna studies from the latter portion of the nineteenth century to the present day. While Ramakrishna's early Western interpreters by and large presumed the superiority of Western religious and cultural traditions, the veracity of the Ramakrishna tradition's source texts and the reliability of insider translations remained unquestioned. Insider interpretations of Ramakrishna were not inherently suspect by virtue of the fact that they were insider interpretations. By the second half of the twentieth century, predictably in the 1960s, the dynamic between the believing community and the academic community changed. By the latter half of the twentieth century, the basic assumption of good faith between the Ramakrishna tradition and the academy was ruptured, for the tradition's source texts, authors and translators were now interpreted through a hermeneutic of suspicion. In many ways Ramakrishna came to embody the various debates and understandings that both India and the West have had of each other. For this reason Ramakrishna has been and continues to be a lightning rod for East/West understanding.

Ramakrishna in Context

Of all India's nineteenth-century religious figures, Ramakrishna (1836–1886) is arguably the most towering. His influence—and the influence of the Order that bears his name—has increased over the years and remains an impressive force to this day. Ramakrishna was an extraordinary mystic who profoundly affected the lives of many who encountered him. Yet had Ramakrishna not been noticed, indeed championed, by prominent Westerners (such as Max Müller and Romain Rolland) and prominent Indians (such as Keshab Chandra Sen and Swami Vivekananda) in the movement's formative early years, it is doubtful whether Ramakrishna would be known today outside India's borders or even throughout India.

It is useful to remember that by the end of Ramakrishna's fifty-year lifespan, British rule in India was firmly entrenched. While mid-nineteenth century Europe was locked in the grip of militaristic nationalism, India was experiencing the upheavals of modernity, carrying with it the birth pangs of nationalism. India's anticolonial nationalism, Partha Chatterjee argues, divided the world into two domains, the material and the spiritual. Included in India's nationalist agenda was its self-definition as essentially "spiritual" in contrast to the West, which was essentially "materialistic" (Chatterjee, 6). As both Europe and India struggled to redefine themselves, each defined itself by steadily observing its European or Indian alter-ego.

For nineteenth-century India, the accumulated influence of generations of colonialism—whether ostensibly benign or aggressive—had its effect. Thrust into modernity through continual association with a culture presumed superior because of its reason and science, many Indians—particularly Bengal's educated, urban middle-class—had accepted and internalized the colonial credo: Indian culture was decayed, contemporary Hinduism was degraded, and reform was needed. Yet hovering over Bengal's educated middle-class was the mounting suspicion that Western science, philosophy, reason, and rationality could not provide them with anything better.

It was into this uneasy set of circumstances that Ramakrishna was born. Ramakrishna's early background scarcely predicted the far-reaching effects his life would have. The early years of Ramakrishna's life were spent in Kamarpukur, a village geographically near yet culturally distant from Kolkata. At his elder brother's request, Ramakrishna moved to Kolkata when he was sixteen. Except for the final year of Ramakrishna's life, the remaining thirty-four years of his life were spent in a temple complex at Dakshineswar, near burgeoning Kolkata, where he initially served as a priest at the Kālī temple founded by Rani Rasmani. Kolkata was not only British India's capital but also India's intellectual metropolis and the city that experienced modernity far earlier than any other Indian city.

If there were to be a single locus at which Ramakrishna's trajectory changed from an unknown Bengali mystic to that of a public figure, it would be his 1875 meeting with Keshab Chandra Sen (1838–1884), the Westernized charismatic leader of the Brahmo Samaj, who was instrumental in thrusting Ramakrishna, very much the traditional Hindu, into history. If the educated middle-class elite who composed Keshab's Brahmo Samaj were discomfited by traditional Hindu culture and religion—deemed irrational, unprogressive and unmanly—they were equally ill at ease with Western culture, religion and the strict rationality that was believed to be the antidote to Hinduism's superstitions. The urban intelligentsia of Bengal were nostalgic for their lost rural past, when their religion was uncontaminated by Western scorn and their lives were free from urban anonymity and complexity.[2]

Ramakrishna's village simplicity, rustic Bengali and complete lack of sophistication thus made him all the more attractive to many of Kolkata's elite. His earthy language and vivid parables were redolent of the rural world long left behind but still longed for. "Through Ramakrishna," Sumit Sarkar writes, "the city *bhadralok* [the educated middle-class gentry] could imagine themselves to be reaching back to lost traditional moorings, in the countryside, in simple faith conveyed through rustic language" (1993, 7).

Without any desire for doing so, Ramakrishna, through his very existence in Dakshineswar, subverted the value system upheld by the British and absorbed by Bengal's elite. Ramakrishna's unapologetic and unaffectedly enthusiastic Hindu identity, combined with his distaste for modern education, was a breathtaking change from the educated Hindu reformers who were defensive about Hindu culture and religion. While Hindu reformers attempted to stave off Christianity by creating a "purified," rational and anglicized Hinduism as embodied in the Brahmo Samaj, Ramakrishna created an impetus for Hindu pride and self-assertion which was more effective against Christian inroads than any of Bengal's reform movements.[3]

Ramakrishna and his followers sang at the drop of a hat, danced ecstatically, wept freely, and laughed often in joyful abandon. Later reminiscences by Ramakrishna's disciples recall them laughing so hard that they rolled helplessly on the ground. No contrast could be more stark than that between Ramakrishna's spontaneous freedom and the formalized, highly structured colonial educational system and the equally structured, formalized and inhibited world of *cākri*, the lowly clerical work in which many Indians were engaged (Sarkar 1993, 23–24).

Keshab Chandra Sen's initial role in making Ramakrishna known both inside and outside India was nearly as significant as Vivekananda's was to be in ensuing years. So influential was Keshab, both through his lectures and his articles, that his admiration for Ramakrishna turned the latter into a well-known personality. "By the early years of the 1880s," Partha Chatterjee writes, "[Ramakrishna] was a frequently discussed personality in the schools, colleges and newspapers of Calcutta" (45).

While Keshab enjoyed enormous popularity in Bengal, of equal or greater significance was the fact that he and his Brahmo Samaj had influential European admirers. For the colonized, the door to success had to be found via appreciation from the West, which both Keshab and Vivekananda had. Indeed, both Keshab's and Vivekananda's luster was geometrically increased in India by the very fact that they were known and admired in the West. Keshab was lionized because, among other factors, he had had breakfast with Prime Minister Gladstone and an audience with Queen Victoria—the latter in India being a near-mythic figure. Vivekananda was even more lionized because he successfully proclaimed Hinduism's greatness to the West and had a good number of Western followers. Most importantly, Vivekananda renewed Hindus' faith in their own religious traditions. Since both these men garnered a significant Western following, it became possible for Ramakrishna to be known in the West.

Keshab's monotheistic Westernized Hinduism, with its strong Christian flavor, was extremely appealing to many who sought a "purified" Hinduism. For the Ramakrishna movement, the most significant among them was F. Max Müller. But before we continue with the Western strand of Ramakrishna studies, we must first investigate the texts which constitute the basic source books on Ramakrishna's life and teachings.

Source Texts

Ramakrishna wrote no books and delivered no lectures. All that we know about Ramakrishna today has come down to us not directly from him but from others through the accounts of his life, his conversations and reminiscences. Some of these biographical accounts, reminiscences and conversations were recorded or written by those who had seen Ramakrishna, lived with him, and knew him closely. All other books on Ramakrishna, written by those who did not meet him, have used these early texts as their source material.

While the *Kathāmṛta* is the best-known source text in Ramakrishna literature, it was not the first publication on Ramakrishna. In Ramakrishna's own lifetime, four books of his sayings were published, several of which also included biographical information. These were written by Keshab Chandra Sen (1878), Suresh Chandra Dutta (1884), and Ramchandra Datta (1885 and 1886). Among the other early books published after Ramakrishna's death were those by Akshaykumar Sen (1896) and Satyacharan Mitra (1897). Unlike the authors mentioned above, Mitra had no contact with Ramakrishna, and some of the material published in his book can be assessed as either wildly exaggerated or fabricated. This would not be unexpected, since by 1896—particularly given Vivekananda's enormous success in the West—Ramakrishna had gained considerable fame, and tales surrounding him had grown exponentially.

Today Ramakrishna scholars primarily direct their attention to the three major source texts on Ramakrishna: *Śrī-Śrī-Rāmakṛṣṇa-Kathāmṛta* recorded by Mahendra Nath Gupta, *Śrī-Śrī-Rāmakṛṣṇa-Līlāprasaṅga* written by Swami Saradananda, and *Śrī-Śrī-Rāmakṛṣṇa-Paramahaṁsadeber Jībanabṛttānta* written by Ramchandra Datta. In addition, the records of conversations with Vivekananda and other disciples of Ramakrishna provide nuggets of valuable information. None of these, however, deal with Ramakrishna exclusively the way the three books mentioned above do. These three books were published with the clear intent of making Ramakrishna more widely known, and they provide considerable information about his life and teachings.[4] All subsequent additions to Ramakrishna literature have used in varying degrees these three books as their basic resource.

Notwithstanding claims of objectivity, every book ever written necessarily has subjective elements in it. Subjectivity plays a major role in determining what makes the author highlight one aspect at the expense of another, or position events in an order or a pattern best suited to conform to the author's agenda or thesis. Every book—even if it is a "translation"—is at some level an "interpretation." This holds true for these three books—*Kathāmṛta*, *Līlāprasaṅga* and *Jībanabṛttānta*—as well. The authors of these books do not merely provide their readers with information but also interpret Ramakrishna for them. Their books can be viewed as both source texts and as being among the earliest Indian interpretations of Ramakrishna's life and teachings.

Śrī-Śrī-Rāmakṛṣṇa-Kathāmṛta

By far the best known among the source books on Ramakrishna is *Śrī-Śrī-Rāmakṛṣṇa-Kathāmṛta* ("The Nectar of Sri Ramakrishna's Words") written by his disciple Mahendranath Gupta (1854–1932), famously known simply as "M." M had a brilliant academic career at Hare School and Presidency College in Kolkata. He taught in a number of schools in Kolkata and was a professor at Ripon College. Reputed to be an excellent teacher, M was well versed in both Eastern and Western philosophy as well as in history, literature and astronomy. Before meeting Ramakrishna, M was a member of the Brahmo Samaj.

M's mother died when he was young and, while in college, he married Nikunja Devi, a cousin of Keshab Sen. Eventually the increasing friction within M's joint family reached the point where he was ready to commit suicide. It was at this critical juncture that M's nephew took him for a walk to the temple garden in Dakshineswar "where a paramahaṁsa. lives." It was here that M met Ramakrishna for the first time. For M, life would never be the same again. Years later, when M was asked what had been the greatest day in his life, he answered without hesitation: "The day I had my first darśan of Thakur [Ramakrishna] in February 1882."[5]

Providentially, M had been a meticulous diarist from childhood. His longstanding habit of maintaining a personal diary now found a serendipitous outlet: beginning with his first meeting with Ramakrishna, M carefully noted every meeting he had with him. M was graced with an eye for detail and a formidable memory and these gifts served him well as he recorded Ramakrishna's words and actions in his diary—a record that finally took the form of a book which became known as *Śrī-Śrī-Rāmakṛṣṇa-Kathāmṛta*.

The book's appearance took a somewhat circuitous route, however. There is no question that when M began to record in his diaries the words of Ramakrishna, M had neither the idea nor the intention of ever creating a "book" from it (Dey, 146). This is evident from the *Kathāmṛta* itself, where we read M's response to Girish Ghosh's request to share the contents of his diary: "I am writing for myself, not for others. . . . You may get it when I die" (KA 2.242). Clearly at this point in his life, M was not in a sharing mood. How M created what eventually was to become his life's greatest project is best described in M's own words:

> Thakur made my condition such that—after hearing him for seven or eight hours and observing him closely—I could remember everything when I returned home at night. I could note down every detail. I could not finish it all in a single day. It would come to my mind gradually. Such was the deep impression he made. I was recording everything for five years and none knew of it. (Nityatmananda, 5.18)

Unlike a stenographer, M did not record the words of Ramakrishna as soon as he heard them. To continue M's story:

> I wrote everything from memory after I returned home. Sometimes I had to keep awake the whole night. What I have presented here is not collected from others. . . . Sometimes I would keep on writing the events of one sitting for seven days, recollect the songs that were sung, and the order in which they were sung, and the samādhi and so on. . . .
>
> On every scene I have meditated a thousand times throughout my life. . . . Many a time I did not feel satisfied with my description of the events; I would then immediately plunge myself in deep meditation on Thakur. Then the correct image would arise before my mind's eye in a bright, real and living form. That is why in spite of the big gap in the physical sense, this story remains so fresh and lifelike in my mind as if it happened just now. (Dey, 143–44)

M began compiling Ramakrishna's teachings within two years of Ramakrishna's death. Once the teachings were compiled, M sought out Ramakrishna's widow Sarada Devi and read them out before her. Significantly, it was from Sarada that M sought confirmation of his writings, since for M there was no question that Sarada was the ultimate authority. Not only did M revere her for her spiritual wisdom but, on a practical level, he also recognized that she had known and lived with Ramakrishna for many years. Though largely hidden in the *Kathāmṛta*, Sarada's influence on the book's creation was quite profound. Not only was M's wife Sarada's disciple, but M himself—although a disciple of Ramakrishna—had also taken mantra initiation from Sarada Devi (Prabhananda 2004b, 346–47). What is also not generally known to readers either of the *Kathāmṛta* or of its English translation was that most of M's diary entries began with the heading "Śrī Śrī Gurudev [Ramakrishna] is the refuge," followed by "Śrī Śrī Mā [Sarada] is the refuge." During Sarada's lifetime, the first four volumes of the *Kathāmṛta* were dedicated at her feet (Prabhananda 2004b, 350). Given this, it is not surprising that M often sought her counsel. As M read out his manuscript to her, Sarada confirmed its accuracy, praising and blessing his endeavor.

M's first publication, issued long before the *Kathāmṛta*, was a twenty-page pamphlet of Ramakrishna's teachings, entitled *Paramahaṁsadeber Ukti* ("Sayings of Paramahaṁsa Dev"), published in 1892.[6] According to the pamphlet, Sadhu Mahindranath Gupta collected the sayings and Satchidananda Gitaratna was its publisher—both names being pseudonyms for M (Prabhananda 2004c, 378). The booklet went into several editions and was warmly received. Vivekananda wrote M in February 1889 with vigorous praise:

> Thanks a hundred thousand times, Master [M]! You have hit Ramakrishna in the right point. Few, alas, understand him!
>
> PS. My heart leaps with joy—and it is a wonder that I do not go mad when I find anybody thoroughly launched into the midst of the doctrine which is to shower peace on earth hereafter. (CW 6.204)

It was not long before M decided to bring out Ramakrishna's teachings in English and in conversational form, publishing them in the English journals *Dawn* and *Brahmavadin* (it was from the latter journal that Max Müller found the source material for "A Real Mahatman"). M also published them separately as two pamphlets entitled *A Leaf from the Gospel of Sri Ramakrishna*, in October and November 1897 (Dey, 147). He sent copies of these pamphlets to Vivekananda, who was extremely enthused and encouraging, writing M: "Everybody likes it here and in the West" (CW 5.140).[7]

However, while M's efforts were greatly appreciated both by the general public and within the young Ramakrishna movement, Ramchandra Datta in his Bengali journal *Tattvamañjarī* criticized M for writing in English rather than Bengali. As to why this struck a particular nerve, we should keep in mind that by the middle of the nineteenth century, English had replaced Persian as the language of bureaucracy. It had become the prerequisite tongue of Bengal's intelligentsia and was the instrument of intellectual influence, of "modern" culture, and of course, colonial domination. Moreover, language is a defining feature of national identity. As Partha Chatterjee points out, the Bengali language belonged "to that inner domain of cultural identity, from which the colonial intruder had to be kept out" (7). Urging M "not to give up the Bengali language," Datta further advised M to publish his material as a book rather than as pamphlets (Dey, 147). Given this spur, M made the decision to write the Bengali *Kathāmṛta* in the conversational style of his English *Leaf from the Gospel.*

By the time M had made the decision to publish the *Kathāmṛta*, portions from his diary had already appeared in several Bengali journals such as *Anusandhān*, *Ārati*, *Ālocanā*, *Utsāha*, *Udbodhan*, *Ṛṣi*, *Janmabhūmi*, *Tattvamañjarī*, *Nabyabhārat*, *Punya*, *Pradīp*, *Prabāsī*, *Prayās*, *Bāmābodhinī*, *Sāhitya*, *Sāhitya-saṁhitā*, and *Hindu Patrikā* (Sunil Bihari Ghosh, 220). And amazingly, while this is quite a formidable list, it is not exhaustive. The first volume of the *Kathāmṛta* was compiled from those extracts which had already been published. This in itself substantiates the fact that M's five-volume work was not pre-planned to be arranged cyclically in order to conceal "a secret," as *Kālī's Child* alleges. The *Kathāmṛta* was printed and published in 1902 by Swami Trigunatitananda, Ramakrishna's disciple, at the Udbodhan Press, the Bengali publishing house of the Ramakrishna Order (220). M's choice of *Kathāmṛta* for the book's title—literally, "nectarine words"—was inspired by a verse (10.31.9) from the Vaiṣṇava text, the *Bhāgavata Purāṇa*.

What we may not realize today is how truly uncharted M's literary territory was. The format and the style which appeared in the Bengali *Kathāmṛta* had never before appeared in print. Instead of a linear arrangement of teachings, M presented Ramakrishna as he had encountered him in the full context of his daily life, with all the atmospheric sounds and visual effects included. In contrast to the formalized language which was deemed mandatory for Bengali writing, M's language revealed to the public a living human being who told funny stories, danced, sang, and went into *samādhi*.

What is nearly impossible to transmit to those who cannot read the Bengali *Kathāmṛta* is how wildly different Ramakrishna's voice is from M's. As Partha Chatterjee has noted, the *Kathāmṛta* "combines two radically different linguistic idioms—one, the rustic colloquial idiom spoken by Ramakrishna, and the other, the chaste formality of the new written prose of nineteenth-century Calcutta" (51). The "new" prose of Kolkata was profoundly influenced by not only the words and syntax of the English language but, as importantly, by the very thoughts and the conceptual framework articulated in the language. Thus Ramakrishna's language and M's language projected entirely different worlds, world-views, value systems and senses of history.

While much has been made of Ramakrishna's "vulgar" language, we need to keep in mind that it was coarse only when compared to the newly minted, urban, English-parturiated Bengali. What is also nearly impossible for readers unfamiliar with pre-modern village Bengali to know is that, as Chatterjee points out, Ramakrishna's language showed

> great conceptual richness, metaphoric power, and dialectical skill. It was the language of preachers and poets in pre-colonial Bengal, and even when used by someone without much formal learning (such as Ramakrishna), it was able to draw upon the conceptual and rhetorical resources of a vast body of literate tradition. (51–52)

That is, of course, one reason why Ramakrishna was such a great source of attraction in late-nineteenth-century urban Bengal. Had it not been so, he—a poor uneducated priest—would hardly have drawn the likes of Keshab Chandra Sen, Girish Ghosh, Bankimchandra Chattopadhyay and other luminaries belonging to Kolkata's cultural elite.

In contrast to Ramakrishna, M was a product of the British educational system. In the *Kathāmṛta*, M navigates between his "English" world and his Bengali one, a contrast made clear not only by Ramakrishna's pre-modern village cadences and M's highly educated, anglicized narrative voice, but also by M's frequent English captions which he employs throughout the *Kathāmṛta*. While Ramakrishna discusses any number of varying subjects, M often places these topics under such English headings as (and here is a short random sampling): "Involution and Evolution" (KA 2.219); "Reconciliation of Free Will and God's Will—of Liberty and Necessity" (KA 4.255); "Identity of the Undifferentiated and Differentiated" (KA 4.34); "The Absolute Identical with the Phenomenal World" (KA 3.67); "Perception of the Infinite" (KA 1.190)—and so on. Significantly, the "Perception of the Infinite" heading provides a footnote which directs the reader to "compare discussion about the order of perception of the Infinite and of the Finite in Max Müller's Hibbert Lectures and Gifford Lectures" (KA 1.190). In so doing, M pointedly places Ramakrishna on the same intellectual platform as Europe's renowned philosophers.

This is significant, especially when we see how Swami Saradananda, author of the *Līlāprasaṅga*, confronts the same issue as M; namely, as English-educated members of the Bengali elite and as disciples of Ramakrishna, should they place Ramakrishna only within the context of India's philosophical history or also within the framework of Western philosophy? Their interpretations could not be separated from the ground reality of India's domination by Western intellectual traditions. While the Brahmos were caught in an uneasy pull between the Western modernity they embraced and India's Hindu religio-philosophical heritage, M would make every effort to place Ramakrishna and European thinkers on the same intellectual footing. To implement this, M also supplements through footnotes Ramakrishna's words with Sanskrit quotations from the Upaniṣads and the Bhagavad Gītā in order to place Ramakrishna in the august company of India's religious and intellectual giants.

The *Kathāmṛta* was originally written in five volumes, which were published over a period of thirty years, the first four volumes published in 1902, 1904, 1908 and 1910 respectively. The fifth and final volume took much longer, as M was elderly and increasingly ill; it was published in 1932 and was at the printers when M died. The volumes are almost—but technically not—a stenographic record of Ramakrishna's conversations from March 1882 to April 1886. As we have already seen, there is no textual evidence anywhere to indicate that M began transcribing his diaries with the express intention of publishing a "book." There is also no evidence to support the idea that M organized the contents of the five volumes of the *Kathāmṛta* in a predetermined manner. In fact, in none of the extensively documented conversations of M, which comprise sixteen volumes,[8] do we find anything to suggest that M had planned in advance the scheme of what is available today as the *Kathāmṛta*.

Since M's day, many have held the *Kathāmṛta* in high regard, and for those devoted to Ramakrishna, the book has become a kind of Bible. As Sumit Sarkar points out: "Today, an average middle or lower middle class Hindu household in Bengal can be expected to have a portrait of Ramakrishna somewhere, along with, quite possibly, a well-thumbed copy of the *Kathāmṛta*" (1993, 2). Such has been the impact of the book that Swami Vijnanananda, a disciple of Ramakrishna, told M: "After inquiring, I have discovered that 80% or more of our monks have embraced the life of renunciation by reading the *Kathāmṛta*, and through contact with you" (Lokeswarananda 1992, 15).

In each of M's *Kathāmṛta* entries, he scrupulously records the date, time and place of the conversation. The *Kathāmṛta* also contains the memoirs of Aswini Kumar Dutta, several secondhand accounts of Ramakrishna's meeting with other devotees, and a description of events at the Baranagore Math, the earliest monastery of the Ramakrishna Order. All of these, however, were placed in the Appendix and not in what M calls "the main text" of the book, because they were not firsthand material recorded on the same day as the event.

When M was told that different versions of what Ramakrishna had said and done had already begun to appear, M replied that he was not at all surprised. Such things had happened before, he said, pointing to the dissimilarities in the four Gospels of the Bible (Dey, 143). M's biblical reference is telling. Considering the odd mixture of awe and resentment with which the religion of their colonial rulers was viewed in British India, it is worth noting that M's choice for his first English title was *A Leaf from the Gospel of Sri Ramakrishna*. Like his contemporaries in Bengal's intelligentsia, M was both familiar with and influenced by the Bible. His choice of the word "Gospel" is understandable, even predictable. In using this scriptural tag, M both affirms Ramakrishna as equivalent to the Christ of the Christians and provides a scripture—the necessary written text—which will endow the young movement with a vital requirement. Again we see M navigating the terrain between his "English" and Bengali worlds. Hence M both acquiesces to the colonial standards for an accepted religion, while inserting a Hindu avatar in place of the Christian savior. For Bengal's nineteenth-century elite, the Bible would represent the religion and the language of the educated. In emulating the biblical model, M aims—even if unconsciously—to validate Ramakrishna among the educated classes of his peers.

It would therefore be entirely expected that M would retain the "Gospel" title when he translated the first volume of the Bengali *Kathāmṛta* into English in 1907. The book was published in Madras by the Brahmavadin Club, founded by followers of Ramakrishna. What is remarkable is the *extent* to which M employed the language of the King James version of the Bible. To a contemporary North American ear, M's biblical language in describing Ramakrishna's samādhi, for example, lies somewhere between hilarious and jarring: "The sweet angelic voice hath become still. . . . . The inner eye looketh within and beholdeth the Vision of Glory. The Blessed Vision the Master enjoyeth for a while. His face shineth with a heavenly luster and at last breaketh into smiles" (Mahendranath Gupta 1912, 61). M's choice of language must have struck an off key with his peers as well, for we find M revising the book four years later and freeing it from its biblical trappings.

Yet even without the "thou"s and "speaketh"s which appeared in the earliest editions, the hovering presence of the Bible as a fundamental model pervades the text. M's penchant for making the *Gospel* similar to the Bible was not limited to the title alone. In several places in the *Kathāmṛta*, we find him going out of his way to demonstrate a connection between Ramakrishna and Jesus (see, for instance, KA 3.210, 3.249, 4.246). Importantly, however, Christ was not the only exemplar. Caitanya (1486–1534), Bengal's ecstatic saint, was the other role model whose similarity with Ramakrishna is invoked throughout the *Kathāmṛta*. It is no accident that M said to Ramakrishna: "I feel that Jesus Christ, Caitanyadeva, and yourself—all three are one" (KA 3.211). What is interesting here is how M balances two models of religiosity as he holds the scale of East and West while reconstructing his diary which later became the *Kathāmṛta*.

M's English version of the *Kathāmṛta* is not a literal translation but his "own rendering of his thoughts rather than language, directly into English with many elaborations and elucidating repetitions" (Dey,

147). He evidently did not undertake to translate the other volumes of the *Kathāmṛta*. The second volume was translated by Swami Ashokananda and published in Madras in 1922 (Gargi, 82). Its second edition was published in 1928 after its language had been "edited and improved mostly by a Western friend" (Dey, 148).

When Swami Nikhilananda finally published in 1942 the more or less complete English translation of *The Gospel of Sri Ramakrishna* in New York, he did not change the title chosen by M. Nikhilananda's translation was well received, *Time* magazine writing that it was "one of the world's most extraordinary religious documents."[9] In 1949 the *New York Herald Tribune* invited eminent literary figures in America to name "three memorable books of the past twenty-five years," and included in that august company was *The Gospel of Sri Ramakrishna*.[10] While Nikhilananda's translation has increasingly come under critical scrutiny in the last two decades, it is worth remembering that it was a groundbreaking book in its era.

In reading the *Kathāmṛta*, one is aware of the constant presence of two people—M and Ramakrishna. Yet M is often seen by his desire to not be seen. By nature quiet and self-effacing, M instinctively avoided calling any attention to himself. Moreover, M wanted to remain invisible so that the reader's focus would be solely on Ramakrishna. While often referring to himself in the *Kathāmṛta* simply as "M," he also used pseudonyms such as "Master,"[11] "Mani," "Mohinimohan" or simply "a devotee."

One other point worth mentioning is that at the time of M's death, he had enough diary material for another five or six volumes. Poignantly and frustratingly, M's diary notations were as sparse as they were cryptic. As a result, M's *Kathāmṛta* project ended with the fifth volume. And, lest there be any misunderstanding, it needs to be said that the sketchy notations which constitute the remainder of M's diary belong solely to M's descendants, not to the Ramakrishna Order. It also needs to be pointed out that, according to Dipak Gupta, M's great-grandson, scholars can, and have, seen these diaries. Gupta's letter which attests to this fact appears in this book's Appendix.

Śrī-Śrī-Rāmakṛṣṇa-Paramahaṁsadeber Jībanabṛttānta

Published four years after Ramakrishna's death, the *Jībanabṛttānta* ("The Life Story of Sri Ramakrishna Paramahaṁsa") was the first major book written on Ramakrishna. Ramchandra Datta (1851–1899) was among the early wave of devotees that came to Ramakrishna in the late 1870s. Ramchandra—his name was often shortened to "Ram" in Ramakrishna circles—inherited his Vaiṣṇava faith from his father, who was a devotee of Kṛṣṇa. Ram briefly became an agnostic in his youth while he pursued his degree in science, becoming an assistant chemical examiner at Calcutta Medical College. Through the writings and speeches of Brahmo leader Keshab Chandra Sen, Ram came to know about Ramakrishna. The deep-seated devotional temperament that Ram had had in his childhood was resurrected in Ramakrishna's company and he became a devout disciple and devotee of Ramakrishna. He was among the first to publicly proclaim Ramakrishna an avatar.

It is ironic that Ram heard of Ramakrishna through Keshab, because Ram's renewed faith in God awakened his Vaiṣṇava heritage and simultaneously killed any appreciation of the Brahmo Samaj that he may have had. In fact, Ram's real antipathy to the movement is unmistakable in the *Jībanabṛttānta* (which is second only to his hostility toward Tantra). Interestingly, Ram, though educated, was unlike either M or Saradananda; his writing showed little sign of the Westernization that had so deeply influenced the other two. While both M and Saradananda felt compelled to address the issues of Western thought and how Ramakrishna fit into those alternative paradigms, Ram had no interest in doing so. He never discusses it, it does not interest him. He found it unimportant, tangential at best. Ram's distaste for the Brahmo Samaj—he was extremely critical of study and lectures, for example, which were the Samaj's strongest suit—is indicative of the low-grade conflict that would be seen within Ramakrishna's disciples, particularly after his death. Like many Vaiṣṇavas, Ram did not believe in *sādhana* (spiritual practice), but in the grace of the avatar. Again, faith in the avatar—not reason—was of prime importance. There was, Ram warned, no hope for the faithless (JB, 234). This outlook would not sit well with a number of Ramakrishna's other disciples, as many of them had previously been members of the Brahmo Samaj and had been nurtured with the belief in the primacy of reason and logic.

Perhaps none of Ramakrishna's disciples had a stronger desire to publish books about Ramakrishna than Ram did, and no one had more problems doing so. In 1884, while Ramakrishna was still living, Ram wrote a brief biography of Ramakrishna. In his Preface to the *Jībanabṛttānta*, Ram writes that he had long desired to write a biography of "Paramahaṁsadeb" [Ramakrishna]. Krishnaprasanna Sen of Varanasi took the manuscript from Ram with the intention of having it printed in Varanasi, but for some reason that never came to pass. Ram writes in the

Jībanabṛttānta's Preface that he does not know why it was not printed. In 1885 Ram collected a number of Ramakrishna's teachings, publishing them in Bengali under the title *Tattvasāra*. A number of devotees disapproved of Ram's publishing venture, however, and mentioned the news to Ramakrishna. According to Swami Chetanananda, Ramakrishna cautioned Ram: "Do not publish my biography now. If you do, my body will not last long" (1989, 88–89).

It was Ram's conviction that Ramakrishna was the embodiment of "eternal and total being of Brahman" (*pūrna-brahma sanātan*) and for this reason all that was necessary for one's spiritual life was to remember Ramakrishna, meditate on him, and propagate his name. Ram was therefore nonplussed by the altogether different attitude of Ramakrishna's other disciples, primarily the younger ones, who saw Ramakrishna as their exemplar. They reasoned that Ramakrishna had set the pattern to follow: faith in Ramakrishna was not enough. It had to be accompanied by personal effort, which would, in time, result in spiritual experience (Mahendra Dutta, 54). Like Christianity's faith versus works or the Hindu tradition's bhakti versus jñāna dispute, this basic difference in approach was a source of strain in the early community of Ramakrishna devotees.

While many of Ramakrishna's young disciples were opposed to Ram's outlook and methods, they certainly were not the only ones who took issue with Ram's way of making Ramakrishna known to the wider public. Many of Ramakrishna's older devotees were equally displeased. Even after Ramakrishna's death, when it became known that Ram was preparing to write Ramakrishna's biography, the majority of them disapproved of the idea. The general consensus among Ramakrishna's followers was that they should first practice sādhana to acquire enough spiritual maturity and stature for others to take them seriously. Indeed, Narendra (who later became Swami Vivekananda) dissociated himself from the project to such an extent that he sent word to Ram through an older devotee, Balaram Bose, not to include him in the new biography. Several others also made similar requests.[12] While this undoubtedly upset Ram, he acquiesced.

A more mundane reason for Narendra's not wanting to be included in Ram's book was Narendra's involvement in a court case against some of his relatives who had claimed ownership of the house in which his widowed mother and young brothers lived. Although already a monk, Narendra took responsibility for managing the court case as he was the eldest son. For that reason, Narendra did not wear his ochre robes or use his *sannyāsa* (monastic) name in public, for that could have complicated his participation in the court case. Under these circumstances, the prospect of Ram's book on Ramakrishna (with the inevitable reference to Narendra as a sannyāsin), would have hurt the lawsuit, hence Narendra's request not to be included in the book. It was only after the court case was settled in 1889,[13] in fact, that Narendra began using his sannyāsa name in public.

We should keep in mind, however, that this disagreement over Ram's biography did not spill over into hostility or antagonism. According to Mahendra Dutta, although these two groups had their differences, they nevertheless had great love and respect for one another (87). Despite their differences, Ram and Narendra maintained a very good relationship with one another. When Narendra returned to India as the lionized Vivekananda, he visited the ailing Ram and did a prāṇam to him in the traditional way, which overwhelmed Ram. Further, even before Vivekananda returned from America, Ram's public lectures included glowing references to Vivekananda.[14]

To return to the *Jībanabṛttānta*, Ram's Vaiṣṇava approach is clearly seen throughout the book. The language and style exude his unquestioning reverence for Ramakrishna. In the preface to the first edition, Ram recognizes his own inability to gauge the depth of a life like Ramakrishna's, but he also does not hesitate to say that "ordinary" (*sādhāran*) people—himself obviously not included—will not be able to comprehend some aspects of Ramakrishna's life. This kind of remark has naturally created the impression that Ram was withholding secret information. Since no one knows what Ram was keeping to himself, it leaves the field open for speculation.

The *Jībanabṛttānta* chronologically describes the events in Ramakrishna's life. The book contains more commentary than events, which is understandable given the author's temperament: Ram was more a devout preacher than a painstaking researcher. Not surprisingly, there are some inaccuracies in his book. However, the *Jībanabṛttānta*'s strength lies not in its historical accuracy but in the devotion of its author and the insight it provides into many aspects of Ramakrishna's life. As the first published biography of Ramakrishna, the *Jībanabṛttānta* is invaluable, for it gives the reader insight into the mind of a devotee who had the opportunity to be closely associated with Ramakrishna for a period of approximately ten years.

The *Jībanabṛttānta* was first published in Kolkata in 1890 and remained relatively unknown even in Bengal. Although Ram's devotion and dedication were unquestionable, he lacked the stature—at least at that time—which would have given his book more authenticity. Years later, after the copyright of the book was transferred to the Ramakrishna Order, the book was published by the Order and it began to acquire the readership it deserved.[15] By that time, however, Saradananda's *Līlāprasaṅga* had already been published and had become a classic in its own right. Although Saradananda's book was—like the *Jībanabṛttānta*—also an interpretation of Ramakrishna's life, the *Līlāprasaṅga* had the added advantage of having been meticulously researched and enriched by the input of several of Ramakrishna's contemporaries.

Śrī-Śrī-Rāmakṛṣṇa-Līlāprasaṅga

Whereas the *Kathāmṛta* is a diary, or a record of Sri Ramakrishna's conversations, the *Līlāprasaṅga* is Ramakrishna's biography written by his disciple Swami Saradananda (1865–1926). Sarat (as Saradananda was known in his youth) came from a middle-class, orthodox brahmin family. An exceptionally good student, Sarat, like M, was a graduate of Hare School and—again, like M—gravitated to the Brahmo Samaj. It was through a friend of his cousin's that Sarat heard about Ramakrishna and visited him in Dakshineswar in October 1883. Eventually, both Sarat and his cousin Sashi took *sannyāsa*, monastic vows of renunciation, upon Ramakrishna's death.

Sarat later joined Vivekananda in the West to help the incipient Vedānta movement. While never attaining the celebrity status that Vivekananda achieved, Saradananda was appreciated for his learning and loved for his sweet, affectionate nature. He developed close friendships with a number of Westerners, which he valued and maintained throughout his life.[16] At Vivekananda's request, Saradananda returned to India to become the first General Secretary of the Ramakrishna Order. His temperament was well suited to being the General Secretary of a growing organization, known as he was for his kindly temperament, unflappability and patience.

Saradananda's magnum opus, the *Līlāprasaṅga*, was not planned as a "biography" in the usual sense of the term. There were a number of overlapping factors which prompted Saradananda to write what he called "the series" on Ramakrishna. What we know today as the *Līlāprasaṅga* is in fact a five-part narrative which deals with Ramakrishna's childhood, his years as a *sādhaka*, and later his years as a teacher training his disciples. As Saradananda wrote to an American friend on June 18, 1914:

> The book [part 3 of the book, which Saradananda wrote first] is not really on the life of Sri Ramakrishna but on Sri Ramakrishna as the spiritual guide and can be counted as a philosophical analysis of that side of his character only … My plan is to present a complete picture of Sri Ramakrishna (the various phases of his character) when the series will be completed. The series is more along the line of writings which has been called in German as Character-build. (Prabhananda 1997, 274)

There were several motivations which prompted the project. In the Ramakrishna Order's Bengali journal, *Udbodhan*, innumerable articles arrived for publication in the early years of the twentieth century, no doubt in response to the growing interest in Ramakrishna's life and teachings. Many of the articles abounded in factual errors. As editor and publisher of the journal, Saradananda felt the need for an authentic biography.

Another motivation for Saradananda's book was his desire to dispel the view, propagated in the early days by M, that many people—primarily Ramakrishna's monastic disciples—had ignored the message of Ramakrishna's life and had pursued a path which was basically counter to Ramakrishna's teachings. M's primary objection was to the ideal of *sevā*, service, which was given considerable attention in the movement. Significantly, it was Sarada Devi who categorically stated that *sevā* was indeed "Thakur's work," thus completely and permanently changing M's mind on the subject (Gambhirananda, 210).[17]

A more down-to-earth reason for the *Līlāprasaṅga*'s publication was to raise funds to pay off at least part of the money borrowed to build a house (*Māyer Bāri*) for Sarada in Kolkata. Finally, there remained the simple fact that many of Ramakrishna's admirers and disciples, lay and monastic, had either died or were on the verge of doing so, and for this reason Saradananda felt it was important to preserve for posterity their reminiscences and memories of Ramakrishna. Accordingly, he issued an appeal in the *Udbodhan* to all who had met Ramakrishna to share what they knew about him. Much of that material, after a careful verification process, later found a place in the *Līlāprasaṅga*.

Saradananda's secretary, Swami Aseshananda, noted that of all Ramakrishna's monastic disciples, only Saradananda kept a diary of day-to-day events. While Hindu sādhus traditionally placed little to no importance on either time or historicity, Saradananda was constituted altogether differently—paying careful attention to historical detail and taking great pains to record in the *Līlāprasaṅga* only those incidents which could be verified. "He would unceasingly encourage me," Aseshananda wrote, "to distinguish what I had seen from what I had heard from others and then to verify the truth of what I had heard. He was a staunch admirer and uncompromising advocate of truth—both historical (*vyāvahārika*) and transcendental truth" (Aseshananda 1982, 49–50).

If that be the case, then Saradananda's situating of careful historical research on his subject against his larger backdrop of the *līlā* of an avatar (*Śrī-Śrī-Rāmakṛṣṇa-Līlāprasaṅga* literally means "incidents from the *līlā* of Ramakrishna") is an example of the conflict between the worldviews in which Bengal's educated middle-class found themselves. As we have seen, M attempted to balance his Western intellectual background with the contrasting worldview which Ramakrishna presents. Ramakrishna and European thinkers are placed together, along with biblical references and Sanskrit verses from the Upaniṣads and Bhagavad Gītā. By contrast, Ramchandra Datta does not address Western intellectual concerns at all.

Saradananda takes an entirely different route by placing Ramakrishna's life in the realm of eternal *līlā*, the divine play of the avatar. While Ramakrishna's life is to be understood as entirely different from ordinary human lives, Saradananda nevertheless simultaneously presents a wealth of carefully acquired data to accurately present the incidents of the avatar's earthly life. It is interesting that Saradananda's contemporary Bankimchandra Chattopadhyay presents Kṛṣṇa in his famed *Kṛṣṇacarita* as an ideal man, not an avatar. Faced with choosing East or West, Bankim veers West, with all that this implied.

Saradananda takes the opposite tack, and this very divergence is symbolic of the larger questions which Bengal's intelligentsia faced. Saradananda presents what are seemingly miraculous elements in Ramakrishna's birth to a presumably skeptical audience. Saradananda addresses these doubts by noting that other avatars—Rāma, Kṛṣṇa, Buddha, Jesus, Caitanya, Śaṅkara—also had miraculous events surrounding their birth, which could not be explained by Western reason.

While the West had made enormous strides in physical sciences, Saradananda writes, its materialistic outlook "could not show the way to the knowledge of the Atman" (LP 1.16). Thus, in the most important area of human life, that of God-realization, India stood above all. Partha Chatterjee discusses this problematic of the material and the spiritual within the context of the nineteenth-century Bengali intelligentsia, who at this point were painfully aware of the "incompleteness of the claims of the modern West to a superior culture." For this very reason, the intelligentsia would assert

> the sovereignty of the nation over the domain of spirituality. . . . Saradananda himself was very much a part of the middle-class culture of Bengal that had, by the turn of the century, come to accept these criteria as fundamental in framing of questions of cultural choice. (Chatterjee, 48)

Thus, it would be a mistake to think that Saradananda (or Vivekananda, for that matter) was exceptional in positing an essentialist East-is-spiritual versus West-is-materialistic argument. This dichotomy was the very basis of the middle-class's dilemma. It was a "cultural choice" which the middle-class had to make in order to navigate their particular world. As Chatterjee notes, "The assertion of spirituality would have to rest on an essential difference between East and West, and the domain of autonomy thus defined would have to be ordered on one's own terms, not on those set by the conqueror in the material world" (49).

Therefore when faced with the same question that M addressed: How would they—as English-educated members of the Bengali elite and as disciples of Ramakrishna—place Ramakrishna within the context of India's religious heritage and India's domination by the West, Saradananda takes his stand on India's religious heritage, placing Ramakrishna squarely in the tradition of the avatar and his *līlā*.

Divided into five parts and published between the years 1911 and 1918, the *Līlāprasaṅga* is a massive book spanning more than 1500 pages. It does not cover the entire story of Ramakrishna's life. It begins with his birth in 1836 and concludes with his stay at Shyampukur in Kolkata for the treatment of cancer. In 1935, eight years after Saradananda's death, his article in the *Udbodhan* which covered a few of the incidents in the Cossipore garden house was added as an appendix to the fourth edition of the fifth part. From the notes discovered among Saradananda's papers it is evident that he wanted to write a sixth part incorporating Ramakrishna's last days. However, with the death of Sarada Devi in 1920, he apparently lost any impetus to complete his magnum opus, and for this reason an account of the last days of Ramakrishna is missing from the book. Instead, Saradananda became involved in the building of a temple to Sarada Devi in her native village of Jayrambati.

From all appearances it would seem that when Saradananda began writing the *Līlāprasaṅga*, he did not envision composing Ramakrishna's complete biography, and for this reason the book was not written in chronological order. Saradananda began with a description of Ramakrishna as the spiritual teacher, which eventually formed the third part of the *Līlāprasaṅga*. Initially, chapters of the book were serialized in the Bengali journal *Udbodhan*. Since incidents from Ramakrishna's life had already appeared in magazine articles and in several books prior to the *Līlāprasaṅga*, Saradananda focused his attention primarily on locating a unifying principle that integrated all the known events of Ramakrishna's life as well as his teachings. Saradananda found that principle in the concept of *bhāvamukha*, "the threshold of consciousness," which is his original contribution to the analysis and understanding of Ramakrishna's life.[18]

Apart from his own firsthand knowledge of many of the incidents mentioned in the book, Saradananda's sources included: the elderly villagers of Kamarpukur who shared with him their knowledge of Ramakrishna's early life; Ramakrishna's nephew and attendant Hriday, who was a direct witness to Ramakrishna's extensive sādhana; Sarada Devi, who was able to share aspects of her husband's life that only she was in a position to do; and devotees and disciples of Ramakrishna, who had met with Ramakrishna on different occasions, in different places, and for different reasons. The most important resource for Saradananda was obviously Ramakrishna himself, who freely shared his spiritual experiences and visions with his disciples.

With such a rich abundance of firsthand sources, the *Līlāprasaṅga* succeeds in taking the reader as close to its central character as any good biography should. Ramakrishna provided his students with the insights and teachings meant to help them in their own particular sādhana. For this reason, it is helpful to study the *Kathāmṛta*, the *Jībanabṛttānta* and the *Līlāprasaṅga* in tandem, along with the very significant views of Ramakrishna that are available through the reminiscences of Sarada Devi and Ramakrishna's disciples.[19] Together, these texts provide a much more comprehensive picture of Ramakrishna's personality and teachings than the study of only one or two books.

Apart from his famed *Līlāprasaṅga*, Saradananda also wrote *Bhārate Śakti Pūjā* ("Mother Worship in India"), which he dedicated to Sarada Devi. This is a significant point since recent interpreters, notably Jeffrey Kripal, have consistently pegged Saradananda as a "renouncer" Vedāntin to the exclusion of other traditions. Saradananda, however, found no conflict between Tantra and Vedānta. A devotee of Kālī, Saradananda undertook the discipline of Tantric worship under the guidance of his uncle, Ishwar Chandra Chakravarty, a Tantric adept (Aseshananda 1982, 81). It is important to note that he underwent this sādhana long after he had taken his sannyāsa vows. Saradananda obviously saw no conflict between the philosophy and practice of Tantra and the philosophy and practice of Vedānta.

Early Interpreters

> There is no discipline, no structure of knowledge, no institution or epistemology that can or has ever stood free of the various sociocultural, historical, and political formations that give epochs their peculiar individuality.
>
> -Edward Said, *Jean François Lyotard: Critical Evaluations in Cultural Theory*

Max Müller

A liberal Christian and a scholar of international renown, Frederich Max Müller (1823–1900) believed in the scientific study of religion, progressive revelation and a universalized, liberal Christianity. Like his earlier Orientalist forebears, Müller held as sacred the Enlightenment ideals of reason, science and, above all, progress. An ardent admirer of Kant, he translated his *Critique of Pure Reason* into English in 1881, and the imprint of Kant's philosophy on Müller can be seen not only in Müller's understanding of Hinduism, but also in his understanding of Ramakrishna and the material he was willing to validate concerning him. That Müller's Vedānta was not necessarily the same Vedānta as understood by Ramakrishna or other Hindus did not give him pause. It merely meant that much work had to be done in educating Hindus as to what Vedānta really was.

Müller was the progenitor of *Religionswissenschaft*, literally, the "science of religion," which he modeled after another newly minted "science," comparative linguistics. As comparative linguistics had aimed at uncovering the lost secrets of Indo-European languages, so Müller believed that a similar comparative methodology would uncover religions' hidden truths. Müller's *Religionswissenschaft* set out to prove this truth. Müller wrote that the "Science of Religion will for the first time assign to Christianity its right place among the religions of the world; ... it will restore to the whole of history of the world, in its unconscious progress towards Christianity, its true and sacred character" (Müller 1869, xx).

Yet despite what Sharada Sugirtharajah calls in this regard Müller's "spiritual colonialism" (Sugirtharajah 2003, 64), for Müller's day *Religionswissenschaft* was a truly radical proposal in that it advocated that Christianity be subjected to the same mode of inquiry as other religions. Equally radical was Müller's belief that truth was available outside Christianity.

From the haven of his Oxford study, Müller maintained a lively interest in the Indian religious affairs of his day and held an abiding concern for "purifying" Hinduism. Müller had taken particular interest in the Brahmo Samaj, whose monotheistic credo and denunciation of image worship fit his Protestant idealism like a glove. Both the Brahmo Samaj and Müller believed that true Hindu worship should consist of pure contemplation.

Along with pure contemplation, Müller longed for the Christianization of Hinduism, hoping that Brahmo Samaj members would eventually designate themselves as Christians, declaring themselves to be either "Christian Brahmos" or "Christian Aryas" (Müller 1902, 419). In that hope Müller was to be disappointed, but he never gave up on purifying Hinduism. In his last, 1894 letter to his friend, the Brahmo leader Pratap Mazumdar, Müller wrote: "When you think of the popular Hinduism of the present day, with its idol-worship, its Pujahs, its temple-service, its caste, its mendicants, surely you do not approve, you rather shrink from them" (428).

It was from Pratap Mazumdar, Müller's trusty correspondent, that he first heard of Ramakrishna. In fact, the first published compilation of Ramakrishna's sayings appeared in a long essay by Mazumdar in the *Sunday Mirror* (April 16, 1876), and Müller read this essay when it was reprinted in *Theistic Quarterly Review* (October–December 1879). Predictably, Mazumdar presented Ramakrishna largely devoid of the vestiges of popular Hinduism that Müller—and Mazumdar—abhorred. Müller's interest was piqued and he established contact with both Keshab Sen and Pratap Mazumdar. The result of Müller's interest and correspondence was his article "A Real Mahatman," which appeared in the *Nineteenth Century* in August 1896. The sayings of Ramakrishna which Müller included in his article were largely taken from the journal *Brahmavadin*.[20] The other sayings apparently had their source in Müller's personal correspondence with Mazumdar (Beckerlegge, 11).

Certainly Müller's commitment to the "science" of religion had much to do with his particular interest in Ramakrishna. Having at his disposal a friendly informant who knew Ramakrishna, Müller had a unique vantage point to witness the early stages of a new religious movement. Yet the mere fact that Müller wrote about Ramakrishna at all was a crossing of the Rubicon. As the best-known Indologist of his time and a scholar of international renown, Müller brought immediate recognition to Ramakrishna and his teachings. For the larger Western world—and particularly in India—appreciation from a man such as Müller bore enormous weight. Further, Müller's standing ensured serious interest from later Western scholars. Ramakrishna would appear again in J. N. Farquhar's classic *Modern Hindu Religious Movements* and, as we shall see, in Romain Rolland's books on Ramakrishna and Vivekananda. Both authors relied significantly on Müller for their background information. More than any other factor, it was Müller's interest in Ramakrishna that plucked the latter from the relative obscurity of Bengal and placed him before the scholars of the Western world as an object of interest.

In April 1896 Müller sent Vivekananda a postcard, thanking him for a pamphlet, and expressing his admiration for "Rama Krishna Paramahansa" (Burke, 170). Vivekananda's response was apparently positive, for that very month Müller again wrote Vivekananda:

> As for your beloved master of blessed memory, Bhagaban Sri Ram Krishan, how can I ever tell you what he is to me, I love and worship him with my whole heart. To think of him makes my eyes fill with tears of gladness that I was permitted to hear of him. His sayings, published in the Brahmavadin, are my greatest delight. . . . If I might only have known him, while he was yet with us! My greatest desire is to one day visit the spot which [was] sanctified by his presence. (Burke, 170–71)

Müller's effusive response arose from his own Westernized perception of a Kantian Hindu exemplar, who simply did not exist. In response to Müller's warm invitation, Vivekananda, then in London, visited Müller at his Oxford home. It is likely that Müller saw Vivekananda as a potential partner in his goal of purifying Hinduism via promoting appropriately deracinated Hindu saints. Müller wrote in his June 22 letter to Vivekananda that he would be "very glad to write a larger and fuller account … if sufficient materials were forthcoming" (Burke, 171). Pleased, Vivekananda immediately asked Swami Saradananda, then also in London, to provide Ramakrishna's biographical material.[21]

When Müller asked for a collection of Ramakrishna's sayings, Vivekananda asked his brother-disciple Ramakrishnananda to provide it, while specifying the tenor of the material to be included: "Max Müller wants all the sayings of Shri Ramakrishna classified, that is, all on Karma in one place, on Vairagya in another place, so on Bhakti, Jnana, etc., etc. You must undertake to do this forthwith. . . . We must take care to present only the universal aspect of his teachings" (CW 6.364). Vivekananda knew that Müller could only appreciate that part of

Ramakrishna's teachings which would meld easily with his pre-existent worldview. Anything too far removed from that graph would only elicit patronizing devaluation or outright dismissal.

Even so, Müller was evidently displeased with the material he received from Ramakrishna's disciples: "I applied ... to one of [Ramakrishna's] most eminent pupils, Vivekananda, asking him to write down for me what he could tell of his own knowledge of his venerable teacher. . . . It will be easily seen, however, that even this account is not quite free from traditional elements" (RLS, 24).

Those "traditional elements"—defined by Müller as the "dialogic process"—were the "irrepressible miraculizing tendencies of devoted disciples" which mythologized the historical facts of a teacher's life (30). Since Europeans had cornered the market on rational thinking, anything incomprehensible to a nineteenth-century European intellectual was branded as foolish. Moreover, progressive Europeans equated truth with historical events. To give credence to anything outside linear time was to endorse mythology over history, fiction over fact. As Müller wrote in his autobiography, "Vivekananda and the other followers of Ramakrishna ought ... to teach their followers how to distinguish between the perfervid utterances of their teacher, Ramakrishna, an enthusiastic Bhakta (devotee), and the clear and dry style of the Sūtras of Bādarāyana. The Vedānta spirit is there, but the form often becomes too vague and exaggerated to give us an idea of what the true Gnānin (knower) ought to be" (1899, 169).

"Ought to be" is the operative phrase here. As much as Vivekananda had attempted to give Müller the material he wished, neither Ramakrishna nor Vivekananda was able to measure up to Müller's expectations. Vivekananda himself was acutely, indeed personally, aware of the West's limits of acceptance, and therefore publicly emphasized only what seemed rational and "scientific" according to the lights of the Western day. Vivekananda's meeting with Müller had been preceded by three years of living in the West, where he had actively defended Hinduism against specious, and often vicious, criticism.

Müller did what he could with what he considered somewhat tainted material: he divided the book between a lengthy introduction and an assemblage of Ramakrishna's sayings, placing Ramakrishna squarely in India's Vedānta tradition. Müller announced: "Vedānta-philosophy ... is the very marrow running through all the bones of Rāmakrishna's doctrine" (RLS, 70). Müller recounts the biographical details of Ramakrishna's life which he received from Vivekananda (written by Saradananda).

Interjected at times are Müller's editorial comments, adding the rational adult voice to neutralize the presumed incipient mythologizing process. Dwelling at length on the "dialogic process," he seems to sigh in resignation at the "childish love of the miraculous" which infects the oral tradition (28). Müller also quotes from a letter from his correspondent Pratap Mazumdar about Ramakrishna's weaknesses: his occasionally "abominably filthy language" (62), his ignorance of Sanskrit, and the "almost barbarous treatment of his wife" (64).

What prompted Mazumdar's letter was Müller's fatal suggestion that Keshab was Ramakrishna's disciple. A deeply committed Brahmo teacher, Mazumdar was enraged by Müller's claim and shot off a letter which enumerated Ramakrishna's flaws (which would then render absurd the notion of Keshab's "discipleship").

Letting out all the stops, Mazumdar accused Ramakrishna—as if his celibacy, his occasional use of "abominably filthy" language and lack of education weren't bad enough—of not showing "sufficient moral abhorrence of prostitutes" and of not honoring "the principle of teetotalism according to Western notions" (67).

Müller, who seemed to enjoy a good fight, defended Ramakrishna against Mazumdar's charges: about language Müller noted that there is "a great difference between what is filthy and what is meant to be filthy" (RLS, 62).[22] Müller did not see Ramakrishna's lack of education as an insurmountable flaw (perhaps because as a Hindu, Ramakrishna would never be expected to measure up to a European in the first place), coolly noting that he never believed Ramakrishna to be the originator of the Vedānta philosophy, nor did Ramakrishna possess "scholarlike knowledge" of the Vedānta philosophy (69). If Ramakrishna did not show sufficient abhorrence of prostitutes, Müller writes, "he does not stand quite alone in this among the founders of religion." As for being tolerant of alcohol (and presumably alcoholics), Müller writes that "no one ... has ever accused him of any excess in drinking" (67).

It is telling that concerning Ramakrishna's relationship with Sarada Devi, Müller declares that it is by no means unusual for such couples to "decline to live *maritalement*" (64). As an aside, it is useful to observe how the Western Zeitgeist has inevitably affected the interpretation of Ramakrishna and Sarada's lack of sexual relations. Müller and later Ramakrishna interpreters, up to the time of Jeffrey Masson, did not perceive Ramakrishna's and Sarada's celibacy as inherently pathological. As Freudian theory gradually percolated throughout Western culture, particularly after the 1960's sexual revolution, Western views on sexuality and Western sexual standards dramatically changed. So, naturally, did interpretations of Ramakrishna's and Sarada's rejection of sexual relations.

Taken as a whole, Müller's book—while often patronizing and chauvinistic—is largely sympathetic. Considering Müller's basic worldview and cultural milieu, *Ramakrishna: His Life and Sayings* is remarkable for its breadth and for its expressed desire to bridge an enormous cultural gap and engage with a radically different man from a radically different religious tradition. While extraordinarily broad in his views, Müller—a pioneer in many ways—remained a man of his era. His outlook was basically one of sympathy and for this he was harshly criticized by many of his contemporaries. Müller did not seem to care what his critics thought. His genuine love for India (which was made far easier by the fact that he never went there), his dedication and heartfelt appreciation of many elements of the Hindu tradition cannot be questioned. If we judge Müller solely from hindsight's high ground, we do both Müller and Indology a disservice.

Should one feel the urge to reproach Müller for cultural and religious chauvinism, the enormous contribution he made to Indology should be equally remembered. It is tempting to congratulate ourselves about how we have advanced in our thinking and how much times have changed. It is easy to dismiss eighteenth- and nineteenth-century Orientalists as conscious or unconscious racists, or European chauvinists with colonialist agendas, but a facile dismissal inhibits further investigation. The inquiry needs to proceed to the point where we ask how much Orientalism and a Western universalizing paradigm have persisted up to this day. The closer we look, the more we discover how much both these elements are still in place, though in more subtle (and therefore more invidious) forms.

Dhan Gopal Mukerji

If Vivekananda was concerned that the Western world receive only the "universal aspect" of Ramakrishna, Dhan Gopal Mukerji (1890–1936) either did not get the message or did not care. *The Face of Silence*, published in 1926, provides a splendid example of a writer sacrificing the banality of historicity for the *frisson* of romantic Oriental ambience. The book also offers an equally splendid example of Westernized Indians assimilating the Orientalist romantic stereotype and mirroring the stereotype back for Western consumption. As with all colonized people, the stereotype was frequently internalized and resubmitted to the colonizers.

"Do you seek the Ramá Krishna history, or the Rama Krishna legend?" was the purported question posed to Dhan Gopal Mukerji by the "Pundit" (clearly meant to be M). Mukerji's reply is significant: "I seek just enough facts to enable me to gather all the trustworthy legends together." The Pundit allegedly replied, "Good! . . . Rama Krishna legends have not been gathered together. They contain more of the truth about him than all the authentic facts that I have written down" (Mukerji, 12–13).

The Face of Silence thus presents a romantic rendering of Hindu holy otherness, tending as much to fable as to fact. Like every good fable, the pattern is predictable, with the particulars embroidered to make the tale more exotic and appealing. Mukerji reports that, following the Pundit's advice, he sought out elderly villagers who knew Ramakrishna in his earlier years (13–14): "In order to study the life of Rama Krishna I began to look for its chroniclers and not the chronicle" (7). One wonders where Mukerji found his chroniclers, since we see little in *The Face of Silence* to indicate the testimonies of the villagers, let alone the testimonies of Ramakrishna's disciples. Apart from basic biography, Mukerji's book is based in romantic Oriental flights of fantasy, coated with the sugared enthusiasms of his close friend Josephine MacLeod, an American student of Vivekananda.

While Kālī is discussed with loving, if detached, appreciation (21–22), the topic is not Mukerji's great interest. If none of Ramakrishna's Tantric sādhanas are discussed, neither are Ramakrishna's Vaiṣṇava sādhanas nor any other sādhana. The omission seems to have little to do with Mukerji's contacts with the Ramakrishna Order: Romain Rolland's journal states that Mukerji's original interest was Śaṅkara.[23] Clearly Mukerji was among Bengal's highly educated elite. Westernized and urbane, he was nostalgic for his native roots but too "civilized" to identify with them.[24] The book predictably dwells upon Ramakrishna's "Hindu reform" milieu, as well as Ramakrishna's forays into Christianity and Islam.

While *The Face of Silence* contains the basic and familiar outlines of Ramakrishna's biography, many details are hilariously creative. In what would work better in a pious tale of a Christian priest's path to sainthood, Mukerji writes of the young Ramakrishna, whose family "decided to dedicate him to the priesthood" because of his earnest devotion (18). Yet Mukerji certainly knew that the priesthood was hereditary—whether Ramakrishna was earnestly devoted or not had nothing to do with the simple fact that Ramakrishna was born into a family of priests. Moreover, Ramakrishna became a priest at the Dakshineswar temple because his older brother had sent for him and had asked for his assistance.

To add interest to his tale, Mukerji paints Rani Rasmani in larger-than-life terms. While Rani Rasmani was undoubtedly a wealthy and intelligent landowner, she was hardly "one of the most able rulers that feudal India has known" (18). Rani Rasmani was from the fisherman caste and, because of her low caste, no brahmin priest would agree to officiate at the temple she had built at Dakshineswar. Indeed, Ramakrishna's elder brother was the only priest whom Rasmani could find who would agree to assume the position. Yet perhaps to make the story redolent of European fables of queens, princes and poor but pious priests, Mukerji refers to Rani Rasmani as "Queen Rash Mani" and her family as "the royal household" (19); Ramakrishna's duties as temple priest are described as "administering a royal chapel" (20). Continuing along these lines, Mukerji writes that in order to live a life of renunciation while serving as a priest in the Kālī temple, the young Ramakrishna

> refused to eat from plates of gold, waited on by a dozen servants ... He moved from his sumptuously furnished residence into the little room near the servants' quarters where he lived for the rest of his life. . . . No more did he put on himself the ceremonial garlands of pearls, dhoti, the vestment of scarlet silk, the chuddar of gossamer blue shot with bits of diamonds like stars. He refused to wave censors of gold before his deity, and gave up reading to the people from a book held between gold-embossed covers. (24)

One must appreciate Mukerji's vivid palette here. No poor Bengali priest would ever eat off a plate of gold nor would he be waited upon by a dozen servants. One also must wonder what book—gold-embossed—Mukerji had in mind that the functionally illiterate Ramakrishna could have read "to the people." As for the "chuddar of gossamer blue shot with bits of diamonds like stars," again, pure Oriental fantasy—Arabian Nights transported to the Ganges. Mukerji grieves that "the commentaries that Rama Krishna made on the New Testament, the Koran, and other holy books have not been preserved" (69). Ramakrishna never produced such commentaries. Equally comical, Mukerji portrays the nahabat where Sarada lived as a high tower (one visualizes a Hindu Rapunzel) (33).

Either despite of, or more likely because of, the fairytale quality of Mukerji's book (he was given the Newbery Medal for Children's literature for a later book), *The Face of Silence* played a major role in making Ramakrishna's life and teachings known to a Western audience.

Pre-digested as it was for Western consumption, it found a ready audience there. Published in 1926, *The Face of Silence* was chosen by the League of Nations as one of the forty outstanding books of 1926 and was chosen for the International Library of Geneva (Prabuddhaprana 1990, 202). At this juncture we again encounter Vivekananda's peripatetic student, Josephine MacLeod: it was MacLeod who gave this book to her friend Romain Rolland, and it was this romanticized Ramakrishna that caught Rolland's attention (Vrajaprana 2006, 1103–104).

As an interesting aside, Mukerji quotes the Pundit as saying that when "[Ramakrishna] spoke of God a light unknown on earth would come on his face; then if he touched anyone with his hand or foot that person would see the whole world bathed in radiance, and *Ananda* (Bliss) for at least three to four days" (Mukerji, 15). Since *Kālī's Child* regards Ramakrishna touching male devotees with his foot "troubling," it is significant that someone as attuned to both high-caste Bengali mores (Mukerji refers to himself as a brahmin more than once) as well as Western sensitivities should write about Ramakrishna touching someone with his foot not only without demur but with positive enthusiasm.

Romain Rolland

In his day, Romain Rolland (1866–1944) was considered the greatest living French writer, having won the Nobel Prize for Literature in 1915 for his magisterial *Jean-Christophe*. As with Müller's imprimatur, the advocacy of Rolland would ensure Ramakrishna's fame and the appreciation of other Western intellectuals. A humanist and idealist sickened by Europe's devastation following World War I, Rolland believed that Ramakrishna's (and Vivekananda's) teachings could bring unity and harmony to a "fever-stricken Europe, which has murdered sleep" (LR, 14). This kind of romanticization, as Richard King has noted, carries within itself "the implicit (and sometimes explicit) criticism of contemporary elements of the Orientalists's own culture" and "for many of the Romantics 'the Mystic East' represented the spirituality that much of contemporary Christian religion seemed to lack" (King 1999b, 97).

Thus, in setting up Ramakrishna as India's restorative to a European dystopia, Rolland settled into a European Romantic fantasy which succeeded in obscuring Ramakrishna as thoroughly as any other Orientalist. Rolland's interest was not Ramakrishna; it was Europe. His interest in Ramakrishna extended only so far as he presumed Ramakrishna could effect a change in Europe's existing modus operandi. Both Rolland and Mukerji exoticized Ramakrishna—a process which exchanges a human being for a blank canvas upon which one applies particular ideals and goals.[25]

World War I was a catastrophic shock to the West following a period of great optimism that had characterized the years up to 1914. To many in the West it seemed clear that somewhere on its march to perfection, the West had gotten lost. For a number of European intellectuals, the East offered directions. Rolland was so enthused about *The Face of Silence* that Josephine MacLeod gave him another book, the *Life of Ramakrishna*, published by the Ramakrishna Order.[26] That provoked Rolland to initiate correspondence with Ramakrishna's disciple, Swami Shivananda, then President of the Ramakrishna Order.

Although he did not acknowledge it, Rolland's humanist ideology was fundamentally at odds with Ramakrishna's worldview, which perceived the world as only temporarily remediable, but intrinsically unfixable. Rolland clearly felt more comfortable with Vivekananda, whose "mournful and heroic obsession of universal suffering" (Rolland 1990, 86) neatly fit Rolland's romantic presuppositions. In reality, however, Vivekananda's views of human suffering had little in common with Rolland's ("To talk of evil and misery is nonsense, because they do not exist outside" [CW 2.137]). By the mid-1930s Rolland gave up his interest in religion, becoming increasingly interested in socialism and combating fascism through armed resistance.

Before realizing he was barking up the wrong philosophical tree, however, Rolland was determined to locate in India's wisdom the antidote for political madness and human suffering. Rolland believed that India's religious teachers shared one universal goal: "human unity through God" (LR, 8). Rolland blithely assumed that this *was* their shared goal, his European humanist presuppositions rolling over any inconvenient Hindu reality. Rolland found the unity he sought, and to this Unity—which he personified as a goddess—he dedicated *La Vie de Ramakrishna* [*The Life of Ramakrishna*]: "The essence is Unity … And it is She whom I adore … To her I dedicate this new book … to the great Goddess, Unity" (1947, 16–17). Heady words indeed.

Unlike Müller, Rolland had a wealth of translated material to use for his research, though he assures the reader that none of this made him abdicate "one iota of my free judgment as a man of the West" (LR, 1). Rolland not only corresponded with Swami Shivananda but also with M, the recorder of *The Gospel of Sri Ramakrishna*, and Swami Ashokananda. Rolland's source material included early editions of *The Gospel*, *The Great Master*, Müller's *Ramakrishna: His Life and Sayings*, as well as Mukerji's *Face of Silence*. Perhaps as importantly, two of Vivekananda's American disciples, Josephine MacLeod and Christina Greenstidel, provided him a large number of contacts and unpublished material (Beckerlegge, 19–20).

Significantly and presciently, Rolland also shared a warm and illuminating correspondence with Freud. Rolland sent Freud his biographies of both Ramakrishna and Vivekananda, asking for Freud's analysis of the mystic's "oceanic feeling" described by Rolland in Ramakrishna's biography.[27] This correspondence was to have far-reaching consequences, for it was Rolland who brought to Freud's attention the forever-famous "oceanic feeling." Marianna Torgovnick writes:

> Romain Rolland wrote a book whose implications staggered Sigmund Freud and shook ... Freud's belief in the inevitability and rightness of civilization. . . . Rolland believed that the experience of dissolved boundaries and the interpenetration of the self with the cosmos is a universal spiritual experience. His model was the life of Ramakrishna, in which the Hindu saint describes himself several times as being like salt dissolved in the great ocean of the universe. (11)

Since that landmark correspondence, this "oceanic feeling" has been an unending source of debate concerning the nature of mystical experience. It is worth remembering that not only did Rolland coin the term, but he also found the oceanic feeling to be, as he wrote Freud, "a source of vital renewal" (1990, 87). For Freud and many others, however, the "oceanic feeling" was a threat to the mature, civilized man. Escaping the norms of controlled behavior in search of the oceanic experience was viewed by Freud as infantile regression (we can connect the dots to the Orientalist view of India being inhabited by irresponsible children). Importantly, Freud further believed that an individual's desire to merge into the cosmic was associated with the death wish. Freud's views will linger with us as we analyze the development of Ramakrishna studies through the twentieth century.

Freud took eighteen months to answer Rolland's letter and his response is telling: "Your letter ... containing your remarks about a feeling you describe as 'oceanic' has left me no peace" (Freud, 388). Freud wrestled with its implications in his landmark work *Civilization and Its Discontents*, a copy of which he sent to Rolland. Despite their warm and intriguing correspondence, in the end Rolland found psychoanalysis fascinating but ultimately deficient when it came to understanding mystical experience.[28] Freud, in his turn, wrote Rolland: "To me mysticism is just as closed a book as music. . . . And yet it is easier for you than for us to read the human soul!" (389).

In contrast to late-twentieth-century scholars, Rolland found Saradananda's biography "the most interesting and the most reliable" (LR, 34). In sharper contrast, Rolland found no reason to question the authenticity of the material he received from his sources. Because of Rolland's international stature, both *La Vie de Ramakrishna* and *La Vie de Vivekananda et L'Evangile Universel*, published in 1929 and 1930, respectively, were soon translated into a number of languages and received wide appreciation. For the young Ramakrishna movement, these were graced days indeed. Instead of the typical view of India as a colonized and therefore powerless country, one of Europe's leading thinkers was actively commending Ramakrishna and Vivekananda as a remedy for Western afflictions.

Rolland's *Life of Ramakrishna* centers on the life of Ramakrishna rather than his teachings. While Ramakrishna's teachings are nestled to a degree within the biography, Rolland's emphasis remains on Ramakrishna's life and what Rolland sees as its larger meaning for humanity. Rolland's book follows the biographical pattern found in the *Life of Ramakrishna* published by the Ramakrishna Order (which is basically a simplified version of Saradananda's *Līlāprasaṅga* with a significant amount of material from M's *Kathāmṛta*), and he enriches this text with the material provided by his insider correspondents.

In its concern with the "subjective reality of living impressions" rather than "objective reality," Rolland's *Life* stands in marked contrast to Müller's, though Rolland commends Müller's "precious little book" written by the "great master of learning" (LR, 21). Compared to Müller's dry, analytical style, Rolland's prose billows with excess—he seeks to inspire as much as to educate. While he addresses introductory notes to both Eastern and Western readers, Rolland basically directs his gaze at the West, stating at the beginning that he sees Ramakrishna as a man, not an incarnation, and places Christ and Buddha in the same rank.

In a letter to Shivananda, Rolland indicates his concern over Ramakrishna's lack of engagement in human suffering, and Rolland answers this concern by writing that as far as he could assess, philanthropy found no essential place in Ramakrishna's teachings (201–2). "But meanwhile humanity is suffering, humanity is dying, abandoned. Is it to be left without help? Certainly not. For that which Ramakrishna never accomplished. . . . he left to his greatest disciple … Vivekananda" (203–4). Rolland concludes his biography of Ramakrishna by directing his readers to Vivekananda, informing them that his next volume will be on Ramakrishna's heir.

Interpretations by Monks of the Ramakrishna Order

Apart from the source books written by Ramakrishna's contemporaries, a number of books were written by monks of the Ramakrishna Order which interpreted Ramakrishna's life and teachings. We will discuss three books in particular which were written on the occasion of Ramakrishna's birth centenary in 1936 and reflect the respective environments of the swamis as well as the concerns of their era. None of these books attracted attention outside the Ramakrishna Order. Each of these books focuses on what the author considers to be the essential message of Ramakrishna. All three writers see Ramakrishna as one who regenerated India and, more importantly, all three swamis see Ramakrishna's life and teachings as having global significance.

Swami Ghanananda's *Sri Ramakrishna and His Unique Message* was written at the request of Ramakrishna's disciple and Ramakrishna Order President Swami Shivananda.[29] First published in 1937 and substantially revised both in 1946 and 1970, the book's third edition contains a foreword by historian Arnold Toynbee. Ghanananda's book takes an overarching view of Ramakrishna, examining his life and teachings in terms of world history. Accordingly there is substantially less biographical material on Ramakrishna, as the book emphasizes his ideas, particularly those on religious harmony. The book's central thesis is that "Ramakrishna is the supreme reconciler of religions, the outstanding teacher of synthesis and harmony. . . . Ramakrishna reconciled the religions and schools, sects and paths of the modern world" (Ghanananda, 115).

Swami Ghanananda (1898–1969) was head of the Ramakrishna Vedanta Centre in London from 1948 through 1969, and the book reflects the needs and concerns of a war-traumatized Europe. Just as Romain Rolland presented Ramakrishna as a prophet of harmony to heal a wounded continent, so did Ghanananda see Ramakrishna's message as the solution to the West's seeming impulse to destruction. Toynbee's Foreword states that "the only way of salvation for mankind is an Indian way. . . . here we have the attitude and the spirit that can make it possible for the human race to grow together into a single family … this is the only alternative to destroying ourselves" (viii).

Ghanananda's book explicitly deals with colonialism, seeing it as a significant factor not only in India's plight but also in the world's disorder. "When one nation conquers another," writes Ghanananda, "it attempts to justify its subjugation of the vanquished by claiming cultural superiority. That is why we hear of 'the White Man's burden' of civilizing the non-white races of the earth. Such a burden means not only the heartless exploitation of the natural resources of the conquered countries, but also the duty of raising them to the level of the rulers in culture and civilization. . . . It may be asked, 'Why do cultures and civilizations clash?' The answer is simple: man is neither able nor willing to recognize that other cultures and civilizations have a value, and are as good and necessary for others as his own is for himself" (4–5).

Swami Nirvedananda's *Sri Ramakrishna and Spiritual Renaissance* (1940) takes a wider, yet more Indian approach than Ghanananda—not altogether surprising since Nirvedananda (1893–1958) remained in India his entire life. According to Nirvedananda, Ramakrishna's particular strength was spiritual realization, which he declares to be the "keynote of Hinduism." It was Ramakrishna's realization, Nirvedananda states, which allowed him to reconcile both the extremely conservative and the radical elements of Hindu society (19). Like Ghanananda, Nirvedananda discusses Ramakrishna's various sādhanas. He pays particular attention to the synthesizing elements in Ramakrishna's life. Ramakrishna, for example, continued to have relationships with his family members after his sannyāsa, against the traditional Hindu norm for sannyāsis. Thus, for Ramakrishna, "the Absolute and the relative were equally divine. It was this position ... on the threshold of relative consciousness [*bhāvamukha*] that enabled him to fuse the apparently contradictory schemes of monastic and householder's life into an undivided synthetic attitude" (112).

Compelling, also, is the book's discussion of Ramakrishna and humanitarian service. Nirvedananda gives the famous example of Sambhu Mallick informing Ramakrishna that he wanted to spend his money on hospitals and schools. Ramakrishna's oft-quoted reply was: "Suppose God appears before you; then will you ask him to build hospitals and dispensaries for you? A lover of God never says that" (KA 1.51). Nirvedananda argues that Ramakrishna's remark should not be construed as apathy toward humanitarian work, as in that case he would not have insisted, on two separate occasions, that Mathur Babu feed and clothe indigent villagers.

Ramakrishna discouraged Shambhu from building hospitals and dispensaries simply because Shambhu's "enthusiasm for charity appeared to be much more intense than that for realizing God" (130). On the other hand, the book reminds the reader that when Narendra stated his desire to remain continually absorbed in samādhi, Ramakrishna quickly reproved him by saying, "Shame on you! I thought you were to be the great banyan tree giving shelter to thousands of weary souls. Instead you are selfishly seeking your own well-being. Let these little things alone, my child" (141). Prominent throughout the book is Nirvedananda's view of Ramakrishna as one who synthesized divergent aspects of Hindu practice to form a cohesive whole.

Swami Gnaneswarananda's *Ramakrishna: The Man and the Power* was published in Chicago in 1936. Swami Gnaneswarananda came to the United States in 1926, living first in New York, then moving to Chicago to found the first Vedanta Society in that city in 1929. A man at ease in the West,[30] he died at the age of forty-four in Chicago in 1937. *Ramakrishna: The Man and the Power* is a small book of 125 pages and is written for "free-thinking minds that seek a solution of present day problems" (5). Where Ghanananda stresses the harmony of religions and Nirvedananda emphasizes wide-ranging spiritual regeneration, particularly in India, Gnaneswarananda sees Ramakrishna in more humanistic and psychological terms: "The world needed a *man* who could prove in his life the potential divinity of man and his inseparable contact with the Divine Reality hidden to the ordinary senses; one who would establish a happy relation between the human faculties of man—his body, mind and feelings—and his deeper spiritual reality, in regard to himself and his fellow men" (7).

Gnaneswarananda sees Ramakrishna's "ministry" as highly significant and a lesson to the "modern aggressive world": rather than using "propaganda and criticism" (read: missionaries and colonizers), he taught through "universal love and service" (54). Compared to the books written by Ghanananda and Nirvedananda, *Ramakrishna: The Man and the Power* is more personal and direct. While all three swamis discuss Kālī, Gnaneswarananda's great personal devotion comes vividly off the page. For example:

> Her long black hair floats in the air, and with raised sword she destroys the evil ones. . . . She is fearlessness itself, and has nothing to hide under covers. She is the climax of beauty and has nothing to add by clothes. The ignorant are terrified by her appearance while the wise, meditating on her on the lotus of their hearts, enjoy heavenly bliss. (25–26)

About Ramakrishna's *madhura bhāva*, Gnaneswarananda writes that Ramakrishna's physical body underwent a transformation as he became immersed in the attitude of Rādhā. "As he dressed like a woman during that period, even his close friends could not recognize him as their own Gadadhar [Ramakrishna's childhood name]. This, and certain other amazing facts in the life of Ramakrishna, open up new avenues for scientific investigation regarding the relation of body, mind and spirit" (37). It is important to note here that although Gnaneswarananda was writing for an American audience in the 1930s, he felt no hesitation in writing about Ramakrishna dressing as a woman. For a Hindu, this was not seen as scandalous or even unconventional; it was an accepted feature of that particular sādhana. There was no question of transgressing societal norms.

In contrast to Ghanananda and Nirvedananda, Gnaneswarananda has not only an extended discussion of Sarada Devi and Swami Vivekananda but also a detailed discussion of Ramakrishna's other disciples. And, while the book concludes with the Ramakrishna Order, the final paragraph of the book returns to the personal: "It must not be forgotten, however, that deeper wisdom of a practical nature has always descended through a line of living sources—from the Guru to the Shishya, or disciple. The special skill of an artist can never be taught and handed on except through direct contact" (125). The importance of "direct contact" was particularly important in the case of Christopher Isherwood, as we shall see below.

Christopher Isherwood

Christopher Isherwood (1904–1986), a homosexual and pacifist (not popular lifestyles at any time, but distinctly not so during times of war), arrived in America from England in 1939. Two years earlier his fellow Englishman and friend Gerald Heard had immigrated to Los Angeles, along with Aldous Huxley. While living in Los Angeles, both Huxley and Heard had become Vedānta enthusiasts. Isherwood had heard of their interest in yoga and, though appalled, nevertheless sought them out because he trusted Heard's judgment and Huxley's pacifist bona fides. Heard introduced Isherwood both to Vedānta philosophy and to Swami Prabhavananda, which proved to be a life-changing encounter.

Heard's and Huxley's enthusiasm for Vedānta eventually cooled; only Isherwood remained a staunch Ramakrishna devotee until his death. Nevertheless, their combined influence in popularizing Ramakrishna is inestimable. Isherwood, in particular, plays an important role in Ramakrishna studies, for while Ramakrishna was taken up by the likes of Tolstoy,[31] Heinrich Zimmer, Joseph Campbell, Pitirim Sorokin, Carl Jung, Arnold Toynbee and even Henry Miller (who would have thought!),[32] it was not until 1965 that Isherwood filled a perceived gap, writing *Ramakrishna and His Disciples*—a full-scale account of Ramakrishna's life—primarily for Western consumption.

What prompted Isherwood to write about Ramakrishna was primarily Swami Prabhavananda's request that he do so. Isherwood had profound love and respect for Prabhavananda, who was "almost entirely free from the puritanism that had so constrained Isherwood," writes Katherine Bucknell, editor of Isherwood's *Diaries*. "In all the years of their friendship, Isherwood never records an instance of the Swami's expressing disapproval toward him. Swami did not regard Isherwood's homosexuality as a sin. . . . Swami simply regarded all forms of lust as obstacles to spiritual progress" (Bucknell, xiii–xiv).

Ramakrishna and His Disciples was thus dedicated to Prabhavananda, "my guru, dear friend and literary collaborator for the past twenty-five years." The book, which took nearly ten years to write, proved to be wearisome and unnervingly difficult to complete. It would nevertheless be inaccurate to assume that Isherwood wrote the book solely to do Prabhavananda's bidding. Nearly twenty years before *Ramakrishna and His Disciples* was published, Isherwood wrote: "[The saint] is the most interesting person to write about. The most interesting and the most difficult" (Isherwood 1946, 61).

If Isherwood found the work galling, he found at least some aspects of it gratifying. Writes Isherwood in his diary entry of June 10, 1957: "I ask myself: What am I fit for, nowadays? What am I accomplishing? What does my life mean? And the answer seems to be I have to write that Ramakrishna book. *That* will sum up what my life has been about since the thirties" (1997, 703). Isherwood's source materials were primarily *Sri Ramakrishna the Great Master* and *The Gospel of Sri Ramakrishna*, though Isherwood's diary says his book is "really a rehash of Saradananda" (787). Prabhavananda's role was to clarify points for Isherwood, not to issue instructions. For example, Isherwood records that when he mentioned to Prabhavananda that he was considering adding some of his own biographical material to the book, Prabhavananda replied, "However you write it will be all right" (691).[33]

Upon completion, each chapter was first read out to Swami Prabhavananda and the devotee audience who attended the weekly *Gospel* reading at the Vedanta Society. Prabhavananda would occasionally correct Isherwood while he was reading out his manuscript, and these corrections were incorporated into the finished chapter, which was then sent to Swami Madhavananda, then President of the Ramakrishna

Order, and considered one of the Order's great scholars. Elderly, ill, and burdened with the affairs of a burgeoning monastic order, Madhavananda agreed only with great reluctance to proof-read the chapters.[34] After reading a chapter, Madhavananda would return it almost immediately. According to Pravrajika Anandaprana, Prabhavananda's secretary, sending the chapters to Madhavananda was a courtesy, not a requirement, and the suggested changes were relatively few.[35] We should also keep in mind that it was not at all unusual to send a manuscript out for double-checking. Prabhavananda had sent the Prabhavananda/Isherwood translations of the Bhagavad Gita, Patañjalī's *Yoga-Sūtras*, and *Vivekacūḍāmaṇī* to Sanskrit scholars in India for double-checking as well.

Given the above, a question then arises about the "censorship" under which Isherwood chafed. Isherwood wrote:

> Prema [later Swami Vidyatmananda, an American swami], with his usual crushing frankness, remarked that he ... doesn't think it's [*Ramakrishna and His Disciples*] really "great." I agreed with him, of course, and added that I could probably give a much more vivid impression of Ramakrishna when talking to a sympathetic stranger in a bar, after several drinks. There is that in me which will never write its best to order. Deep down, I have always resented the censorship of the Math. (Isherwood 1980, 266)

No one knows how Isherwood would have written about Ramakrishna had Prabhavananda not asked him to do so. It is important to keep in mind, however, that the Ramakrishna Order did not ask Isherwood to write "to order," nor did the Order suggest the book be written in the first place. Furthermore, the entire publishing enterprise of the Order is not only decentralized but thoroughly unorganized. There is no question of the Order having a *nihil obstat*.

It was Prabhavananda alone who asked Isherwood to write the book, without consulting anyone at Belur Math (nor would such a consultation have ever been done by anyone within the Order). Once Prabhavananda *did* tell members of the Order about the project, they were extremely enthused. It had been a long time since a good biography of Ramakrishna had been written. As with Romain Rolland's book, it was hoped that *Ramakrishna and His Disciples* would attract a good amount of positive attention and there would be a resurgence of interest in Ramakrishna in the West. It is not surprising, then, that Prabhavananda wanted the book read by Madhavananda, both for fact-checking and for his blessings, before it was published.

Nevertheless, by sending the book out of the direct orbit of Swami Prabhavananda (who never once criticized Isherwood and whom Isherwood trusted without question) and into the purview of Swami Madhavananda (who, as President of the Order, embodied "organized religion"), the freedom which Isherwood felt with Prabhavananda was effectively removed. This affected not only the kind of material Isherwood addressed in the book, it also affected *how* the material would be addressed. Throughout the course of his long life, Isherwood had two focal role models, twin compasses, whose influence cannot be overestimated: E. M. Forster and Swami Prabhavananda. Isherwood placed such great store by these men that their opinions served as inbuilt censors. Indeed, Isherwood's reverence for Prabhavananda was such that he delayed coming out for many years simply because he did not want to do anything that might embarrass Prabhavananda.[36]

Ramakrishna and His Disciples thus stands out from the rest of Isherwood's literary output not only due to the nature of its content but also in its style and approach. Like any good writer and particularly a homosexual writer living in a homophobic society, Isherwood was exquisitely tuned to his audience's sensibilities. The knowledge, therefore, that part of his audience would consist of "devotees" inevitably constrained him. Isherwood's diary is revealing on this point. While in India with Prabhavananda, Isherwood found himself an object of quasi-reverence, a situation that made him acutely uncomfortable:

> As long as I quite unashamedly get drunk, have promiscuous sex, and write books like *A Single Man*, I simply cannot appear before people as a sort of lay monk. Whenever I do, my life becomes divided and untruthful—or rather, the only truth left is in my drunkenness, my sex, and my art. (There are, of course, dozens of audiences which would be ready to accept the drink, sex, and art. To these I could also talk about God without falseness. They might be embarrassed but they would listen. Such audiences are not to be found within the Vedanta Society, however). (Isherwood 1980, 271–72)

Yet it was precisely this audience who, Isherwood knew, would be reading his book. Isherwood had a lifelong antipathy to organized religion—the joyful spontaneity and freedom which so appealed to Isherwood, and which Ramakrishna and Prabhavananda manifested in their personalities and in their actions, were the very things tamped down by an organization.[37] Further, as one of the great prose writers of the twentieth century, Isherwood would have found any suggested changes to his writing demeaning—an artistic slap in the face from (worst of all nightmares) "organized religion."

Isherwood writes that he would have liked to discuss Ramakrishna dressing as a woman ("getting into drag"), but he knew that doing so was "out of the question," for while "many of Madhavananda's comments and corrections were helpful ... I was made aware that there were limits to his permissiveness" (1980, 249). If there were limits to Madhavananda's permissiveness, there were also limits to the permissiveness of the Vedanta Society during that time. More likely than not, any perceived unseemliness would have ended up on the cutting room floor long before it reached Madhavananda. We should keep in mind that *madhura bhāva*—mentally and physically assuming the attitude of a female lover of God—was a normal and accepted part of India's religious discourse, particularly among Vaiṣṇava sects. Neither Madhavananda nor Prabhavananda would have blinked at a long discussion of Ramakrishna dressing as a woman. "Getting into drag" would have made no sense to them, no blip on their radars, unless they managed to cross an entire ocean of culture and history.

To return to *Ramakrishna and His Disciples*, Isherwood knew that the book's audience would consist of Ramakrishna devotees along with a much larger proportion of skeptical Western readers. With this in mind, Isherwood wrote the book assuming a skeptic's point of view, employing biblical cadences throughout the text. From the first sentence, one sees Isherwood accommodating the readers' incredulity: "This is the story of a phenomenon. . . . A phenomenon is always a fact, an object of experience. This is how I shall try to approach Ramakrishna" (1). Isherwood presents Ramakrishna in as straightforward a manner as possible, aligning his prose with the "scientific" mood of the era. Isherwood characteristically puts his own cards on the table, stating that he believes Ramakrishna to be an avatar. Aware that many in his audience viewed Hindu mysticism as commensurate with séances and ouija boards, Isherwood emphasized the ordinary in order to remove any whiff of the spooky. Bucknell notes that Isherwood "freighted the book heavily with quotidian detail, attempting ... to approach as near as possible to the borderline between ordinary reality and the transcendent" (Bucknell, xliii).

Moreover, by highlighting the ordinary, Isherwood was replicating his own experience with Prabhavananda. Isherwood's knowledge of mysticism was accessed through Prabhavananda. In a way, for Isherwood Ramakrishna was Prabhavananda writ large.[38] Isherwood's long years of association with Prabhavananda proved to Isherwood that mystical experience was an extension—certainly a vast extension—of what was inherent in ordinary human life. Isherwood wanted to demonstrate that Ramakrishna's mystical experiences were an extension of the divinity inherent in all human life, available to everyone. In this aspect, at least, Isherwood's outlook dovetailed with Rolland's belief that the "oceanic feeling" is a universal experience available to every human being.

In biographical details *Ramakrishna and His Disciples* follows much the same structure as Saradananda's *Great Master*. In every other aspect, however, Isherwood's book takes very much its own tack. Isherwood writes for the West and addresses twentieth-century Western concerns. Considering the nature of the book, perhaps the most central concern is the very nature of a "spiritual" experience. Isherwood dryly observes: "Roget's *Thesaurus* gives 'vision' as a synonym for 'hallucination.'" He continues: "As the result of these vague definitions, the reader gradually comes to rely on Matter as the only reality and to think of Spirit as a shadowy and dangerous hinterland of deceptions and illusions" (Isherwood 1965, 14). In the same vein, Isherwood gives a spirited defense of the visions associated with Ramakrishna and his parents (22–23), criticizing Müller for his refusal to take Hindu spiritual experiences seriously while sanctioning those associated with Christianity (33–34).

Isherwood's assumption of his readers' skepticism was not misplaced. While there was some critical appreciation for *Ramakrishna and His Disciples*,[39] most American and British reviews were unfavorable. Isherwood remarked: "One recurring objection to the book was that I, who had written such worldly novels, was its author" (1980, 287). The contrast between Isherwood-the-earnest-devotee and the louche Isherwood of the *Berlin Stories* was too much for most reviewers to stomach. More importantly: "Many of the reviewers—including even some who were themselves unbelievers—felt offended by the suggestion that Ramakrishna could have been an avatar, since this was a denial of the uniqueness of Jesus as Son of God" (288).[40]

Legendary critic Frank Kermode's lengthy, acid review in the *New York Review of Books*—replete with references to "queer circles" and the book's "inevitable contamination" by feather-boa—provides another telling example of the kind of disparagement Isherwood's book received. Kermode's subtext throughout the review is that Isherwood had sold out his finely trained British sensibilities for something undignified and unworthy. As for the book itself, Kermode writes that it "lacks all irony, all criticism. . . . One would have liked an account of [Ramakrishna] free of all the uncriticized Aberglaube" (1965a, 20). One wonders if, in those days, "irony" would have been considered an appropriate response when assessing a religious subject in the Western monotheistic tradition. Interestingly, what particularly provoked Kermode's ire was not merely Hinduism, but Hinduism "adapted by Western participants in the flight from reason" (1965b, 27).

It is telling that both Kermode's review and George Woodcock's review of the book in *Commonweal*[41] chide Isherwood for being taken in by "superstition." If Isherwood was attacked as a credulous believer, the intolerance of his critics toward a belief system alien to theirs was equally visible. Predictably, many of Isherwood's critics viewed their reaction as one of "reason," while Isherwood was seen as having succumbed to the lure of Hindu fantasy. As with earlier Western assessments of Ramakrishna, we again see the undercurrent of Western "reason" versus Hindu "superstition." In general, the negative reviews of *Ramakrishna and His Disciples* take for granted Western secular, humanist values and their presumed superiority over anything found in the Hindu tradition.

In fairness to Isherwood's critics, it is understandable how they estimated *Ramakrishna and His Disciples* to be one of Isherwood's lesser writings. Since it is the only book Isherwood wrote in this genre, it stands alone. It cannot be fairly compared to any of his other writings in which he directly engages and beguiles the reader. (*What happened to the man who brought us the Berlin Stories?*) In *Ramakrishna and His Disciples*, Isherwood stands back, far back, out of the way, and as a result, *Ramakrishna and His Disciples* has an unusually flat affect. Given Isherwood's mighty skills as a writer and stylist, however, we have to assume that he intended this effect. Isherwood consciously removed himself from the text so that Ramakrishna could be more clearly seen. We can also assume, however, that because Isherwood felt as if he were writing with an organization reading over his shoulder, the book lacks the spontaneity, the richness—born of the extraordinary polarities of his life—and gem-like clarity of his other writings.[42] In fairness to Isherwood, however, he was critiqued for all the wrong reasons. His personal beliefs were savaged, not his prose.

Of particular interest in these reviews is the stinging critique of Isherwood's empathetic approach and the preference for the distanced "outsider" stance. The relationship and balance between these two approaches has guided much of the history of Religious Studies and has been a matter of consistent debate. To a large degree the history of

Ramakrishna scholarship has been accompanied by a parallel history of that very debate.

Later Interpreters

> In reading through the mass of material available, one fact stands out: there is severe psychopathology in Ramakrishna.
>
> —Jeffrey Masson, *The Oceanic Feeling*

> Thus [Ramakrishna's] neurosis or psychosis accounts for his theosis.
>
> —Narasingha Sil, *Rāmakṛṣṇa Paramahaṁsa*

In contrast to the interpreters of Ramakrishna discussed so far, a different dynamic comes into play with Ramakrishna's more recent interpreters. Compared to the more sympathetic approach of earlier interpreters, Walter Neevel's two studies, the latter one in particular, inaugurate a change in the academic interpretation of Ramakrishna, reflecting concomitant changes occurring in the academic study of religion. Neevel's studies and those of later, Western-educated scholars present an entirely different tone from the admiring studies of Mukerji, Rolland, Isherwood and, to a large degree, Müller. None of these earlier interpreters questioned the authenticity of the material made available to them by Vivekananda and his successors. None of the earlier writers questioned Saradananda's legitimacy nor did they find him a less accurate or trustworthy source than M. Neevel's essay signals the first departure from these assumptions, and it is at this point that we begin the transition from the hermeneutic of empathy to the hermeneutic of suspicion.

Concerning this change in approach, Beckerlegge notes: "A far wider gulf exists between the understanding of the comparative study of religion shared by Müller, Rolland and the Ramakrishna movement and the intentionally value-free 'pure historical science' employed by more recent academic practitioners of the comparative study of religion in North America and Europe" (25). Significantly, there has been a post-modern turn in recent years which recognizes that a value-free approach does not and cannot exist. The claim of "scholarly objectivity" only serves—consciously or unconsciously—to cloak one's own agenda. For this reason a number of scholars have found it helpful to aim at transparency, discussing their own attitudes towards their subject matter in an attempt to clear the interpretive air.[43]

Walter Neevel

Walter Neevel's lengthy article "The Transformation of Sri Ramakrishna" was published in 1976. His second article, published in 1997, presents a renewed look at his subject matter. Typical of the earlier Orientalists' *solà scriptura* approach, Neevel argues that M's *Gospel of Sri Ramakrishna* is the "major source and the authority against which all other sources must be judged"; it is this text in which the reader comes "closest to Rāmakrishna" and it is here "where the overlay of traditions is least significant" (1976, 58). (One hears the echoes of Müller's "dialogic process" in the background.) While Neevel mentions the biographies and biographical sketches written by Ramakrishna's disciples, these, he asserts, "have been heavily influenced by the later systematic reinterpretation of the tradition" (62).

Through a close reading of the English *Gospel*, Neevel attempts to discover "Rāmakrishna's own position" (90). Yet by forcibly confining Ramakrishna to one text, he obviates other valid and important source books on Ramakrishna. Neevel goes on to argue that to understand Ramakrishna, who was "consummately Hindu," one must understand not his universality, but his particularity as a Hindu (1976, 54). Noting that earlier interpretations emphasized his universality, Neevel states, without irony, that "with the current shift in the cultural winds ... it is now possible to present Śrī Rāmakrishna in his own Hindu garb" (55–56). To think that an American scholar—reading one source text to the exclusion of all others, and that too in translation, while employing exclusively Euro-American methodology—can be exceptionally qualified (even more qualified than Ramakrishna's contemporaries) to understand Ramakrishna *as a Hindu*, seems unduly optimistic.

Neevel gives a drubbing to the reliability of Swami Saradananda, who resolved the question of Ramakrishna's birth date via horoscopic reconstruction. For Neevel this raises "the question of how the many other uncertainties" concerning Ramakrishna's life were "resolved" by Swami Saradananda. Neevel suggests that Saradananda restructured the ordering of Ramakrishna's sādhana in his *Līlāprasaṅga* in order to create the impression that his final realization was Advaita rather than Tantra (81–83).

Neevel contests Saradananda's accuracy, yet finds both Müller and J. N. Farquhar authoritative sources on Ramakrishna—a piquant irony since, first, the primary source for Müller's biographical information on Ramakrishna was Saradananda himself. Secondly, it is confounding that

Neevel would find Farquhar a particularly reliable source on Ramakrishna since Farquhar's 1913 book, *The Crown of Hinduism*, promotes Christ as the fulfillment of Hinduism. (Farquhar's analysis of Ramakrishna drew from Müller's work as well as the 1912, single-volume edition of the *Gospel of Sri Ramakrishna* and Vivekananda's "My Master.")

Neevel is the first scholar to contest Saradananda's accuracy regarding the chronology of Ramakrishna's life, and his skepticism concerning Saradananda's reliability will be repeated in *Kālī's Child.* As with the issue of Saradananda's reliability regarding Ramakrishna's sādhanas, Neevel advances some basic theses on Ramakrishna which other scholars will follow in later years. First, Neevel moves away from Ramakrishna's previous interpreters by asserting that Tantra, rather than Advaita Vedanta, was the central religious focus of Ramakrishna's life. According to Neevel, Ramakrishna's followers have "overemphasized the significance" of attaining nirvikalpa samādhi (1997, 293).

For Neevel, the Advaita experience of nonduality is hardly something one would wish for. In Ramakrishna's life, Neevel states, it was a "life-threatening excursion." This hazardous event was precipitated by Totapuri, who "ruthlessly forced Rāmakrishna to concentrate on the point of a broken piece of glass pressed painfully into his forehead." The unfortunate result was Ramakrishna's mind being "torn from the Divine Mother's form and plunged into the trancelike state of *nirvikalpa samādhi*"(1997, 292–93).[44] But Ramakrishna himself called the Advaita plunge the equivalent of being in an "ocean of immortality"—a fly in a cup of nectar (KA 1.130–31). Ramakrishna similarly tells M that meditating on the formless aspect of God is equivalent to fish swimming joyfully in the ocean of bliss and consciousness (KA 4.27). There is no evidence that Ramakrishna's experience of samādhi was anything other than profoundly joyful.

Neevel writes that Ramakrishna "often talks as if he accepted *kevalādvaita* [absolute nondualism], and his disciples have emphasized his seeming acceptance" (1976, 87). In other words, Ramakrishna did not genuinely accept nondualism—his acceptance was only "seeming."[45] Because Ramakrishna's disciples did not understand him correctly, they could not interpret his teachings correctly. To authenticate his claim, Neevel quotes from the *Gospel of Sri Ramakrishna*, citing Ramakrishna's well-attested declaration that the path of jñāna is extremely difficult. This is a tenuous conclusion, however: Ramakrishna said that the path of jñāna is difficult, *therefore* he did not accept that path. The Kaṭhopaniṣad (1.3.14) also points out that the path is extremely difficult, as does the Bhagavad Gītā (12.5), as does Śaṅkara's bhāṣya on the Gītā. Following Neevel's argument, one would be tempted to conclude that neither the Upaniṣads nor the Gītā nor Śaṅkara himself advocated the path of jñāna.

Neevel's thesis rests on several unstated presuppositions. The first is that a Western-trained scholar possesses the rationality, intellectual tools and emotional distance that Ramakrishna's disciples lacked. Included also is the presupposition that Ramakrishna's monastic disciples were inherently unreliable witnesses. Finally, Neevel shares the earlier Orientalists' emphasis on the crucial significance of the proper understanding of one central text. The unstated but presumed assumption is that differences of culture and language are minor obstructions, easily overcome with a good English translation. Yet not only was Neevel working with translated texts, he was also working with untranslatable cultural and religious values, overarching concepts that are difficult to grasp and convey. Further, in the Hindu tradition, words themselves are seen as incapable of fully expressing the experience the language attempts to convey.

Neevel's essay marks an important shift in scholarly perspective on Ramakrishna in several areas. First, whereas earlier interpretations viewed Tantra as one of Ramakrishna's sādhanas but not the paramount one which surpassed all other sādhanas, from this time forward, scholars will generally privilege Tantra over every other sādhana. If earlier interpreters hastened to gloss over the less reputable elements of Tantra, later interpreters will accentuate them.

The second major shift in Ramakrishna studies is a near consensus among Western-trained academics that Vivekananda's (and to a large degree, Saradananda's) interpretation of Ramakrishna is flawed. By and large, the Western academy will agree that Vivekananda's emphasis on jñāna was at the expense of Ramakrishna's true emphasis upon bhakti. Neevel's essay will also prove prescient in his belief that while M's recordings of Ramakrishna's conversations were accurate, the writings of Ramakrishna's monastic disciples could not be considered as reliable as M's.

Finally, in a crucial development which begins with Neevel and will profoundly affect Ramakrishna studies, psychoanalysis as a hermeneutical tool for interpreting Ramakrishna will be increasingly employed. Yet the issue of psychoanalysis vis à vis non-Western figures is potentially problematic since "psychoanalytic theory and practice is profoundly related to Northern European and North American cultural values and philosophical assumptions involving individualism" (Roland 1996, 5). The issue of psychoanalysis figures prominently in what could be seen as a latter-day incarnation of Orientalism, as psychoanalytic theory presumes Western values and social norms to be universal human values and norms. Some will see this development as yet another manifestation of Western cultural domination, masked under the guise of scientific or scholarly detachment.

The turn toward psychoanalysis in Religious Studies, coming into full flower in the 1960s, was a sign of the times. Psychoanalysis had become a pervasive, dominating presence in Western society, and psychoanalytical interpretation was considered an appropriate, indeed indispensable, tool for understanding humanity—Hindu religious figures included. As psychoanalyst Alan Roland (2002) points out: "Psychoanalysis has played a surprisingly major role in South Asian studies, much more so than in other area studies, not to mention many other intellectual disciplines."

It is worth noting that, as an intriguing article in the *New York Times* points out, psychoanalysis "is alive and well in literature ... and just about every other subject in the humanities," but it is treated as a "historical artifact" within American universities' psychology departments. The primary reason for its marginalization is that "while most disciplines in psychology began putting greater emphasis on testing the validity of their approaches scientifically," this has not been the case with psychoanalysis. "Psychoanalysts haven't developed the same evidence-based grounding," Alice Eagly, chairperson of the psychology department at Northwestern University, asserts. Thus, the article observes, "most psychology departments don't pay as much attention to psychoanalysis." Yet this disconnect between what is taught in psychology departments and in other branches of the humanities has far-reaching effects:

> Given how psychoanalytic ideas have shaped the culture, the issue reverberates far beyond the tiny cluster of psychoanalysts. They worry that the gradual disappearance of psychoanalytic theory from psychology curriculums means that those ideas are bound to be applied incorrectly as new advances are neglected.[46]

If Neevel's essays reveal the first imprints of psychoanalytic interpretation in Ramakrishna studies, the work of Jeffrey Masson, to whom we now turn, reveals its effect in full flower.

Jeffrey Masson

In 1980 Jeffrey Moussaieff Masson, trained as a Freudian psychoanalyst in Toronto and for some time the director of the Freud Archives, wrote *The Oceanic Feeling: The Origins of Religious Sentiment in Ancient India*. The book applies classical psychoanalytic techniques to various figures within the Hindu tradition, Ramakrishna among them.

Masson's book was prefigured by two articles which indicated the direction his work would take. His first, "Sex and Yoga: Psychoanalysis and the Indian Religious Experience," declared that "hallucination and states bordering on the psychoses are likely to develop" as a result of yoga. Not only individuals are at risk, however: "When such delusional states are not only egosyntonic, but acceptable to the culture as well, we find ourselves with much larger problems … of the psychodynamics of an entire culture" (1974, 311). Given Masson's cultural insularity, it is not surprising that he refers in the same article to Ramakrishna's "transvestite activities" (312), which we can assume means Ramakrishna's *madhura bhāva* sādhana when he moved, walked, talked and dressed like a woman. By this time, Masson's conclusion about Ramakrishna is almost anticipated: "There *is* an element of homosexuality in … Ramakrishna" (310). That *madhura bhāva* sādhana has a significant place in the Vaiṣṇava tradition does not deter Masson's diagnosis. "Psychoanalysis," Masson writes, is "always skeptical of … 'spiritual' explanations of … what we cannot understand" (309).

Yet Masson seems equally skeptical, and intolerant, of non-Western intellectual categories and cultural values. His 1979 article "Indian Psychotherapy?" takes strong issue with the views of Indian psychiatrist J. S. Neki, then Head of the Department of Psychiatry at the All-India Institute for Medical Science in New Dehli. Neki had written several articles which discussed the "lack of cultural relevance that makes orthodox Western psychotherapies especially ineffective in India" (Masson 1979, 327). Masson's response is to universalize human motivation, values and behavior, presuming that whatever psychiatric issues any human being might have, Freudian analyses and therapies would be culturally universal. Masson assails Neki for his "easy cultural relativism" and writes: "If psychoanalysis is a valid theory of the human mind, then it applies to all people, of all times" (328). Quoting Freud liberally throughout his article, Masson makes it clear that "the traditional procedures of classical analysis" are the rules to go by, and any deviation from that—by, for example, incorporating indigenous Indian techniques—is intellectually puerile and doomed. According to Masson, the attempt of Indian psychiatrists "to overthrow Freud holus-bolus in favor of some generally unnamed syncretistic approach" would "fail utterly" (329).

In *The Oceanic Feeling*, Masson assigns Ramakrishna a prominent place in the Hindu traditions by saying that "Ramakrishna can be said to be second in religious importance only to ... Śaṅkarācārya." Masson continues, "And yet, if one studies any of the biographies, one is struck by just how deeply disturbed Ramakrishna was" (1980, 9). Ramakrishna is discussed in a chapter devoted to the origin of the term "oceanic feeling," which also discusses Rolland's correspondence with Freud. Another chapter discusses the oceanic feeling within the earliest Sanskrit texts and its psychological implications. About these texts Masson writes: "The whole of Vedānta philosophy, from the Upaniṣads forward ... can be said to be a paean of praise to the pleasures of depersonalization and derealization" (60). Equally, in a story of Nārada and Viṣṇu from the Purāṇas he again finds "narcissism, depersonalization, derealization" (58). The book includes a chapter entitled "Kubjā the Hunchback and Kṛṣṇa, with Some Observations on Perversions." The chapter's title is self-explanatory: "Kṛṣṇa's attraction to a hunchback, then, is a defect in loving of universal application. By examining some of the possible motives for such a love," Masson suggests, "we can better understand normal sexuality" (118–19). One is tempted to add "whatever that may be"—yet the suggestion that there is one normative standard of sexuality, departures from which are "perversions," says much about the authorial stance throughout the text.

Masson expresses surprise that, comparatively speaking, there had been so little psychoanalytic work done on the Indian tradition. This he finds "puzzling, since there is nothing inherent in Indian culture, past or present, that would make it refractory to psychological investigation." After all, Masson continues, "the insights Freud derived ... belong to the structure of the human mind, and are the property of mankind in general" (1). Thus we again encounter the unquestioned assumption of universalism and its intellectual Eurocentrism. We encounter the familiar Orientalist protocol, which presumes European "logic" to be a universal human phenomenon and the assumption that certain rational procedures (which include such "scientific" endeavors as psychotherapy) contain within them scientific "laws" which are universally applicable to all societies.

From the book's introductory essay to the book's conclusion, Indian religious traditions are summarily pathologized. They demand a "retreat from the emotions" and instill a "dread fear of human feeling" which,

Masson writes, is "one of the fundamental disguised themes of almost all ancient Indian writing" (4). Buddha was "severely depressed," which is why "he made *duḥkha* … the cornerstone of his ethical teaching" (6).

Ramakrishna has the cards stacked against him from the start since Masson states in the book's Introduction: "I consider the states of feeling manifest in the practice of mysticism to be basically defenses against depression" (x). Ramakrishna, Masson writes, clearly suffered "delusions and hallucinations" but, interestingly, "Ramakrishna's worldview was not judged psychotic, because it was shared by his culture" (8–9).

Anticipating the judgment of Jeffrey Kripal some years later, Masson writes that "we can assume, hypothetically but correctly" that Ramakrishna suffered "specific traumata in his childhood" (9–10). In *The Oceanic Feeling*, Masson repeats his assertion that Ramakrishna's behavior was indicative of homosexuality. Masson finds it "astonishing that Romain Rolland could so overlook the blatant homosexual concerns of Ramakrishna." The evidence Masson husbands is found in Saradananda's *Great Master*, where Saradananda relates that Ramakrishna would look at the chests of his male disciples and would carefully "examine the tongue, the chest, the working of the organs. . . . He preferred them young … and unmarried, 'not yet caught in the net of desire'" (46). Adding more ammunition to his armory, Masson then quotes Nikhilananda's *Gospel*, in which Ramakrishna, discussing the younger Naren, says:

> "He is totally unaffected by worldliness. He says he doesn't know what lust is. (To M.) Just feel my body. All the hair is standing on end." The Master's hair actually stood on end at the thought of a pure mind totally devoid of lust. (47; quoting GSR, 952)

If Saradananda's and M's reports reveal Ramakrishna's "blatant homosexual concerns," it is interesting that neither they nor, as far as we know, anyone else in India were aware of it. By superimposing Euro-American standards of behavior on Indian practices and presuming that they alone are normative, Masson again pathologizes an entire culture. He concludes by making short work of his analysand: "In reading through the mass of material available, one fact stands out: there is severe psychopathology in Ramakrishna" (34).

Alan Roland has criticized Masson by saying that he

> asserted reductionistic strategies *ad absurdum* in the area of Indian studies by drawing upon the full psychoanalytic armamentarium of

> psychopathology. His seeming meticulous Sanskrit and psychoanalytic scholarship is unfortunately flawed by his wild methodology of speculating loosely on ancient Indian texts as well as on modern Indian biography, such as on Ramakrishna. (Roland 1997, 3)

While Masson's interpretation may lack nuance, it nevertheless requires serious attention since his work is widely quoted as an authority by Jeffrey Kripal, Narasingha Sil, Malcolm McLean, and other Ramakrishna scholars.

While the work of Neevel and Masson will lead Ramakrishna studies in a direction not heretofore seen, recent interpretations of Ramakrishna from within India—from both inside and outside the Ramakrishna Order—will follow a markedly different course. Although a number of insiders have written about Ramakrishna, three authors will be particularly examined, as their writings represent significant scholarship on Ramakrishna from within the ranks of the Ramakrishna Order. It also should be mentioned that there are a number of nonmonastic writers who have made significant contributions to Ramakrishna literature: M. Sivaramakrishna, Dinesh Bhattacharyya Shastri, R. K. Das Gupta, and others. While their writings have greatly enhanced Ramakrishna literature, by and large they have not done the considerable original research which the three swamis of the Ramakrishna Order whom we discuss below have done.

Recent Interpretations by Monks of the Ramakrishna Order

While *Kālī's Child* has made much of "the tradition" or "the doctrine" (KC, 204) espoused by the Ramakrishna Order, there has been little examination of the Order's intellectual activity in order to assess what such a "tradition" might be. First, it is important to note that there has been, from the Order's inception, a great deal of discussion, argument and debate over any number of issues pertaining to the Ramakrishna Order. There has never been an established orthodoxy or orthopraxy to keep members' thoughts and actions in line. Indeed, it would be unusual, more likely impossible, to find two members who share precisely the same outlook and spiritual ideals. Such questions as the role of Ramakrishna in the world, the role of Ramakrishna vis-à-vis Hinduism, the role of Vivekananda, and whether his teachings formed an organic whole with those of Ramakrishna, the role of Sarada Devi, whether the Ramakrishna Order is a "new" religious movement or a regeneration of the ancient Hindu tradition, whether the Vedānta of the Ramakrishna Order is the same as the Vedānta of Śaṅkara, whether Ramakrishna was an Advaitin or a Śākta Advaitin or a Viśiṣṭādvaitin—these subjects have long been discussed, debated and written about. And this is just a small sampling of the kinds of issues that are discussed. Since, mercifully, there is no "doctrine" offered by the Ramakrishna Order, there has been in its stead a long tradition of open-ended discussions in which ideas are freely brought up, examined and debated.

It is significant, however, that the questions which will become increasingly central to recent Western-educated scholars on Ramakrishna—Neevel, Masson, McLean, Sil, and Kripal—were, as far as we are aware, never debated or discussed within the Ramakrishna Order. It is not that the topics were forbidden or so shocking as to be only whispered under one's breath—they were simply so fatuous as to never have been seriously considered in the first place. The issue, for example, of whether Ramakrishna was "homosexually oriented"—a view endorsed by Masson, McLean and Kripal—was never an issue nor a point of debate: Ramakrishna's heterosexual orientation was so obvious to those who were familiar with Bengali culture and to those who had read the source texts in the original Bengali that the issue itself was a non-issue.

Should this be construed as a cover-up or a case of universal cultural homophobia, it is worth noting that even Ashok Row Kavi, one of India's most prominent gay rights activists and spokesmen, does not agree with *Kālī's Child*'s conclusions about Ramakrishna. Row Kavi, who had joined the Ramakrishna Order in Mumbai, left the monastery in order to freely explore and express his homosexuality. Since that time, he has had nothing but praise for the Ramakrishna Order and for the senior monk who encouraged him to lead as honest and happy a life as possible. Row Kavi writes: "I am ever grateful to the monks of the Ramakrishna order for making my coming out so painless and worthy of all that is great in man's heritage" (Row Kavi, 15).[47] Row Kavi has also been highly critical of *Kālī's Child*. He asserts that the book's assessments regarding Ramakrishna's "alleged sexuality are wrong." He further critiques Kripal for his "derisive attitude towards Ramakrishna" and also asserts that Kripal is "culturally condescending."[48]

We must again emphasize that the issue at stake in *Kālī's Child* is not homosexuality per se. There is nothing intrinsically problematic or "wrong" with being homosexual any more than there is anything intrinsically problematic or "wrong" with being heterosexual. What is at stake is whether Ramakrishna was living an unconscious life, a deeply fractured life, or a deceitful life. The issue is whether Ramakrishna was "incapable of deciphering the homoerotic images … in his visions and language" and whether he "was not fully aware of his own homosexual desires" (KC, 320). In other words, was Ramakrishna unaware of the contents of his own mind? Was Ramakrishna "incapable" of understanding his own visions and language? There are a large number of testimonies by those who knew Ramakrishna and spoke, unanimously and convincingly, not only of his purity, straightforwardness and guilelessness, but also of his deep insight and wisdom. Did every one of them get it wrong? Perhaps. According to Kripal, for many the truths are "just too difficult to accept." They are also "quite literally traumatic" (2004, 195). He continues:

> How many times have I heard something like the following between the lines, as it were, of my offended critics: "How could *this Westerner* see something that we Hindus have not seen for the last 130 years? What hubris!"
>
> On one level, I can only agree with them—it does indeed seem quite preposterous. But what am I to do? I cannot cognitively or morally deny the conclusions of my intellectual labors. (201)

A couple of points: First, the issue of "Westerner" is a bit of a red herring since two of his most noted and vocal critics—Swami Atmajnanananda and Pravrajika Vrajaprana—are Westerners as well. Second, the crucial point is that the issue is not about homosexuality or heterosexuality. The issue at stake here is whether Ramakrishna was spiritually and psychologically fragmented or whole.

Again, while Ramakrishna will be accused of misogyny by Masson, McLean, Olson and Kripal, this has not been the subject of debate in the Ramakrishna Order. It is not that such debate was discouraged or inhibited, but simply that for those who understand Hindu traditions and culture, it was a non-issue—particularly for those who have read the source material on Sarada Devi and Ramakrishna's other women disciples.

The three monks of the Ramakrishna Order upon whose work we focus have largely been ignored by Western-educated scholars. Of these three, Swami Prabhananda's work—primarily his in-depth historical research on Ramakrishna and other figures in the Ramakrishna tradition—has made an occasional appearance in academic footnotes. The other two monks, Swamis Dhireshananda and Bhajanananda, have not, as far as we are aware, been noted at all. Their writings have discussed philosophical aspects of Ramakrishna, the Ramakrishna Order and the Hindu traditions in general.

Swami Dhireshananda

A second-generation monk of the Ramakrishna Order—that is, a disciple of one of Ramakrishna's monastic disciples—Swami Dhireshananda (1907–1998) was a disciple of Swami Saradananda. Dhireshananda studied Sanskrit and Vedānta scriptures from traditional scholars and later taught them to a cross-section of at least two generations of monks of the Ramakrishna Order. Dhireshananda's literary output was relatively small; apart from his Bengali translations of the *Yoga-vāsiṣṭha-sāra* (1972), *Vairāgya-śatakam* (1985), *Vedānta-saṁjña-mālikā* (1985), *Aṣṭāvakra Gītā* (1988), and *Adhyātma Rāmāyaṇa* (1994), he also wrote several thought-provoking essays in *Udbodhan*, the Ramakrishna Order's Bengali journal published from Kolkata.

Two of Dhireshananda's outstanding essays, both published in *Udbodhan*, merit special attention, as he has raised in them several key issues and has provided compelling insights. "Swami Vivekananda o Advaitavād" ("Swami Vivekananda and Advaita Philosophy") was published in 1962 and "Nānā Dṛṣṭite Śrī Rāmakṛṣṇa" ("Sri Ramakrishna through Different Lenses") was published in 1980. In these two essays, Dhireshananda attempts to analyze Ramakrishna's words against the backdrop of the Hindu traditions.

Dhireshananda's 1962 essay was written on the eve of Vivekananda's birth centenary and, while its focus was on the role Advaita played in Vivekananda's life and teachings, it analyzes the kind of Advaita he learned from Ramakrishna. The second essay deals directly with Ramakrishna and highlights what is probably one of the most significant features of his life: namely, that any attempt to force Ramakrishna's life into the straitjacket of a single philosophy or tradition is bound to produce distortion. Indeed, this was pointed out in the very first biography of Ramakrishna, Ramchandra Datta's *Jībanabṛttānta*, in which he wrote that in Ramakrishna's life one sees the fulfillment of all spiritual ideals (*bhāva*) (JB, 52). To Vedāntins he was a paramahaṁsa, to devotees he was an avatar, and to Tāntriks he was a *kaulaśreṣtha*. He has also been called *rasīkacuḍāmaṇi* by those in the Navarasika sect, *sāi* by the Bāuls, *gosvāmī* by the Vaiṣṇavas, and *ālekh* by the Kartābhajās (Dhireshananda 1980, 220). Dhireshananda points out that Ramakrishna was "the embodiment of infinite *bhāvas*" (*anantabhāvamay*). Having practiced the disciplines of many spiritual traditions, Ramakrishna demonstrated both the authenticity and the effectiveness of their practices in the lives of qualified students (*adhikārī*).

Another significant feature to which Dhireshananda draws our attention is the method of Ramakrishna's teaching. Although Ramakrishna himself embodied a number of different ideals in his life, he taught only what was suitable to the person who sought his guidance. As Vivekananda once remarked: "Generally he used to teach dualism. As a rule he never taught Advaita. But he taught it to me" (CW 7.414). Dhireshananda quotes profusely from the *Kathāmṛta* and points to Ramakrishna's words that teach, at different times and to different students, the insights derived from the Advaita, Viśiṣṭādvaita, and Dvaita traditions. For most beginners in spiritual life, Ramakrishna taught the path of devotion.

Dhireshananda raises a question regarding the nature of Ramakrishna's experience of the Divine Mother. What kind of an experience was this? According to him, this vision of Ramakrishna can be understood only from the perspective offered in the Śāktādvaita tradition of the Tantras.[49] Giving a brief exposition of Śāktādvaita and quoting from scriptural texts, Dhireshananda points out that Śāktādvaita pushes the inquiry into the nature of Reality beyond the inherent duality of the Sāṁkhya tradition and, philosophically, can be considered to be only a step away from the nonduality of Vedānta (1962, 76).

The conversations in the *Kathāmṛta*, generally recorded on weekends when most people frequented Dakshineswar, reflect the insights of Śāktādvaita to a considerable degree. Ramakrishna's life revolved around his chosen ideal (*iṣṭa-devatā*) Kālī and he used to say: "Looking upon God as Mother is a very pure approach" (*matṛbhāb baḍo śuddhabhāb*). In the *Kathāmṛta* the reader finds repeated emphasis on the motherhood of God, the interchangeability of both the *saguṇa/nirguṇa* and *līlā/nitya* aspects of the divine in the unitary Consciousness that manifests as Mother, and many references to kuṇḍalinī and its movement.

Dhireshananda cautions his readers, however, about jumping to the conclusion that Śāktādvaita was the one and only philosophy that guided Ramakrishna's life. If it were, he says, Ramakrishna would not have taken so much care in teaching Vivekananda and others alternative ways of understanding life and reality. Once when a person asked Ramakrishna to give him one teaching that would produce knowledge (*ek kathāy gyān*), Ramakrishna told him: "'Brahman is real and the world is an appearance'—meditate on this" (*'brahma satya jagat mithyā'—ei-ṭi dhāraṇā karo*). After saying this, Ramakrishna then remained silent (Dhireshananda 1980, 223). This is as clear an Advaitic teaching as one can get. Dhireshananda provides many other instances of similar teaching which are found in the *Kathāmṛta*:

> The forms and aspects of God disappear before Vedāntic reasoning. The ultimate conclusion of that reasoning is this: Brahman is real and the world of name and form is illusory. It is possible to see the forms of God or be conscious of God as a Person only as long as there is the awareness "I am a devotee." Through the lens of reason, the devotee's "I" keeps the devotee a little away from God. (KA 1.61)

> But *līlā* is by no means the last word. After experiencing all the *bhāvas*, I said, "Mother, in all these states there is separation. Keep me in a state where there is no separation." That is how I remained for some days absorbed in indivisible Saccidānanda. (KA 2.192)

> God has shown me that only the Paramātman, who is called in the Vedas as the pure Ātman, is one, immovable like Mount Meru, unattached, and beyond joy and sorrow. (KA 3.71)

> When one begins to reason, one sees that all this is like a dream. Brahman alone is real; everything else is unreal. Even Śakti is like a dream, unreal. (KA 1.41)

Why did Ramakrishna's teachings, as they have come down to us, seem to reflect a bias toward Śāktādvaita? Quantitatively, a significant portion of the *Kathāmṛta* has teachings that are clearly Śāktādvaitic when compared to the teachings on bhakti, Viśiṣṭādvaita, or Advaita. Dhireshananda suggests that Ramakrishna felt that "worshiping the cause of the universe as Mother was the best practice or way for spiritual liberation of the people of the modern age whose minds were polluted with worldly desires" (1980, 224). Thus Ramakrishna generally recommended *santāna-bhāva* (looking upon oneself as child of the Divine Mother). Quoting copiously from the *Kathāmṛta*, Dhireshananda further writes that, according to Ramakrishna, after the state of enlightenment (*vijñana*) the person continues to live in the world holding either a Śāktādvaitic or Viśiṣṭādvaitic worldview, for in the nondual state of samādhi, negotiating the external world is neither possible nor necessary (1962, 142).

Citing many references from the *Kathāmṛta* and the *Līlāprasaṅga*, Dhireshananda points out that Ramakrishna showed the inherent harmony in—as well as brought about a synthesis of—all the Vedic as well as non-Vedic sādhanas (1962, 78). Dhireshananda emphasizes that every student of Ramakrishna understood him in the light of the teachings that he or she received. We can extend that observation today by stating that any study on Ramakrishna is a reflection of how Ramakrishna appears to the interpreter and not necessarily of what Ramakrishna really was. As such, how a person sees Ramakrishna is often an indicator of the person's frame of mind which processes and interprets the information about Ramakrishna. Dhireshananda's two essays have made a significant contribution toward understanding the multifaceted spirituality of Ramakrishna by putting into perspective the remarkable variety which is seen in both Ramakrishna's mystic experiences as well as in his teachings.

Swami Prabhananda

Swami Prabhananda is considered the Ramakrishna Order's foremost researcher and historian. Prabhananda's first book, *First Meetings with Sri Ramakrishna*, was published in 1987 and discusses thirty-nine significant figures in Ramakrishna's life, while providing information about their first encounters with Ramakrishna. In so doing, Prabhananda provides a wealth of new biographical data on his subjects, material he uncovered through years of meticulous research.

The first person discussed is Ramakrishna's first guru, the Bhairavi Brahmani, who first met Ramakrishna in 1861. "Bhairavi" was not her name; the term merely indicates that she was a nun of a Tāntrik order. The Bhairavi's given name was Yogeswari, but Ramakrishna simply referred to her as "Bamni"—the brahmin woman (since it is rude to address one's guru by his or her given name). While little has been written about the Bhairavi in academic literature on Ramakrishna (apart from the fact that she was Ramakrishna's "Tāntrik guru"), few Ramakrishna scholars have noted that the Bhairavi was a deeply learned woman, a scholar of both Vaiṣṇava and Tāntrik scriptures (Prabhananda 1987, 8). It is also not well known that the Bhairavi was a devotee of Viṣṇu, her *iṣṭa-devatā* being Raghuvīr, to whom she offered cooked food daily.

Prabhananda's chapter on Totapuri tells us that Ramakrishna was thirty when Tota arrived in Dakshineswar, and he was probably in his fifties. Tota was tall and robust with matted hair and an untrimmed beard. Prabhananda notes: "Typical *paramahaṁsa* (the highest order of monks) that he was, his only possessions were a pair of tongs, a brass water-pot, a coarse wrapper [shawl], and a piece of [animal] skin to sit on" (27–28). A sannyāsī from a young age, Tota belonged to the Puri order of the Daśanāmīs, which was founded by Śaṅkara in the seventh century, C.E. Tota's monastery was in Haryana state and its monks lived notably ascetic lives. Most memorably, they were "clothed in the sky"—i.e., completely naked—and hence were called "nāgā" sādhus. They observed personal poverty and performed hard manual labor. Ramakrishna recalled what Tota had told him about his monastery and his training as a sādhu:

> There were seven hundred naked spiritual aspirants. . . . Those who were beginning to learn meditation were asked to do so on cushions, for they might feel an ache in their legs if they were to sit and meditate on hard seats, and their unaccustomed minds might come to think of their bodies instead of God. Then afterwards, the deeper their meditation became, the harder were the seats on which they had to sit. And at last they had to sit on pieces of skin only or on the bare ground to practice meditation. They were also made to observe strict rules regarding everything, viz., eating, drinking, etc. As fetters of shame, hatred, fear, egoism regarding one's birth, lineage, custom, pretentiousness and so on, they were taught to give them up one by one. Afterwards when they developed deep concentration of mind they had to go and travel from one place of pilgrimage to another, at first with other monks, and later alone, and then return. (30–31)

Apart from the fact that this offers a fascinating insight into the training of sannyāsīs—imagine seven hundred at once—it is worth noting that particular attention is given to removing the fetters of "shame, hatred, fear, etc." Let us remind ourselves that this is strict training in the Vedānta, not Tantric, tradition. While *Kālī's Child* goes to great lengths to declare that Tantra's onus is to remove these fetters, it ignores the fact that every liberative tradition within the Hindu fold seeks to remove these same fetters.

More About Ramakrishna, published in 1993, was Swami Prabhananda's subsequent book. It presents in-depth articles on various topics, including Ramakrishna's interactions with other religious traditions, his visit to East Bengal, his final days, and a history of the early days of the Ramakrishna Order. "The Gospel of Sri Ramakrishna and the Life of M" recounts the fascinating history behind M's *Kathāmṛta* and offers little-known details about the author and his book. For example, M records in the *Kathāmṛta* Ramakrishna's statements about M himself. These statements, fifty-two in number, were regarded by M as *mahāvākyas*. One example: In the thirty-sixth statement, Ramakrishna said regarding M: "Illumine him, Mother, otherwise how will he illumine others in turn?" (219). Apart from these mahāvākyas concerning M himself, Ramakrishna also issued directives to M, eighty-five in number, which

M took as holy commandments. For example: "Meditate on God, you have much work to do," and "Advise the youths who call on you" (220).

Also of interest in this article is how Ramakrishna discouraged M from becoming a monk. While much has been said about Ramakrishna's preference for those who renounced "woman and gold," little has been said about how Ramakrishna encouraged the great majority of his householder devotees to remain in the world. M is no small example. When M had a strong urge to renounce the world, Ramakrishna prevented him from doing so by telling him: "Mother has told me that you have to do a little of Her work—you will have to teach 'Bhagavata,' the word of God, to humanity. The Mother keeps a Bhagavata pundit bound to the world." When even this did not pacify M's desire to renounce the world, Ramakrishna said to him: "Let nobody think that if he does not do Mother's work, it would remain undone. The Mother can turn even a straw into a teacher" (221). With this, M renounced his desire for monastic life. Fittingly, as time passed, M became a leading figure in the Ramakrishna movement, his room continually teeming with people, both monastic and lay, while he spoke unendingly of Ramakrishna.

Prabhananda's most recent book, *Journeys with Ramakrishna*, provides exhaustive research about Ramakrishna's pilgrimages and journeys. While some of his journeys are well known—to Varanasi and Vrindaban, for example—others, such as the one to Bali-Diwanganj in West Bengal, are not. Yet Bali-Diwanganj is of great interest to Ramakrishna scholars since this is the only known pilgrimage in which Ramakrishna and Sarada Devi traveled together. As Sarada told her disciple Nikunja Devi: "We [Ramakrishna and herself] traveled together by boat to Bali [Diwanganj] and from there to Kamarpukur. On this trip we ate together, we sang songs in chorus, and we shared prasad [offered food]" (2001, 149).

Journeys also mentions another, lesser-known incident, which occurred in 1870. It is well known that while on pilgrimage in Deoghar, Ramakrishna, seeing the desperate situation of the tribals, refused to budge until Mathur had clothed and fed them. Prabhananda reveals a second occasion in which Ramakrishna had accompanied Mathur to the latter's estates in Kalaighat, near Ranaghat, now in Bangladesh. The villagers, Mathur's tenants, were poverty-stricken and Mathur had come with the expectation of extracting money from them. Appalled at their miserable condition, Ramakrishna persuaded Mathur to remit their taxes and give them clothes, food for a week, and oil for their hair (105–110). It is worth noting that while Vivekananda has been credited with inaugurating social service while Ramakrishna purportedly had little use for it, these incidents are often invoked to demonstrate that Ramakrishna himself was concerned about ameliorating human suffering.[50]

While *Kālī's Child* portrays Mathur in sinister terms, referring to him as Ramakrishna's "boss" or the "temple boss" who "may have forced" himself upon Ramakrishna (KC, 2), Prabhananda spends some time discussing Ramakrishna's and Mathur's unique relationship. As Prabhananda notes, sometimes Mathur would be like a child, depending entirely upon Ramakrishna. At other times, Mathur looked after Ramakrishna as one would a child. Prabhananda writes:

> But here too there was a difference. . . . [Mathur] strongly believed that Baba [Ramakrishna, whom Mathur called "Baba," the Bengali word for "father"] had the power to direct his destiny. It was therefore no wonder that Mathurmohan made extravagant arrangements for the Master's visits to different temples and other places. Whenever the Master went out, someone would hold an umbrella, ornamented with silver, over his head; and servants would carry silver maces and other paraphernalia. (2001, 18–21)

Apart from the silver maces and ornamented-silver umbrellas, the fact that Mathur put up with feeding villagers, foregoing his taxes—what to speak of going on an extended pilgrimage in the first place—shows that Mathur had no small regard for Ramakrishna.

The events of Ramakrishna's 1868 Varanasi pilgrimage are well-known. Less known is the fact that the Bhairavi Brahmani was living in Varanasi at the time, and Ramakrishna met her at her request. When the pilgrimage continued on to Vrindaban, the Bhairavi accompanied him and there she passed away, after Ramakrishna had returned to Dakshineswar (28). While in Vrindaban, Ramakrishna began to practice Vaiṣṇava sādhana. About this, Ramakrishna later remarked: "Once I thought, 'Why should I be one-sided?' Therefore I was initiated into Vaiṣṇavism in Vrindaban and took the garb of a Vaiṣṇava monk" (62–63; KA 5.82). Prabhananda notes that Ramakrishna took initiation from a Vaiṣṇava priest by the name of Catura in a place near Radhakunda, and he probably lived in that locality for some time as well.

It was also in Vrindaban that Ramakrishna met Gangamata or Gangamayi, a woman in her sixties who was renowned for her holiness. She and Ramakrishna apparently had an instant rapport, developing a deep attachment for one another—so much so that Ramakrishna decided to stay with her and live in Vrindaban. Everything had been arranged for his permanent residence in Vrindaban—he would stay in Gangamayi's small hut, with his bed on one side and Gangamayi's on the other. So intent was he on remaining in Vrindaban that Gangamayi and Hriday got into a tug of war, with Ramakrishna being pulled from side to side. "But just then," Ramakrishna later remarked, "I remembered my mother. . . . She was old. I said to myself: 'My devotion to God will take to its wings if I have to worry about my mother. I would rather live with her. Then I shall have peace of mind and be able to meditate on God'" (68).

Ramakrishna has been criticized, by Jeffrey Kripal among others, for having his mother as his primary motivation in returning to Dakshineswar, with no mention of his wife, Sarada. One needs to remember, however, that in Indian culture a man is expected to have a much stronger and more intense attachment to his mother rather than to his spouse. Not to have such love and sense of responsibility would be seen as immoral and unnatural. Noted Bengali psychologist/sociologist Ashis Nandy writes that "the mother-son relationship is the basic nexus and the ultimate paradigm of human social relationships in India" (Nandy 1980, 37). Alan Roland has observed that in Indian cultural norms, "it is expected that [the son] remain deeply attached to his mother and deeply involved with his original family throughout life" (Roland 1996, 137).[51] Finally, Narasingha Sil has noted the same:

> Kripal betrays his ignorance of Bengali culture and social habits when he considers Ramakrishna's hurrying back home from Vrindaban on learning of his mother's illness somewhat reprehensible because he never mentions his wife Sarada left behind at home. . . . Anybody who is familiar with a Bengali household will know that it is quite common and even praiseworthy for a son to remember his mother more than his wife.[52]

In returning to Ramakrishna's journeys, we find that in 1874 Ramakrishna traveled to Khardah, a Gauḍīya Vaiṣṇava pilgrimage site, approximately twenty miles north of Kolkata. There seems to have been a strong bond of affection between Ramakrishna and Khardah's Goswami family. Prabhananda reports that reminiscences from the Goswami's descendants indicate that Yadavkishore and his brother Harikishore took a small boat to Dakshineswar and found, much to their surprise, that Ramakrishna was ready to go to Khardah. Though there had been no previous arrangement, Ramakrishna seemed to know they were arriving. The brothers took him to Khardah, where he visited the Śyāmsundar temple. When Ramakrishna was brought before the deity, he said: "Mā, you're playing the flute?" and went into deep ecstasy. According to the printed account given by Shrishkishore Goswami, grandson of

Yadavkishore, Śyāmsundar always assumes the form of Śyāmā (Kālī) on the night of Kālī worship (141–43). This is significant as another example of a culture in which it is entirely possible to worship both Kālī and Kṛṣṇa, without conflict and apparently even within the same image.

Prabhananda's article entitled "Śakti-sādhanā o Śrī Rāmakṛṣṇa" ("Śakti Worship and Sri Ramakrishna") was published in the Bengali journal *Udbodhan* (September 1999). Prabhananda begins by stating that "the idea of Śakti is intrinsically connected with Śakti sādhana" (1999, 549). It is important to keep this in mind since the implications of Śākta philosophy can be manifested only through sādhana.

Prabhananda discusses Tantra's ancient pedigree by noting that at one time both Vedic and Tantric sādhana were prevalent in Indian society. He quotes Kulluka Bhatta, the commentator on the *Manu Smṛti: vaidikī tāntrikī caiva dvividhā śrutiḥ*, "Vedic and Tantric are the two types of revealed scriptures (*śruti*)." By placing Tantra within the purview of śruti, Prabhananda locates Tantra in the realm of the sacred—hardly the view of Tantra the reader encounters in *Kālī's Child*, in which Tantra is reduced to "magical power, strangeness, seediness, and sex" (KC, 28). Prabhananda goes on to note the various unresolved debates concerning Tantra: whether or not Tantra was derived from the Vedas or was an independent tradition; whether or not Tantra was indigenous to India; whether or not Hindu and Buddhist Tantras are different and which of the two is more ancient. Prabhananda himself expresses no opinion on any of these debates.

Asserting that at one time Śakti worship was prevalent worldwide, Prabhananda goes on to state that only in India has there been an unbroken tradition of Śakti worship, and this has deeply and permanently influenced the Indian mind. Prabhananda quotes Swami Saradananda who wrote: "Śakti worship, especially the worship of Śakti as Mother, is the native treasure of India" (1999, 549). Prabhananda categorically declares: "The importance of Tantra in Śakti sādhana is undeniable. *Tanyate vistāryate jñānam anena iti tantram*, 'Tantra is that which broadens and deepens knowledge'" (549). This is again a far cry from what we read in *Kālī's Child*, which would have the reader believe that the Ramakrishna Order more or less rejects Tantra.[53]

Prabhananda reminds us that, according to Ramakrishna, a person cannot entirely follow the Vedic path in the Kaliyuga, and thus: "The path of Tantra is suited for the Kaliyuga" (*kolite tantrokto mot*; KA 2.66). But it is only through spiritual practice that anything can be achieved and therefore sādhana is given the utmost importance in the Tantras. In introducing the basic patterns of Śakti worship, Prabhananda writes that Kālī is the principal deity of both Śākta and Tantric sādhana, though Kālī has various forms which are represented by the Daśa-mahāvidyās, the ten aspects of Devī. Prabhananda notes that Tantra sādhana is open to all, with no barriers regarding caste, color or race. Yet "there is the shadow of *adhikāra-vāda*, or the required fitness of students" (1999, 550). Only one who is initiated, that is, has received *mantra dīkṣā*, is fit for Tantra sādhana.

Prabhananda notes that according to the Tantras, "the characteristics present in the universe are also present in the body" and for that reason the body is esteemed as the home of great spiritual power. The body, however, is not the goal of the Tantras; the goal is to develop and express the divine power housed within the body. Tantric sādhana is eclectic: it integrates "elements of yoga, prayer, worship, and meditation on the identity of the individual and the Absolute" (550). Śakti sādhana is primarily for householders: "A householder devoted to the supreme ideal described in the scriptures is called *gṛhāvadhūta*, a householder-mendicant" (550). Thus, if all aspects of Śakti sādhana have not been followed by those within the Ramakrishna Order, it has been for the simple reason that not all aspects of Śakti sādhana are either suited to or practicable for monastics.

Critically, however, Prabhananda asserts:

> From a liberal perspective, Śakti sādhana may be seen as a sādhana of nondual Brahman. Swami Saradananda says, "The enlightened Tantric, like the Advaitin, sees no difference between mud and sandal[paste], friend and foe, a dwelling house and the cremation ground." (550)

Again we see that, in a fairly significant way, there is no hard and fast division between Advaita and Tantra. In many aspects the paths converge and in many ways their views are complementary. Case in point: both Advaita and Tantra assert that consciousness is one and nondual. Advaitins state that Brahman is pure consciousness. Quoting the *Durgā Saptaśatī* (5.17): *Yā devī sarvabhūteṣu cetanety-abhidhīyate*, "[Salutations to the] Goddess who, present in all beings, is called Consciousness," Prabhananda notes that while modern science views power as unconscious, Tantra sees it as filled with consciousness (550).

During the time of Ramprasad (1720–1781) there were "two streams of Śakti sādhana: (1) secret sādhana and (2) worship of the clay image of Mother Kālī with full pomp and glory" (552). Ramprasad integrated both streams, "lifted Kālī worship above its sectarian bias, and gave it a universal appeal." While the Tantras emphasized internal purification, Ramprasad emphasized *bhāva*. Prabhananda quotes Ramprasad: "She is known through bhāva; can She be grasped in the absence (*abhāva*) of bhāva?" Ramprasad's goal was to attain Brahman, which he did by "holding on to Mother Śyāmā [Kālī]." To that effect Ramprasad sang, "My [Mother] Tārā is formless" and, when his spiritual heart opened, he sang: "Mother dwells in every being" (552).

The final section of Prabhananda's article addresses Śakti worship in relation to Ramakrishna's life. He mentions that Ramakrishna, under the direction of Yogeswari Brahmani, practiced all sixty-four Tantric disciplines. "There is," Prabhananda writes, "a subtle intermingling of bhāvas in the sixty-four Tantras. Gradually [Ramakrishna] scaled the highest pinnacle of bhāva sādhanas" (552). After his Tantric sādhana, Ramakrishna then pursued Advaita sādhana under the direction of Totapuri. Rather than seeing these as contradictory sādhanas, Prabhananda sees them as complementary: "Firmly established in nondual knowledge and with the bhāva of a vijñānī as his support, Ramakrishna lived joyfully as a child of the Universal Mother. Coming down from nirvikalpa samādhi, he enjoyed *līlā* with devotion and with devotees." Prabhananda confirms this by quoting Pratap Chandra Mazumdar's recollection of Ramakrishna: "He worships Śiva, he worships Kālī, he worships Rāma, he worships Kṛṣṇa, and is a confirmed advocate of Vedantist doctrines" (553).

Prabhananda observes that Ramakrishna's sādhanas are tinged with the ideal of harmony. That is, Ramakrishna practiced various sādhanas and saw all manifestations of the divine as valid and efficacious. As Ramakrishna famously said, *Jato mot tato poth*, "As many faiths, so many paths." More to the point, Prabhananda points out that Ramakrishna repeatedly said that Brahman and Śakti are one and the same (KA 1.202–3).

As for the practical application of Ramakrishna's Śākta sādhana, Prabhananda writes that Ramakrishna's Śakti worship had established him on the pinnacle of nondual knowledge. Further, while both Ramakrishna and Vivekananda attained nirvikalpa samādhi, neither of these experiences made them turn away from humanity. Finally, Ramakrishna's Śakti worship culminated in the worship of his wife, Sarada Devi. "If one wishes to understand the Śakti sādhana of Sri Ramakrishna," Prabhananda writes, "one has to look deeply at the significant role played by his two principal companions, Sri Sārada Devi and Swami Vivekananda" (554).

Prabhananda concludes that, in contrast to earlier times, people now want concrete examples of the utility of Śakti sādhana and how that manifests in terms of social benefit. Further, in contrast to earlier times, where individual liberation was the only goal, Śakti sādhana has also become an instrument of social good, and has now become easily accessible to all people.

Swami Bhajanananda

From 1979 through 1986, Swami Bhajanananda, now a trustee of the Ramakrishna Order, was editor of the most widely read journal of the Ramakrishna Order, *Prabuddha Bharata.* While Bhajanananda has written a number of articles for various publications of the Ramakrishna Order for many years, none of his major writings have been compiled into a book. His most respected writings are his *Prabuddha Bharata* editorials. A monk since the early 1960s, Bhajanananda is widely regarded as one of the leading intellectuals of the Ramakrishna Order.

While Swami Bhajanananda has written comprehensively on a number of subjects, we will consider here only his writings dealing directly with Ramakrishna. In March 1979 Bhajanananda wrote "Sri Ramakrishna the Unknown," in which he discusses the question Ramakrishna occasionally asked his devotees: "What do you think of me?" Ramakrishna encouraged a spirit of inquiry among his closest disciples, and he asked the question for two complementary reasons: first, to gauge the disciple's mind so that he could assess the disciple's belief patterns; second, to stimulate his disciple's mind in order to more fully understand him.

Ramakrishna said: "The devotees who come here may be divided into two groups. One group says, 'O God, give me liberation.' Another group, belonging to the inner circle, doesn't talk that way. They are satisfied if they can know two things: who I [Ramakrishna] am; second, who they are and what their relationship to me is" (KA 4.99). As we shall see, *Kālī's Child* takes a very different view of both Ramakrishna's "inner circle" as well as Ramakrishna's question "What do you think of me?" In contrast to the explanation given above, Kripal asserts that Ramakrishna "did not ask the question because he was already absolutely certain of the answer. Rather, he asked the question to be reassured that the answer that he had already been given many times before was in fact the correct one." Kripal goes one step further to declare: "*Ramakrishna the incarnation was socially created through human interaction and the process of interpretation and debate*" (KC, 219; italics in text).

Seeing the matter in an entirely different light, Bhajanananda returns to his original question "Who is Ramakrishna?" by noting that "an aura of mystery surrounds Sri Ramakrishna's life right from his very birth" (1979, 88). It is interesting to compare the "mystery" as understood by those within the Ramakrishna Order to "the secret" according to *Kālī's Child*. As we shall see, these two terms come from two entirely different worldviews. Apart from this overarching divergence, two entirely different ways of translating words, concepts and cultural meanings are at work here. The "mystery" of Ramakrishna begins with his father's dream of Viṣṇu at Gaya, in which Viṣṇu informs Ramakrishna's father that he will be born as his son. Ramakrishna's mother, on the other hand, had the experience of celestial light emanating from the Śiva temple, which then entered her womb. "This," Bhajanananda writes, "raises the interesting question, whose manifestation Sri Ramakrishna really was—whether of Viṣṇu or of Śiva. Or, was it a case of religious harmony right in the mother's womb?" (88–89). *Kālī's Child*, by contrast, declares: "No one has noted the obvious, that both Viṣṇu and Śiva are identified … as the divine source of Ramakrishna's conception" (KC, 55). One wonders how Kripal could assume that no one had noticed something so obvious, which, of course, many had. They simply did not find it problematic. This is what Bhajanananda and other Ramakrishna devotees simply subsume into the category of "mystery"—just as tens of millions of Christians, Jews, Muslims, Hindus, Buddhists and everyone else under the sun have similarly done with divine legends since the beginning of time.

Asserting that "the historical aspect of an incarnation is only the temporal dimension of his eternal spiritual reality," Bhajanananda goes on to say that the real Ramakrishna is to be sought in the depths of one's soul. "The real Sri Ramakrishna is unknown but *not* unknowable. He can be known only if he reveals himself. And he reveals himself to the sincere aspirant in the secret depths of his heart and fulfills the beginningless yearnings of his soul" (1979, 91). Bhajanananda commends the reader to engage in a deeper and more intense mystical life with a deeper relationship with Ramakrishna. Such a stance, not uncommon in insider literature, obviously takes for granted a number of presuppositions which would be difficult for most academics to swallow. Nevertheless, since many of the core ideas of the Ramakrishna tradition will be dissected and dismissed by those outside the Ramakrishna tradition, it is important to see how some of these central beliefs have been viewed by those within the tradition.

According to Bhajanananda, the Vedic seers (*ṛṣis*) felt no conflict between work and knowledge; many ṛsis lived in cities and advised kings. This ṛsi ideal was revived by Ramakrishna through his life and teachings (87) and he "recaptured the integral vision of the Vedic seers who saw divinity shining through every object in the universe" (1986, 498–99). Instead of avoiding marriage, Ramakrishna not only chose his own bride but also allowed her to live with him and be his helpmate in his larger mission. Quoting distinguished sociologist G. S. Ghurye, Bhajanananda points out that Ramakrishna also gave a wholly new orientation to the monastic ideal and "effected an all-round rejuvenation of monastic life in India" (499).[54]

Ramakrishna recovered for the modern world the "idea of the divinity of the soul and the sacredness of nature" (1980, 87). In place of the Vedic worship of nature, Ramakrishna encouraged the worship of Śakti. His worship of Kālī is "one of the most significant—if not the most significant aspect—of Ramakrishna's life" (1986, 501). By this declaration, Bhajanananda unknowingly counters what will become one of academia's more prevalent (and persistent) myths—that Kālī has been "marginalized" by those within the Ramakrishna tradition. Those within the tradition would be astounded to hear about such "marginalization." Devotion to Kālī continues to find expression in the succeeding generations of the Ramakrishna tradition, both monastic and lay, through not only prayer and worship but also meditation with Kālī as the *iṣṭa-devatā* ("chosen deity").

Ramakrishna's worship of the Divine Mother is deeply significant, first, because such worship of the Divine Mother, who is the Primal Energy, brings in its wake "a great spiritual upsurge everywhere" (501). Second, by regarding "the Godhead as feminine," Ramakrishna elevated the status of women everywhere. By worshiping God as Mother, Ramakrishna, through the force of his own example, brought to the world the spiritual attitude of regarding God as Mother. This is the highest spiritual mood for Ramakrishna, according to whom the "attitude of regarding God as Mother is the last word in sādhana. 'O God, Thou art my Mother and I am thy child'—this is the last word in spirituality" (504).

Of critical importance was Ramakrishna's own intense spiritual aspiration, or *vyākulatā*. Significantly, during the Ṛg Vedic period, the primary forms of spiritual discipline were prayer and worship. "But these were animated by the power of blazing aspiration. Sri Ramakrishna has brought back that fire of aspiration (which he called *vyākulatā*) and has revitalized prayer and worship as much as he rejuvenated the Upaniṣadic spirit of meditation, inquiry and self-analysis" (1980, 88). The term—often used by Ramakrishna to describe the intense longing that one should have for God—has, since the controversy over *Kālī's Child* arose, been a matter of intense debate. *Vyākulatā* was translated by Nikhilananda as "yearning" or "longing" while *Kālī's Child* renders it as a homoerotically oriented "anxious desire."

Bhajanananda states that Ramakrishna's teaching of religious harmony was a reinterpretation of the Ṛg Vedic "Truth is one, sages call it by various names."[55] More importantly, he observes that while traditional Advaitins followed the path of jñāna to negate the world in order to realize Brahman, Ramakrishna advocated going a step further. The path of negation (*neti, neti*—"not this, not this") "should be followed by the realization of Brahman in the manifested world through a process of affirmation. This fuller knowledge he termed 'vijñāna'" (1980, 88). Since there has been impassioned debate over Ramakrishna's root practice—whether he was a Vedāntin or Tāntrik or Vaiṣṇava—with much of the debate centered around Ramakrishna's advocacy of vijñāna or "fuller knowledge," it is significant that Bhajanananda sees vijñāna within the purview of Vedānta, stating that Ramakrishna's vijñāna was the basis for Vivekananda's doctrine of social equality. Refusing to characterize vijñāna as dualistic or nondualistic, Bhajanananda contends that, having established the "multidimensional and integral nature of religious experience," Ramakrishna showed that there was no conflict between dualism and nondualism (1986, 496).

According to Bhajanananda, Ramakrishna had experienced the highest knowledge, knowledge of Brahman, and also experienced the bliss of communion with the Supreme Self in different ways. While normal human love is tinged with selfish or instinctual motives, of which one may not be aware, Ramakrishna's love was utterly unselfish and unique in its intensity. Bhajanananda points out that "so great was [Ramakrishna's] love for Naren, Rakhal, Baburam and other disciples that he would weep for them when they were away" (1982a, 88). While *Kālī's Child* will assert that this indicates the homoerotic basis of Ramakrishna's attitude toward his male disciples, Bhajanananda does not see any sexual component in Ramakrishna's attitude. Indeed, he goes out of his way to make Ramakrishna's intense love and longing for his disciples—*vyākulatā*—a central point of his editorial in the most widely read journal of the Ramakrishna Order. To strengthen his point, he quotes Vivekananda on this score: "It was [Ramakrishna's] unflinching love for me that bound me to him forever. He alone knew how to love another" (88).

Bhajanananda sees Ramakrishna's message as one of harmony on various levels, one being between the ideals of the Personal God and the Impersonal God. He quotes Ramakrishna's words: "Brahman and Śakti are identical. If you accept the one you must accept the other" (1982b, 168–69). Ramakrishna harmonized, through his own experience, the issue of whether God was formless or had form, which was one of the great hot-button issues of nineteenth-century Bengal. In the interreligious field also, Ramakrishna's message was one of harmony: "The God of Hindus is not different from the God of Christians or Muslims, but he appears to be different because of the religious 'language' (that is, the symbols, images and myths) employed in describing him varies from religion to religion" (1982b, 169).

While the ultimate goal of all spiritual paths, Bhajanananda writes, is the one God, the paths are diverse. "But this does not mean that they are discordant. All spiritual paths—jñāna, bhakti, yoga and karma in Hinduism and the various paths in other religions—are valid means to realizing God. This [Ramakrishna] learned through his own experience" (1982b, 170). Moreover, Ramakrishna "never allowed any of his followers to criticize any religious path. He encouraged each to stick to his own path and guided him along that."

The most pressing need in contemporary life "is an incontrovertible assurance of the existence of the transcendent Reality and the possibility of realizing it. This assurance Sri Ramakrishna gave through his life" (1986, 493). Such realization is possible through "the transformation of consciousness." Ramakrishna demonstrated that by transforming human consciousness, every person could attain higher spiritual experience (493). Bhajanananda also discusses the state of bhāvamukha, of which we will see more in *Kālī's Child*. Bhāvamukha, that threshold between the Absolute and the relative world, is a state of consciousness which Bhajanananda defines as "a kind of vestibule with doors opening to all the different levels of consciousness" (496). It is important to keep this definition in mind when we again encounter bhāvamukha (which Kripal defines as "remaining in existence") in *Kālī's Child*.

Ramakrishna's greatest contribution to the world, Bhajanananda asserts,

> is he himself. By the very birth of such a person ... humanity has enriched itself and has its dignity raised to the highest level. He may be adored as an avatar. . . . But, more than that, he is the embodiment of love. . . . For many people life would be unthinkable or insupportable without him. His birth on earth is for them the greatest blessing that the Supreme Spirit has conferred on humanity. (505)

We have closely examined Swami Bhajanananda's writings on Ramakrishna in order to provide a glimpse into the alternative universe of the Ramakrishna insider community. While there are insiders who may differ with Bhajanananda on a few issues, on the whole Bhajanananda's views on Ramakrishna may be taken as a representative sample of the insider view of Ramakrishna. As we have mentioned earlier, Bhajanananda is widely respected and his writings are closely followed.[56] If nothing else, an investigation into such thought provides a variant interpretation of a number of contested issues which we shall soon encounter in *Kālī's Child— vyākulatā*, for example, the nature of Ramakrishna's love, and of course, the nature of Ramakrishna himself. While no one would seriously suggest that an outsider Ramakrishna scholar regard Ramakrishna as an avatar or assume that he was divinely inspired, one would hope that the scholar could at least glimpse how deeply Ramakrishna is loved and revered. Simply understanding this fact alone would go far in making some sense of the tumultuous reaction which *Kālī's Child* provoked when it was published.

Amiya Sen

A historian specializing in nineteenth-century India and the intellectual history of modern Bengal, Amiya Sen serves in Deshbandhu College's Department of History at the University of Delhi. In the mid-1990s Sen was the Agatha Harrison Fellow at St. Antony's College in Oxford and Visiting Fellow at the Indian Institute of Advanced Study, Shimla. Sen's *Hindu Revivalism in Bengal*, published in 1993, examines the great change or "revival" which transformed Bengal, beginning in the early 1870s and extending through the first years of the twentieth century. It is important that, in contrast to his Western contemporaries, Sen comes to significantly different conclusions regarding Ramakrishna, remarking that "reading the original five-volume Bengali *Kathāmṛta* has been quite rewarding" (1993, 8). Importantly, he does not restrict his research on Ramakrishna to one sole dominating text. He culls information not only from M's *Kathāmṛta* but also from Saradananda's *Līlāprasaṅga*, Sarada Devi's recorded conversations which appear in *Śrī-Śrī-Māyer*

Kathā, Swami Saradeshananda's reminiscences of Sarada in *Śrī-Śrī-Māyer Smṛtikathā*, Vivekananda's works, and the biographies of Swami Adbhutananda and Durga Charan Nag, as well as the biographies and reminiscences of other contemporaries of Ramakrishna. In discussing Ramakrishna, Sen also addresses (and occasionally disputes) some of the issues raised by Sumit Sarkar in his *Kathāmṛta as Text*.

Hindu Revivalism in Bengal comprises a detailed examination of Bengal's social, intellectual and religious life between 1872 and 1905. In the closing years of the nineteenth century, Sen observes, notions of a "Hindu revival" had gained acceptance. Instead of a direct trajectory, however, this "Hindu awakening" underwent several stages of construction and transformation (3–4). From this vantage point, Sen provides an investigation and reappraisal of Ramakrishna.

In contrast to Neevel and Kripal, Sen does not conclude that Ramakrishna was a Tāntrik rather than a Vedāntin. Observing that "Ramakrishna would not ultimately listen to the Bhairavi who tried hard to dissuade [Ramakrishna] from being instructed in Vedanta by ... Totapuri," Sen concludes that "Ramakrishna did not evidently find Tantra and Vedanta to be mutually irreconcilable."[57] Addressing what might seem counter-intuitive to a Euro-American audience, Sen explains: "Hindu religious philosophy ... speak[s] of an inner unity between the highest conclusions of both Tantra and Vedanta—after all Ramakrishna did speak of Brahman and Sakti as only two manifestations of the same Cosmic Power. Secondly, Ramakrishna found endorsement of his social and religious views in both these forms of sadhana" (298).

Sen asserts that it is "clear from an examination of [Ramakrishna's] life that in the ultimate analysis, Ramakrishna held the Vedantic idea of oneness between God and man and of a *Nirakar-Nirguna* Brahman to be the ultimate road to God-realization although he rarely prescribed this to his followers" (298). Why, if such were the case, would Ramakrishna rarely prescribe the *jñāna marga*—nondualistic path—to his followers? Because of Hinduism's "concept of *adhikarbheda*—worship commensurate with the spiritual potential of individuals," Sen writes, which "Ramakrishna helped to ... popularize in modern Bengal" (299–300).

It is also significant that Sen discusses Ramakrishna dressing as a woman without assigning pathology to Ramakrishna. "Gadadhar," Sen writes, "appears to have been greatly influenced by the playfulness of the child Krishna and also the mystical relationship between Radha and Krishna—themes that were very important in popular Vaishnavism. . . . In later life Ramakrishna was to interpret this as the *Madhur-bhava* ...

and such experiments in early life ... may have eventually contributed towards his personal conquest of sex which he held to be so important to success in spiritual life" (295). Sen sees no reason to raise a red flag here.

Also in contrast to what we will increasingly see in Western interpretations of Ramakrishna, Sen does not see Ramakrishna exhibiting either fear or hatred of sex. "It is ... certain," Sen writes,

> that [Ramakrishna] was not against sexuality per se but against sexual over-indulgence. It was here that he made a valid distinction between the code of conduct of *grihasthees* (householders) and those initiated into *sanyas* (in this context monastic life). While sexual continence was a lifelong vow for the monk, the rules for the lay disciples were obviously more liberal.

Ramakrishna, he continues, "was trying to use a normal and healthy sexual relationship with the wife as the best offensive against sexual promiscuity or extra-marital relationships" (303).[58] Importantly, though, Sen reports that Ramakrishna suggests husband and wife live together as brother and sister after they have two or three children. Sen (perhaps because of his own cultural background and his comprehensive understanding of Ramakrishna's historical background) sees nothing extraordinary about it.

It is remarkable that so many of Bengal's profoundly important religious, social, political and cultural leaders in these crucial years had associated with Ramakrishna. Some were particularly close—Vivekananda, of course, and Keshab Sen, as well as the founder of modern Bengali drama, Girish Ghosh. Less known in the West but extremely significant in Bengal's history are others who also knew Ramakrishna to a greater or lesser degree: Brahmo leader Shivanath Shastri, Vaiṣṇava spiritual leader Vijoy Krishna Goswami, novelist Bankimchandra Chattopadhyay (who later became a disciple of Vijoy Krishna Goswami), epic poet and playwright Michael Madhusudan Dutt, nationalist leader and philanthropist Aswini Kumar Dutta, Devendranath Tagore (who was not only Rabindranath's father, but also Keshab Sen's predecessor as leader of the Brahmo Samaj), scholar, social reformer and philanthropist Ishwar Chandra Vidyasagar, Hindu revivalist leader Pandit Shashadhar Tarkachudamani, the celebrated actress Binodini, as well as many others. One can observe these characters appearing throughout the pages of the *Kathāmṛta* and, with a few exceptions, for most Western readers these are personalities of no great significance. But for Indians, and Bengalis in particular, it is akin to reading a roll call of the founders of modern Bengali society. Their contribution to Indian history, particularly to

Bengal, should not be underestimated. What also should not be underestimated is the fact that these extraordinarily influential people—all (with the exception of Binodini) members of Bengal's forward-thinking intelligentsia—were influenced, some minimally, some profoundly, by Ramakrishna.

Sen's final conclusion on Ramakrishna himself is that he was a "many-layered personality" with "diverse possibilities latent in his life and message." Ramakrishna was "an ingenious story-teller with fairly well-developed skills of communication; a man conservative to the core but possessing an amazing breadth of personality; a rustic, paternal figure distinctive for his kindness and compassion and a greatly inspiring religious teacher. . . . Many aspects concerning his life or human qualities are capable of being interpreted in radically different ways" (310).

The accuracy of Sen's last statement can be dramatically seen in the section that follows. Malcolm McLean, although reading the *Kathāmṛta* in the original Bengali, will nevertheless use Western paradigms for evaluating Ramakrishna. Further, he will use the *Kathāmṛta* to the exclusion of all other source documents in his interpretation. As a result, McLean's view of Ramakrishna will be radically different from Sen's. McLean's work will also be a precursor to future Western interpretations of Ramakrishna.

Malcolm McLean

Malcolm McLean's unpublished Ph.D. thesis, "A Translation of the *Śrī-Śrī-Rāmakṛṣṇa-Kathāmṛta* with Explanatory Notes and Critical Introduction" was submitted to the University of Otago in 1983, the same year that Sen's *Hindu Revivalism* was published. McLean's thesis was his translation of the entire *Kathāmṛta*, which is preceded by his lengthy introduction. The first Western scholar to seriously examine the Bengali *Kathāmṛta* rather than its English translation, McLean nevertheless appraised Ramakrishna according to Western cultural norms.

While it is far too facile to construct Amiya Sen's and Malcolm McLean's opposing views of Ramakrishna as an East/West binary, certainly their respective cultural locations strongly influenced their conflicting interpretations. In contrast to Sen's appraisal of Ramakrishna, McLean writes in his introduction: "What kind of a man was he? I think it is fair to say that he would today be regarded by westerners as a little mad, if not actually psychotic, because of his great insecurity, his need for disciples and adulation, his need to be the center of attraction wherever he went" (McLean 1983, lxxi–lxxii).

McLean easily pronounces Ramakrishna a homosexual, finding evidence in Ramakrishna's statement that he has a feminine nature (KA 2.125). A number of points need to be addressed here: first and obviously, not all male homosexuals are "feminine" and what passes for "feminine" according to contemporary Euro-American standards is not a pan-cultural phenomenon. Even were such a thing to exist, it would neither define nor constitute homosexuality. The current obsessive concern with "masculinity" did not exist in rural India.[59] More critically, the "feminine nature" which Ramakrishna attributes to himself was not indicative of sexual preference. It is a deeper indication of a person's psychic structure. Importantly, a feminine identification would not be interpreted in India as a symptom of homosexuality or pathology. A male sādhaka's "feminine nature" would be viewed as an exemplary quality and, in fact, as an indication of holiness. We can recall that according to the Gauḍīya Vaiṣṇava tradition, there is only one male—and that one male is Kṛṣṇa. Even within some Tantric schools, the goal of Tantra sādhana is to become the goddess. About this N. N. Bhattacharyya writes, quoting R. G. Bhandarkar: "The ambition of every pious follower of the [Vāmacāra Tantra] system is to become identical with Tripurasundarī." The followers of Śakti believe that "it ought to be the aim of all to become a woman." Bhattacharyya goes on to quote M. M. Bose, who states that the Sahajiyās "believe that at a certain stage of spiritual culture the man should transform himself into a woman, and remember that he cannot have experience of true love so long as he cannot realize the nature of woman in him." Bhattacharyya further notes: "The *Ācārabheda Tantra* prescribes that the Parā Śakti should be worshiped only by becoming a woman." Finally in this connection, Bhattacharyya tells the legend of Brahmā, Viṣṇu and Śiva who were transformed into women before being allowed to see Devī in her highest form (Bhattacharyya, 292).

Ramakrishna's admonition about worldliness as embodied in "woman and gold" (*kāminī kāñcana*) is also seen as an indicator of his homosexuality. Declares McLean: "I think [Ramakrishna's] ambivalence tending on dislike of women, this fear of their presence and their power, stems from his homosexuality" (1983, lxxxv). Finally, McLean judges Ramakrishna's wearing of women's attire during his *madhura bhāva* as evidence of "transvestitism and female impersonation" (lxxiv). It bears mentioning that while McLean was the first Western scholar to seriously examine the Bengali *Kathāmṛta*, literally millions of Bengalis—including numerous indigenous scholars—had read the same material for nearly eight decades and had not come up with a similar assessment.

As far as philosophy is concerned, McLean finds Ramakrishna unequal to the task: "Ramakrishna has strayed … into the realm of philosophy without the background or the tools to succeed there. His use of language is imprecise, his use of concepts confused and contradictory, like his claim that God both has form and is formless." Continuing, McLean wonders why Ramakrishna attempted his task: "He should have realized that a qualified non-dualism is a dualism, that one has to choose between dualism and non-dualism, and that there is no position between them or beyond both … nor can the two co-exist so that man can move between the two like someone going up and down a ladder to the roof of his house" (xxiv–xxv; referring to KA 5.58). If such remarks seem hauntingly familiar and raise the specter of a latter-day Orientalism, it is perhaps due to the author's insistence upon European univalent logic and methodology as the ultimate determiner of truth.

McLean was the first scholar to take issue with Nikhilananda's English translation of the *Kathāmṛta*. While Nikhilananda had written that he had "made a literal translation, omitting only a few pages of no particular interest to English-speaking readers" (GSR, vii), McLean writes that "more than a few pages has … been omitted" (1983, i). Kripal extends this charge by claiming that the omitted portions "contain some of the most revealing and significant passages of the entire text" (KC, 4). The website associated with this book (http://interpretingramakrishna.com) contains the material that Nikhilananda did not include in his translation of the *Kathāmṛta*. Readers may judge for themselves the veracity of these claims and counterclaims.

On a different note and prefiguring Jeffrey Kripal's criticism of *The Gospel of Sri Ramakrishna*, McLean correctly observes that M "began publishing his recollections of Ramakrishna piecemeal," its five, nonchronological volumes appearing over a twenty-nine-year span. Nikhilananda's 1942 translation "collapsed all these into one whole," McLean argues, and this presents "serious disadvantages for the scholar interested in the reliability of Gupta's material." Apparently McLean finds M's reliability potentially as problematic as Nikhilananda's, because, as McLean writes, "This material [in the *Kathāmṛta*] came from three different sources, of different standards of reliability" (1983, ii).

This is puzzling. M writes in his Preface, which McLean reproduces in full (ii–iii), that there are three classes of evidence: first-class evidence is that which is "direct and recorded on the same day." Second-class evidence is also direct but was not immediately recorded and was recollected long after Ramakrishna's death. Third-class evidence is, like the second, unrecorded, and was heard secondhand from Ramakrishna's contemporaries after Ramakrishna's death. M makes it extremely clear that in the main body of the text he has *only* included material from the first class of evidence, that is, words spoken by Ramakrishna and heard directly by M himself,[60] and McLean faithfully translates this. It is thus utterly perplexing that McLean writes: "It may be possible … to recover the material from Gupta's diary … and distinguish from the other two types [i.e., types 2 and 3]. But this will only be possible if the distinguishing marks (day, date, year and phase of the moon) are not excluded, as they are from Nikhilananda's translation" (iii).

First, while Nikhilananda removes the phases of the moon, he has retained the day, date and year in the translation. Second, and more importantly, Nikhilananda's *Gospel* also notes that the material translated in the *Gospel* was heard firsthand by M; an appendix to his *Gospel* includes "several conversations which took place in the absence of M, but of which he received a first-hand record from persons concerned" (GSR, vii).

Like Neevel, McLean finds that, for Ramakrishna, bhakti had primacy over jñāna and "Ramakrishna's monism is Tantric monism rather than Vedantic Advaita" (McLean 1983, xxxi). He also observes that "Ramakrishna does not use even Tantric language consistently" (xvii). Stating that Ramakrishna was a Tantric devotee, McLean notes that "Ramakrishna always insisted that … [his] sādhana was of the right-handed variety. There is no reason why, even though his guru was a woman, we should doubt what he says. And the fact of his homosexuality … would lend support to this theory" (lxv).

Should one wonder why we would concern ourselves with an unpublished Ph.D. thesis, the answer is that McLean is respected as a Ramakrishna scholar and his views have been widely cited by other scholars. Moreover, McLean's thesis reflects the tenor of his time in terms of the way Western-trained scholars analyzed religious figures from the Hindu tradition.

Malcolm McLean's 1989 article "Women as Aspects of the Mother Goddess in India: A Case Study of Ramakrishna" continues much the same pattern seen earlier in his Ph.D. thesis. McLean's particular hypothesis in this article is that, rather than seeing women respectfully—as embodiments of the Divine Mother—Ramakrishna had an essentially negative view of women. "Ramakrishna seemed to see women predominantly in sexual terms," McLean writes (17), yet McLean neither investigates nor discusses what Ramakrishna's women disciples had to say about the matter.

As a person competent in Bengali, McLean could have found a wealth of literature concerning Ramakrishna's women disciples, not the least of which are the recorded conversations of Sarada Devi (*Śrī-Śrī-Māyer Kathā*), Sarada's attendant Swami Saradeshananda's reminiscences (*Śrī-Srī-Māyer Smṛtikathā*), Ramakrishna's disciple Gauri-Ma's biography (*Gaurī-Mā*), Binodini's autobiography (*Āmār Kathā*) as well as a large number of reminiscences of women associated with Ramakrishna which have been published in Bengali journals. McLean largely confines his source material to the *Kathāmṛta* (with an occasional nod to Saradananda's *Līlāprasaṅga*), but his interpretations lean heavily on the analyses of G. M. Carstairs, Wendy Doniger O'Flaherty, Sudhir Kakar, Jeffrey Masson, and Manisha Roy, who, by and large, presuppose the Euro-American psychosocial model to be the normative (i.e., healthy) standard, thus assuring that departures from this "norm" are considered deviant.[61] Given McLean's presumption that Euro-American societal models form the basis of the normative standard against which all other paradigms are to be assessed, he necessarily sees Ramakrishna, the Hindu religious traditions, and nineteenth-century Indian social norms through a distorted lens.

McLean denigrates Śāktas by writing: "Devotion to the Mother … involves a regression to infancy, based on the inability to cope in an adult fashion with the dual nature of the natural mother, and its subsequent transference to other women" (1989, 16). McLean also pathologizes Ramakrishna's "strong desire for *moksha*," reading it as "a way of escape from the world and avoidance of sexual contact with women." He goes on to argue that "this explains his retirement to the temple complex at Dakshineswar" (19).

Indeed, the thesis of McLean's article centers on Ramakrishna's "anti-woman stance." Treating women as embodiments of the Mother Goddess, he writes, "masks a number of anxiety states which made normal relations with women difficult, if not impossible" and, in fact, "may be a cheap way of covering up the fear of or denigration of women so that it is not recognized for what it is" (21). Here again, by the phrase "normal relations" the familiar Euro-American model is presumed to be normative and any deviation from it is pathologized and denigrated. From the standpoint of a Hindu sādhaka, looking upon women (indeed, everyone) as manifestations of the divine would be normative, praiseworthy, emulatory. But according to McLean, it is—at least for Ramakrishna—a cheap cover-up tactic.

June McDaniel

June McDaniel's insightful *Madness of the Saints* (1989) sees Ramakrishna as a model of divine madness. Interestingly, the very qualities which in Bengal would identify Ramakrishna as a holy person possessed by divine madness, are the same symptoms so often pathologized by most Western-trained scholars. In fact, McDaniel points out that "writers such as Jeffrey Masson ... emphasize the psychopathology of ecstatic and mystical states, assuming Western paradigms to be normative" (280).

Based on her field work in Bengal, McDaniel observes: "Several holy men listed four qualities as the hallmarks of the saint: he is inert, *jaḍa* (he becomes lost in meditation, appearing like a corpse or a stone statue); mad, *unmāda* (he acts irrationally, for he is always in ecstasy); ghoulish, *piśāca* (he does not discriminate between pure and impure things, feeling love toward all); and childlike, *bālaka* (he acts like a child between four and eight years old). As a holy man interviewed in Bākreswar stated, the one who has attained Kālī is eternally in a state of apparent madness (*pāgal bhāva*)" (9–10). McDaniel further notes that "in [Ramakrishna's] visions and identifications with the Divine Mother, his roles fit those of both Vaiṣṇava and tantric madmen" (100).

According to McDaniel, in Bengal's religious context, "to call Caitanya, Nityānanda, and Rāmakṛṣṇa mad was not to insult them, but to compliment them and show them respect; theirs was a 'good' madness" (250). One remembers here Ramakrishna's telling remark: "The thought of God makes me mad (*īśvarer bhābe āmār unmād hoy*) (KA 1.254).

Carl Olson

Carl Olson's 1990 *Mysterious Play of Kālī* uses the concept of Kālī's *līlā*, divine play, as a hermeneutical key for understanding Ramakrishna (Olson 1990, 15). Olson's book has been characterized by Narasingha Sil as "situated squarely in the well-known hagiographic tradition" (Sil 1991, 4). On this point not only do we disagree but certainly Olson would disagree as well, albeit for different reasons. While not entirely unsympathetic, Olson's work nevertheless displays a prodigious amount of applied psychopathology and cultural misinterpretation. It needs to be mentioned, however, that Olson's study of Ramakrishna was made much more difficult by the fact that Olson was denied permission by the publisher—the Ramakrishna-Vivekananda Center in New York City—to make extensive quotations from *The Gospel of Sri Ramakrishna*. Olson reports: "A committee at the center thought that this work does not depict Rāmakrishna in the best light." Although he tried to persuade "my implacable and ardent censors," his attempts were fruitless (Olson 1990, x). One cannot help thinking that had there been positive communication between publisher and scholar, a more balanced book would have been produced and the publisher (and by extension, Vedanta Societies) would not be viewed as would-be censors.

This regrettable occurrence aside, Olson's *Mysterious Play of Kālī*—in contrast to McDaniel's culturally nuanced interpretation—comes across as culturally blinkered:

> Wide mood swings, memory lapses, sitting immobile, having conversations with no visible persons, laughing and dancing with an inanimate object, personal identity and sex-role confusion, hearing sounds and voices, apparent hallucinations in the form of various kinds of visions, and loss of normal consciousness. . . . Did Rāmakrishna suffer from an affective disorder? Or did he have schizophrenia? (48)

Olson rightly asserts that even if Ramakrishna *were* insane, the madness would have to be placed within a Hindu religious context. He nevertheless continues by stating:

> Rāmakrishna did exhibit many symptoms associated with schizophrenia and affective disorder. But given the distance between the present moment and this late nineteenth century figure, it is difficult to determine with any accuracy from which disease he suffered. (49–50)

Apparently uninformed regarding Indian cultural norms, Olson writes that a few actresses "touched the Master's feet as part of their obsequious greeting" (40). Continuing, Olson writes: "Sāradā Devī played the role of the obsequious wife by massaging her husband's feet, rubbing oil on his body and preparing nourishing and palatable meals" (41–42). Yet those with even a rudimentary background in Indian cultural behavior will know that touching the feet is an extremely common way of showing respect: a person touches the feet of his or her parents, a younger brother or sister will touch the feet of an elder sibling, and it would be considered improper *not* to touch the feet of a holy person. Further, it is not unusual for an Indian wife to massage her husband's feet, oil his body and cook nourishing meals. She will do the same for her children. Within the Indian context—especially in the India of the late nineteenth and early twentieth centuries—these actions were far from obsequious. We need to remember that women of that era often found fulfillment in a number of tasks which today may be considered oppressive. Nor would anyone, one would hope, consider making "nourishing and palatable meals" debasing.

Olson perseveres in applying a Western psychoanalytic model to his stubbornly non-Western subject (the reader will find in later pages more square pegs unhappily coupled with round holes). Using Wendy Doniger O'Flaherty's *Women, Androgynes and Other Mythical Beasts* as his compass, Olson surmises that Kālī's sword "bears a remarkable similarity to the *vagina dentata* (vagina-with-teeth) that possesses the ability to castrate penetrating males" (34). Discussing Saradananda's assertion that Ramakrishna's "sexual organ would shrink instantaneously [in] ... reaction to the touch of lewd women" (LP 4.289), Olson deduces that Ramakrishna suffered from fear of castration (Olson 1990, 39).

Olson identifies Ramakrishna as a misogynist, but also suggests: "Because Ramakrishna was a product of his culture, he inherited and espoused many of the negative attitudes toward women in general gained from his cultural heritage" (38). As should be apparent, the author seems blind to the fact that the Bengali cultural heritage is radically different from the Euro-American model and therefore has to be assessed on its own terms, without using Western cultural norms as a universal paradigm.

Ramakrishna, Olson notes, dressed like a woman on occasion and also mimicked women to entertain his disciples. Olson speculates that this could be interpreted as "a manifestation of Ramakrishna's confused sexual role." He adds, however: "We must ... remember the religious context in which he lived his life" (43). Despite this cautionary note, Olson suggests: "The frolic of a male turned female alleviates unconscious male fears of an overpowering, threatening, mysterious, female figure. This especially makes sense, if we consider the male sexual anatomy ... [which renders] the male penis vulnerable to attack." By assuming the role of a woman, Olson concludes, "Ramakrishna's unconscious fears were dispelled and enabled him to play with and serve the Goddess without concern to his sexual anatomy" (44). One can only wonder how a contemporary North American could intuit "unconscious fears" of a nineteenth-century Bengali mystic (when, by definition, a person is not aware of his/her own "unconscious fears" let alone the fears of someone else who belongs to another culture). By assuming that this male fear is necessarily universal, Olson obviates any possibility of cultural divergence between Bengal and North America, thus elevating the contemporary American male psychological model to the status of the basic blueprint of human experience.

What also needs to be recognized is that for Ramakrishna, Kālī was never an "overpowering, threatening" figure. Again and again, in every source book on Ramakrishna, we see Ramakrishna describing Kālī or addressing her directly as *Ānandamoyī*, "Blissful Mother." Not only does Ramakrishna not fear Kālī, he teases her, chides her, laughs with her. He addresses her as *tui*, the most intimate form of address in Bengali. He touches her chin—a gesture indicating utter trust and intimacy, hardly fear. Fear would perhaps be an appropriate reaction for someone ill at ease with the Śākta tradition, but it would not be the reaction of a Kālī devotee. Yet as if to counter the above, Olson also notes that "to usurp the feminine mood benefits one on the path to salvation. The feminine mood can help one conquer one's passions" (44).

Sudhir Kakar

In 1991 Ramakrishna scholarship brought forth two books which employed psychoanalytic theories: Sudhir Kakar's *The Analyst and the Mystic: Psychoanalytic Reflections on Religion and Mysticism* and Narasingha Sil's *Rāmakṛṣṇa Paramahaṁsa*. Interestingly, both authors are Indians and both are trained in the Western academy. Kakar's book takes issue with the often pathologized psychological assessment of mystical experiences. Unlike many other psychoanalysts, he has a refreshing openness to mysticism. That he did so long before such openness became accepted is a testimony not only to Kakar's own creativity but to his professional courage as well. "The earlier equation of the mystical state with a devalued, if not pathological, regression comparable to a psychotic episode is ripe for radical revision," Kakar writes (1991, 3). Kakar sees creativity rather than pathology at the root of mystical experience. In fact, mysticism can be the prime venue of experiencing creativity: "Mystical experience [is] ... in some cultures and at certain historical periods—the preeminent way of uncovering the vein of creativity that runs deep in all of us" (29).

Both Freud's and Ramakrishna's presence hovers throughout the book: Freud's, because as a Freudian-trained analyst Kakar addresses the conclusions that Freud came to regarding mysticism and religion, and Ramakrishna's because, as Kakar writes: "I have tried to organize my observations and understanding of mysticism around the person of a single mystic ... Ramakrishna" (x).

Kakar makes a clear break with Freud, whose view of mysticism Kakar does not share. He also criticizes Masson for following Freud's lead and viewing mysticism in terms of psychopathology (56). In other important areas also Kakar views Ramakrishna through a much wider, more culturally accommodating lens than had earlier been used by his colleagues. Significantly, Kakar does not regard Ramakrishna's dressing in women's clothes as either transvestism or as something problematic. "[Ramakrishna] loved putting on women's clothes and ornaments. . . . In his mature years, talking to his disciples, there was a certain wry pride with which he related, and occasionally enacted to their surprised delight, incidents from his youth which showed his ability to mimic women's gestures and movements to perfection" (10).

Discussing Ramakrishna's period of madness during his sādhana, Kakar writes: "Later in life, he would wonder at some of his behavior during this phase [*unmāda*]—worshiping his own phallus as that of Shiva, being seized by ecstatic visions while he defecated, and so on" (13). Yet even this *unmāda* phase remains only a phase, a phase violently shaking the old foundation, only to create a new, psychologically integrated man. About Ramakrishna's *bhāvas*, divine moods, Kakar writes:

> Psychologically speaking, I would tend to see *bhavas* as more than psychic looseners that jar the soul out of the narcissistic sheath of normal, everyday, self-limiting routine. . . .
>
> ... In a *bhava*, Ramakrishna rekindled the world with fresh vision, discovering or rather endowing it with newfound beauty and harmony. (18–19)

Far from seeing Ramakrishna's practice of *madhura bhāva* as symptomatic of a deeper psychological disorder, Kakar sees Ramakrishna's behavior as belonging to a long tradition of mysticism:

> The renunciation of adult masculinity is not only a feature of Hindu devotional mysticism but is also a feature of Christian emotional mysticism of medieval and early modern Europe. Affective prayer or Bernardine mysticism ... possesses a striking affinity to its Hindu counterpart. . . . The message of the European emotional mystics seems to be the same as that of Ramakrishna: the actual gender of the mystic is not important for his practice. It is, however, vital that the mystic accept and cultivate his or her femininity to the point that the female-self part becomes dominant in his or her inner psychic reality. (30–31)

Yet despite the real insights that Kakar provides, his views concerning human nature and mysticism inevitably become reductive to the extent that he largely accepts European psychological categories as universally valid. Kakar, for example, sees mystical experiences as regression—a "deeper regression," no doubt, but regression nonetheless. "The mystical regression is akin to that of the analysand," Kakar writes (x).

About Ramakrishna's maddened quest for the vision of the Divine Mother, Kakar writes: "The unity Ramakrishna aimed for is ... not the mergerlike states of the infant at the breast ... but the ending of separation striven for by the toddler" (26–27). Like his fellow Western-educated colleagues, Kakar sees the Western model of individuality as the healthy, normative model, thus inevitably making the Indian social model inferior in comparison to that of Europe and North America. For this and other reasons, Kakar's application of psychoanalytic insights to Indian settings has been critiqued by Stanley Kurtz and Alan Roland.[62]

In 1993 Kakar co-authored with French philosopher Catherine Clément *La Folle et le saint*, a book which takes the form of a lengthy conversation between the two authors, whose discussion centers around East/West understandings of religious experience and madness. Clément and Kakar juxtapose the "folle" (madwoman) Madeleine with the "saint" Ramakrishna. Madeleine was a nineteenth-century Frenchwoman who had numerous mystic visions, bore marks of the stigmata, and was deemed insane. She was institutionalized for twenty-two years in La Salpêtrière under the care of Dr. Pierre Janet. While Ramakrishna and Madeleine were more or less contemporaneous, their cultures were vastly different. Had Madeleine lived in India, would she have been venerated as a saint? Both Madeleine and Ramakrishna used unusual metaphors, including sexual ones, in their relating of spiritual experiences. Kakar argues, however, "And yet, no, this is not sexual." He continues: "It is that we are touching fragile, permeable ground, on which our vocabulary, whether Hindi, Bengali, English, German, or French, constantly slips . . . Even if they [Madeleine and Ramakrishna] use metaphors that are ostensibly sexual, they are so for us, not for them. For these two singular beings, there is no longer a difference between male and female, between body and soul, between sex and spirit, between real and unreal" (Clément/Kakar, 18–19). Thus as Kakar and Clément point out, while Ramakrishna's language *could* be interpreted as sexual, the language he used to describe spiritual experiences does not lend itself to a facile psychoanalytic decoding of hidden sexual meaning.

Clément and Kakar also discuss the question of Ramakrishna's sexual identity. Kakar mentions that Ramakrishna felt more comfortable with those of his own gender. But, he continues, when Ramakrishna sought physical contact with his young disciples, did he have real sexual excitement? "Nothing," Kakar concludes, "confirms this" (177–78). Interestingly, Clément says that to speak of homosexuality in this context is simply insufficient. "That," she declares, "is not the issue at all!" (178). Agreeing with Clément, Kakar says that in Ramakrishna's case, it is more accurate to say that he felt more secure in the company of his own gender, but "this is not the usual definition of what people call homosexuality." Kakar goes on to state that on this point, Ramakrishna had a defect. According to Kakar, Ramakrishna was not entirely liberated; Ramakrishna said that he was freed from all sexual determinations, yet he felt ill at ease in the company of women. "From which I conclude," Kakar states, "that even an authentic mystic, fully realized, is not independent of sexuality. Sexuality always counts, even in a negative way" (178).

It is a testament to Ramakrishna's continuing power of appeal that other interpretations of Ramakrishna have continued to appear—including films and novels based upon his life. It is remarkable that Sudhir Kakar, having already written nonfiction interpretations of Ramakrishna, turned to fiction and wrote *Ecstasy* in 2001. Kakar writes in the book's preface: "Many incidents in Gopal's [the book's protagonist] story are based on events in the life of the great Bengali mystic, Ramakrishna Paramahamsa." In addition, Kakar tells us that the character of Vivek has "a number of parallels with … Swami Vivekananda."

Kakar's appreciation and affection for Ramakrishna are apparent throughout the book. Unfortunately, however, the book fails both as an interpretive device and as a novel in revealing a deeper understanding of Ramakrishna. The novel's first sentence: "Gopal's visions ended when he grew breasts" is a portent of what is to follow. Gopal is hermaphroditic, a subtle-as-a-hammer metaphor for sexual ambiguity. If one is seeking to discover any hidden springs of Ramakrishna's life either as a mystic or as a human being, we are alerted that the author may not be successful in his venture.

Further character development begins quickly. "Gopal," Kakar writes, "had always looked like a pretty girl, and the other boys had tormented him with coarse remarks and indecent gestures which made his eyes sting with hot tears of shame" (2001, 7). There is no point in quibbling over the fact that there is nothing in Ramakrishna's life to indicate that before his father's death, his childhood was, from all accounts, happy and uncomplicated. There is no source material to hint at anything different, but Kakar is, after all, writing a novel, and in seeking to uncover the mystic's quest, his source material is his own creative stores, not the literal nuts and bolts of a person's life. Kakar states in the preface that he is far from being a mystic himself, which seems unarguable, and from that angle (as Kakar mentions in his Preface) the book "presents itself in the name of an incompetence."

Ecstasy shows the marked influence of *Kālī's Child*. One example is "Gopal's" problem with the village women. It was only with the publication of *Kālī's Child* that the allegation of sexual abuse by village women gained currency. There is nothing to indicate anything of the kind in the source texts, as we shall discuss at length in later chapters. However, in *Ecstasy*, Gopal suffers the torment of their sexual attention. Gopal, Kakar writes, "had begun to be wary of the village women. . . . They touched him, too. Feathery, light brushes of their fingers on his groin from which he recoiled as if they were lances pressing into his skin" (9).

Again we hear echoes of *Kālī's Child*, with Kakar's rendition of the young Ramakrishna's encounter with a Tāntrik sādhu. "Take off your clothes," the Tāntrik ordered. Kakar continues:

> What the tantrik's puja had done ... was to awaken his Kundalini from where she slept at her seat above the anus. He had felt alternating currents of keen elation and piercing pain begin in his rectum and shoot up the rope of his spine. The latter were so painful that he had to contract his anal muscles tight to withstand the torture. The spontaneous movements of the Kundalini subsided ... leaving behind a dull ache in his anus which persisted all the way home. (36–37)

This sounds like sexual violation, not a spiritual experience. Needless to say, there is nothing to indicate that Ramakrishna's kundalini experiences were anything other than profoundly joyful—at least this is what every known source text indicates. Nor was there any indication in any source text to imply that Ramakrishna was subject to any sort of sexual abuse. Mystical experiences, kundalini or no, have nothing to do with rectal pain. The passage seems to indicate that Kakar, at least to some extent, entertained Kripal's speculation that Ramakrishna was sexually abused by the wandering sādhus who frequented his village.

Ultimately, the book does not bring an understanding of Ramakrishna, though it is interesting in illuminating how Kakar views Ramakrishna and mysticism in general. As a novel the book fails because of weak characterization; moreover, the dialogue is often so awkward as to seem ironic or even camp. Baba says to Vivek, for example: "Perhaps you are not destined to know that desperate love for the Lord which sends storms of rapturous feeling snaking through the body, making the very marrow in your bones beat as wildly as your pulse" (248). Vivek's embrace of Hindu nationalism reads as woodenly as Gopal's kundalini experience. In the end, one does not quite see the point of *Ecstasy*. It neither illumines mystical experience nor successfully plumbs the sources which provoke its characters to make the choices they do.

Narasingha Sil

In contrast to the nuanced interpretations found in Kakar's works of nonfiction, Narasingha Sil's 1991 *Rāmakṛṣṇa Paramahaṁsa* and his later revised edition (1998) of the book, *Ramakrishna Revisited*, begins with the premise that mystical experience itself is inherently pathological. Sil avers that Ramakrishna had a "mother-fixation" and notes that, according to Freud, this "involves an unconscious desire to return to the mother's womb and ... to castrate oneself to become a woman" (Sil 1991, 15). Sil grew up in Kolkata and admits: "My evolution from adolescence to adulthood was marked by a growing detachment—worse, disenchantment—with prophets and Godmen." An academic historian, Sil writes that his "study is an exercise in psychobiography or ... psychohistory" (xi). He describes his tone as "neo-Freudian" (5). Sil's assessment of Ramakrishna's samādhi is simple enough: "His trances were pathological rather than spiritual" (99).

Sil claims that the "most noteworthy feature of Rāmakṛṣṇa's spirituality ... is an obsession with human sexuality" (5). In view of the tone and language in both *Rāmakṛṣṇa Paramahaṁsa* and *Ramakrishna Revisited*, the remark would appear to be a classic case of transference.[63] It is worth noting that as a Bengali not favorably disposed to the Ramakrishna Order, Sil judges Swami Nikhilananda's *Gospel of Sri Ramakrishna* to be a "masterful translation." Nevertheless, Sil finds "occasional problems with his translation." According to him, Nikhilananda "frequently excised Rāmakṛṣṇa's vulgar expressions with explicitly sexual connotation and reference and occasionally, albeit unintentionally, distorted the meaning of the crude words Rāmakṛṣṇa used" (8). As we have already seen, Ramakrishna's "filthy language" was nothing out of the ordinary for a Bengali villager unschooled in what was considered appropriate language. There was a great distinction between the language of Kolkata's educated middle class and the earthy dialect of a Kamarpukur villager. While the middle-class gentry had been taught that certain words and certain bodily functions should not be discussed in public, Ramakrishna had been spared such instruction. Indeed, it was this very quality of linguistic innocence that the gentry found so appealing.[64] Yet while Bengal's nineteenth-century intelligentsia found Ramakrishna's language authentic and refreshing, Nikhilananda's 1940s American audience would not have been so favorably disposed. Such openness would not be possible in America until the 1960s.

While Jeffrey Kripal has noted that *Kālī's Child* is but the latest example of "a long line of scholarly consensus" concerning Ramakrishna (KC, xx), it is only when reading *Rāmakṛṣṇa Paramahaṁsa* that it becomes apparent how much *Kālī's Child* has benefited from the work of preceding scholars.[65] Indeed many—though certainly not all—of Kripal's conclusions, as well as the extensive source material, were foreshadowed by Sil. Had Sil's book been more widely read, there is little question that the controversy would have centered on Sil's book rather than Kripal's.

Sil refers back to Masson's proposal that early childhood trauma was "most probably" responsible for Ramakrishna's adult behavior. Like Masson, Sil begins with the assumption that Ramakrishna's behavior exhibits symptoms of psychopathology, then works backward to find ratifying evidence.[66] Sil ponders various childhood possibilities:

> What the women of Kāmārpukur did with the ecstatic boy by treating him as their Kṛṣṇa while pretending to be his *gopīs* ... is anybody's guess. . . .
>
> ... [Ramakrishna's] skepticism ... [about women ensnaring young men] must have been caused by the unconscious experiences of his own childhood. Then, the old man Śrīnīvas' overtures might very well have been the only one of many such unrecorded episodes. Gadādhar's intimacy with the rough upcountrymen who were, on his own admission, hemp-smoking *sādhus*, could very well lead to his physical abuse which the boy, easily seduced with food ... and awed as he was by the mystique of the monks, could not comprehend. (1991, 28–29)

Throughout *Rāmakṛṣṇa Paramahaṁsa* and its 1998 revision, *Ramakrishna Revisited*, Sil consistently uses a catch-all approach, replete with the habitual usage of "possibly," "quite probably," "most likely," "most probably," while suggesting highly sexualized scenarios without providing corroborating data to back up his theses.

The caption above, for example, provides us with "hemp-smoking sādhus" whose potential actions "*could very well lead* to his physical abuse" [emphasis added here and through the remainder of the paragraph]. Other examples: "[Ramakrishna] *probably* fantasized his admiring patron Mathurā Mohan as a sex maniac trying to molest him sexually" (1991, 32). Then there is: "It is *quite possible* that the women of Kāmārpukur ... worshiped young Gadāi's genitals." Sil suggests: "Either due to [Ramakrishna's] deliberate repression or ... *most probably* ... bodily malfunctioning (caused by excessive masturbation), Rāmakṛṣṇa really became incapacitated for any normal sexual activity." Sil further claims: "[Ramakrishna] *must have been* fascinated by the naked physique of the big Punjabi monk, Totāpurī. . . . Totāpurī's nudity *may have had* something to do with Rāmakṛṣṇa's penile obsession" (51). And again: "*Most probably* the naked phallus of the big man made an abiding impression on Rāmakṛṣṇa" (66). We will re-encounter the excessive drumbeat of speculative phraseology as well as the enforced association between Tota's nudity and Ramakrishna's presumed fixation on his penis later in *Kālī's Child*.

Sil's revision of his 1991 *Rāmakṛṣṇa Paramahaṁsa* was published in 1998 under the title *Ramakrishna Revisited: A New Biography*. While maintaining nearly all his earlier theses, *Ramakrishna Revisited* is fascinating in its vehement response to *Kālī's Child*. Sil declares that *Kālī's Child*

> reflects more the genius of its author less of Ramakrishna the man. . . . The simple soul, fun-loving, funny and exceedingly witty man . . . is lost behind the psychocultural hermeneutic that bypasses Ramakrishna's Bengali idiosyncrasies. Especially Kripal's portrayal of Ramakrishna as a homosexual Tāntrika is not only misleading but downright false. Kripal's *KC* resembles the portrait of the Master by the Czech artist Frank Dvorak—a mystic with well-defined, bright and bold features—very Western but hardly authentic. (Sil 1998, 6–7)

We have seen that from the latter part of the nineteenth century to the present day, "finding the explanation" of Ramakrishna absorbed the attention of a wide variety of interpreters, both East and West. The first interpreters were Ramakrishna's immediate disciples, one of whom meticulously recorded his words and two others—one lay, one monastic—recorded the story of his life. These writings have formed the source texts of the Ramakrishna tradition. In addition to these writings, there were also notable works by monastics of the Ramakrishna Order who also sought the meaning of Ramakrishna's life through their own interpretations, which, though varying in detail, nevertheless presumed Ramakrishna's tremendous significance not only to India in particular, but to the world and humanity in general.

It is not unusual for a revered teacher's disciples and their successors to presume the great significance of their spiritual lineage. What was remarkable about Ramakrishna was that he also captured the imagination of others, including a number of well-known intellectuals in Europe and North America in the late nineteenth century. As we have seen, the interest Ramakrishna evinced would most likely not have occurred had it not been for Keshab Chandra Sen's promotion and Vivekananda's later success. Because of Keshab's enthusiasm, Max Müller undertook his own study. With Max Müller's imprimatur, doors opened from India to Europe to North America, returning again to India with the patina of Western endorsement.

Those seeking to "find the explanation" to Ramakrishna have produced interpretations which have served as a bellwether of their own culture's preoccupations and their own personal concerns as well. For this reason, interpretations of Ramakrishna have frequently provided more insight into the interpreters and their cultural presuppositions than into Ramakrishna himself.

In this overview we have observed that if there is one common issue in the history of Ramakrishna scholarship, it has been the tendency to privilege a Western intellectual paradigm and assume it to be universal. That said, interpretations of Ramakrishna from the late nineteenth century up through the mid-1960s were largely dominated by either those sympathetic to the insider view of Ramakrishna or those who found some of their own views corroborated by Ramakrishna. Until the second half of the twentieth century there was no yawning chasm between the interpretations of those inside the Ramakrishna Order and those of outsider scholars.

It was only in the mid-1960s that Ramakrishna studies dramatically changed course from its earlier, tame trajectory. The first significant rift between the insider view of Ramakrishna and the outsider view appeared with the work of Walter Neevel. This rift, beginning slowly but insistently, set in motion a long, steady rip in the seam that had held together insiders and outsiders on some basic premises of Ramakrishna literature. If the earlier interpreters of Ramakrishna had viewed Ramakrishna according to their own predetermined cultural values, they had at least accepted the basic source texts as valid sources of information. If the earlier interpreters of Ramakrishna had found the authors of the source texts not the intellectual equals of their European counterparts, they at least did not consider the authors manipulative or deceitful. Yet by the end of the twentieth century, the hermeneutic of suspicion hovered over

North American Ramakrishna studies (and, indeed, over the study of religion in general), and that suspicion was eventually returned by the insider community in response to the publication of *Kālī's Child* and the subsequent praise it received. How this came to pass will be discussed in the following chapter.

In looking back over the recent scholarship on Ramakrishna, we can see several persistent trends. We have seen that—with the notable exception of the scholarship on Ramakrishna done by those within the Ramakrishna Order as well as by Amiya Sen and June McDaniel and, to a certain extent, Sudhir Kakar—the social, cultural and intellectual trends which deeply influenced the course of North American and European life during this time made inevitable inroads into Ramakrishna scholarship. As in the work of the early Orientalists, there remained in recent decades persistent presumptions of the universality of contemporary Euro-American social and cultural values, mores, and expectations, which would serve as an unexamined pattern for interpreting Ramakrishna and other Hindu figures. Psychoanalysis as a hermeneutic tool came to be widely utilized in Ramakrishna scholarship during these years and only rarely was that approach questioned. Indeed, so pervasive was this methodology that its cultural presuppositions were almost never examined.

Moreover, even culturally defined models such as gender roles, social and sexual norms, definitions of masculinity, etc., were taken from a contemporary Western perspective and superimposed on nineteenth-century Hindu figures. It is no accident that this sort of heavy-handed hermeneutic stance has been increasingly viewed as a sort of neo-Orientalism, in the sense that the presumption of the universality of Western values and standards can be seen as yet another form of Euro-American cultural domination, albeit more subtle and more invidious than its earlier blatant incarnations.

As we close this chapter on Ramakrishna's past interpreters, we open the door to *Kālī's Child* and the subsequent scholarship on Ramakrishna which it engendered. With the publication of *Kālī's Child*, Ramakrishna studies would cross a threshold of sorts, for, with few exceptions—notably those books on Ramakrishna published by the insider community—nearly all subsequent scholarship on Ramakrishna would show the influence of *Kālī's Child*. For this development we turn to a new chapter in Ramakrishna scholarship with the publication of *Kālī's Child*, the honors it received, and the uproar it created.

2

Approaching *Kālī's Child*

> Precisely what I have distorted and what I have clarified I leave to colleagues and the historical record to decide.
>
> —Jeffrey Kripal, *Kālī's Child*

As we have seen in our examination of Ramakrishna studies up to the close of the twentieth century, a number of *Kālī's Child*'s theses were anticipated by previous scholarship. No work is ever created in a vacuum, and *Kālī's Child* is no exception. When the book was published in 1995, it arrived nestled in a worldview which would, to a large extent, presume the universality of Euro-American sociocultural values and mores. Moreover, the book was presented to a reading public with little or no knowledge of Bengali language or culture. It was thus not surprising that when *Kālī's Child* was published, it was the recipient of great acclaim within the academy. What was not anticipated was the fierce controversy and wholesale condemnation it engendered from the insider community.

As we have noted earlier, in the years between *Kālī's Child*'s publication and our present discussion, *Kālī's Child* became more than just a book. It became shorthand for a number of hot-button issues: freedom of speech juxtaposed with the issue of who was credentialed and what credentials were required to interpret Hindu religious figures. Charges of Hindutva political agendas were juxtaposed with charges of anti-Hindu prejudice; charges of homophobia were juxtaposed with charges of Orientalism; to these were added charges of racism from both sides of the controversy. Given the poisonous atmosphere, it has been extremely difficult to unhook *Kālī's Child* from the controversies which have engulfed it. This has presented no small difficulty for the present authors, who have found themselves unwillingly identified with homophobia and Hindutva. Yet in order to unravel *Kālī's Child* and to pull out the text from its subsequent accretions, we need to return to simpler days, before the book was published.

Entering into the Text

It is helpful to put *Kālī's Child* in perspective by beginning the study with a look at what is known about its author. One need not look far, as Kripal himself has published a good deal of autobiographical material. Jeffrey J. Kripal, born in 1962 and raised in Nebraska, describes his childhood as "idyllic," a childhood which was "filled with love and happiness and emotional warmth" (Kripal 2001a, 91). As he writes:

> It was this very happiness that set me up for an adolescent crisis, for this was an "Eden" I had absolutely no desire to leave. But the "fruit" of sexuality would come … and with it the shame and guilt of this newfound knowledge. Freud's oedipal theory … was not just another piece of speculation for me: it was the most obvious and healing of truths.

Kripal relates that from the onset of puberty through the next six years, he engaged in "various ascetic practices, mostly involving different forms of fasting." Kripal continues: "In the meantime, I would enter a Benedictine seminary and begin to consider the monastic life my chosen vocation." Kripal states that the monks (in Conception Seminary College in Missouri) recognized his need for therapy. He writes: "I entered psychoanalysis with a professionally trained monk at the beginning of my junior year … and, on the point of starvation, began to dream dreams" (2001a, 91). The dreams, he writes, were of "women, women bearing milky, rich food," which he felt guilty about accepting.

Kripal continues: "At some point in the course of our sessions, it suddenly 'hit' me: on some unconscious level, I was making the symbolic, and incestuous, equation: food = mother = sex." Therapy had given Kripal the insight that to "cope with my unacknowledged oedipal feelings, I had effectively attacked the source of my illicit desires, the body, with a piece of deadly symbolic logic: you desire the mother, the mother is food, you cannot have the mother, you cannot have food." Once he had gained that knowledge, Kripal writes, he was able to eat, gaining seventy pounds in five months. Freud, Kripal continues, "literally saved my life" (91–92).

Should the reader wonder why Kripal felt compelled to engage in such public revelation or why it should be further discussed here, it is because he asserts that his "interest in the erotic nature of certain forms of religious experience is largely a function of my own mystico-erotic experiences and my subsequent attempts to make some sense of them through the history of mysticism" (2001a, 12). Furthermore, Kripal writes that he sees "the entire process [of writing *Kālī's Child*] as a function of my own autobiographical trajectories" (203). Moreover, as we stated in this book's Preface, one of the driving motivations behind this book is to ask (even if the question does not necessarily imply that there is a simple, unambiguous answer): Why do we see what we see? Why do we interpret the way we interpret? In order to gain another's vision, we also need to try to gain the area where the other stands so we can try to catch that person's view of reality.

Of profound significance to Kripal was a dream he had while living in the seminary, though as he writes, "it was more of a vision" or a "myth-dream." The dream involved Kripal, a young, attractive maiden dressed as a Greek or Roman woman, and a winged unicorn with a burning body that appeared "like brilliant black lightning" (92). Kripal writes:

> The maiden said nothing but simply smiled and led me to the edge of what looked like a very deep, very turbulent black sea. Just below the waters burned the fires of a terrifyingly beautiful winged horse with a single horn coming out of its head. . . . I instinctively knew that it was my task to get this mysterious being out of the water, and so I entered the waves and tried to pull him up, but to no avail. The scene then shifted and I saw myself as a youth riding naked on the now fully winged and fully horned being into the sky. (92–93)

How this dream relates to what would later engage Kripal emotionally, spiritually and professionally is explained by him: "I realized that the dream was structured around a profound *coincidentia oppositorum* that would engage me for years to come, that between the mystical and the sexual, or what I would later call the erotic." In another augury of what we shall see in *Kālī's Child*, Kripal writes that the unicorn could be read as a self-representation, the fearful waters represented the Mother, and the maiden "was a transitional figure between the Mother and the Lover. Accordingly, the dream's resolution would depend ultimately on my facing and resolving these same oedipal themes" (93).

During Kripal's seminary years, his interest in bridal mysticism intensified, and he attempted to pray the Song of Songs. As Christian mystics have done over the centuries, "the Song was employed and commented on in order to imagine the feminized Church or human soul wedded to Christ in a variously conceived mystical marriage" (Kripal 2000/2001a, 14). Yet for Kripal, this was deeply problematic:

> How, I asked myself, was I supposed to imagine myself as a woman and, even more puzzling, as one married to another male? This was no good at all.

> . . . It was as if there simply was no genuinely established place in the Catholic tradition for a modern heterosexual male who desired to use erotic language to effect and express his embodied religious experience. (14)

Further, Kripal's unicorn dream troubled him deeply, "for as hard as I tried, I could not discover any adequate resources in my inherited religious tradition to appropriate the truths I had seen that night." At this point, Kripal writes:

> I had to admit that there simply were no adequate symbolic resources within Christianity to nurture and eventually realize the union of the mystical and the sexual I had known intuitively in the dream-vision. . . . Symbolically, the male nature of God made a heteroerotic approach to the divine through this eros equally impossible. (2001a, 94)

Kripal first encountered Tantra in the seminary's library. The subject intrigued him because the tradition "allowed the male mystic to be heterosexual and approach the divinity as female, that is, as a goddess" (2000/2001a, 14). After graduating from the seminary, Kripal attended the University of Chicago to study the history of religions, with a special focus on Hinduism and the comparative study of mysticism. It was at the University of Chicago, where he wrote his Ph.D. dissertation under the direction of Wendy Doniger, that Kripal found his intellectual home. "The historian of religions, and especially the historian of mysticism," he writes, "almost by definition it seems, is someone who deals in the exotic and the erotic" (2001a, 4).

Indeed, far from being drawn to the seemly garden-variety mysticism of, say, W. T. Stace, Schleiermacher, Swedenborg or Underhill, Kripal emphasizes the significance of the transgressive and excessive—offhandedly informing the reader that "extreme illness, car wrecks, and sexual abuse are particularly effective inducers of the mystical" (2001a, 29). It needs to be said that the association of sexual abuse with mystical states is troubling. There is a dissociative state that is the result of sexual trauma and there is a dissociative state that comes with mystical transcendence, in which the mystic's self-identification is no longer locked into the body/mind locus. One cannot equate one experience with the other. Sexual boundary violations are not infrequently interpreted as mystical experience by abuse survivors, but to accommodate that interpretation and equate the mystical experience with violation is deeply unhealthy for the trauma victim. To conflate the two experiences is damaging to both sides of the equation.

Kripal's interest in Tantra and Tantra's long history in Bengal grew in graduate school, and it was there that he began to study Bengali. In 1989 he went to Kolkata for eight months, staying at the Ramakrishna Mission Institute of Culture, where he intensified his study of Bengali and worked on source texts on Ramakrishna. In the midst of this visit, Kripal made a return visit to the United States. Suddenly, a visit to the airport bathroom unexpectedly reawakened "a powerful memory" which had lain quiescent for ten years. In his words:

> The memory involved a waking fantasy that used to torment me as an adolescent. . . . The fantasy was constructed out of the symbols of my Catholic culture: I would see a naked ithyphallic Jesus on the cross with myself and the Virgin Mary standing beneath him. I felt terribly guilty about this fantasy as a boy, but I could never quite shake it. . . . In that bathroom stall in JFK I finally understood its original meaning and the ominous announcement it was making: at puberty I was about to "crucify" my sexuality for its unresolved oedipal dimensions. The divine erection, I realized, was aimed, if always unconsciously, at (the Virgin) Mother, and for this it had to be crucified, it had to be killed. (2001a, 90–91)

In *Roads of Excess, Palaces of Wisdom*, Kripal acknowledges that "while researching Ramakrishna's secrets in Calcutta, I encountered not a few of my own." Of particular importance was

> a series of highly symbolic ecstatic experiences that were unmistakably sexual and mystical and whose meanings seemed to point in powerful, if still hidden, ways to the ontological identity of human sexuality and the psychological realities experienced in ecstasy, vision, and mystical union. This is what I would later call "the erotic." . . . But with this series of mystical experiences in Calcutta and my simultaneous discovery of Ramakrishna's own "secrets" in the texts, this union of the mystical and the erotic also became the central thesis of my research on Ramakrishna. The lives of the researcher and the researched had begun to mingle in strange, confusing, and wonderful ways. (200)

As he looked back over the process that became *Kālī's Child*, Kripal observed that it was "not just a research project. It is also an integral part of my own biography. Looking back, I can see clearly that my methods were not simply linguistic or theoretical; they were also experiential" (201).

Kripal returned from India a changed man.[1] Back at the University of Chicago, he discussed with Wendy Doniger his project of determining how sexual energies were employed in mystical experience. Far from being contradictory elements, Doniger asserted, *"they are the same"* (205; italics in text). Kripal would have found no reason to disagree with her declaration, for he maintains that Ramakrishna speaks of the same reality when he says in the *Kathāmṛta: "tāke pete gele bīrja dhāran korte hoy"* ("in order to attain [God], the semen must be retained") (KA 4.85). Enlarging upon this, Kripal explains:

> That which you are attaining is precisely that which you are retaining, transmuted now into another type of sexual experience—the erotic. The English rhyme (not to mention the Bengali text) signals an ontological identity between the semen (or better, the libidinal energies that accompany its release) and God. (2001a, 205)

It is important to note this, as this is the hermeneutical lens through which Ramakrishna was interpreted and with which *Kālī's Child* was written. Yet such facile equations are deeply problematic. Why this is so will be discussed at length in the course of this book, along with a wider discussion of mystical experience and sexuality.

Before we leave Kripal's self-revelations in *Roads of Excess* to dwell for the remainder of this book on *Kālī's Child*, one telltale aside which appears in *Roads of Excess* needs to be addressed. Kripal's notation from July 8, 2000, again discusses his Kolkata experience ("that Night") which was "both erotic and noetic .... its energies carried both an unbearably intense pleasure, which I can still feel in my body, and an intuitive grasp of the texts and their doctrinal content, which still often almost physically overwhelms me" (254). Kripal goes on to say that his experience reminds him of a story told in Saradananda's *Līlāprasaṅga* (which Kripal references as LP 1.2.1 but is in fact LP 2.8):

> Narendra had already developed what the text calls the power to transmit religion (*dharma-śakti-saṃkramana*) to others through touch. . . . Narendra asks the brother [Ramakrishna's disciple Kali, the future Swami Abhedananda] to touch his knee. The disciple does and feels a distinct shock. . . . This allows the disciple to meditate more deeply, but, unfortunately, he is not ready for such an ontological revelation and, consequently, cannot assimilate the energy's innate doctrine. Ramakrishna scolds Narendra for giving to the disciple something for which he was not yet intellectually and religiously ready (interestingly, he compared Narendra's attempted *śakti-pāta* (initiatory transmission) to a forbidden sexual act, that is, the impregnation of a woman already six months into her pregnancy—such an act, we are told, destroys the delicate development of the pregnancy and ruins everything). Saradananda then informs us that, because the teaching came too

> suddenly and without the proper preparation, the disciple misunderstood the doctrine of nonduality and used it in an immoral fashion (we are told no details). The story fascinates me, both for what it clearly implies and for what it does not quite say, namely ... that these energies possess definite erotic dimensions—hence their "immoral" use in what I suspect was a sexual practice of some sort (and that is not at all clear, but "immoral" is often a euphemism for "sexual" in the texts). (2001a, 254)

There are a number of problems with the above passage, which may have to do with Kripal's "intuitive grasp" of the text. First, the assertion that Ramakrishna compared Narendra's attempted *śaktipāt* to "a forbidden sexual act" is not correct. Ramakrishna simply says: "He (Abhedananda) was progressing until now along one *bhāva* and that is now fully destroyed. It is as if a six-month old fetus were aborted" (LP 2.9–10). This clearly implies that just as a six-month old fetus is well on its way to "birth," Abhedananda, too, was well on *his* way to birth, or fruition, in his own particular bhāva, along which he was moving quite well. Because of Narendra's interference, however, this had been "aborted." Ramakrishna makes no mention of *how* the fetus was aborted. That it was as the result of "a forbidden sexual act" is pure imagination since abortions are not performed via sexual acts. An abortion is an abortion, not a "forbidden sexual act."

Further, the claim that Saradananda indicates Abhedananda behaved in an "immoral fashion" is based upon a faulty translation. Saradananda's words are: "sometimes he did actions contrary to good behavior (*sadācār*)." Though Kripal is predisposed to equate *improper* behavior with sexual impropriety or transgression, there is nothing in the text which reflects this. (The Bengali word *anaitik* is equivalent to "immoral" and does not appear in this context.) There have been absolutely no allegations regarding Abhedananda's transgressions in sexual matters. Had there been the slightest whiff of such allegations he would never have been treated with reverence by either the monks or lay devotees associated with the Ramakrishna Order.

The behavior that Abhedananda *was* criticized for, was his insistence upon eating chicken even after returning to India after his many years in the West. This was bad enough considering that he was a sādhu, but that he did so even on pūjā days, even on the day that Swami Brahmananda (then the President of the Ramakrishna Order) died, placed him beyond the pale. Furthermore, for Hindu Bengalis in India, until well into the mid-twentieth century, eating chicken at all was completely unacceptable.[2]

Further, it was rumored that while he was in the West, Abhedananda had drunk alcohol. Neither of these constitutes "immoral" behavior and no acts of sexual impropriety are in evidence. Yet all of these fall under the rubric of "actions contrary to good behavior." Thus the same carelessness—or bias—regarding translation and the same sexual preconceptions that guided Kripal's interpretation of Ramakrishna in *Kālī's Child* make a further appearance in *Roads of Excess*. With all these factors in place, we can now make a reverse segue into *Kālī's Child*, unspooling the book's thread as we go along.

Kālī's Child's Introduction presents the reader with a microcosm of the book as a whole, displaying a collection of issues which will be systematically addressed as *Kālī's Child* progresses. Apparent in the Introduction are not only *Kālī's Child*'s central theses but also a glimmer of the way in which they will be presented. The book's Introduction is fittingly titled "Approaching the Secret."

Kālī's Child informs the reader that it would be difficult to overestimate Ramakrishna's importance within the Hindu tradition. While this seems indisputable, the statement is made while noting that Ramakrishna's face "grins over stall after stall in the markets and streets of Calcutta" (1). The verb choice is significant. Throughout the *Kathāmṛta* and other source texts, we frequently see Ramakrishna "smiling" (*sahāsya*—which literally means "with smile" or "smilingly") or laughing (*hāsitechen*); we frequently find everyone in the room laughing (*sakaler hāsya*). But the Bengali equivalent of "grin," which normally requires an adjective to qualify *hāsya*, does not appear in the *Kathāmṛta*. This is not to say that Ramakrishna never grinned; what this does say is that M did not portray a "grinning" Ramakrishna in the *Kathāmṛta*. There is, as we know, a world of shading which separates "smiling" from "grinning."

Appearing on *Kālī's Child*'s first page, a grinning Ramakrishna begins the book on a vaguely belittling note, a tone which reappears at various points throughout *Kālī's Child*.[3] The author was not incognizant of his word choice: in a later article published in the *Harvard Divinity Bulletin* (written primarily as a response to Tyagananda's "*Kali's Child* Revisited"), Kripal writes of Ramakrishna "smiling at me" (2000/2001, 14) from those very Kolkata stalls where he had earlier "grinned." Also carrying a whiff of disdain is the book's opening paragraph, in which Kripal remarks that Ramakrishna "entertained the belief that he was the latest of the incarnations of God" (KC, 1). The reader is to understand that entertaining such a belief is risible (we can remember how Isherwood was savaged on this score), which works well with the verb choice "grin."

Though worth noting, more important than the author's tone is the statement, thrust like a proverbial gauntlet into the opening paragraph, that "Ramakrishna is everywhere, and everyone seems to know him. And yet, I would argue, no one really does" (1). Except, perhaps, the promising student of History of Religions, specializing in comparative mysticism, who was convinced he could uncover the mystic's sexual "secrets." Many of these "secrets" had been hidden in plain sight—Kripal was reading, after all, the *thirty-first* edition of the *Kathāmṛta.* Yet of those literally millions who had read the same texts as Kripal, none apparently had acquired the hermeneutical expertise to tease out of the texts the darker elements which fueled Ramakriṣhna's mysticism. This, too, despite the author's limitations in Bengali: Aditi Sen, Kripal's Bengali tutor, whom he acknowledges in his Preface, writes that Kripal's Bengali was initially "fairly elementary" and after eight months of study in India, he did not advance "beyond the intermediate stage." Sen also noted his lack of knowledge of Indian culture.[4]

Nevertheless, an outsider to language and culture *can* offer a fresh vantage that insiders can either consciously or unconsciously overlook. With this in mind, we can examine those hidden elements of Ramakrishna's mysticism which the *Kathāmṛta*'s earlier readers had theoretically missed.

"Terror" and the Goddess

In any book, the opening sentences provide clues as to where the author will lead the reader. *Kālī's Child* generously fulfills this expectation. In the Preface to the book's first edition, the opening sentences give the author's rendition of Ramakrishna's vision of Kālī:

> Ramakrishna once saw the goddess in a vision. She emerged from the dark waters of the river, gave birth to a child before the saint's eyes, and then proceeded to eat it. As a terror-stricken Ramakrishna watched the horrible sight, he noticed that the child became "empty" as it entered the goddess's mouth. On the outside, as a creature, it was solid enough. Inside the goddess, however, it was merely a relative moment in a flurry of mystical "emptiness" (*śūnyatā*). Ramakrishna came out of the dreamlike vision and confidently advanced his own interpretation: "Everything is empty!" (xxv)

A dramatic vision indeed, except for the fact that there is nothing in the *Kathāmṛta*—or any other source text on Ramakrishna—to indicate that Ramakrishna was "terror stricken." Nor is there anything in the text to indicate that Ramakrishna found it a "horrible sight." On the contrary, this is what appears in the *Kathāmṛta* (4.259–60):

> Thakur again entered into samādhi. He returned to normal consciousness after a while and again began speaking with M.
>
> "My state is changing again. I cannot take prasād anymore. The real and the appearance are becoming one. Do you know what I saw? A divine form (*īśvarīya rūp*)—the form of the Divine Mother (*bhagavatī mūrti*). She had a child in her womb. She gave birth to it and then swallowed it. As much of it as went inside became empty. She showed me that everything is empty (*śūnya*)."
>
> "It was as if she were repeatedly saying, 'Let the magic begin!'"
>
> M thought about Thakur's words: "The magician alone is real and everything else is an appearance."

With this, Ramakrishna changes the subject. No terror, no "horrible sight"—at least in Ramakrishna's eyes and, presumably, in M's eyes as well. What *Kālī's Child* also neglects to inform the reader is that Ramakrishna had *wanted* to see the "deluding power of the Mother of the universe" (*mohinīmāyār darśan*) and it was this desire which precipitated the vision (LP 2.214). While this fact is mentioned in texts which Kripal apparently cites, it is kept hidden in *Kālī's Child*.

Kālī's Child's opening words alert the reader to the possibility that the author may not be translating the text as conscientiously as one would hope. The reader may further question whether the author is able to make the metaphysical leap necessary to grasp another culture's view of divinity. For Ramakrishna and his followers—as well as millions of other Hindus—the Divine Mother not only creates and preserves but also destroys.[5] The Divine Mother—the "magician"—casts her spell as all beings turn on the relentless cycle of birth, death and rebirth. All these changes, however, are *śūnya*, empty. Only the Divine Mother, who casts the spell, is real. The spell may seem "horrible" to one not accustomed to thinking of divinity in these terms, but for those in the Hindu tradition, it is an embraced part of a lived reality. Further, it seems peculiar that *Kālī's Child* would characterize Ramakrishna's words to M about the vision as having "advanced his own interpretation." Any vision necessarily being subjective, whose interpretation would he have provided?

The opening vision and Kripal's interpretation of it (in contrast to Ramakrishna's own) is particularly significant since the remainder of the book will follow a similar pattern: according to *Kālī's Child*, Ramakrishna was not aware of his own drives and motivations. Kripal suggests that *Kālī's Child* "is meant to function in ways not unlike those of Ramakrishna's vision," which, Kripal writes, may "initially horrify some of its readers." What is perhaps more accurate is that *Kālī's Child* will be like the author's interpretation of Ramakrishna's vision of Kālī writ large—Ramakrishna's "own interpretation" of his life and spiritual experiences will be at variance with that of *Kālī's Child*. While this in itself is neither unusual nor problematic—no one expects a biographer to interpret the subject's life the way the subject would care to have it rendered—what *is* problematic is that *Kālī's Child*'s interpretation is at variance with what Kripal states the texts say and what the texts themselves actually *do* say.

Kripal places the finishing touches on *Kālī's Child*'s basic theses by adding: "I can only hope that the book … is nuanced and sophisticated enough to carry [Ramakrishna devotees] beyond their initial shame, disgust, and fear (and the anger such emotions might encourage)." Stating that his intent is not to offend or anger, he seeks to "surprise, shock, or awe" (xxv). Shock and awe perhaps having lost their savor by now, the problem with the book's reception was not the book's sophistication or readers' lack thereof, but rather readers who knew the source texts and the Bengali language better than the author. Narasingha Sil is particularly thanked in the Preface to the book's first edition, and Sil's influence can be seen not only in the book's choice of citations but also in the insistent drumbeat of questionable evidence which, after initial speculation, is subsequently presented as fact.

In *Kālī's Child*'s Preface to the first edition the reader can discern a trend—not previously seen in Ramakrishna studies—of self-revelation and confessionalism. It is worth mentioning that we are at a point of departure in Religious Studies, where the earlier "scientific" investigations are being replaced by deeply personal considerations. At a time and in a culture where psychology and self-help groups have manifested in many ways like a religion, it is significant that Kripal writes:

> I cannot help but think that Ramakrishna has deeply affected me. In my more imaginative and bolder moments, I also allow myself to think that if Ramakrishna were alive and could fully understand what follows, this work would deeply affect *him*, for he could then read his life

> through the lens of mine and see things he never saw before. Perhaps something here might clear up a particular vision or help him deal more adequately with some of his painful emotional reactions. (xxvii)

Tellingly, Kripal writes that his "imaginal world" has "given me a genuinely human way of understanding Ramakrishna *and, through him, myself*" (xxvii; emphasis added).[6] We have seen, from the time of Neevel to the present day, an increasing use of psychoanalysis in interpreting Ramakrishna and other figures from the Hindu tradition. However, this is the first time that we see the scholar turning the lens into a mirror for himself: "As such," Kripal continues, "the book is an act ... of friendship, sympathy, and a deep compassion" (xxvii).[7] While the Hindu tradition has long beckoned the West for its perceived palliative applications—yoga for fitness, meditation for relaxation, and Tantra for delivery from sexual repression—this sort of academic therapeutic-confessional marks a new trend in Religious Studies.

Much Ado about the Foot

Ramakrishna's foot is discussed at length in *Kālī's Child*'s beginning, and indeed, Ramakrishna's feet and their actions are invoked throughout the pages of the text. So significant is Ramakrishna's foot that Kripal writes that it serves as a symbol for the entire study, advancing the thesis that Ramakrishna's foot points to a secret of which he himself was not aware, namely, that his mystical experiences and visions were constituted by erotic energies he neither fully accepted nor understood. (238)

For our purposes here, Ramakrishna's foot, as represented in *Kālī's Child*, serves well as an indicator of the book's failings. According to Kripal, Ramakrishna's feet "constituted a problem" (238). In introducing them, *Kālī's Child* states that when Ramakrishna went into mystical absorption, "he would sometimes place this foot 'in the lap' (*kole*) of a male disciple or visitor." Inexplicably, the reader is told that "Ramakrishna saw 'the lap' as a normally defiled sexual space" (2)—news to everyone in India, particularly in Bengal, where the lap is associated with love, trust and care. When, for example, one of Sarada Devi's devotees died while repeating Ramakrishna's name, Sarada remarked: "He has attained the lap of the one [Ramakrishna] whose son he is" (Purnatmananda, 194). There are a vast number of Bengali songs to the Divine Mother in which the devotee asks to be taken onto her lap.[8]

It is also not clear why Kripal felt compelled to put "the lap" into scare quotes, except to suggest that "the lap" really is not a lap.

While the first edition of *Kālī's Child* states that "lap" indicates "on the genitals" (KC 1995, 2), the second edition internalizes the allusion by deleting "on the genitals" and inserting the statement that the lap is "a normally defiled sexual space" (KC, 2). What is puzzling is how the author presumed a lap would necessarily be equated with genitals or how a lap would normally constitute "a sexually defiled space" in the first place. Sometimes a lap is just a lap. Similarly, the first edition of *Kālī's Child* states that Ramakrishna would sometimes place his foot on "a young boy disciple" (KC 1995, 2), yet in the three *Kathāmṛta* citations provided (KA 3.172; KA 4.245; KA 4.278), only one (KA 3.172) points to a disciple, Nityagopal, who was young but at the age of twenty-three, was hardly a "boy".[9] *Kālī's Child*'s second edition corrects the text from "young boy disciple" to "male disciple or visitor" (2). What both editions of *Kālī's Child* avoid mentioning, however, are references to the women whom Ramakrishna touched with his foot, even when they are mentioned in the *same paragraph* from which another citation has been taken. Because Ramakrishna's foot is so central to *Kālī's Child*'s basic thesis, it will be fruitful to investigate the examples the book has provided.

Ramakrishna's Foot and Nityagopal's Lap

In *Kālī's Child*'s first example (KA 3.172), Ramakrishna places his legs—or foot, or feet—on the lap of Nityagopal. It is important to keep in mind that the Bengali text is completely ambiguous regarding whether it was Ramakrishna's feet or legs which were either *on* or *in* the lap. The Bengali word *pā* can mean either "foot" or "leg"—therefore either translation is possible. Similarly, *kole* can either mean *on* the lap or *in* the lap. The translator must take into consideration the context, then assess the words that best recreate the situation M presents in the *Kathāmṛta*.[10]

The context which M presents is as follows: On May 23, 1885, there is a room full of people with a kīrtan about to begin. Upon hearing the sound of the *khol*, Ramakrishna goes into samādhi, placing his legs—or leg or foot—either *on* Nityagopal's lap or *in* Nityagopal's lap. Nityagopal himself was weeping in a state of *bhāva*, ecstasy, leading one to assume that, at least from M's account, Nityagopal was neither distraught nor scandalized nor traumatized. About the reactions of the others who were in the room with Ramakrishna and Nityagopal, M reports: "Speechless with wonder, all the devotees were looking at that state of samādhi with one-pointed attention" (KA 3.172). It thus seems equally clear that those observing Ramakrishna's actions were neither shocked nor scandalized.

Ramakrishna's Foot and Pandit Shyamapada's Lap

The second example presented by *Kālī's Child* occurs on August 27, 1885, when Pandit Shyamapada Bhattacharya, whom Ramakrishna had never met, arrived from Antpur. M, Rakhal, Latu and others are in the room. The pandit, M informs the reader, experienced amazing visions while he performed his worship on the bank of the Ganges river. Ramakrishna is immediately impressed by the pandit, telling M that the pandit is "very nice" (*ekjon beś lok*). Then, directing his comments to the pandit, he says, "Where the mind finds peace by practicing *neti, neti,* there one finds it [Brahman]" (KA 4.243).[11] Ramakrishna and the pandit discuss various religious topics, and the pandit—who informs Ramakrishna that he hates being called a pandit (because of the egotism implied)—recites verses from the Bhagavad Gītā. Then, after more religious discussion, the pandit chants a hymn from the *Bhāgavata*. M writes that while listening to the hymn, Ramakrishna—who is standing—goes into samādhi. Pandit Shyamapada is seated. Ramakrishna—still in samādhi and smiling—places his foot on the pandit's "lap and chest" (*kole o bokkhe*). The pandit holds Ramakrishna's foot and says, "O Guru, give me enlightenment!" (*Guro caitanyaṁ dehi*). When the pandit leaves the room, Ramakrishna remarks to M that just as he had earlier predicted, those who sincerely practiced meditation and japa (*dhyān jap*) must come here—that is, to Ramakrishna (KA 4.245).

Ramakrishna's Foot and Dr. Sarkar's Lap

In the third example cited in *Kālī's Child*, Ramakrishna places his foot on Dr. Sarkar's lap. While this occurs on October 31, 1885 (KA 4.278), Dr. Sarkar's reaction to Ramakrishna's foot begins earlier, on October 27, 1885. On this earlier date, Dr. Sarkar joins a large group of devotees in Ramakrishna's room. After a long discussion on religious topics and after much singing, Ramakrishna tells Dr. Sarkar that he should give up concern for money, honor, and lecturing (*tākā, mān, lekcār*). Now he should direct his mind to God, visiting now and then so that by hearing of God, his spiritual feeling can be enkindled (*uddīpan hobe*) (KA 1.252).

After some time, Dr. Sarkar prepares to leave, when Girish Ghosh enters the room, bowing low before Ramakrishna. Apparently deciding to stay longer, Sarkar discusses the Science Association with Girish, Dr.

Sarkar telling Ramakrishna that if he were to go there, he would lose consciousness upon seeing in there the wonders of God (*īśvarer āścarjjo*). At this point, Sarkar turns to Girish and says (combining both English and Bengali): "Do everything else but do not worship him as God. Why are you turning the head of this good man?" (*Ār sab koro*—but do not worship him as God. *Emon bhālo lokṭār māthā khāccho?*) (KA 1.253).

The conversation thus turns to the devotees' attitude toward Ramakrishna—Girish staunchly maintaining that he has no alternative *but* to see Ramakrishna as God, since Ramakrishna has taken him across the ocean of the world. Girish continues by saying that there is nothing in Ramakrishna which he does not find sacred, including his excrement. Sarkar retorts that excrement does not disturb him at all—he knows there is no difference between himself and the scavenger (*methor*) (KA 1.253). Then Sarkar says: "Can't I take the dust of his [Ramakrishna's] feet? See, I can take it" (*Āmi ki em̐r pāyer dhulā nite pāri nā? Ei dekho nicchi*), placing his forehead on Ramakrishna's feet. When Girish expresses jubilation over this development, Sarkar proceeds to take the dust of everyone's feet. At this point, Narendra suggests to Sarkar that the devotees do not look upon Ramakrishna *as* God, but someone *like* God (*īśvarer moto mone kori*), to which the doctor declares that "one should suppress one's personal feelings" (*nijer nijer bhāb cāpte hoy*). The doctor, a firm believer in the primacy of reason, goes on to confess that even his best friends think of him as cruel and hard-hearted because he suppresses his feelings. The doctor confesses that his feelings get "worked-up" and tells Narendra: "I shed tears in solitude."

It is at this point in the conversation that Sarkar turns to Ramakrishna and says: "When you are in ecstasy, you put your foot on others' bodies. That is not good" (*Tumi bhāb ho'le loker gāye pā dāo, śeṭā bhālo noy*). Note that the context of the conversation is the importance, at least in Sarkar's mind, of restraining one's emotions. Reason—and reasonable behavior—should never be overwhelmed by one's emotions. Note also that the doctor does not specify gender in his complaint: Sarkar tells Ramakrishna that he puts his foot on the body (*gā*)—not lap—of people (*lok*)—not solely males or "boys." Sarkar's word choice reflects the fact that Ramakrishna placed his feet on both males and females, young as well as old.

Ramakrishna replies to Sarkar's complaint by saying that when he is in samādhi, he does not know whether he touches anyone's body with his foot. To this Sarkar retorts: "You have at least some awareness, haven't you, that it is not right (*oṭa bhālo noy, ekṭu to bodh hoy*)?" Ramakrishna replies that he cannot explain to Sarkar what he experiences in samādhi; the thought of God makes him mad (*īśvarer bhābe āmār unmād hoy*). Ramakrishna concludes with "What can I do (*ki korbo*)?" Seizing upon that remark, Sarkar declares that now Ramakrishna accepts his viewpoint and "expresses regret for what he does." Ramakrishna, Sarkar declares, knows that the act is "sinful" (*ānyāy*) (KA 1.254). While the doctor uses the English word "sinful," it is M who adds in parentheses the Bengali word *ānyāy*, which means improper, wrongful, unreasonable, or unjust. Significantly, M does not use the Bengali word *pāp*, which means "sin" in the sense of an ethical wrong. While *Kālī's Child* sees the doctor's objection to Ramakrishna placing his foot on others as evidence of the "scandal" surrounding Ramakrishna's purported homoerotic behavior, there is nothing in the texts to indicate either that Ramakrishna's actions were homoerotic or that there was a "scandal" anywhere concerning Ramakrishna.

If the above seems an unduly long examination of one particular incident concerning Ramakrishna's foot and its actions, it is important to provide the background details to contextualize the situation in which Dr. Sarkar is speaking. *Kālī's Child* lays great stress on Dr. Sarkar's characterization of Ramakrishna's foot being placed on others as being "sinful," so it is imperative that we investigate precisely what Sarkar had in mind when he was speaking.

Where the conversation goes from here is significant, for at this point Girish explains to Dr. Sarkar that Ramakrishna places his foot on others' bodies for their spiritual benefit. Interestingly, Sarkar quickly withdraws his objection and says: "I confess my defeat at your hands. Give me the dust of your feet." And with that, Sarkar took the dust of Girish's feet (KA 1.254). There is nothing in the text to indicate that Dr. Sarkar was being sarcastic or merely giving up the fight. He could be quite argumentative, and he often was.

What was so "sinful" about Ramakrishna touching others with his foot? To understand Dr. Sarkar's reaction, we need to remember how strong were the winds for Hindu reform at this time, particularly with the elite Kolkata intelligentsia. Dr. Sarkar—as evidenced by his very frequent use of English—belonged to the highly Westernized, educated elite. Partha Chatterjee notes that Mahendralal Sarkar (1833–1904) was "the most eminent practitioner in his time of Western medicine in Calcutta and founder of the first Indian institution for modern scientific research, [and] … the only one of those close to Ramakrishna to openly voice his skepticism about Ramakrishna's preaching" (Chatterjee, 60). While Sarkar obviously had love for and appreciation of Ramakrishna, he did not believe in the possibility of God incarnating as a human being. Disgruntled by those whom he termed "religious reformers" such as "Jesus, Caitanya, Buddha and Mohammed," Sarkar dismissed the entire bunch by saying that they "were filled with egotism" (KA 1.255). Sarkar found Ramakrishna's behavior with his foot objectionable for two reasons: first, in India touching another with one's foot is considered disrespectful. It is indeed *ānyāy*, improper. Second, as a proud, self-declared "man of science" who worshiped reason above all else, Sarkar found the Indian habit of touching the feet of holy or highly respected people irrational and undemocratic. We may recall that Sarkar told Girish that he knew there was no difference between himself and the scavenger (KA 1.253). Interestingly—and somewhat paradoxically—Dr. Sarkar affirmed his democratic credentials by touching not only the feet of Ramakrishna but also of everyone in the room, as we have already seen.

Further, what stuck in Sarkar's craw the most was not so much the actions of Ramakrishna's foot but the reverence accorded Ramakrishna. These two complaints of Dr. Sarkar's are interrelated, as we shall see. We can remember Sarkar's admonition: "But do not worship him as God." Why was this so objectionable? Primarily because, for Sarkar, such a belief was antithetical to reason. Secondly, Dr. Sarkar feared that if Ramakrishna were treated by his disciples as an avatar, he could become as egotistical as those "religious reformers"—Jesus, Caitanya, et al. Again, we may recall that Sarkar told Girish that he was "turning the head of this good man" (KA 1.253). If Dr. Sarkar considered Ramakrishna's actions truly "sinful"—in terms of unethical or immoral rather than improper—then he hardly would have referred to Ramakrishna as "this good man" (*bhālo lok*) nor would he have spent untold hours with Ramakrishna to the detriment of his medical practice—a fact Sarkar repeatedly mentioned.

Two days later, we find Dr. Sarkar in Dakshineswar, rebuking Ramakrishna for allowing others to take the dust of his feet. It is significant that while Sarkar objected to Ramakrishna touching others with his feet, Sarkar objected most strongly when others touched *Ramakrishna's* feet. Dr. Sarkar thus tells Ramakrishna: "It hurts me to see people salute you (*namaskār kore*) by touching your feet (*pāye hāt diye*). I say to myself, 'They are spoiling such a good man'" (*mone kori emon bhālo lokṭāke khārāp kore dicche*) (KA 2.219). Again, this is the issue of the reverence accorded Ramakrishna—in Sarkar's mind, reverence unnervingly close to divine worship, which engenders egotism.

What is most significant is that when Dr. Sarkar again visits Ramakrishna on October 31, five days after Sarkar's "sinful" comment, Sarkar does not object when Ramakrishna places his foot on Sarkar's own lap (KA 4.278). In fact, for all of Sarkar's much-vaunted reason, we find the doctor "almost ecstatic" (*bhābābiṣṭoprāy*), after having listened to Ramakrishna's rendition of a song. Ramakrishna, lost in ecstasy, places his foot on Sarkar's lap. The context of this incident is important as well, for after returning to a normal state of consciousness, Ramakrishna says to the doctor: "Ah! What a wonderful thing you said: 'We lie in the lap of God'" (*Uh! Tumi ki kathā-i bolecho! Tām̐r-i kole bośe āchi*). It is at this point that Ramakrishna says to the doctor, "You are very pure! Otherwise I couldn't have placed (my) foot!" (*Tumi khub śuddha! Tā nā hole pā rākhte pāri nā!*) (KA 4.278).

Ramakrishna's Foot and *Kālī's Child*

The context now fleshed out, let us examine how *Kālī's Child* views the same incident. We read: "In one scene, [Ramakrishna] explains that a visiting male must be very 'pure' ['pure' is placed in scare quotes] since he [Ramakrishna] was able to place his foot 'there,' that is, in the man's lap" (KC, 2). However, there is no "there" in the text; the word has been added and placed in quotation marks even though it does not exist in the *Kathāmṛta*.[12] Kripal adds to his evidence by noting: "In one scene … a visitor declares the saint's habit of placing his foot 'on people's bodies' while in ecstasy to be 'sinful' (significantly, the English word is used)" (2). But as we have seen, Dr. Sarkar is both the "visitor" *and* the "visiting male" in these instances, and he apparently had no objection to Ramakrishna placing his foot on *him*. To recap: the "sinful" comment predates the doctor's own experience of Ramakrishna's foot by five days. Despite this fact, *Kālī's Child* invokes Dr. Sarkar's reaction to Ramakrishna's foot yet again, a mere three pages later, when this time Sarkar is referred to as "a troubled observer." Thus the same incident is recycled and made to look as if negative reactions to Ramakrishna's foot (which *Kālī's Child* characterizes as "the controversial actions of Ramakrishna's foot") were commonplace—or at least were not the reaction of one sole individual, Dr. Sarkar. Instead, the reader is told about the "shocking connection between the mystical and the sexual that the observer seemed to see in his foot" (5).

In the central portion of the book, *Kālī's Child* returns again to the subject of Ramakrishna's foot and *again* brings up Sarkar's characterization of Ramakrishna's foot's actions as sinful. Kripal also reiterates Ramakrishna placing his foot on Dr. Sarkar's lap, again quoting the *Kathāmṛta* and, unfortunately, again adding his own word "there," placing it in quotation marks even though it does not exist in the Bengali text: "You're very pure! Otherwise I wouldn't be able to place my foot there!" Even worse, at this point Kripal adds a further commentary: "The reader can only smile" (239–240; quoting KA 4.278).

The reader does not smile, however, if the reader is familiar with the *Kathāmṛta*. Those conversant with the *Kathāmṛta* are appalled, first, by the insertion of a word to make it appear as if Ramakrishna had, in fact, said it. Second, they may well be more appalled at the sniggering comment that followed. Were that throwaway barb not enough, Kripal adds that "Ramakrishna never denied that he stuck his foot in strange places" (KC, 238). Aside from the "when did you stop beating your wife" quality of this statement, what is meant by "in"?

If we are returning to the "genitals" argument (the first edition of *Kālī's Child* states that "lap" indicates "on the genitals" [KC 1995, 2]), then the reader would have to keep in mind that it requires some real excavation to locate the genitals of a person sitting cross-legged on the floor through the many layers of cloth that Bengalis typically wear—especially since the foot is attached to someone who is standing and unconscious of his external surroundings. Among his other achievements, Ramakrishna would also have had to be more of an acrobat than he is given credit for. *Kālī's Child* continues on the same tack by adding: "We see a whole range of opinions focused on Ramakrishna's foot 'there'" (240). First, one does not find any range of opinions. Second, apart from adding his own material and implying it to be Ramakrishna's—and this happens time and again throughout *Kālī's Child*—the author also insinuates where the "there" is located in order to give weight to the argument that Ramakrishna was homoerotically motivated.

One of the most telling aspects of *Kālī's Child*'s foot thesis is the book's omissions. In *Kālī's Child*'s Introduction, the reader is told that Ramakrishna announced to his disciple Niranjan that Niranjan was his father (*āmār bāp*) so that he could sit on Niranjan's lap (implying that this was a homoerotically motivated act). Yet Kripal neglects to tell the reader that *in the same paragraph* of the *Kathāmṛta*, M discusses two women who had come to visit Ramakrishna: "This morning [Ramakrishna] blessed two women devotees as well. In a state of samādhi he touched their hearts with his foot. They started shedding tears and one of them, weeping, said: 'You are so full of compassion.' The atmosphere was filled with love" (KA 4.280). We also read in the *Kathāmṛta* that Ramakrishna put his foot on his sister's head (KA 4.45). This never appears in *Kālī's Child*. As a brief aside it should also be mentioned that while *Kālī's Child* makes much of Ramakrishna sitting in Niranjan's lap, the book never mentions the fact that Ramakrishna sat in Aghoramani Devi's (Gopaler-Ma's) lap as well (LP 4.242).

Ramakrishna's Foot and Narendra

Kālī's Child declares that Ramakrishna's foot constituted a "problem" for Narendra, for Ramakrishna, and for Saradananda (209). But was it so? While Kripal is critical of Saradananda's *Līlāprasaṅga*, Kripal nevertheless finds in that text evidence of Ramakrishna's foot being placed on Narendra in a troubling manner. While Kripal claims to find his evidence in the original Bengali texts, he strangely enough references the Bengali *Līlāprasaṅga* while using the numbering system of Jagadananda's English translation (*Sri Ramakrishna: The Great Master*). Yet the purpose of referencing one text by using the numbering system of another is not only bizarre but also entirely useless for those attempting to check the Bengali sources.[13] The reader, however, is led to believe that the material quoted is taken from the Bengali *Līlāprasaṅga* as the citations indicate "LP" or *Līlāprasaṅga*, rather than Jagadananda's English *Great Master*, which is indicated in the pages of *Kālī's Child* as "GM."

In turning our attention to Narendra and Ramakrishna's foot, we also turn our attention to the *Līlāprasaṅga*, which relates the story of Narendra's first meeting with Ramakrishna. When Narendra first met Ramakrishna, the latter took him aside and, taking Narendra's hand, wept with joy, and spoke to him warmly in familiar terms as if he had known him for a long time, simultaneously complaining that Narendra had taken too long to come. Then, with palms folded in reverence, Ramakrishna addressed the bewildered Narendra with the words: "I know, my Lord, that you are the ancient *ṛṣi*, Nārāyaṇa in the form of Nara. You have incarnated again in order to remove the misery of *jīvas*" (LP 5.64). Of course, Narendra thought Ramakrishna must be insane, though Ramakrishna was able to extract a promise from Narendra to come back again.

To Narendra's amazement, Ramakrishna, upon returning to the group of people gathered in his room, acted in a totally normal manner. "I sat down and began to observe him," Narendra later reported, "and I began thinking. I saw that there was nothing that looked like madness in his bearing, behavior and conversation with others. Seeing his holy conversation (*sadālāp*) and bhāva-samādhi I felt that he had truly renounced everything for God (*īśvarārthe sarbatyāgī*) and had himself practiced what he preached" (LP 5.65).

What were those words which so greatly impressed Narendra, the words that Narendra felt Ramakrishna had personally practiced? Narendra reports that Ramakrishna said: "God can be seen and talked to, just as I am seeing you and speaking with you. . . . Distressed at not having seen God, if anyone calls on him with longing (*vyākul hoiyā*), God certainly reveals himself to the person" (LP 5.65).

Narendra was impressed with what he encountered, but perplexed at how this man, who spoke so convincingly about God, could be the same person who not long before had behaved like a madman. Thus he concluded that Ramakrishna must be a "monomaniac" (*ardhonmād*).[14] The use of the Bengali word *ardhonmād*, with "monomaniac" in parentheses, is significant since *ardhonmād* literally means "half crazy" or "eccentric."

Ramakrishna was thus temporarily pigeonholed into the "monomaniac" slot, but unsatisfactorily so, for Narendra says that he "could not forget the greatness of his wonderful renunciation for God." He continues:

> I thought, "He may be mad, but only a rare person in this world can renounce everything for God in this way. In spite of his madness, this person is very pure (*mahāpavitra*), a great renunciant (*mahātyāgī*), and truly worthy of reverence (*śraddhā*), worship (*pūjā*), and respect (*sammān*) by the human heart." With these thoughts, I bowed down at his feet, took leave of him and returned to Kolkata that day. (LP 5.66)

While *Kālī's Child* assesses Narendra's "monomaniac" label to be "pathologizing Ramakrishna" (210), this is not altogether accurate, for Narendra himself was not entirely at ease with his diagnosis. While Ramakrishna did indeed strike Narendra as mad when he spoke to him privately, Narendra makes it equally clear that he was greatly impressed with Ramakrishna's purity and renunciation. Narendra also noted that Ramakrishna seemed completely normal around everyone else. Further, the word *ardhonmād*, half-crazy or eccentric, is not a term that ascribes pathology.

Narendra's second visit to Ramakrishna did not occur until the following month. According to Saradananda, Narendra's delay was due to a number of factors: first, he suspected Ramakrishna was a monomaniac. Second, Narendra was also busy with his college studies, music and athletic practice as well as his own meditation practice. Even apart from that, he was involved with organizing prayer and discussion meetings of the Brahmo Samaj (LP 5.90–91).

Kālī's Child flattens Saradananda's text by stating: "Saradananda believes that Narendra waited so long to return a second time because he believed that Ramakrishna was a 'monomaniac'" (210). By suppressing Narendra's other reasons and implying that his first impression of Ramakrishna as a monomaniac was the *only* reason, *Kālī's Child* distorts both Saradananda's text and intent.

The texts indicate that Narendra's impressions of Ramakrishna were much richer and more varied than the simple monomaniac tag. In the text cited by Kripal, Narendra also found Ramakrishna—apart from being a "monomaniac"—to be a "rare person" (*biral byakti*) and a "great renunciant" (*mahātyāgī*) who "personally practiced what he preached" (LP 5.66). Narendra obviously had conflicting impressions of Ramakrishna, which were concurrently running against each other in his mind. To strip away Narendra's other impressions of Ramakrishna in favor of one sole "monomaniac" diagnosis serves to validate *Kālī's Child*'s thesis that Narendra was "pathologizing" Ramakrishna. Yet, apart from the fact that this is not faithful to the source texts, such a thesis also makes one wonder why Narendra would go out of his way to see Ramakrishna again, an issue which *Kālī's Child* does not address. Kripal frequently refers to Narendra as being "nervous" in Ramakrishna's company: "Mad men, after all, make people nervous. They are not normally sought out as conversation partners" (211). But Narendra *did* seek out Ramakrishna and Narendra was not "nervous," he was nonplussed.

Narendra's second visit to Ramakrishna was delayed until the following month and, as Narendra later relates, since he had not realized how far Dakshineswar was from Kolkata, he took great time and trouble in locating Ramakrishna. At last Narendra found him, sitting alone, absorbed in thought (*ekākī āpon mone bośiyā āchen*) (LP 5.91). Ramakrishna greeted him joyfully, Narendra reports, asking him to sit at one end of his bed. Narendra sat, but found Ramakrishna immersed in a kind of reverie (*ekprakār bhābe ābiṣṭa hoiyā poḍiyāchen*) (LP 5.92), speaking indistinctly to himself. Ramakrishna looked steadily at Narendra, then began moving towards him. Narendra remembers:

> I thought the crazy man (*pāgol*) would do something crazy (*pāglami*) yet again like the earlier time. Scarcely had I thought so when he came near and placed his right foot on my body, and in the very next moment

> by that touch I had an extraordinary experience (*apūrba upalabdhi*). With my eyes open I saw that all the things in the room together with the walls were rapidly whirling and disappearing somewhere and my ego, together with the whole universe, was as if about to merge in the all-devouring great void (*sarbagrāsī mahāśūnye*). I then became overwhelmed with a terrible fear. I thought that the destruction of the "I" was death and that death was before me, very close. Unable to restrain myself, I blurted out aloud, "Ah! What have you done to me? I have my parents." The wonderful crazy man (*adbhut pāgol*) laughed heartily when he heard my words and, touching my chest (*bokkha*) with his hand, he said, "Let it now stop; it doesn't have to be done all at once. It will all happen in time." It is astonishing that no sooner had he touched and spoken in that manner than my extraordinary revelation (*apūrba pratyakkha*) disappeared. I returned to a normal state of consciousness and saw the things inside and outside the room as they were before. (LP 5.92)

In describing Ramakrishna, Saradananda frequently uses the Bengali word *adbhut*, which literally means "unprecedented," but in ordinary usage means "wonderful," "remarkable" or "extraordinary." Kripal occasionally translates *adbhut* as "unprecedented" but more often than not as "strange." For example, in the section above, Kripal says that when Ramakrishna placed "his own foot" on Narendra's body, Narendra "had an unprecedented experience at his touch." Yet later in the same paragraph when *abdhut* is used again referring to Ramakrishna, Kripal translates this as "the strange crazy man"; the Bengali *adbhut pāgol*, would be better translated as "wonderful crazy man" or "remarkable crazy man."

As he later related this experience, Narendra states that although the occurrence itself was of short duration, "it produced a great revolution in my mind. Stunned (*stabdha*), I kept thinking about what it was that happened. I saw that the experience came suddenly and went suddenly by the power of this wonderful person (*adbhut puruṣ*)" (LP 5.92–93). Narendra wondered whether Ramakrishna had hypnotized him into having this experience, but could not accept this hypothesis since Narendra saw himself as strong-minded and strong-willed, not the type to fall under the sway of unwilling hypnosis. Narendra said what came to mind in terms of an explanation was: "In the words of the great poet (*mahākavi*): 'There are more things in heaven and earth than are dreamt of in your philosophy.'" (That Shakespeare's words would come to Narendra at this time shows the extent of his Westernization.)

At this point, Narendra began to doubt whether Ramakrishna really *was* mad, for how could a madman, Narendra later recalled, "shatter to pieces the structure of a mind like mine, possessed of strong will power (*prabol icchāśakti-sampanna*) and filled with firm impressions (*dṛḍha-saṁskāramoy*), making it like a ball of clay and reshaping it in his own way?" (LP 5.93–94). Nothing added up. Ramakrishna, Narendra says, was "pure and simple-hearted like a child," but that during their first meeting, Ramakrishna's words to him were nothing short of insane. Baffled, Narendra was determined to find out what was going on. Again Ramakrishna extracted a promise from Narendra to return to Dakshineswar, and again Narendra agreed (LP 5.95).

In reading *Kālī's Child*'s version of Narendra's experience, the reader is told that "a nervous Narendra was certain that this 'crazy man' was about to create another embarrassing scene." Further, "the madman treated Narendra like a dear relative or friend—it all made Narendra very nervous" (211). But the *Līlāprasaṅga*—the text *Kālī's Child* cites—makes it clear that there was no "embarrassment," and whatever Narendra experienced in the way of "anxiety" (*cintā*) was the result of Narendra's inability to make sense of either Ramakrishna or Ramakrishna's ability to change Narendra's perception of reality with a mere touch.

According to *Kālī's Child*, "Narendra left, confused, troubled, and upset. The problem remained unsolved" (211). *What* problem? In reading the *Līlāprasaṅga*, we find no "problem." At least part of the "problem" seems to lie in Kripal's reliance on Jagadananda's English translation. In Jagadananda's *Great Master* we read, in Narendra's words: "I left Dakshineswar musing on what had happened and on how to solve the problem" (GM, 735). But the word "problem" does not occur in the Bengali text. Why Jagadananda used it in his translation is anyone's guess. Why Kripal used "problem" is anyone's guess as well, except to indicate that he did not use the Bengali text.

Did Narendra have a "problem," and if so, was it Ramakrishna's foot? Was Narendra anxious (*cintā*) because of Ramakrishna's physical proximity or intimations of familiarity? Narendra makes it clear that his "anxiety" was due to his inability to make rational sense of the situation:

> I could not come to any definite conclusion (*sthiraniścay*) about this person, pure and simple-hearted like a child. From the time I began to think on my own, I could never remain content until I reached, with the help of philosophy, investigation, reasoning, and debate (*darśan, anusandhān o jukti-tarka-sahāye*), a settled conclusion about any thing or person. That nature of mine, receiving a severe shock (*dārun*

> *āghāt*) that day, produced pain in my heart (*prāne ekṭā jantranā*). As a result, there again arose a firm determination in my mind to understand in any way I could the nature and power of that wonderful person (*adbhut puruṣ*). (LP 5.94)

Like Dr. Sarkar, Narendra was very much a member of the educated elite, who believed Western reason and science to be the apotheosis of human endeavor. Unlike Dr. Sarkar, Narendra was becoming painfully aware that his carefully organized worldview was being demolished. Yet one would not know this by reading *Kālī's Child*. In contrast, Kripal writes that after Narendra's extraordinary experience, "Narendra left, confused, troubled, and upset" (KC, 211). The reader does not see that Narendra is equally impressed by Ramakrishna's character. The reader also does not see Narendra's determination to figure things out, but instead is shown a rather passive Narendra who is "troubled," "upset," and "nervous." The reader is told: "it all made Narendra very nervous" (211). But this is not the impression one gets after reading Saradananda's *Līlāprasaṅga*, the cited source.

One also does not get this impression when reading the reports of Ramakrishna's other disciples. For instance, Sashi (later Swami Ramakrishnananda) reports that during Narendra's second visit to Dakshineswar, Ramakrishna leaned over and touched Narendra's heart through the front of Narendra's shirt, which was unbuttoned. About Narendra's experience with Ramakrishna, Sashi said:

> Naren told me afterwards: "The walls of the room began to recede and disappear. Then the river and all of Calcutta vanished. The floor of the room seemed to sink down into the earth, until at last I seemed to be in a vast vacuum in which there was nothing but this brahmin [Ramakrishna] standing before me." . . .
>
> Later, when I [Sashi] asked Sri Ramakrishna whether there was a God, he told me to go to the boy Narendra and ask him. I went and asked him. Then Naren told me this story, and added that for fifteen or twenty days after this he seemed to see God everywhere. Everything seemed to be living—the ground, the wall, everywhere there was life. So he came to know that this brahmin was no ordinary paramahaṁsa. (Chetanananda 1990, 149)

If this experience was initially terrifying for Narendra—who was, at this point, a die-hard rationalist—it ended up becoming exalting and transformative. The reader does not see anything like this in *Kālī's Child*, however, which endlessly repeats that Narendra was "nervous." If one wonders why "nervous" has been repeatedly invoked, along with other words such as "troubled" and "upset," an endnote attached to Narendra's statement that Ramakrishna "placed his own right foot on my body," provides clarification. Kripal writes:

> The "body" (*aṅga*) is a rather safe term to explain the object of Ramakrishna's foot, despite the fact that the term can also mean "limb" and in another passage (LP 1.4.8) is used to describe Śiva's phallus. In any case, the "body" (usually *gā*) is used a number of times in the early volumes of the *Kathāmṛta*. In the later volumes ... the term is sometimes replaced by a more precise one, the "lap" (*kola*). It is quite possible that Ramakrishna's foot was placed in Narendra's lap, although this cannot be established with any certainty. (KC, 355)

Thus the reader is given the hint that the "body" is not really Narendra's *body*—which is a mere "safe term" for what very well may be the "lap." Perhaps, too, the "lap" really means "on the genitals," as the first edition would have it. Thus, innuendo intact, Narendra is "nervous," "troubled" and "upset." However, translating *aṅga* as "limb" and interpreting it as "Śiva's phallus" is not only wrong but also unintentionally funny. The particular passage in the *Līlāprasaṅga* uses the word *śrī-aṅga*, "holy image," which *Kālī's Child* mistranslates as both "the great limb" (55) as well as "Śiva's phallus" (355).

Saradananda writes that what happened during Narendra's third meeting with Ramakrishna was "inconceivable" (*abhābanīya*) and informs the reader that he provides "the reader here what we have heard from both Thakur and Narendra" (LP 5.95). Narendra, now well steeled for those unusual events which seemed to occur when he visited Ramakrishna, was on guard. As the Kālī temple compound was crowded that day, Ramakrishna suggested that they walk along the bank of the Ganges in the neighboring garden of Jadu Mallick. As they walked and talked, Ramakrishna came to Jadu's parlor, then sat down and went into samādhi. Narendra sat near him while he "calmly observed" (*sthīrabhābe lakkha koritechilen*) Ramakrishna's samādhi. At this point, Ramakrishna reached over and touched him "as on the earlier occasion" (*pūrbadiner nyāy*). With Ramakrishna's touch, Narendra completely lost consciousness. As he was regaining consciousness some time later, Narendra became aware of Ramakrishna passing his hand over his chest (LP 5.96). Narendra had no memory of what had transpired, but Ramakrishna related the following to his disciples:

> When Narendra lost his normal consciousness, I asked him that day many questions, such as who he was, where he came from, why he came (why he took birth), how long he would live here (in the world)

> and so on. . . . [His] answers confirmed what I had thought and seen about him. It is forbidden (*niṣedh*) to narrate all those things. But I have known from all these that, on the day he knows who he is, he will not stay in this world. Using his strong willpower, he will give up his body immediately through the path of yoga. (LP 5.97)

Saradananda's version of these events is echoed by other disciples and associates of Ramakrishna, who had also heard it from Ramakrishna, and to whom also he insisted that it remain secret. Of course one can easily contest Ramakrishna's story, assuming him either to be insane or having ulterior motives for any number of less-than-enlightened reasons, whether sexual predation or the desire for spiritual renown or the desire to tell a fabulous story. What we can definitely verify is that while Narendra himself had no memory of what he had said to Ramakrishna, Ramakrishna nevertheless repeated the incident to his other disciples who, in later years, repeated it to their own disciples in turn.

Saradananda informs the reader that with Narendra's third visit to Ramakrishna, Narendra no longer believed Ramakrishna to be a "monomaniac"—thus any presumed "pathologizing" of Ramakrishna by Narendra on this score had ended. However, this did not stop Narendra from arguing and disagreeing with Ramakrishna, and it certainly did not prevent Narendra from telling Ramakrishna that his visions were hallucinations. As Narendra later said: "Let none regret that they were difficult to convince! I fought my Master for six years with the result that I know every inch of the way! Every inch of the way!" (CW 9.411).

Nivedita writes that the source of Narendra's battle with Ramakrishna was Narendra's refusal to accept Kālī. Narendra, proud of his rational mind and modern "scientific" outlook, was also a member of the Brahmo Samaj, which rejected image worship. Ironically, in the ensuing years, Vivekananda came to embrace Kālī unreservedly. Nivedita writes what Vivekananda said to her about his change of heart:

> How I used to hate Kālī! . . And all Her ways! That was the ground of my six years' fight—that I would not accept Her. But I had to accept Her at last! Ramakrishna Paramahaṁsa dedicated me to Her, and now I believe that She guides me in everything I do, and does with me what She will. . . . Yet I fought so long! I loved him [Ramakrishna], you see, and that was what held me. I saw his marvelous purity. . . . I felt his wonderful love. . . . His greatness had not dawned on me then. . . . At that time I thought him a brain-sick baby, always seeing visions and the rest. I hated it. And then I, too, had to accept Her! (CW 8.263)

This is a long digression, but it points out several significant factors. First, while Narendra initially thought Ramakrishna to be a "monomaniac," the characterization was short-lived. As the texts have indicated, Narendra did not "pathologize" Ramakrishna. Second, even from his first visit, Narendra was impressed by Ramakrishna's purity and renunciation. Even during the period when Narendra accepted neither Ramakrishna nor Kālī, Narendra's genuine respect for Ramakrishna was in place. Ramakrishna's nephew Ramlal recalled that once Ramakrishna had asked him to go to Kolkata and bring Narendra some food. When Ramlal arrived at Narendra's home, Narendra—concerned that Ramlal had walked the entire distance from Dakshineswar—washed Ramlal's feet and fanned him. Ramlal told Narendra: "You told the Master that you would visit him on Wednesday, but you didn't. He was worried about you and has sent me with these things." To this Narendra replied, "Yes, Brother, I always plan to visit the Master, but the pressure of my family does not allow me to go anywhere. I shall go with you right now." Ramlal reports that Narendra changed his clothes immediately and off they went to Dakshineswar. When they arrived, Narendra bowed low before Ramakrishna, who greeted him with great affection (Chetanananda 1990, 51–52). This is not the behavior of one who is "nervous" around Ramakrishna.

Despite *Kālī's Child*'s repeated accusations, there is not a hint of "scandal" to be found in any of the source texts—even if one expends a great deal of effort reading between the lines—concerning Ramakrishna's character or motives. If *Kālī's Child* sees a "problem" with Ramakrishna's foot being placed upon Narendra's body, Narendra does not share this concern. Narendra's "problem" was not Ramakrishna's foot but the wholesale destruction of his previously held worldview and his inability to make sense of the alternate reality he experienced when Ramakrishna touched him—either with his foot or with his hand.

Ramakrishna's foot will take on a life of its own as it goes into service to provide a homoerotic drumbeat, from *Kālī's Child*'s inception to its conclusion. Even before the Introduction is completed, readers will be reminded yet again of Ramakrishna's "foot extended onto the bodies of young males" (36)—predictably not mentioning the foot extended onto older males or females. Nor is subtlety Kripal's strong suit when it comes to indicating the motives stimulating Ramakrishna's foot, which, he writes, was "extended … onto the bodies of his disciples in order to awaken their phallic love" (243).

This recurring anthem will continue even after the book's conclusion, where in the Appendix, Ramakrishna's foot is referred to as "that sexually charged organ" (335). Yet from the material *Kālī's Child* has presented and from the source material extant on Ramakrishna, one is hard pressed to make a case for the "curious habits" of Ramakrishna's foot. These "curious habits"—which Kripal describes as one of Ramakrishna's "techniques of arousal" (238)—serve as one of *Kālī's Child*'s key bulwarks for the book's homoerotic thesis.

If Ramakrishna's foot was not used as a technique of arousal, then what *was* he doing with his foot? Those in the Hindu tradition, and particularly those within the Ramakrishna tradition, would interpret Ramakrishna's foot placed on the bodies of devotees (whether male or female) as an act of grace. This is completely consonant with the Hindu religious tradition. In contrast, *Kālī's Child* asserts that Ramakrishna was "not at all sure why he [did] such things," nor was Ramakrishna "willing to take any blame" for sticking "his foot in strange places." While Kripal admits that Ramakrishna's feet "evoked great devotion and faith" (238), he nevertheless concludes that "Ramakrishna's foot points to a secret of which he himself was not aware, namely, that his mystical experiences and visions were constituted by erotic energies that he neither fully accepted nor understood." Significantly, Kripal declares: "Ramakrishna's foot placed provocatively in the lap of a young male disciple" is "a symbol for the entire study" (238). We would suggest looking at Ramakrishna's foot in another way altogether, seeing it as a symbol for how treacherously difficult cross-cultural interpretation can be.

In the Hindu tradition, the feet of a deity or holy person are sought for their darśan. Hindu sacred literature—Vaiṣṇava, Śākta, Śaiva, Tantra, Advaita, Sikh—is replete with references to the sacred feet of the deity, the feet of one's guru and the feet (or, more likely, "the lotus feet") of other spiritual personalities. The vertical line placed on the forehead by Vaiṣṇava devotees is a representation of Viṣṇu's foot. In Hindu mythology, the Ganges is said to have emerged from Viṣṇu's feet. Hindu devotees actively seek the dust from a holy person's feet and "taking refuge at his (or her) feet" is an extremely common expression of Hindu piety, an expression which is common to every tradition in the Hindu fold. To be touched by the feet of the Lord or by a particularly holy person is considered a great blessing.[15]

Given this powerful religio-cultural background, Ramakrishna's devotees and admirers not only were not shocked by Ramakrishna's placing his feet upon others, they actively sought touching his feet themselves. For example, once when Swami Akhandananda was visiting Dakshineswar, Ramakrishna asked him to massage his feet. Akhandananda recalled:

> I drew his legs onto my lap and was passing my hands over them when he began to tell me with a smile many beautiful things on spiritual life. . . . While massaging his feet I rubbed his two big toes on my forehead, as if I were drawing the Vaiṣṇava marks.
>
> The Master smiled, "What are you doing, my boy?". . .
>
> [Akhandananda replied:] "Today I am putting the sāttvic marks on my forehead. What is there on earth more sacred than your holy feet?" (Chetanananda 1990, 242)

Again, Ramchandra Datta in his *Jībanabṛttānta* describes the celebration that the devotees arranged every year in Dakshineswar on Ramakrishna's birthday. Datta paints a vivid portrait of Ramakrishna in bhāva samādhi in the company of devotees singing kīrtan. When Ramakrishna gradually returned to normal consciousness

> he tore the garland around his neck and threw it away, wiped the sandal paste on his forehead with the corner of the cloth he was wearing, but he could never wipe the sandal paste on his feet. . . . How could he? The feet don't belong to him. What right has he over something that he has given away? The feet now belong to the devotees. His feet are the treasure of their hearts, so he could not destroy their beauty [by wiping off the sandal paste]. (JB, 166)

As we have seen in this rather exhaustive discussion of Ramakrishna's foot and its actions, the evidence presented in *Kālī's Child* does not withstand critical scrutiny. *Kālī's Child*'s treatment of Ramakrishna's foot is a microcosm of the many problems exhibited throughout the book.

Secrecy, Censorship and Cover-up

Secrecy and scandal are the hallmarks of *Kālī's Child*, and the first building blocks of this supposed conspiracy to hide Ramakrishna's "secrets" are placed in the book's Introduction. Concerning earlier books on Ramakrishna published by the Ramakrishna Order, Kripal argues that they "hide as much as they show." The "tradition" has produced books that are "historically naive" and "translations that are not translations" to the point where "talk (and more talk) about Vivekananda [has] effectively buried that foot and its meanings beneath a mountain of pious ink, touched-up images, bowdlerized books, and wordy words" (KC, 2). What would provoke the Ramakrishna Order to bury, touch-up and bowdlerize? The reason, according to *Kālī's Child*, is that "Ramakrishna's mystical experiences ... were in actual fact *profoundly, provocatively, scandalously erotic*" (2; italics in text).

Another gauntlet having been thrown down, *Kālī's Child* hits its stride as Kripal concisely presents the book's central theses:

> I will demonstrate that even though Tantra, *not* Vedānta, structured the saint's ecstasies, visions, and teachings, Ramakrishna was emotionally torn by the tradition and its heterosexual symbolism; he could not be forced to complete the Tantric ritual of *maithuna* or "sexual intercourse" with a woman, for example, *not* because he had somehow transcended sex (the traditional claim) but because the ritual's heterosexual assumptions seriously violated the structure of his own homosexual desires. His female Tantric guru and temple boss may have forced themselves ... on the saint for both personal and Tantric reasons, but Ramakrishna remained ... a lover not of sexually aggressive women or even of older men but of young, beautiful boys, those "pure pots," as he called them, that could hold the "milk" of his divine love.[16] Finally, I will show ... how the saint ... fashioned out of his experience ... an impressive "spirituality of secrets" that could speak, and yet not speak, about the pain of his past, affirm the joys of his present, and transmute it all into a life of ecstasy and vision. (2–3)

Kripal concludes by declaring Ramakrishna to be "a conflicted, unwilling homoerotic Tāntrika" who was "uncomfortable in [Tantra's] symbolic world." Kripal states that he supports his claims with "Bengali texts, many of which, having been threatened, denied, and systematically censored, have remained untranslated to this day" (3).

At this point Kripal walks the reader straight into the edifice of *Kālī's Child*'s conspiracy theory: according to him, the *Kathāmṛta*, the central text of the Ramakrishna tradition which forms the centerpiece of *Kālī's Child*, is "the source of much nervousness within the tradition" (3). This is, as one may suspect, a revelation to those within the tradition, for whom the *Kathāmṛta* is a revered, much-loved and probably thumbworn text. It is not the kind of book that one generally associates with "nervousness," either inside or outside the tradition.

According to *Kālī's Child*, in order to uncover Ramakrishna's secrets, the text must be "recovered" (3)—an unintended echo of those early Orientalists whose stated goal was also to "recover" the text. The question is, recovered for whom? Obviously not for the large majority of the text's readers who have read the book in its original Bengali, in which every word remains just as M had written it.

In keeping with *Kālī's Child*'s secrecy thesis, Kripal speculates that the *Kathāmṛta*'s volumes were "arranged cyclically" in order to "conceal … a secret." As we have seen, the *Kathāmṛta* was written in five volumes and published over a period of thirty years. Kripal's thesis—and it is important to note that this is one of *Kālī's Child*'s truly original postulations—is that M "held back" the secret in the first volume, "hinted at" the secret in the second, "toyed with" it in the third, and "revealed" it in the fourth. Then, according to Kripal, M found that he had hardly any material left for the fifth (4). Yet as we have seen, there is no textual evidence to indicate that M began transcribing his diaries with the express intention of publishing a "book." Just as importantly, there is no evidence that M had any predetermined plan to divide his work into five volumes, however elegant Kripal's theory may appear to be. On the other hand, there is abundant evidence that M had hoped to complete more volumes before his death.[17]

Interestingly, even while contending that the *Kathāmṛta* is a source of "nervousness" within the tradition, Kripal nevertheless asserts that "from [the] renouncer point of view," M's *Kathāmṛta* "is little more than a collection of 'Sunday notes'" (12). One would think that a trifling collection of "Sunday notes" would not raise enough interest for "much nervousness." Yet from here, Kripal goes on to make a rousing defense of the major source text of the Ramakrishna tradition. "I am arguing that, despite the claims of the renouncers," Kripal writes, "M's *Kathāmṛta* is a legitimate and relatively accurate source for approaching and understanding the secret of Ramakrishna's life and teachings" (14). For those inside the Ramakrishna tradition—either monastic or lay—this is one of the weirdest statements in the entire book.[18] Kripal is arguing a non-argument. The *Kathāmṛta* is indisputably the core text of the Ramakrishna tradition and it is deeply loved and revered, and just as much by "renouncers" as "householders." The text is central to every monastic center of the Order and many, if not most, centers have time set aside for reading it. Swami Madhavananda, one of the greatest scholars of the Order and translator of the Bṛhadāraṇyaka Upaniṣad, read nothing but the *Kathāmṛta* in his last years and he was not exceptional in that practice.

In returning to *Kālī's Child* and to what it categorizes as the "political dimension" of the "secret," Kripal alleges that the Ramakrishna

Order has zealously guarded M's original diaries from the probing eyes of researchers. "No Western researcher has ever seen," Kripal asserts, "and may never see, the original manuscripts of M's diaries." The reason? "They contain a secret that is kept hidden from the public's eye" (i.e., that Ramakrishna was a "conflicted, unwilling, homoerotic Tāntrika"). For this reason, they "are kept under lock and key." Kripal adds in a confidential tone: "Anyone who has tried to locate M's diaries knows what I mean. The researcher soon discovers that the powers that control the archives and historical documents do not want these texts to be studied too closely" (311). Yet these charges are patently untrue. M's diaries are not the property of the Ramakrishna Order. M's diaries belong to M's descendants, as they always have. According to Swami Prabhananda, the Order's current General Secretary as well as its most respected scholar and historian: "The diaries, which are in the possession of the descendants of M, are their family property." Kripal, Prabhananda continues, "has accused M's descendants and the Ramakrishna Order for not disclosing the diaries to the Western scholars. Swami Prabhananda or for that matter the Ramakrishna Order has nothing to do about 'carefully' photocopying the diaries. None of the diaries or their copies are in the archives of Belur Math."[19] A simple inquiry about the original diaries would have elicited this information, which is hardly secret.

As this book's Appendix shows, Professor Dipak Gupta—the present controller of M's archives—attests that many scholars have *already* seen those diaries, even photographed them, without undue difficulty. Since Dr. Gupta emphatically denies that anyone has ever been prevented from seeing M's original diaries, one must wonder whom Kripal asked when he asked to see them. Perhaps the request was not given to the appropriate person or perhaps the request was never received at all.

Given the above, for those in the insider community, the "political dimension" of Ramakrishna's "secret" is clear: erroneous allegations created out of whole cloth were manufactured without anyone being interested in ascertaining the correct information. The simple truth was pedestrian, nothing as spicy as a conspiracy of lurking monks who engaged in "this hiding, this refusal to submit to public scrutiny" (KC, 311).

Kripal extends his conspiracy theory to Nikhilananda's English *Gospel of Sri Ramakrishna*, which he condemns as a "bowdlerized" text. Nikhilananda is accused of "ingeniously mistranslating many of the secrets; those passages for which he could not find a suitably safe enough 'translation,' he simply omitted" (4). There is no small irony in this accusation since Kripal's own staggering mistranslations and *additions* of his own material into his translation profoundly distort not only the letter but also the spirit of the original text.

Nevertheless *Kālī's Child* purports to unearth Ramakrishna's "secret," said to be previously concealed. This Kripal does through analyzing Ramakrishna's "secret talk" or *guhya kathā*, which consists of "eighteen passages dealing with visions and confessions Ramakrishna thought too troubling or important to reveal to any but his most intimate disciples" (3–4). One immediate problem is that Kripal associates, then equates, "secret" with "sexual." Yet secret teachings have historically been associated with the world's mystical traditions. As Elaine Pagels has written about Christian gnostic texts:

> Many regarded these secret gospels not as radical alternatives to the New Testament Gospels, but as advanced-level teaching for those who had already received Jesus' basic message. Even the Gospel of Mark tells us that Jesus explained things to certain disciples in private, entrusting to them alone "the mystery of the Kingdom of God."[20]

"Secret teachings" are as old as religion itself. As Kripal himself has noted, the Upaniṣads are associated with secret teaching: they were originally intended for only those few people who were spiritually fit to understand them. Ramakrishna's "secret teachings" are similarly directed to those students whom he considered capable of understanding higher spiritual truths.[21] Yet higher spiritual truths are not what is uncovered in *Kālī's Child*, since "secret" quickly slides into "sexual."

The most problematic aspect of *Kālī's Child*'s analysis of Ramakrishna's "secret talks" is its extremely narrow scope. Kripal restricts the category to eighteen isolated passages from the *Kathāmṛta*—the sole determinant for what constitutes the category of "secret talks" being whether the Bengali phrase *guhya kathā* has been used or not. Not only is this an artificial device, it is capricious as well, since much of what is included in the "secret talk" is repeated on other occasions without the *guhya kathā* tag. Thus what is labeled a "secret" on one day ceases to be "secret" on another day. Ramakrishna has a number of conversations with his disciples which constitute what normally would be considered "secret teachings"—that is, talks or instructions directed to those qualified students (*adhikārins*) who are advanced in spiritual practice. Yet these conversations do not fall under the purview of "secret talks" since the "*guhya kathā*" label was not applied.

Further, limiting and defining Ramakrishna's *guhya kathā* by what has been published in the *Kathāmṛta* presents a difficulty in itself. M's record of Ramakrishna's conversations—limited to the days and times when M was present—is obviously not the entirety of Ramakrishna's teachings. Sarada Devi was certainly an authority on Ramakrishna's teachings and her discussions of them should be taken into account. Similarly, the reminiscences of Ramakrishna's other disciples provide a wider body of knowledge, which needs to be incorporated into the corpus of Ramakrishna's *guhya kathā*. For example, as Ramakrishna's disciple Swami Premananda (whom we meet as "Baburam" in the *Kathāmṛta*) said:

> Thakur's teaching depended upon the audience—the teachings for the householders and the would-be monks were different. He never disturbed anyone's faith, he taught what was suitable to the person concerned. He taught the householders and the would-be monks in different ways. When there was no householder devotee in his room, he would shut his door and instruct us with burning ideas of renunciation and discrimination. Again, in between the talks, he would peep outside to see if any householder devotee was coming. He presented those ideas with illustrations to help us develop a strong dispassion for women and the world. (Omkareshwarananda, 28)

In order to get a comprehensive view of Ramakrishna's teachings—which he tailored to the audience in front of him—it is necessary to read a wide variety of accounts: the accounts of those who sought him out as the famous "paramahaṁsa from Dakshineswar" as well as the accounts of those who were closely associated with him. While M is indisputably a member of the latter category, he did not receive exactly the same teachings that others did—whether they be married women, Sikhs, actresses, Vaiṣṇavas, Christians, Brahmos, or future monastics. Whether or not the words *guhya kathā* were invoked in his teachings is too arbitrary a device to cull out the constituents of Ramakrishna's "secret teachings."

Tantra and Psychoanalysis

The stated goal of *Kālī's Child* is to "offer a nonreductive, psychoanalytically informed reading of Ramakrishna's mystical eroticism" (KC, 6). In this endeavor, the book draws upon the previous studies of Ramakrishna by Jeffrey Masson and, selectively, from Sudhir Kakar as well as other psychoanalytic interpreters of the Hindu tradition.[22] *Kālī's Child* endeavors to interpret Ramakrishna's mystical experiences through two hermeneutic strategies, one being Tantra, and the other, psychoanalysis. Kripal assures the reader that he offers "a historically accurate, psychologically nuanced reading of the Hindu Tantra as it was practiced by Ramakrishna" (2). Unfortunately, the book does not live up to its promise, for neither is it historically accurate nor is its reading of Tantra psychologically nuanced.

"Tantra," we read early on in *Kālī's Child*, "was Ramakrishna's secret." Kripal also makes the remarkable claim that "if Ramakrishna was a Tāntrika, it seems that either he was not willing to admit the fact" or "he himself was not fully aware of his own Tantric identity." Indeed, *"Ramakrishna's secret was secret even to himself"* (5; italics in text). We have seen other scholars, notably Walter Neevel, who have identified Ramakrishna with the Tantric tradition. What is novel in this case is the suggestion that Ramakrishna could be a Tāntrik without being aware of it. While the supposition that a Euro-American scholar would have fuller knowledge than the native practitioner is hardly a new phenomenon, *Kālī's Child*'s hypothesis belongs to a tradition of shorter duration: psychoanalytic interpretation.

Kripal writes: "I have attempted to use psychoanalytic categories, but only *within* Ramakrishna's Tantric world" (38). Yet readers might well question how Kripal would know what was "within Ramakrishna's Tantric world." As we delve further into *Kālī's Child*, it becomes apparent that the contents of Kripal's Tantric world have been misconstrued for Ramakrishna's Tantric world. One of *Kālī's Child*'s philosophical missteps is its conflation of Tantra with Vāmācāra, "the left-handed path," while Vāmācāra itself is exoticized into "magical power, strangeness, seediness, and sex." In so doing, *Kālī's Child* seriously diminishes the philosophical and ontological range of the Tantric tradition. If magical power, strangeness, seediness, and sex were indeed Tantra's primary constituents, then there is no doubt that Ramakrishna would surely not be "aware of his own Tantric identity." Yet *Kālī's Child* avers that it is *Ramakrishna* who did not correctly understand Tantra, since Ramakrishna denied the "basic Tantric equation of the mystical and the erotic" (5).

Apart from the issue of *Kālī's Child*'s version of "the Hindu Tantra," Kripal's psychoanalytic skills are not sufficient to provide a deeper understanding of a nineteenth-century Bengali mystic. Even while admitting that "human psychology is ... variable, and radically so" (38), Kripal maintains that "human psychology ... is relatively consistent across cultures" (37), despite a significant body of evidence which contests this assertion.[23] Further, though Kripal writes that his "use of psychoanalysis is fairly light," he goes on to say that it is restricted to "Freud's most basic ideas (the unconscious, repression, sublimation, condensation, the Oedipus complex, the whore-virgin split, upward displacement, etc.)" (38). This is more than enough to misread any nineteenth-century Hindu, particularly when such analysis is in the hands of one who is not professionally trained in psychoanalysis and is insufficiently familiar with Bengali culture and language. As a result, the armchair psychoanalysis employed in *Kālī's Child* reveals presuppositions based on culturally biased Freudian models, while it remains debatable whether Freudian psychoanalysis can be applied to Ramakrishna at all. Were it viable, then a deep knowledge of the cultural context and language of nineteenth-century Bengal would be an absolute prerequisite.

Kripal argues that "psychoanalysis ... *can* be used to interpret non-Western cultures," but it must be, à la Stanley Kurtz, "'reshaped' to fit each and every cultural context in which it is applied" (38). While that seems quite reasonable, this is, in fact, what does not happen in *Kālī's Child*. Had Ramakrishna's cultural context been better understood, it is doubtful whether *Kālī's Child* would have been written in the first place.

We should mention in passing that Kripal's prescriptive treatment of Ramakrishna becomes evident here. Throughout *Kālī's Child*, Kripal will point out a number of areas in which Ramakrishna needed improvement. In this instance, not only was Ramakrishna unaware of his own Tantric identity, but he also did not get Tantra right—he denied the "basic Tantric equation of the mystical and the erotic." Furthermore, Ramakrishna did not enact Tantra as it should have been enacted, hence he was a "failed Tāntrika." Harking back to the prescriptive notions of the early Orientalists, Kripal's dressing-down of Ramakrishna concerning Tantra reads like a twentieth-century reprise of Max Müller. While Müller's Ramakrishna was not "what the true Gnānin (knower) ought to be" (Müller 1899, 169), Kripal's Ramakrishna is not what the true Tāntrik ought to be. Whether falling short of either Müller's or Kripal's expectations, Ramakrishna does not measure up to the pre-existing bar set by his interpreters. As we have seen with Müller and we shall see with Kripal, there is an agenda which first discredits the subject's knowledge or abilities, then shows how the subject should have thought and behaved in order to get it right.[24]

Ramakrishna is thus dismissed in *Kālī's Child* as a "failed Tāntrika" who "could not consciously make it through the Five M's" (129)[25]—as if the literal performance of the "Five M's" were in and of itself the purpose of Tantra. What are the Five M's *for?* Citing both Sanjuka Gupta and Aghehananda Bharati, Amiya Sen reminds us that Tantra's "eschatological goals … are no different from that found in other schools of Hindu philosophy; the release from the *karmic* cycle of rebirths" (2001, 128). Thus, like every other Hindu liberatory tradition, the goal of Tantra is the attainment of union with the ultimate Reality. Whether the sādhaka can attain this union by means of one M or Five M's or through the use of symbolic M's alone, the Five M's are themselves secondary to the issue of whether liberation has been attained. The Five M's are the means, not the goal.

Should the reader wonder how Ramakrishna could be not fully aware of his own Tantric identity, a psychoanalytic explanation is offered:

> For Ramakrishna … the experience of Tantra was intimately and uncomfortably bound up with *emotional* reactions, with "shame, disgust, and fear," that in turn were psychologically connected to troubling memories of his own vague past. . . . He was … struggling with the horrors of his past and the challenges of his present through the rituals and symbolic states of Tantra. If he became a Child, it was at least partly because he *feared* women. . . . If he brought Kālī's sword to his own throat, it was at least partly because he felt *shame* for phallic desires. . . . And if he consistently associated Tantra with the latrine, it was because he himself had experienced and was *disgusted* with the dark abusive side of the tradition. All these emotional reactions, and many more, made Tantra for Ramakrishna a thing of almost limitless, and so terrifying, power. (KC, 32; italics in text)

What is remarkable about the passage above is how much biographical and psychological knowledge about Ramakrishna is presumed by the author—knowledge to which Ramakrishna himself was seemingly not privy, nor his disciples, nor those succeeding generations who carefully studied Ramakrishna's life. It is remarkable that, after wading through pages of Ramakrishna's many failings as a Tāntrik, that he is suddenly deemed to be "the greatest of Tantric mystics" at the book's conclusion (apparently even a failed Tāntrik can be the greatest Tāntrik). Yet despite such ascribed greatness, Ramakrishna "nevertheless remained quite unaware of the latent or 'hidden' themes that structured much of his own experience" (327).

It is not uncommon for biographers to assume that they can understand more of their subjects than the subjects themselves. Is this the case with Ramakrishna? Can we say, for example, that "Tantra for Ramakrishna [was] a thing of almost limitless, and so terrifying, power"? There is no evidence for this. Indeed, Ramakrishna's reactions to Tantra are quite domesticated. In the *Kathāmṛta* Ramakrishna tells Ishan: "The path of Tantra is suited for the Kalīyuga (*kolite tantrokto mot*)" (KA 2.66). This looks like at least a mild endorsement, not a statement of fear, disgust or horror. Importantly, however, Ramakrishna does not recommend *Vāmācāra* to Ishan. Ramakrishna speaks approvingly of "the path of Tantra." On the other hand, Ramakrishna warns Narendra that the Tantric practice performed with women "is not a good path. It is very difficult and often causes a sādhaka's downfall" (KA 2.8). As we have noted, Ramakrishna geared his teachings to his listeners' aptitudes. While he encouraged jñāna for Narendra, he did not encourage Tantra, or more accurately, he discouraged the *vīra* or heroic aspect implicit in Vāmācāra.

Nevertheless, when Girish Ghosh (of all people) told Ramakrishna that he was going to write a book denouncing the Vāmācāra practices of the Kartābhajās, Ramakrishna dissuaded him, saying: "It is also a path. Some people have made progress in spiritual life through that path" (Chetanananda 1990, 105). Again, when Narendra denounced Vāmācāra practices, Ramakrishna gently reminded him that this path was also a spiritual path.[26]

Yet despite Ramakrishna's noncondemnatory approach, *Kālī's Child* presents what it takes to be Ramakrishna's "Tantric world" in an atmosphere of ripe exoticism. Kripal asserts that the *Kathāmṛta*, for example, is "peppered with graphic Tantric visions and descriptions of seedy midnight rituals. An occasional visiting Tāntrika even appears here and there ... ready to offer a sexy interpretation of a particular symbol or metaphor" (30). One wonders if Kripal is reading the same text as the rest of us.

The *Kathāmṛta* pays particular attention to the visits of only two Tāntriks. If they offer a "sexy" interpretation of anything, we may be dealing with a new definition of "sexy." The first Tāntrik we meet in the *Kathāmṛta* (KA 5.56–57) visits Ramakrishna on June 17, 1883, arriving in the middle of a discussion about the characteristics of a paramahaṁsa. When the Tāntrik asks whether a paramahaṁsa is aware of virtue and vice, Ramakrishna replies that good and bad, virtue and vice, the real and unreal are the splendors of God's māyā (*e sab tāṁr māyār aiśbarjjo*). The Tāntrik asks Ramakrishna about the law of karma, and after more singing and discussion, Ramakrishna tells the Tāntrik that when a person has attained God, then he or she cannot retain sinful tendencies. The Tāntrik tells Ramakrishna that today he has destroyed many of their doubts, to which Ramakrishna replies, "All doubts disappear when one realizes the Ātman" (*ātmār sākkhātkār hole sab sondeha bhañjon hoy*). Ironically, the Tāntrik's final question to Ramakrishna is: "Why don't the rituals of Tantra bear fruit now?" (*tāntrik kriyā, ājkāl keno phale nā?*). Ramakrishna replies that it is because the rituals are practiced neither correctly nor with devotion (*sarbāṅgīṇ hoy nā, ār bhaktipūrbak hoy nā*). It is clear that our Tāntrik did not find Ramakrishna a "failed Tāntrika," since—apart from the fact that the Tāntrik sought out his counsel in the first place—he declares that Ramakrishna has destroyed many of their doubts. If there is anything "sexy" in this interchange, it is very subtle indeed.

The second Tāntrik who appears in the *Kathāmṛta* (KA 5.103) visits Ramakrishna on January 2, 1884. In discussing the Tantric practice of drinking wine from a skull, Ramakrishna begins the conversation with the Tāntrik by saying: "All these are parts of Tantric sādhana, such as drinking wine from a skull. That wine is called 'causal water' (*kāraṇbāri*), isn't it so?" The Tāntrik replies, "Yes, sir." Nikhilananda does not translate the following two lines, in which Ramakrishna goes on to say, "Eleven cups, no?" The Tāntrik replies, "A measure of three *tolas* for the sādhana while meditating on [i.e., sitting upon] a corpse (*śab-sādhana*)." This may be a mildly interesting detail which Nikhilananda omitted, but the omission does not seem tantamount to either bowdlerization or censorship. Nor do the untranslated lines appear to be sexy.

Ramakrishna goes on to state that he cannot drink wine at all. The Tāntrik's reply to this is telling: "You have spontaneous bliss (*āpnār sahajānanda*). If I were to have this bliss, I wouldn't want anything else (*śe ānanda h'ole kicchui cāi nā*)." Obviously the Tāntrik does not find Ramakrishna remiss in not drinking wine; Ramakrishna already has spontaneous bliss, the Tāntrik declares. Once the goal of Tantra sādhana is attained, there is no need for performing the Five M's or any other kind of formalized sādhana. It is in keeping with this idea that Ramakrishna then tells the Tāntrik that he does not like japa and austerity (*jap-tap*), but he does have constant remembrance of God (*sarbadā smaraṇ-manan āche*).

Ramakrishna then asks the Tāntrik, "When they speak of the six chakras, what do they mean?" The Tantrik replies that the chakras are "like different holy places" (*śab nānā tīrther nyāy*). "In each of the chakras," he adds, "Śiva and Śakti dwell, but they can't be seen with physical eyes" (*ek ek cakre śibśaktiḥ cokkhe dekhā jāy nā*). Nikhilananda does not translate what the Tāntrik now says, which is apparently what Kripal believes to be "sexy": "The stem of the lotus is the *Śivaliṅga*, and the vulva-shaped primal power dwells in the pistil" (*padmer mṛṇāl śibliṅga, padma karṇikāy ādyaśakti yonirūpe*). Ramakrishna then asks the Tāntrik (and here Nikhilananda resumes his translation) whether one can attain perfection without the *bīja* mantra. The Tāntrik replies that a person can, if he or she has faith in the words of the guru (*gūrūbākye biśvās*); Ramakrishna then turns to M and repeats, "Faith!" (*biśvās!*). The Tāntrik then takes leave of Ramakrishna.

As we can see, the drift of Ramakrishna's and the Tāntrik's conversation concerns itself with the deeper aspects of Hindu spiritual life and, as with Ramakrishna's conversation with the first Tāntrik, there is little in the way of "sexy interpretations" unless one's definition of "sexy" is very broad indeed. The conversation is not even tangentially about vulvas and phalluses but with the fact that Śiva and Śakti dwell within the human being, the chakras themselves being *tīrthas*—places of pilgrimage. This is why the conversation naturally moves toward a discussion of *bīja* mantras, the role of the guru and the importance of faith. Just as importantly, the conversation also reveals the Tāntrik's admiration for Ramakrishna as one who has achieved "spontaneous bliss" and thus neither wanted nor lacked anything in his spiritual life.

Yet according to *Kālī's Child*, the Tāntrik's remark revealed Ramakrishna's "secret"—which is why Nikhilananda did not include the Tāntrik's description of the chakras ("The stem of the lotus is the Śivaliṅga, and the vulva-shaped primal power dwells in the pistil") in his *Gospel of Sri Ramakrishna*. That writing about anything which was "vulva-shaped" (unless it was in a medical textbook) was thoroughly unacceptable in 1942 America does not seem to have occurred to Kripal. This is, of course, why Nikhilananda and his editorial assistants—Joseph Campbell, Margaret Woodrow Wilson and John Moffitt—opted not to include the phrase. In 1942 such language was considered highly offensive and inappropriate.[27] (We should mention in passing that *yoni* can be translated either as "vulva" or "vagina"; since a lotus arguably resembles a vulva more than a vagina, we have translated *yoni* as "vulva."). Further, by not including the physical description of the chakras, Nikhilananda did not detract from the purport of the conversation, which was concerning the chakras themselves, their manifestation as holy places within the body, and the presence of Śiva and Śakti there. Finally, since the great majority of the text's readers do not read the English translation but rather M's original Bengali text, where every word remains just as he wrote it—including "vulva-shaped"—the "secret" could hardly be a secret for those millions of readers who have taken the adjective for what it is—an adjective—and have taken it in their stride. Nor do they think of the Śivaliṅga as "Śiva's phallus." For Hindus, the liṅga *is* Śiva, Śiva in all his greatness and splendor, not merely his phallus.

It would appear, however, that as far as *Kālī's Child* is concerned, the most significant part of the conversation is the Tāntrik's physical description of the lotus and what this purportedly conveys. Kripal writes: "A Tāntrika ... one day visited Ramakrishna and pointed out that the 'stem' and 'lotuses' of kundalini yoga represents Śiva's phallus (*liṅgam*) and the goddess 'in the form of a vagina' (*yonirūpa*) (KA 5.103), establishing the very same symbolic equation that Ramakrishna's secret vision had established twenty-five years earlier" (128). *Kālī's Child* gives no indication of the basic tenor of the conversation—the chakras being places of pilgrimage, of Śiva and Śakti dwelling within the body, and certainly no indication of the Tāntrik's deep respect for Ramakrishna. Far from it—in fact, Kripal uses this conversation as a springboard to bring forth his speculation that Ramakrishna, whom the Bhairavi "failed to take ... through the fifth M" (126), performed ritual cunnilingus with the Bhairavi. Evidence for this bizarre conjecture is found, Kripal asserts, in the "secret vision" from twenty-five years earlier.

Kripal refers to Ramakrishna's famed "lotus vision" as the "secret vision," a mystical vision which detailed the awakening of the six chakras. As we discuss this vision at length in Chapter Four, we will address this only briefly here. In this vision, Ramakrishna sees a twenty-two or twenty-three-year-old young man who resembles himself, and who, with the touch of his tongue, arouses each dormant vulva-shaped lotus (chakra) into full bloom. It goes without saying that this mystical vision uses vivid erotic imagery—particularly since Ramakrishna uses the word *ramaṇ*, which has a wide cascade of meanings: sport, enjoyment, sexual intercourse, communion. In its adjectival form *ramaṇ* can mean delightful, charming, pleasing. Nikhilananda translates *ramaṇ* as "commune," which Kripal sees as a whitewash. We would argue that, on the contrary, to literalize this mystical vision, which is what happens in *Kālī's Child*, is to diminish it and remove its real meaning. Erotic imagery has often been used to convey the ineffable and profound. It attempts to express what ordinary language cannot convey, and for that reason, mystical experiences are often placed in erotic terms because of their obvious power. Kripal persists in translating *ramaṇ* in purely sexual terms, but in doing so he does serious injustice to the range of meanings implicit in this very rich word. One obvious example: Ramana Maharshi, whose name is an abbreviation of Venkataramana—"one who delights in Veṅkaṭa (Viṣṇu)." His name does not mean "one who has sex with Veṅkaṭa."

In contrast to Nikhilananda's translation of *ramaṇ* as "commune" or our preference for "have intercourse with," *Kālī's Child* interprets Ramakrishna's lotus vision as his "secret cunnilingus vision" (271). "Secret" is the operative word here, for this "secret" is purportedly obvious to our second Tāntrik: "For the Tāntrika," Kripal writes, "the secret was evident, the latent was manifest" (128).

But is there any evidence to support this "secret cunnilingus vision" hypothesis? Kripal states that the "Ramakrishna-*homunculus*" in the "secret vision" is about the same age that Ramakrishna would have been when he was under the Bhairavi's tutelage. Further, both the lotus vision and the second Tāntrik employ the adjective *yonirūpe*, vulva-shaped. It is, Kripal writes, "the same term that Ramakrishna uses to describe the 'vaginal shape' of the lotuses in KA 4.238 [the lotus vision]" (349). *Kālī's Child* also tells us, by way of offering more evidence in favor of the cunnilingus speculation, that the "association between the vagina and flowers is common enough in Indian culture" (127). Kripal then provides several references from the *Kālī Tantra, Bṛhadyonitantra, Yonitantra* (all of which, we can be sure, Ramakrishna never read and probably never heard of). *Kālī's Child* goes on to declare that the "*Kathāmṛta* is just as rich in symbolic equations between the vagina and flowers" (128). That is news for those of us who know the *Kathāmṛta* well. Kripal backs up his bold claim by providing an endnote that points to six references from the *Kathāmṛta* for "lotuses and their symbolic associations" (KC 349). Yet not even one of these deals with "vagina and flowers."[28]

What other evidence is offered to support this speculation? *Kālī's Child* offers as evidence Ramchandra Datta's adjectives from the *Jībanabṛttānta*'s description of Ramakrishna's Tantra sādhana: "horrific" and "filled with obscenities" (JB, 31). Datta's characterization of Tantra is not surprising because, as one with powerful Vaiṣṇava leanings, he had an antipathy for Tantra. There are aspects of Ramakrishna's Tantra sādhana that could be construed as "horrific" and "filled with obscenities"—meditating on an altar under which are buried five skulls (jackal, snake, dog, bull and man); touching rotting human flesh with his tongue; sitting on a naked woman's lap while doing japa—yet none of these suggest that Ramakrishna performed ritual cunnilingus. Kripal also writes that the *Kathāmṛta* describes Tantra as "bizarre." Yet when one turns to the reference which describes Ramakrishna's sādhana under the Bhairavi's direction (KA 3.24), one merely finds the phrase *bhāri utkaṭ*, which simply means that the sādhana was "extremely difficult" or "extremely severe."

Apart from these factors, there is also what Amiya Sen describes as *Kālī's Child*'s "gross confusion over chronology." In discussing Kripal's thesis concerning Ramakrishna performing cunnilingus on the Bhairavi, Sen notes that the *Kathāmṛta* places the lotus vision in 1858, around the time of Hriday's arrival in Dakshineswar (KA 4.237–38). But as Sen points out, according to the usually accepted chronology of Ramakrishna's life, Hriday arrived as early as 1855, a fact acknowledged by *Kālī's Child* as well (KC, 61). "But even allowing for some inaccuracy with this date," Sen writes, "this is still far removed in time from Ramakrishna's meeting with the Bhairavi, sometime in 1861" (2001, 142). As should be obvious by now, the evidence to support Kripal's speculation that Ramakrishna engaged the Bhairavi in ritual cunnilingus is somewhere between preposterously thin and nonexistent.

Why, given such thin evidence, would Kripal go out on a limb to propose such a speculation? Because of the "failed Tāntrika" dictum. If Ramakrishna "could not make it through the Five M's" and "failed" particularly with the fifth M (*maithuna*), then this line of reasoning apparently goes, the Bhairavi must have wanted Ramakrishna to engage in *some* kind of sexual activity. Hence, even if the cunnilingus speculation is baseless and Ramakrishna did not *physically* engage in cunnilingus with the Bhairavi, then—the reasoning continues—he performed this erotic act in his visionary state:

> The Ramakrishna-*homunculus* was ... engaging in a mystical form of oral sex, arousing vagina-shaped lotuses into ecstatic blossoms with a playful Tantric tongue. The secret vision thus accomplishes in its obscene, if still symbolic, form what Ramakrishna could not accomplish in his Tantric practices with the Bhairavī, namely, the breaking

of the bonds of "shame, disgust, and fear" and the transcendence of society's notions regarding purity that they represent. (KC, 129)

There are a number of problems with this, but we will address only two here. First, the point of Tantric sādhana is not merely the transcendence of society's notions of purity, but to transcend *everything*, including the Five M's, including the body and the mind as we know it. The goal of Tantra sādhana is not to perform the Five M's, but to attain divine union. It was for this very reason that *both* our Tāntriks sought out Ramakrishna as an adept, as one who had reached the goal, one who was filled with spontaneous bliss (*sahajānanda*), attaining which a person desires nothing else.

Second, despite the assertion that the "Bhairavī clearly tried to employ sexual intercourse as one of her means to teach Ramakrishna Tantric truths" (KC, 120), there is no evidence that she wanted or expected Ramakrishna to physically engage in *maithuna*, the fifth M. And there is certainly no evidence that she saw Ramakrishna as "failed" in any way. Indeed, she was quite proud of her student—it was she, after all, who said that Ramakrishna had the same signs of divine madness as Caitanya. It was the Bhairavi who convened a conference of spiritual leaders who determined that Ramakrishna's madness was not ordinary madness but divine madness, and deemed him to be an avatar. Far from being disappointed by Ramakrishna going into samādhi while sitting on a young, beautiful woman's lap or entering samādhi while observing a couple having sexual intercourse, the Bhairavi was deeply gratified. She declared: "My child, you have attained perfection in *anandāsana* and have become established in the divine state (*divyabhāva*). This is the final sādhana of this path (*vīrabhāva*)" (LP 2.206). The Bhairavi did not see samādhi as an escape mechanism; she saw it as the culmination and fulfillment of Ramakrishna's sādhana.

Kripal writes that the *Kathāmṛta* is "peppered with graphic Tantric visions," yet despite the enticement, there is little to show for it. The only "Tantric visions" to be had—which do not offer much in the way of "graphic" descriptions—are two visions in particular, one of which is the "lotus vision" (discussed in Chapter Four) and the other is Ramakrishna's vision of the paramahaṁsa boy (discussed in Chapter Five). While the lotus vision can certainly be seen as Tantric, since Ramakrishna's vision is about the awakening of his chakras, assessing Ramakrishna's vision of the paramahaṁsa boy as "Tantric" is a real stretch. Other visions such as the bearded Muslim (KC, 165), which Kripal defines as "Tantric," are simply laughable.

Ramakrishna and Sexual Abuse

In returning to Kripal's use of psychoanalytic categories within "Ramakrishna's Tantric world," we should note the language of victimization which *Kālī's Child* employs to interpret Ramakrishna. Kripal first speculates, then assumes, then presents as fact that Ramakrishna was sexually abused both as a child and an adult. *Kālī's Child* is unburdened by evidence, textual or otherwise, to back up its claims. It initially offers these claims as speculations about Ramakrishna's past, then the dominos fall backward and the claims assume the mantle of fact within a short number of pages. For example, we read that Ramakrishna's "female Tantric guru and temple boss *may have forced themselves* ... on the saint for both personal and Tantric reasons" (2; emphasis added), but within thirty pages we are already encountering Ramakrishna being "*disgusted* with the dark abusive side of the tradition," with nothing presented in the entire text to establish evidence of this purported abuse. What *abusive* side? Instead of evidence, the reader encounters a steady trickle of erroneous information, inaccurate translations and sexually laden insinuations, which are endlessly repeated, then slowly built into an edifice of presumed sexual abuse and alleged sexual reenactment patterns.

What are Ramakrishna's "troubling memories of his own vague past"? There is no evidence presented apart from presumption. Under normal circumstances, a lack of evidence is taken seriously when weighing the veracity of an accusation. Yet Kripal sees this lack of evidence as *itself* evidence of childhood sexual abuse. With evidentiary rules such as these, Ramakrishna can't win for losing:

> We must admit that there are no clear indications of early sexual abuse in the biographies. But why should there be? . . .
>
> ... Is it just a coincidence that repeated traumatic events, . . . that, in the words of one psychiatrist, "simultaneously conceal and reveal their origins ... [and] speak in [the] disguised language of secrets too terrible for words?" It is indeed remarkable that the vast, if young and still debated, literature on sexual trauma suggests that individuals who have experienced abuse often become adept at altering their state of consciousness ... lose control of their bodily, and especially gastrointestinal, functions, experience visions and states of possession, become hypersensitive to idiosyncratic stimuli (like latrines), symbolically reenact the traumatic events, live in a state of hyperarousal ... become hypersexual in their language or behavior, develop hostile feelings toward mother figures, fear adult sexuality, and often attempt suicide. This list reads like a summary of Ramakrishna's religious life. (KC, 298–99)

One would hope that not everyone's religious life would include a laundry list consisting of losing control of gastrointestinal functions, living in a state of hyperarousal or developing hostile feelings toward mother figures, etc. Thus, without evidence—since there is none that indicates Ramakrishna ever suffered from "hyperarousal" or that he harbored "hostile feelings toward mother figures" (though it must be admitted that Ramakrishna, along with much of the country, suffered from gastrointestinal problems)—Kripal forges ahead with his hunches about Ramakrishna as his modus operandi.

It is illuminating to analyze several examples of what *Kālī's Child* takes to be Ramakrishna's troubled and "vague past." We need to first mention, however, that there is nothing "vague" about Ramakrishna's past. Ramakrishna spoke about his early life often and much of his language reflected his life and experiences of that period. Further, Saradananda amassed a great deal of data from the villagers who knew Ramakrishna long before he became a public figure. Ramlal (Ramakrishna's nephew) and other members of Ramakrishna's immediate family also provided a good deal of information to Saradananda and others who wished to know about Ramakrishna's early history. In brief, until the death of his father, Ramakrishna's childhood was happy and fairly carefree. He says so himself; his relatives and neighbors agree. Some thought he later became insane; others thought he became too religious; at least one believed him to be an avatar. But all agree that his childhood was untroubled.

Yet even in describing fairly neutral aspects of Ramakrishna's early life, *Kālī's Child* inserts a sexualized context which is not in the original texts. For example, in describing Ramakrishna's childhood Kripal writes that Ramakrishna and his friends acted out scenes from Hindu mythology in their own dramatic troupe. Citing the *Līlāprasaṅga*, Kripal writes that in the village mango grove, "[Ramakrishna] and his friends acted out the erotic exploits of Kṛṣṇa and the milkmaids in Vrindavana" (56). Yet when one checks the referenced text, one instead finds that Ramakrishna and his friends were "acting in the plays about Śrī Rāmacandra and Śrī Kṛṣṇa" (*Śrī-rāmacandra o Śrī-kṛṣṇa biṣoyak jātrābhinoy*). There is no mention of "erotic exploits," there is no mention of "milkmaids," there is not even a mention of *līlā* here. We should note that Kripal *excised* "Śrī Rāmacandra" since one would have difficulty associating "erotic exploits" with him. The irony is that while Kripal repeatedly censures Nikhilananda for "censoring" and "bowdlerizing" his translation of the

Kathāmṛta, Kripal is more than willing to excise what may detract from his theses. Further, while Nikhilananda did not translate every word (though he certainly did translate the vast majority of them), he did not *add* material that was not in the *Kathāmṛta*. Kripal cannot make the same claim. Again and again, as we shall see in upcoming pages, Kripal adds words and phrases that are neither present nor implied in the *Kathāmṛta*.

One of *Kālī's Child*'s prominent allegations about Ramakrishna's early years is that he was sexually abused by the itinerant sādhus who visited his village. As is well known, Gadadhar (the young Ramakrishna) enjoyed spending time with the monks who often stopped by his village en route to Puri. Purportedly quoting the *Līlāprasaṅga* (LP 1.108–9), Kripal writes that Ramakrishna's mother "began to worry about such visits, especially when the boy returned home with his clothes torn into a simple loin-cloth and his nearly naked body covered with ashes, but Gadadhar assured her that nothing was wrong." To this Kripal adds ominously, "But something *was* wrong" (KC, 57). This does sound alarming until one checks the *Līlāprasaṅga* and finds that the boy's *clothes* were not torn, but rather his *cloth (dhoti)* was torn into a loincloth (LP 1.108–9). This distinction is extremely important, for it is obvious that Kripal is unaware of the nature of a loincloth (*kaupin*) and how much material it requires.

There is nothing the slightest bit unusual about cutting a portion of the dhoti and making it into a kaupin. It is a *very* common thing for monks to do. This fact is mentioned in the *Ādi Kathāmṛta* by Girish Chandra Sen, an author whom Kripal quotes. Sen writes: "Whenever [Ramakrishna] met any mendicants, he would associate with them; and like them, he would wear a loin cloth, even if it meant tearing up his own cloth" (Chetanananda 1990, 401). There was no "naked body" anywhere, which makes sense, since the phrase referring to the young Gadadhar's "near naked body" does not appear anywhere in the *Līlāprasaṅga*. The phrase was, unhappily, newly minted for *Kālī's Child*, giving us yet another example of Kripal adding his own material to the original text. Further, in India it is not at all unusual for males to wear only a kaupin; it is not considered "naked," unless genitals are exposed. There are many photos of Ramana Maharshi wearing only a kaupin. When Vivekananda returned to India from the West, he was relieved to be released from Western clothing and he could be free to wear just a kaupin. In *Ramakrishna for Children*, there is an illustration—on the very cover of the book—of young Ramakrishna wearing only a kaupin during his *upanayana* ceremony.

Continuing our investigation into this purported incident of childhood sexual abuse, we read in the *Līlāprasaṅga* that Gadadhar would "tell his mother everything" (*tāhāke samasta kathā nivedan korilo*) (LP 1.108). When he returned from his visit to the monks, the boy would tell his mother, "Look mother, how the monks have adorned me" (*mā, sādhurā āmāke kemon sājāiyā diyāchhen, dekho*). It was *then* that Gadadhar showed her the kaupin. In *Kālī's Child*'s skewed account, the reader is led to believe that the boy returned home with "his nearly naked body" covered with ashes. Moreover, the *Līlāprasaṅga* keeps these events quite distinct. Gadadhar was smeared with sacred ash (*vibhūti-bhuśitāṅga hoiyā*) on some days (*kono din*), and on some days (*kono din*) he returned home with a sacred emblem on his forehead (*tilak dhāran koriyā*), and on some *other* days (*ābār kono din*), he returned home using a part of his dhoti as a loincloth (LP 1.108). *Kālī's Child* throws these distinct elements together while adding words that do not exist in the text which is allegedly quoted: "torn clothes" and a "nearly naked body."

What is particularly interesting here is that Kripal chooses *not* to mention the nature of Ramakrishna's mother's fear. In the *same paragraph* which Kripal quotes, it is made quite clear by Saradananda that Ramakrishna's mother was "afraid that one day the mendicants might tempt her son to go away with them" (*sādhura tāhār putrake kono din bhulāiya soṅge loiyā jāibe nā to*). She mentioned this fear to her son, who tried to pacify her. When the monks eventually heard of this, they came to her house and "assured her that the thought of taking away Gadadhar in that way never crossed their minds, and that they considered it kidnapping, a great crime unbecoming of sādhus, to take away a tender-aged boy without the permission of his parents. At this, not even a shadow of her earlier anxiety remained in Chandradevi's mind and, at the request of the sādhus, she gave her permission to the boy to visit the sādhus as before" (LP 1.109).

Much of this information is excluded in *Kālī's Child*, leaving the readers with Chandradevi's ambiguous "fear" and the impression of a helpless young boy with torn clothes and a nearly naked body. Finally, by the time we approach the conclusion of *Kālī's Child*, we are told in a hand-wringing tone about the "holy men stripping a trusting little boy" (303)! So sure is Kripal of his child abuse thesis that Ramakrishna's childhood ecstasies are discussed as "troubling trances" (57), thus creating the background necessary for *Kālī's Child*'s interpretation of Ramakrishna's ecstasies as an escape mechanism.

Sādhus were not the only ones whom *Kālī's Child* regards as child abusers. The village women of Kamarpukur were also apparently unable to keep their hands off the "trusting little boy." While Kripal wonders why Ramakrishna "was letting [the village women] worship him as a male lover" (58), there is nothing in either the *Life of Ramakrishna* (which Kripal references as his source) or the *Kathāmṛta* or the *Līlāprasaṅga* to indicate anything which remotely resembles this. The texts all state that the village women looked upon Ramakrishna as Gopāla, the child Kṛṣṇa. Interestingly, Kripal quotes the *Life of Ramakrishna* as saying, "the boy actively sought the company of the pious women of the village because they reminded him of the milkmaids of Vrindavana, who had realized Kṛṣṇa as their husband *and had experienced the bliss and pleasure of his love*" (58; emphasis added).

Yet when we check the reference cited in the *Life* we find: "The pious young women of the village, who were mostly devotees of Viṣṇu, reminded him of the Gopis of Vrindaban, and, therefore, he sought their company. He knew that the Gopis were able to realize Krishna as their husband and *feel the bliss of his eternal reunion*, because they were women" (*Life*, 30; emphasis added). Note the difference between the "bliss and pleasure of his love"—laden with sexual innuendo—and what is actually in the text. Yet since it is cited as a reference to the *Life*, the reader naturally expects the words, or at least an honest summary of the referenced passage, to be there. And it is not. In fact, *Kālī's Child* declares with no apparent irony: "The texts agree" (58). Kripal further opines that "Gadadhar … entered his trances at least partially to escape these women and their worship," quoting Narasingha Sil to clinch his thesis: "Indeed what the women of Kāmarpukur did with the ecstatic boy … is anybody's guess" (58, quoting Sil 1991, 28). In this way, a steady drip of innuendo is created through the accumulation of the images of a nearly naked young boy with torn clothes, predatory sādhus, voracious village women, and troubling trances.

Again, concerning Ramakrishna's childhood, *Kālī's Child* states: "Gadadhar's effeminate nature and womanly ways did not go unnoticed by the villagers. Observing the boy's friendship with Ram Mallick, a seventeen-year-old teenager, the villagers used to say that, if Gadadhar were a woman, the two of them would be married (KA 3.184)" (59). What the *Kathāmṛta* actually says, however, is: "People used to say, if either of these [Ramakrishna or Ram] had been a woman, they would have been married" (*loke bolto, eder bhitor ekjon meyemānuṣ hole dujoner biye hoto*). Nowhere does it say, in any source text, that Ramakrishna was "effeminate" or that any of the villagers ever appraised him as such. Despite this, *Kālī's Child* declares that Ramakrishna "desired to be a woman" and adds that "all the evidence suggests that he did" (58). Yet the same source Kripal quotes, the *Life of Ramakrishna* notes that the young Ramakrishna liked to play the part of Kṛṣṇa (who cannot be accused of being "effeminate").

The young Ramakrishna said that if he were to be born again, he would like to be born as a poor child widow with a spinning wheel, a cow and a plot of land where the days could be spent in singing devotional songs and making sweets for Kṛṣṇa, who would enter her hut to steal the sweets (*Life*, 27). There is nothing here to suggest that Ramakrishna in his present incarnation felt uncomfortable in his present gender. It is also important to remember that for those who take reincarnation as a given, it is assumed that one does not maintain the same gender birth after birth. One who assumes a male body in one incarnation may well assume a female one in the next.

As Ramakrishna moved into adulthood, *Kālī's Child* similarly suggests that he experienced sexual abuse at the hands of the Bhairavi, Mathur Babu and Tota Puri. These speculations are gingerly invoked at the book's inception ("His female Tantric guru and temple boss *may have forced themselves* ... on the saint" [2; emphasis added]), yet within seventeen pages, the tentative speculation is treated like documented fact: "Ramakrishna ... entered ecstatic states to escape the sexual advances of his boss" (19). Yet nowhere within these seventeen pages and nowhere else in the text is any evidence presented to support this thesis. We are similarly told of the "traumatic treatment he received from Mathur" (109) with no credible evidence presented, only an insistent accusation. Larded throughout the text are many such repeated insinuations and accusations which are presented without benefit of substantiation.

In the example given below, Kripal garners evidence for Ramakrishna's purported abuse at the hands of Mathur by improbably quoting from Swami Chetanananda's book on Ramakrishna's close associates, *They Lived with God*. The excerpt quoted below (pointed out to Kripal by Narasingha Sil [KC, 347]), has its origin in Swami Turiyananda's reminiscences of Ramakrishna. Turiyananda (whom we meet as "Hari" in the *Kathāmṛta*), was a monastic disciple of Ramakrishna. The purport of the incident, at least as far as Turiyananda and Chetanananda were concerned, was to show the power of Ramakrishna's ecstatic visions. Indeed, so powerful were they that they affected the carriage's horses, provoking an accident:

> One day Mathur Babu was returning to Jan Bazar in his deluxe phaeton and was bringing Sri Ramakrishna with him. When the carriage reached Chitpore Road, the Master had a wonderful vision. He felt that he had become Sita and that Ravana was kidnapping him. Seized by this idea, he merged into samadhi. Just then the horses, tearing loose from their reins, stumbled and fell. Mathur Babu could not understand the reason for such a mishap. When Sri Ramakrishna came back to the normal plane of consciousness, Mathur told him about the accident. Sri Ramakrishna then said that while he was in ecstasy he had perceived that Ravana was kidnapping him and that Jatayu [the great bird who had attempted to rescue Sita] was attacking Ravana's chariot and was trying to destroy it. After hearing this story Mathur Babu said, "Father, how difficult it is even to go with you through the street!"[29] (Chetanananda 1989, 29)

This incident appears in *Kālī's Child*, partially quoted and out of context (KC, 105). Before the incident is related, however, the reader has already been informed of Ramakrishna's "cross-dressing" which caused "'scandalous' interpretations of the Master's 'austere renunciation.'" Yet there was no "scandal" concerning Ramakrishna's dressing as a woman, i.e., practicing the sādhana of *madhura* bhāva. Whatever criticism there was about Ramakrishna's behavior concerned the costliness of his apparel. A holy man, the opinion went, should not wear expensive fabric. Kripal associates Ramakrishna's practice of *madhura* bhāva with Mathur (referred to here as the "temple proprietor"), which, Kripal asserts, "involve[d] unusually intimate contact with Mathur and his family" (KC, 104–5). Yet Kripal's understanding of what constitutes "unusually intimate contact" is not based upon nineteenth-century Bengali social mores but rather contemporary North American social standards. According to the standards of nineteenth-century Bengal—and those standards are not very different even today—there was nothing "unusually intimate" about Ramakrishna's living situation.

Even before Ramakrishna's vision is described, it is referred to as "an interesting fantasy"—"fantasy," of course, carrying the undercurrent of sexual fantasy, especially when associated with scandal, cross-dressing, and "unusually intimate contact." After Ramakrishna's vision is briefly described, Sītā's abduction is referred to as a "sexual abduction" and her captivity as "a series of attempted seductions" by her "devilish captor" Rāvaṇa. Thus Mathur becomes quickly and simplistically identified with Rāvaṇa, with no corroborating evidence, while material which would dissuade the reader from such a premise is never presented—such as the obvious fact that a phaeton—that is, a light, open-air carriage, drawn by horses—no doubt reminded Ramakrishna of a chariot. *Kālī's Child*'s final assessment of Ramakrishna's vision is that Ramakrishna's "fantasy" allowed him to "deal with the traumatic event," which in *Kālī's Child*'s first edition is described as a "painful yet pleasurable abduction" (KC 1995, 106), the language of which comes straight from the literature of childhood sexual abuse. (*Kālī's Child*'s second edition removes the word "pleasurable" from the description.)

The accusation that Mathur abused Ramakrishna is bewildering since there is no evidence that Mathur ever treated Ramakrishna with anything other than warmth, affection and reverence. Moreover, Mathur was exuberantly heterosexual in his appetites, his visits to female prostitutes not being well disguised. Yet even before *Kālī's Child*'s Introduction is complete, the reader is informed that Ramakrishna was "struggling with the horrors of his past"—i.e., his purported abuse at the hands of a raft of sexual predators. The accusation is first insinuated, then declared—all without any evidence upon which to base this charge except for cultural miscues and innuendo. One example of the latter is Kripal's insistence upon giving Mathur the sinister appellation "the temple boss." Mathur was the temple *manager*, but "manager," with its white-collar overtones, does not carry the menacing tone that *Kālī's Child* wishes to convey. Hence Mathur is the "temple boss." We have already seen how Mathur is simplistically identified with Rāvaṇa, thus making "Rāvaṇa-like Mathur" (106) Ramakrishna's "devilish captor" (105). Ramakrishna is also referred to, in a subheading no less, as "Mathur's Handmaid" (103), and just to make sure the point is made, the reader is told that Ramakrishna is "commanded by his boss" (134). One wonders how Mathur, who is so affectionately characterized in the *Kathāmṛta*, *Līlāprasaṅga* and *Jībanabṛttānta*, came out looking like a sadistic prison guard, who had "unchallenged authority over the boy" (KC, 300).

Mathur, as the *Līlāprasaṅga* and all the subsequent source texts on Ramakrishna state, was immediately attracted to Ramakrishna, because of his "pleasing appearance, tender nature, steadfastness in dharma, and youth." To this Kripal adds: "Saradananda tells us, seemingly completely unaware of the homosexual dimensions of his own description, a 'sudden loving attraction' arose in the mind and heart of the temple boss" (61). The "homosexual dimensions" found in the *Līlāprasaṅga*, of which Saradananda (and apparently millions of others) were unaware, are quoted here: "It is often seen that when a very close and lasting relationship is established with anyone in life, the loving attraction (*prītir ākarṣan*) towards them is felt right away (*sahasā*), at first sight (LP 2.87)." This is given as proof of the "homosexual dimensions."

But does a "sudden loving attraction" imply a sexual attraction? Can males not bond with each other unless it be through sex? All of us have had the experience of meeting people—male and female—with whom we immediately establish a warm rapport. Even though we have just met them, we nevertheless feel drawn to them. We may even feel as if we have known them all our lives. In the Hindu worldview, this phenomenon is understood to be completely natural. It is often assumed that such rapport and attraction indicates that there had been a relationship in a previous life, thus our attraction to a person is a kind of "recognition" from a previous existence. This presupposes neither a homosexual nor a heterosexual dimension to anything. It simply means that there are some people to whom we feel very drawn from the minute we meet them.

To add to the creepy atmospherics surrounding Mathur and Ramakrishna, *Kālī's Child* remarks upon "Mathur's practice of dressing Ramakrishna in expensive women's clothes" (300). But Mathur never "dressed" Ramakrishna, what to speak of making it a "practice."[30] Mathur provided Ramakrishna with clothing, jewelry, and other articles necessary for his *madhura* bhāva sādhana—just as he provided all the material which Ramakrishna needed for all of his other sādhanas. Ramakrishna frequently spoke of Mathur as one of his *rasaddārs*—one of his five "suppliers of provisions" who was appointed by the Divine Mother to look after his material needs. Even less subtly, immediately following the remark about "dressing" Ramakrishna, Kripal informs the reader: "not everyone was naive"—implying that those who do not see a sexual abuse scenario here *are* naive. "Naive" is invoked again when we read about "holy men stripping a trusting little boy" and "a boss whose 'demonic' presence could send a young priest into prolonged states of unconsciousness." Of course this "unconsciousness" is samādhi, believed to be the highest state of consciousness and joy, which is now summarily pathologized. Kripal lets the reader know that he is not gullible about what really went on with Ramakrishna and his purported abusers: "I have refused to be naive about such things" (303).

Kālī's Child also presents several quotations from the *Jībanabṛttānta* as evidence for Mathur's sexual abuse. But if readers check those references, they will find that the cited texts were either mistranslated or clearly misinterpreted. Or they will find nothing there at all. For example, Kripal writes that Ramchandra Datta "describes Sītā's sufferings at Mathur's Janbajar home in some detail" (107). But Datta does not mention Sītā at all. *Kripal* makes this connection to create the facile equation: Ramakrishna = Sītā, Mathur = Rāvaṇa.

What Datta does describe in some detail are aspects of Ramakrishna's life with Mathur and his family, and there is no "suffering" described there at all, unless, of course, one assumes that Ramakrishna "suffered" when Mathur's daughters bathed him and applied oil to his body. Ramakrishna had no objection; neither did Mathur nor his wife nor his daughters. Datta writes:

> After coming to Janbazar, Paramahaṁsa Deva [Ramakrishna] always stayed in the inner apartment (*antaḥpur*). All the women residents of the inner apartment viewed him as a greatly loved treasure (*ati ādarer dhan*). No one felt shy even though Paramahaṁsa Deva was a man and no one felt hesitant to come in front of him. Among the women of the family, some saw him as their child and some saw him as a holy man. Often it was Mathur's daughters who bathed him after giving him an oil massage. On some occasions, Paramahaṁsa Deva would, in a state of bhāva, lose external consciousness and lie naked. But that did not bother anyone. On the other hand, they themselves dressed him with clothes. (JB, 48–49)

And this is Datta describing "Sītā's sufferings at Mathur's Janbajar home in some detail"? Many would like to sign up for such "sufferings"! Kripal writes that Ramchandra Datta records "an unusually explicit scene"—we can note the subtext here—in which "Ramakrishna enters Mathur's bedroom at an inopportune time, angering Mathur and his wife and leading them to exclaim: 'Father! Now that you've watched us, why are you leaving? Do you have something else in mind?'" (JB, 49). Yet when we read the *Jībanabṛttānta* this is what we find:

> Whenever Paramahaṁsadeva wished to go some place, he would go there without bothering about the appropriateness of the place, the time or the people. He would immediately retreat after entering the room if Mathur and his wife were sleeping on the bed. Mathur and his wife would become dismayed and say, "Father! Why do you go away after seeing us? Do you have any different way of thinking (*bhāb*)? Father, you don't even have the 'knowledge' that children have." On some days, when a spiritual feeling (*bhāb*) would rise in Mathur's mind (*mone kono prokār bhāboday hoito*), he would invite Ramakrishna to sleep near (*nikaṭ*) him. Paramahaṁsadeva did not object to that. (JB,49)

Far from being "angry" with Ramakrishna, Mathur and his wife do not want him to leave. This is not to suggest a ménage à trois, but rather that they felt no sense of hesitation or shyness in his presence. In their eyes, Ramakrishna's purity surpassed even that of a child who, perhaps, could be embarrassed by the sight of a man and woman together in bed. Hence when Ramakrishna uncharacteristically retreated from their room, they felt compelled to assure him that they were not disturbed by his presence.

Not surprisingly, *Kālī's Child* finds something sinister afoot in the last two sentences of the citation above, where we read: "In this next scene, after 'a certain kind of mood' comes upon Mathur, he asks Ramakrishna to lie down next to him. Ramakrishna makes no objections to his boss's request" (KC, 107). Yet as we can see from the above citation, the "certain kind of mood" is not the concupiscent one implied by Kripal. *Kālī's Child* asserts that "*bhāva* can also be used to refer to a person's sexual orientation or intention" and gives the above example of Ramakrishna and Mathur (KC, 353). The Bengali "*bhāb*" (*bhāva*) can be translated in a number of ways depending on the context of the situation. The *bhāb* in Mathur's mind indicates spiritual feeling, not a randy mood.

Even apart from this, inviting Ramakrishna to sleep "near" is vastly different from "lying down with Ramakrishna." Furthermore, inviting someone to sleep near them in India was not unusual at that time; it is not unusual now. It is more common than uncommon, particularly in non-urban areas. India has very different standards of personal space than those of Western cultures. We should also note the sinister undertone of "his boss's request"—which is an attempt to establish proof of sexual abuse by virtue of innuendo, whereas the actual texts have nothing in them to suggest such an allegation. Other insinuations regarding the purportedly wicked Mathur appear in the text. For example, when Ramakrishna returned from Kamarpukur to Dakshineswar, Kripal quotes Romain Rolland's words: "Kālī was waiting for him." To Rolland's words, Kripal provides his own addendum: "So, no doubt, was Mathur" (112). No specific accusation is made here, just the implication of a menacing, predatory presence hovering over Ramakrishna, the young priest bending to the boss's demonic lust.

Kālī's Child states that Ramakrishna lived in the *kuṭhi*—Rani Rasmani's commodious bungalow in the temple compound—for sixteen years. The *kuṭhi* was not Mathur's primary residence, which was in Kolkata. When in Dakshineswar, the *kuṭhi* was concurrently occupied by Rani Rasmani (during her lifetime) and Mathur's entire family, along with attendant guests. Yet simply because Ramakrishna and Mathur were often under the same roof, *Kālī's Child* spins a web of speculations without any factual basis. About Mathur's and Ramakrishna's respective bedrooms, Kripal suggests: "Their bedrooms were no doubt very close." By the next paragraph Kripal asks: "Was Mathur 'keeping' him there?" (175).

While Kripal suggests that Ramakrishna left the *kuṭhi* (moving to what became his permanent room in another building) because of Mathur's death, Ramakrishna himself states that he left the *kuṭhi* because Akshay—his much-loved nephew—died there. Though *Kālī's Child* asserts that it is "the tradition" which "explains Ramakrishna's move … by connecting it to the death of his nephew, Akshay" (175), the "explanation" comes from Ramakrishna himself: "After a long time," Saradananda wrote, "referring to that incident [Akshay's death], he [Ramakrishna] told us on various occasions that although in bhāva he could view death as only a change of state, when the bhāva ended and he returned to normal consciousness, he deeply felt the absence of Akshay as a result of his passing. Since Akshay had died in that house, he could no longer stay in Mathur Babu's house after Akshay's death" (LP 2.343–44). Thus whenever convenient, *Kālī's Child* cites the *Līlāprasaṅga* and uses it as a valid source. When inconvenient, the *Līlāprasaṅga* is brushed aside as "the tradition," and not deemed a source of valid data.

There are many other insinuations and allegations regarding Mathur in *Kālī's Child* which could be addressed, but the point has been made. Similar charges are made against the Bhairavi, although she is portrayed in more sympathetic terms than the "temple boss." Thus, we are to understand that while Ramakrishna experienced abuse at the hands of Mathur because of Mathur's predatory nature, the Bhairavi's "abuse" could well have been for Ramakrishna's spiritual betterment: "The Bhairavī clearly tried to employ sexual intercourse as one of her means to teach Ramakrishna Tantric truths," Kripal writes (120). But neither is this true nor does *Kālī's Child* supply any evidence to support this contention. Instead, *Kālī's Child* consistently mistranslates the source texts in an attempt to hypersexualize both the Bhairavi and her relationship with Ramakrishna.

We are told, for example, of the incident when the Bhairavi leaves Dakshineswar for good. She had broken caste restrictions, created an ugly scene and lost a showdown with Hriday. The latter was a particular source of humiliation. Realizing that she had acted badly because of her anger and pride, the Bhairavi asked Ramakrishna for pardon and, garlanding him, left for Varanasi. *Kālī's Child*'s version of this incident is: "Finally, when the Bhairavī broke a village custom, a verbal battle ensued that led to her eventual defeat and humiliation. She apologized to

Ramakrishna, rubbed his body with sandal-paste, and left for Benares" (166). There is nothing to suggest that the Bhairavi "rubbed his body with sandal-paste." While *Kālī's Child* provides no reference, the *Līlāprasaṅga*—which is the only source text that mentions this—is quite clear about the Bhairavi's actions: "with devotion she made garlands of various flowers and smeared them with sandal-paste, and having beautifully adorned the Master as Śrī Gauraṅga, asked his forgiveness with all her heart" (*tini bhakti-sahakāre vividh puṣpamālā svahaste racanā o candana-carcit koriyā śrī-gaurāṅga-gyāne ṭhākurke manohar-beśe bhūṣita korilen evaṁ sarvāntaḥkaraṇe kkhamā-prārthanā korilen*) (LP 2.325). It is quite clear that it was the garland of flowers (*puṣpamālā*) that was "smeared" (*carcit*) with sandal-paste, not "Ramakrishna's body" that was "rubbed."

Even in the simplest matters, Kripal seemingly goes out of his way to translate the Bengali into as highly a sexualized language as possible. As a result, his translations are not only incorrect but also unintentionally funny. For example, in an encounter between Mathur and the Bhairavi, Mathur asks her, "Where is your Bhairava, O Bhairavi?" When she pointed to the Śiva lying supine at Kālī's feet, Mathur said, "But that Bhairava doesn't move." To this the Bhairavi quickly retorted, "If I cannot make the immovable move, why did I become a Bhairavi (*jodi acal-ke sacal korite-i nā pāribo, tobe ār bhairabī hoiyāchi keno*)?" (LP 3.228). As we can see, the Bhairavi uses the rhyming *acal* and *sacal*—unmoving and moving—to make her point. Kripal, however, translates "*sacal*" as "arouse": "Why have I become a Bhairavī if I cannot arouse the unmoving" (KC, 115), which is not only bizarre but also quite funny (and completely lacking in linguistic accuracy). Both *acal* and *sacal* are from the verb root *cal*, to move or to go. There is simply no way to get "arouse" out of *sacal*. Nor is there any way to make the non-ithyphallic Śiva that the Bhairavi pointed to, ithyphallic.

Again Kripal, purporting to translate from the *Līlāprasaṅga*, writes that the Bhairavi "now and then would enter into the mood of the milk-maids of Vraja and begin to sing songs filled with erotic sweetness" (116; quoting LP 2.14.3, which is actually LP 2.263). But the *Līlāprasaṅga* merely states that she sang *madhura-rasātmaka-saṅgīta*, "songs filled with *madhura*-rasa"—songs imbued with the mood of the gopīs of Vraja, which in any standard translation would mean that the songs were infused with the deep yearning the gopīs had for Kṛṣṇa. While Kripal, among others, may view this longing as simply erotic, many would object to such a reductionistic interpretation of *madhura* bhāva. A soul's yearning for the divine, even when the divine is Kṛṣṇa the divine lover, cannot be reduced to a simple erotic attraction. That said, it is clear that many of *Kālī's Child*'s dubious translations are done as much for the sake of hypersexualized atmospherics as they are to advance the book's hypotheses.

As for examples of the Bhairavi's "sexual abuse" of Ramakrishna, *Kālī's Child* neglects to give the reader explicit information, let alone documentation. Perhaps suggestive of "sexual abuse" is *Kālī's Child*'s speculation that the Bhairavi attempted "to engage her disciple ... through a ritualized form of cunnilingus or through the oral consumption of sexual fluids" (128). Yet, as with Mathur, there is nothing to actually indicate sexual abuse, unless one considers the difficult course of Tantra sādhana which Ramakrishna underwent under the Bhairavi's guidance (sitting on a naked young woman's lap, for example) to be "abusive."

As we continue our lengthening list of sexual predators, Tota Puri, Ramakrishna's Vedānta guru, is also presumed to have been one. As with our previous examples, there is nothing to indicate that this claim has any basis in fact. Again, as with the previous examples, all Kripal provides the reader are insinuations propped by speculations. Taking as a given that Ramakrishna was "homosexually oriented," Kripal also takes as a given that Ramakrishna was relentlessly preoccupied with Tota's naked body, his penis in particular.[31] However, this preoccupation seems to be Kripal's as well, since he characterizes Tota as "a phallic guru" (303)—whatever that may be. We may recall that Tota was a Nāgā sannyāsi, belonging to an austere sect of the Daśanāmi Order. Uncompromising followers of Vedānta, Nāgā monks are *digambara*, clothed in space, refusing to accommodate the body with comforts or enjoyments.

One would think that the more interesting story would be the encounter between Tota, the Vedānta monk, and Ramakrishna, the ecstatic worshiper of Kālī. This is not what Kripal finds interesting. Instead, he whispers: "One can only imagine what it must have been like for Ramakrishna, a homosexually oriented man, to be shut away for days in a small hut with another, stark-naked man. Vedantic instruction or no, it was this man's nudity, and more specifically, his penis, that naturally caught Ramakrishna's attention. How could it *not*?" (160; emphasis in text). In other words, *because* one must accept that Ramakrishna is homosexual, then the only thing that would interest Ramakrishna about his Vedānta guru was his penis. "How could it *not*?" But there is no reason to assume that this might be true unless one were to assume that

Ramakrishna was not only homosexually oriented, but also not much interested in attaining nirvikalpa samādhi. It also needs to be said that the presumption that a homosexually oriented man would be necessarily preoccupied with his guru's penis is denigrating. One assumes that a genuine sādhaka would find more of interest in his guru than his genitals.

Kālī's Child responds head-on to those who would question this line of reasoning:

> Of course, there are no passages in the texts that state clearly that Ramakrishna was attracted to the paramahaṁsa's penis. There are, however, a number of powerfully suggestive texts that say just about everything else. (160)

First, before looking at the "powerfully suggestive texts," which consist of references from the *Kathāmṛta*, we should note that *Kālī's Child* is much more preoccupied with Tota's nakedness than Ramakrishna ever was. In fact, Kripal has difficulty invoking Tota's presence without also invoking his nakedness. The first sentence of *Kālī's Child*'s section on Ramakrishna's Vedānta sādhana thus begins: "When a naked monk arrived on the banks of Dakshineswar" (151). In the same paragraph, Tota is referred to as "the naked Vedāntin." Within two paragraphs "Ramakrishna finally sat down with the naked man in a small hut tucked away in the trees and began his Vedantic training. The Naked One began by commanding Ramakrishna to give up the unreal world" (152). Again we have "Tota Puri, the naked paramahaṁsa" (159) and three sentences later: "the naked form of the wandering paramahaṁsa" (160). The next sentence reminds us "Ramakrishna called Tota Puri 'the Naked One' because the monk used to remain nude." And so on. The reader has been thoroughly drilled that Tota is *naked*.

But does this make him, or Ramakrishna, concupiscent? Apparently it does, for—circular reasoning intact—Kripal makes this very assumption. Nor does it end here. More than a hundred pages later, the topic reappears with even more insistence. This time we read that—scare quotes intact—"something more than 'Vedantic instruction' went on between Ramakrishna and the naked Tota Puri in the small hut tucked away in the trees" (299). By now, *Kālī's Child* is discussing "Tota's abusive presence," yet, predictably, there is no evidence to back up this charge, while a wealth of evidence mitigates against it.

Kālī's Child implies that if Ramakrishna is "shut away for days in a small hut with another, stark-naked man" and if Tota and Ramakrishna are together in "a small hut tucked away in the trees," then this is an inevitable equation for sexual abuse. Except that it isn't. In fact—even apart from the dubious inevitability of sexual abuse—the entire scenario is a clear misrepresentation of what the source texts state. Every source text indicates that after Tota had given Ramakrishna sannyāsa vows, Tota began teaching him Advaita Vedānta, eventually sticking a shard of broken glass between Ramakrishna's eyebrows in order to aid his concentration. With that, Ramakrishna went into nirvikalpa samādhi. The texts tell us that Tota, upon seeing Ramakrishna's samādhi, remained seated by his side for some time, then silently got up and left the hut, locking the door behind him lest someone enter the hut and disturb Ramakrishna. Tota himself went to the Panchavati, where he waited for three days for Ramakrishna to summon him. When after three days Ramakrishna still had not called him, Tota went back to the hut and found Ramakrishna exactly as he had left him, in deep nirvikalpa samādhi. Astonished, Tota brought him back to ordinary consciousness by loudly chanting "Hari Om" (LP 2.294–97; *Life*, 158–62). This does not portray an abusive living situation or relationship.

What, then, about Kripal's allegation of what those "powerfully suggestive texts" have to say about Ramakrishna and Tota's relationship? The "texts" referred to here are the *Kathāmṛta*'s description of Ramakrishna's mystic vision of the paramahaṁsa boy as well as Ramakrishna's description of how, in his period of divine madness, he worshiped his own phallus "looking upon it as a *Śiva-liṅga*" (KA 4.106). As we address these visions in depth later in this book, we will not go into detail here. In brief, Ramakrishna describes his vision of the paramahaṁsa boy by saying: "A naked person used to be with me—I would touch his penis and make fun. I would then laugh a lot. This naked form used to come out of me. It was the form of a paramahaṁsa, like a boy" (KA 4.231). Kripal finds the vision "powerfully suggestive" of a sexual relationship that "no doubt existed between Tota and the young Ramakrishna." Thus we go in circles again: the vision suggests a relationship; and the relationship, which "no doubt" existed between the two, explains the vision of the paramahaṁsa boy. Kripal reasons:

> The vision ... sets up clear linguistic connections between the nudity of the two paramahaṁsas. The vision, however, does more than hark back to the memories of the hut in the trees: it also *answers* those memories by reversing the relationship that no doubt existed between Tota and the young Ramakrishna. (160)

The aforementioned speculation now leaves "no doubt" as to what really transpired between Ramakrishna and Tota Puri. The mention of "memories of the hut in the trees" evokes a subtext of the half-buried memories of sexual abuse survivors. As to what Ramakrishna and Tota were doing in that hut in the trees—even though the source texts indicate that Ramakrishna was in the hut by *himself* for three days—Kripal speculates that Tota "taught" Ramakrishna "to worship his own *liṅgam* as if it were Śiva's" (161). This kind of "worship" resulted in "teasing a precious 'pearl' of seminal fluid" from the penis (161), which sounds more like masturbation than nirvikalpa samadhi.

Where would this bizarre conjecture come from? Ramakrishna's words make it clear that he was never "taught" to worship his own phallus. In the context of the conversation (in the referenced "powerfully suggestive texts"), Ramakrishna discusses how a paramahaṁsa often behaves like a madman. He then states that when he himself was in a state of divine madness (*unmāda*), he worshiped his own phallus, looking upon it as a *Śiva-liṅga* (KA 4.106). Ramakrishna was not *taught* anything—his actions were utterly spontaneous and they were done as worship, not for sexual gratification. *Kālī's Child* throws aside any potential for worship, what to speak of Ramakrishna's three days of samādhi where, the texts indicate, "his face was calm and serene and full of effulgence" (LP 2.296). Instead of samādhi, then, it all comes down to sexual activity.

"Clearly the saint [Ramakrishna] was sexually excited by these memories," *Kālī's Child* asserts (161), referring, of course, "back to the memories of the hut in the trees."[32] Kripal thus takes his speculation and makes of it a pronouncement: there *was* sexual abuse and there were memories of it, which, though lacking evidence, can be presumed. Should the reader look for further substantiation, it can be found in the use of the adjective *nyāṅṭā*, "naked," which according to Kripal, is "the very same term that Ramakrishna used to dub his nude Vedantic teacher 'the Naked One" (*nyāṅṭā*) (160). "Ramakrishna," *Kālī's Child* declares, "explicitly associated Tota with nudity" (161).

We should keep in mind, however, that Ramakrishna referred to Tota as Nyāṅṭā or "Naked One" for the same reason he called the Bhairavi *Bāmni*—"the Brahmin Woman." (The Bhairavi's given name was Yogeswari.) It is considered extremely disrespectful to refer to one's guru by his or her given name, hence appellations are used instead. None of Ramakrishna's disciples ever referred to Ramakrishna by his given name either.[33] We should also keep in mind that whenever Ramakrishna spoke about Tota, which was often, it was always with respect and affection, as can be easily seen by reading the source texts.

The other evidence which is offered to suggest that Ramakrishna was the victim of sexual abuse at the hands of Tota was that after Tota's eventual departure from Dakshineswar, Ramakrishna went into nirvikalpa samādhi for six months. While nirvikalpa samādhi is generally viewed as the highest state of spiritual realization, in *Kālī's Child* this state is pathologized into an "almost catatonic state" (153). Thus the samādhi that Tota worked for forty years to achieve (and which had already been attained by Ramakrishna in three days), is interpreted—when Ramakrishna experienced it without interruption for six months—as a trauma-based reaction, one "that looks ... as much like a death as it does a realization" (154). Yet what *Kālī's Child* pathologizes others see as spiritual attainment. M, for example, said of Ramakrishna's six-month samādhi: "The Master was absorbed in the formless aspect of the Mother for six months at the time of his sadhana" (Chetanananda 1990, 293).

The reader cannot be sure whether the trauma-cum-samādhi is due to Tota's purported abuse or because Ramakrishna mourned the monk's absence. Ramakrishna, Kripal writes, "most likely experienced Tota's presence as both pleasurable and abusive" (KC, 162)—and again, the reader is fed language which comes straight out of the literature of sexual abuse. Yet there is nothing to suggest this conjecture to be true; all evidence mitigates against it. Nevertheless, Tota's eventual departure from Dakshineswar is strangely referred to in *Kālī's Child* as "a tragedy of immense proportions" since "Ramakrishna's six-month *samādhi* is explicitly connected to Tota's departure, something Saradananda has a hard time explaining" (153–54). But Saradananda does not have a hard time explaining it at all. Saradananda states quite explicitly that "a strong determination arose in the Master's mind to remain incessantly thenceforward in the nondual plane of consciousness" (LP 2.298).

The real issue here is why there is "no doubt" that there existed a sexually abusive relationship "between Tota and the young Ramakrishna." (Ramakrishna was then thirty.) According to Kripal, there was "a fascination on Ramakrishna's part with naked paramahaṁsas, penises and boys" and all these "stem back to Tota, the naked paramahaṁsa" (162). The clincher is found in the paramahaṁsa vision.

"If," Kripal continues

> [Ramakrishna] once was sexually manipulated by males, including Tota, the naked paramahaṁsa, he would later relive the experiences by uncontrollably rubbing sandal-paste on the penises of boys, by playing with the penis of a visionary paramahaṁsa youth, by worshiping his own erect penis. . . . The pattern, although admittedly speculative in

> its attempt to move backward from known biographical events to the *if* of alleged childhood and early adult scenes, is too consistent and too suggestive to be ignored. The pattern, moreover, is only strengthened and confirmed when we can remove the *if* and discuss with confidence both the childhood scene and later adult acts. (301)

This is convenient. If the label of speculation is removed and confidence asserted in the thesis of childhood sexual abuse and adult sexual reenactment patterns, then it all makes sense. Except that it makes sense only *if* one takes for granted certain presuppositions which neither are true nor can they be substantiated in a way that can withstand critical scrutiny. One simply cannot ascertain patterns of childhood sexual abuse and adult reenactment patterns by presuming they are correct to begin with and then moving backwards and pathologizing the person's early history. If one begins by removing the *if* of alleged and early adult scenes, then one can summarily dismiss samādhi as an escape mechanism or a trauma-based response, and indeed one can pathologize any and all aspects of a mystic's life. But this process does not work if we require evidence for these facile assumptions and insist that these insinuations be held up to critical scrutiny. No one can be exempt from these basic requirements of scholarship.

Mysticism and the Unconscious

As *Kālī's Child* equates "secret" with "sexual," so also does it conflate the workings of the unconscious with mystical experience. Noting that there is a connection between "secrecy" and "mysticism" the book makes a troubling leap:

> But the mystical is also "hidden" in a psychological sense, for it lies in the depths of human consciousness in a psychic space that is not easily accessible and not commonly known. In most instances, we might say that the human being is "unconscious" of its reality and presence. (20)

We are dealing with false analogies here. Simply because something is secret—a text, spoken words, an experience—does not make it mystical, nor does the fact that something is secret make it sexual.[34] Nor does something sexual—a text, spoken words, an experience—make it either mystical or a secret, for that matter. Simply because mystical experience does not operate on the level of the rational mind and is unavailable to cognitive analysis does not locate mysticism in the realm of the unconscious. Mystical experience is unmediated through the mind and senses and is thus, according to the Hindu tradition, a superconscious experience, not an unconscious one.

Kālī's Child defines the unconscious as

> *a secret dimension or dimensions of the human person of which he or she is not aware*. . . Some of these dimensions clearly witness to repressed memories and childhood conflicts. Others, however, speak of godlike states of consciousness, patterns of divine energy, unions with the cosmos, and ecstatic flights of the soul. Pathology finds its roots in this unconscious, but so also does the mystical, for it too is "that which is secret" (*mustikos*). (43)

We are perhaps dealing with different understandings of the word "mystical." In the tradition in which Ramakrishna—and later his followers—were nurtured, the mystical is associated with the realm that transcends speech and mind (*avāṅmanasagocaram*). That realm is the "superconscious"—not the unconscious, as *Kālī's Child* presumes. The mystical is *beyond* the mind, both conscious and unconscious.

Kālī's Child correctly reports that the *Kathāmṛta* is replete with hundreds of instances of Ramakrishna being established in samādhi or ecstasy (*bhāva*). While this is true enough, it does not lead to the following assertion: "Ramakrishna's secret visions appear to him in the brilliant darkness of these 'unconscious' states" (39). The Hindu traditions are in agreement that these spiritual experiences transcend normal consciousness, thus the claim that Ramakrishna experienced them in "'unconscious' states" displays either ignorance or an attempt to diminish the spiritual nature of his visions. Further, why is the word "unconscious" placed in scare quotes? To imply that "unconscious" can just as well mean "mystical"? Moreover, where does this "brilliant darkness" come from, apart from atmospherics? Yet from this contrived depiction, another perplexing leap is taken: "Ramakrishna and his disciples ... operated with cultural and religious assumptions about the hidden or secret dimensions of the human being that are, at least on the surface, similar to Western notions of the unconscious" (39).

This is completely erroneous. Just as catatonia is qualitatively different from nirvikalpa samādhi, so the Western notions of the unconscious are entirely different from the Hindu concept of *anubhūti*, the direct apprehension of the ultimate Reality, which is unmediated by the mind and senses. This direct experience of the divine is understood to be the highest state of perception and has nothing to do with the unconscious.

Again, Kripal asserts that the "pure consciousness event" of mysticism is "profoundly influenced by numerous ... psychological, physical, social, and doctrinal conditionings." He then builds upon this questionable hypothesis by adding that his method of approaching Ramakrishna "refuses to separate the specific forms of Ramakrishna's life, however seemingly bizarre, from the famous formlessness of his ecstasies" (19). Kripal makes a point of emphasizing that "the contextual forms and the formless content of his states are in fact inseparable." In this context Kripal quotes, oddly enough, the Buddhist text *Prajñāpāramitāsūtra*: "Form is emptiness, emptiness is form," which has nothing to do with Ramakrishna, but has a great deal to do with the thesis *Kālī's Child* would like to establish. From here another great disquieting leap is taken:

> So too with Ramakrishna, who knew the formless joys of *samādhi* while looking at the cocked hips of a beautiful English boy, experienced trance at the exact moment the "secret door" of his anus opened to defecate, and entered ecstatic states to escape the sexual advances of his boss. (19)

While we will later address the particulars of these claims, the larger issue of conflating the highest mystical experience with a dissociative response concerning unresolved sexual trauma and sexual conflict is more troubling than any specific example. *Kālī's Child* blurs this distinction by asserting that "the formed contexts—the boy, the physical opening of the anus, the boss—and the formless content of these mystical states cannot be facilely equated, but neither can they be artificially separated" (19–20). What does "*artificially* separated" mean? It is clear that if these elements are not *equated* in *Kālī's Child*, then they are certainly conjoined. Tellingly, after alerting the reader to his thesis that the "formed contexts"—anus, boy, boss—cannot be "artificially separated" from the "formless"—samādhi—Kripal then purports to quote Ramakrishna: "These, Ramakrishna would say, are states 'beyond form and the formless.' They are both and they are neither" (20). Let us step back to examine this more closely since the most basic hypotheses which underlie *Kālī's Child* are presented here.

While *Kālī's Child* informs the reader that the cocked hips, the anus and Mathur cannot be facilely equated with Ramakrishna's mystical states, they are nevertheless presented in a cause-and-effect sequence. However, neither the boy, the anus nor Mathur have anything to do with Ramakrishna's words regarding form and formlessness and what lies beyond them both. Throughout the *Kathāmṛta*, Ramakrishna speaks of God (*īśvar*) both as being formless and as having form. As the reader can see by going through the *Kathāmṛta*, the question of whether God was formless or endowed with form was, at that time, a controversial, hotly debated item. M's early discussions with Ramakrishna were centered on that very topic.

In March of 1883, we find Ramakrishna saying to Kedar, what he also said on a number of other occasions: "God has form and he is formless too. Further, he is even beyond both form and formlessness. No one can limit him" (*Īśvar sākār ābār nirākār, ābār sākār-nirākārer-o pār. Tam̐r iti korā jāi nā*) (KA 2.20). That God (*īśvar*) cannot be limited, can both have form and be formless as well, and is also beyond the limits of form and formlessness has nothing to do with English boys, Mathur, and Ramakrishna's defecation. Yet *Kālī's Child* insinuates that Ramakrishna's words ("Ramakrishna would say") about form and formlessness, and what lies beyond them both, refer to samādhi and patterns of sexual attraction/sexual abuse—the formless and the formed contexts—"they are both and they are neither." They are not, nor did Ramakrishna ever imply anything even remotely similar to what *Kālī's Child* suggests.

Yet even more crucially, the most troubling issue here is the larger question about linking mystical experience with unconscious drives of which the mystic himself was ignorant. Can one enter into samādhi as a way to escape a predatory "boss"? Can one enter into ecstasy as an avoidance mechanism due to "shame for his phallic desires"? Can one enter a state of rarefied mystical awareness while defecating because the opening of the anus brings back troubling memories of sexual abuse? Not unless one redefines what constitutes a mystical experience. While Kripal assures the reader that he does not facilely equate what he calls these "formed contexts" with mystical states, it is clear that Kripal *does* equate trauma-based dissociative response with mystical experiences. Dissociative response is the very antithesis of samādhi; the psychological numbness which trauma victims suffer as a result of sensory overload cannot be equated with samādhi which, in the Hindu tradition, is understood to be the highest experience of joy.

As *Kālī's Child* progresses, mystical experience is repeatedly conflated with an unconscious experience, whereas these two areas of consciousness are neither equivalent nor interchangeable. As for the particulars, let us look at the English boy, at the sight of whom Ramakrishna purportedly went into samādhi "while looking at the *cocked* hips of a *beautiful* English boy" (19; emphasis added). We should note the felicitous choice of adjectives. This is repeated later as an example of the "homoerotic dimensions" of Ramakrishna's samādhi. Seeing an English boy, Ramakrishna is reminded of Kṛṣṇa. Kripal writes that, like Kṛṣṇa, "the English boy is thrice-bent in a seductive pose. Stunned by the cocked hips of the boy, Ramakrishna falls into *samādhi*" (66). Yet neither of the references cited by the author (KA 2.49; KA 2.110) mention "cocked hips" or a seductive pose. It simply states that the boy was *tribhaṅga*—bent in three places in Kṛṣṇa's traditional pose—bent at the knee, waist and elbow, with flute in hand. Neither citation indicates the English boy to be "beautiful" and, perhaps obviously, there is no mention of "cocked" hips either. Again, Kripal adds what is not there (yet implying that it is) in the *Kathāmṛta*. The *Kathāmṛta* merely states that Ramakrishna went into samādhi upon seeing a boy who was—as Kṛṣṇa is depicted in Hindu iconography— *tribhaṅga*, bent in three places. It is clear that the boy—standing in a pose traditionally ascribed to Kṛṣṇa—reminded Ramakrishna of Kṛṣṇa and, as a result, he went into samādhi. Yet *Kālī's Child* continues his "stunned by the cocked hips of the boy" train of thought by following in the very next sentence:

> Again, [Ramakrishna] looks at the boy Rakhal and becomes "all excited" (*uddīpana*). Why? Because Rakhal reminds him of Gopāla, the child Kṛṣṇa (KA. 4.5). In still another passage, he looks at the boy Kedar and is reminded of Kṛṣṇa's sexual exploits with the milkmaids (KA 4.7). (KC, 66)

Why, we might ask, is *uddīpan* translated as "become 'all excited'" and why is "all excited" put into scare quotes? First, *uddīpan* (from *dīpa*, "light") means to be enkindled, to be lit, or occasionally more prosaically, to be reminded. "All excited" is obviously a mistranslation but done so, apparently, for a reason: to provide sexual content for Ramakrishna's relationship with Rakhal. Remember, we have encountered Ramakrishna "stunned by the cocked hips of the boy" as he was reminded of Kṛṣṇa, and, in the next sentence, Ramakrishna becomes "all excited" seeing "the boy Rakhal" (who was twenty years old and married). Why was Ramakrishna "all excited"? Because Rakhal reminded Ramakrishna of Gopāla, the child Kṛṣṇa (who, in *Kālī's Child* is known for nothing other than his "erotic exploits"). Of course, Rakhal *did* remind Ramakrishna of Gopāla, but there is no reason to presume that this indicates an erotic attraction. If we check the *Kathāmṛta*, we find Ramakrishna in an ecstatic mood. Looking at Rakhal, M writes that suddenly, "Ramakrishna was flooded with the feeling of parental love (*vātsalya*)" (*Rākhālke dekhite dekhite bātsalya rośe āpluto hoilen*) (KA 4.4). *Vātsalya*, by definition, is a non-erotic relationship. Ramakrishna himself tells the devotees why he is enkindled (*uddīpan*) at the sight of Rakhal: it is because the more one advances toward God (*īśvar*), the less one sees aspects of divine power. Beginning with a vision of the goddess with ten arms, the next vision is the goddess with two arms. Then one sees the form of Gopāla (*tārpor Gopāl mūrti darśan*). Significantly, Ramakrishna continues with his description and goes on to say that there are other visions as well—then the sādhaka sees only light (*er-o pāre āche—kebol jyotiḥ darśan*) (KA 4.4). Of course, *Kālī's Child*'s readers have no idea that Ramakrishna will end the conversation on the topic of the vision of light. All they know is that Ramakrishna gets "all excited" seeing "the boy Rakhal."

To continue Kripal's train of thought regarding Kedar (Ramakrishna "looks at the boy Kedar and is reminded of Kṛṣṇa's sexual exploits with the milkmaids"), when we check the *Kathāmṛta* we find the "boy Kedar" to be a fifty-year-old government accountant who had walked into the room wearing office clothes. M says that Kedar is a devotional person (*premik lok*) who maintained the attitude of the gopīs (*antare gopīr bhāb*). M tells us that seeing Kedar enkindles in Ramakrishna the [thought of the] Vrindaban *līlā* (*Kedārke dekhiyā Ṭhākurer ekbāre śrībṛndābon-līlā uddīpan hoiyā gelo*) (KA 4.7). Again, no sexual exploits and again no milkmaids.

To recap, *Kālī's Child*'s Introduction contains a rich distillation of what the reader will encounter in the book's succeeding five chapters, followed by an epilogue and conclusion. As each chapter unfolds, other "secrets" come to the fore. Each chapter is organized around an aspect of Kālī's iconography, associating aspects of it with aspects of Ramakrishna's life and giving an analysis of Ramakrishna's teachings and mystical experiences. Hence the first chapter, entitled "Kālī's Sword: Anxious Longing and the First Vision," discusses Ramakrishna's childhood and adolescence, his first vision of Kālī (which *Kālī's Child* characterizes as "Ramakrishna's initial mystico-erotic crisis") and his *vyākulatā*, which is idiosyncratically translated as "anxious desire" and "erotic torment." The second chapter discusses Kālī as Mother and Lover, associating these aspects with the years of Ramakrishna's Tantric sādhanas. "Kālī on Top of Śiva," the book's third chapter, concerns itself with Tantra and Vedānta in Ramakrishna's teachings and experiences.

Intriguingly, Kripal writes that his own Kolkata nocturnal erotic/mystical experiences were reified in the structure of *Kālī's Child*. Each of the book's five chapters

> was structured around a particular iconographic feature of Kālī erotically astride the supine Śiva. . . Taken together, from chapter 1 on Kālī's sword, which inflicts death and grants liberation, to the oedipal themes of chapter 2 on Kālī as Mother and Lover, to the final three chapters on various aspects of her erotic position "on top" of Śiva, the chapters unconsciously recreated... the phenomenological shape of that Night [of his mystico-erotic experience in Kolkata]. (Kripal 2001a, 202)

The book's fourth chapter, entitled "Kālī's Feet," discusses Ramakrishna's relationship with his male disciples, specifically Ramakrishna and his "homoerotic community, united through an erect passion that was at once profoundly religious and provocatively sexual" (KC, 231). Chapter Five, "Kālī's Tongue," discusses "shame, disgust, and fear in a Tantric world" along with Ramakrishna's last days, when his "secret" was both "revealed and concealed."

The publication of *Kālī's Child* provoked intense debate and raised a number of questions, which will be addressed in this book's following chapter. It also raised questions of interpretation, which will be considered in Chapter Four. On a more basic level, questions regarding issues of translation, documentation and language were raised, and these will be taken up in Chapter Five. The larger issue which *Kālī's Child* provoked is the question of whether it is valid to take subjective experiences and universalize them to create a larger paradigm which is presumed applicable to everyone else's experience, regardless of language, culture and history. *Kālī's Child* raised the issue of whether, for example, a Euro-North American psychotherapeutic model can successfully be employed for understanding the deeper motivations of a nineteenth-century Bengali mystic.

While Kripal correctly notes that many of the issues he raises were broached by previous scholars (KC, xx–xxi), none of the works of these earlier scholars entered the larger public forum. For better or for worse and for a variety of reasons, *Kālī's Child* changed the way a large number of people thought not only about Ramakrishna but also about the Western academy. How *Kālī's Child* emerged from the confines of the academy into the public forum will be examined in our next chapter.

3

History of the Debate

> After revealing the secrets associated with the life of Ramakrishna, it would be a crime for [*Kālī's Child*] to remain a secret.
>
> —Carl Olson, *International Journal of Hindu Studies*

Until the last decade of the twentieth century, the mutually exclusive, self-sustaining environments of academia and Ramakrishna devotees, outsiders and insiders, hummed along in their own way, their paths rarely intersecting. This dramatically changed with the publication of *Kālī's Child* in 1995. While portions of the book appeared as early as 1992 in separately published articles (which were later revised when published in *Kālī's Child*),[1] these earlier articles never brushed against the community of Ramakrishna devotees. An early harbinger of the upcoming controversy appeared in the Summer 1995 edition of the *Journal of the American Academy of Religion*. That issue contained two noteworthy contributions: Kelley Ann Raab's article "Is There Anything Transcendent About Transcendence? A Philosophical and Psychological Study of Sri Ramakrishna" and its counterpoint, Jeffrey Kripal's book review of Richard Schiffman's *Sri Ramakrishna: A Prophet for the New Age*.

Raab observed that Ramakrishna had been primarily studied either from the perspective of a devotee or from a psychoanalytic perspective. Raab's aim was to approach Ramakrishna from a psychoanalytic *and* a philosophical perspective, both of which are sympathetic to mysticism.[2] A philosophical approach, Raab suggested, "offers terms for study of these phenomena upon which psychologists can also agree" (Raab, 326).

Raab noted that Ramakrishna's "cross-dressing" and feminine attitude have often been deemed pathological by psychological interpretations. Philosophical interpretations "place it within the accepted theology of the Hindu tradition, particularly that of Indian mysticism." Raab quotes Tantra scholar Ajit Mookerji: "The masculine adept of Sakti-worship becomes 'ideal' if by ritual techniques he can arouse his own feminine quality. It is even suggested he should undergo a process of transvestism. . . . Men wear the clothes and ornaments of women, and even observe a few days' monthly retirement-period" (332). Raab concluded that "Ramakrishna's visions and behavior were in keeping with his culture and tradition. . . . Dressing as and imitating a woman, Ramakrishna broke through dualistic thought patterns defining gender, humanity and God" (338).

In a lively bookend to Raab's article, Jeffrey Kripal's review of Richard Schiffman's *Sri Ramakrishna: Prophet for the New Age* arrived like a cherry bomb ready to detonate. Schiffman's book—written by a non-academic for a non-academic audience and published six years before Kripal's review—had raised little interest and garnered few reviews. Basically modeling his book after the *Life of Sri Ramakrishna*, Schiffman also relied upon *Sayings of Sri Ramakrishna* and Nikhilananda's *Gospel* and *Holy Mother*. A devotee of Mata Amritanandamayi, to whom the book is dedicated, Schiffman wrote the book at her suggestion.[3] The book had low-level sales, which were largely confined to a "New Age" readership and the small community of Ramakrishna devotees.[4] Yanked from relative obscurity, *Ramakrishna: Prophet for the New Age* was reviewed by Jeffrey Kripal for the academic readers of the *JAAR*, apparently for the sake of savaging it. Kripal's challenging tenor and more challenging assertions foretold the collision course soon to come.

Schiffman's book, Kripal's review declared, was the latest example of a "dubious tradition" which is "marked by the same tiresome list of *naivetés*: an uncritical acceptance of the tradition's Ramakrishna, an assumption that the English translations are faithful reflections of the Bengali originals, an unfounded reliance on a neo-Vedāntic hermeneutic, and an embracing of Vivekananda's Orientalist equations of the 'materialistic West' and the 'spiritual East'" (Kripal 1995b, 363). Noting with no lack of distaste that Schiffman is "a self-confessed 'spiritual seeker,'" Kripal accuses Schiffman of "a simplistic perennialism," among other failings:

> Never mind Kali's positively gruesome and graphically sexual history and myth and ritual; she is a "doting spiritual Mother" to those who see her true nature. . . . According to Schiffman, Ramakrishna had a peaceful and idyllic childhood, practiced Tantra for a page, finally found his "Realization" in an entire chapter on Vedanta, worshipped the Ganges as a physical incarnation of the Divine second only to Kali, married Sharada in a "match made in heaven," and was "never seriously troubled" by sexual temptations. (364)

At this moment Kripal throws into the greater arena his basic theses concerning Ramakrishna: "Anyone who has looked carefully at the historical records knows that these are all gross simplifications based more on the tradition's censoring Swamis than on the texts themselves. The Bengali texts suggest, when they do not loudly proclaim … Ramakrishna's childhood was punctured by pain and tragedy; his religious states were also psychological symptoms; his relationship to Sharada was often marked by a flagrant misogyny; and many, if not most, of Ramakrishna's ecstasies and religious states were shaped and driven by his profound homoerotic desires." Books such as Schiffman's, Kripal writes, "rely exclusively on the same old translations, most of which have been seriously bowdlerized and censored." *Sri Ramakrishna: Prophet for the New Age*, Kripal concludes, "confirms everything the tradition holds. Unfortunately, this 'everything' has virtually 'nothing' to do with the Ramakrishna of history, that strange and somehow tragic being who graces the Bengali texts" (365). Thus condensed, we can see Kripal's salient and controversial points as well as the combative tenor directed toward what Kripal calls "the tradition." This combination would prove to be incendiary when it reached Kolkata a little over a year after this review was published.

Meanwhile, *Kālī's Child* was published and greeted with largely positive reviews from Western academics. As we shall see, Western scholars would generally accept Kripal's thesis that Ramakrishna's disciples and their successors suppressed Ramakrishna's Tantra and elevated Vedānta. *Kālī's Child* would also convince a large number of Western readers that Nikhilananda's *Gospel* was "sanitized" and "bowdlerized." It needs to be mentioned, however, that the great majority of those who accepted the latter thesis were not in a position to assess the translation since most of the reviewers were not Bengali readers. Moreover, it is extremely unlikely that any reviewer did a close or extensive comparison of the Bengali *Kathāmṛta* with Nikhilananda's *Gospel* and checked them against Kripal's translations. For that reason, even the best scholar would have no idea of the extent to which Kripal himself both censored and distorted the original texts he purported to quote. In the scholarly appraisals that follow, we shall see that other conclusions which *Kālī's Child* endorses—the validity of Western psychoanalysis in interpreting a Hindu saint, for example, as well as the homoerotic nature of Ramakrishna's mysticism—will be more contested.

In 1996 the American Academy of Religion conferred upon *Kālī's Child* its History of Religions prize for the best first book of 1995. Yet the mutually sustaining worlds of academia and the believing community still had not crossed each others' trajectories. It was only with the publication of Narasingha Sil's inflammatory book review—"The Question of Ramakrishna's Homosexuality," which appeared in Kolkata's newspaper, *The Statesman*, in January of 1997—that the worlds of Western academia and the insider community collided with a vengeance. Many belonging to the insider community, who had never had any knowledge of or interest in Western academia's understanding of Ramakrishna, were suddenly confronted with a vision of Ramakrishna totally alien to their own. The devotee community was nearly universally outraged and wounded. On the other side of the fence, even scholars with little knowledge of or interest in Ramakrishna were quickly made aware of the controversy not only because of the amount of outrage it engendered but also because of the crucial issues which were to arise later—free speech, "book banning," and the discussion concerning the degree of responsibility, if any, that scholars bore toward the insider community. Since the publication of Sil's *Statesman* review, the debate—initially explosive, tempered of late—has continued to simmer. Even by June 2004, nine years after the book was first published, John S. Hawley observed that the "furious debate … persists unresolved today" (Hawley 2004, 369). Nor has the issue eased since that time, as recent publications such as Martha Nussbaum's *The Clash Within: Democracy, Religious Violence and India's Future* have shown.[5]

Early Reviews

Jeanne Openshaw

The first reviews of *Kālī's Child* appeared almost immediately after its publication. In December of 1995, Edinburgh University's Jeanne Openshaw wrote a generally unfavorable review for the *Times Higher Educational Supplement*, which received little attention from American academics. A Bengali specialist, Openshaw found Kripal's familiarity with a variety of Bengali texts impressive. However, as a Bengali reader she was troubled by serious errors in Kripal's translations. For example, Openshaw notes that Kripal gives evidence of Ramakrishna's "homoerotic dimensions" on the grounds that "he 'liked to look at pictures of men, for they aroused in him feelings of "tenderness" and "love."' But the word translated here as 'men' is *mānuṣ*, which means 'human being' without gender specificity. In fact, despite his initial differentiation of the erotic (as the sexual plus the sacred) and the purely sexual, Kripal himself falls into a reductionistic trap by sexualizing his language in a way quite inappropriate to the material."

Openshaw further remarks: "More serious than these lapses and tendentiousness is the sleight of hand by which strained or confessedly speculative arguments are subsequently transformed into a firm base for further such arguments." Openshaw uses Kripal's example of Ramakrishna's foot to illustrate her point:

> While in mystical absorption, the saint would sometimes place his foot on the body or in the lap of others, an act disapproved of by his doctor but not his devotees. For no reason that I could discern, Kripal has taken "body" (*ga-* or *an+ga*) and "lap" (*kol*) to mean "genitals." The act therefore becomes one of homoeroticism, which naturally evoked an adverse reaction. There are many arguments against this interpretation. First, in an almost identical passage ... the *Kathāmṛta* specifies that the relevant portion of the body is the chest (*buk*). Second, with the exception of divine feet (of a guru or "incarnation") which are a source of blessing, there is a prohibition against touching a person or revered object with the feet. The doctor saw Ramakrishna neither as a guru nor an "incarnation." Above all ... it is highly unlikely that any act considered "homosexual" would have been defended by the disciples (homosexuality was rigorously repressed in Indian society of the time), let alone immortalized in print by a devotee. (22)

Openshaw finds Kripal's arguments for Ramakrishna's "Tantric" world convincing and she appreciates his "appropriate skepticism towards the sources." She adds that "Kripal displays a welcome agnosticism about the status of the texts he uses, likening the *Kathāmṛta* to a 'play' and emphasizing that he is drawing from them one possible 'story.'" She continues: "In the light of this it is surprising to find him attempting to reach not just the 'real' Ramakrishna, but an even deeper Ramakrishna of which the saint himself was probably not aware. . . . On the whole," she writes, "this reader was not convinced."

Openshaw scores a salient point which other reviewers missed vis à vis Kripal's Vedānta versus Tantra argument. Writes Openshaw: "The effect of contextualizing most of the discussion in terms of 'Vedanta' and 'Tantra' is to present many of Ramakrishna's traits as idiosyncratic or even aberrational by Bengali cultural standards. Had the contextualizing backgrounds been the paths of knowledge (jñāna) and devotion (bhakti), rather than 'Vedanta' and 'Tantra,' the saint would have seemed less extraordinary."

Finally, Openshaw critiques Kripal on grounds of cultural ignorance:

> In the context of devotional Bengali Vaishnavism, where femininity represents the highest attainable condition, the cultivation of femininity

> by men in various ways is not necessarily abnormal. Nor can it necessarily be taken as a sign of what we would call "homosexuality," that is, love between men. Many other traits that Kripal sees as indications of "homoerotic" tendencies are not uncommon in heterosexual Bengali men. Unlike our own society … male celibacy, in the sense of conservation of vital seminal essence, is highly prized in rural Bengal. Male fear of women, the attempt to see all women as mothers rather than as sexual partners, and, in its extreme form, a cultivated sense of revulsion for the female body—all these stem precisely from the attractive power of women, rather than from "homoerotic" tendencies. (22)

André Padoux

André Padoux's review in *Archives de Sciences Sociales des Religions* is generally appreciative and Padoux accepts *Kālī's Child*'s basic assertions. He nevertheless makes a significant critical assessment: "The defect of the book … is that his [Kripal's] approach is too Western. If J.J.K. [Kripal] better understood the Indian religious traditions (notably Tantra), if he understood the link [the religious traditions] always create between sex and asceticism … if he had taken better account of these matters if, in fact, he was aware of them, he would have considered Ramakrishna in a fairer and more nuanced way" (1996, 85–86).

Laurie L. Patton

Laurie L. Patton's favorable 1996 review in the *Journal of the History of Sexuality* notes that the "debate about whether Ramakrishna was a Vedāntan philosophical teacher or a *bhakta* (devotional) teacher misses the real center, however ambivalent, of his religious life: Tantra focused on Kālī, the goddess who is both mother and lover. The best lens with which to view Ramakrishna's religious teachings is neither doctrine nor devotion, but desire" (287–88). Patton questions, however, the "easy charges of textual 'bowdlerization' without giving the 'bowdlerizer' his own religious due. The practices of omission and rewriting in the construction of a mystic's life are fascinating activities worthy of study in their own right." That said, Patton continues, "This is an understandable distortion; the book is, of course, attempting to tell a secret, and like all tellers of secrets (and all good Tantrics), Kripal must first dismantle the propriety of its protectors." In conclusion she finds *Kālī's Child* "a fundamental contribution to the history of mysticism and of human sexuality, and as an extraordinarily creative synthesis of the relationship between the two" (289).

Malcolm McLean

Malcolm McLean's review of *Kālī's Child* in *South Asia: Journal of South Asian Studies* finds the book "very important, very exciting, and very well written" (1996, 117). As we have already seen, McLean's Ph.D. thesis was his translation of the *Kathāmṛta*. McLean's thesis had already put forward several presuppositions which would be promoted later in *Kālī's Child*: Ramakrishna's homosexuality and misogyny as well as Nikhilananda's flawed English translation. McLean begins by observing that Ramakrishna has fascinated students of religion since the time of his death, and much of the nature of this fascination was due to "the almost bizarre nature of his religious experiences" (116). Earlier writing by the tradition on Ramakrishna "amounts to hagiography," McLean writes. He continues: "It is only now, with Kripal's book, that we have a full detailed and critical study of Ramakrishna's life and experience."

McLean places particular importance on Kripal's use of the *Jībanabṛttānta* to deconstruct both the *Līlāprasaṅga* and the *Kathāmṛta*. The core of Kripal's analysis, McLean writes, is the "secret teaching" which takes the reader to "the essentially Tantric nature of Ramakrishna's experience." In Ramakrishna's case, this "manifested itself as a homoerotic infatuation for the young men and boys who surrounded him as his disciples. This was in turn the basis of his mystical experiences." Yet this "story was complicated by the fact that Ramakrishna himself was probably barely aware of what was going on within him."

McLean was prescient in his assurance that *Kālī's Child* "will certainly prove to be controversial, and will probably not convince every reader." Nevertheless, he concludes that it "will have to be considered very carefully from now on" (117).

Hugh Urban

Hugh Urban's 1996 review in *Chicago South Asia Newsletter*, while generally quite positive, also provides a telling critique. Urban represents the views of a number of scholars when he writes that "Kripal's book penetrates through the layers of pious obfuscation and reverential distortion surrounding Ramakrishna, to recover the original Bengali texts (above all, the key text of the *Kathamrta*) which had been mistranslated and censored by later disciples." One of the generally accepted credits given by Western academics to *Kālī's Child* is that it succeeded in "recovering the text." As we have already noted, the irony is that the *Kathāmṛta*, the "real" text, has always been widely and readily available for the majority of its readers, since the great preponderance of the book's readers are Bengali. Thus "recovering the text" makes one question who the text's "recovery" is for. The implication is that English readers are the only readers whose opinion and scholarship matter. The irony continues in that Kripal, in translations found in *Kālī's Child*, grossly distorts the original Bengali texts, not only by mistranslations and excising inconvenient portions from the original texts, but also by adding material of his own which does not exist in the cited sources. For this reason it is painfully ironic that Urban writes: "By recovering the original text and the 'secret talk' passages of the *Kathamrta*, Kripal sheds new light on the saint's relations with the mysterious female Tantrika, Brahmani Bhairavi, and his initiation into the forbidden five M's."

In what may appear to be a niggling point but is actually quite important, Urban notes that the book is "often very funny." This is a point which will be made in a number of reviews—significantly, always by "outsiders"—and it is also pointedly made in *Kālī's Child* itself. In a number of places, the book is meant to provoke laughter or at least a wink and a nod.[6] This, however, was understood by the insider community as "laughing at" (no possibility of "laughing with"), and they felt mocked and disparaged.

After declaring the book's "undeniable importance," Urban then discusses some of the book's shortcomings:

> Kripal's work also bears some rather troubling problems. Perhaps most striking is Kripal's ambivalent and unclear use of psychoanalytic categories. The book is filled with psychological terminology, Freudian readings, and the heavy influence of theorists like Kakar and Obeyesekere, while Ramakrishna is diagnosed as a man torn by his repressed homoerotic and pedophiliac desires. Yet Kripal resists applying psychoanalytic categories in a rigorous way. . . . A second problem arises from Kripal's understanding of "Tantra" and his identification of Ramakrishna as a "Tantrika". . . . He ignores the fact that … the category of "Tantra" as a singular, unified entity is itself an imaginary construction of 19th century British Orientalists. Ramakrishna and his disciples were themselves an important part of the way in which Tantra came to be defined in Western discourse. Second, Kripal lapses all too often into a very popular misconception of Tantra as something "scandalous," "seedy," "sexy" and "dangerous," which is defined primarily by the equation of eroticism and mysticism. . . . Sexuality is in fact but one, rather limited, and not necessarily the most important element of the diverse texts and traditions we label collectively as "Tantra."

Urban writes that "perhaps the most problematic aspect of Kripal's work is its lack of attention to social and historical context. . . . He never asks ... just what homoerotic and pedophiliac impulses would mean in 19th century Bengali culture—other than to say that they are 'scandalous,' fraught with 'shame, disgust and fear.'" Nevertheless, Urban concludes that "despite these weaknesses ... this work stands out as an enormous contribution to our knowledge of Ramakrishna and to the study of Indian Tantra."

Glen Hayes

Glen Hayes's short review of *Kālī's Child* in *Religious Studies Review* was entirely laudatory. Describing the book as an "entertaining, informative, and richly provocative study," Hayes praises Kripal for his "skillful analysis of texts" and for his "scholarly brilliance, sensitivity, and humor" which reveal the "'secrets' lurking within the complex (and conflicted) godman" (95). Hayes notes that Kripal "suggests intriguing relationships" between the mystical and the erotic "in the troubled life of a renowned religious figure" (96).

David Haberman

Finding *Kālī's Child* to be "impressively documented and well written," David Haberman contends in *Journal of Asian Studies* that "Kripal demonstrates that homosexual desire was the major driving force of Ramakrishna's mystical life." Haberman writes that his appreciation for Ramakrishna was "enhanced immensely" after reading the book. In lieu of the earlier "bland" Ramakrishna, Kripal's Ramakrishna is "Kali's passionate child, a sexually abused child who found a great deal of joy, love, and ecstasy in the very world that abused him." Accepting Kripal's theses without demur, Haberman praises Kripal's "fairly detailed picture of a particular and lived understanding of Hindu Tantra that promises to flesh out the more textual and ideal representation found in most books on Tantra" (Haberman 1997, 532).

Carl Olson

Carl Olson's review in *International Journal of Hindu Studies* judges *Kālī's Child* to be a "model of clarity, sensitivity, single-minded pursuit of the truth, a joy to read, an example that textual studies need not be boring and deserves to be widely read by everyone in the field of religious studies, Indian studies, and among educated readers in general." Were that not enough, Olson goes on to declare that "after revealing the secrets associated with the life of Ramakrishna, it would be a crime for this book to remain a secret" (1997, 202). Clearly no need to fear on that score. More perplexing and more interesting is the disconnect between Olson's perception of Kripal's "sensitivity" (and Olson is hardly alone in this perception) and that of the devotee community, who perceived insult and slur rather than sensitivity and clarity.

One year later in the same journal, Olson's essay "Vivekānanda and Rāmakṛṣṇa Face to Face: An Essay on the Alterity of a Saint" places blame squarely on Vivekananda for allegedly expunging certain events from his portrait of Ramakrishna. Olson makes this astonishing claim based upon Kripal's speculations in *Kālī's Child*, which are unsupported by any of the source texts. For Olson, this lack of evidence does not point to the questionable nature of Kripal's conjectures, but rather to the suppression of facts by later followers. That there is no evidence for this suppression other than the claims made in *Kālī's Child* does not seem to have disturbed Olson. He writes: "[Ramakrishna] was a failed Tāntrika with respect to his conscious awareness ... but he was a genuine Tantric hero by means of his unconscious vision in which he performed cunnilingus upon the goddess, according to Kripal's scholarship, although neither the *Kathāmṛta* of Mahendranāth Gupta nor the *Līlāprasaṅga* of Sāradānanda mention this dream" (1998, 51).

William Parsons

William B. Parsons's lengthy review essay, "Psychoanalysis and Mysticism: The Case of Ramakrishna," in *Religious Studies Review* discusses three books on Ramakrishna: Sil's *Rāmakṛṣṇa Paramahaṁsa*, Kakar's *Analyst and the Mystic*, and Kripal's *Kālī's Child*. Each book, Parsons writes, corresponds to three distinct psychological models which have been used in interpreting religious figures: the classic mode associated with Freud, the adaptive model used by Erikson, and the transformative model found in Kohut and Lacan. Noting that the nexus between religion and psychology is well-trod—beginning with Freud's correspondence with Romain Rolland—Parsons writes that in recent times there has been an "explosion of essays in psychology, religion, and gender studies."

Parsons sees Sil's work as a "paradigmatic example of the classic psychoanalytic approach to mysticism," which views mysticism as regressive and pathological. Parsons sees it also as reductive. The Ramakrishna Sil portrays, Parson writes, is "infantile, antisocial, vulgar, and crude" (355). By contrast, Parsons sees Kakar's *Analyst and the Mystic* as exemplifying the adaptive psychological model, one which views mysticism as therapeutic and which perceives religious practice as alternative therapeutic techniques. Parsons outlines Kakar's critiques of earlier Ramakrishna studies: that a "simple reading of Ramakrishna's sexuality as homoerotic or his mysticism as pathological betrays the prejudices of a Western-bound ethnoscience." Parsons continues by noting that Kakar "demands empathic resonance with socially constructed concepts like 'desire.'" In addition, Kakar "shows how physiological and cultural factors relativize the complex issue of saintly eroticism." Finally, Parsons finds Kakar's book "revealing a culture that tolerates males experiencing their femininity and advocates 'being' and 'receptive absorption' over 'doing' and 'active opposition'" (357). In Parsons's estimation Kakar's work is flawed because of "his failure properly to contextualize the totality of Ramakrishna's visions" in addition to Kakar's "lack of textual expertise (he takes for granted the legitimacy of bowdlerized biographies of the Master)" (358). Parsons apparently assumes that all works on Ramakrishna published by the Ramakrishna Order are "bowdlerized"; Kakar used for his study the *Śrī Rāmakṛṣṇa Vacanāmṛta*, the Hindi translation of the Bengali *Kathāmṛta*.

Parsons holds the best book until last: "Jeffrey Kripal blesses us with what is to date the most sophisticated and thorough interdisciplinary study of Ramakrishna" (358). *Kālī's Child* (which, as Parsons appreciatively notes, is "highly entertaining") is "an extraordinary book that makes an invaluable contribution to Ramakrishna studies" that "should become a classic" (359). It is ironic that Parsons finds tremendous significance in Kripal's alleged uncovering of the original *Kathāmṛta*, the Ur-text of Ramakrishna studies. Parsons writes: "At the heart of Kripal's study is the restoration of the text," adding that Kripal displays "a masterful command of the text" and "the net result is an accurate descriptive and historical account of Ramakrishna's mystical practices" (358). Parsons reiterates: "The text reinstated, Kripal shows how sexuality, mysticism, and significant others are related in Ramakrishna's life and thought" (359).

On the psychoanalytic front, Parsons finds Kripal's hermeneutic strategy multidisciplinary, building upon Sil and Masson. According to Parsons, Kripal best exemplifies "a true psychology-comparativist dialogue" and "one can only look forward to the new advances such scholarship will inspire" (360).

The people of Kolkata begged to differ.

The Storm and Its Aftermath

"The Question of Ramakrishna's Homosexuality," screamed the banner headline of one of Kolkata's premier newspapers, *The Statesman*.[7] "Kripal's Ramakrishna is a gay tantric mystic," Narasingha Sil's article began, "who, like a modern day drag queen, often cross dressed and lay down with his employer Mathur Nath Biswas and who also let himself be sodomized by his naked Vedantic guru from Punjab, Totapuri" (Sil, 1997). The looming controversy exploded with a vengeance, and Ramakrishna studies, as well as the academic study of Hinduism, has never been the same since. While Sil's review article was intentionally provocative, with language generally deemed unprintable,[8] even a gentler rendition of *Kālī's Child*'s theses would have provoked a firestorm. The icing on this volatile cake was the prominent display of photos of Kālī, Ramakrishna surrounded by his disciples, and Mathur Babu included in the full-page article. What is surprising is not that a firestorm ensued, but rather that anyone was taken aback by it.

The basic tenets of *Kālī's Child* would have been offensive enough to provoke outrage, particularly in Kolkata, where Ramakrishna's visage is ubiquitous and devotion to him is common. In *The Statesman* review, however, Sil inserted his own inflammatory comments, which added to the intensity of the outrage. For example, Sil writes: "Probably Ramakrishna's premature impotence … made him averse to hetero-sexual practice though not thoughts. Only in his advancing years, when he was growing older and uglier … he developed a longing for young men … the only option for an erotic and impotent male." Yet while Sil and Kripal set themselves to overturn the traditional insider's view of Ramakrishna, Sil's review makes it abundantly clear that he finds little in *Kālī's Child* to appreciate. The book, Sil writes, is

> a fascinatingly misleading interpretation of the sources, an interpretation that is at once highly schematized, tendentious but provocative. [Kripal] is ever apologetic of Freudian reductionism but has little qualms in trampling evidence for the sake of the integrity of what he labels Ramakrishna's symbolic universe. . . .
>
> Kripal takes Swami Nikhilananda … to task for his bowdlerized translation of Mahendranath's Bengali, but he himself has doctored the meaning of numerous Bengali words and terms with gay abandon to suit his purpose. Kripal would insist on Ramakrishna's tantric world-view and would unhesitatingly adduce spurious evidence with highly concocted interpretation of his behavior.

Sil ridicules Kripal's book on a number of fronts. Sil writes: "In spite of [Kripal's] scholarly attempt to define 'the ontological status of the Hindu unconscious' and explain 'how this ontology might affect a psychological method,' his agenda consists in pronouncing the Master gay and then validating his spiritual experiences on the basis of his alleged homosexuality." Sil derides Kripal for his claim that Pandit Vaishnavacharan was a Tāntrik when, in fact, he was a Vaiṣṇava belonging to the Kartābhajā sect; Sil also mocks Kripal's speculation that the women of the Vaiṣṇava Navarasika sect were eunuchs when they are described as *strīlokera* (women) in the source. Another issue which rouses Sil's ire was the fact that Kripal "references the *Lilaprasanga* from the English translation supplying different words, apparently for no reason."

Ramakrishna does not capture Sil's interest as much as Kripal, whose

> enterprise is a classic example of what happens when an author's clever use of dictionary, index card and intelligence without an understanding of the history and culture of people other than his ethnic group but with a pretension to insider's knowledge through the back door, as it were, produces a psychoanalysis of the mystical-spiritual experience of a saint from another religion and culture.

In short, it was in Sil's final words on the subject, "plain shit." While Sil had little use for Ramakrishna as a saint, he had even less use for someone with little knowledge of Bengali language or culture.

Outraged letters, telephone calls and cancellation notices flooded *The Statesman*. Of the thirty-nine letters published in response to Sil's review (thirty-three written from Kolkata), only one reader had actually read *Kālī's Child*—and that particular reader had read the book in the United States.[9] All the letters published were extremely critical of *Kālī's Child*. Letters published by *The Statesman* appeared under such titles as: "An Affront," "Perverted Piece," "Abuse of Power," "Grievous Hurt," "Desecration of a Saint's Memory," "Preconceived Ideas," and "A Mirror." All published letters, with the exception of one, were extremely critical of *The Statesman* for publishing the review in the first place.[10] While Sanjib Kumar Sanyal's letter of February 7, 1997, praised Sil's review as "a specimen of what a book review ought to be" for "patiently [going] over the ground traversed by Dr. Kripal and ... deliver[ing] his knock-out punch in the very last paragraph," other letters were not so sanguine. Two letters requested the book be banned. M. K. Mukherjee's letter of February 5th declared that the book "hurt the sentiments of millions who look upon Sri Ramakrishna as God Incarnate. We, Hindus, are tolerant but there is a limit. This is a sacrilege. Through this column I would earnestly appeal to all right-thinking people to put pressure on the Union Government to proscribe the book in India." Letters from non-Hindus were also on display. Jaffar Halim wrote to *The Statesman* on February 2nd: "A semi-ignorant writer with a perverted mind purposefully maligns a saint and you give the author's delirious view such wild publicity?" Ratna Viswas Ray's February 6th letter questioned "which scholar directed and supervised Kripal's thesis and what research into primary sources was conducted by him to satisfy his putrid propensity and to meet the strict standards of a scholarly work?"

The Statesman was taken aback by the outpouring of indignation from its readers. In its February 18, 1997, editorial "Now Let It Rest," *The Statesman* waved an editorial white flag:

> In the past fortnight, this newspaper has seen more reaction from its readers than as far back as memory serves. Most of the mail, the telephone calls and a substantial share of the personal contact that the members of the staff have had with our public ... have been critical of Dr. Narasingha P. Sil's review. . . . [Kripal] has been questioned on his credentials and the quality of his research. . . . The greatest criticism has however been reserved for *The Statesman*—for having allowed its editorial judgment to be suspended by publishing a review of such a book at some considerable length. . . . If a vote were taken, on the evidence and we concede this, our judgment went askew.[11]

And with that, *The Statesman* dropped its hot potato.

T. G. Vaidyanathan

In May of 1997, T. G. Vaidyanathan's "Kripal and *Kālī's Child*" appeared in India's Chennai-based newspaper, *The Hindu*. The review, nestled inside a two-page extract from *Kālī's Child*'s Introduction, begins by invoking the furor initiated by *The Statesman*, mentioning those readers "calling upon the Home Ministry to ban Kripal's *Kali's Child*." This, Vaidyanathan declares by the end of his first paragraph, is "a sign of the deterioration of basic values in Indian life." By the next paragraph, Vaidyanathan has moved on to Stanley Wolpert's controversial book on Nehru and Salman Rushdie's *Satanic Verses*. Vaidyanathan sees the negative reaction to *Kālī's Child* in a similar vein: "Apparently many right thinking Indians are baying for Kripal's blood after *Kālī's Child*."

Vaidyanathan, co-editor with Jeffrey Kripal of *Vishnu on Freud's Desk: A Reader in Psychoanalysis and Hinduism*, writes that he can "only marvel at the extent and scope not only of Kripal's formidable scholarship but of his compassion as well, in documenting and analyzing the life of the great Bengali saint." Yet this review makes apparent Vaidyanathan's own lack of knowledge concerning Ramakrishna and Ramakrishna scholarship. For example, Vaidyanathan writes that Kripal deconstructs "the heavily bowdlerized 'Kathamrta' in the only version hitherto available to us thanks to the pioneering, if entirely misplaced, efforts of Mahendranath Gupta's monumental 5-volume 'The Gospel of Sri Ramakrishna.'" Such a statement leaves those even vaguely familiar with the texts scratching their heads. Apart from the obvious confusion of the *Kathāmṛta* with the *Gospel*, Nikhilananda's English translation was not the "only version available." Vaidyanathan concludes on a surer note: "One fervently hopes that good sense will prevail and the Home Ministry will remain impervious to the siren calls of a belated and totally misplaced local patriotism."

Swami Atmajnanananda

In August 1997, Swami Atmajnanananda, an American-born monk of the Ramakrishna Order, published a refutation of *Kālī's Child* in the *International Journal of Hindu Studies*. Fluent in Bengali with a Ph.D. in Oriental Studies from the University of Pennsylvania, Atmajnanananda has lived in India and Bangladesh for extended periods of time. In his review entitled "Scandals, Cover-ups, and Other Imagined Occurrences in the Life of Rāmakṛṣṇa: An Examination of Jeffrey Kripal's *Kālī's Child*," Atmajnanananda closely compares the *Kathāmṛta* with Kripal's translations in *Kālī's Child* and writes: "For those who take the trouble to check his references and compare his translations with the original texts ... there are some basic problems with Kripal's thesis ... problems which ... go to the very heart of his assertions" (401). Accusing Kripal of circular logic and biased translations, Atmajnanananda states: "Time and again [Kripal's] translation of terms presupposes the very attitudes he is trying to prove. Kripal consistently misreads situations, takes events out of their cultural context, assumes attitudes and beliefs without justification, and allows his fertile imagination to conjure up incidents for which there is no concrete evidence" (402).

Atmajnanananda first examines Kripal's analysis of Ramakrishna's foot, asserting that Kripal ignored both cultural and religious implications in order to provide a sexualized reading. He goes on to discuss Kripal's treatment of the Bengali word *uddīpana* as an example of the book's "prejudicial translation work and circular reasoning." Correcting

Kripal's translation of *māg-chele* (which Kripal translates as "bitch and kids"), Atmajnanananda asserts that the phrase "is actually nothing more than the colloquial equivalent of the more formal expression, *strī-putra*, "wife and children" (405).[12] Atmajnanananda contends that while Kripal levels extremely harsh criticism at Swami Nikhilananda, whatever few omissions Nikhilananda employed were the result of "his sensitivity to Western decorum … not fear of revealing hidden secrets. Had this been the case, he certainly would have eliminated far more of Rāmakṛṣṇa's remarks than he did. In each case also, we find Kripal's translation of the missing portion more misleading than Nikhilananda's omissions" (409).

Challenging Kripal's suggestion that Ramakrishna was the victim of early sexual abuse, Atmajnanananda contends that there is no evidence provided in *Kālī's Child* and none is found in the source texts (409–10). Atmajnanananda disputes Kripal's assertions regarding Ramakrishna's sexual relationships with the Brahmani and Mathur Babu, while also addressing Kripal's claim of Ramakrishna's homoerotic desires for his disciples. In every case Atmajnanananda points out Kripal's dubious translation as well as cultural ignorance. Finally, concerning Kripal's assertion that the *Jībanabṛttānta* was "suppressed" by the Ramakrishna Order, Atmajnanananda points out that it was, in fact, *published* by the Ramakrishna Order (415).[13]

Rajat Kanta Ray

Kālī's Child was icily received by a number of Indian academics. Rajat Kanta Ray's unfavorable review in the October 1997 edition of *Indian Economic and Social History Review* criticizes Kripal's ignorance of Indian culture and psychiatry. Ray, professor and head of the History Department at Presidency College, Kolkata, does not seem appalled by Kripal's speculation of an erotic crisis which led to Ramakrishna's mystical experience: "The suggestion is not unreasonable," Ray writes, "but what erotic crisis?" (101). A Bengali himself, Ray pulls apart the book's tenets by demonstrating Kripal's considerable ignorance of Bengali language and culture. "The historical evidence Kripal offers in favor of Ramakrishna's homosexuality seems to me to be shaky; some of his own evidence seems to contradict it, and opens up the possibility of an alternative interpretation. A number of his translations from the primary text—*Ramakrishna Kathamrita*—are wrong; his psychoanalytical proceedings with the text … fills me with doubt, especially as regards his identifications of some Tantrik symbols" (102).

Ray gives specific instances of critical translation errors which bias the interpretation of the text: "Kripal translates 'Kamini' as 'lover'—why not 'woman'? He derives Ram, son of Dasrath, etymologically from 'sexual delight,' but the root verb ... means 'to please.'" Kripal translates "Janani is Ramani" as "she who gives birth," is "she who makes love"—"the Mother is the Lover." Ray contends: "The average Bengali reader of the *Kathamrita* will, however, understand the line thus: 'Mother is a woman.'" Ray gives particular attention to what he terms Kripal's "doubtful translation" of *uddīpana* as "sexual excitement" as it is "critical to Kripal's interpretation." Ray observes that Kripal renders *uddīpana* "as 'religious enlightenment,' 'mythical remembrance' and 'sexual excitement'; it is the last alternative that he plays on. Etymologically, however, 'uddipana' means 'enkindling,' and the ordinary reader of the *Kathamrita* will understand that Ramakrishna's mind was enkindled in the presence of his young disciples" (102–3).

Ray takes umbrage at Kripal's mention "of a 'once glaring scandal' concerning Ramakrishna and his fourteen-year-old disciple, Purna." "Yet," Ray contends, "the historical record contains no such 'glare.'" Ray then takes several instances of Kripal's translations to show an unwarranted homosexual bias. One example: "every Bengali knows 'māthā khāwā' (eating the head) means just 'misleading someone,' it has absolutely no sexual connotation. It is on the basis of such evidence that [Kripal] builds his case" (103). Ray critiques the absence of the psychoanalytic work of Girindrasekar Bose, founder of the Indian Psychoanalytic Society, in *Kālī's Child* and concludes his review by stating: "Ramakrishna might have had a considerably more complex sexual personality than Kripal has supposed" (104).

Gerald Larson

An entirely different critique emerged from the American academy, this one from Gerald James Larson, whose "Polymorphic Sexuality, Homoeroticism, and the Study of Religion" was published in the *Journal of the American Academy of Religion*. Larson begins his review by saying that his first reaction to *Kālī's Child* was an "Aha! experience." He observes that *Kālī's Child*'s reviews in the secular academy have been largely favorable while those in what Larson terms "the believing community" have been negative ("running the gamut from anger, even fury, to disappointment, sadness, bemusement, personal hurt, and betrayal") (1997, 656). Larson frames his "Aha!-experience" thus: "What is the relation, if any, between our modern secular intellectual communities, on the one hand, and the target believing communities or persons whom our scholarly and creative work seeks to interpret and characterize, on the other?"

Before delving into that issue in depth, Larson specifically addresses *Kālī's Child*, stating that "the book … unlocks an important dimension of the manner in which sexual fantasies, and especially homosexual fantasies, relate to our understanding of the mystical and/or religious experience of Sri Ramakrishna. It must also be said, however, that the treatment overall lacks balance and proper contextualization and in the end falls into the trap of monocausal reductionism" (658). By this he means: "Ramakrishna's mystical experience is reduced to his homoerotic fantasies. . . . The homosexual desires explain the entire life of a saint including his mystical or spiritual experience" (659).

Kripal's assertion that Ramakrishna was unaware of his own homosexual desires and the further assertion that Ramakrishna (and earlier interpreters) lacked the hermeneutical key to understand his behavior, is characterized by Larson as "remarkable hubris." Larson goes on to say that Kripal's declaration that Ramakrishna's

> "homoerotic energies … *were* his mysticism," or that "Ramakrishna's homosexual tendencies … deeply influenced, indeed determined the manner in which he created his own self-defined 'states' out of the symbols of his inherited religious tradition," is thoroughly implausible and does not follow from the evidence presented in the book. None of the evidence cited in the book supports a cause-effect relation between the erotic and the mystical (or the religious), much less an identity! (660)

The larger picture, Larson states, is more complex and nuanced. Moreover, citing Kakar and Sil, Larson attests that "all of this puzzling data about Ramakrishna's eccentric sexuality has been widely known for many years," adding that there has not been

> any shortage of articles and books that make clear Ramakrishna's syncretistic Gauḍīya Vaiṣṇava, Śaiva, Śākta and Tāntrika predilections. For anyone even casually acquainted with Bengali spirituality and cultural life many of the symbolic visions and fantasies of Ramakrishna, which appear bizarre and even pathological when construed only in isolation or individually, become much less so when one relates the visions and fantasies to nineteenth-century Bengal. (662)

Larson returns to his "*Aha!* Experience," which centers on "the various attitudes or perspectives we have in the academy regarding the relation between modern secular intellectual communities, on the one hand, and believing communities, on the other." He suggests that *Kālī's Child* "would have been much more balanced and would have avoided reductionism had [Kripal] taken the trouble to engage in a frank intellectual exchange about his interpretation with the community about which and in which much of his material centers." Larson takes pains to add: "I am not suggesting that he should have allowed the members or followers of the Ramakrishna Mission and Math to exercise any sort of veto or censorship over his material." Larson further notes: "I am also inclined to think that the book would have achieved greater balance and would have avoided reductionism had it been vetted by professionals within the psychoanalytic community" (663). Larson thus concludes: "It is important for all of us in the modern academy to be in frank and open conversation with the communities we study and with other scholarly communities in the academy. . . . I am, therefore, personally persuaded that the relation of symmetrical reciprocity ... is the only way to go if we wish our studies to be taken seriously and if we wish our studies to be properly nuanced and persuasive" (664).

One year later the readers of the *Journal of the American Academy of Religion* would have a reprise of the *Kālī's Child* debate with Jeffrey Kripal's response to Larson's article and Larson's rejoinder to Kripal. Kripal begins by noting that psychoanalytically inclined historians of mysticism attempt to understand "'the secret'(*mustikos*), the hidden, the concealed, and subsequently, the censored, even the persecuted." Those historians of religions who choose to "reveal the secret" suffer "the moral outrage of those, scholar and believer alike, who would prefer to keep 'the hidden,' well ... *hidden*" (1998b, 627). Apparently Kripal saw Larson's critique as part of a larger movement since Kripal speaks of "the hermeneutical revenge that seeks to silence (or at least domesticate) the scholar who 'speaks the secret.'"

Regarding Larson's point that earlier scholars had raised the issue of Ramakrishna's sexuality, Kripal argues that "no one followed up on these themes" (of Tantra and sexual orientation) though "one could speak of a consensus on the homosexual issue, at least among academics trained in historical-critical and analytic methods" (628).

Concerning Larson's charge of "monocausal reductionism," Kripal states that Larson has misread the book, stating his "own consistent rejection of a Freudian reductionism ... and the logical impossibility of reducing the mystical to the sexual in a radically monistic universe." Kripal states that "Larson wants to argue that I am advancing a single cause, when in fact I mapped out two primary levels (the Tantric and the incarnational) and *eight* different dimensions ... in the production and process of Ramakrishna's secret" (1998b, 629).

Kripal goes on to state that "many scholarly reviews have noted, if not highlighted, this multi-dimensional, nonreductive element of my work with warm and enthusiastic appreciation, as have even some devotees in personal correspondence. I mention this not to commit the logical fallacy of appealing to authority but to ask simply: Why does as sophisticated a reader as Larson completely miss what other scholars have so easily seen? Why must he so seriously misrepresent what I have written?" (629–30). Kripal voices his suspicions by saying, "I suspect that Larson's own relationship to the Ramakrishna Mission and his role here as a defender of the tradition were influential in both the original conception and final negative conclusions of the review" (630).

Kripal strongly contests Larson's suggestion that he should have engaged the tradition in a more explicit fashion by saying,

> I did in fact explore, both anecdotally and historically, the limits of the tradition's willingness (if not in the way Larson proposes). One Bengali friend would only whisper to me about the censored passages. . . . Another felt uncomfortable talking about the issue in a restaurant. . . . I also spoke to Indian intellectuals in Calcutta, whose responses could be summarized as follows: "You are right, but we cannot say that here. You, however, can and should say it *over there*."

Kripal then follows with a sentence of particular significance: "It was my willed distance and cultural otherness that gave me a perspective, a voice, and an emotional freedom that my Indian colleagues and friends either lacked or refused to claim as their own" (630). In other words, Kripal's outsider status provided him the distance necessary to see and interpret what others—cultural and religious insiders—could not see or would not acknowledge.

Kripal continues by suggesting that "there is nothing particularly new about this. Ramakrishna has always been a scandal." Among other points, Kripal states that Ram Chandra Datta's *Jībanabṛttānta* "became the object of a possible lawsuit"[14] and that Nikhilananda "systematically censored Gupta in his 1942 translation of the *Kathāmṛta*" (630–31).

What is astonishing, however, is Kripal's next point: "An old friend of Isherwood's stood up after I finished delivering a paper on Ramakrishna's cross-dressing at the annual AAR meeting in Washington, DC, and said to me with a warm smile, 'Chris would be very pleased'" (631). Yet this "old friend of Isherwood's" approached Swami Tyagananda at the November 2000 annual meeting of the American Academy of Religion and declared that he had been completely misquoted. In fact, he said that he had never even *met* Christopher Isherwood, so he could hardly be considered "an old friend"![15]

Equally problematic, Kripal finishes his list of people supposedly censored by the Ramakrishna Order by adding Sumit Sarkar's 1991 publication "Ramakrishna and the Calcutta of His Times."[16] Kripal writes: "Sumit Sarkar's provocative socio-economic reading of the saint was only published in a considerably altered, 'censored' form." Yet this is completely untrue. Sumit Sarkar categorically denies ever having been censored or pressured in any way. When questioned on the matter, Sarkar states that there was "absolutely no pressure" from the Ramakrishna Mission—or anyone else for that matter—and he was not in any way prevented from writing or publishing or saying exactly what he wished.[17] Sarkar's 1991 essay bears a strong resemblance to his 1993 *An Exploration of the Ramakrishna Vivekananda Tradition*, which he seems to view as a more accurate reading of the *Kathāmṛta* than his unpublished 1985 essay.[18]

Kripal accurately records that "the Ramakrishna-Vivekananda Center in New York denied Carl Olson permission to quote from Nikhilananda's *The Gospel of Sri Ramakrishna* in his (AAR published) *The Mysterious Play of Kālī*," and the reason was, as Kripal states: "A committee appointed by the Center disagreed with Olson's interpretation" (631). This idiosyncratic decision was not directed by the Ramakrishna Order, which, we can be sure, never heard of either Olson's request or its subsequent rejection by the New York committee. The decision was directed solely by a committee of New York's Ramakrishna-Vivekananda Center, for which the rest of the Ramakrishna Order can bear no responsibility. Whatever the process that led to the committee's decision, it was clearly short-sighted and ultimately self-defeating. Decisions of these kinds are local in the extreme and do not involve the Ramakrishna Order as a whole. Scholars have frequently requested permission from other publishing centers of the Ramakrishna Order and have not experienced any difficulties. Obviously the committee seems to have confused the difference between giving permission to quote and endorsing the book's findings.

Kripal goes on to write that since the publication of *Kālī's Child*, he has engaged "the tradition" through various devotees "and one talented and eloquent swami (Swami Atmajnanananda)," whose critique of

Kālī's Child resulted in correcting "a few minor, tangential errors" for the book's second edition (631–32). Kripal concludes his response to Larson's article by arguing:

> Had I engaged the culture earlier in an open fashion and learned what I know now (after the hate-mail and a movement to have the book banned in India), I indeed would not, *could not*, have written this book. . . . I simply would have been too afraid. . . . [Censorship] was an all too real possibility. I simply was not willing to take that risk. . . .
>
> I have not abandoned or rejected dialogue with the tradition. . . . [but] I chose to practice my dialogue with the official tradition only *after* I had published my work. (632)

In the same issue of the *Journal of the American Academy of Religion*, Larson provides a spirited refutation. First clarifying points from his earlier article, Larson states that Ramakrishna's "mystical experiences and his severe emotional disorders" were "old news" and that the general discussion between mystical experience and psychopathology had been discussed and analyzed since the time of Romain Rolland (637). Larson reiterates his appreciation for Kripal's "unpacking of the homoerotic dimension in the saint's life." Larson goes on to state that his belief in the value of engaging with the tradition with "considerable openness, critical exchange, and healthy feedback" was his own personal approach, not a matter of ethics: "I fully recognize that many in our field are inclined to take quite different interpretive stances along the lines of a 'hermeneutic of suspicion' ... I have no 'ethical' problem with those stances, although I do not favor such stances in my own intellectual work" (638).

The strongest element in Larson's riposte is his answer to Kripal's claim that Larson was taking material from *Kālī's Child* out of context. "*Pace* Kripal," Larson writes, "these lines were not taken out of context. They are at the core of the final six or seven pages of his text and are good examples of what Whitehead called the 'fallacy of misplaced concreteness,' that is, taking one motif and thinking that one has given a satisfactory interpretation" (639). Countering Kripal's claim that *Kālī's Child* is not reductionistic, Larson ups the ante by stating that the book's "concluding analysis is doubly reductionist. First, it analyzes Ramakrishna's religious experience almost exclusively from the perspective of sexuality and the 'erotic.' Second, from within the remarkable range of sexual evidence, much of which goes quite beyond the homoerotic, the book focusses almost exclusively on the homoerotic" (638). Larson concludes his response by stating that an erotic reading "only brings us to the threshold of a substantive problem to be explored, namely, the manner in which our religious or mystical experience relates to all of the dimensions of our ordinary experience, including our sexuality" (639).

Up to this point in history, the focus of the *Kālī's Child* controversy was centered upon the Hindu community's anger at the perceived denigration of its saint and the distortion of its culture. From this point forward, the focus changed to the claims of a national movement to ban the book and the suppression of academic freedom.

Reframing the Debate

The year spanning Larson's first critique and Kripal's response was a momentous one, both for Hinduism scholars and for Hindus feeling the need to defend their tradition from those they believed to be ill-willed interlopers. This goes a long way to explain why the *Kālī's Child* controversy increased both in size and temperature and why the controversy remains a critical issue today. The earliest calls for banning *Kālī's Child* came from two angered readers of *The Statesman*.

On April 6, 1997, the *Sunday Times of India* noted that the "newspapers carrying the review have been inundated with angry letters" (although only one newspaper, *The Statesman*, carried the review) and D. P. Bagchi, the additional secretary and financial adviser in the commerce ministry, had written to the home ministry asking for a ban on the book.[19] The article further notes that "Senior home ministry officials, admitting to having received Mr. Bagchi's letter, said they had written to the Intelligence Bureau and the West Bengal government asking for their comments on the possible impact of the book on people's sensitivities. The ministry ... will give its verdict after a thorough reading of the book and on the basis of the IB [Intelligence Bureau] and West Bengal government's assessment." The article also added that Mr. Bagchi suggested that "India take up this matter with the U.S. government and ask it to impress upon the publishers to disallow the publication of 'such trash, totally devoid of a sense of history.'" Predictably, nothing happened in response to this initiative, as the issue was raised by only one incensed government official. When the present authors inquired about what had finally happened with the controversy, Tapan Roy, a Deputy Secretary assigned to the Rajya Sabha, India's upper house of Parliament, investigated the issue and "drew a blank."[20] Nothing at all happened, at least at this time. The debate would again blaze from Indian political embers, but not until 2001, and that, too, in a very different context.

Yet from this time forward the debate would be framed under the rubric of "censorship," "book banning," "death threats," "Hindutva," and "academic freedom." The second edition of *Kālī's Child*, published in 1998, quickly acquaints the reader with these topics in the book's Preface. Kripal discusses Sil's review, the readers' outraged responses and the requests that the book be banned. About these "devotional and Indian readers," Kripal writes: "[They] may begin by rejecting an author … for wanting to talk openly and honestly about the homosexual roots of Ramakrishna's mysticism only to find themselves … rejecting some of their own brothers and sisters … and, ironically, their own saint" (xiv). Kripal bemoans the fact that the heat which the controversy generated "tended to erase the larger textual, psychological, ontological, and mythical concerns of my work" (xix), yet, concurrently, he uses the argument of Hindus' angry reaction to confirm the truth he has told. The rage was due to a "deep cultural rejection of homosexuality" (xxi); thus, the furious response was a predictable reaction to exposing the "secret" of "Ramakrishna's homoerotic desires" (xv).

Why did those readers not see what Kripal saw? "Not because of any inherent fault in the book's arguments or evidence," Kripal writes, "but because there are at present simply too few social, cultural, psychological, and religious support structures available in such contexts to render its ideas widely thinkable." Tellingly, Kripal notes that as far as his detractors are concerned, it is difficult to "change one's world." Nevertheless, they should understand that *Kālī's Child* offers "a warm, liberating revelation of a shared humanity" (xxii).

Yet we find this "shared humanity" taking on all the characteristics of a Western humanism that speaks to Western secular values—values which are not necessarily shared by the rest of the world. Again we find a universalizing Western paradigm, with a Western scholar promoting a worldview which is presumed to be universal. If the "devotional and Indian" readers do not see what he sees, then their social, cultural, psychological, and religious support structures are at fault.[21] We can see this attitude crystallized in Kripal's correspondence with a Ramakrishna devotee who "*had learned to reread his own tradition*," Kripal writes, "in the new light of [*Kālī's Child*'s] theses and methods" (xxiii–xxiv, emphasis added). For the Hindu community, this scenario was all too familiar.

Kālī's Child's second edition marshals additional ammunition to back up its theses regarding Ramakrishna's sexuality as well as the Ramakrishna Order's "censorship" of the same. Kripal attempts to invoke Christopher Isherwood for support, declaring that the author was "quite frank about his homosexual reading of Ramakrishna" (xiii). Kripal further insists that Isherwood "was prevented by the tradition from writing about Ramakrishna's homosexual dimensions" (xiv). What are we to make of these allegations?

About "censorship," we may recall that Isherwood felt constrained while writing *Ramakrishna and His Disciples*. He had wanted to discuss Ramakrishna dressing as a woman in terms of "getting into drag," but knew that doing so was "out of the question" (Isherwood 1980, 249). Nevertheless, it is clear from Isherwood's writings that he did not believe Ramakrishna was homosexual. Unlike most people at the time, Isherwood was not shocked by the idea and was able to easily ponder its possibility. Yet having seriously examined the question, Isherwood concluded that Ramakrishna was not homosexual. In fact, Isherwood states in *My Guru and His Disciple* that accusations concerning Ramakrishna's homosexuality were "irresponsible" (247). Despite this, Kripal surmises that it was Isherwood himself who "wrote (autobiographically, I suspect) about a person who in 1962 had written about Ramakrishna as a 'homosexual who had had to struggle hard to overcome his lust for his young disciple later to be known as Vivekananda'" (KC, xiii).

Had Kripal done serious research, however, he would have discovered that the book referred to here was not written by Isherwood at all. It was written by Ann Marshall under the title *Hunting the Guru in India* (London: Victor Gollancz, 1963).[22] About this book and Prabhavananda's reaction to it, Isherwood writes:

> Swami somehow got to hear about a book. . . . The author [Marshall] had at first felt attracted by Ramakrishna's personality but had decided against him on the ground that he was (I quote) a homosexual who had had to struggle hard to overcome his lust for his young disciple later to be known as Vivekananda. (1980, 247)

On this point Isherwood is particularly illuminating:

> It didn't surprise me that someor reading about Ramakrishna for the first time should be disconcerted by the extremely emotional way in which he expressed his love for his young male disciples—and that such a reader should also fail to realize that Ramakrishna's kind of love feels no inhibitions because it makes no demands. Most of us are familiar only with the kind of love—be it parental or romantic—which does demand something in return. So we suspect Ramakrishna's love of having ulterior homosexual motives.

> There is another excuse for accusing Ramakrishna of homosexuality; he sometimes dressed in woman's clothes. As a boy, he did this for a joke; he was a talented impersonator and mimic. As an adult, he wished to experience every sort of religious mood, including the mood of a female devotee of Krishna. He used to say that one "should make the outside the same as the inside"; and so, when he took part in certain pujas, he wore woman's clothes, with ornaments and a wig, to complement his devotional mood. This naturally scandalized the conventionally pious. Ramakrishna regarded the distinction between the sexes as a part of *maya*, the cosmic illusion; therefore, he can't have thought of himself as being exclusively masculine or feminine. (248–49)

Thus it seems fairly obvious that the allegations presented in *Kālī's Child* regarding Isherwood's "homosexual reading of Ramakrishna" are simply not true.

To provide further proof of Ramakrishna's homoerotic inclinations, Kripal musters Shivanath Shastri's reminiscence of Ramakrishna where, in a carriage en route to see the lions in Kolkata's Zoological Gardens, Ramakrishna covered his head with a chaddar in the fashion of married women, put his arm around Shivanath's waist, and said, "Don't you see I am a woman for the time being; I am travelling with my lover." Shastri continues by stating that Ramakrishna "threw his arm around my waist and began to make a sort of dancing movement, seated as he was, as a mark of his great pleasure. At this point there came on his fit or trance. . ." This (minus the portion referring to the fact that Ramakrishna was seated) is where Kripal leaves the quotation (KC, xxiii).

Yet had Shivanath been allowed to finish his sentence (and complete the paragraph), the reader would discover that Shivanath went on to say something quite significant:

> and then I witnessed a scene that I shall never forget. His whole countenance was aglow with a strange spiritual light, and before he became fully unconscious, he began to pray with incoherent words, in the following fashion—"O Mother, my beloved Mother, do not make me unconscious. O Mother, I am going to see the lions in the Zoological Gardens. O Mother, I may have a fall from the carriage. Do, do let me be all right till the journey is finished." At this point he became thoroughly unconscious, leaning on my arm for some minutes. After consciousness had returned he once more began conversation in his usual childlike and simple manner. (Mookerjee, 25)

There are several points here worth noting. Most significant is that while Kripal sees Ramakrishna's actions as indicative of homoerotic behavior, Shastri himself did not. Rather, he confirms Ramakrishna's spiritual experience. Shastri tells us that he saw Ramakrishna's "countenance ... aglow with a strange spiritual light" and it was a scene that he would never forget. Shastri does not give any indication anywhere that he was the recipient of Ramakrishna's erotic attraction.

What we *do* see is Ramakrishna jubilant over the prospect of seeing the lions in the zoo and happy that he is being accompanied by Shivanath, a man he often praised. In this joyous, playful mood, Ramakrishna does what he often did with his disciples in Dakshineswar: he entertained and played by mimicry. There is no sign that Shivanath found this odd or unseemly, and he was a Brahmo highly sensitive to elements indecorous. In fact, Shivanath informs the reader, as he did Ramakrishna himself, that he visited Ramakrishna less frequently in later years because Shivanath disapproved of the "objectionable characters, such as the actors of the Indian theaters" who visited Ramakrishna. "I did not like to be associated with such men," Shivanath writes (Mookerjee, 25). Such a rarefied moral weathervane as Shivanath saw no problem with Ramakrishna's behavior in the carriage. In fact, he tells us that it was an experience he would never forget.

Not only that. The *Jībanabṛttānta* records Shivanath's words regarding Ramakrishna:

> Who has his kind of love for God which made him fall on the bank of the Ganga and cry "Mother! Mother!"? Caitanya had that kind of love; he used to pull out his hair and rub his face on the ground for the vision of Kṛṣṇa. Jesus had that kind of love; he remained without food for forty days. . . . Paramahaṁsadeva [Ramakrishna] belongs to that category. When a spiritual soul like him is born in a country after a gap of four hundred years [i.e. after Caitanya], that country never lacks in spirituality. (JB, 213)

After Ramakrishna's death, Shivanath wrote that "[Ramakrishna's] memory is now feeding hundreds of earnest souls." Shivanath concludes by noting that while his association with Ramakrishna was short, its effect was "strengthening many a spiritual thought in me. He was certainly one of the most remarkable personalities I have come across in life" (Mookerjee, 26). We find no "troubled," no "conflicted," no "homoerotic" saint here.

Implicit in *Kālī's Child*'s selective quotations from Shivanath Shastri is the assumption of uniform gender roles which are consistent over time and culture. Indeed, if there is one obvious fact which is repeatedly overlooked in *Kālī's Child* and a number of other studies on Ramakrishna which precede and succeed it, it is that male and female gender roles and gender expectations were vastly different in nineteenth-century Bengal from contemporary North American and European models. Thus what may appear in the contemporary West as sexualized behavior on Ramakrishna's part was not seen as such by his contemporaries. As Ruth Vanita and Saleem Kidwai point out in *Same-Sex Love in India*: "Ideas of what is sexual and what is not change with place and time" (xiii). While this should be obvious, when it comes to Ramakrishna and his behavior with his disciples, these facts are not addressed. Several contemporary scholars have noted Ramakrishna's physical intimacy with his male disciples: he touches their chin, he feeds them with his hands, etc. He expresses his longing to see them. While a North American reader may find this abnormally close and perhaps even unsettling, this behavior would not have been considered at all unusual in nineteenth-century Bengal. Vanita and Kidwai further remind us that in many societies, a person's primary emotional attachment could well be to a friend of his or her own gender, which is perfectly compatible with marriage and procreation. They write:

> It is only relatively recently in human history that the heterosexual monogamous relationship has come to be viewed as necessarily a married person's chief emotional outlet. Although this view is dominant today, in many parts of the world, including many parts of India, the earlier view still coexists with it. (xiii)

Today's Western monolithic view of gender roles has not only stigmatized other cultures' gender roles and expectations, but it has also proved destructive in the West to the emotional ties which can be provided by close friendships. By the nineteenth century, Freud and others labeled these close relationships "homosexual," and thus in Europe and North America by the twentieth century, "the heterosexual couple became more exclusively romanticized in movies and fiction as the individual's primary source of social support, cutting him or her off from kin and friends" (xiv). By apotheosizing the heterosexual couple, Western rigid gender norms served to condemn other gender roles to the status of deviancy.

While this topic could be discussed at further length, we would do well to move on to other areas that also need discussion. In *Kālī's Child*'s second edition, Kripal argues that the history of religions, psychoanalysis, Christian mysticism and India's Tantric traditions "all ... know that the secret of the mystical is the erotic" (KC, xviii). He further contends that his "dialectical category of 'the erotic' has been misread by some as flatly monodimensional, as if it meant simply 'sex,' when in fact the erotic only begins with physical sexuality and moves out (really 'up') from there into the sublime, 'sublimated' realms of symbolic vision, mystical experience, mythology, and theology" (xv). Yet as more than one critic observed, for all intents and purposes Kripal's use of the term "erotic" nearly always refers to the purely sexual. Kripal again takes up the subject of "the erotic":

> To speak of the erotic ... as a dialectical phenomenon that develops only through ... spirals of regression and progression, of sexual expression and spiritual experience, of neurotic suffering and liberative healing, and which finally culminates in a transethical psycho-physiological transformation of genuine ontological significance—is not to practice a prurient sensationalism (or more bizarrely, a misplaced "orientalism"). Nor is it to reduce the quite genuine mystical experiences of Ramakrishna to simple sex. (xviii)

We argue that, in *Kālī's Child*, we are indeed looking upon Orientalism, of which "prurient sensationalism" has often been a boon companion.

The second edition of *Kālī's Child* notes the corrections that were done as the result of Atmajnanananda's critique. Kripal apologizes for "any emotional pain" that he may have caused his readers by his errors—in particular, translating *māg* as "bitch." Kripal further acknowledges his embarrassment in discovering that Datta's *Jībanabṛttānta*—far from being suppressed by the Ramakrishna Order—was actually published by it (xix). Kripal reports that these errors have been corrected for the book's second edition. More importantly, Kripal declares that "nothing that has been advanced so far has convinced me that my hermeneutical model is wrong or misguided or even exaggerated. Quite the contrary, numerous events—from my revisiting of previous scholarship to my personal correspondence with a number of appreciative devotees ... have convinced me of the correctness of my original model." Kripal is assured of the soundness of his thesis because it is contextualized within "a long line of scholarly consensus." Further, there is "support from within the tradition" for his thesis, which problematizes "any simplistic dichotomy between my conclusions and the tradition itself" (xx).

That said, Kripal announces: "The case of Ramakrishna's homosexuality ... seems to be closed" (xxi). But for the insider community, there was never a "case" to begin with. Again, one has to ask, Why does he see what he sees, and why do we see what we see? Kripal's "long line of scholarly consensus" consists of Jeffrey Masson, whose pathologizing interpretation of Ramakrishna (as well as Buddha, Hinduism, Tantra, etc.) we have already seen. Kripal also invokes Malcolm McLean's unpublished translation of the *Kathāmṛta* and mentions Sumit Sarkar's 1985 *Kathāmṛta as Text*. Yet Sarkar's later writings on Ramakrishna do not suggest Ramakrishna was homosexual and Sarkar himself indicates that *Kathāmṛta as Text* is not representative of his final thought.[23] It is no doubt for this reason that *Kathāmṛta as Text* remained an unpublished manuscript, not because the Ramakrishna Order was "suppressing" it—the mention of which Sarkar found absurd.

Intriguingly, Kripal adds Sudhir Kakar's name to the list because "Kakar pointed out that Ramakrishna could be identified as a 'secondary transsexual'" (xxi). But in fact, Kakar writes something altogether different: "Just as the writings of medieval European female mystics ... have been analyzed as expressions of a pathological, hysterical sexuality, it would not be difficult to diagnose Ramakrishna in traditional Freudian terms as a secondary transsexual." Kakar goes on to say something radically at odds with what Kripal suggests: "Any transsexual or homosexual labels may obscure [Ramakrishna's] sense of comfort and easy familiarity with the feminine components of his self. It may hide the fact that the freeing of femininity from repression or disavowal in man and *vice versa* in a woman may be a great human achievement rather than an illness or a deviation" (Kakar 1991, 33).

Equally intriguing is Kripal's statement of "support from within the tradition." Upon being personally questioned about this point, Kripal said that "monks" within the Ramakrishna Order had agreed with his thesis.[24] When questioned more closely about the "monks" who supported it, "they" turned out to be "one"—the one referred to as "the open-minded, open-hearted monastic who found real inspiration in [*Kālī's Child*]" (KC, xxiii). That one monk changed his opinion about *Kālī's Child* after reading Atmajnanananda's and Tyagananda's rebuttals. In fact, this monk enthusiastically distributed Tyagananda's rebuttal at the November 2000 American Academy of Religion meeting and would have liked to publish Tyagananda's rebuttal in book form. The monk in question is American, does not read Bengali, and admittedly does not have extensive knowledge of the source texts.[25]

Kripal's later writings on the controversy invoke Parama Roy's writings on Ramakrishna as well. Parama Roy is not a Ramakrishna scholar. Her writings have neither influenced *Kālī's Child* nor has she particularly contributed to the debate surrounding the book. Yet Roy does merit passing discussion, since Kripal's later writings concerning the *Kālī's Child* controversy (Kripal 2002, 2004) invoke her chapter, "As the Master Saw Her," as indigenous verification of his theses.[26]

Parama Roy

Parama Roy's 1998 *Indian Traffic: Identities in Question in Colonial and Postcolonial India* includes one chapter which centers on Swami Vivekananda's Irish disciple, Nivedita. In discussing Nivedita, Roy includes a lengthy discussion of Ramakrishna and Vivekananda. One significant problem with Roy's chapter is that her writing on Ramakrishna is extremely derivative, leaning heavily on secondary sources such as Sumit Sarkar, Partha Chatterjee, Gayatri Spivak and others. As a result, her research on Ramakrishna is thin: there are no citations from Bengali primary texts such as the *Kathāmṛta* or the *Līlāprasaṅga*, for example. Yet as problematic as her derivative scholarship may be, more problematic are Roy's pronouncements concerning Ramakrishna and Vivekananda.

Roy claims, for example, that Vivekananda "had been erotically solicited for discipleship by Ramakrishna" (111), and consequently Vivekananda "remained always ambivalent about his guru" (105). Roy then adds that Vivekananda "was nonetheless unable and unwilling to shake him off completely." Roy refers to Ramakrishna's "erotic solicitations" of Vivekananda more than once, but gives no indication of what such a "solicitation" might be. Would it be inducing Vivekananda's ecstasy? Feeding him with his own hands? Touching him? The reader is not informed.

It would appear that much of Roy's assumptions regarding Ramakrishna as well as Vivekananda's relationship with him hinge on Ramakrishna's earlier sādhana of *madhura* bhāva (which Roy defines as "becoming woman"), along with Ramakrishna's statement, which she cites from Nikhilananda's *Gospel*. Roy quotes:

> A man can change his nature by imitating another's character. By transposing on to yourself the attributes of woman, you gradually destroy lust and other sensual drives. You begin to behave like women. I have noticed that men who play female parts in the theatre speak like women or brush their teeth like women while bathing. (97; citing GSR, 176)

Though Roy cites Nikhilananda's *Gospel* here, her quotation from Nikhilananda is inaccurate. The quotation from Nikhilananda is as follows:

> A man can change his nature by imitating another's character. He can get rid of a passion like lust by assuming the feminine mood. He gradually comes to act exactly like a woman. I have noticed that men who take female parts in the theatre speak like women or brush their teeth like women while bathing. (GSR, 176)

As we can see, Roy changes the "he" to "you" and she adds "transposing on yourself," which is not in Nikhilananda's text. Whether this is done to mislead or is simply the result of sloppy scholarship, is impossible to tell. Roy continues by stating that "this 'transvestic' discipline ... was not enjoined upon Narendranath Dutta ... whom Ramakrishna identified at several points as firmly fixed in a masculine identification" (97). With this Roy concludes: "It was clearly [Narendra's] masculinity that had attracted the guru" (115).

Several points: First, *madhura* bhāva is not about "becoming woman." The purpose of this sādhana is to become identified as one of Kṛṣṇa's gopīs, Kṛṣṇa being the sole male in Vrindaban, everyone else being female.[27] How this manifests via external dress and behavior is entirely secondary to the internal identification as a gopī, which defines one's relationship with Kṛṣṇa. Merely "becoming woman" does not constitute a spiritual practice. Roy writes of Ramakrishna's "conquest of desire through becoming woman" (99)—as if "becoming woman" were the only practice necessary to remove desire and as if it were the only spiritual practice Ramakrishna ever suggested, which, as we know, is inaccurate.

Throughout *Kālī's Child*, Kripal effectively pathologizes the sādhana of *madhura* bhāva, rejecting the possibility of it being a valid sādhana by identifying it as a trauma-based response associated with Mathur Babu. It appears that Parama Roy misinterprets *madhura* bhāva just as thoroughly as *Kālī's Child* does. As we know, Ramakrishna was profoundly influenced by Bengal's Gauḍīya Vaiṣṇava tradition. In this tradition, as David Haberman writes, "even men must somehow emulate the gopīs . . . to attain the highest state." He continues:

> Gauḍīya Vaiṣṇavas agree that the ultimate religious goal is to be transformed into a character in Vraja, usually a *gopī*, by imitating the original characters of Vraja ... or rather, since one's true identity is a *gopī*, to overcome—by imitating the original *gopīs*—the ignorance which keeps one from realizing that fact. (2001, 95)

How one actually goes about doing this has been a matter of dispute. Haberman writes that those religious traditions which suggest imitating divine models face certain problems. He asks: "Is the imitation to be literal or symbolic, external or internal?" (94). Ramakrishna, as we know, was quite literal in all his sādhanas, imitating Hanumān by affixing a tail to himself, eating bananas with their skins on and living in a tree while he practiced the *dāsya* bhāva sādhana. Ramakrishna was clearly a man who threw himself into external observances when he thought they would produce results.

Thus the fact that Ramakrishna would dress as a woman while practicing *madhura* bhāva is both in keeping with Ramakrishna's temperament as well as in keeping with the practitioners of *rāgānugā* bhakti sādhana, who "physically imitate the *gopīs* in all ways—dress, external behavior, and so forth" (Haberman 2001, 96). While this practice is rare today, though certainly not unheard of, it was frequently practiced in earlier years. It is worth remembering that the famed Gauḍīya saint and disciple of Caitanya, Rūpa Gosvāmī, gave instructions to the effect that the imitation of gopīs was to be done both mentally as well as "with the *sādhaka-rūpa*"—with one's own physical body (96–97). Those literal adherents of rāgānugā bhakti sādhana "physically imitate the *gopīs* by taking on the dress and behavior of a woman. They believe that since their true and essential identity is a *gopī*, they should dress and act the part" (98). To dismiss or reduce these aspirations to "cross-dressing" or interpreting them through the lens of a presumed calamity does injustice to a large number of Gauḍīya practitioners as well as to the tradition itself.

Apart from her profound misunderstanding of *madhura* bhāva, what is striking about Roy's chapter is her presumption that Ramakrishna's *madhura* bhāva sādhana was the most significant aspect of his sādhana and his advice about acquiring feminine characteristics was the signal point of his spiritual teachings. But any serious study of Ramakrishna would make it clear that this was not the case. Again and again Ramakrishna returned to *īśvar lābh*, attaining God, no matter which tradition one followed, no matter which sādhana one practiced. The tangential recommendation of assuming female characteristics to remove lust was simply that—tangential, absolutely peripheral, the point being to remove any desire which stood in the way of the ultimate goal of *īśvar lābh*. Moreover, while Ramakrishna generally suggested assuming the characteristics of another gender to overcome lust, there is no record of anyone whom he actually instructed to do so.

As is well known, Ramakrishna said that he could not speak of himself as a man: *Āmi āpnāke pū (pūrūṣ) bolte pāri nā* (KA 2.155). He also said on occasion that he had the nature of a woman. Significantly, however, this "nature" does not indicate or constitute his desired gender or his sexual preference. It is a deeper indication of a person's psychic structure and emotional integration. It is apparent from the source texts that when Ramakrishna speaks along these lines, no one is surprised, shocked or repelled. There were plenty who argued with Ramakrishna on a number of occasions and a number of individuals felt quite free in contesting his actions and statements. Narendra, Dr. Sarkar, and Hazra come to mind, but there were a number of others as well. Yet feminine identification was not a point of interest or contention. It is noticeably unnoticed. As Bengali psychologist and sociologist Ashis Nandy writes:

> "Bisexuality" in India has always been considered an indicator of saintliness and yogic accomplishments. Perhaps it is considered an indicator of having successfully coped with or transcended one's deepest conflicts about femininity and masculinity. . . . One who is close to godliness is expected to show ... a little more ability to transcend the barriers imposed by one's own sexual selfhood. He is expected to subscribe to values which are unfettered by society's prevalent sexual identities. (1980, 38)

It is important to keep in mind that for Nandy, as even Parama Roy has noted, the term "bisexuality" "has everything to do with identification and nothing at all with object choice" (Roy, 98). Nandy's assessment is seconded by psychoanalyst Alan Roland, who reminds us: "Indian men incorporate much more of maternal-feminine qualities than is characteristic of Western men, have a greater degree of bisexuality in terms of these more maternal-feminine components" (Roland, 1996, 137). It is no accident that sexual impropriety was not among the criticisms leveled against Ramakrishna by his contemporaries.

Roy's assertion that Vivekananda remained ambivalent about Ramakrishna is unsupported by any evidence and, in fact, all source texts argue to the contrary.[28] Even when the young Narendra was arguing endlessly with Ramakrishna, even when Narendra told Ramakrishna that he was delusional, Narendra's love and respect for Ramakrishna kept bringing him back to Dakshineswar. Roy attempts to persuade the reader that Vivekananda was repelled by Ramakrishna's "infatuated pursuit," but she neglects to tell the reader that Narendra kept coming back to see Ramakrishna even when Ramakrishna purposely ignored him.[29]

Roy backs up her "erotic solicitation" premise by citing the following quotation from Sumit Sarkar's *Kathamrita as Text*: "Girish Ghosh confessed that seeing Ramakrishna 'playing' with a young disciple made him recall a 'terrible canard' that he had once heard about the saint" (Sarkar 1985, 103). While several contemporary Ramakrishna scholars, including Jeffrey Kripal, have referred to Sarkar's quotation, others now cite this quotation from *Kālī's Child*, which quotes Sarkar who quotes yet another source. But no one has bothered to look at the original quotation—everyone seemingly content to quote Sarkar or Kripal. But who and what, after all, was Sarkar quoting?

The book Sarkar cites is *Śrī Rāmakṛṣṇa o Baṅga Raṅgamañca*, written by Naliniranjan Chattopadhyay, a college lecturer who was a close devotee of the Ramakrishna Order. Chattopadhyay's book quotes from Girish Ghosh's reminiscences, in which Girish recalls one of his first encounters with Ramakrishna. One evening Ramakrishna visited the Star Theater and began speaking with Girish on many subjects. "I felt as if a big current were rising to my head and falling," Girish remembered. "In the meantime, [Ramakrishna] became immersed in bhāva. In that state of bhāva, it looked as if he were playing with a devotee boy" (*ekṭi bālak bhakter sohit bhābābasthāy jeno krīḍā korite lāgilen*). The word "play" (*krīḍā*) means just that in Bengali. Play. A playground, for example, is *krīḍāṅgan*. Girish continues:

> Long back, I had heard criticism (*nindā*) of Paramahaṁsadev from a very wicked person (*durdānto pāṣaṇḍa*). Seeing this play with the boy, the thought of that criticism rose in my mind. Paramahaṁsadev's *bhāva* came to an end. He looked at me and said, "There is crookedness (*bāṁk*) in your mind." I thought, there are, of course, many crookednesses [in my mind] but I did not understand which crookedness he was referring to. I asked him, "How will crookedness go?" Paramahaṁsadev said, "Develop faith" (*biśvās koro*). (Chattopadhyay, 41)

While Sumit Sarkar has translated *nindā* as "terrible canard," there is no word in the Bengali text which suggests the adjective "terrible" before *nindā*, which means criticism, slander or vilification. Girish simply states: *Paramahaṁsadeber nindā śuniyāchilām*: I had heard criticism (or vilification or slander) of Paramahaṁsadev. Further, Sarkar's sentence, "Girish *confessed* that seeing Ramakrishna 'playing' with a young disciple," makes it appear as if Girish was unwillingly admitting something about Ramakrishna. Yet the "confession" we find here is Girish's own reminiscence, as he tells the world that the minute the slander about Ramakrishna came to his mind, Ramakrishna instantly came down from his bhāva to a normal state of consciousness and made a comment on the crooked (*bāṁk*) state of Girish's mind. Girish readily concurred with Ramakrishna's assessment: Girish's concern was how to remove those many "crookednesses," not about the *nindā* he had heard about Ramakrishna.

We have no idea of the nature of the criticism or slander that Girish heard "long ago." We only know that seeing Ramakrishna in bhāva, playing as it were (*jeno*) with a devotee boy, Girish remembered the *nindā* that he had heard long ago. We can, however, speculate about the nature of the criticism or slander which Girish heard. One possibility is that since Girish writes that he heard the criticism "long ago," the criticism could very well have been that Ramakrishna was insane; after all, when in bhāva Ramakrishna often seemed to be conversing with an imaginary person. This was the most common criticism of Ramakrishna, especially before Ramakrishna became popular in later years. There were more than a few people who believed that Ramakrishna's visions and extreme longing for God were the result of simple insanity. Swami Prabhavananda recalled that when he was growing up in Vishnupur, a village located not far from Kamarpukur, the old village women still spoke of *pāgal Gadai*, crazy Gadai (Ramakrishna's childhood name).

Another strong possibility concerning the nature of the slander is a memory of Girish's own. Before Girish had been introduced to Ramakrishna, Girish was invited by his neighbor, Balaram Bose—a close householder disciple of Ramakrishna—to visit his home to see Ramakrishna. Girish accepted Balaram's invitation and found Ramakrishna already there, seated next to Bidhu, a nautch (dancing) girl who was singing devotional songs. "I used to think that those who consider themselves paramahaṁsas or yogis do not speak with anybody," Girish said. "They do not salute anybody. If strongly urged, they allow others to serve them." Girish continues:

> But the behavior of this paramahaṁsa was quite different. With the utmost humility he was showing respect to everybody by bowing his head on the ground. An old friend of mine, pointing at him, said sarcastically: "Bidhu has had a previous intimacy with him. That's why he is laughing and joking with her." But I did not like his insinuations. (Chetanananda 1990, 330)

This does indeed seem to be a likely source of the *nindā*. Another possible "slander" was that Ramakrishna was epileptic and his religious experiences were the result of epileptic seizures; this "slander" also had some currency in earlier years as well. While there are endless speculations that can be made about that mysterious *nindā*, we would do well to keep in mind that while Ramakrishna had any number of critics, there is no record of his contemporaries ever having questioned his sexual orientation, though they certainly did question his sanity.

In conclusion, Kripal's claim that Roy's work was proof of indigenous acceptance of *Kālī's Child* may have more to do with her recommendation of *Kālī's Child* "for a careful and fascinating reading of the relationship of Ramakrishna's 'homosexuality' to his mysticism" (Roy, 195) than to Roy's own merits as a Ramakrishna scholar.[30]

Later Reviews

Though the dust from *Kālī's Child* had largely settled in Kolkata, reviews in Western journals continued to appear, brought about, one suspects, by increased interest due to the unexpected appearance of Hindu furor.

Hugh Urban

In April 1998 Hugh Urban wrote another review of *Kālī's Child*, this time for *Journal of Religion*. In this review, Urban refers to the "intense controversy among both Western and Indian audiences," and goes on to make a point which begged for further investigation: "The same work that won a major award from the American Academy of Religion has also been the target of scathing attack by Bengali readers outraged at Kripal's suggestion that their national hero may have had homosexual inclinations." Urban characterizes the book as "truly original, often scandalously provocative, and perhaps revolutionary" and adds: "Kripal's book penetrates the layers of pious obfuscation … to recover the original Bengali texts … which had been mistranslated and censored by later disciples" (Urban 1998, 318). Urban nevertheless observes that the book has troubling problems: "Perhaps most pervasive of these is Kripal's tendency toward sensationalism." Urban goes on to say that it is not "difficult to understand why some Indian critics should regard Kripal's work as yet another example of neocolonialism and the West's exploitation of the 'exotic Orient'" (319).

Steven F. Walker

Steven F. Walker's review in *Religion* questions a number of Kripal's theses while praising the author for "locating … the ways in which the image of Ramakrishna in the West was made to seem more respectable to potentially censorious Occidental eyes through the omission or bowdlerization of potentially offending references to the sensual and the sexual" (211). Kripal is persuasive, Walker states, "when he foregrounds the role that Tantrism played in Ramakrishna's mystical *sadhana* and later teachings." He observes that the book appears at a time "when interest in Tantrism is running high in the West" (210). Conversely, Walker finds that the book's "psychoanalytic foundation is shaky" and

Kripal "heavy-handed in his diagnosis of unconscious homosexuality as the key to some of Ramakrishna's 'secrets'" (209). Kripal "succumbs too quickly to the pleasures of armchair psychology, providing facile explanations of complex phenomena" (210). "The problem," Walker states,

> is that he has got it wrong.... Kripal seems to have no particular theory as to what might constitute homosexuality and its characteristics. He simply assumes we know what it is.... This casual approach is fine for beach reading, for which repressed homosexuality is an entertaining, if somewhat pleasantly old-fashioned, topic, but it is more than a bit thin for a scholarly book. (210)

Walker goes on to say that "even if [Ramakrishna's] spiritual practice of cross dressing were to be interpreted as betraying the presence of unsublimated sexuality, it would still be no clear indication of unconscious homosexuality. Many other such examples ... fail to convince this reader that Ramakrishna, who ... as an adept of the Tantra, was singularly free from shame and aversion, would have been unable to recognize homosexual tendencies in himself and would have been fortunate if only Kripal had been born soon enough to enlighten him about them." Walker notes that "there is much [in Ramakrishna] that points toward a pronounced feminine gender self-image. This was an indicator of unconscious homosexuality is dubious." Preferring Kakar's view of Ramakrishna to Kripal's, Walker states that "after reading Kripal in the light of Kakar, I would say that Ramakrishna was not so much 'Kali's Child' as 'the Child *as* Kali' or (to amend Kripal's title even further) 'Kali's Self'" (211).

William Radice

William Radice's 1998 favorable review in the *Bulletin of the School of Oriental and African Studies* mentions the storm *Kālī's Child* produced "in the still quite prudish atmosphere of Calcutta, where Ramakrishna is deeply revered and the Ramakrishna Mission ... is widely respected." Proficient in Bengali, Radice observes that "the praise and prizes [*Kālī's Child*] ... received, if anything worsened the outrage." Radice largely blames Sil's "lurid review" for provoking the strength of the outburst, though he notes that with "the growing emphasis on the erotic aspects of Ramakrishna's visions" such a reaction "was inevitable." While Radice characterizes Sil's *Ramakrishna Paramahamsa* as "mischievous," Radice finds Kripal's approach "subtle and respectful. . . . Whereas Sil set out to capsize Ramakrishna, Kripal wishes to rescue him" (160).

Radice discusses the "intriguing possibility" that more of M's diaries are in existence, "preserved under lock and key by the Ramakrishna Mission and are still 'off limits to questioning minds'" (160). As we have already seen, however, this assumption is not correct. Radice quotes Kripal as his authority, but M's diaries are not, nor have they ever been, "under lock and key by the Ramakrishna Mission."

Not an issue, Radice writes, is "the saint's homosexual leanings and his horror of women as lovers"; the more interesting question is "would Ramakrishna's visions have been as rich and intense if he had not been so constituted? Can one imagine a heterosexual Ramakrishna? Kripal's resounding answer is 'No'" (160)—a point with which Radice appears to concur. Finding Kripal more persuasive than Kakar, Radice sees Kripal's most important achievement as "his successful reconciliation of Tantra with psychoanalysis" (161). Radice asks whether Kripal makes "a mountain out of a molehill" with his emphasis on Ramakrishna's *guhya kathā* —"secret talks"—which only number eighteen. Radice responds: "Not if one accepts his [Kripal's] view that these passages take one to the core of Ramakrishna's mysticism, and are therefore a lens through which one can validly read the whole *Kathāmṛta*" (160). Radice concludes with the hope that in the future, Kripal will "give equal attention to the vastly greater proportion of [the *Kathāmṛta*] that was *not* secret," adding that "the erotic-Tantric lens is not the only one through which the *Kathāmṛta* can be read" (161).

John S. Hawley

In his review of *Kālī's Child* which appeared in *History of Religions*, John S. Hawley boldly declares: "Only a few books make such a major contribution to their field that from the moment of publication things are never again quite the same. *Kālī's Child* is such a book" (1998, 401). Hawley points out that Kripal is the first author to focus persuasively "on Ramakrishna's sexuality as being religiously significant" (402). He asserts that "Kripal offers ample proof that Ramakrishna ... had a very significantly homosexual side" (401). Hawley then questions: "Why should Ramakrishna's homoeroticism be so disturbing?" Hawley suggests that this is partially due to Kripal's subversion of "the disembodied Vedantin reading of Ramakrishna" that was presented through *The Gospel of Sri Ramakrishna*, the "sanitized, bowdlerized translation" of the *Kathāmṛta*. In describing a visit to New York's Vedanta Society and what he observed there, Hawley locates what he believes to be the animus behind the visceral rejection of *Kālī's Child*: the book's theses run utterly contrary to the tradition that has grown around the personalities of Ramakrishna, Vivekananda and Sarada Devi. For Ramakrishna devotees, the position of Sarada would become especially problematic. A homoerotically oriented Ramakrishna would make Sarada's celibacy a matter not of choice but of necessity, effectively removing her from the pedestal upon which the tradition has placed her. In this case, Ramakrishna and Sarada's "partnership cannot have been founded on the idealized, mutually shared sexual self-abnegation that sectarian writers wanted to believe, though it is possible that Sharada Devi thought it was" (402). Hawley seems to suggest here that Sarada herself may not have been aware of her husband's presumed sexual orientation.

Hawley notes that some of the followers of Ramakrishna were "struggling" to assimilate Kripal's analysis. This is reminiscent of Kripal's appreciation for a Ramakrishna devotee who "had learned to reread his own tradition" as a result of "the new light" provided by *Kālī's Child* (KC, xxiv). In both cases, the suggestion is that the tradition's own interpretative model falls short, its light being comparatively dim. By contrast, Hawley sees *Kālī's Child*'s strength in that it "bathes psychoanalysis in the light of Tantra" and Kripal, by revealing Ramakrishna's "homoerotic secret," is able to turn "that secret into a searching beacon" (Hawley 1998, 404).

Nodding to the controversy swirling about *Kālī's Child*, Hawley states that the book has been "a bit of a bombshell" (401). That said, he finds it to be "a wonderfully exuberant book—spirited, sympathetic, complex" (404). He does point out, however, that in his own university, students of South Asian descent questioned *Kālī's Child*'s presence on the syllabus, at least without a "balancing" text to offer another view of Ramakrishna (401).

Brian Hatcher

Brian Hatcher's 1999 article, "Kālī's Problem Child: Another look at Jeffrey Kripal's Study of Śrī Rāmakṛṣṇa," was published in the *International Journal of Hindu Studies*. The article states that Hatcher and his student Andrew Busch journeyed to India in order to have the student learn about Ramakrishna. During an informal gathering which consisted of "another university professor, a novelist, a couple physicians, and a journalist" who were "admittedly not a representative cross-section of Calcuttan society," the discussion turned to *Kālī's Child*.

None of those in the room were offended by Kripal's theses; one physician laughed, and exclaimed, "What a marvelous idea!" (165). From this group of five Bengalis, there were questions for Kripal, such as: "What could it mean to speak of homosexual behavior in Rāmakṛṣṇa's world?" Yet we are also told that "there was no defensiveness and certainly no outraged Bengali pride." Hatcher tells us of this scenario while informing the reader of the article's purpose: "In light of the wildly varying responses to Kripal's book, it may be worthwhile to consider some of the issues surrounding its critical reception" (166).

While Kripal asserts that "Brian Hatcher ... travelled to Calcutta to do fieldwork on the reception of my work there, [and] found support for it among Bengalis" (Kripal 2002, 199),[31] Hatcher and Busch had a very different story to tell. There is, in fact, nothing in the preliminary report filed by Hatcher and Busch which suggests that the book "found support among the Bengalis." On the contrary, Busch's and Hatcher's report states:

> The planned project was not able to work for the simple fact that I underestimated the amount of hostility that the Bengali people, especially people affiliated with the Mission, had towards Kripal and his book. . . . I found that the only people who were willing to speak with me about the book were scholars, and they were generally not open to Kripal's thesis, save for two who have been living in the West for an extended period of time. . . .
>
> I have recently completed a rough draft of a paper that questions a scholar's rights and motives in using his or her own cultural constructs to analyze something that has no similar constructs. This is the case with Kripal and "Kali's Child." . . . Overall, my experience in India made me question what it means to have academic freedom, and how truth has different meanings for different people. (Busch and Hatcher, 1998)

Hatcher frames the first portion of his essay under the subheading: "What Kripal Was Up Against," which does not suggest so much critical analysis as it does circling the wagons. Hatcher asserts that Ramakrishna *was* Kālī's Child—universally confirmed both by scholars and popular Kolkata posters—yet upon entering the Ramakrishna Mission Institute of Culture in Kolkata, Hatcher complains, Kālī is not to be found. Hatcher compares the Kālī temple in Dakshineswar with "the almost compulsive cleanliness of the Rāmakṛṣṇa folks" who "have thrown the mother out with the bath water," and have left Ramakrishna orphaned, "packed off to the stern and orderly confines of the Order" (Hatcher, 167).

It seems unfair, however, to compare Dakshineswar's Kālī temple with the Ramakrishna Mission Institute of Culture. The Institute of Culture is, after all, an educational facility with auditoriums and classrooms. It is not a temple. Further, it was specifically planned with Western guests in mind—particularly Western scholars and students—in the hope that they could reside there in relative ease. Of course it will not resemble the Dakshineswar Kālī temple. Moreover, the criticism of the alleged banishment of Kālī from the Ramakrishna Order, an idea currently prevailing in Western academia, does not take into account the strict and elaborate rituals required when Kālī's presence is invoked through a picture or image. Kālī is considered an *ugradevatā*, and any failure in her ritualistic service is understood to be extremely inauspicious. Placing Kālī on an altar is very different from placing a Buddha or a Ganeśa as a decorative piece in one's household. It is precisely because the Order understands Kālī to be very real indeed that her presence is taken very seriously and she is worshiped only in specific places at specified times and always with the greatest care and devotion.[32]

Hatcher suggests that since Ramakrishna "was more a Tantric devotee than an Advaitin" (167), there has been an attempt to "'reform' the problem child," Ramakrishna (168). We can see here a Western binary that is not intrinsic to the Hindu tradition—that is, if one practices Tantra, one cannot be an Advaitin or the reverse—and that one affiliation precludes the other. Hatcher nevertheless goes on to caution the reader: "If one is going to join Kripal in his work, one is going to have to join in an uphill battle. Every inch of ground will be contested" (168). Hatcher avers that there is a great challenge to have one's arguments heard "when confronting a century-old institution whose origins amid the vortex of colonial power/knowledge and nascent nationalism more than account for its curious philosophy of dogmatic toleration and inflexible apologetic. . . . The followers of Rāmakṛṣṇa are not just touting a *sādhana*, they are defining and defending a cultural tradition. For better or worse, the linchpin for that defense is the figure of a rather crude, if charismatic, mystic" (168). If this linchpin is found to be motivated by Tantra and "the dynamics of homoerotic desire," then one is "threatening to reveal a secret that has been kept carefully guarded for a century" (169).

Having presented the opposing armies on the battlefield, Hatcher marshals the forces of the Western academic army to bolster Kripal's defenses, noting that *Kālī's Child* has been praised by scholars of religion and by experts on South Asian culture. Despite the fact that some reviewers have had misgivings, "their overall verdict has been an approving, and at times highly laudatory, one" (169). Ranged against the laudatory reviews are ones who have questioned Kripal's competence in Bengali. Hatcher, himself proficient in Bengali, certifies that Kripal is competent in Bengali, and whatever errors he made in the book's first edition were corrected for the second (170).

Admitting that Kripal gives "a degree of prominence" to the so-called secret-talk passages in the *Kathāmṛta*, Hatcher suggests that these passages allow Kripal "to develop the hermeneutical key that unlocks the mystery of the entire *Kathāmṛta*" (171). He also upholds Kripal's psychoanalytic reading of Ramakrishna and defends him against charges of "reductionism" made by other scholars. Coming down heavily upon Gerald Larson for attributing monocausal reductionism to Kripal's analysis and suggesting that Kripal should have engaged with the tradition, Hatcher agrees with Kripal that Larson quotes him out of context and suggests that Larson "selected his quotations for maximum effect" (173). Hatcher defends Kripal's "fixation on secrecy" as "a function of what he experienced as a scholar attempting to discuss theories and propose conclusions" that were not openly discussed within the Ramakrishna Order (176).

Perhaps to provide a sense of balance to his generally laudatory review, Hatcher suggests that *Kālī's Child* "does not give adequate consideration to a whole host of issues, not the least of which concern the origin, development, and continuing agency of the Order within modern Bengal." He argues that as a historian of religion, Kripal should have directed more attention to "the cultural ethos and religiopolitical context of colonial and postcolonial Bengal." Hatcher goes on to write that he has one misgiving about Kripal's book and "it is that it treats Rāmakṛṣṇa and his followers in a sort of historical and political vacuum; it seems benignly unconcerned, for instance, with issues of colonialism and representation" (177). Hatcher also questions Kripal's claim that "Ramakrishna's secrets have been concealed by his followers" since the Bengali utterances of Ramakrishna are easily available at the centers of the Ramakrishna Order and "are not passed under the counter with a wink" (178). A more sensitive attention to "the dynamics of cultural formation that gave us both Rāmakṛṣṇa and the Rāmakṛṣṇa Order might have given a Bengali reader, at least, the sense that Kripal had more on his mind than a smear campaign" (178).

While the *Kālī's Child* controversy was simmering away in the Western arena, it was assumed that the controversy was being hotly replicated in India. Kripal in his Preface to the Second Edition of *Kālī's Child* writes that the book is "wished away in an entire country" (xxiv). Yet this was not the case; the vast majority of the population had never heard of it, even in West Bengal, even among Ramakrishna devotees. As we have seen, Sil's review in *The Statesman* elicited an outraged response to both the review and *Kālī's Child*. Yet we should remember that this was the response of a very small urban, English-speaking elite in Kolkata and Delhi, which is hardly representative of India or the general milieu of Ramakrishna devotees throughout India. Further, the majority of Ramakrishna devotees in India do not read *The Statesman*, which—with editions only in Kolkata and Delhi—has a substantially smaller readership than other major Indian newspapers.

Swami Tyagananda, for example, stationed in Chennai as editor of the *Vedanta Kesari* during these years, had only heard of *Kālī's Child*—long after its publication—through an American correspondent. Had Tyagananda's position not necessitated contact with English-speaking Westerners—which in itself is a fairly unusual position—it is likely that he might never have heard of the book at all. It was not that the book or the controversy was suppressed, it simply was not an issue to begin with. Even now, many years after the book's publication, there are any number of Ramakrishna monastics and devotees who have never heard of the book or the controversy. A book about Ramakrishna written by a Western academic does not evoke much interest on the part of the general Hindu population, particularly those who do not belong to the educated cosmopolitan elite. For most Hindus, a sādhu's words will carry authority, not those of a scholar who is not a sādhu or at least a practicing Hindu. To assume, therefore, that there was a uniform response of burning outrage to *Kālī's Child* is to presuppose that the book garnered more attention within the ranks of the Ramakrishna Order (what to speak of the general population) than it actually did.

A fair and accurate statement would be that those Vedanta Societies and branches of the Ramakrishna Order that have historically interfaced with Western scholars were aware of *Kālī's Child* and their reaction to the book was uniformly negative. Within these Centers, however, there were two general views concerning the *Kālī's Child* controversy. By far the most prevalent opinion was that the book was trash and there was no point in trying to correct the misinformation printed in it because to deal with trash was a waste of time and energy. The book was so obviously full of misinformation and mistranslations that one could not take it seriously. Truth would inevitably prevail, so there was little point in tarring one's hands or wasting one's time on a book that was not based on documented facts and a book which would not stand the test of time. The minority view was that misinformation produced by academia tended to replicate itself and unless the misinformation was corrected, the theses presented in *Kālī's Child* would be presumed accurate. Further, while the misinformation about Ramakrishna in *Kālī's Child* was only an issue in the West, not in India where the vast majority of Ramakrishna devotees lived, it was an injustice to allow misinformation to stand uncorrected. Again it should be stressed that there was no uniform viewpoint either on the part of those who are in the governing body of the Ramakrishna Order or on the part of its monastics or devotees. And again, for the large majority of people associated with the Order, it never was an issue at all.

We have seen that Swami Atmajnanananda took the view that a published rebuttal was necessary, as did Pravrajika Vrajaprana, whose negative review of *Kālī's Child* was published in the *Hindu-Christian Studies Bulletin* in 1997 (59–60). Most significant of all the responses coming from inside the tradition was Swami Tyagananda's photocopied rebuttal, "Kali's Child Revisited or Didn't Anyone Check the Documentation?" which was informally distributed at the November 2000 American Academy of Religion meeting. As Arvind Sharma noted: "Tyagananda ... questioned [Kripal's] linguistic competence in Bengali on which the whole thesis hinged. . . . Kripal did not respond to Tyagananda's critique in any detail, and to date still has not. Such perceived indifference to an obviously credible critic was noticed by the Hindu community, and independent scholars within the community took it upon themselves to explore the matter further" (Arvind Sharma, 2004). Tyagananda's response to *Kālī's Child* inaugurated what would become a cascade of responses from the insider community, critiquing what it perceived to be the prejudicial treatment of Hindu religious figures. This response has continued to gain both social and political momentum as time has passed. Meanwhile, Hindu academics were continuing to respond to the issues raised in *Kālī's Child*.

Renuka Sharma

Renuka Sharma's stinging review, "The Foot in the Lap or Kripal's Discontent," was published in *Sophia* in 2001, and critiques a number of the basic theses which constitute the framework of *Kālī's Child*. Sharma, before her untimely death in 2002, was a psychotherapist, feminist philosopher, and social activist in Australia and India. Sharma wrote that there is no evidence based upon ethnographical work corroborating

Ramakrishna's homosexuality. Neither is there valid psychoanalytic evidence, nor has the issue been "debated with scholars of the rich Indian exegetical scholarship." Sharma characterizes the appreciation of North American scholars as spurious: "Among the reasons advanced are: the inexorability of the connection between 'sexuality and spirituality' (universalized to the Indian subcontinent)" along with the use of "the new-found strategic template of psychoanalysis" and "the as-it-were-constitutional right of the outsider-scholar to interrogate the workings of (an)other's cultural productions" (77).

Sharma comes down heavily upon Kripal's "veneer of psychoanalysis and symbolic deconstruction. . . . The imperialistic use of some outdated dogmas of psychoanalysis perpetuates a kind of psycho-orientalism that, indeed, Indian feminists ... argue are a construct of masculinity as a well-known colonial ruse" (78). As a psychoanalytic-trained psychiatrist, Sharma is dubious about the use of psychoanalysis as a valid interpretive device, since there is "growing reflection within psychoanalysis of its own doubtful status as a science" (78–79).

From this vantage point, Sharma defines a critical issue in the debate: the political and social location of the analyst and the analysand. This, Sharma writes, opens a new theoretical space from within the practice of psychoanalysis, and it is from this space that she wishes to interrogate Kripal: "Might the tome be actually autobiographical, while the publishers and untutored readers have taken it to be simply about Sri Ramakrishna's life?" Sharma goes on to suggest that "this auto-analysis is enacted through the medium of the construction of the hagiography of a ... saint (*sant*) in another tradition." With this, Sharma places *Kālī's Child* squarely in the "whole tradition of colonial psychoanalysis which neatly defines 'the Indian personality'—as being homophobic, mother-hating, [and]... deeply feminized" (80).

At the heart of the *Kālī's Child* debate lies an issue which is rarely addressed, and it is this issue which Sharma directly confronts: "Which culture's homosexuality or homophobia ... is precisely at stake here or put on the couch?" In Sharma's estimation the issue is clearly not Ramakrishna's sexuality but the problems Western scholars have with personal and cultural transference. About Ramakrishna's sexuality, Sharma questions: "Why did this question even come up? What motivates one to fly cross thousands of miles away from home to probe this matter? Is the agenda controlled from elsewhere or by an overdrive within a particular mode of late (still de-orientalizing) Western scholarship?" (81). Sharma's review makes it clear that, in her view, the de-orientalizing process in Western scholarship has a long way to go.

What were the issues behind this protracted debate? With the specter of "censorship" and the perceived threat of "book banning," the most immediate issue arising within the academic community was that of academic freedom. Should a scholar avoid speaking what she or he feels to be true simply to avoid offending the insider community? Scholars of religion can walk an uneasy tightrope between speaking the truth as they see it and abiding by any responsibility they might feel toward the religious community. On the other hand, the insider community often feels powerless, believing its voice to be either silenced or disregarded by the secular academy. Moreover, the insider community has had the bitter experience of being mocked or patronized—raising the ancient specter of racism (either correctly or incorrectly perceived), and this dynamic has created frustration and anger against those who would like to remove the debate from their playing field. For the insider community, it was not a question of an unlevel playing field; their perception was that the playing field was being removed altogether from their neighborhood. A small example: In her Foreword to *Kālī's Child*, Wendy Doniger assesses the book to be a "fair-minded formulation" (ix)—to which the insider community response was: "Who defines what is 'fair'?" In his Preface to the second edition of *Kālī's Child*, Kripal writes: "The case of Ramakrishna's homosexuality ... seems to be closed" (xxi)—to which the insider community response was: "Who gets to be the arbiter? Who is qualified to make those judgments?"

To make matters more complicated, each community—whether academic or insider—tended to visualize the conflict in terms of its own history. While Western scholars tended to see a Hindu replay of the American conservative/liberal debate over "family values" versus personal choice or of sexual repression versus sexual liberation, these issues are far from universal, though their universal validity is often assumed in Western secular communities. To the devotee community, the debate brought back memories of colonial domination, racial discrimination and having one's religion belittled.

Given the enormous differences between Hindu religious culture and the secular Western academy with the intellectual standards it is expected to uphold, it is not surprising that there would be intrinsic difficulties in translating language, culture, cultural values and religious ideals from one language/history/culture to another. The scholar automatically faces difficulties in deeply understanding radically divergent worldviews and the attitudes which attend these worldviews. Historically, Western scholars have often pathologized the cultural and religious practices which are at variance with those already familiar and considered normative. In recent years there has been a move toward a conscious awareness of cross-cultural issues when addressing the concerns inherent in teaching the religious traditions of non-Western cultures. The secular Western university system is, after all, a product of the Enlightenment, which was profoundly influenced by Europe's Christian heritage. In discussing this issue, Richard King has observed that "religious studies as a cognitive discipline may actually distort or reduce that which it is claiming to investigate and explain." King continues, noting that

> the secular framework upon which the modern discipline of religious studies is founded may actually subordinate religious phenomena and emic explanations of it to a secular meta-discourse. In other words, to what extent does the secular study of religion subvert or devalue religious beliefs and explanations of the world? (King 1999b, 42–43)

With King's remarks kept in mind, we now move to a related discussion of the role translation plays in the debate.

Translations and interpretations cannot be separated from worldview—whether secular or religious. Every translation presupposes a worldview and every translation is also an interpretation, a view through the lens of someone else's world. In the next two chapters of this book, we will address the problematics and issues behind this cross-cultural procedure along with the question of accurate documentation, since no translation can be freed from the original source materials from which it is taken.

4

Interpretation in Cross-cultural Contexts

> Using secular tools to interpret sacred materials is not an innocent enterprise.
>
> —Huston Smith. *A Magic Still Dwells*

Translating and interpreting are two distinct processes, yet they are so intimately related that any attempt to pull them apart becomes an act of futility. In her article "Translating into English," Gayatri Spivak leads off with an abrupt fiat: "I'd like to begin with what should be an obvious point. That the translator should make an attempt to grasp the writer's presuppositions." But there, as we know, lies the rub. Spivak continues by stating the obvious: "Translation is not just the stringing together of the most accurate synonyms" (Spivak, 93). This is the case because translation always involves interpretation. The translator needs to interpret the sense in which a word or a phrase is used in the original text in order to choose its most appropriate equivalent in the language of the translation. By its very nature, "interpretation" is subjective and is dependent upon the perspective, knowledge and purpose of the interpreter.

Translation is intrinsically problematic because of the very nature of language and culture. In *Nation, Language and the Ethics of Translation*, Sandra Bermann writes that "if language is not a simple nomenclature for pre-established and universally recognized 'meanings,' as most contemporary language philosophers agree, translation can never be a complete or transparent transferral of semantic content" (5). Yet translate we must, as frustrating a task as it is, as incommensurable as languages are, translate we must. But when we translate, we do so knowing the task to be delicate, subtle, extraordinarily difficult and laden with ethical responsibility. To again quote Bermann: "[Translation] requires attention to cultural values, to economic and political inequalities, to individual choices and, perhaps most obviously, to otherness in its linguistic and cultural forms. In the process, it foregrounds some explicitly ethical questions" (5).

Because of the otherness inherent in languages and cultures other than our own, there can be no translation that is purely "objective." Furthermore, interpreting the sense of a word or a phrase in a text involves interpreting the event that is being described or the context in which it occurs. When more than one interpretation is possible, as is frequently the case in cross-cultural contexts, a scholar must address these questions: Do I interpret the event from my perspective or from the perspective of those who were direct participants in the event? In the case of a historical text, do I interpret the event as it was perceived at the time of its occurrence, or do I interpret it from the standpoint of the present time? What is gained—and what is lost—when we try to understand an event that occurred in one cultural setting by using categories and applying theories from a vastly different cultural setting? If interpretation is necessarily subjective, are there any objective standards which the interpreter needs to uphold?

All of these questions become relevant when examining the issue of interpretation in *Kālī's Child*, which uses categories and theories alien to the cultural and religious settings in which the principal events described in the book took place.[1] In this chapter we shall focus on only three of the major issues: the mystical/sexual connection, liṅga/yoni symbolism, and Ramakrishna's alleged misogyny.

Kālī's Child informs the reader that Ramakrishna was "a lonely young man despairing of his life" (KC, 325), who suffered "tormenting shame ... for his homosexual desires" (344). These "homosexual desires ... [were] the driving, shaping force of his mystical life" (324). Kripal contends that Ramakrishna's mysticism was the direct result of his sexuality. On this point he pulls no punches: "These homoerotic energies ... *were* his mysticism." Just to make his point completely unambiguous, he adds: "Let me be very clear: without the conflicted energies of the saint's homosexual desires. . . . there would have been no 'Ramakrishna'" (322). To add religio/cultural weight to his thesis, Hinduism's liṅga/yoni symbolism is appealed to in an attempt to demonstrate that it played a major role in Ramakrishna's life and teachings (230–31). Finally, Kripal contends that Ramakrishna's sexual orientation and past experiences with women largely explain why he "hated and feared women as Lovers and worshiped them as Mothers" (280). These three issues are related but need to be analyzed separately.

But first some general observations: *Kālī's Child* asserts that the writings of Vivekananda and Saradananda "fail miserably to meet the standards of historical accuracy and scholarly objectivity" because they were "created in a particular social context" and were "intended for a specific audience" (171). Since *Kālī's Child* claims both historical accuracy and scholarly objectivity, one must assume it to be unique in that it was not created in a particular social context and not intended for a specific audience.[2] Sheldon Pollock, however, reminds us that "disinterested scholarship in the human sciences, like any other social act, takes place within the realm of interests ... its objectivity is bounded by subjectivity." The only form of scholarship that *appears* value-free "is the one that conforms fully to the dominant ideology, which alone remains, in the absence of critique, invisible as ideology" (Pollock, 96).

Let us examine the assertion that Vivekananda and the other monks of the Ramakrishna Order were not only incapable of being objective but also had personal and political reasons not to be accurate in their representations of Ramakrishna. If Vivekananda, Saradananda and others in the Ramakrishna Order can be assumed to have some personal and ideological axes to grind (indeed, they are accused of manipulating information about Ramakrishna), then it is not outrageous to question if Kripal may not have carried his own axe along, consciously or unconsciously. Whether we notice the existence of others' axes may very well depend upon our own cultural norms and prejudices.

While presenting *Kālī's Child* as a model of scholarly objectivity, Kripal blames Vivekananda and others for having "cleaned up Ramakrishna"—Ramakrishna's disciples being either unable or unwilling to present the "'original' Ramakrishna" (KC, 171). The unwitting hubris (Kripal can locate the "original" Ramakrishna while those who lived with him cannot) displayed here is second only to the author's assurance that his own writing is free from such drawbacks. He assures his readers that he is offering "a historically accurate, psychologically nuanced reading" (2). In attempting to retrieve the "original" Ramakrishna, *Kālī's Child*'s Ramakrishna is carefully constructed not to be "cleaned up," yet in doing so Kripal creates a Ramakrishna of his own making—a kind of reverse-Pygmalion—via his own cultural and psychological presumptions.

How "objective," after all, can anyone be? The presumption that as insiders, both Vivekananda and Saradananda were incapable of being objective, while Kripal, as the outsider scholar, *is*, begs examination. If insiders can routinely be dismissed as incapable of being objective in evaluating or describing their own traditions, how objective can outsiders be in representing a tradition of which they are not a part?

The representation of the Other's religion carries within it a problematic, for there is intrinsically an unequal power dynamic between the one who is allowed to represent and those who are represented. There is an even greater problematic in representing a tradition which has historically been exploited by colonialism and Orientalism. One of the ways in which Hinduism traditionally has been exploited is through dismissing the native voice while assigning the power of representation to those who are presumed to understand the tradition better because of their status as "objective" outsiders. Yet no matter how objective we may feel our appraisals to be, our interpretations are necessarily informed by our historical location, culture, values, religious background, political persuasion and socio-economic level. No interpreter can bring a tabula rasa to his or her interpretation. "No representation is a neutral or innocent activity," Sharada Sugirtharajah points out. "It functions as an interpretive act at the same time" (2003, 69). Which brings us back to our original conundrum of pulling apart translation from interpretation. Whenever we translate, we interpret; whenever we interpret, we necessarily include the shadow of a self-portrait. As David Richards has written: "The representation of other cultures invariably entails the presentation of self-portraits, in that those people who are observed are overshadowed or eclipsed by the observer" (Richards, 289).[3]

We can begin with the thesis that Ramakrishna was "not fully aware of his own Tantric identity"—in fact, "*Ramakrishna's secret was secret even to himself*" (KC, 5; italics in text). The book provides the italics in order to emphasize the significance of its thesis that Ramakrishna did not understand the basis of his own spiritual life, nor did he understand his own motivations, nor did he understand the relationship between the erotic and the mystical. Indeed, one of the book's central theses is "that *Ramakrishna's mystical experiences were constituted by mystico-erotic energies that he neither fully accepted nor understood*" (4; italics in text). Again, these italics are in the text to emphasize their significance to the book's central thesis as a whole. We are told that Ramakrishna "even denied this basic Tantric equation of the mystical and the erotic" (5). Nevertheless, Kripal declares that Ramakrishna *was* a Tantric, though he was not aware of it. Ramakrishna was equally mistaken about his lived experience as a mystic, though he apparently was not aware of that either.

If Ramakrishna "denies" the connection (or at least the connection that the book has made) between the erotic and the mystical, then Ramakrishna must either be invincibly ignorant or suffering from psychopathology. For the insider community, this sort of Hobson's choice is as frustrating as it is offensive. Kripal rubs salt into the wound by stating that those disagreeing with his understanding of Ramakrishna suffer either from homophobia or racism[4] or are kowtowing to the "politics of 'identity correctness' and 'cultural purity'" (2004, 203). We are told in the Preface to the book's second edition: "What we are seeing in the controversy surrounding the book is not a balanced scholarly debate. . . . [but] a deep cultural rejection of homosexuality" (KC, xxi). How can there be even conversation, let alone "balanced scholarly debate," if those who question the book's theses are so insouciantly dismissed?

If Ramakrishna was ignorant about himself, it was due to the fact that he "lacked the hermeneutical key" to understand his visions and behavior (KC, 327). Yet the privileged position of holding the hermeneutical keys seems to be allocated—at least as far as Ramakrishna studies is concerned—to outsiders alone. In the *Kathāmṛta* Ramakrishna describes the following vision:

> There was a fog of bliss all around. A thirteen or fourteen year old boy rose from within it. The face was visible. He looked like Purna. We were both naked. Afterwards both of us ran in the field and played in great delight. After running Purna felt thirsty. He drank water from a glass and came forward to offer me the rest. I said, Brother! I can't take your leftovers. Then he laughed and after washing the glass brought me fresh water in it. (KA 4.259)

About this vision, Kripal writes that he doubts whether "Ramakrishna himself grasped the meaning of his fog of bliss vision. It was too close to him, too immediate. He himself was lost in the fog" (KC, 309). Yet while Ramakrishna was "lost in the fog"—along with Vivekananda, Saradananda, the Ramakrishna Order, along with literally millions of Bengalis and Bengali readers who, for five generations, have closely studied the *Kathāmṛta*—the outsider trained in the Western academy suffers no such debility.[5] There is no fog with which to contend since, as Kripal writes, "the historian of religions is outside it" (309).

Asserting that the images in the above vision "did not make sense to the saint," Kripal writes that, by contrast, the historian of religions "encounters them in the light of his waking reason and its interpretive powers" (309). While Kripal insists that "misplaced 'orientalism'" is not to be found in *Kālī's Child* (xviii), for the insider community, the idea that the Western academic has a corner on the market of rationality appears very much like the old, familiar orientalism of earlier generations.

If there is a danger of subjectivity when insiders interpret their own texts, there is also a danger of subjectivity when an outsider to the tradition translates and interprets the same texts. This "danger"—if, in fact, there is one—becomes more acute when there is the possibility of an emotional involvement by the translator/interpreter in question. While such involvement is expected and perhaps natural for insiders, in many cases it is natural and expected for outsiders as well. *Kālī's Child* is a case in point: Kripal writes that his prior experience in a Benedictine seminary sparked his interest in Ramakrishna. Unable to relate to the mystical writings of John of the Cross and see himself as a bride of Christ, Kripal attributed his discomfort to the "structural dilemma" of being in what he defines as a homoerotically structured religious world of Catholic bridal mysticism. Turning to what he perceived to be heterosexually structured Hindu Tantra, Kripal discovered Ramakrishna. "Whereas I had been a heterosexual aspirant in a homoerotically structured religious world (Catholic bridal mysticism)," Kripal writes, "[Ramakrishna] had been a homosexual mystic in a heteroerotically structured religious world (Hindu Tantrism)." Remembering his own "structural dilemma," Kripal had little difficulty in locating one in Ramakrishna: "We were both in very similar structural dilemmas, if for exact opposite reasons. I understood him precisely because I was and was not like him" (2000/2001, 15).

But maybe not. If, for example, I suffer from a cold and someone complains to me about a nagging cough, I easily assume the person also has a cold. But perhaps this person does not have a cold at all. Perhaps the cough is symptomatic of an allergy or tuberculosis or lung cancer. My easy diagnosis was the result of my projection—the diagnosis was all too easy since it readily sprang from my own experience. When we interpret the actions, thoughts and motivations of the other, the possibility of personal projection is always present. We all work within the confines of our own minds, with their attendant memories, impressions, reactions and prejudices, both conscious and unconscious.

When we carefully examine the source texts, we find no evidence that Ramakrishna experienced a "structural dilemma." For our purposes here it is enough to know that Kripal was intrigued by Ramakrishna's life because it resonated with his own dilemmas. Kripal makes his personal interest quite clear, speaking of the book as "only a part" of a "larger personal project." This, he says, is "my own life," mentioning Ramakrishna's vision of emptiness "on a specifically autobiographical plane" (KC, xxvi). Kripal further acknowledges that he was "intrigued" when he encountered Tantra and "hopeful" that he might be able to find something in Hinduism "that seemed to exist nowhere in [his] own Catholicism" (2000/2001a, 14). Which is why, he says, he chose to study the History of Religions with a special focus on Hinduism. Given this, it is not unreasonable to assume that there was a strong element of personal motivation behind Kripal's choice of study, and at this point the reader may wonder whether the historian of religion is automatically exempt from being "lost in the fog."

There is nothing unusual, of course, about being emotionally involved in a particular subject and having a personal reason for focusing on it. Many, if not most of us, do just that. It is futile, however, to deny the element of subjectivity which accompanies that interest. While the risk of subjectivity can be kept to a minimum in approaching the physical sciences (where it intrudes as well), subjective intrusions are more or less inevitable when addressing the complex issues surrounding religion. Should we question why subjectivity is "inevitable," Eugene Nida, in his pioneering study on translation, asserts that subjectivity is unavoidable when dealing with religious issues since religion involves a deeper part of the human personality.[6]

Subjectivity plays an even more central role when an author employs a psychoanalytic approach—such as we see in *Kālī's Child*—because no one undertakes a journey of the psyche without carrying along personal baggage. According to psychoanalyst Alan Roland, this is even more evident "when investigating the psyche of persons from vastly different cultures from one's own, such as India and Japan" (1988, ix). In addition to our own psychic baggage, every investigative journey also has its beginning, that is, "its reasons and motives for going." Roland notes that we are all drawn—pulled, as it were—to specific places, locations and areas of study. What we look for, what we perceive, how we perceive it and the meanings we attach to our findings are all strongly influenced by our reasons and motives for going in the first place. For this reason, Roland writes that the "subjectivity of the psychoanalytic observer is thus an integral part of the field" (ix).

When we translate, we inevitably translate our mental landscapes around the words we attempt to capture and tame, making foreign words and concepts our own. No matter how much care we may take in consciously maintaining objectivity, no translator/interpreter can avoid a certain degree of personal involvement in her or his work. "The human translator is not a machine, and he inevitably leaves the stamp of his own personality on any translation he makes," Eugene Nida writes. He continues:

> In [the translator's] interpretation of the source-language message, his selection of corresponding words and grammatical forms, and his choice of stylistic equivalents, he will inevitably be influenced by his overall empathy with author and message, or his lack of it. It is quite understandable that the behavioral and intraorganismic meanings employed by the author will affect and be affected by the translator's corresponding values—which in no instance will be exactly the same as the author's. (Nida, 154)

This is apparent from even a casual study of different translations of the same text done by various people. All creative work bears the stamp of the author's personality, occasionally revealing more of the observer than the observed, presenting—however unconsciously—an illuminating self-portrait. It should be clear by this point that *Kālī's Child*'s claims to objectivity can only be seen as compromised. This is not to say that the book is purely subjective, but only that the author's personal history, psychoanalytic approach and translation/interpretation strategies are factors which necessarily detract from the book's self-declared objectivity.

Having presented a general overview of the problematics involved in a cross-cultural interpretation such as *Kālī's Child*, we will now deal with specifics, analyzing three of the core issues in the text: the mystical/sexual connection, liṅga/yoni symbolism, and Ramakrishna's purported misogyny.

The Mystical/Sexual Connection

To understand the mystical/sexual connection propounded in *Kālī's Child*, we need to examine three key terms employed in the book. Two of these—"the mystical" and "the erotic"—occur in the subtitle, and the third term—"the Tantra"—appears intermittently throughout the book. For the present purpose, what these terms mean to the reader is less important than how the author of *Kālī's Child* interprets them, because only through *his* understanding of these three terms can we hope to make sense of the conclusions he reaches vis-à-vis mysticism and sexuality in Ramakrishna's life.

"The Mystical"

According to *Kālī's Child*, "the mystical" has three components: (1) The mystical is a hidden dimension of human consciousness; (2) in it the dichotomies of normal awareness are transcended; and (3) it is an intense experience of unity with a hidden reality (KC, 20). Kripal provides a good exposition of these three areas. Explaining the second component that deals with transcendence, he rightly recognizes that in the mystical states of Ramakrishna, Brahman is "beyond good and evil." But from here his definition of "transcendence" goes awry when he continues with:

> the impure becomes pure, God becomes the world, the "I" becomes "you," formlessness has form, and man becomes woman, who in turn unites with man. The dichotomies of normal awareness have been transcended. (KC, 21)

"Transcendence" has now reincarnated into "transformation." In the act of transcendence, the impure does not *become* pure, rather the person's consciousness transcends notions of purity and impurity. God does not *become* the world but the duality of God *and* world is transcended. "I" does not *become* "you," but the notion that "you" and "I" are separate and different is transcended. "Formlessness" does not *have* "form," but the ideas of "form" and "formlessness" are transcended. "Man" does not *become* "woman" but gender difference is transcended. After invoking Brahman, who is "beyond good and evil," the author then switches gears, instructing his readers that the transcendence of dichotomies means "man becomes woman, who in turn unites with man." With this startling non sequitur, the generally good description of "the mystical" in *Kālī's Child* takes a bizarre turn.

"The Erotic"

Kālī's Child introduces a category called "the erotic," which Kripal defines as

> *a dimension of human experience that is simultaneously related both to the physical and emotional experience of sexuality and to the deepest ontological levels of religious experience.* (23; italics in text)

Kālī's Child reminds us that in Platonic and Christian mystical discourse, the term "eros" carries mystical connotations, while in contemporary American culture, "erotic" implies "sexual fantasy and arousal." In *Kālī's Child*, however, "erotic" is used in yet another sense—as a dialectical term that refuses "to separate the sexual and the mystical." It is a term that forms an integral part of Kripal's "contextually focused method" (KC, 23), a term that represents at once "the palpably sexual and the genuinely mystical" (Kripal 2000/2001a, 14).

Although the book clearly distinguishes the use of the term "erotic" from its other uses—historically in Christian mystical literature and popularly in contemporary American culture—the reader discovers that in the book the word does not always remain confined within the clear definition offered by the author. Although Kripal denies that his dialectical category of "the erotic" means "simply sex" (KC, xv), his use of the term often implies just that.

The subtitle of the book itself is a prime example. What does "the erotic" mean in "The Mystical and the Erotic in the Life and Teachings of Ramakrishna"? If "the erotic" refers to something which is "at once sexual and mystical" (KC, 24), then what are we to make of "the mystical *and* the erotic" in the subtitle? Since the book does not recognize that there is anything purely *mystical* in Ramakrishna's life,[7] "the erotic" in the subtitle is clearly used in the sense of, in Kripal's own words, "sexual fantasy and arousal." It has nothing to do with the specially created category of "the erotic."

The book approaches Ramakrishna's religious experiences "as manifestations of Kālī's mystico-erotic *śakti*." (KC, 24). Mystico-erotic? If "the erotic" itself is supposed to refer to something that is mystico-sexual, then what is "mystico-erotic"? The explanation that the phrase means "at once mystical and sexual" (192) again shows that the word "erotic" is being assigned its popular meaning rather than the specialized sense which was earlier proposed. Many such instances can be cited where "the erotic" means just that—the erotic or, to use the author's own words, "the palpably sexual."[8] This begs the question of the legitimacy of any proposed definitional reworking of "the erotic."

"The Tantra"

Another term that requires examination is "the Tantra." If ever there was a word that defies definition or classification, this is it. As David Gordon White points out in *Tantra in Practice*, any understanding of Tantra needs to take into account both the etic view (outsider's assessment) and the emic view (insider's view) in order to get a relatively complete picture (White 2000, 5). White draws our attention to another difficulty in defining Tantra by noting that if we take an exclusive view, then "those elements of Tantric doctrine and practice that are not found anywhere else in the Asian religious traditions ... would provide us with a sharply defined but very limited account of Tantra." White calls this "hard core" Tantra. A more inclusive, "soft core" Tantra will include many doctrines and practices found in nearly all forms of the various Asian religions, and the "category loses its specificity" (6–7).[9]

Acknowledging the difficulties involved, White offers a good working definition of Tantra as

> that Asian body of beliefs and practices which, working from the principle that the universe we experience is nothing other than the concrete manifestation of the divine energy of the godhead that creates and maintains that universe, seeks to ritually appropriate and channel that energy, within the human microcosm, in creative and emancipatory ways. (9)

He concludes the essay after drawing the reader's attention to what he calls "the broken world of Tantra"—"the one transcendent and quietistic and the other pragmatic and 'shamanistic.'" Intriguingly, these two worlds, White states, appear to have little or no relationship to one another (35).

What kind of Tantra, then, is "the Tantra" that we find in *Kālī's Child*? Does it represent the unbroken Tantric world or the broken variety? If "the Tantra" is the broken variety, then which of its two segments? Is it hard-core Tantra or soft-core Tantra? Unhappily, "the Tantra" of *Kālī's Child* resembles none of these. The Tantra presented is utterly singular, and probably unrecognizable to the tradition's wide variety of practitioners. Since much of the book is "concerned with uncovering and ordering this Tantric universe," Kripal acknowledges that he must spell out clearly how he uses the term (KC, 30). But when we see the peculiar version of "the Tantra" that emerges from his definition, we also see that the universe the author hopes to uncover is not only precariously small but also seen through a distorted lens.

In *Kālī's Child*, Tantra is defined as an Indian mystical tradition with the following six characteristics. It is: (1) a tradition that is at once anti-Vedic and Vedic; (2) a tradition that employs the "Five M's"; (3) a tradition that simultaneously provides both "pleasure" (*bhukti*) and "liberation" (*mukti*); (4) a tradition that is steeped in secrecy; (5) a tradition in which "shame, disgust, and fear" are shunned; and (6) a tradition whose followers are called Śāktas (KC, 30–32). The book uses Ramakrishna's own words, culled from different books and divested of their contexts, to highlight these six characteristics of "the Tantra." This Tantra, then, is a tradition in which "human eroticism and religious experience are intimately related, even identical on some deep energetic level" (5). Interestingly, the "human eroticism" mentioned here has nothing to do with the category of "the erotic" described above.

Included in the discussion of "the Tantra" are repeated references to the "Five M's"—the *pañca makāra*—the five transgressive ingredients whose Sanskrit names begin with the letter "M."[10] The steady repetition of the Five M's throughout the book gives one the impression that it is one of the most prevalent characteristics of a unified, static practice and philosophy which is "the Tantra," but this is not at all the case. Under the general umbrella term of "Tantra" there is an enormous variety of philosophies and practices. Even within the broad category of Vāmācāra Tantra, there are "no less than six different interpretations of *Vamachar* Tantra, each of these originating in the work of acknowledged authorities on the subject" (Amiya Sen 2001, 113).

The "Tantric universe" Kripal both creates and analyzes in *Kālī's Child* shrinks even further with the declaration that he is "more interested in what Tantra *feels* like in Bengali than in what it *thinks* like in Sanskrit" (KC, 29)—and his primary Bengali source for Tantra, it turns out, is Ramakrishna's words in the *Kathāmṛta*. Never mind that Ramakrishna was "not fully aware of his own Tantric identity" (5) and "in his external life" he was "a failed Tāntrika" (129). By discounting Tantra philosophy and its Sanskrit texts, Kripal further reduces his ability to access Tantra's wide variety and, by depending on an obviously secondary source, he effectively eliminates the barrier of scholarship from his path and presents a purely subjective picture of an entity that "feels like" Tantra to him.[11] Thus Tantra is a tradition known for "its stubbornly 'impure' ways" (KC, 29), associated with "magical power, strangeness, seediness, and sex." This exoticized view is not universally shared by other scholars and certainly not by Tantra practitioners.[12] Rachel McDermott, for example, writes that no matter how awed the outsider may be by the literal use of ritual substances like wine, meat and sex, the Bengali Tantra tradition itself devalues it: "Meditation takes precedence because Bengali Tantra places the 'divine path,' the path of mental worship, highest in the spiritual hierarchy" (McDermott, 173).

Kālī's Child's Tantra flattens an ancient, rich tradition to create a simulacrum which may exist in popular Western sensibilities but is a world apart from the tradition's depth and breadth. Thus, Kripal can assert that Tantra's "radical nondualism" fuses both the pleasure one seeks within the world (*bhukti*) and liberation from the world (*mukti*). Tantra practitioners can "have it both ways"—they can have their cake and eat it too, so to speak. Further, in this rendition of the Tantric world, the pleasurable particulars of form and the liberating reality of the formless are "graphically, intimately, sexually united" (KC, 31). The book continues in this vein by misappropriating Ramakrishna's words concerning Īśvara ("beyond form and the formless"), giving readers the erroneous impression that these words were used in connection with the "Tantric world."[13] As a parting shot, the book dismisses as "dualistic" the basic Hindu tenet that one cannot concurrently get both pleasure in the world and liberation from the world.

Those within the tradition say the desire for sexual pleasure and the desire for spiritual liberation are not mutually compatible in the same person at the same time. It is true that the power (*śakti*) that fuels the quest for sexual pleasure and the power that fuels the quest for spiritual liberation are not different. They are, without question, one and the same. But, importantly, one is called to choose *where* that power should be directed. One cannot have it both ways. On this point, the Hindu tradition is exceptionally clear.

A personalized envisioning of Tantra, an ambivalent and misleading use of the term "erotic," coupled with an idiosyncratic notion of "transcendence" and "nondualism," set the stage to establish the mystical-sexual connection in the book. It is true that ontologically the same energy that drives the lower chakras also drives the upper chakras and that "it is all one life force" (KC, 44). No Hindu tradition, including the Tantra, would disagree with this. What *is* problematic in this formulation is the extension of the idea: "Sexuality, as a potent expression of *śakti*, is realized as essentially mystical" (45) or, as we read in the Preface to the second edition, "the secret of the mystical is the erotic" (xviii).

This equation leads *Kālī's Child* to connect mysticism and sexuality in a way unintended by any of these traditions. While the author denies reducing mystical experience to sexuality, that is precisely what happens throughout the book. For example: "[The] mystical flower that blossoms in the pure light of consciousness ... draws its life, sustenance, and beauty from the dark, muddy bottom of the world and the body" (KC, 44).

Neither Tantra nor Yoga nor any other Hindu tradition would agree that sexuality is essentially mystical, or vice versa. Sexuality is "a potent expression of *śakti*"—as much as mystical experience is—but that does not make sexuality essentially mystical. It makes both sexuality and mystical experience two potent expressions of *śakti*. In fact, all Hindu traditions, including Tantra, are in agreement that if *śakti* is expressed in one direction, it cannot simultaneously be expressed in another direction. This is why Hindu traditions stress the value of *brahmacarya* in the quest for mystical experience. Simply because the same force powers both the urge for sex and the urge for transcendence does not mean that one is the cause of the other. Nor does it mean that mystical power depends on sexual power for its "life, sustenance, and beauty" (KC, 44). The force is one and the same but what makes all the difference is the direction in which that force is employed. Releasing the force in service of one urge makes it unavailable to power the other urge. This is why a key element in the left-handed Tantric practice of ritualized sex is *coitus reservatus*, which is replaced in the right-handed forms of Tantra by the mystic union of *śakti* with Śiva within one's own body through arousing of the psychic power (kundalini), or by the "sublimation of sex into a child-like love for the mother-goddess" (Sarkar 1993, 43).

Kripal correctly points out that "everything depends upon our ontological understanding of human sexuality" (KC, 326).[14] Thus it goes without saying that his view of Ramakrishna's mystical experiences is dependent upon *his* ontological understanding of human sexuality. What is open to debate is whether that understanding has anything to do with the understanding of sexuality in the Tantric tradition. But meaningful debates are possible only if there are commonly accepted sources of knowledge (*pramāṇa*).[15] Unfortunately there are none in the present case because Kripal relies upon what Tantra "feels like" to him. Under the circumstances, all that one can say is that there are many, certainly the present authors among them, to whom Tantra does *not* "feel like" the way it feels like to the author of *Kālī's Child*.

Liṅga/Yoni Symbolism

Two words, "liṅga" and "yoni," appear often in *Kālī's Child* and require further exploration.

Yoni

One of Ramakrishna's mystical visions, related to the awakening of the six chakras, provides a good starting point. Ramakrishna described the vision to a group of devotees on August 9, 1885:

> A little before I attained this state I was shown how, when the kundalini becomes awake, all the lotuses bloom one after another and samādhi is attained. This is a great secret. I saw a twenty-two or twenty-three year old young man, who looked like me, entering inside the suṣumnā nerve and having intercourse with the vulva-shaped lotuses with his tongue. First the anus, the penis, the navel—the lotuses with four petals, six petals, ten petals, which had been drooping, became erect.

> When he came to the heart—I remember this clearly—after having intercourse with the tongue, the drooping twelve-petaled lotus became erect and bloomed. Then the sixteen-petaled lotus in the throat and the two-petaled lotus in the forehead. In the end the thousand-petaled lotus bloomed. From that time, I have been in this state. (KA 4.238)

Undeniably and obviously, this vision contains strong sexual imagery. English translations of this "lotus vision" fall broadly into two categories: those done by academics (generally outsiders) and those done by non-academics (generally insiders). Non-academic translators have ignored the adjective "vulva-shaped" (*yonirūp*), interpreting the Bengali verb *ramaṇ* as "commune," and have focused on what they perceived to be the essential meaning of the vision.[16] Generally speaking, academics have chosen to translate every word literally, directing their gaze, it would seem, as much on sexual imagery as on the mystical implications of the vision itself.[17] *Kālī's Child*'s translation of the passage belongs to the second category, and the book comes down heavily on Nikhilananda's purportedly "bowdlerized" translation.[18] Blind to any other possible explanation, Kripal accuses the Ramakrishna Order of censorship (KC, 311). The "secret," he alleges, has been kept hidden under lock and key, away from the public eye by "the political forces of Vivekananda's community of renouncers"—bringing to mind an ochre-clad, cloak-and-dagger plot.

It is easy to manufacture a *Kathāmṛta*-gate scenario from the material given above, but it is completely erroneous. "Vivekananda's community of renouncers" never possessed M's original diaries, let alone kept them under lock and key. They are, and always have been, in the possession of M's family, the Guptas. What is interesting about this manufactured plot and "secret" is the presumption necessary to create such a scenario in the first place. Apart from the obvious hermeneutic of suspicion, only one reared in a highly organized, centralized religion with a long history of intellectual and social repression could presuppose that sort of organizational will and organizational capability. This is the Hindu tradition, after all. By Indian standards the Ramakrishna Order is well organized and disciplined, but it is composed of Hindu monastics who are, by their very nature, extremely independent and averse to being organized. For a Hindu to leave the family structure to become a sādhu, a strong element of independence—if not sheer cussedness—must already exist in order to flout powerful family and social expectations. To concoct a plot requiring a century-long, organized effort on the part of Hindu monks to hide organizational "secrets" reveals a profound ignorance of

Hinduism's long history of intellectual freedom, which is mirrored in the Ramakrishna Order. It also reveals a profound ignorance of the workings of the Ramakrishna Order.

Why, then, did Nikhilananda remove "vulva-shaped" from his translation? Of the *Kathāmṛta*'s millions of readers, perhaps 80% or more read it in the Bengali original, and they have no problem with *yonirūp padma*, "the vulva-shaped lotuses." What, then, would provoke Nikhilananda to remove its English translation?

While words can be translated from one language to another, they often do not carry the same timbre or coloration. The weight and resonance a particular word carries in one language and culture may be entirely different in another language and culture. Those who have wrestled with translating the subtleties and nuances of one language and rendering them into another know this only too well. Much of the translator's wrestling involves issues of cultural values and cultural differences, and how much of these can be—or indeed should be—communicated to the reader. About these issues Sandra Bermann has written:

> Translators have long agreed that the effort to render one language system into another requires a keen awareness of broad cultural as well as specific linguistic values. It also requires existential choices that are bound to have wide-ranging repercussions for the text and its audience. How much of the "otherness" of the "foreign" should the translator highlight? How much of the foreign should he mute or erase in order to make texts easier for the "home" (target) audience to assimilate? The problems posed demand judgment calls as ethical as they are practical or cognitive. (Bermann, 5)

There is no single, easy answer to these issues and every translator will address them in a different way. "Translation," Gayatri Spivak remarked, "is as much a problem as a solution" (Spivak, 95). The "problem" becomes much more complex when rendering South Asian languages into English, not only because of the vast cultural gulf involved, but also because of the hegemonic linguistic status of English as today's global lingua franca. Every translator faces these issues when rendering words and meanings from another language into English. The result is dependent upon the translator's individual choice along with, one can only hope, an abundance of cultural sensitivity and sense of ethical responsibility.

That said, "yoni" is a perfect example of the problems inherent in translating Bengali into English. The word in Bengali, Sanskrit and other

Indian languages carries an enormously wide range of meaning that stretches from the purely biological to the metaphysical. Neither "vulva" nor "vagina" (Kripal translates *yonirūp padma* as "vagina-shaped lotuses") have a similar range. By using the word "vulva" or "vagina" the translator is automatically manacled to an anatomical or biological meaning. While *yonirūp padma* does not sound offensive, an English rendering as "vulva-shaped lotuses" seems crass and oddly graphic. There is simply no good way of translating the phrase. Nikhilananda obviously preferred omission rather than a translation which would have been not only bad but also, to his 1942 audience, offensive.

In translating the *Kathāmṛta*, Nikhilananda was introducing Ramakrishna to English readers, primarily those in the Western world. While Nikhilananda himself was aware of Western sensibilities and mores, he also sought the advice of his Western editorial assistants. They would have taken great pains to make sure Nikhilananda committed no cultural faux pas in his manuscript. Moreover, as a Hindu practitioner, Nikhilananda's translation strategies were necessarily different from those of McLean, Sil and Kripal. Literal accuracy is absolutely vital for scholars and practical application is equally vital for practitioners. Usually and ideally, these two goals are not in conflict with one another. When they occasionally are, the purpose of the translation determines what gets precedence, the word or the meaning that it is meant to convey. It is not uncommon for a stubbornly literal translation to provide a wildly inaccurate meaning.

In books written by practitioners, the focus is on the context and the idea—not simply on the words. The shape of the lotuses in Ramakrishna's vision is not as important as the fact that the six centers of consciousness can be "opened" (represented by the blooming of the lotuses) one after another by directly "touching" each center with the light of awareness (represented by the tongue erotically engaging the lotuses), leading to the superconscious experience of samādhi (represented by the blooming of the thousand-petaled lotus).

The purpose of erotic imagery is to convey the experience of intense joy that accompanies the opening of every psychic center (chakra). Although joy can be experienced in any number of ways, the most intense joy of everyday human experience is sexual pleasure. Most people can immediately understand and relate to the joy experienced through sexual activity. This is why erotic imagery is often used in many traditions, including those within Hinduism, to convey the idea of both intense joy and intense longing. For example, a much-loved mystic from Tamil Nadu, Āṇḍāḷ, describes her love and longing for Kṛṣṇa in the following way:

> So great is my desire to unite with the Lord
> who rests upon the turbulent Milk Ocean
> that my breasts rise and fall and tremble,
> hurting me, and so do you,
> oh lovely koel bird —
> what do you gain by hiding from me?
> If you summon Him who holds conch, discus and mace,
> great indeed is that good thing you'll do. (*Nacciyar Tirumoli* 5.7)[19]

Contrary to what *Kālī's Child* suggests, the erotic imagery found in the *Kathāmṛta* does not necessarily indicate or imply erotic activity. This does not, of course, mean that the omission of certain words from the translation is acceptable or should be condoned. What it *does* mean is that, seen through another perspective, Nikhilananda's translation has not distorted what, for a practitioner, is the essence of the text. A doggedly literal translation certainly has value (and for scholars is a necessity) but for many—and at least for practitioners—a word-for-word translation is not the only way to comprehend a religious text.

As we have mentioned earlier, it is important for us to keep in mind the oppressive social atmosphere that Hindus faced in 1940s America. One also has to remember that in those years—and to some extent, even now—Hinduism was a distinct religious minority viewed with great prejudice, suspicion and often undisguised animosity by a sizable percentage of the population in North America. Many if not all of the Ramakrishna Order swamis in the West faced racial prejudice and hostility. At least one Vedanta Society was under F.B.I. investigation for a decade. A number of Ramakrishna swamis were prevented from buying property for Vedanta centers. Until relatively recently, even Catholics and Jews were discriminated against, what to speak of Hindus.

Let us also not forget that American culture, and what was acceptable *to* that culture, is vastly different today from American culture in the 1940s. During those years, America was much more homogenized and parochial than it is today. It was also more intolerant in social, religious and sexual matters. What was considered acceptable for public (and even private) discussion was radically different from today's norm. In contrast to our current free-wheeling standards, words and phrases considered inappropriate were kept out of print, radio and television. We may forget what it was like a few short decades ago, but even on

1960s television, "Laura and Rob Petrie slept in separate beds on 'The Dick Van Dyke Show,' Lucille Ball could not use the word 'pregnant' on her show, and Barbara Eden could bare her midriff but not her navel on 'I Dream of Jeannie.'"[20] Henry Miller's *Tropic of Cancer* was banned and confiscated at the borders until it was vindicated by the Supreme Court in 1964. It is worth remembering that while *Kālī's Child* portrays the Ramakrishna Order as being composed of censorious prudes, Henry Miller found both welcome and refuge with one of the swamis of the Ramakrishna Order—as did Isherwood and many others who were not accepted in other places of worship.[21]

Clearly, an ideal translation is one which offers literal accuracy without distorting the meaning of a text. In translations which span widely divergent cultures and languages, this can be sometimes difficult to achieve. Every translator has sometime or other faced situations where, on the one hand, translating a text literally may either make no sense or even distort the sense of the original. On the other hand, translating accurately the sense of the text may involve compromising literal accuracy. In such cases, it is the translator's burden to make the choice between the "letter" and the "spirit." The choice is usually dictated by the purpose of the translation and the needs of the audience. Typically, most translations done for a general, nonacademic audience give priority to translating the idea over translating the word when it is not possible to do both simultaneously.

Considering all these factors, it is not surprising that the description of the shape of the lotuses as *yonirūp*, "vulva-shaped," does not appear in Nikhilananda's 1942 translation. Far from participating in a plot to conceal dark secrets, Nikhilananda was attempting to respect the cultural sensitivities of the times and the audience for whom it was intended, without compromising the basic message of the original text. A 1942 American audience would have been literally *stunned* by any mention of "vulva-shaped lotuses," and the resulting horror and fascination would have succeeded in bringing their attention, not to Ramakrishna's mystical experience, but to vulvas.

Let us also keep in mind that whatever modifications or deletions Nikhilananda did, the English text has always remained a resource to only a minority of the *Kathāmṛta*'s readers—Bengalis taking *yoni* and *ramaṇ* in their cultural stride. It should seem obvious that if the Ramakrishna Order were in the business of orchestrating furtive cover-ups, then it has done a spectacularly poor job. If there were scandals to be hidden, then the evidence should have been excised in the *Kathāmṛta*, not the

English *Gospel of Sri Ramakrishna* with its relatively small readership.[22] For nearly one hundred years there have been millions of readers of the *Kathāmṛta* who have pored over the text. It was in the widely available copies of the *Kathāmṛta*, in its *31st edition*, that Kripal found the "secret talks" of Ramakrishna—not in some classified documents squirreled away under lock and key or unearthed in an archeological find. These talks were no great secret when they were given—Ramakrishna's room was always full of people when he imparted these "secrets." And these talks are no secret even today: the *Kathāmṛta* is well-stocked in bookstores and widely available in Bengal.[23] Every word and every phrase in the Bengali original—including *yoni*, *ramaṇ* and *liṅga*—has remained unchanged and has been available to millions of Bengali readers, as well as to readers of the *Kathāmṛta* translations into other Indian languages.

The alleged secret was never a "secret" at all until *Kālī's Child* came along and conjured a conspiracy theory of censorship and cover-ups. What is utterly astonishing is Kripal's unquestioned privileging of the English translation with its limited audience over the Bengali original read by a vastly larger audience. It is not only he who discusses "recovering the text" in *Kālī's Child* but also, as we have seen, many academics in their glowing reviews. The text was never "lost" in the first place; the unspoken message, however, is that the English translation and its audience are the only ones that matter.

That brings us to the third, and probably the most important, point that deserves consideration. For most readers, the shape of the lotuses and the significance of the Bengali *ramaṇ* (whose meaning spans from sexual intercourse to enjoyment to communion) is less important than the meaning behind the mystic vision itself. Ramakrishna's purpose in telling his listeners about his vision was not to belabor the shape of the lotus, but to emphasize that the lotuses (chakras) *open* as a result of the awakening of the kundalini. For nearly a century, Bengali readers have closely read the *Kathāmṛta* to understand the genuine significance of the lotus vision—and have found nothing untoward, unless one is credulous enough to believe that Bengalis are too benighted—or perhaps too unschooled in "contemporary gender studies, queer theory, psychoanalysis or feminism"[24]—to understand the genuine significance of the lotus vision. The Orientalist assumptions here are too pronounced to ignore: Is it only the Western-trained academic who has the ability to see the real meaning, whereas Hindus lack the intellectual acuity and background to do so?

Were we not already crossing difficult cross-cultural terrain, the problematics of translation and interpretation become even more complex if peculiar speculations are thrown in to muddy the waters. Not only does Kripal condemn Nikhilananda's translation of Ramakrishna's lotus vision, but he also speculates that the vision could be the result of Bhairavi's attempt to engage Ramakrishna "in the fifth M through a ritualized form of cunnilingus or through the oral consumption of sexual fluids" (KC, 128). Urging his readers to take this "possibility seriously," Kripal proceeds to suggest that Ramakrishna was engaging in "a mystical form of oral sex" and this "unconscious vision was necessary because Ramakrishna could not consciously make it through the Five M's" (129). Later in the book Kripal reverts to his cunnilingus speculation, but by this time what was a "possibility" has transformed itself into an established fact, a pattern consistently followed in *Kālī's Child*. Yet of the book's many academic reviews, only one (Openshaw, 1995) specifically noted and critiqued this process. What, then, is going on in Ramakrishna's lotus vision?

Sudhir Kakar characterizes some of Ramakrishna's visions as "conscious"—"symbolic representations of an ongoing psychic process, the symbols taken from the mystic's religious and cultural tradition" (1991, 22). This is the case, Kakar believes, of Ramakrishna's "lotus vision":

> Ramakrishna's vision of his "enlightenment," which he "saw" in the traditional Yogic imagery of Kundalini, the coiled serpent energy rising through the different centers (*chakras*) of his body and opening up the "lotuses" associated with these centers, [is] a specifically Hindu metaphor for mental transformation and the opening up of the psyche to hitherto inaccessible psychic experience. (22)

According to Kakar, in the lotus vision, "self-representation is split into observing and participating aspects." The vision "can also be seen through psychiatric glasses as a heutroscopic depersonalization which occurs particularly among individuals with tendencies toward self-contemplation and introspection." Kakar refuses to pathologize the vision and makes the following observation: "Yet in the absence of any associated painful or anxious affect and the fact that this kind of vision was only one among Ramakrishna's vast repertoire of visions with very different structures and qualities, I would tend to see its ground in a creativity, akin to the heightened fantasy of an artist or a writer, rather than in pathology. Goethe and Maupassant are two instances of creative writers who also experienced the phenomenon of their doubles" (22).

S. S. Sankaranarayanan, Chennai's highly respected scholar of Tantra, points out startling similarities between Ramakrishna's lotus vision and the traditional Tantric understanding of how the kundalini rises:

> The *mūlādhāra* centre is also known as *kulakuṇḍa*, the pit of the *kula*. Ku in Sanskrit represents the earth, the gross physical *kula* is where this element is concentrated. Kundalini starts from here as kula kundalini. She is verily the *śakti*, the Time principle, Kālī for the Tāntrik. She travels upwards towards the summit and becomes united with the Śiva there. . . . the way, the kundalini licks the other centers with its tongue, makes them fully blossomed to their potentialities before meeting Śiva at the *sahasrāra*.[25]

According to Sankaranarayanan, the young man in the lotus vision represents Ramakrishna who, "with his intense love and devotion, gets identified with his mother Kālī, who is none other than the kundalini *śakti*." Mystically united with the kundalini *śakti*, Ramakrishna "enters the suṣumnā nerve and communes with the lotuses, touching them with his tongue. He is also able to stand apart and watch this experience." Continuing, Sankaranarayanan approvingly quotes from Aurobindo's *Savitri*:

> A mighty movement rocked the inner space / As if a world were shaken and found its soul: / Out of the Inconscient's soulless mindless night / A flaming Serpent rose released from sleep. / It rose billowing its coils and stood erect / And climbing mightily, stormily on its way / It touched her centres with its flaming mouth; / As if a fiery kiss had broken their sleep, / They bloomed and laughed surcharged with light and bliss. / Then at the crown it joined the Eternal's space.[26]

These alternative ways of understanding the lotus vision are a far cry from the cunnilingus speculation found in *Kālī's Child*.

We also find in the *Kathāmṛta* another reference to yoni, which is associated with Brahman: literally, the "womb of Brahman" (*brahmayoni*), which is predictably translated in *Kālī's Child* as "cosmic vagina" (KC, 128). *Brahmayoni*, however, is used in this context as a way of conveying the idea of Brahman as the "source" (*yoni*) of everything:

> Kṛṣṇa himself did many spiritual practices with the Rādhā-yantra. A yantra is the womb of Brahman—it is that which is worshiped and meditated upon. It is from the womb of Brahman that millions of universes (*brahmāṇḍa*) are produced. This is very secret. I used to have darśan under the bilva tree—it flashed (*lak lak korto*) [like a flame]. (KA 4.232)[27]

Unlike other scholars who have translated this passage, Kripal interprets the onomatopoeic Bengali phrase *lak lak* as the lolling sound of a tongue (although it can just as easily and, given the context, perhaps more accurately, mean flashing like fire or flame) and connects it to "Ramakrishna's tongue," associating it with "oral sex, with tongue-like lolling vaginas" (KC, 129). It is difficult to see Ramakrishna's tongue here since there is nothing in the text to suggest that. Intriguingly, throughout the book the connotations continue to change in a recurring reference to this same passage: what was a cosmic vagina lolling like "Kālī's tongue" (128) is later transformed into the "goddess's cosmic vagina" (250) and finally into "Rādhā's cosmic vagina" (334)—when the text itself speaks simply of *brahmayoni*. Literally translated, it could mean either "Brahman-womb" or "Brahman-source."

Liṅga

The word *liṅga* occurs in the *Kathāmṛta* sometimes in isolation and sometimes in conjunction with the word *yoni*. Not unexpectedly, *Kālī's Child* relentlessly privileges the sexual meaning of the term—in the book *liṅga* nearly always means "Śiva's penis"—even where the context calls for a different meaning. As we have seen, *Kālī's Child* takes great pains to portray Śiva in erotic terms, no matter in which context the term occurs. When one reads the *Kathāmṛta*, however, the reader will search in vain for any association of Śiva with the erotic, unless one wildly stretches the definition of erotic.

This is not to deny the sexual connotation of the term *liṅga* but to affirm that it is by no means the only connotation (or even the primary connotation), and certainly no practicing Hindu connects the *liṅga* to a penis in his or her daily devotions. The *liṅga* has a complex history and the concept is reinforced by a finely nuanced theology. To see nothing but "Śiva's penis" in *liṅga* demonstrates not only ignorance but also enormous cultural and religious insensitivity. Among several prominent symbols from the Hindu tradition which have captured the imagination of non-Hindus, *liṅga* is a prime candidate, to which a kind of Rorschach test can be applied. What comes first to mind when we hear the word *liṅga* or visualize the *liṅga* being worshiped in a Hindu temple may either indicate our ignorance about Hindu worship or perhaps tell us more about our way of perceiving symbols sacred to "the other" than about the *liṅga* itself and what it symbolizes.

The Purāṇas abound in myths about Śiva. We read in them the stories that describe the churning of the ocean, the rising of the *kālakūṭa* poison, and Śiva swallowing the poison to save the world. When he emerged from the waters, he tore off his phallus (*liṅga*) in fury and cast it on the earth, where it fell in the forest of deodar trees. Śiva appeared there as a naked yogi smeared with ashes, holding out his begging bowl for alms. Irresistibly fascinated, the wives and daughters of the *ṛṣis* rushed to bring him fruits and other food. Seeing them attracted to the strange mendicant, the *ṛṣis* were bewildered and infuriated. Śiva's visit to the forest was an act of grace at Umā's request. Failing to recognize him, the *ṛṣis* failed the test. When Śiva's phallus fell on the earth, it burned everything in its path. It became transfigured as the cosmic pillar, without end or beginning, flaming upward and spanning the entire universe. The mystery of this metamorphosis reverberated in the liberating sound of OM. When the celestials saw the sign (*liṅga*) of the Great God (*mahādeva*), they bowed to him. The vision of that flaming pillar seen by the celestials and the legend of the establishment of the stone *liṅga* in the Samnihatya lake introduced the worship of the *liṅga*.[28]

Through these overlapping and yet diverse myths, it is clear that *liṅga* is not just "Śiva's penis." As Stella Kramrisch points out in her classic *The Presence of Śiva*:

> The *liṅga* of Śiva has three significations. They are *liṅga* as sign; *liṅga* as phallus; and *liṅga* as cosmic substance (*prakṛti or pradhāna*), which is the subtle body (*liṅga śarīra*) of Śiva, who is the absolute reality. . . . The original meaning of the word *liṅga* is "sign," a mark that proves the existence of a thing. (Kramrisch, 166–67)

Paradoxically, the first recorded use of the term associated with Śiva tell us that Śiva has no *liṅga* or mark, meaning that he is transcendent, beyond any characteristic that would mark him as a part of the created world.[29] As a distinguishing mark, *liṅga* can refer to the sign of gender or sex, whence comes the popular equation: *liṅga* = phallus. The word "liṅga" is used to denote not just the characteristic of perceptible things but also the potentiality inherent in the imperceptible essence of a thing. For instance, in contrast to the visible form (*rūpa*) of fire, the potential of fire, its imperceptible essence, is the *liṅga* of fire. Thus the subtle body (*sūkṣma-śarīra*), imperceptible to the senses and ontologically preceding the gross body, is also called the *liṅga* body (*liṅga-śarīra*) (Kramrisch, 167). So easily taken for granted is the *liṅga* = phallus equation that Narasingha Sil went so far as to translate *liṅga-śarīra* as "body with genitalia" (1991, 30)! The references to the *liṅga* in *Kālī's Child* ignore the theologically rich and religiously meaningful Hindu symbol of the divine, crassly reducing it to nothing more than "Śiva's penis."

Some scholars have even called into question the supposition that the *liṅga* has a phallic origin. Departing from the convention that holds *liṅga/yoni* symbolism as non-Vedic, Mahamahopadhyay Krishna Shastri Ghule, a highly respected Vedic scholar, has found clear evidence in Brāhmaṇa texts to identify Śiva with Vedic sacrificial fire, and the *liṅga*, with the *araṇis* that produce the sacrificial fire. Ghule maintains that one must interpret a complex symbol like *liṅga/yoni* consistently and comprehensively. Identifying it simply with the male and female sex organs does not, for instance, explain why the *liṅga* is traditionally installed facing north. This practice makes sense if the *liṅga's* Vedic origins are accepted: some of the Vedic altars were indeed shaped like the *liṅga* and had to face north. More interestingly, the altars were often preserved even after the rite was over. The *Baudhāyana-śrauta-sūtra* even prescribes the installation of a bull-shaped image on the altar (Deshpande, 227–28).

One can endlessly debate the origin of *liṅga/yoni* symbolism and it is doubtful whether the controversy about its Vedic or non-Vedic origin will ever be settled. The tension between Vedic and non-Vedic traditions is seen by some social scientists as the divide between the "great" and the "little" traditions: the former usually has written texts and wider acceptance whereas the latter can be accessed through oral legends, folk songs and stories, local customs and ceremonies. In the Indian context this divide is usually represented by the Sanskritic traditions, on the one side, and the vernacular traditions, on the other. These two traditions have been in dialogue with one another for centuries and, in the process, have been profoundly influenced by one another. Some historians view the phenomenon as hegemonic and oppressive with the vernacular traditions gradually being "Sanskritized" and swallowed by the Vedic tradition. Other historians reject the idea that the vernacular traditions are any less powerful and thus see the process of assimilation as mutual and interactive, strengthening both the Sanskrit as well as the vernacular traditions (Vanita and Kidwai, xvi).[30]

This perhaps explains why written texts in India rarely speak with one voice. Almost all originate in oral traditions and were built up in layers over time. On the basis of what knowledge is available to us, it seems reasonable to conclude that the *liṅga* as it survives today—and, specifically, as it was understood in the mid-nineteenth century when Ramakrishna lived—is a complex symbol formed with layers of meaning, which are reinforced through a rich mythology. To render it simply as "Śiva's penis" is not only simplistic but profoundly distorting. Yet such is the fascination for the phrase that Kripal interprets even the reference to "Śiva" as a reference to "Śiva's penis." For example, we read in the *Kathāmṛta* (3.68):

> *Ekdin pūjār śomay śiber māthāy bojra dicchi emon śomay dekhiye dile, ei birāṭ mūrti-ī śib. Takhon śib gode pūjā bondha holo. Phūl tulchi haṭhāt dekhiye dile je phuler gāchguli jeno ek ekṭa phuler toḍā.*
>
> [Ramakrishna:] One day at the time of worship, when I was offering a bilva-leaf on the head of Śiva, it was shown to me that this Virāṭ, the universe, itself is Śiva. After that my worship of Śiva through the image came to an end. When I was plucking flowers, it was suddenly revealed to me that the flowering plants were so many bouquets.

Now let us compare the translation/interpretation of the same passage in *Kālī's Child*:

> This then reminds him of another time when, just as he was about to worship the Śiva-*liṅgam*, he was shown that "this universe is the very form of Śiva," that is, he was shown that the entire cosmos was a Śiva-*liṅgam* (KA 3.68). The phallic dimensions of this experience are significant. (KC, 109–10)

In the *Kathāmṛta* selection quoted above (KA 3.68) there is no mention whatsoever of a *Śiva-liṅgam*. What we find instead is the mention of Śiva. Although "*liṅgam*" is not part of the quoted text in the above example, placing a reference after "Śiva-*liṅgam*" makes a significant difference in the way one reads the text, especially when one considers that almost no reader of *Kālī's Child* would be sitting with the *Kathāmṛta* nearby for immediate verification. We can see how the word "*liṅgam*" has been deliberately inserted twice into the sentence above when it does not exist at all in the referenced selection from the *Kathāmṛta*. Why this was done becomes apparent when we read the concluding sentence: "The phallic dimensions of this experience are significant."

Phallic dimensions? They may be "significant" if the goal is to build a particular thesis in *Kālī's Child*, but they are not a part of the experience of those *within* the tradition. Certainly, those who pray to, worship, and meditate on Śiva are not concerned with any "phallic dimensions." Nor are the "phallic dimensions" hinted at, even indirectly, in the *Kathāmṛta* section that is cited. *Kālī's Child* seems oblivious of the simple truth that all symbols have a history and, like all bearers of meaning, their semantics change with time.

As we can see, the book creates a distorting lens which reveals a "phallic dimension" that is unsupported by the text. But in the incidents where the "phallic dimension" *is* obvious, this lens reveals something altogether different. Take the case of Ramakrishna's worshiping, in a state of divine madness, his own penis as "a living *liṅgam*" (KA 4.106) or the penises of boys with flowers and sandal paste (KA 4.232). While students of Ramakrishna's life have seen these recorded events as further evidence of Ramakrishna's vivid awareness of the all-pervading, tangible divine reality, *Kālī's Child* takes them as evidence of "a tendency on Ramakrishna's part to take a Vedantic figure or category ... and to eroticize it, to awaken it out of its abstract slumber and engage it in erotic acts" (KC, 163).

If these passages are seen as the *eroticization* of a Vedantic category, students of Ramakrishna's life see in the very same passages the *divinization* of a part of the body that is associated with erotic acts. Perhaps everyone finds what they are looking for: Kripal sees a penis in a *Śivaliṅga* whereas Ramakrishna saw *Śivaliṅga* in a penis. It is ironic, however, that Ramakrishna should be portrayed as eroticizing Śiva (KC, 163), since *Kālī's Child*—not Ramakrishna—seems to be doing precisely that, through not only the relentless translation of "*liṅga*" as "Śiva's penis" but by describing Śiva himself as "Śiva's penis."

Clearly both—the *eroticization* of a Vedantic category and the *divinization* of a physiological category—are interpretations. Only Ramakrishna knows what exactly he saw and what made him do what he did. All that his interpreters can hope to do is to make an educated, informed guess. The best guess would be one that, first, depends less on speculation and more on verifiable evidence and, second, is in harmony with the rest of Ramakrishna's life as well as with the culture and the times in which he lived. The worth of every interpretation can be tested on the basis of at least these two requirements. *Kālī's Child* suffers on both these counts: first, it relies heavily on speculation, and the sparse "evidence" it provides is created from questionable translations, circular logic, and other strategies. Second, the interpretation does not provide answers to other features in Ramakrishna's life, which are either side-stepped or minimized.

The two interpretations—the *eroticization* of a Vedantic category and the *divinization* of a physiological category—proceed from two very different worldviews. A Hindu practitioner will assert that one's identification with the body (*deha-buddhi*) manifests in many ways but perhaps most strongly through one's sexuality. The Hindu worldview accepts the possibility that the body/mind-centered identity can be transcended consciously and, when this happens, one's true, spiritual identity is regained, resulting in freedom (*mokṣa*) from the cycle of birth and death.

Many students of Ramakrishna's life see him, at the very least, as an enlightened soul, one who is "living-free" (*jīvanmukta*) and find his life consistent with the characteristics described in Hindu texts. It is not clear whether the worldview which forms the backdrop of *Kālī's Child* can accommodate the spiritual freedom (*mokṣa*) which is an integral part of the Hindu worldview because of the presumption that Ramakrishna could not have transcended sexual desire (KC, 2).

Further, by claiming that Ramakrishna himself was not aware of his thoughts, motivations and actions—his so-called secret being a secret "even to himself"—all possible refutations are preempted. Ramakrishna himself cannot contest the book's theses, what to speak of others. Any complaint on that score is preempted with denials of "misplaced 'orientalism'"—even while the book's modus operandi is consistent with the Orientalist history of presuming that only the Western expert can correctly assess and interpret the Hindu, who will always remain incapable of self-understanding.[31]

Given the above, it should come as no surprise that *Kālī's Child* mocks Saradananda's interpretation of Ramakrishna (KC, 316). How could the disciple have known the meaning of Ramakrishna's visions when the saint himself was incapable of understanding them? The irony eludes Kripal that his own claim to understanding the meaning of Ramakrishna's visions can be similarly questioned. To again invoke Sheldon Pollock, we tend not to notice any cultural assessment "that conforms fully to the dominant ideology" (Pollock, 96). For example, when we read Max Müller's interpretations, we can clearly see the deep Christian overlay which infused Müller's understanding of Ramakrishna. When we read Romain Rolland, we can see the humanist preoccupations in his interpretation of Ramakrishna. What we cannot so easily see are our own cultural overlays, since they appear self-evident and "reasonable." Yet contemporary North American culture is deeply steeped in its own peculiar dogmas and credos such as secular humanism, individualism, democracy, and a thousand other presuppositions we take for granted. In contemporary North America, the basic assumptions of psychoanalysis are so widely accepted that they are assumed to be as true as the Word of God was in earlier centuries. This is perhaps one of the major reasons why the basic theses of *Kālī's Child* were, more often than not, left largely unchallenged except by those outside that cultural paradigm.

Kālī's Child informs the reader that "if Ramakrishna were alive and could fully understand," the book would "deeply affect" him and would "help him deal more adequately with some of his painful emotional reactions" (xxvii). Which, hubris intact, first questions whether Ramakrishna *could* understand the book, then presumes that Ramakrishna actually experienced these "painful emotional reactions"—a presumption based on the verities of contemporary psychoanalysis under the aegis of circular logic. Characterizing the book as an act of "friendship, sympathy, and a deep compassion," Kripal in effect claims that he is not merely "interpreting" Ramakrishna—he implies that he is aware of the contents of Ramakrishna's mind. So sure is the author of his knowledge of Ramakrishna's mind that he warns his readers that rejecting his thesis would amount to a rejection of Ramakrishna himself (KC, xiv). An interpreter needs the mind and insight of a prophet to be so confident of knowing the inner motivations and promptings of a person he or she has never met, someone who lived in a vastly different culture and in an altogether different century, a person whom the interpreter knows only through textual records in a language that he can neither speak nor thoroughly comprehend. When an interpreter assumes the mantle of a prophet, the interpretation is bound to suffer.

Misogyny

When it comes to Ramakrishna's relationships with women, there are, according to *Kālī's Child*, two interpretive camps: the first is "the devotional camp ... populated almost solely by devotees and swamis." This camp sees Ramakrishna as "an infallible saint who loved all human beings and who worshiped women as embodiments of the divine." The second camp sees Ramakrishna as "a misogynist who hated and feared women." The latter camp is inhabited by "scholars, both Western and Indian, [who] usually have sided with some version of the misogynist reading" (KC, 278). The latter interpretation has echoed in a number of *Kālī's Child*'s reviews. While Kripal promotes this view, he is not the first scholar to have criticized Ramakrishna for his attitude toward women. In fact, the first criticism Ramakrishna received vis-à-vis women came from one of his admirers and contemporaries, the Westernized Bengali Pratap Mazumdar.

Ramakrishna and Women

Kālī's Child points out that Mazumdar found Ramakrishna's treatment of Sarada "almost barbarous" (KC, 278). It also refers to Mazumdar's letter to Max Müller, which mentions that there was "another side" to

Ramakrishna which was "not edifying," implying that what was unedifying about Ramakrishna was his misogyny and the sexual nature of his "secret." Yet as we have seen, the letter indicates that Mazumdar was offended by Ramakrishna's insufficient abhorrence of prostitutes, his indifference to "the principle of teetotalism according to Western notions," and his occasionally "abominably filthy" language (which was basically no different from the language of any other unschooled Bengali villager). Yet as Sumit Sarkar has pointed out, it was this very quality of Ramakrishna which attracted many of the middle class elite to him. *Because* Ramakrishna was unvarnished, unlettered, un-Anglicized and hopelessly unsophisticated, he was deeply attractive to those Anglicized middle-class Bengalis who mourned their own loss of identity (Sarkar 1993, 6–7).

According to Mazumdar, Ramakrishna's "almost barbarous" treatment of Sarada consisted of Ramakrishna's and Sarada's lack of sexual relations. But this, after all, was a decision strongly endorsed by Sarada herself. Indeed, her husband's celibacy and lack of "worldliness" were a matter of great pride to her. We must remember that in the Hindu value system of that era, *brahmacarya* was nearly universally regarded as praiseworthy, a value in and of itself. Sarada frequently invoked Ramakrishna's renunciation and set it as a standard by which the renunciation of others could be assessed: "Renunciation (*tyāg*) alone was his glory (*aiśvarjja*)," she said, adding, "People think that his devotees also must be very great, as he was a man of such great renunciation (*boḍo tyāgī*)" (MK, 214). On another occasion when a devotee suggested that Ramakrishna's religious universality was his particular gift, Sarada replied: "What you should note, my dear, is that renunciation (*tyāg*) is his specialty (*biśeṣattva*) in this age. Did anyone see such natural renunciation any time before?" (Gambhirananda 2004, 352). It is difficult to envision Sarada as a frustrated, sexually unfulfilled wife after reading Sarada's lengthy conversations, teachings and the copious reminiscences of her disciples and devotees. Yet these important source texts are never quoted, never referred to, with the result that Sarada and other women disciples of Ramakrishna are never permitted to speak for themselves—at least not in *Kālī's Child*.

Ramakrishna's behavior found an unlikely supporter in Max Müller, who declared that it was by no means unusual for such couples to "decline to live *maritalement*" (RLS, 64). It would be difficult to find an equally ranked defender today. Nor would there be many couples who would let it be known that they declined to live *maritalement*. What appeared "by no means unusual" to Müller a century ago in Europe, now appears bizarre if not pathological in contemporary North America. We must keep this in mind when we assess the values of nineteenth-century Bengal and the marriages which accommodated those values.

As we have already seen, some contemporary Ramakrishna scholars—Malcolm McLean, Carl Olson, Narasingha Sil and at least the early Sumit Sarkar—also have characterized Ramakrishna as a misogynist.[32] Conversely, other scholars and the insider community believe such allegations to be misplaced. While Kripal construes these opposing views as "a long history of controversy and concealment," the "controversy"—such as it is—has only occurred recently with the unerring certainty bestowed by cultural monovision and modernity's hindsight.

A good deal of the controversy has focused on the correct translation and interpretation of a vexing Bengali idiomatic phrase, *kāminī kāñcana*, "woman and gold." As we approach the subject, however, we would be wise to remind ourselves that the phrase was not found vexing at all until it was seen through the eyes of the late twentieth century.

Ramakrishna and Kāminī Kāñcana

In going through the *Kathāmṛta* the reader often finds Ramakrishna using the phrase *kāminī kāñcana*. Today an oft-repeated "woman and gold" strikes a jarring note, especially when one reads the English translation and most especially if the reader is unaware of the phrase's history or intent. What precisely did Ramakrishna mean by *kāminī kāñcana* and what was his intent in repeating it?

In attempting to interpret *kāminī kāñcana* for a Western audience, Nikhilananda translated the phrase as "woman and gold," with a lengthy footnote appearing under its first usage in *The Gospel of Sri Ramakrishna*. "Woman and gold," Nikhilananda writes, "has been used throughout in a collective sense [and] ... designate the chief impediments to spiritual progress." *Kāminī kāñcana*, Nikhilananda continues,

> has often been misconstrued. By it he [Ramakrishna] meant only "lust and greed." . . . He used the word "kāminī" or "woman," as a concrete term for the sex instinct when addressing his man devotees. He advised women, on the other hand, to shun "man." (GSR, 82)

In contrast, Jeffrey Kripal translates *kāminī kāñcana* as "lover and gold"—one of *Kālī's Child*'s signal theses being that Nikhilananda's "woman and gold" is a "false translation" of *kāminī kāñcana* (KC, 280). Obviously on a different wavelength, Vivekananda—who heard *kāminī kāñcana* innumerable times directly from Ramakrishna—translated the phrase as "lust and greed." A new translation of the *Kathāmṛta* by Dharm Pal Gupta also renders *kāminī kāñcana* as "lust and greed" as well as "lust and gold."[33] Interestingly, M's own English translation of his diary, written in King James English, translates *kāminī kāñcana* as "lust and gold." For this offense, Kripal accuses M of having "participated in the cover-up" since his translation "is conspicuously silent on the topic"—the "topic" and "cover-up" being Ramakrishna's presumed misogyny intrinsic in *kāminī kāñcana* (KC, 278).

"Lover" and Gold?

Kripal asserts that the alleged cover-up process "begins in the last entries of M's diaries, where the brother monks reflect back on Ramakrishna's teachings on *kāma-kāñcana*, 'lust-and-gold'" (KC, 357). Rather than viewing "lust and gold" as M's considered decision of the best translation of his own words into a foreign language, Kripal accuses M of participating in an elaborate cover-up.

Yet translating *kāminī* as "lover" can be seen as idiosyncratic at best and perverse at worst. One could also argue that Kripal's translation is not only wrong but also self-serving. Rajat Ray, chair of the History Department at Presidency College in Kolkata—and hardly an insider—wondered about the mystifying word choice in his review of *Kālī's Child*: "Kripal translates '*kāminī*' as 'lover'—why not 'woman'?" (Ray, 102). How "woman-and-gold" forms part of the "secret" is explained in the first edition of *Kālī's Child*. There we read that Nikhilananda's "woman and gold"

> is a false translation, yet another strategy in the concealing of Ramakrishna's secret. The word *kāminī* does not mean "woman." Literally, it could be translated as "lusty woman" or "sexy woman." It certainly is not an abstract term for woman. (KC 1995, 280)

The book's second edition modifies this bold declaration, no doubt in response to Atmajnanananda's published critique of the accuracy of Kripal's Bengali.[34] Thus we read in the second edition that Nikhilananda's translation was

> yet another strategy in the concealing of Ramakrishna's secret. The word *kāminī can mean* simply "woman." Literally, however, it *could be* translated as "lusty woman" or "sexy woman." It is hardly an abstract term for woman. (KC, 280; emphases added.)

With either translation, however, we encounter a problem. Translating *kāminī* as "lusty woman" is convenient—provided one accepts *Kālī's Child*'s thesis that Ramakrishna related to women either as

"Lovers" (whom he hated and feared) or as "Mothers" (whom he worshiped) (280; capitalizations in text). But this either/or binary is not only grossly reductionistic, it also thoroughly misrepresents Ramakrishna's attitude toward women, which was, as he repeatedly said, that he saw them as manifestations of the Divine Mother. In the pages that follow we shall delineate the problems with *Kālī's Child*'s Mother/Lover dyad and we will show that Ramakrishna's attitude towards women was neither misogynistic nor contradictory. To do this we will return to *Kālī's Child* to examine *kāminī kāñcana* and the linguistic and philosophical impediments to *Kālī's Child*'s theses.

One fundamental philosophical problem with *Kālī's Child*'s *kāminī kāñcana*/homoerotic-secret theses is that it ignores the simple truism that an aversion needs to be developed only toward those things to which one is attracted. One need not needlessly browbeat someone about the dangers of smoking, for example, if the person has no attraction to cigarettes in the first place. Jeanne Openshaw zeroed in on this point in her book review of *Kālī's Child*: "Male fear of women, the attempt to see all women as mothers rather than as sexual partners, and, in its extreme form, a cultivated sense of revulsion for the female body—all these stem precisely from the attractive power of women, rather than from 'homoerotic' tendencies" (Openshaw, 22).

Linguistic Misconstructions and Kāminī Kāñcana

In translating an idiomatic phrase such as *kāminī kāñcana*, Kripal runs into a problem anyone could encounter while attempting to translate from a language not adequately understood. It is quite true that the Sanskrit word *kāminī* is related to *kāma*, lust, therefore *kāminī* could mean a lusty woman or one that evokes lust in others. But in Sanskrit, *kāminī* could just as well refer to a beautiful, sensual woman. When used in Bengali, however, *kāminī* can simply mean a woman. Not necessarily a sexy woman, just a woman. Further, its usage in Bengali is very rare, *kāminī* being largely restricted to poetry and songs (including at least two to the goddess Durga).[35] The more commonly used Bengali words for woman are *strī* or *mahilā*. Should one wish to say "lusty woman" in Bengali, an adjective would have to be added to *stri*, such as *kāmātura strī* or *kāmāsakta strī*. One would not use the phrase *kāmātura kāminī* at all; it would sound ridiculous. Given all this, why would Ramakrishna use an uncommon word such as *kāminī* in his decidedly unliterary Bengali conversations? Because of its alliterative qualities when combined with its companion, *kāñcana*, "gold."

It is significant that whenever Ramakrishna used the word *kāminī*, it was almost always in conjunction with *kāñcana*. Ramakrishna frequently used rhyming phrases such as *lok na pok* (people are like worms); *jato mot, tato poth* (as many opinions, so many ways to the divine), *grantha granthi* (scriptures can be binding knots); *mānuṣ man-huṁś* (the person whose consciousness is awakened is a worthy person). More examples could be provided, but hopefully the point has been made. The alliterative quality of these phrases made them memorable, which is why alliteration is one of the oldest teaching devices in the world. Crucially, when Ramakrishna spoke of "woman" not in conjunction with *kāñcana*, "gold," he generally used an altogether different word for "woman"—*strī* or *meye*.

Ramakrishna and Kāminī

What precisely did Ramakrishna have in mind with the *kāminī* element within *kāminī kāñcana*? To begin with, it is important to remember that Ramakrishna's usage was hardly unique. During its long history, Hinduism's epics, Purāṇas and *dharmaśāstras* have consistently reflected a deep mistrust of women's power of sexual attraction as well as an equally deep mistrust of men's ability to resist that attraction. Sharada Sugirtharajah has written that the *dharmaśāstras* "reflect a profound sense of ambivalence in their attitude to woman. On the one hand, she is elevated to the status of a goddess, but on the other, she is seen as a temptress and seducer" (1998, 66).

A random opening of Kamala Subrahmanian's translation of the *Bhāgavata*, for example, reveals the following passage:

> It has been said that the indriyas are powerful, so powerful that they will pull even a wise man into the snare of sin. That is why the wise have said that one should not sit on the same seat with his sisters or even daughter. Such is the power of the senses that man may forget himself in the blindness of the moment. (275)

This is not an atypical text, and as we can see, the real root of the problem is not the woman (though often enough the texts blame the woman as well). More than anything else, it is the man who fears his inability to resist his sexual attraction to the woman. This is not out of the ordinary; it is prevalent throughout the Hindu—and especially the Hindu ascetic—tradition. As Sumit Sarkar has written:

> Ramakrishna's constant warning to his disciples about the danger of *kamini* do not seem [sic] to pose much of a problem, for they are deeply rooted in the Hindu religious tradition (and indeed, with

> variations, most other religions). . . . An equally deep-rooted notion in Hindu culture is the assumption that *biryapat*—ejaculation—enervates the male, while conversely continence in the midst of temptation is a potent source of spiritual energy. . . . Ramakrishna stood four-square within this tradition. (1985, 99)

Other purported evidentiary claims for Ramakrishna's misogyny center around Ramakrishna's many warnings to his male disciples about women and his graphic descriptions of the contents of women's bodies. Evidence for Ramakrishna's misogyny is presumably found in his statement: "It is not good for a sannyāsi to sit in the company of a woman devotee, or even to talk to her. . . . There are eight kinds [of sexual intercourse]. To listen to a woman and enjoy her conversation is one kind; to speak about a woman is another kind" (GSR, 701).

Yet this injunction is hardly peculiar to Ramakrishna. Strict standards for a sannyāsi are ancient and fairly universal across Hinduism's renunciant traditions. Both Sudhir Kakar and Parama Roy are surprisingly shortsighted on this topic. Kakar writes, for example: "For a renunciate, he [Ramakrishna] felt, to sit with a woman or talk to her for a long time was a kind of sexual intercourse of which there were eight kinds" (Kakar 1991, 31).[36] Yet Kakar and Roy should know that Ramakrishna did not make this up himself: those "eight kinds of sexual intercourse" which Ramakrishna recounts belong to a longstanding Hindu tradition. Ramakrishna would not have had to look far, since it is found in Bengal's Gauḍīya Vaiṣṇava tradition, which, as we know, deeply influenced him.[37] The "eight kinds of sexual intercourse" are discussed in the *Vairāgya Mārtaṇḍa* (12.144–45),[38] which has been attributed to Jīva Gośvāmī as well as to Śrīdhara Svāmī. This text cites the more ancient *Dakṣa Smṛti* (7.31–32) regarding these eight kinds of intercourse. Śaṅkara himself discussed the eight kinds of sexual intercourse in his *Sarva-vedānta-siddhānta-sāra-saṁgraha* (109–110)[39] and an almost similar list appears in the *Kaṭharudropaniṣad* (8.9) as well. Even the *Nārada Bhakti Sūtra* (#63) warns that "descriptions about women, wealth and atheists are not to be heard." Before (mis)ascribing misogyny to Ramakrishna, it would be more fruitful to contextualize Ramakrishna's statement within the renunciant tradition. Admonitions about *kāminī kāñcana* are hardly limited to Ramakrishna.

Saral Jhingran has written in her study of Indian morality: "All Hindu philosophic systems believe in the duality of self and body, and assert the transcendent nature of the self. . . . The thinkers of the tradition of liberation have given very vivid descriptions of the loathsome constituents of the body, such as blood, bone, urine, etc." (Jhingran, 218). Ramakrishna was solidly within the Hindu ascetic tradition when he invoked these "loathsome constituents," particularly when addressing young men who were potential sādhus. For example, in remembering the course of his own sādhana, he says:

> I saw clearly before me heaps of money, shawls, a plate of sweets, two girls with rings in their noses. I asked my mind, what do you want? Do you want enjoyment? The mind said, "No, I don't want anything. I don't want anything other than the lotus feet of God." I saw the inside and the outside of the women just as you can see from outside all the things inside a glass house! I saw inside them—entrails, blood, excrement, worms, phlegm, saliva, urine, etc. (*tāder bhitare dekhlām—nāḍībhuḍi, rakto, biṣṭhā, kṛmi, koph, nāl, prosrāb*). (KA 3.139)

It is worth mentioning that translating the above paragraph is a microcosm of the problems the translator faces in attempting to translate between languages and cultures. How does one translate, for example, *biṣṭhā*, excrement, and *prosrāb*, urine? "Shit" and "piss" carry, in the English language and particularly in print, a harshness and shock value not found in village Bengali. On the other hand, "urine" and "excrement"—what to speak of "feces"—is too fastidious for Ramakrishna. "Pee" and "poop" are infantile. Since there is no completely accurate translation for those words, one must opt for the least inaccurate translation. Interestingly, Majumdar—a native Bengali who translated the entire *Kathāmṛta*—translated "nāl" as "tubes" since the word can mean either "saliva" or "veins." In the rural Bengali dialect, however, it is more likely to mean saliva than veins, and considering Ramakrishna's intent, he probably meant saliva since it is considered more repugnant than veins.

While a word can be looked up in a dictionary and assigned a translation, it is much more difficult to translate the culture, history and religious values that undergird the word *in the context of the culture*. As Gayatri Spivak acidly notes: "The implicit assumption [is] that all that 'third world' texts need is a glossary" (Spivak, 95). While overstated, Spivak has a point: if the translator only has a limited understanding of the multi-layered nature of a language and its culture, then his or her translation will inevitably be faulty. All of which brings us back to the question of Ramakrishna's "misogyny," which Kripal qualifies by writing that "his misogyny was not so much a misogyny, a 'hatred of women,' as it was a 'disgust' (*ghṛṇā*) of female bodies" (KC, 286). Yet as we have seen, this is perfectly in keeping with the ascetic tradition within Hinduism, and from that perspective, it makes perfect sense.

We would do well to remember this point when we encounter some of Ramakrishna's more emphatic statements on women—that women are tigers, ogresses with large pores, etc.—which seem difficult to reconcile with his oft-repeated statement that he looks upon all women as embodiments of the Divine Mother. Ramakrishna admitted that in his early years he was afraid of women (*āge bhārī bhoy chilo*) and would not allow them to come near him. But when we see him in the *Kathāmṛta*, he had reached the stage where he saw them all as "forms of the blissful Divine Mother" (*mā ānandamoyīr ek ekṭi rūp*) (KA 4.201). Thus we find no difficulty reconciling these apparently conflicting views, especially when we remember that Ramakrishna's talks in the *Kathāmṛta* were directed to a variety of different individuals at varying stages in their lives, all going toward very different futures.

We often forget in reading the *Kathāmṛta* that an extremely diverse array of people visited Ramakrishna on a daily basis. Most of Ramakrishna's meetings with other people are not recorded in M's diaries since M did not live with Ramakrishna. Though M was an especially close disciple who spent as much time as possible with Ramakrishna, he was, for the most part, able to visit him only once or twice a week, occasionally staying in Dakshineswar for longer stretches of time. While the *Kathāmṛta* is without question the best single record we have of Ramakrishna and his teachings, this record is nevertheless incomplete since it can only reflect what M heard and observed on those days when he was with him. Sumit Sarkar has noted:

> It is easy to slip into an assumption that Ramakrishna's teachings in the early 1880s constitute a single bloc. But speech is inherently "dialogic," modulated by contexts and audiences—and Ramakrishna's devotees included many apart from the middle-aged householders who tend to predominate in Mahendranath's text. The *Kathamrta* does not give an equivalent direct access to other groups: the very young men who later become *sanyasis* (they are often present, but not possibly in their more intimate conversations with the saint) ... the wives and widows, the prostitutes-turned-actresses. (1993, 60)

The accounts that we have from these other groups—the future sannyāsis, wives and widows, prostitutes-turned-actresses, along with a wide assortment of others—attest to the fact that Ramakrishna directed his words to the particulars of his audience. Ramakrishna's talks to his women disciples were necessarily different from those he gave to his male disciples, and both of these were quite different from the teachings he gave to future sannyāsis. Swami Premananda (whom we meet as "Baburam" in the *Kathāmṛta*) said that a wide variety of people sought out Ramakrishna and each person was taught differently, "according to their different temperaments and their capacity of understanding." Ramakrishna's teachings to his future monastic disciples "were given in private." Premananda said that Ramakrishna taught them how to discriminate and analyze the body which is "made up as it is of flesh, blood, and bones, so that our minds would not run after the enjoyments of the flesh" (Prabhavananda, 114).

On the other hand, to his householder disciples, who perhaps feared they might be asked to abide by unattainable standards, Ramakrishna said:

> For a person who pursues the path of knowledge, it is not harmful to have occasional conjugal relations with his own wife. The emission of semen is like the elimination of urine and feces. You eliminate and do not think of it anymore. It is like eating a sweet. It is not so harmful for a householder. (KA 4.68)

Ramakrishna told his disciple Bhavanath, whose time with his wife was spent in spiritual conversation, to "have a little fun with your wife" (KA 3.115). *Kālī's Child* distorts the tenor of this conversation by stating that Ramakrishna "complains" about Bhavanath talking with his wife all night. There is no complaint in Ramakrishna's words. He seemed pleased that the couple shared spiritual conversations with each other and was clearly amused by Bhavanath's incensed retort to Ramakrishna's suggestion that they "have a little fun." Seeing it as a concession made to the worldly-minded, Bhavanath replied to Ramakrishna's suggestion with a huffy "Shall we too remain immersed in that kind of fun?"

Ramakrishna gave the same advice to Hari, telling him to go to his father-in-law's house, talk to his wife "and have a little fun with her if you like." With this, Ramakrishna turned to M and said, "What do you say?" (KA 4.206). At this everyone laughs, enjoying the joke. Not surprisingly, *Kālī's Child* paints this scene with a pejorative brush, depicting M as "grinning" (284), which, predictably, is not in the text. The *Kathāmṛta* depicts a scene of light-hearted fun, the participants enjoying an easy conversation.

Kālī's Child states that Ramakrishna offered a "double message—the family is at once a pile of shit and a convenient fort—[which] produced great ambivalence and doubt in Ramakrishna's disciples" (284). First, we find no evidence of "great ambivalence" in any of the source texts. Second, as we have seen, Ramakrishna did not give a double message but two distinctly different messages for two distinctly different groups of people. There is one message for householders and another message for future sādhus.

In contrast to householders, the rules for sādhus were more severe. Ramakrishna said:

> A sannyāsī must not look even at the picture of a woman. For a sannyāsī to have relations with a woman is like eating what has been spat out. A sannyāsī must not sit and talk with women even if they are greatly devoted. He should not talk to them even when he has mastered his passion. A sannyāsī renounces both *kāminī* and *kāñcana*. Just as he should not see even a picture of a woman, he must not touch *kāñcana*—money. (KA 4.68)

If we find this to be absurdly negative and restrictive, we should remember that Sarada was often more severe than Ramakrishna on this score. She said to one of her women disciples who was trying to lead an exclusively spiritual life: "Never trust men. What to speak of strangers, don't trust even your father or brother. Even if God comes to you in the form of a man, don't trust him" (MK, 118). To another disciple she said: "A monk must not lower the ideal of renunciation. Even if a wooden image of a woman lies upside down in the road, he must not turn it the other way, even with his foot, to look at its face" (Nikhilananda 1962, 181). Neither Ramakrishna's nor Sarada's guidelines for sādhus were unduly harsh in the context of Hindu religious culture, particularly during that time. Their attitudes were very much in keeping with the expected standards of behavior for sannyāsis. We may remember the fifteenth-century ecstatic saint Caitanya (who even in nineteenth-century Bengal was still a presence to be reckoned with) being a severe disciplinarian when it came to sannyāsis. When Caitanya's disciple, the younger Haridās, merely *spoke* to an elderly widow devotee after Caitanya had forbidden him to do so, Haridās was banished without a second thought. Incidents such as this were part of the everyday consciousness of Bengalis such as Ramakrishna and Sarada. Ascetics were given a set of rules, entirely separate from that of householders, by which to abide and through which they could traverse the world of *saṁsāra*.

In assessing Ramakrishna's attitude toward women, we therefore need to keep in mind that when Ramakrishna spoke of women in seemingly pejorative terms, he was addressing a specific audience consisting of determined sādhakas and future sannyāsis. The intent behind

Ramakrishna's pungent words was to decrease their desire for sex and instill in them an increased desire for God. As we have seen, Ramakrishna was just one in a long line of spiritual teachers to have done so with bracing effect. To a different audience at different times, Ramakrishna often spoke of the advantages of a married life, especially when people asked whether they could succeed in spiritual life as householders. Comparing the situation of the householder to fighting a battle from inside the fort, Ramakrishna said:

> Why should you renounce? Since fight you must, it is better to fight from a fort. You must fight against your senses and things like hunger and thirst. It is better to fight this battle from within the world. . . . Why should you renounce? It is more convenient to be at home. . . . Whatever and whenever the body needs something, it will be near at hand. (KA 1.153)

On another occasion Ramakrishna said: "In the world one has to fight against lust (*kām*) and anger (*krodh*), against different kinds of desires (*bāsonā*), and against attachment (*āsokti*). It is convenient if the battle is fought from a fort. The fight from home is good" (KA 1.173). When asked whether it was possible to live in the world once the mind became filled with God, Ramakrishna answered: "Why not? Where will you go leaving the world? I see that wherever I live, I am in Rāma's Ayodhya. This world is Rāma's Ayodhya" (1.173). While *Kālī's Child* interprets this statement as depicting "the ontological silliness of renunciation" (KC, 284), this disparaging assessment only serves to muddy the issue's waters without providing clarity. Ramakrishna spoke approvingly of householder life to those who were already leading a householder life. He encouraged them to practice more sādhana, to spend some time in solitude or in the company of the holy (*sādhusaṅga*), and he told them that they need not renounce physically but only mentally. To young future sādhus, Ramakrishna spoke enthusiastically of both inner and outer renunciation.

While *Kālī's Child* belabors Ramakrishna's presumed horror at his young disciples' contact with women (82–83), Ramakrishna actively encouraged his young disciple Rakhal (who was considered Ramakrishna's spiritual son and later became the first President of the Ramakrishna Order) to return home to his wife. Rakhal did just that and, while living at home, his wife became pregnant and bore a child.[40] *Kālī's Child* briefly mentions the fact that Ramakrishna suggested that Rakhal return home to his wife, yet the book does not come to terms with its significance. Kripal's explanation for Ramakrishna's suggestion was that he had "throw[n] his previous cautions to the wind." Kripal adds: "The life of the renouncer, Ramakrishna seems to be saying, is not all that it is cracked up to be" (KC, 284). In other words, there *is* no explanation for Ramakrishna's suggestion since it would be inconsistent with *Kālī's Child*'s assertion that Ramakrishna did not want any of his disciples to have anything to do with women (82–83).

Ramakrishna had great regard for Rakhal's spiritual potential and yet Ramakrishna had no qualms about Rakhal returning home. As we read in the *Kathāmṛta*: "Rakhal now understands what is knowledge and what is ignorance; he now discriminates between the real and the unreal (*sot asot bicār hoyeche*). Now I say to him, 'Go home. You may come here sometimes and spend two or three days'" (KA 4.93). On the other hand, Ramakrishna was alarmed about Rakhal and *kāñcana*, telling him: "I would rather hear that you had jumped into the Ganges and died for the sake of God than hear that you had become someone's slave or accepted a job under someone" (KA 2.201). Here we find Ramakrishna not bothering about *kāminī* but extremely concerned about *kāñcana*.

Interrelated Triad of Bondage: Kāñcana, Marriage, Employment

It is remarkable that while a great deal of dust has been raised over Ramakrishna's purported misogyny as reflected in *kāminī*, there has been precious little interest in *kāñcana*—to which *kāminī* is attached like a Siamese twin—and about which Ramakrishna is equally biting. Like "woman," Ramakrishna also speaks of "gold" separately from the *kāminī kāñcana* dyad. When discussing *kāñcana* separately from *kāminī*, Ramakrishna generally used the common Bengali word for money, *ṭākā*, instead of the more ornate term, *kāñcana*. While a number of contemporary Ramakrishna scholars have tried to pull *kāminī* away from *kāñcana*, doing so misrepresents Ramakrishna and distorts his multi-layered approach to what he viewed as the major impediments to a serious spiritual life. Simply put, as Ramakrishna repeatedly said: "Maya is *kāminī kāñcana" (kāminī kāñcana māyā)* (KA 3.33).

Partha Chatterjee correctly observes that the "figure of a woman often … stand[s] for concepts or entities that have little to do with women in actuality" (68). In his extended discussion of *kāminī kāñcana* in the *Kathāmṛta*, Chatterjee writes: "The figure of woman-and-gold signified the enemy within: that part of one's own self which was susceptible to the temptations of ever-unreliable worldly success" (69). Ramakrishna often discussed the interrelated nature of *kāminī kāñcana*, which begins with a wife, followed by children, and the necessity of a job for their maintenance. Included in this package are ever-increasing distractions, worry, loss of freedom and loss of autonomy. In order to keep the job for the sake of money to maintain the family, the husband will have to endure any number of humiliations from his superiors. He will feel compelled to flatter their egos and pander to their whims in order to keep the job. He may be pressured to lie or cheat or accept bribes. The ability to keep his mind on God becomes an increasingly remote possibility. Ramakrishna says in the *Kathāmṛta*: "*Kāminī kāñcana* create bondage for the soul (*jīva*) and it loses its independence. It is woman that creates the need for gold. That, in turn, necessitates servitude to others (*porer dāsatva*). That takes away one's independence. You can no longer do what you like" (KA 1.72).[41]

Sumit Sarkar writes of "Ramakrishna's triad of *kāminī-kāñcan-chakri*"—that is, the interdependent alliance of woman-gold-clerical job. Sarkar writes that the central link of this bondage is "between *kamini* and the *dasatva* of *chakri* (bondage of the office-job), mediated by *kanchan*." To this point Sarkar quotes Ramakrishna in the *Kathāmṛta*: "Look, how many educated people trained in English, with so many degrees, accept *chakri* [clerical job] and receive kicks from their master's boots every day. *Kāminī* is the sole reason for all this" (1993, 29; quoting KA 3.143 and 1.73). Partha Chatterjee also observes that "woman as *kāminī* and the identification of this figure with *kāñcan* (gold) produced a combination that signified a social world of everyday transactions in which the family man was held in bondage." Chatterjee goes on to say that "the specific semantic content of this idea in Ramakrishna's sayings could well be traced to a very influential lineage in popular religious beliefs in Bengal" (68).

Not just Bengal. There are any number of examples throughout the history of Indian literature. In thumbing through an English rendering of the *Bhāgavata* by Kamala Subrahmanian, for example, we find the following passage: "Gold will propagate avarice, untruth, arrogance, lustfulness, ruthlessness and hatred. . . . This is why the wise say that *Kamini* and *Kanchana* are the two dread enemies which are lying in wait to destroy man" (31).

Those who find Ramakrishna's perspective unnecessarily negative will find Sarada speaking in exactly the same vein, which is not surprising since these ideas are an integral part of the Hindu ascetic tradition. When Sarada was asked by a woman devotee to order her unwilling daughter to marry, Sarada responded with a counter-question: "Is it any less miserable to remain subservient to someone for life and to dance to his tune?" She further said that, though there is a possibility of problems in unmarried life, it is wrong to force an unwilling person into a life of worldliness through marriage (MK, 164).

There is a strong tradition within Hinduism which views marriage as a fearsome bondage which steals away the sādhaka's body, mind and freedom. When speaking from that tradition's stance (which they often did) Ramakrishna's—and Sarada's—words were not out of the ordinary.

Marriage: Con and Pro

Kālī's Child reports that Ramakrishna viewed the householder life as "scary, dangerous, and dirty" (140), and had "general disgust with women" (141). However, further investigation shows that an apprehension of the snares of householder life is fairly universal among those who advocate renunciation, whether male or female. We find Sarada, for example, taking the same attitude when her niece Maku criticized her for encouraging young men to become monks. Annoyed, Sarada gave a spirited reply, making those in the room "hang their heads in shame":

> These [potential future monks] are all God's children. In the world they will remain pure like flowers. Is there any happiness greater than that? You have seen what sort of happiness there is in the world. You have also seen the happiness of living with a husband. Are you not ashamed to go to your husband again and again? What have you learned after living with me for so long? Why is there still so much infatuation and carnality? What joy do you find in that? If you go back to your husband, I won't keep you here. Can you not hold a pure thought even in your dreams? Can you not stay even now like a brother and a sister? Do you want to live like a pig? My bones burn in the fire of your worldly life.[42] . . . Whether a person calls on God or not, one who has not married is already half-liberated. When the mind of such a person is drawn to God, he will make quick progress. (MK, 282–83)

Does the above indicate that Sarada also had a "general disgust with women"—or men for that matter? Sarada's many disciples, both men and women, numbering in the hundreds, have attested to the great love they felt from her, just as Ramakrishna's women disciples have attested to the great love they felt from him. One of Ramakrishna's women disciples, Yogin-Ma—who was one of Sarada's closest companions for many years—said in response to a devotee who was discussing Sarada's compassion: "Mother [Sarada Devi] certainly loves us all very much, but her love doesn't have the intensity of Thakur's. What concern and love he had towards his disciples! We saw it with our own eyes. Words cannot describe it" (MK, 349).

Sarada's fiery words to her niece—and Ramakrishna's words concerning *kāminī kāñcana*—were meant to burn an imprint of *vairāgya*, renunciation, into the minds of their devotees. The extent to which they succeeded was due to the fact that *vairāgya* and *brahmacarya* were accepted and esteemed virtues in the Hindu milieu of the nineteenth century. Surprisingly, to a limited degree, they remain so even today. Psychoanalyst Alan Roland has written extensively on Indian psychotherapy and observed that even today in India: "Sexuality is ... not experienced as a liberating force. . . . Rather, sexuality is associated with even greater family enmeshments and obligations" (Roland 1996, 138). This is not too far of a cry from Ramakrishna's *kāminī kāñcana*. Roland adds:

> Since in India, sexuality connotes greatly increased family obligations rather than personal autonomy as in the West, the striving for *brahmacharya*, or sexual abstinence and renunciation in adulthood in the service of spiritual disciplines ... can also be viewed as a step in the loosening of the intense personal attachments and obligations in extended family-communal relationships and a reaching toward personal autonomy in the spiritual sphere. (143)

If this is true of modern India, with all the Westernization that has taken place, think of what the normative values were for Hindu India over a century ago. Of course one can pathologize these values and presume they are psychosexual disorders. To do so, however, would diminish the core values of Hindu religious culture and would misapprehend a vital facet of that tradition. This should not be done lightly. Clearly, those in the room with Sarada took her words quite seriously. Were that not the case, they would not have been moved to "hang their heads in shame."

Perhaps, we may wonder, Sarada's negative words about marriage were the result of her marriage to Ramakrishna, which had left her either embittered or brainwashed. To consider this hypothesis, however, we would need to accept the premise that Sarada found marriage to be generally undesirable. But neither Sarada nor Ramakrishna was against marriage per se. They were against marriage for those with the potential of renunciation, and they were particularly against marriage when addressing sādhus, potential sādhus and those who would impede or criticize sādhus. For example, Sarada said to one of her disciples who wanted to be a monk but whose father vehemently opposed it: "Just see how a father wants to strike at his own boy's head with an axe!"

(Saradeshananda 1981, 102). On another occasion, when a woman complained to Sarada that it was difficult to find suitable bridegrooms for her daughters, Sarada replied that the reason boys were not marrying was that "they have learnt now that the world is transitory" (*cheleder ekhon gyān hocche soṅgsār je anitya*) (MK, 11). At another time Sarada said: "Is there any happiness in this world living with one's wife and children? They have lost themselves in *kāminī* and *kāñcana* (*Soṅgsāre māg chele niye ki ār sukh āche? Kāminī ār kāñcan, otei bhule royeche*) (MK, 223). It is worth noting that Sarada uses not only *kāminī kāñcana* here but also *māg chele*—a colloquial expression for "wife and children"—which, when mistranslated as "bitch and kids" in *Kālī's Child*'s first edition, was seen as proof of Ramakrishna's misogyny. As we can see, *māg chele* was so common a colloquialism that even Sarada used it. While Kripal removed references to Sarada as "bitch" in the book's second edition, he did not remove it in other instances. As a result, even the book's second edition has a subhead entitled "Cleaving the Bitch in Two," which informs the reader that "the saint had split the goddess into a pure sexless Mother and a despised Lover bitch" (KC, 142). This is a catastrophic mistranslation, based upon inadequate knowledge of the language and culture.

Despite Sarada's words on the pitfalls of marriage, it would be incorrect to characterize her (or Ramakrishna's) attitude as anti-marriage. To those who worried that they were unfit sādhakas because they were married, Sarada assured them that they could certainly live a spiritual life while living in the family. After all, she said, was she not also living in the midst of her family? When one of her male disciples, who did not want to marry, expressed such a concern, she said: "Who says it is not possible to be virtuous if one is married? It is through the mind that everything is accomplished. Didn't Thakur marry me?" (MK, 338). While both Ramakrishna and Sarada showed a marked appreciation for renunciation (an appreciation also shared by their culture), they nevertheless praised married life and both advised various people to follow that path rather than that of sannyāsa unless the person in question was not only eager but also qualified for it. We can remember the case of the man who wanted to live with Ramakrishna, leaving his wife and their many children at her father's home. Outraged, Ramakrishna said: "Will people from the neighborhood feed them and bring them up? Isn't he ashamed that someone else is feeding his wife and children, and he has dumped them at his father-in-law's house? I scolded him very hard and asked him to look for a job. Then he was willing to leave here" (KA 1.19).

Ramakrishna's Attitude toward Women

If Ramakrishna was not a misogynist, then what *was* his attitude toward women? The following passage from the *Kathāmṛta* is particularly illuminating, as it puts into perspective Ramakrishna's own attitude towards women as "parts of the Divine Mother." Moreover, the passage also brings to light the basic philosophical problem with *Kālī's Child*'s analysis of *kāminī kāñcana*. Ramakrishna begins by saying:

> When God is attained (*īśvarlābh*) through intense dispassion (*tībro boirāgya*), there is no longer any attachment toward women. There is neither attachment nor fear even if one is married. If there is a very large magnet and another small one, then which one will pull a piece of iron toward it? It is the large one that will do so. God is the large magnet; compared to him, a woman (*kāminī*) is a small magnet. What can a woman do?
>
> A DEVOTEE: Sir, should we hate (*ghṛṇā*) women?
>
> SRI RAMAKRISHNA: One who has attained God does not see women with lustful eyes and so has no fear. He sees clearly that women (*meyerā*) are parts of the Divine Mother (*mā brahmamoyīr aṅgśa*) and, addressing them as "mother," he worships them all. (KA 1.73)

As we can see, Ramakrishna says that a person without lustful attachment has no fear. What does a man fear? Not the woman: "What can a woman do?" He fears his own weakness, his own wavering will, his own "lustful eyes" in the face of temptations. This is the point which Kripal (and others) have missed: the major misstep of *Kālī's Child*'s *kāminī kāñcana* thesis is that Ramakrishna's cautionary words about *kāminī* are not directed to the woman *outside* the man. The source of the problem is lust-identified-with-woman *inside* the mind of the man, which is then projected onto the woman *outside*. Ramakrishna's many warnings about women were directed to the *kāminī* hovering inside his male disciples' minds, and it was this interior *kāminī* (as well as the interior *kāñcana*) that needed to be tamed. According to Ramakrishna, once the lust located in the mind (which for men is usually identified with woman) is overcome by the attainment of God (*iśvarlābh*), then any external woman will have no effect on the mind. With the attainment of God, māyā is removed, allowing the once-deluded man to see a woman as she is, a part of the Divine Mother.

This point was reiterated by Ramakrishna's disciples. After Ramakrishna's death, M often visited the Baranagore monastery to spend time with the young monks. In his diary he recorded Brahmananda's words on the subject of women: "Many think it is enough if one does not look at a woman. What good will it do if you just lower you head when you see a woman? Last night Narendra said it very well, 'A woman exists as long as there is lust. Without it one feels no difference between a man and a woman' (*jatokkhan āmār kām, tatokkhan-i strīlok; tā nā h'le strī-puruṣ bhed bodh thāke nā*)" (KA 2.255). As long as lust *inside* the mind is not conquered, the sādhaka must be extremely cautious about the objects of lust *outside* the mind. Ramakrishna repeatedly used the example of a young tree that needs to be fenced in to protect it from cattle. Once the tree is thick and strong "the tree won't be hurt even if an elephant is tied to it" (KA 1.47).

Puruṣa Kāñcana—"Man and Gold"

It is because Ramakrishna saw *kāminī kāñcana* as an interior problem lodged within the sādhaka's mind that he could be equally vehement about *puruṣa kāñcana*, "man and gold," with his women disciples. Because both the *Kathāmṛta* and the *Līlāprasaṅga* were written by men—women for the most part being illiterate—the texts' language generally reflects Ramakrishna's spiritual instructions to men. Had a woman been the main recorder of Ramakrishna's talks, we would have had a better idea of Ramakrishna's teachings to women and would have heard repeated references to *puruṣa kāñcana*, "man and gold."

Gauri-Ma, one of Ramakrishna's prominent women disciples (and to whom he gave the ochre cloth of sannyāsa), said the following about *kāminī kāñcana*:

> [Ramakrishna] has uttered this note of warning, against gold and sensuality, against a life of enjoyment, but surely not against women. Just as he advised the ascetic-minded men to guard themselves against women's charms, so also did he caution pious women against men's company. The Master's whole life abounds with proofs to show that he had not the slightest contempt or aversion for women; rather he had intense sympathy and profound regard for them. (Gauri Mata, 93)

In the *Līlāprasaṅga* we read what Yogin-Ma, one of Ramakrishna's women disciples, said about Ramakrishna:

> Everyone now says that he did not allow women to touch him or to go near him. We laugh when we hear this and think, "Ah, we are not dead yet!" How will anyone understand how kind he was! He treated women and men the same way. But it is true that if women stayed near him for long, he would say, "Please go now and have darśan in the temples." We have heard him ask men also to do the same." (LP 3.34)

Silencing Women: Why Does This Seem So Familiar?

This brings us back to the baffling omission of women's voices in *Kālī's Child*. This kind of omission is remarkable when we consider that Kripal included in his sources even obscure writers who had never met Ramakrishna and who only provided secondhand information from other sources. Given that he refers to such sources, it is strange indeed that *Kālī's Child* does not discuss the extensive literature concerning Sarada Devi and Ramakrishna's other women disciples. Unlike some of Kripal's sources, these books are hardly obscure. They are widely available, in Bengali and in faithful English translations, and they contain a great deal of information not only about Sarada, but also about Ramakrishna—and these sources, critically, are firsthand. These sources were known to Kripal, since in a later article on Sarada he discussed the "daunting body of devotional literature in both English and Bengali," and he quoted extensively from two of the major source texts on Sarada, *Śrī-Śrī-Māyer Kathā* and *Śrī-Śrī-Māyer Smṛtikathā* (2001b, 174). Indeed, since he stayed at the Ramakrishna Mission Institute of Culture in Kolkata for eight months, he would have found literature on Sarada, as well as on Ramakrishna's other women disciples, difficult to avoid. Yet these critical sources were pointedly avoided in *Kālī's Child*. Such an omission would be excusable if *Kālī's Child* did not discuss any of the women in Ramakrishna's life and their relationships with him. But to indict Ramakrishna on charges of misogyny and then not allow these women to speak for themselves on their personal relationships with Ramakrishna, ranks somewhere between incomprehensible and unconscionable.[43]

It is ironic that *Kālī's Child* accuses Ramakrishna of being a misogynist when it was Ramakrishna who insisted that Sarada and Gauri become spiritual teachers. Yet the one who accuses Ramakrishna of misogyny effectively silences the women associated with Ramakrishna, taking away their words and speaking for them—presuming to understand their relationship with Ramakrishna better than they did themselves. For Hindu women, it is (à la Yogi Berra) déjà vu all over again.

Sarada and Ramakrishna

Had *Kālī's Child* not avoided Sarada's reminiscences of Ramakrishna (as well as all the reminiscences of his other women disciples), it would have been extremely difficult for Kripal to sustain his misogyny thesis. To begin with, Ramakrishna had no problem touching Sarada's body. Sarada told her disciple Sarayubala Devi: "Thakur showed me how to massage by massaging my own body" (*ṭhākur āmār gā ṭipe dekhiye diye bolten—emni kore ṭepo*) (MK, 49).

Sarada repeatedly spoke about Ramakrishna's tenderness: "Ah, how he treated me! Not one day did he say anything that would hurt my mind" (MK, 63). If we feel tempted to roll our eyes about a husband who never said anything to hurt his wife and ask, "Is that all? What about love?" In that case we must recognize the enormous power of our own cultural upbringing, which determines our suppositions about marriage. Alan Roland has written that in India even today, what to speak of over a century ago, "the marital relationship does not assume the same importance or intensity that it does in the American nuclear family" (1996, 137). Roland also observed: "Traditionally, wives and husbands refrain from any displays of affection before other family members. . . . Indian women in psychoanalytic therapy seem far more preoccupied with how they are getting along with their female in-laws than with their husbands" (140).

Sarada often said: "I was married to one who never addressed me as *tui*." To clarify, this pronoun is generally used for those lower in the social hierarchy—a servant, a child, a younger brother or sister. One would not use *tui* with one's husband or wife (*tumi* would be used) unless one were mightily irritated or displeased—at which point *tui* would be used to good effect to show one's anger or disgust. In other words, Sarada indicates that Ramakrishna never showed any displeasure with her—on the contrary, he was consistently loving, kind and respectful. The story of Ramakrishna accidentally calling Sarada *tui* is well known: Sarada brought food into Ramakrishna's room. Thinking the person in his room was his young niece Lakshmi, Ramakrishna said, "close the door behind you (*tui*)." To this Sarada replied, "Yes, I am closing it." Hearing Sarada's voice, Ramakrishna was aghast and said, "Ah! It's you! I thought it was Lakshmi. Please don't mind." However, this unintentional slight disturbed Ramakrishna so much that the following morning he told Sarada, "The whole of last night I couldn't sleep, worrying about how I spoke so rudely to you" (MK, 246).

Moreover, Ramakrishna had deep respect for Sarada's potential as a spiritual teacher, and he insisted that she continue his teachings after he died. Not long before his death, Ramakrishna said to Sarada in an aggrieved voice, "Well, my dear, won't you do anything (*hyām̐ gā, tumi ki kichu korbe nā*)? Should this (pointing to his body) do everything single-handedly?" To this Sarada replied, "I am only a woman. What can I do?" To which Ramakrishna answered, "No, no, you will have to do a lot (*nā, nā, tomāke anek kicchu korte hobe*). Some days later Ramakrishna repeated his instruction to her: "See, the people of Calcutta appear to be crawling like worms in the dark. Look after them." When she again protested, "I am a woman. How is that possible?" Ramakrishna responded by pointing to his own body and said, "What after all has this one done (*e ār ki koreche*)? You will have to do much more (*tomāke er anek beśi korte hobe*)." When Sarada attempted to change the course of the conversation, he refused to let the topic go, saying: "Is this my responsibility alone (*śudhu ki āmār-i dāy*)? It is yours also" (*tomār-o dāy*)" (Gambhirananda, 96).

Ramakrishna taught Sarada all the mantras which she later used for giving initiation after his death. Sarada later told one of her disciples: "Do you know that these mantras are all given to me by Thakur? These mantras possess great power (*siddhamantra*)" (MK, 296). In fact, Sarada gave mantra *dīkṣā* (initiation) to several of Ramakrishna's disciples after his death, and the initiation of at least one of them, Swami Yogananda, was at Ramakrishna's behest, according to both Sarada and Yogananda.[44] Nor was it just mantras that Sarada learned from Ramakrishna. Sarada said to one of her disciples: "Thakur with his own hands drew for me a picture of the kundalini and the six chakras" (*Ṭhākur nija hate āmāke kula-kuṇḍalinī, ṣaṭcakro em̐ke diyechilen*) (MK, 33).

Ramakrishna's interest in Sarada was not limited to her spiritual capacities. Ramakrishna was particularly concerned about how Sarada would be cared for after his death. As she told her disciple Swami Saradeshananda: "Even Thakur, who wouldn't know whether his wearing cloth was on or off, had so many worries about me!" She told Saradeshananda that Ramakrishna was concerned about "where she would stay after his death, [and] how she would manage to have her food and clothing." He would ask devotees: "If one has six or seven hundred rupees, could a woman maintain herself in a village?" Sarada then told Saradeshananda: "For this purpose Thakur had collected some money and given it to me" (Saradeshananda 1981, 98).[45] Saradeshananda continues:

> One day [Ramakrishna] asked her, "Where have you kept the money?" On the Mother replying, "In the pot where I keep the condiments," the Master was perturbed and asked, "Is it how money is to be kept?" It is said that about six hundred rupees were collected. The money was later deposited in the Zamindari account of Balaram Bose, and it collected an interest of six rupees per month for her. In speaking on these matters, the Mother would say with a smile, "Now see how much money is coming and is being used by his will!" (98)

There is an abundance of evidence in the literature on Sarada that Ramakrishna was loving and deeply concerned for her welfare. He was concerned about her health and suggested that she get some exercise, moving out of the confines of her small hut. Ramakrishna told her: "A wild bird, if kept within a cage day and night, gets rheumatic. So now and then you should take a walk in the neighborhood" (MK, 193). Even such an ordinary occurrence as Sarada getting a headache made Ramakrishna anxious about her. He repeatedly asked Ramlal, "O Ramlal, what may have caused her headache?" (Gambhirananda, 65).

Though he was famed for his utter indifference to "worldly" life, Ramakrishna was greatly concerned about Sarada's welfare not only after his death but also very much while he was alive. Knowing, for example, that Sarada liked ornaments, Ramakrishna spent three hundred rupees having a pair of bracelets made for her. When Ramakrishna saw Sītā in a vision, she wore a pair of bracelets with tiny facets, making the gold appear to be flecked with diamonds. It was in imitation of these bracelets that Ramakrishna had Sarada's bracelets made, the bracelets she wore until the end of her life (Saradeshananda 1982, 14). Sarada remembered: "[Ramakrishna] used to say, 'Her name is Sarada. She is Sarasvatī. This is why she loves to adorn herself.' He told Hriday, 'See how much money is in your box. Have a pair of nice gold armlets made for her.' He was ill at that time and still he arranged to have the ornaments made for me at the cost of three hundred rupees. And remember, he himself could not touch money" (MK, 54).

While much has been made of the fact that Sarada lived in a tiny room in the music tower (*nahabat*) near Ramakrishna's room, spending her time cooking for him and his visitors and watching him through a window when he sang, danced and spoke of spiritual life, Sarada herself repeatedly asserts that her years with Ramakrishna were the happiest in her life. "I always felt as if a pitcher filled with bliss (*ānander pūrṇaghoṭ*) were kept in my heart" (Gambhirananda, 28). Of course it is possible to discount her words as a pitiful attempt to put a brave face on a miserable life, but only if we ignore the fact that there is more evidence to verify her words than there is to dismiss them. If Sarada felt great happiness in her living situation—and she repeatedly said she did—then why should we attempt to impose upon her Western modernity's standards for a woman's happiness? With all the voluminous literature available on Sarada, there is not the slightest hint that she was anything other than happy during her years in Dakshineswar. We may choose to disregard the testimonies of those who knew her, but on what grounds should we ignore *her* testimony? Because we ourselves cannot imagine being happy under such circumstances?

Binodini Dasi

If, according to *Kālī's Child*, Ramakrishna hated and feared the "Lover," that is, the untamed woman who was not "rendered pure, sexless, devout" (286), then certainly Ramakrishna would have hated/feared women like the actress Binodini (though Binodini was devout). In nineteenth-century India, actresses were generally viewed as prostitutes, and to a large degree they were drawn from the ranks of Kolkata's prostitute quarters. As far as public opinion went, "even those who were not directly recruited from prostitute quarters were regarded as public women" (Bhattacharya, 12).[46] One evening when Ramakrishna went to the Star Theatre to see Girish Ghosh's play *Caitanya Līlā*, Ramakrishna went backstage after the play was over. As Binodini reminisced, this meeting was "the source of greatest pride in all my life." She continued in her autobiography:

> It was after seeing me perform in *Chaitanya-Lila* that the most divine of beings granted me refuge at his feet. When the performance was over I would present myself and sit at his feet, in the office room. He would rise and begin to dance joyously, singing as he did so: "Our Guru is Hari! Hari is our Guru!" He asked me to sing this along with him. He would place his hands on my head and cleansing with his touch my sinful body, he blessed me, "Ma, may you have *chaitanya!*" Poignant indeed was the sight of his gentle and compassionate image before an inferior creature such as myself. The *Patitpaban* ["purifier of the fallen"—which is how Binodini referred to Ramakrishna] himself was reassuring me. . . .
>
> And once when he lay ill in the house at Shyampukur I had gone for a *darsan*. Then, too, his body had radiated a calm contentment. "Come, sit down, my child," he said to me. How affectionate were his words; as though he was truly reaching out to forgive this creature of hell. . . . My body that was dedicated to the theatre had truly been blessed. If the world looks upon me with contempt, it does not matter to me, for I know that he who was the most worthy of worship, Ramakrishna Paramhansadeb, has been kind to me.[47] (Bhattacharya, 95–96)

As Binodini related above, she visited Ramakrishna during his last illness, at a time when his disciples were vigilantly protecting him from unwelcome visitors. In Swami Prabhavananda's unpublished reminiscences, we read how Binodini eluded Ramakrishna's caretakers:

> Binodini, the famous actress and Girish's mistress, came to see Thakur during his last illness. She was disguised as an English boy and was let in to see him. Atul, Girish's brother, brought her. When she took her hat off, her hair fell over her shoulders. Thakur laughed. He put his foot on her heart and went into samadhi.[48]

There is no hate, no fear, no contempt anywhere here. There clearly is affection, however, for a woman whom many people shunned. Contrary to what we read in *Kālī's Child* ("it was flesh-and-blood women whom Ramakrishna *literally* could not touch" KC, 281), Ramakrishna did not hesitate to touch her, even a "fallen woman." Interestingly, Binodini refers to Ramakrishna as one of her two "protector figures"—the other being Girish Ghosh (Bhattacharya, 29). It is no accident that Ramakrishna's photograph is found backstage in nearly every Bengali theater. Sumit Sarkar writes that Ramakrishna

> allowed actresses, recruited from prostitutes, to touch his feet. . . . Ramakrishna's unexpected blessing of theater women gave a new respectability to a profession despised by many. . . . he became in fact, in course of time a kind of patron-saint for the Calcutta public theater. (1993, 64)

Gauri-Ma (Mridani Chattopadhyay)

One could argue that Ramakrishna felt compelled to be agreeable to his wife and to the women in society's lower echelons who did not constitute a threat, yet basically he had little liking for the other women he encountered. Ramakrishna's women disciples would disagree with this thesis, however. While one can dismiss the accounts of Ramakrishna's women disciples by suggesting that their reminiscences were the result of wishful thinking, there is enough evidence provided by these women to at least merit the possibility that their accounts of Ramakrishna are accurate. Since we have no evidence that these accounts are falsified, we will assume that they, as firsthand accounts of Ramakrishna, are valid. They are certainly more valid than the secondhand sources quoted in *Kālī's Child*—the only merit of those apparently being that they provided a viewpoint with which Kripal could agree.[49]

Gauri-Ma's writings further counter any idea of Ramakrishna's "general disgust for women." Gauri-Ma was one of Ramakrishna's women disciples and he had a particularly high opinion of her. In fact, Ramakrishna gave her the ochre cloth of sannyāsa, and she later founded the Saradeswari Asram, a monastic organization for women that is still active in Kolkata. Gauri-Ma was profoundly influenced by Ramakrishna, especially by his instructions to her regarding women. One day Gauri-Ma was picking flowers in Dakshineswar, when Ramakrishna came near her with a pot of water. While holding a branch of the bakul tree with one hand, he began pouring water with the other. He then said to her: "Gauri, let me pour water and you knead the clay" (*ami jol ḍhāli, tui kādā coṭkā*). Surprised, Gauri replied: "There is no clay here. How can I knead it? This place is filled with chipped stone." Ramakrishna smiled and said:

> I meant one thing and you understood quite another. I was referring to the condition of our women. They are greatly suffering. They are drowned to their necks in the darkness of ignorance, unable to see their own path. They have no idea what the purpose of life is. You must take up the burden of educating them. Light the lamp of knowledge before them. (Guharoy, 49)

According to Gauri-Ma, when she heard these instructions of Ramakrishna, she was completely taken aback and replied: "What are you saying! This is not my work. I cannot get along with worldly people. Instead, give me a few girls and I shall take them to the mountains and mold their character." Gauri-Ma said that Ramakrishna replied with a smile: "Oh no. No going to the mountains. Here, in this city, you will have to do work for women. You have practiced enough spiritual disciplines. Now you have to consecrate your life which is purified through austerities. Set yourself to work for the sake of the women of this country" (Guharoy, 49).[50]

Yogin-Ma (Yogindramohini Biswas)

We have already seen that Yogin-Ma attested to the intensity of Ramakrishna's love. She was also extremely close to Sarada, to the extent that when the latter went on an extended visit to Kamarpukur, Yogin-Ma wept. Seeing this, Ramakrishna had Yogin brought to his room where, she wrote in her reminiscences,"to console me he began telling me about the sādhanas he had practiced in Dakshineswar. He said, 'Do not reveal these things to anyone.' That day I sat very close to him while we talked. I was a housewife and until that day used to feel shy" (MK, 132).

Swami Aseshananda, who as Saradananda's secretary lived with both Yogin-Ma and Golap-Ma for five years at the Udbodhan House in Kolkata, often spoke of these women with reverence and great affection. They were held in very high esteem not only by Aseshananda but also by all the monks of the Ramakrishna Order. In his published reminiscence of Yogin-Ma, Aseshananda writes that Yogin-Ma had said: "The ideal of purity, which I cherished in my inmost heart, was not only reflected in Sri Ramakrishna's character, but surpassed by far all my conceptions" (1954, 56). Ramakrishna gave her many spiritual instructions, both general and detailed, and kept close watch on her spiritual development. Yogin-Ma told Aseshananda: "Although it is natural for us to feel a certain shyness before men, we had no such feeling in Sri Ramakrishna's presence ... we [were] free to open our hearts to him. We used to speak to him about very intimate things without any scruple or hestitation. And how kind, how affectionate the Master was to us! When strangers, casually reading the life of Ramakrishna, sometimes jump to the conclusion that he did not like women, we simply laugh" (59).[51]

When Yogin was in Dakshineswar, she was picking flowers one day, holding them in a corner of her cloth. Seeing her, Ramakrishna approached her and asked: "What are you carrying?" Yogin-Ma showed him the flowers and then, bowing down, offered them at his feet. With this, Ramakrishna went into ecstasy and placed his foot on her head (Chetanananda 1989, 144).

We can recall that *Kālī's Child* places great emphasis on Ramakrishna's foot being placed "onto the bodies of young males" (KC, 36), which Kripal sees as a homoerotic act, claiming that it was one of Ramakrishna's "techniques of arousal" (238). Yet as we can see from Binodini's and Yogin-Ma's reminiscences, Ramakrishna had no difficulty with placing his foot on women. Ramakrishna states in the *Kathāmṛta* that he placed his foot on his sister's head as well. Without a doubt, if Ramakrishna's other women devotees had been literate and had left their own reminiscences, we would have heard of many other instances.

When Ramakrishna attended the great Vaiṣṇava festival in Panihati, a number of women devotees accompanied him, Yogin-Ma among them. A few days later the women again joined him at Balaram Bose's house for the Jagannath *ratha-yātrā* ("chariot festival"). As he was preparing to leave for Dakshineswar, Yogin-Ma continued to follow him. In an ecstatic mood, Ramakrishna kept repeating: "Mā Ānandamoyī! Mā Ānandamoyī!" (Blissful Mother, blissful Mother). So reluctant was Yogin-Ma to leave Ramakrishna that he suggested she accompany him on the boat to Dakshineswar—which she did, along with another woman devotee, both of them madly running down the streets of Kolkata in order to catch the boat before it departed (LP 4.217-18).

It is worth mentioning that after Ramakrishna's death, both Saradananda and Yogin-Ma were given *pūrṇa abhiṣeka*, Tantric initiation, by Iswar Chandra Chakrabarty. Both Saradananda and Yogin-Ma practiced Tantric sādhana under Chakrabarty's guidance. Some years later, Yogin-Ma was given Vedic sannyāsa by Swami Saradananda in the presence of Swami Premananda (Aseshananda 1954, 63). While Kripal accuses the Ramakrishna Order of hiding Ramakrishna's Tantric background, it is difficult to maintain that argument in the light of such information.

Other Women Disciples of Ramakrishna

There are a number of other women disciples of Ramakrishna—among them, Gopaler-Ma (Aghoramani Devi), Golap-Ma (Golapsundari Devi), Nikunja Devi (M's wife), Lakshmi Devi (Lakshmimani Devi), Krishnabhavini Basu, Nistarini Ghosh—whose recorded reminiscences of Ramakrishna consistently speak of a man who was loving and caring. While *Kālī's Child* harshly critiques Ramakrishna's attitude toward M's wife Nikunja Devi (KC, 285), we find a very different story when we read the account of Devamata (an American woman closely associated with Sarada and Ramakrishna's monastic and householder disciples). According to Devamata, when Nikunja Devi visited Ramakrishna,

> he would sit for two or three hours at a time talking over with her the ailments of her children and the failings of the servants. She sought his advice about the best food to bring from the bazaar, how she should discipline the children when they were naughty, and what she could do to make her husband more comfortable and happy. Sri Ramakrishna listened and answered with grave interest. He never showed the least impatience or inattention. (Devamata 120–21)

Sumit Sarkar notes that Ramakrishna had, in "his last years a considerable number of women devotees" (1985, 105). Sarkar finds this ironic because of the negative images of women which are portrayed in the *Kathāmṛta.* Yet we must bear in mind that when Ramakrishna spoke to women, he spoke just as forcefully about the danger of lust and greed—using the phrase *puruṣa kāñcana*, "man and gold"—in spiritual life. The other more obvious point is that these women—whose reminiscences indicate that they were spirited, intelligent and often quite independent—would not have gone out of their way (and often in very difficult circumstances) to seek Ramakrishna's company if he had hated or feared them or had had "a general disgust" for them. Swami Aseshananda spoke often of a number of Ramakrishna's women disciples whom he encountered at Udbodhan, and he made it quite clear that these women were formidable in every way.[52] There was not one meek woman in the lot. The reminiscences of Ramakrishna's women devotees indicate that they found him a nurturing presence, with whom they felt not only inspired but also at ease.

Moreover, not only did Ramakrishna receive women visitors but he also visited them. He went, for example, to Yogin-Ma's house, to Golap-Ma's house and no doubt to the homes of others as well. When Ramakrishna visited his householder disciples, he would also spend time in the "inner apartments" with the women of the family. According to Devamata, Ramakrishna's visits to his women disciples "were occasions of great rejoicing. Sometimes fifty or sixty ladies would congregate to listen to the Master and he would talk to them in his simple informal way for several hours" (Devamata, 118-19).[53] Sumit Sarkar confirms that Ramakrishna "won the devotion of many women. We even have accounts of women casting off inhibitions and *parda* to go to Dakshineswar in a spirit of almost joyous abandon" (1993, 63). This is not the sort of reaction a man who hates and fears women generally receives.

Problematics of Interpretation

What we have discussed so far in this chapter—even though it relates specifically to *Kālī's Child*—provides a context in which to explore the problematics of interpretation across cultural and linguistic borders. We have focused primarily on only three of the major themes which course throughout *Kālī's Child*: the relationship between the mystical and the sexual, the significance of liṅga/yoni symbolism, and Ramakrishna's alleged misogyny. The difficulties involved—and the distortions possible—have also been explored at length in Chapter Two through an examination of what *Kālī's Child* describes as "the curious habits of [Ramakrishna's] foot" (KC, 2), where we also discussed the question of "censorship" and "cover-up" as well as what constitutes "secret" and "scandal."

We have seen that total objectivity—achieved by eliminating all subjective elements from one's interpretation—is virtually impossible. This basic truism of human existence necessarily contributes to the number of varying interpretations we find regarding any particular subject. Other elements that color one's subjectivity include the interpreter's worldview, her or his life experiences which, in turn, inevitably produce biases and prejudices, likes and dislikes. Another factor which will inevitably generate varying interpretations is the status of the source material. If the sources are in a language different from the one in which the interpretation is offered, the role of translation becomes enormously important. The problem becomes vastly more complex if the difference is not limited merely to language but extends also to culture and time. Apart from the quality of translation, the "coloring" of any translation further depends on the kind of interpretation strategies employed. When these existing variables are then factored into existing problems such as inaccurate documentation, unjustified speculation, and conscious or unconscious omissions—it is then hardly a surprise when wildly diverse interpretations abound regarding a particular subject, theme or human being. It is to these factors of documentation and translation that we now turn in the following chapter.

5

Documentation and Translation of the Texts

> Words differently arranged have a different meaning, and meanings differently arranged have different effects.
>
> —Blaise Pascal, *Pensées*

There is something special about a published book. It somehow seems more authentic than an unpublished manuscript or a newspaper or magazine. But simply because a statement can be traced to a published book does not necessarily make the book's information reliable. Errors often slip in through oversight when facts or references are not checked in a systematic way. The onus is generally on the author; publishers typically limit their responsibility to checking spelling and dates of key events. No publisher has the time to duplicate years of research in cross-checking every fact or claim, nor is it practical.

Notwithstanding the enormous burden of delivering an error-free manuscript, no author can guarantee a perfect book. While errors are inevitable and understandable, they pose a question if their number is unusually high and, more importantly, if they are pivotal to the central theses of the book. The textual problems in *Kālī's Child* present just such a scenario. Some of the documentation and translation issues in the book are serious; many others may seem insignificant. But it is the collective force generated by stringing together questionable translations in a seemingly logical way that has made *Kālī's Child*'s theses appear sustainable.

This chapter provides a textual analysis of *Kālī's Child* through a few representative examples of problematic passages in the book. It would have hardly mattered if the book possessed only a few minor errors in translation and documentation. Such errors are understandable in any human undertaking and, by themselves, would not have hurt *Kālī's Child*'s theses or have made its conclusions untenable. In fact, that is exactly what Kripal claimed after errors in his book were pointed out in several of *Kālī's Child*'s reviews. After conceding that "a few translation errors" (Kripal 2002, 192) had indeed been present and thanking the reviewers for pointing them out, he went on to say that none of those errors would warrant "altering the substance or conclusions of the book" as the "big picture" would remain unaffected (193).

Unfortunately that is not true. *Kālī's Child*'s "big picture"—the book's central theses—would be seriously affected if all the errors were acknowledged and corrected. These errors are neither "few" nor insignificant. Many of them are extremely serious. Others, although seemingly minor, are sprinkled throughout the book, on nearly every page. The result is a steady drip of misinformation that succeeds remarkably in its goal of navigating the discussion toward the author's predetermined conclusions. The strategy can be detected only by careful readers well versed in the source texts. Addressing these problems brings to light considerable issues that need to be confronted in studies that span cultural, linguistic and religious boundaries.

Methodological Problems

How did *Kālī's Child* maintain a steady drip of misinformation? Primarily through inaccurate translations of the Bengali texts. But there are other factors as well which helped to maintain the flow of misinformation: speculations are presented as facts, information not supportive of the author's thesis is suppressed, contexts in which Bengali quotes appear are altered, and the author's own comments are slipped in within the purported paraphrases of documented Bengali texts. All of this raises questions related to methodology.

Mistranslation

Languages differ radically from one another. Some insist that we can never communicate adequately in one language what has been expressed in another. Sandra Bermann has written that "language can never be viewed as a simple mental tool, or as a transparent medium of representation. . . . language remains radically impure, haunted by endless semantic contexts and … insuperable undecidability" (Bermann, 4).[1] Nevertheless, adequate or not, translations are indispensable because that is the only way through which communication across linguistic borders becomes possible. Bermann writes that if we must translate, "we must do so while attempting to respond ethically to each language's contexts, intertexts, and intrinsic alterity" (7).

Given this, it is obvious that the translator faces a number of challenges and is called to make choices between conflicting options: Should the "word" be translated or the "idea" that it is meant to convey? What is primary—being faithful to the letter or to what the translator believes to be the spirit of the text? The decisions of the translator are often dictated by the purpose for which the translation is undertaken. Another challenge is posed by the dynamic nature of language. Languages evolve and translating a text that is a century or more old involves knowing the subtle connotations of a particular word or phrase as understood by the people of that period.

Moreover, every translation—particularly between languages that originate in radically different cultures—is an act of interpretation. Should the text be viewed from the translator's perspective, which is shaped by a different time and culture, or should an attempt be made to view it from the perspective of the time and culture in which the text originated? The second option involves a double interpretation: interpreting another's perspective from the translator's perspective. This raises, in a roundabout way, the issue of potentially conflicting perspectives of insiders and outsiders, and privileging of one over the other.

It is difficult to discern in *Kālī's Child* any consistency in the policy used in translating from Bengali sources. Sometimes the translation is literal, sometimes it is interpretative, and sometimes it is just wrong. Sometimes a Bengali passage is translated and at other times it is conveniently paraphrased. The choice in every instance seems to be dictated by the sole concern that the source texts appear to support the author's theses. Since the portions that are not amenable to such a strategy have been suppressed in *Kālī's Child*, the conclusions reached in the book have the aura of being evident and unarguable.

Speculation

No matter how extensively documented the subject of one's research is, some degree of speculation is unavoidable in order to fill in the blanks that almost always exist in any research work. Such speculation may even be necessary to make sense of what the texts say. If the book is not meant to be categorized as fiction, then the speculations in it need to meet certain criteria, at least two of which seem basic. First, the speculation must fit the blank it is meant to fill; in other words, it needs to be in harmony with the information already available from the source texts. Second, the speculation must be clearly acknowledged to be a speculation.

In *Kālī's Child* both of these requirements have been flouted. Although faulty translations abound in the book and may seem to be the central problem, those translations were done to support speculations that support fragile theses. The "translations" were designed to give legitimacy to speculations and, in many instances, even to mask them.

The speculations presented in *Kālī's Child* contradict the evidence in the source texts; this difficulty is overcome for the most part by ignoring and occasionally dismissing any contradictory evidence. The speculations do not support what is already known about Ramakrishna. Kripal overcomes this difficulty through contrived translations, selective quotations, and studious omissions. Moreover, the speculations in the book are only occasionally acknowledged to be speculations. In many instances, the speculative portions of *Kālī's Child* are inserted into the body of a supposed paraphrase or "translation," giving the impression that it has textual support. Even in those places where the speculation is initially acknowledged as such, it is thereafter treated in the rest of the book as if it were an established fact—and these "facts" are used to draw the book's central conclusions.

Misdocumentation and Context-Tampering

Identifying the sources of direct quotations and of any facts or opinions "not generally known or easily checked" is what documentation is all about, and it is required as a matter of "ethics, copyright laws, and courtesy to readers."[2] Just as important is the placement of the source-reference, which should leave no ambiguity or create the wrong impression in the reader's mind about what exactly is being cited from a source. When the line separating a quotation (or paraphrase) from another book and the author's own comments becomes blurred, we have a serious problem. It is unfair to the source being cited, because it is not being cited honestly and clearly. It is also unfair to the readers because, if they are unfamiliar with the source being cited, they cannot distinguish between the quoted text and the author's gloss, or between the citation and the commentary.

In the section which follows, several examples are given of the ambiguities created by misdocumentation in *Kālī's Child*. Whether the misdocumentation that occurred was by design or not is not for us to answer. We can only point out instances where Kripal's own interpretations and speculations were presented as though they had textual support when, in fact, they had none. There are also many instances in *Kālī's Child*, only a few of which have been presented in this book, where the reference cited leads nowhere; there is nothing in the referred text to justify that reference. Of course, typos are always possible, if not inevitable, in a research work that has to handle hundreds of references. Mistakes of some variety are nearly impossible to avoid. But there is no way to distinguish in *Kālī's Child* between sloppy documentation and conscious presentation of dead-end references.

Words and sentences lifted out of context can deliver a different meaning, sometimes a meaning that is even opposed to what the word or sentence meant in the original context. An accurate translation and proper documentation are no guarantee that the original text is properly represented if the quotes are divorced from the specific context. The following section also presents examples that illustrate how *Kālī's Child* used Bengali sources out of context and sometimes fused together quotes from different contexts to create a new context to bolster its theses.

It is our hope that this analysis will highlight not merely the problems in *Kālī's Child*, but also the dangers that lurk in studies which cross cultural, religious, and linguistic boundaries—and the precautions which need to be taken to preserve intellectual honesty and integrity without sacrificing academic freedom.

A Brief Analysis

In order to sustain *Kālī's Child*'s theses, it was first necessary to question the validity of existing translations; accuse the Ramakrishna Order of censorship and harboring "secrets"; diminish Ramakrishna by creating a pattern of derision and trivialization; accentuate the distinctions between Vedānta and Tantra in order to define Ramakrishna as a Tāntrik and claim that his followers had recreated his image as a Vedāntin; manufacture an issue of Ramakrishna's "confused sexuality," and focus on Ramakrishna's love for "boys" in order to strengthen the allegedly homoerotic dimension of his life.

The following brief analysis presents a glimpse of how the steady drip of misinformation was manipulated in order to fulfill the objectives necessary to sustain the book's theses.

The "Secret" and Its Censorship

Kripal claims to be a "digger" (KC, 303), the uncoverer of "a secret that is kept hidden from the public's eye" (311). To substantiate this assertion, Kripal claims that the original diaries of M, the source of his *Kathāmṛta*, have been hidden in order to protect scandalous "secrets." He further claims that Nikhilananda's English translation of the *Kathāmṛta* is "bowdlerized."

We believe that it is both inaccurate and unfair to characterize Nikhilananda's 1942 *Gospel of Sri Ramakrishna* as "bowdlerized," as can be seen by examining the portions which Nikhilananda either excised or did not fully translate. These selections are available online at: http://www.interpretingramakrishna.com. Readers can decide for themselves whether what was omitted constitutes "bowdlerization" and what kind of "secrets" were kept hidden. We have also seen that the Ramakrishna Order does not possess the diaries, and M's descendants, who possess those diaries, have affirmed that scholars have access to them.

Given the above, it seems incredible that Kripal could refer to the "reluctance" of the Ramakrishna Order to help Western researchers (KC, 311) when it was, in fact, a monk of the Ramakrishna Order, Swami Prabhananda, who shared with Kripal the photocopies of the pages of M's diary. Kripal was also welcomed by another monk of the Order, Swami Lokeswarananda, who extended his hospitality to Kripal and allowed him not only to stay in a Kolkata branch of the Order but even to use its extensive library. "Reluctance" of the Ramakrishna Order, indeed!

What are these "secrets" that the Ramakrishna Order is accused of hiding? According to *Kālī's Child*, the "secrets" are both textual and psychological. The textual secrets are the passages that were specifically introduced with the phrase "secret talk" (*guhya kathā*) either by M or by Ramakrishna himself. It was apparently to hide these secrets that M ordered "his [*Kathāmṛta*] volumes in a cyclical pattern"—so that he could "tuck the more explicit 'secret talk' passages away in the later volumes" (KC, 310). The logic behind this reasoning is unfathomable, considering that the "later volumes" are as easily available as the earlier volumes. Furthermore, as we have already seen, there is no basis for *Kālī's Child*'s purported cyclical pattern theory of the *Kathāmṛta*. Another dimension of the textual secrets is the "bowdlerization" of texts: according to Kripal, Nikhilananda mistranslated or simply omitted those passages "that he found personally troubling or that he considered unfit for a Western audience" (310).

As we have already discussed, *Kālī's Child* asserts that Ramakrishna's "secret" can be unearthed by analyzing the *guhya kathā*—the so-called "secret talk" of Ramakrishna, which consists of "eighteen passages dealing with visions and confessions Ramakrishna thought too troubling or important to reveal to any but his most intimate disciples" (KC, 3–4). The passages which form the "secret talk" are identified by Kripal with the help of one sole determinant: the use of the Bengali phrase *guhya kathā* in the *Kathāmṛta*. This is both a mechanical and inadequate device since many of the topics included in the *guhya kathā* are also repeated on other occasions *without* the "secret talk" tag.

One impenetrable obstacle to *Kālī's Child*'s interpretive process is Kripal's reductive understanding of the term *guhya*, which Kripal generally takes to mean either a secret of a sexual nature or a reference to the anus (while *guhya* can mean anus, it is not the most generally understood meaning or use of the word). It is important to keep in mind that the word *guhya* occurs with great frequency in nearly all Hindu religious texts, including the Bhagavad Gītā, the Upaniṣads and a great many others. For example, in the first verse of the eleventh chapter of the Bhagavad Gītā, Arjuna says to Kṛṣṇa: "Your instructions on the highest mystery (*paramaṁ guhyam*), given to me out of your infinite grace, have dispelled my delusion." In the Kaṭha Upaniṣad 1.3.17, we read about knowledge that is both great (*paramam*) and secret (*guhyam*). The Śvetāśvatara Upaniṣad (6.22) employs the same adjectives—great (*paramam*) and secret (*guhyam*)—while referring to the knowledge of the supreme.[3]

The deeper meaning of a scriptural passage is known as *guhyārtha*. The word *guhya* means mysterious, hidden, mystical, but is most frequently used in the sense of "esoteric." That is, "something likely to be understood by only those with a special knowledge or interest." Or taken another way, that which is *guhya* is the knowledge which only the spiritually adept (*adhikārī*) can apprehend. In other words, unless one is religiously trained and prepared, *guhya* is something quite likely to be misunderstood by the untrained. It is "secret" because of the sacredness and the sanctity attached to it and the very real danger of it being misunderstood. One could well argue that *Kālī's Child* is a case in point.

In returning to Ramakrishna's "secret talks," Kripal asserts, in his response to criticism regarding *Kālī's Child*, that those passages "symbolically witness to the homoerotic dimensions of Ramakrishna's mystical life and teachings." Kripal goes on to declare that this is "definitely still 'secret' within the tradition." That is, while "the texts themselves are not secret, but their interpreted meanings certainly are" (Kripal 2002, 196). Implied in this charge is the idea that the "secret" of Ramakrishna cannot be understood—or accepted even after understanding—by those within the tradition. Kripal cites several reasons why his critics would find his homoerotic thesis unacceptable: one, the long-held religious worldview of "the normal believers"; two, cultural differences "about what can and cannot be said in public"; and three, homophobia and the consequent "projection" upon the author's intentions (194–97). Yet Kripal fails to recognize, or refuses to acknowledge, the possibility that those who critique his work may have reasons other than merely competing worldviews, cultural differences, or their own personal neuroses, what to speak of the possibility (using Kripal's own reasoning) of his own "projection" upon the intentions of his critics.

There is irony in Kripal's accusation that the Ramakrishna Order is hiding "secrets." For even while he was enjoying the hospitality of the Order and using its library in Kolkata, he was at the same time accusing the Order in his writings of hiding Ramakrishna's "secret." Yet it was in fact Kripal who was hiding a "secret": he admits to consciously not divulging to his hosts the nature of his research. Of course, he did not have to and no one in the Ramakrishna Order expected him to divulge the particular nature of his research. Scholars staying at the Order's guesthouses have complete freedom to pursue their research in their own way. Kripal's reason for keeping his research secret was, according to him, a virtual necessity:

> My work on the historical textual tradition proceeds only through a hermeneutical recovering of that which has been suppressed, censored, and denied by the tradition. There is thus no way in which work like mine could *not* be controversial; to the extent that it reveals esoteric truths that have been concealed by the tradition, it must be contested and ultimately rejected by that same tradition. (Kripal 1998b, 630)

In other words, even if his work is contested, that only goes to prove that it is accurate. Like Ramakrishna, the Ramakrishna Order can't win for losing.

The "Troubling" Atmospherics

Nearly as important as the specific instances of the book's mistranslations, misdocumentation and unjustified innuendo is the general tenor of the book itself. From the book's beginning to its conclusion, the careful reader will notice how *Kālī's Child* manipulates language in order to create a sex-soaked atmosphere for the sake of lending subliminal credence to the book's theses. Even in describing the temple compound in Dakshineswar, we can see a carefully calibrated word choice: Kālī is described as "seductive in her black immanence" while adding that in *other* images of Śiva (i.e., those that are not in Dakshineswar), "Śiva's penis stands erect, aroused out of its quiescence by the goddess's erotic presence" (15).

In the Dakshineswar temple—where Ramakrishna lived and worshiped nearly his entire life—Kālī stands on a *non*-ithyphallic Śiva. Kripal does not tell us this directly. Instead, he notes that in *other* images, Śiva *is* ithyphallic. Since this was not the case in the Dakshineswar temple, and since, as the author informs us, the Dakshineswar temple "defined the contours of Ramakrishna's religiosity," one wonders why *Kālī's Child* contains so many references to ithyphallic Śivas. In the book's Introduction, for example, we are told of "Śiva's erect penis, aroused by the goddess's frenzied dance on his breast" (22). In the book's first chapter, Kripal writes that at the touch of Kālī's feet, "Śiva's pale penis stands erect." The "ithyphallic corpse [is] ... aroused by the goddess" and Śiva is now, predictably, "Śiva, the erotic ascetic" (50).

If one were to read only *Kālī's Child*, one would never know that Śiva is not always ithyphallic. Indeed, *Kālī's Child*'s Śiva is so priapic that if anyone were to read the *Kathāmṛta* or any other source text on Ramakrishna in the hopes of finding an erotic Śiva, she or he would be sorely disappointed.[4] Yet throughout *Kālī's Child* the reader will encounter every variety of ithyphallic male, mortal and immortal. Ramakrishna is "no ordinary mortal," Kripal writes. "His mystical, essentially divine nature is as obvious as Śiva's erect *liṅgam*." Should that be not obvious enough, Kripal continues: "For Ramakrishna ... his was a homoerotic community, united through an erect passion" (231). So central is the image of the ithyphallic male to *Kālī's Child* that even the last paragraph of the book will carry a reference to "ithyphallic boys," without any discernible reason for its being there (336).

Apart from Śiva, Kālī is described in *Kālī's Child* as having a "sexy waist," with a citation given purportedly quoting the poems of Ramprasad (50). Yet if one checks Ramprasad's poem, one finds Kālī described as having a "slender waist, covered by a girdle of human hands with tinkling bells" (*kṣīna kaṭipar, nṛkar nikar, ābṛta kato kiṅkini*), rather than *Kālī's Child*'s "tinkling ornaments dangling around her sexy waist." The "round sexy thighs" are similarly not to be found in Ramprasad's poetry either.[5] *Kālī's Child* also notes that Kālī's skirt is "strategically, almost seductively, placed over the goddess's buttocks and sexual organs, creating a 'bikini' of human hands that reveal as much as they conceal and conceal only to seduce" (51). This version of Kālī speaks more to contemporary sexual preoccupations than it does to those characters we find on the pages of the *Kathāmṛta* and other source texts. On the same page where we find Kālī's "round sexy thighs," we are told of the "voluptuous milkmaids of Vrindavana" (51) whereas the referenced text merely refers to them as "the women of Vrindavana." There was no reason for such gratuitous sexualization of these descriptions—none of them are central to *Kālī's Child*'s theses—except to heighten the sexual atmosphere surrounding Ramakrishna and his environment.

If there is one operative word that is used throughout *Kālī's Child*, and one used to great effect, it is "troubling." This is second only to its alternate form, "troubled." The reader is endlessly clubbed with these modifiers, yet nowhere in the source documents can we find any material which would justify the usage. A number of *Kālī's Child*'s academic reviewers have referred to Ramakrishna as "troubled" as well, yet nowhere in the source documents do we find anything to support this assessment. Indeed, every source document—and there are hundreds of them—states precisely the opposite. Sarada said on a number of occasions that Ramakrishna was a joyful person. She states: "I never saw Thakur unhappy (*nirānanda*). He was joyous in the company of everyone, whether he was a five-year-old boy or an old man. I never saw him unhappy" (MK, 192). Vivekananda told Sara Bull that "he had expected the 'holy' to be so different" before he knew Ramakrishna. Since Ramakrishna was known as a holy man, Vivekananda assumed that he would be serious and sober. To his surprise, Vivekananda told Sara Bull that Ramakrishna "was full of gaiety and merriment." Ramakrishna, Vivekananda explained, "had become *identified* with holiness" (Prabuddhaprana 2002, 346–47). Ramakrishna was joyful because he lived in joy. Every single one of Ramakrishna's disciples, to a person, both male and female, describes being with Ramakrishna as a joyful experience.

Further, the firsthand documents not written by Ramakrishna's disciples—by members of the Brahmo Samaj, for example—describe Ramakrishna as "wreathed in smiles." Pratap Mazumdar, whom we have already encountered, describes Ramakrishna as possessing a "childlike tenderness … an unspeakable sweetness of expression and smile that I have seen in no other face that I can remember" (Mookerjee, 3–4). Nationalist leader Aswini Kumar Dutta wrote that his "whole life has been sweetened by what I got from [Ramakrishna] . . . . The memory of that elysian smile is still with me, shedding unending bliss" (Mookerjee, 32). Ramchandra Datta, author of the *Jībanabṛttānta*, recalled: "Although the Master was in terrible pain [because of throat cancer] he was always joyful. We never saw him sad or worried" (Chetanananda 1990, 277). A Brahmo writing in *The Indian Mirror* describes Ramakrishna's nature as being "marked by … humor and humility" and further described him as "profound, respectable, sincere and affectionate" (Mookerjee, 124-25). There are no firsthand sources which suggest anything "troubled" or "troubling" about Ramakrishna. Yet these records which attest to his sunny disposition are either disregarded or denigrated.

While there were those—particularly earlier in Ramakrishna's life—who believed Ramakrishna to be mad, there was never any question of Ramakrishna behaving in a "troubling" way toward other people. Moreover, by the time Ramakrishna's disciples arrived, he was by and large accepted as the famed and respected "paramahaṁsa of Dakshineswar"—which is why his room was crowded with people much of the time. There is no evidence of anyone being "troubled" by Ramakrishna's own behavior or by his behavior toward his young male disciples. Nor should we see this lack of evidence as indicative of nineteenth-century Indian psychological cluelessness or cultural naiveté: there was no lack of people who would have merrily pounced upon any perceived character flaw on Ramakrishna's part, particularly given the intense nature of religious rivalry in Kolkata during those years.

Nevertheless, despite a wealth of evidence which argues entirely to the contrary, *Kālī's Child* endlessly repeats that Ramakrishna's behavior was "troubling," people were "troubled" by Ramakrishna and Ramakrishna himself was a "troubled mystic." Thus without any evidence provided, the characterization of Ramakrishna as "troubled" with "troubling" behavior patterns is repeated over and over until the steady drip of misinformation creates a cumulative effect of disquiet.[6]

In keeping with this manufactured unease, *Kālī's Child* repeatedly invokes the specter of "scandal." We read, for example, that Ramakrishna's "sexual behavior mounted to a scandal," a charge which is completely unjustified. To this we are presented another "when did you stop beating your wife" scenario when Kripal adds: "But even given the scandal of Ramakrishna's homosexual behavior…" (79). *What* scandal? *What* homosexual behavior? As with the "troubled" tag, "scandal" is similarly drummed into the reader throughout the pages of *Kālī's Child*, without any basis in fact, without any textual support. It is simply reiterated again and again, and, by dint of repetition, begins to present itself as fact.[7] "Scandal" is occasionally upgraded to more serious charges: "The families [of Ramakrishna's male disciples] object to an unspecified crime" (80). *What* unspecified crime? There is no crime, no charges, just unsubstantiated accusations in *Kālī's Child*.

Kripal similarly writes that parents were "shocked by [Ramakrishna's] eroticized language" (79), which again is untrue and without justification. There was *one person*—and he was not a "parent" whose son visited Ramakrishna—the anglicized Brahmo Pratap Mazumdar, who criticized Ramakrishna's occasional use of "abominably filthy language," but this was by no means "eroticized language." It means the language that any unschooled nineteenth-century Bengali villager would use. Sumit Sarkar and Partha Chatterjee characterize this language as "rustic" and "colloquial," in contrast to the chaste formality of the language of the Westernized middle-class elite. There is no record of anyone objecting to Ramakrishna's "eroticized language," because his language was not "eroticized." Earthy, yes; eroticized, no.

Again, *Kālī's Child* declares that many people criticized Ramakrishna for his "mistreatment of women" (244). Who constitutes this "many people"? There is only *one* known instance of criticism regarding Ramakrishna's "mistreatment of women," and this again is from our friend Pratap Mazumdar, who criticized Ramakrishna for "the almost barbarous treatment of his wife"—that is, Mazumdar criticized Ramakrishna for not having sexual relations with Sarada. Does Mazumdar constitute "many people"? And does Mazumdar's criticism of Ramakrishna's and Sarada's lack of sexual relations translate into a generalized Ramakrishna's "mistreatment of women"?

It is important to note that what we see here is the universalizing of one element—for example, a solitary example of Mazumdar—and creating from it a general statement about Ramakrishna's behavior and the reaction it received. This pattern is a common thread which can be found throughout the course of *Kālī's Child*. We have already seen how Dr. Sarkar's sole negative reaction to Ramakrishna's foot was multiplied into "visitor," "visiting male," and "troubled observer," and this one negative reaction was universalized into "the controversial actions of Ramakrishna's foot."

This pattern of both repeating unfounded accusations as well as universalizing (and misinterpreting) sole incidents into nonexistent behavior patterns is one of the most serious problems found in *Kālī's Child*. Thus we read of Ramakrishna's "originally suspect sexual desires" (85). *What* "suspect" sexual desires? Suspected by whom, apart from the author of *Kālī's Child*? Time and again the reader is presented with what is initially offered as the author's hunch, only to have the hunch quickly transformed into a purported biographical "fact" of Ramakrishna's life. The only problem is that these "facts" do not exist except as the author's own suspicions, with no authentic evidence provided to back up his allegations. When the citations provided as evidence are checked, they are shown to be mistranslated, misdocumented, distorted, or even nonexistent. While Kripal prides himself on being "a digger," when one digs into the allegations and the citations which supposedly provide support for his theses, they evaporate into the mist of smoke and mirrors. In a page taken from Goebbels, we see how the endless repetition of disinformation sets up its own alternate reality system: an untruth repeated enough times becomes not only believable, but appears to be truth itself.

The Trivialization of Ramakrishna

In order to present an alternative view of Ramakrishna which seems plausible, it is necessary to show that earlier views are either in need of revision or are dispensable. Estimates of Ramakrishna cover a wide spectrum: from an avatar to a saint to a good man to a madman. *Kālī's Child* adds a new view to this mix and broadens the spectrum, projecting Ramakrishna to be a homoerotically driven, troubled man. As a first step toward making this view appear credible, the author takes considerable pains to trivialize the events and spiritual experiences in Ramakrishna's life. A few examples:

> **KC, 55:** "On another day while I was talking to Dhani in front of the Śiva temple of the Yogis, I saw a divine light come out of the great limb of Śiva. . . . " (LP 1.4.8)
>
> ... Then Śiva, known for his erotic exploits, impregnates the aging woman as she walks by his "great limb," most likely a reference to the Śiva-*liṅgam* enshrined in the temple.

A look at the referenced text reveals something very different:

> **LP 1.4.8:** *Ār ek din Jugīder Śiva-mandirer sammukhe dām̐ḍāiyā Dhanir sohit kothā kohitechi, emon somay dekhite pāilām, Mahādeber śrī-aṅga hoite dibya-jyoti nirgata hoiyā mandir pūrna koriyāche...*
>
> **Translation:** "On another day while I was talking to Dhani in front of the Śiva temple of the Yugīs, I saw a divine light emanating from the holy image of Mahādeva and filling the temple..."

This passage describes, in the words of Ramakrishna's mother, a vision she had before Ramakrishna's birth. *Kālī's Child*'s translation of *śrī-aṅga* as "the great limb" is neither literal nor contextual. The word *śrī* means "holy" or "auspicious," not "great." While the literal translation of *aṅga* can be either "limb" or "part," in combination with *śrī*, the accurate translation is "holy form" or "holy image." By characterizing Śiva as someone "known for his erotic exploits," it is easy to see why *śrī-aṅga* was mistranslated as "the great limb." Kripal's ignorance of the language and Bengali culture are apparent from his translation: "of the Yogis" (*Jugīder*). Yugī (pronounced in Bengali as "Jugī") is, in fact, the name of a caste of weavers.

Another example of the author's ignorance can be found in this endnote, following the name of Ramakrishna's father, Kshudiram Chatterjee: "Chatterjee becomes 'Bhattacarrya' [sic] in some contexts" (KC, 342). The answer should have been obvious to anyone with a basic knowledge of Bengali language and culture: while "Chatterjee" is the last name, "Bhattacharya" simply means a "priest" when applied to Ramakrishna. It is not the name "Chatterjee" that *becomes* "Bhattacharya." Many such examples can easily be cited from *Kālī's Child*.

The author's disdain for Ramakrishna's parents' religious experiences is again revealed when he conflates Ramakrishna's father Kshudiram's "auspicious dreams and visions" with his sister's possession by a ghost and his aunt's purported "cataleptic fits," pointedly noting how most of his family seemed open to "such experiences" (KC, 54). Kripal refers to Ramakrishna's mother Chandramani's religious dreams as "nocturnal encounters" and "erotic encounters," and the luminous deity (*jyotirmay devatā*) she saw in her dream as a "nocturnal visitor." The vision Chandramani had in front of the Śiva temple, when she saw a flood of divine light (*dibya jyoti*) entering into her, was in fact, a "diurnal rape" by, who else, "Śiva, known for his erotic exploits" (55). In order to set the stage to describe a sexually abused, troubled and confused Ramakrishna, the author subverts the notion that there was anything even potentially "religious" in the experiences of Ramakrishna's parents that preceded his birth. Not surprisingly, Kripal questions whether some of these experiences even occurred or whether they were "simply the products of Saradananda's pen and stylized rhetoric" (63).

Trivializing the experiences of Ramakrishna's parents is merely a precursor to trivializing Ramakrishna's own experiences. Ramakrishna reports in the *Kathāmṛta* that he "entered into samādhi" (*samādhistha hoye gelām*) (KA 4.74); Kripal paraphrases the passage, telling his readers that "Ramakrishna falls over unconscious" (KC, 66). Kripal subjects the crowning spiritual experience that Ramakrishna is reported to have had in the Kālī temple to a seemingly thorough analysis in the book in order to arrive at the conclusion that, far from being a religious experience, it was, in fact, "some sort of erotic crisis" (73). Ramakrishna's longing for God was nothing more than "anxious desire and pain" produced by "the dark forces of sexual desire" (73).

How does the author arrive at this interpretation? The modus operandi is a familiar one. First, he mistranslates the Bengali *vyakulatā*, deep longing, as "anxious desire," and then discards Saradananda's account, which goes counter to the author's thesis. *Kālī's Child* then isolates four accounts in the *Kathāmṛta* in which there is either a mention of a knife or putting an end to one's life. Kripal speculates that those accounts "seem to be" based on actual events (KC, 70) and "might in fact" be referring to the same event (71). The author feels that it is "perfectly possible, indeed likely" that Ramakrishna was working from a fallible memory and did not remember the exact order of his sādhanas (71). That, according to him, has resulted in the "chronological confusion" in the different accounts. The trouble with this reasoning is that the *Kathāmṛta*, from where these accounts are extracted, does not make any attempt to offer a chronological account of the events in Ramakrishna's life. Thus the "chronological confusion" is more contrived than real.

As for the ordering of Ramakrishna's sādhanas, *Kālī's Child* states that Saradananda contradicts himself since, in the fourth volume of the *Līlāprasaṅga*, he "states in passing, perhaps not noticing it himself, that Ramakrishna's Vaiṣṇava practices preceded his Tantric practices, which in turn preceded his Vedantic practices (LP 4.2.24)" (KC, 98). Yet even a casual look at the text by anyone who understands Bengali will make it clear that there is no contradiction. The paraphrase that Kripal provides and attributes to LP 4.2.24 either shows ignorance of the Bengali language or reveals yet another example of faulty documentation.[8] At LP 4.2.24, Saradananda points out an interesting coincidence: whenever Ramakrishna engaged himself in a specific meditation and practice (*upāsanā o sādhanā*), followers and devotees of that specific tradition (*sampradāy*) would arrive in Dakshineswar, and he was able to spend time with them in discussions (*ālocanā*). There is no attempt at all in this section to provide any chronological order. The chronological order that Saradananda does offer in the *Līlāprasaṅga* (LP 2.1–384) is rejected in *Kālī's Child* for no convincing reason, leaving the discerning reader to wonder whether it was done out of necessity to clear the way for an account that conflicts with the source texts.

A similarly flawed strategy is adopted in *Kālī's Child* to present what Kripal calls the "*Kathāmṛta* version" of the chronology (KC, 91–94). What is his source for this version? Incredibly, merely two quotes of Ramakrishna (KA 4.175 and 2.132–33), in which there is no attempt to describe the order in which the sādhanas were practiced. Ramakrishna's words are misconstrued in *Kālī's Child* to neatly categorize "mystical practices" into three kinds, which are centered around three textual sources (the Purāṇas, the Tantras, and the Vedas) and associated with three places (the Panchavati, the bel tree, and the portico). The problems inherent in this formulaic exercise become evident when Vedānta—which is consistently disparaged in *Kālī's Child*—is reduced to Ramakrishna's sitting in the portico and eating rice. Instead of a serious spiritual endeavor, Kripal writes, Ramakrishna's Vedānta practice was "more of a game" and the "only significant thing" about his practice of Vedānta "is the fact that it is not significant" (93). It is "not significant" only if one chooses to ignore and suppress—as *Kālī's Child* does—the enormous information available in the source texts about Ramakrishna's Vedānta practice and teachings.[9]

Kripal discards Saradananda's *Līlāprasaṅga* account by privileging the *Kathāmṛta*, when it suits him, as a "legitimate and relatively accurate source" (KC, 14). But after using the *Kathāmṛta* to discount *Līlāprasaṅga*, he then discounts the authenticity of both books, which, he writes, "ultimately depend on Ramakrishna's memories, which he related to his followers in a most haphazard fashion at a distance of twenty to thirty years" (71). Moreover, Ramakrishna's memories were "usually ambiguous, sometimes contradictory, and often vague" (71). Finally Kripal ends up privileging his own speculations over the material found in the source texts. We are, in effect, asked to believe that *Kālī's Child* got the ordering of Ramakrishna's sādhanas right; while neither the source books nor Ramakrishna himself knew the correct order.[10]

Let us now take a brief look at the four passages that, *Kālī's Child* claims, refer to the same event.

> **KC, 71:** The first passage is simple and short. It occurs in volume 4. Ramakrishna has just told the story of a son forcing his demands on his father by threatening to cut his throat with a knife. He then, almost casually, adds: "I used to do this when I called on Ma" (KA 4.65).

Now let us look at the referenced Bengali text:

> **KA 4.65:** [After the story of the son demanding his share of the property, Ramakrishna continues] *Byākul hole tini śunben hi śunben. Tini je kāle janma diyechen, śe kāle tām̐r ghare āmāder hissā āche. Tini āpnār bāp, āpnār mā—tām̐r upor jor khāṭe. "Dao poricay. Noy golāy chūm̐ri dibo."*
>
> *Kirūpe māke ḍākite hoy, Ṭhākur śikhāitechen—"Āmi mā bole eirūpe ḍāktām—'Mā ānandamoyī!—dekhā dite je hobe!' Ābār kakhono boltām,—Ohe dīnanāth—jagannāth—āmi to jagat chāḍā noi nāth! Āṃi gyānhīn—sādhanhīn,—bhaktihīn—āmi kichui jāni nā—doyā kore dekhā dite hobe."*

> **Translation:** "God will certainly listen if you feel restless for him. Since he has given us birth, we have a share in the inheritance from him. He is our own father, our own mother. We can force our demand on him. We can say, 'Reveal yourself to me or I shall cut my throat with a knife.'"
>
> Thakur is teaching the devotees how to call on the Mother: "I used to pray to her in this way: 'O Mother! O Blissful One! Reveal yourself to me. You must!' Again, sometimes I would say: 'O Lord of the lowly! O Lord of the universe! I am not removed from the world, O Lord. I am without knowledge, without spiritual practice, without devotion. I know nothing. Be compassionate and reveal yourself.'"

Kālī's Child's translation, "I used *to do this* when I called on Ma," is radically different from what the Bengali says: "I used *to pray to her* in this way." This is the first part of a sentence *in another paragraph*—words that, Kripal would have us believe, were added "almost casually." These words preface how Ramakrishna prayed to the Mother; they clearly do not refer to his threat to the Mother to cut his own throat. After juxtaposing sentences from two different paragraphs, with a misleading gloss ("almost casually"), Kripal makes the amazing claim that "it is likely" that these words refer to the First Vision, which occurred at a period when Ramakrishna was passing through "troubled states" (KC, 71). There is no textual evidence to support either of these claims. The context is clearly different.

In the second passage which *Kālī's Child* presents as referring to the same event, Ramakrishna is talking about how his longing for God—his "divine madness"—increased to such an extent that, unable to bear the separation, he was going to cut his throat with a knife when it was revealed to him that he was only a machine and Kālī was the operator (KA 5.23). To this, *Kālī's Child* provides the following gloss:

> **KC, 72:** But here Ramakrishna adds that this crisis led to the realization that he was controlled by external forces, that he was not in control, an ambiguous sign warning of madness but also promising divine possession.

What does the Bengali text say?

> **KA 5.23:** *"Tāi boli Mā āmi jontra, tumi jontrī; āmi roth, tumi rothī; jemon cālāo temoni coli—jemon korāo temoni kori."*
>
> **Translation:** "That is why I say, Mother, I am a machine and you are the operator. I am a chariot and you are the charioteer. I act as you make me act—I do as you make me do."

Ramakrishna's words testifying that the Divine Mother controls every aspect of a person's life is an ancient formulation in the Hindu tradition that sees the Divine as the "inner controller" (*antaryāmī*) and are taken from one of Ramakrishna's favorite Ramprasad songs. But those words are made to sound ominous when *Kālī's Child* claims that "Ramakrishna adds ... that he was not in control"—a statement which is not in the text—and interprets awareness of the divine presence as "the promise of divine possession"—also a statement not in the text. The negative connotation implied in this allows the book to claim that Ramakrishna realized that "he was being controlled by external forces." There is also no indication in the source text that this passage refers to the First Vision, as *Kālī's Child* claims. But, more importantly, a spiritual experience of Ramakrishna has been trivialized and reduced to "an ambiguous sign warning of madness" (KC, 72).

> **KC, 72:** In our third passage, this time in volume 3, Ramakrishna clearly associates the act with a specifically Tantric approach to Kālī: "There is such a thing as dark (*tāmasika*) mystical practice—practice which relies on the dark aspects of human nature. *'Victory to Kālī!* What? You'll not show yourself to me! If you don't show yourself, I'll cut my throat with a knife.' In this type of mystical practice, as in Tantric practice, there's no concern for purity" (KA 3.138).

This is what we find in the *Kathāmṛta*:

> **KA 3.138:** *Tāmasik sādhan—tamoguṅ āśray kore sādhan. Joy Kālī! Ki, tui dekhā dibini! Ei galāy churi debo jodi dekha nā dis. E sādhanāy śuddhācār nāi—jemon tantrer sādhan.*
>
> **Translation:** The *tāmasika* spiritual practice is the practice done with the help of *tamas*. [The attitude of a *tāmasika* devotee is:] "Hail Kālī! Won't you reveal yourself to me? If you don't reveal yourself, I'll cut my throat with a knife." In this practice, there is no observance of conventional purity, as in the practice of Tantra.

Kālī's Child's translation of *tāmasika* as "dark" is certainly one of the literal meanings of the word *tamas*. It is, however, by no means an accurate translation when the word *tamas* is used in a specialized sense, such as in this case, where it clearly refers to one of the three attributes of *prakṛti*.

But what is more significant here is that nowhere in this passage does Ramakrishna say that this is what he *did* before he had the First Vision. Thus, in short order we are served yet another speculation: "The passage is most likely autobiographical" (KC, 72). Yet there are no reasons given to support this speculation. Typical of the methodology used in the book, the author then begins to draw conclusions based on this speculation. With weak-link logic intact, he builds upon his thesis by showing how in some secondary texts the "dark aspects of human nature" are connected with Tantric practices. The suggestion is far from subtle: Ramakrishna's experience was an erotic crisis and, in a similar sounding phrase, caused by the "dark forces of sexual desire" (73). Never mind that the text itself does not refer to any incident or experience of Ramakrishna's life, but merely the attitude of a tāmasika devotee.

The fourth passage to which *Kālī's Child* draws our attention addresses Ramakrishna's reminiscence about the upsurge of lust (*kāma*) in his heart and how he cried to the Divine Mother for it to be removed (KC, 72; KA 3.131). This was so anguishing to Ramakrishna that, were it to continue, he said he would cut his throat with a knife. Again, other than the mention of a knife and threatened self-destruction, there is nothing here to suggest that this incident is identical with the First Vision experience that Ramakrishna had. But this does not prevent the author from advancing the theory that this passage "may" hint at a "secret dimension to Ramakrishna's anxious longing" (KC, 72–73).

As we can see, not one of those passages discussed above refers to the experience that Ramakrishna had in the Kālī Temple. Nevertheless, *Kālī's Child* repeatedly ties these passages together and claims that they refer to the same event, with a subtle disclaimer that "perhaps they all refer to separate events." Despite the disclaimer, the book insists that the passages are "psychologically speaking, indistinct, virtually identical" (KC, 73). Thus the reader is to understand that Ramakrishna's First Vision was not a religious experience but a suicide threat triggered by psychosexual angst.

In keeping with the objective of trivializing Ramakrishna, a lighthearted incident described in the *Kathāmṛta* is reinterpreted to show that Ramakrishna was "a show to laugh at" even for his own disciples:

> **KC, 70:** Indeed, Ramakrishna's habit of threatening to cut his throat with a knife was so common and so well-known that, after he was dead, at least one disciple made fun of him by imitating his *vyākulatā* and faking his dramatic gestures. . . . Ramakrishna apparently was a melodramatic figure, a show to laugh at.

There are only two instances in the *Kathāmṛta* when Ramakrishna uses the expression "I will cut my throat with a knife" with regard to himself. Therefore this can hardly be called Ramakrishna's "habit." The expression is a common form of threat used in Bengali to express one's intense opposition to or desire for something, and it is rarely taken literally. Despite this, *Kālī's Child* suggests that the colloquialism is "a rather immature way of forcing one's demands" (KC, 70). There are two speculations at work in this incident: first, Ramakrishna's disciples—"at least one disciple," at any rate—made fun of him and, second, Ramakrishna was "a show to laugh at." Both of these contradict the source (KA 2.248) from which Kripal quotes.

The replaying of the knife incident is a lighthearted occasion; it is unambiguously clear from the text that the disciples are not "making fun" of Ramakrishna. Regarding the second speculation, Kripal censors what happened soon after the knife incident by neglecting to inform the reader that after purportedly "making fun" of Ramakrishna, his disciples joined in worshiping him: ringing bells and waving lights (*ārati*), standing reverently with folded hands before the picture of one who was "a show to laugh at." Elsewhere in the book, Kripal refers to Ramakrishna as "a fink" (KC, 107) and further intuits that Ramakrishna, after going to Benares, was not recognized as the "the paramahaṁsa he thought he was" (166). While it is entirely within an author's purview to disparage the subject of her or his book, one nevertheless should not be surprised that devotees of Ramakrishna were offended by what appeared to be the book's gratuitous slights.

Other questionable techniques which *Kālī's Child* employs are the promotion of invalid material from a secondary text and dismissal of valid material from a source text. As an example of the former, Kripal uses Bipinchandra Pal as a source on Ramakrishna, yet Bipinchandra never met Ramakrishna. It is from Bipinchandra's book *Saint Bijayakrishna Goswami* (Bipinchandra Pal Institute, 1964) that Kripal unearths a bizarre report about Ramakrishna, which serves to confirm *Kālī's Child*'s thesis about the mystical and sexual in Ramakrishna (KC, 51). *Kālī's Child* thus discusses "Ramakrishna's reported technique for conquering the powers of lust: he would stand before a naked prostitute with a noose hung around his neck and tighten the rope when he became sexually excited, a curious practice indeed if the head is not recognized as a symbolic phallus" (51). Yet in the endnote detailing the information about this incident, Kripal admits: "I doubt seriously that Ramakrishna ever practiced this technique" (341). Inexplicably, twenty pages later in the body of the text (77), the incident is referred to again to strengthen the mystical/sexual hypothesis, despite his own admission that the information was probably dubious. Thus, while Kripal admits using an unreliable source, he only admits it buried in an endnote, while allowing the reader to assume its veracity by using it twice in the body of the text.

Kālī's Child's dismissal of valid material from the source texts occurs when it interferes with portraying Ramakrishna as a troubled man, one who is conflicted and unaware of his deeper motivations. For example, the source texts mention that at the age of ten, Ramakrishna experienced his first samādhi. As he walked through an open field while eating puffed rice, he saw a line of white egrets flying against the sky, which had been darkened by storm clouds. His mind soared beyond normal consciousness at the beautiful sight, and he entered into samādhi. Yet this experience, discussed in all the source texts, is deemed inauthentic by *Kālī's Child*. This vision, Kripal writes, "may be apocryphal" (57–58). Why? Because the account given in the *Kathāmṛta* (5.25) does not mention "the egrets and the storm clouds."

> **KC, 57-58:** Another passage referring to an ecstatic state at the age of ten, again minus the egrets and storm clouds of the more classical account, suggests that the egret and storm cloud vision may be apocryphal.

The "another passage" in the quote above occurs at KA 5.25, in which Ramakrishna refers to the state of samādhi after "I saw something." On this occasion he does not describe what he saw. But on other occasions he *did* describe what he saw and this has been extensively documented in the *Līlāprasaṅga* (2.43–44) and the *Pum̐thi* (Akshaykumar Sen 2000, 9). Kripal ignores or dismisses the evidence in these books. While he does not indicate that Ramakrishna saw something *other* than "the egrets and the storm clouds," he nevertheless precludes the possibility for no explicable reason while speculating that the vision is "apocryphal." It seems fairly obvious that the reason for dismissing the vision is simply to deny and trivialize Ramakrishna's mystical experiences. One can hardly make a case for Ramakrishna going into samādhi because of his suppressed sexual desire for egrets. The examples given here are only a small sampling to show how the source texts are carelessly dismissed in *Kālī's Child* while the author's own speculations are promoted as "recovering the text."

Vedānta versus Tantra

A basic thesis of *Kālī's Child* is that Ramakrishna was a Tāntrik and, because of Tantra's "troubling" aspects, his disciples—notably Vivekananda and Saradananda—staged a makeover and made Ramakrishna a teacher of "boring Vedānta." Vedānta is not merely "boring." According to *Kālī's Child*, Ramakrishna has "disgust for Vedānta" (183), an amazing thesis for anyone who has seriously read the *Kathāmṛta*. M himself writes that Ramakrishna was a worshiper not only of God with form (*sākārbādi*) but also of the Impersonal (*nirākārbādi*) (KA 1.37), a fact which flies in the face of one of *Kālī's Child*'s signal theses: the "ontological dominance of Tantra over Vedānta in Ramakrishna's world" (33). *Kālī's Child* establishes this dominance by setting up an opposition between "boring" Vedānta—which is inexplicably referred to more than once as "the foreign path" (146, 152)—versus "Tantric truths."

The other nonexistent dichotomy which is set up in *Kālī's Child* is between Ramakrishna the "Tantric" Kālī worshiper and Vivekananda the Vedānta "renouncer." Ramakrishna often spoke on Vedānta, as even a cursory reading of the *Kathāmṛta* makes obvious. Ramakrishna's teaching that God alone is real and all else is unreal, is repeated in various forms and in various ways throughout the *Kathāmṛta*. Ramakrishna continually admonishes the devotees to always discriminate between the real and the unreal. If this does not qualify as "Vedānta," then what does? One small example: Ramakrishna says in the *Kathāmṛta*, "When one begins to reason, one sees that all this is like a dream. Brahman alone is real; everything else is unreal. Even Śakti is like a dream, unreal" (KA 1.41). Is this not Vedānta?

In an attempt to minimize the influence Vedānta had in Ramakrishna's life, Kripal writes that Ramakrishna's tutelage under Tota Puri is dealt with in only one paragraph in the *Jībanabṛttānta* (KC, 98). But what does that paragraph in the *Jībanabṛttānta* say? It says that Vedānta practice is the "highest practice in Yoga" (*joger uccatama sādhan*) (JB, 21) and nirvikalpa samādhi is the "ultimate state in Yoga" (*joger caramāvasthā*) (22).

Manomohan Mitra, one of Ramakrishna's close householder devotees, recalled that once he went to visit Ramakrishna with Keshab Sen. The devotees asked Ramakrishna to give a spiritual talk but Ramakrishna replied: "What can I tell you? However, I can tell you one thing that I say to everybody, but very few people appreciate it. I don't know whether you will like it or not." When repeatedly requested to speak, Ramakrishna said, "Brahman alone is real, and whatever you see around you is māyā." With this, Ramakrishna went into samādhi (Chetanananda 1990, 286). Again, if this is not Vedānta, then what is?

According to Ramakrishna's disciples, Ramakrishna wanted his disciples to study Vedānta texts as well. Baburam (later Swami Premananda) said that Ramakrishna "encouraged us to read the scriptures and holy books and kept some books such as *Mukti o Tāṁhār Sādhan* ["Liberation and Its Sādhana," a Vedānta text] in his room and sometimes asked us to read them to him" (Chetanananda 1990, 113). Ramakrishna made the same suggestion to Abhedananda and to other disciples as well. One of Ramakrishna's favorite books, and one he often quoted, was the *Adhyātma Rāmāyaṇa*, a nondualistic interpretation of the *Rāmāyaṇa*. If Ramakrishna thought so little of Vedānta, why did he keep such Vedānta books in his room—especially since so few books were kept there? We can also recall that Ramakrishna persistently requested an unenthused Narendra to read aloud the *Aṣṭāvakra Saṁhitā*, a classic Advaita text, which Ramakrishna kept in his room.

Despite this infusion of "boring Vedānta" and despite what one reads in *Kālī's Child*, Vivekananda became an ardent devotee of Kālī. One would never know this by reading *Kālī's Child*, however, since the book presents the proto-"renouncer" Narendra as rejecting Kālī and bhakti in favor of "Sanskrit hymns and Vedānta talk" (KC, 26):

> Ramakrishna knew that Narendra did not accept Śakti (KA 4.121 [plus endnote 38 (KC, 339) which references LP 5.8.2.19]). After Ramakrishna's death, this rejection of the goddess resulted in a radical transformation of the young movement. (26)

Yet the reference that is given to support his first sentence has nothing to do with the second sentence. On August 3, 1884, Ramakrishna said that Narendra did not accept Śakti. Later Narendra *did* accept Śakti and this fact is amply documented in all Ramakrishna literature (See, for example, LP 5.222–26). Interestingly, in his endnote Kripal cites *Līlāprasaṅga* 5.8.2.19, but he does not quote the *very next* paragraph which describes Narendra's acceptance of Śakti. This information is suppressed since the text conflicts with one of *Kālī's Child*'s core theses, which renders Kripal's accusation of the Ramakrishna Order's "censorship" more than a little ironic. The paragraph which *Kālī's Child* avoids mentioning says: "The Master's face was beaming with delight. . . . [and he said, 'Narendra] never accepted the Divine Mother before; it was only yesterday that he did so . . . Narendra has accepted the Mother; it is very good, isn't it?'" (LP 5.225–26).

Nor was this acceptance of Kālī just a fluke. Vivekananda's Irish disciple Nivedita writes that Vivekananda was always singing Ramprasad's Kālī bhajans. Nivedita reminisced:

> [Vivekananda] told some of us once, that wherever he turned he was conscious of the presence of the Mother, as if She were a person in the room. It was always his habit to speak simply and naturally of "Mother." (1983, 106)

Alice Hansbrough, one of Vivekananda's American disciples, similarly recalled that Vivekananda often sang Kālī bhajans. In San Francisco, she said, Vivekananda "talked a great deal of Divine Mother." According to Hansbrough, Vivekananda told his disciples that the Divine Mother "was here as a form, but was not tied to that form. . . . She would reach for people, though they did not know it, and gradually she would draw them to her" (Hansbrough 2007b, 385). Numerous examples could be provided to flesh out both Ramakrishna's Vedānta as well as Vivekananda's devotion to Kālī.[11] Neither of them saw devotion to Kālī as incompatible with Vedānta; they understood these attitudes to be complementary, not antagonistic.

Kripal makes the boundaries which demarcate Vedānta and Tantra so rigid in *Kālī's Child* that he creates a hard-and-fast separation between them—one that has never existed. For example, *Kālī's Child* presents the Ramakrishna Order as "renouncers" who eschew Ramakrishna's Tantric background. Yet the forms of meditation and daily pūjā—performed in nearly every Ramakrishna/Vedanta center throughout the world—are heavily influenced by Tantra. This fact is indisputable. Even if we look to Śaṅkara, the arch-Vedāntin himself, we find him writing: "Only when joined with Śakti is Śiva able to exercise his power; otherwise he cannot so much as move."[12] Tantra itself is thoroughly suffused with Vedic mantras and practices. Thus the boundary between Vedānta and Tantra has always been more porous than is often portrayed.

According to Amiya Sen: "Whether or not Ramakrishna was a Vedantist or Tantrik, is at one level, a redundant question and follows from a somewhat unproblematized view of the saint's teachings and the religious traditions they reflected." Sen continues:

> Neither Vedanta nor Tantra are homogenized, well-defined schools of thought or practice although much effort has been made in the past to give them this character. Being fairly open-ended categories, both these allow for subtle differences as well as overlaps and this is evident not only within each of these traditions but across them. . . . Given such complexities, it is rather difficult and even misleading to suggest that in the religious philosophy of Sri Ramakrishna one of these traditions was necessarily more important than the other. Ramakrishna as we know, borrowed from both and did not worry over the possible logical and semantic problems following from this act. (2001, 113–14)

This integrated vision is not what we find in *Kālī's Child*, however. We find neither a faithful depiction of Ramakrishna's or Vivekananda's words nor the attitudes they represented. We read instead:

KC, 26: Ramakrishna's usual response to Narendra's Sanskrit hymns and Vedānta talk was emphatic: "It's all so boring!" (KA 3.253).

Only one instance is provided in the book, so we can hardly call this "Ramakrishna's usual response." Nowhere in this solitary citation do we find Ramakrishna "emphatically" declaring the "Vedānta talk" to be "boring." Ramakrishna instead said that such ideas are "very ordinary" (*ati sāmānya*). This, if anything, is only a mild expression of displeasure. The incident occurs on March 15, 1885. Requested by Ramakrishna, Narendra sings the Sanskrit hymn "Unsteady is water on the lotus leaf / Likewise is the transience of life" (KA 3.253). Ramakrishna's response to Narendra is, "Ah, what is that? This idea is very ordinary."

We can recall that Ramakrishna consistently taught that approaching the ultimate Reality merely through the attitude of negation—"neti, neti"—is not enough: the attitude of *vījñāna* (accomplished through "iti, iti" [this, this] *after* having practiced "neti, neti") is a higher state.

Kālī's Child neglects to mention that after Ramakrishna expressed his displeasure with the Sanskrit hymn Narendra had begun to sing, Narendra *then* sang devotional songs describing the love of Kṛṣṇa, through the eyes of a gopī (*sakhī bhāber*) (KA 3.253). The *Kathāmṛta* tells us that Ramakrishna and the devotees are very moved by the song (*gān śūniyā Ṭhākur o bhakterā mugdha hoiyāchen*).

Even more to the point, the *Kathāmṛta* states that Narendra is intoxicated with the love of the gopīs of Vraja (*brajagopīr bhābe mātoārā hoiyā*) as he sings, "O [Kṛṣṇa]! You are mine, my friend, what can I say" (KA 3.254).[13] Narendra had no problem singing those songs—he sang devotional songs quite often—but *Kālī's Child* neglects to mention it since it would not help sustain its characterization of Narendra and the "renouncers" as followers of "boring" Vedānta.

We should also keep in mind that Narendra did not generally sing Sanskrit hymns in the first place. The *Kathāmṛta* records Narendra singing songs 86 times—second only to Ramakrishna in the amount of times he burst into song. Of those songs, only three are Sanskrit hymns, and of those three, only two songs refer to Brahman. In the *Kathāmṛta* Ramakrishna shows no sign of displeasure on hearing them. In fact, when Ramakrishna hears the line, "Day and night who dwell in the joy of Brahman," Ramakrishna says in a very low voice, "Aha," then shows by a sign: "This is the characteristic of the yogi" (*eiṭi jogīr lakkhon*) (KA 2.235). This hardly constitutes: "It's so boring!" No sign of displeasure here.

Yet by the time the reader finishes *Kālī's Child*, the oft-repeated refrain of "boring" Vedānta, with its life-denying "renouncers" has had its effect. The consistent belittling of Vedānta and its aloof "renouncers" fits well with *Kālī's Child*'s other premise, that of "renouncers" versus householders—Narendra being the chief architect of the "renouncers" who rode roughshod over both Ramakrishna's Tantric world and householders as well. While *Kālī's Child* posits a "primordial split" between householders and renouncers (8), with the "renouncers" gaining the upper hand after Ramakrishna's death, such a bifurcation is not borne out by the source documents. Apart from M's *Kathāmṛta*, there are also voluminous records of M's talks which were transcribed after M died. This multi-volume edition, recorded by his attendant Swami Nityatmananda, show an enormous amount of back-and-forth between the two communities as well as a great amount of mutual appreciation and true reverence.[14]

Just as there was much more commonality between Ramakrishna's householder devotees and monastic disciples than *Kālī's Child* recognizes, so also there is much more commonality between Vedānta and Tantra than is recognized—unless one reduces Tantra to a caricature of "magical power, strangeness, seediness, and sex" (28). *Kālī's Child*'s either/or dyads may work well on paper but they do not exist in the lived tradition; they are simplistic and basically misleading. But such characterization becomes necessary in *Kālī's Child* to support its claim that the "renouncers" were followers of dry, boring Vedānta. Associated with *Kālī's Child*'s Vedānta contra Tantra motif is a related theme which courses throughout the text: the effeminate/masculine dyad, which focuses on the "manly" nature of Narendra in order to contrast it with Ramakrishna's "womanly" nature, pitting one against the other:

> **KA 3.269:** *Ekdin bolechilen, tui jodi mone koris Kṛṣnake hṛday madhye dekhte pās. Āmi bollām, āmi Kiṣta-phiṣta māni nā.*
>
> **Translation:** One day he [Ramakrishna] said to me, "If you want, you can see Kṛṣṇa in your heart." I said, "I don't believe in 'Kṛṣṇa-fiṣṇa.'"
>
> **KC, 26:** Knowing full well that Ramakrishna had described himself as having a woman's nature and went so far as to dress like one, Narendra now confesses that he never believed all that "Kṛṣṇa-fiṣṇa nonsense" (KA 3.269).

As the reader can see, the first half of the sentence in *Kālī's Child* has absolutely no textual connection with the second half. *Kālī's Child* makes it appear as if Narendra declared his disbelief in the Kṛṣṇa "nonsense" *after* Ramakrishna's death ("now confesses"), whereas—as is clear from the source text—that is what Narendra told Ramakrishna himself. Narendra's response was fully in keeping with the particular stage in his life when he did not accept a personal aspect of God. But, more importantly, his reply had nothing to do with Ramakrishna's having described himself as having a "woman's nature." Juxtaposing two contextually separate events is a typical strategy employed throughout *Kālī's Child* to promote its theses.

We are further told that Ramakrishna referred to Narendra as Kamalākṣa, meaning "one with lotus eyes." About this Kripal speculates: "One can imagine how upset poor Narendra must have been with Ramakrishna's desire to call him Kamalākṣa, one of those effeminate Vaiṣṇava names" (KC, 26). Narendra *must have been?* There is no indication anywhere in the source texts that Narendra disliked this description. Nor is there any reason why he would have been upset with it. There is nothing particularly effeminate about the term since the epithet is routinely applied to most Hindu male deities as well, including Śiva.

As we have seen earlier, *Kālī's Child* often goes out of its way to suppress material which would counter its theses. One prime example of this is the following passage from the *Kathāmṛta*, in which Ramakrishna affirms one of Vedānta's most basic principles:

> **KA 2.237:** *"Joḍer sottā caitanya loy, ār caitanyer sottā joḍ loy. Śarīrer rog hole bodh hoy āmār rog hoyeche."*
>
> **Translation:** "The attributes of matter (*joḍer sottā*) are superimposed on consciousness (*caitanya*), and the attributes of consciousness (*caitanyer sottā*) are superimposed on matter (*joḍ*). That is why when the body is ill, a person says, 'I am ill.'"

Why is this significant passage never mentioned? Because it would sabotage the thesis that Ramakrishna had no use for Vedānta and that the Vedānta leanings of the movement were initiated by the "renouncers" after Ramakrishna's death. To strengthen both his "boring Vedānta" and householder/renouncer divide theses, Kripal attempts to formulate a rupture which occurred during and after Ramakrishna's life:

> **KC, 27:** The "I only eat, drink, and make merry" chant of Ramakrishna is replaced by an almost desperate "Renounce!" (KA 3.271).

In the *Kathāmṛta* reference cited above (KA 3.271), we see nothing "desperate" about the call for renunciation. Since the author has provided a reference from the Bengali *Kathāmṛta*, the reader assumes that there is something in the text to support the author's assertion. But there is not. Ramakrishna's statement "I only eat, drink, and make merry" became possible only because of his total renunciation of the ego at the feet of Kālī. Those familiar with the *Kathāmṛta* know how often Ramakrishna remarked, "First God, then the world" (*āge īśvar, tārpor jagat*) (KA 4.55). On the same note he often exhorted his devotees to spend time in solitude and, renouncing all else, to weep for God with a longing heart (*śob tyāg kore nirjone gopone byākul hoye keṁde keṁde īśvarke ḍākte hoy*) (KA 4.55).

Thus the effort to pit Ramakrishna's "mansion of fun" against Vivekananda's call for renunciation—which is attempted through sarcasm and, ironically, bowdlerization—is completely misplaced. More serious is the problem that, on occasion, changes are also made to what is found in the citation. For instance, Ramakrishna's "red-bordered cloth" (KA 3.196–97) is transformed into "black-bordered clothes" in *Kālī's Child* in order to claim that Ramakrishna indulged in "luxuries" (KC, 26). *Kālī's Child* effectively suppresses information about Vivekananda's devotional songs to Kṛṣṇa and the Divine Mother in order to claim that songs dear to Ramakrishna are replaced by "songs of manly renunciation" (27). Further, Vivekananda is seriously misrepresented by describing him with words that are Kripal's own creation and are not translations from the sources he cites—such as Narendra "growled" (26) and "brags" (27)—verbs not found in any of the source texts. But readers would never know this unless they pored over the Bengali texts and compared them with *Kālī's Child.*

Let us now turn to a few examples of the distorted version of Tantra that is presented as "the Tantra" throughout the book:

> **KC, 27:** M records Vivekananda's categorical rejection of Tantra in an appendix in volume 5: "Give up this filthy Vamachara that is killing your country."

The word Tantra appears twice in the quote recorded by M, and *both* times Vivekananda qualifies the word with the adjective "Vāmācāra." What Vivekananda condemned was *Vāmācāra* Tantra. Thus, the prefatory statement in the above quote, "Vivekananda's categorical rejection of Tantra," is inaccurate. Or perhaps it is not, at least from Kripal's perspective, for it does reflect Kripal's own view of Tantra. As we have seen in *Kālī's Child*, Tantra almost always *means* Vāmācāra Tantra, and even Vāmācāra Tantra is not accurately represented.

To further shore up his theses regarding Ramakrishna and Tantra, statements are frequently lifted out of context and given a startlingly new interpretation. For example:

> **KA 3.230:** *E tāntrik upāsanā. Jananī ramanī.*
>
> **Translation:** This is Tantric worship: looking upon a woman as mother.
>
> **KC, 85, 142:** This is the meaning of Tantric ritual. The Mother is the Lover.

The context here is important. This statement by Dr. Sarkar comes at the end of a story narrated by Ramakrishna. Bilvamaṅgala (a character in the story) learns an important lesson from his prostitute-lover, hence he looks upon her as his teacher. Addressing her as "mother," he goes forth in search of God. After hearing this story, Ramakrishna's physician Dr. Sarkar says that this approach—of looking upon a woman as one's mother—is a Tantric practice. *Kālī's Child* makes precisely the opposite equation and, sadly, the entire second chapter of the book is nothing but an attempt to prove a fallacious, mistranslated equation in order to reach the predetermined conclusion that "in Tantric culture, the goddess is understood to be a gentle, consoling Mother *and* a wild, uncontrollable Lover" (KC, 87).

Interestingly, having mistranslated this phrase in the body of the text after invoking "a certain poetic license" (KC, 87), Kripal tries to deflect the charge of mistranslation by including in an endnote an alternative translation: "The Lover is (actually one's own) Mother" (346). Unfortunately, even this alternative bypasses the context.

To lend credibility to *Kālī's Child*'s Ramakrishna-as-Tāntrik thesis, words which were not Ramakrishna's are presented as his, and the context in which the words were spoken is changed. For example:

> **KC, 87:** In another passage, the saint adds a specifically erotic dimension to this brilliant blackness by associating it with the love-play of Kālī and Śiva (KA 2.25).

This is erroneous. In this passage from the *Kathāmṛta*, it is not Ramakrishna's but M's words which describe the new moon night as *ramaṇ* between Mahākālī and Mahākāla. In fact, on the entire page from which the citation was taken, Ramakrishna does not speak one word (KA 2.25).

One of *Kālī's Child*'s recurring problems is its tendency to lift words and phrases out of context, then quote them in order to substantiate a preordained thesis—a thesis which would not stand up were the given examples properly contextualized. For example:

> **KC, 252:** The shy housewife, biting her tongue in a public act of restraint, controls by that act an immense reservoir of power capable, at any moment, of dissolving what Ramakrishna called the "bonds of shame, disgust, and fear" and returning the culture to that Tantric midnight "where all jackals howl in the same way" (LP 4.4.30).

In the *Līlāprasaṅga* citation given above, the phrase which mentions all jackals howling alike refers to the shared highest experience of all enlightened beings. Since their "experience" of the truth is identical, their essential teaching is also identical. *Kālī's Child*'s segue from a "Tantric midnight" to jackals howling alike is perfectly breathtaking.

Another problematic aspect of *Kālī's Child*'s use of "Tantra" is that nearly anything qualifies as "Tantric" if sufficient ambiguity can be created around an incident to make it appear "immoral." See, for example, the citation below:

> **KC, 112:** Hriday, Ramakrishna's nephew, paid an especially heavy price for his Tantric practices. He was expelled from the temple for worshiping the feet of Mathur's young granddaughter in some unspecified immoral way (LP 2.APP.26).

The *Līlāprasaṅga* merely says: "Hriday foolishly (*buddhi-hīna-vaśataḥ*) worshiped the feet of Mathur Babu's granddaughter of tender age." There is nothing "unspecified" here and there is nothing "immoral" either. Yet whatever the original text lacks in sexual interest, *Kālī's Child* more than makes up for with imagination and innuendo. Worshiping young girls as embodiments of the Divine (*kumārī pūjā*) is not an exclusively Tantric practice; it is part of the Śākta tradition as well. Nor is it something connected only with the worship of Kālī. As a part of the autumnal Durgā Pūjā in Bengal, the kumarī pūjā draws thousands of devotees even today.

Moreover, from the way the incident is discussed in *Kālī's Child*, it appears as if Hriday was expelled because of "the unspecified immoral" nature of his act. The *Līlāprasaṅga*, however, is quite clear about why Hriday was expelled. In the very next sentence which follows the above citation, we read: "Her father, apprehending that evil might befall the child, became much annoyed and dismissed Hriday from the service in the Kālī temple" (LP 2. 409). Trailokyanath, the child's father, was apprehensive because Hriday was a brahmin whereas Trailokyanath belonged to a lower caste, and the custom in kumārī pūjā is to worship a young girl born in a brahmin family. A brahmin worshiping one belonging to a lower caste was believed to bring calamity.

Another perplexing feature of *Kālī's Child* is the erratic placement of references, which makes the author's own comments appear to be translations and/or a paraphrase from the source text—and in the process, bestows upon them an undeserved legitimacy. For example:

> **KC, 191:** The milkmaids' love was free from lust, he says repeatedly, as if to reassure himself. [KA 2.110; 5.52]

In the above example, "as if to reassure himself" is Kripal's comment and is not found in the *Kathāmṛta*.

> **KC, 132:** "Have you attained [a] Kṛṣṇa?" their guru would ask them. "Yes, I have attained," they would answer, uniting religious achievement and sexual pleasure in a single ambivalent phrase (KA 4.164).

The final phrase: "uniting religious achievement ..." belongs to Kripal, not to Ramakrishna, and it is not found in KA 4.164.

> **KA 2.142:** *Kāśite jakhon āmi gelum, takhon ekdin bhairabīcakre āmāy niye gelo. Ekjon kore bhairab, ekjon kore bhairabī. Āmāy kāran pān korte bolle. Āmi bollam, "Mā, āmi kāran chum̐te pāri nā." Takhon tārā khete lāglo. Āmi mone kollām, eibār bujhi jop dhyān korbe. Tā noy, nṛtya korte ārambha korle. Āmar bhoy hote lāglo, pāche Gaṅgāy poḍe jāy. Cakraṭi Gaṅgār dhāre hoyechilo.*
>
> **Translation:** When I went to Kashi, I was one day taken to a bhairavī circle. There were both bhairavas and bhairavīs. They asked me to drink alcohol. I said, "Mother, I can't touch alcohol." Then they started drinking. I thought, maybe now they would practice japa and meditation. But no, they started dancing. I was worried that they may fall into the Ganges. Their meeting was held on the bank of the Ganges.
>
> **KC, 167:** It was in this holy city that Ramakrishna ran into his old Tantric guru, the Bhairavī. She somehow managed to take him to another of her Tantric circles, this one held under the cover of darkness on the bank of the Ganges (KA 2.142).

Note that there is no mention of the Bhairavi escorting Ramakrishna to the circle and, again, the circle being held "under the cover of darkness" is speculation. It may well have been held in the dark; we do not know. But the text to which *Kālī's Child* refers says nothing about the time. To support his claim, Kripal directs his readers to an endnote (KC, 352) which references *Līlāprasaṅga* 4.4.39, but we find there no mention of the Bhairavi and no mention of the time and the day when the circle was held. On the contrary, the text he cites states that "they had invited Ramakrishna." Again, there is no mention anywhere of the Bhairavi escorting Ramakrishna there.

> **KA 4.60:** *Ei pañcabaṭite bostām. Kāle unmād holām!—tāo gelo! Kāla-i brahma. Jini kāler sohit raman koren, tini-i Kālī—ādyāśakti! Aṭalke ṭaliye den.... Ċidātmā ār cit-śakti. Cidātmā puruṣ, citśakti prakṛti. Cidātma Śrīkṛṣṇa, citśakti Śrīrādhā. Bhakta ei citśaktir ek ekṭi rūp.*
>
> **Translation:** I used to sit in this Panchavati. In time I became mad!—even that stage passed! Time (*kāla*) itself is Brahman. One who sports with Time is Kālī, the Primal Power! She moves the Unmovable.... There is Consciousness-self and Consciousness-power. Consciousness-self is the *puruṣa* and consciousness-power is *prakṛti*. Śrī Kṛṣṇa is the consciousness-self and Śrī Rādhā is consciousness-power. The devotee is one form of this consciousness-power.
>
> **KC, 181:** I used to sit in this Panchavati. In time I became mad! O what happened! *Kālī is brahman*. She who has sex with Śiva is Kālī, the Primordial Power! She arouses the Unmoving .... There is the Self of Consciousness and the Power of Consciousness. The Self of Consciousness is a man, the Power of Consciousness is a woman. The Self of Consciousness is Kṛṣṇa, the Power of Consciousness is Rādhā. The devotee is a particular form of this Power of Consciousness (KA 4.60).

Note especially how Kāla is Brahman has been changed to "Kālī" is Brahman. It is puzzling how "Śiva" enters into *Kālī's Child*'s translation. There is no mention of Śiva in the Bengali. *Puruṣa* and *prakṛti* are ontological principles derived from Saṁkhya philosophy and have no sexual identity. *Kālī's Child*, however, finds it expedient to translate these terms as "man" and "woman."

> **KC, 142:** Ramakrishna the Child remained a child. As he had counselled his tempted disciples to do, the saint had successfully "cleaved" the goddess in two: "You bitch! You're going to ruin my ideals! I'll cleave your body in two!" (KA 3.86).

This passage seems designed to mislead. The quoted words are *not* addressed to the goddess. When we check the *Kathāmṛta* reference we find that Ramakrishna tells Mani Mallick and others that a person should not remain quiet in the face of untruth and injustice. He gives the example of an immoral woman (*naṣṭa strī*) who tries to drag a man away from his highest goal. At such times, a person should be strong (*bīrer bhāb*) and say, "You wretch (*śāli*)! You are going to ruin my ideals. I'll cut your body in two!" (KA 3.86). *Kālī's Child*'s quote from the *Kathāmṛta* misleads the reader into believing that the "you" in the quote is addressed to the goddess.

Another persistent translation issue appearing in *Kālī's Child* is the appropriate translation for *prosrāb* and *biṣṭhā*—as well as other words for urine and excrement—which are consistently translated as "piss" and "shit." While this is not literally incorrect, the mood it conveys into English *is* incorrect. For example, when Ramakrishna speaks of worshiping a little girl as the Divine Mother in the kumarī pūjā, he uses the expression: *hāgā mota meye* (KA 2.97), which *Kālī's Child* translates as a "shitting, pissing girl" (KC, 136). This translation conveys an element of disdain, even repugnance, which is not there at all in the Bengali. The Bengali words are meant to convey the fact that the girl is so small and so young that she has not yet been toilet-trained. It is a statement of the girl's age, not a disgust for her gender. If anything, the expression *hāgā mota meye* would, for a Bengali villager, be endearing.[15] Kripal rightly notes that Nikhilananda does not translate those words. Again, this is understandable considering how difficult it is to translate these ideas from culture to culture. As *Kālī's Child* has demonstrated all too well, the translated words can be literally correct but the ideas they convey can be grossly inaccurate.

Ramakrishna's Sexual Confusion

The source texts are unanimous in their view that Ramakrishna was so filled with love for God that he achieved remarkable self-transcendence, which is characterized by the absence of lust and greed, or—in the words of Ramakrishna, who often used tangible symbols in his teaching—the conquest of desire for "woman and gold" (*kāminī kāñcana*). By contrast, *Kālī's Child* asserts that Ramakrishna's lack of sexual engagement reflects a "sexual conflict" (40). In an attempt to find confirmation in a source text, Kripal writes:

> **KC, 40:** For others in the texts, however, it does indeed point to a sexual conflict, for it is a perfect example of Ramakrishna's "destroyed masculinity" (JV[5], 36).

Pointing to others in "the texts," only one passage in one text is cited—and in it there is nothing to suggest "a sexual conflict." Again, the author's speculation is masked to appear as documented information from a source text. Note also the comically literal but distorted translation of *puruṣatva-hānī* as "destroyed masculinity" in preference to the simple and accurate translation, "impotence." Seeing Ramakrishna's unusual response to sexually stimulating situations, it was natural for some people to wonder if he was impotent.

Who are these "others in the texts"? The referenced text, the *Jībanabṛttānta*, describes in no uncertain terms how Rani Rasmani, Mathur and others at the Kālī temple saw Ramakrishna as a spiritually enlightened person (*siddhapuruṣ*) and had high regard (*ati ucca bhāb*) for him (JB, 34). Ramchandra Datta, the author of the *Jibanabṛttānta*, then observes that such is the weakness of the human mind (*manuṣyer durbol mon*) and the skepticism in the heart (*abiśvāsī hṛdoy*) that even a childlike, divinely mad (*bālakavat, unmādavat*) Ramakrishna was subjected to a test. Mathur arranged to bring a prostitute to seduce Ramakrishna, who was then about twenty-five years old. Seeing a beautiful young woman left alone in the room with him, Ramakrishna bowed down to her saying, "Blissful mother! Blissful mother!" (*Mā Anandamoyī, Mā Anandamoyī*). When the news about this "test" was heard by others, some were wonderstruck (*keho āścharja hoilo*) and some began to criticize in various ways (*keho bā nānāprakār doṣārop korite lāgilo*) (34–35). It is this second group that Kripal refers to as "others in the texts." Interestingly, however, *Kālī's Child* carefully omits the referenced section in the *Jībanabṛttānta*, which concludes by pointing out that after more such tests, everyone's misconception was removed (*sokaler-i bhrom bidurita hoilo*) (37).

> **KC, 59:** Observing the boy's friendship with Ram Mallik, a seventeen-year-old teenager, the villagers used to say that, if Gadadhar were a woman, the two of them would be married (KA 3.184).

Two points: first, both Ramakrishna and Ram were of the same age. So referring to Ramakrishna as "boy" and Ram as "a seventeen-year-old teenager" skews the context. Second, the text says: *eder bhitor ekjon meyemānuṣ hole*, "if *one of them* were a woman" (KA 3.184), *Kālī's Child* changes this to "if Gadadhar were a woman," to fit it into the build-up of Ramakrishna not being comfortable with his gender and wishing he were a woman.

> **KC, 91–92:** "At that time, while I performed the worship, I would wear silk garments [like a woman] and would experience such bliss—the bliss of worship!" [KA 4.175]

To the reference to "silk cloth" (*garader kāpad*) is added the author's own gloss in parentheses: "[like a woman]." Earlier (KC, 75) Kripal criticizes M for adding in parentheses *īśvara* after the word *puruṣa*, because Kripal would prefer to translate it as "man." He speculates that M was perhaps "troubled by this revelation" and dismisses it as a "flimsy set of parentheses." In this example, Kripal adds his own "flimsy set of parentheses"—perhaps anxious for references to prove Ramakrishna's "womanly nature." The gloss is clearly distorting, because it is a common practice for men in India to wear a silk cloth at the time of worship.[16] Wealthy people in India wore silk clothes at other times as well. It is by no means a practice associated only with women.

Having inserted his own words into the translation, Kripal now feels free to make this comment: "Granted, he does refer to this period as one in which he dressed up as a woman" (KC, 92). However, Ramakrishna makes no such reference in the *Kathāmṛta* (4.175).

The author, however, has not yet finished with "silken clothes." He brings them up yet again, and this time he connects Ramakrishna's sādhana with the speculation that it was done in order to conquer his sexual desire for his wife. For a moment Ramakrishna's alleged hatred of women as "lovers" and his love for "boys" is forgotten:

> **KC, 104:** Here we see the same worship context and the same silken clothes, but here Ramakrishna becomes a "Handmaid of the Mother," not to live with Mathur and his household but to conquer his sexual desires for his wife back at the temple (KA 5.140).

In the *Kathāmṛta* 5.140 we merely see this:

> *"Āmi dāsī bhābe ek botsor chilām—brahmamoyīr dāsī. Meyeder kāpoḍ oḍnā ei sob portām. Ābār noth portām. Meyer bhābe thākle kām joy hoy."*
>
> **Translation:** "I spent one year as handmaid—the handmaid of the Divine Mother (*brahmamoyī*). I used to wear women's clothes. I used to put on a nose-ring. One can conquer lust by assuming the attitude of a woman."

These words of Ramakrishna are preceded by his teaching that, as long as one has the ego, one must establish a definite relationship with God. Then he describes his own practice and the benefit such practice can bring. There is no mention here of "silken clothes" or his practicing this discipline "to conquer his sexual desires for his wife back at the temple." Placing the citation at the end of the phrase masks the author's speculation as a paraphrase from the *Kathāmṛta*.

> **KA 4.201:** *Āmi meye baḍo bhoy kori. Dekhi jeno bāghinī khete āsche. Ār aṅga, pratyaṅga, chidra sob baḍo baḍo dekhi. Sob rakkhasīr mato dekhi.*
>
> **Translation:** I am very afraid of women. I feel as if a tigress is coming to eat me. And I find that their bodies, their limbs, and their pores are very large, like those of an ogress.
>
> **KC, 138:** And he frankly confesses that he is terrified of women, that they remind him of female demons with their appendages and huge "holes" (*chidra*) (KA 4.201).

Interestingly, the first edition of *Kālī's Child* translated the last phrase as "they remind him of female demons with their huge vaginal and mammary 'holes'" (KC 1995, 138). While the second edition of *Kālī's Child* eliminated this egregious translation error, it nevertheless retained its subtext of Ramakrishna's hatred and fear of women as "Lovers."

The words of Ramakrishna quoted above may indeed seem to support the allegation that he hated and feared women, but this idea is soon dispelled when we continue to read the text of the conversation and realize that Ramakrishna was, in fact, pointing out how lustful desires can divert a person's mind away from God (cf. KA 4.202). Furthermore, the statement in the present tense ("I am very afraid of women") is immediately superseded by Ramakrishna himself, saying "Earlier I had great fear (*āge bhārī bhoy chilo*) and would not allow anyone to come near me." But now, he says, he sees women as "different forms of the blissful, divine mother" (*mā ānandamoyīr ek ekṭi rūp bole dekhi*). This is not to deny that Ramakrishna suggested that women disciples go see the temples in the Dakshineswar compound if they had remained in his room too long. Here, however, Ramakrishna—as a spiritual teacher—was setting an example for other, less advanced sādhakas, male and female. He often gave the example of a physician who was unable to recommend not eating molasses until his own molasses was removed from his room.

When occasional visitors who were not spiritually inclined visited Dakshineswar, often dragged there by devotees, Ramakrishna would notice their restlessness and ask them to "go look at the temples." *Kālī's Child* claims that "this was an especially popular move when the guests happened to be women" (KC, 11), and cites three references from the *Kathāmṛta* as evidence: KA 3.125, 4.164, and 4.202. When these references are checked, one discovers that KA 3.125 points to Tarak's male friend, not a woman, who is asked to "go look at the temples." The remaining two references—KA 4.164 and 4.202—point not to any incident, but to

Ramakrishna teaching about the importance for monastics about keeping their distance from members of the opposite sex to protect their spiritual practice. To set an example, he says, he too asks women visitors, after they have met him for a while, to go have darśan in the temples; "others will learn after seeing me" (*āmār dekhe ābār sobāi śikhbe*) (4.164).

Gender is associated with the body and conquest of the senses (*jitendriya*), a prime requirement for a God-centered life, involves transcending gender identities. It was in this context that Ramakrishna said the following:

> **KA 2.155:** *Āmi āpnāke pu (puruṣ) bolte pāri nā.*
>
> **Translation:** I cannot speak of myself as a man.
>
> **KC, 234:** True, he became a woman when he lived with his wife, Sharada, in order to conquer his desire for her. And he succeeded: "I'm not able to call you a he," she confessed (KA 2.154–55).

Note that in *Kālī's Child*, Ramakrishna's words about himself have been changed and made to appear as if they were Sarada's words about him. This is done so that Kripal can now, having set the stage, claim: "But he also took on the nature of a woman to live with and lie down with Mathur" (KC, 234).

In the following citation we can see how a misleading translation has been used in an attempt to support *Kālī's Child*'s Ramakrishna-as-homoerotic-Tāntrik thesis, which includes none-too-subtle pederastic undertones:

> **KA 5.31:** *Ṭhākurer rākhāler sambandhe gopāl bhāb. Jemon mā'r koler kāche choto chele giyā bośe, rākhāl o ṭhākurer koler upar bhor diyā bośiten. Jeno māi khācchen.*
>
> **Translation:** The Master looked upon Rakhal as his child. Rakhal would sit leaning on the Master's lap as a young child leans on its mother while sucking her breast.
>
> **KC, 141:** Again, the motherly Paramahaṁsa puts the boy in his lap and tries to nurse him with his strangely full breasts (KA 5.31).

As we can see, a simple comparison of *Kālī's Child* with its *Kathāmṛta* citation reveals how flawed and prejudicial *Kālī's Child*'s translation is. It is repeated several times in the book, phrased differently to suit different contexts, until the twenty-year-old Rakhal, "the boy," is miraculously transformed into "a thirteen-year-old boy sitting in the lap and nursing at the breasts of" Ramakrishna (KC, 301).

We can see further misrepresentation of the source texts when different, unassociated sentences from the *Kathāmṛta* are pieced together to create a hybridized, unintended version of the text.

> **KC, 235:** Narendra in particular has a man's nature and so naturally tends to a "very high state," to a formless state (KA 4.228).

In the *Kathāmṛta* citation (4.228) we find that these are two entirely different sentences. To connect disparate sentences with "and so" is to intentionally distort the text. This is done to contrive a connection between having "a man's nature" and being in "a very high state."

In the example given below, we find not only two disparate passages wantonly forged together, but also Ramakrishna creating metaphors that were never made, implying words that were never spoken:

> **KC, 138:** In a similar vein, Ramakrishna's metaphors equate "analytic reason" (*vicāra*) with the Child's cry. When the Mother comes and offers her breasts, that too will stop (KA 2.35). Unlike the Mother's breast, reason is "dry" (*śuṣka*) (KA 5.131).

Again the author has connected two separate passages from different contexts after inserting his own comment. In the *Kathāmṛta* (5.131), we merely see Ramakrishna telling Hazra that he [Hazra] is "dry" because he only resorts to reason. But *Kālī's Child* presents us with an invented metaphor supposedly given by Ramakrishna: "Unlike the Mother's breast, reason is dry." But when we check the citation, there is no reference whatsoever to a breast.

We will see more textual additions in the following example, which the author implies, via the citation, are in the source text. They are not.

> **KC, 237:** But Narendra, Ramakrishna reports with an excited exclamation point, was in the middle of the thousand-petaled lotus in the head, where Śiva sits waiting for his lover, the goddess Śakti (KA 4.228).

In the *Kathāmṛta* (4.228) we merely find this: *anya padda kāru daśa-dal, kāru ṣodaśa-dal, kāru śata-dal kintu padda-madhye Narendra sahasra-dal!*—"some are ten-petaled lotuses, some are sixteen-petaled, some hundred-petaled, but Narendra is a thousand-petaled lotus!" Everything other than this is Kripal's commentary alone and is not found in the *Kathāmṛta*.

Kālī's Child spends a good deal of time addressing the issue of Ramakrishna and *bhāva* as well as Ramakrishna and the Divine Mother's command for him to remain in *bhāvamukha*. How *Kālī's Child* analyzes *bhāva* is worth noting in the example given below:

> **KA 4.2–3:** *"Haladhārī bolto tini bhāb-abhāber atīt. Āmi māke giye bollām—mā, Haladhāri e-kathā bolche, tā hole rūp-ṭup ki sob mithyā? Mā ratir mā beśe āmār kāche ese bolle, 'Tui bhābei thāk.' Āmi-o Haladhārike tāi bollām.*
>
> *"Ek ekbār o-kathā bhule jāi bole kaṣṭa hoy. Bhābe nā theke dāt bheṅge gelo. Tāi doibabānī nā hole bhābei thākbo—bhakti niye thākbo. Ki bolo?"*
>
> **Translation:** "Haladhari used to say that God is beyond both being and nonbeing. I told the Mother, 'Mother, this is what Haladhari says. Then is the divine form an illusion?' Mother appeared to me in the form of Rati's mother and said, 'You just remain in bhāva.' I repeated this to Haladhari.
>
> "Now and then I forget her command and suffer. Once I broke my tooth because I did not remain in bhāva. So I shall remain in bhāva unless I get a divine command to the contrary. I shall hold on to devotion. What do you say?"
>
> **KC, 155:** "Haladhari used to say that God is beyond existence and non-existence. I went to Ma and said—'Ma, Haladhari is saying these things. So are all forms and things false?' Ma came to me dressed as Rati's mother and said, 'Remain in existence, my child.' I also told Haladhari this. Occasionally I forgot these words and suffered for it. Not remaining in existence, I broke a tooth. And so, when I don't hear divine words or see things, I'll remain in existence—with devotion I'll remain!" (KA 4.2–3)

Kālī's Child's translation of *tui bhābei thāk* as "remain in existence" is ridiculous—as if one could live in nonexistence! This incomprehensible translation provides *Kālī's Child* the opportunity of decoding the meaning for the baffled readers: "Remain as you are, on this side of the dialectic. Go on worshiping forms. You are fine" (KC, 156).

In this passage the word *bhāb* (Sanskrit, *bhāva*) is used in two senses: the first occurrence—used in conjunction with *abhāva*—means "being" (*abhāva* is its opposite, "nonbeing"), but later in the passage the word is used in a different sense, as a word that signifies a specific mode, approach or relationship. It is not easy to find an accurate English word to translate this sense of *bhāva*. David Haberman's definition of *bhāva* as "an emotional state … that allows a higher perception of reality" is helpful for readers unfamiliar with the concept (1994, 228). The concept of *bhāva* has been extensively developed in the Vaiṣṇava tradition, especially in the Gauḍīya school of Bengal. Without this background, it is easy to mistranslate that word as "existence."

Given the context, especially given the reference to Ramakrishna's broken tooth when he fell down while in *samādhi*, it seems reasonable to conclude that the command to "remain in *bhāva*" may have implied: "Do not merge your identity with the Absolute, but continue to remain in a devotional relationship with God."

Kālī's Child's gloss of the following passage from the *Kathāmṛta* shows just how treacherous cross-cultural translations and interpretations can be.

> **KA 4.231:** *"Ekjon nyangṭā soṅge soṅge thākto—tār dhone hāt diye phackimi kortum. Takhon khūb hāstum. E nyangṭā murti āmār-i bhitar theke beruto. Paramahaṅsa mūrti—bālaker nyāy."*
>
> **Translation:** "A naked person used to be with me—I would touch his penis and make fun. I would then laugh a lot. This naked form used to come out of me. It was the form of a paramahaṁsa, like a boy."
>
> **KC, 160:** Ramakrishna is describing a vision he used to have of another naked paramahaṁsa: "A naked person used to stay around—I would play with his little penis with my hand. Then I would laugh a lot. This naked form used to come out of me. It was in the form of a paramahaṁsa—like a boy" (KA 4.231).

To many, the vision points to the innocence and purity of the paramahaṁsa state which transcends the socially and culturally constructed notions of what is appropriate and what is not. It is obvious that Ramakrishna himself had no embarrassment about it and did not invest it with any particular sexual meaning. Moreover, despite this being labeled a "secret talk," the talk was not all that secret: Ramakrishna describes his vision to a roomful of people: Mahendra Mukherjee, Balaram, Haripada, Girish, M and other devotees are present (KA 4.231).

As one might suspect, the vision appears differently in *Kālī's Child.* It is not the paramahaṁsa's childlike state that is the focal point of this passage: it is the paramahaṁsa's penis. Little wonder, then, that Kripal translates the Bengali word *dhan* (literally, "treasure," a euphemistic and endearing term for penis, with no coarse connotation) as "little cock" in *Kālī's Child*'s first edition (KC 1995, 160) and, later in the second edition, as "little penis" (KC, 160). In the endnote of the second edition, the author preempts the charge of mistranslation by admitting: "But it is also meant to be affectionate and funny, something a mother might jokingly say when talking to or about her little boy" (351).

Tellingly, in the book's first edition, the translated sentence is: "I would teasingly fondle his little cock with my hand" (KC 1995, 160). *Fondle?* The Bengali verb *phackimi* can in no way be translated as "fondle"; there is no sexual connotation in the word, it is associated with childish pranks, with young children playing mischievously with one another. We must keep in mind the Bengali culture from which Ramakrishna came. In this environment it is quite common, as common then as it is still today, to see young children running around naked. The children play with one another by grabbing each other's ears, noses, fingers, toes, genitals—anything that can be grabbed. A young boy will mischievously touch or grab another boy's penis in impish, mischievous play. There is no sexual connotation. There is, however, a strong association with the innocence and joy of childhood, which is completely absent in *Kālī's Child.* In its stead the reader is told that "powerfully suggestive texts" point toward a homoerotic relationship which "no doubt existed between Tota and the young Ramakrishna" (KC, 160). No *doubt?* Thus we go in circles: the vision explains the homoerotic relationship, and the relationship explains the vision.

As we have seen on earlier occasions, *Kālī's Child* inserts verbs not found in the source texts in order to lend support to the book's theses—in this case, to convince the readers of the "troubling possibility" that Ramakrishna had unresolved sexual conflicts. Just as Narendra was shown growling and bragging—with nothing in the source text to give support to such usage—so Ramakrishna is similarly provided verbs that are unsupported by the citations given. For example, Ramakrishna is shown "shouting" about the "Gopāla state." This, *Kālī's Child* informs us, "clearly hints at another unresolved conflict in Ramakrishna's child state, namely, the possibility that even the relationship between the Mother and the Child might become sexualized" (KC, 140).

KC, 140: "Beware of the Gopāla state!" he would shout (KA 2.154).

At this point, we are not even surprised when we do not find Ramakrishna "shouting" and, what is more, we do not even see him saying, "Beware of the Gopāla state!" Unfortunately, the disconnect between what the *Kathāmṛta* says and how the text is translated in *Kālī's Child* has almost become anticipated. Yes, there is a discussion in KA 2.154 about the danger of sexual desire masquerading as love of mother for her child, but neither the words quoted nor the description ("he would shout") are found there.[17]

Another aspect of Ramakrishna to which *Kālī's Child* pays especial note is Ramakrishna's anus as well as his defecation habits. Ramakrishna, Kripal writes, "experienced trance at the exact moment the 'secret door' of his anus opened to defecate" (KC, 19). Indeed, Ramakrishna's "wildly swinging 'back door'" is part of Ramakrishna's secret (297). "Homoerotic feelings," Kripal declares, "both excited the saint (he entered *samādhi*) *and* blocked the secret door of the anus" (296). In sum,

> given the text's [*Kathāmṛta*'s] play on the "secret" nature of the anus, the consistently contorted nature of Nikhilananda's handling of the passages, and the hinted realities of Ramakrishna's troubled past, I cannot help but believe that this latrine and this wildly swinging "back door" are part of what I have called Ramakrishna's secret. (KC, 297)

As we have mentioned earlier, *guhya* can mean "anus," though it is not generally used in that sense. We can also note in passing the prejudicial use of language here: "the hinted realities of Ramakrishna's troubled past." There are no "realities" provided anywhere in *Kālī's Child*, only speculations. Kripal himself refers to these very notions as "speculations" which are "a pattern, but only a pattern" (KC, 296). Yet, on the very next page of the book, these speculations have become the "hinted realities" of Ramakrishna's past, which Kripal insists on characterizing as "troubled."

Ironically, as we can see below, the "secret" is dependent upon an erroneous translation.

> **KA 1.178:** *Āmi ek din or bāḍite paikhānāy beṁhuś hoye gechi. O to ato ācārī, paikhānār bhitar āmār kache giye pā phaṁk kore bosiye dey. Ato ācārī, ghṛnā korle nā.*
>
> **Translation:** One day at his house I became unconscious in the latrine. He [Viswanath Upadhaya—generally referred to as "Captain" in the *Kathāmṛta*] is so particular about his orthodox habits, but he helped me sit in the latrine with my legs apart. In spite of his orthodox habits he did not show any disgust.
>
> **KC, 291:** One day I became unconscious in the latrine of his house. He's so concerned about purity, and yet he sat down with his foot in the hole [of the latrine] and pulled me out (KA 1.178).

Kālī's Child builds its interpretation upon the faulty translation given above. It suggests that Ramakrishna became unconscious *while defecating* and Captain had to help him get up. However, in studying the Bengali text we see that Ramakrishna became unconscious inside the room where the latrine was located and Captain had to help him sit so he could defecate—which makes it clear that he became unconscious in the room *before* defecating. When we see how diametrically opposed to the original text the "translation" is, the commentary that follows is hilarious: "The fact that the Captain had to put his foot in the hole of the latrine to lift the saint out suggests that Ramakrishna was frozen in a defecating posture, squatting over the hole. He 'became unconscious,' in other words, in the very act of defecation" (KC, 291). This distortion was necessary for the author to focus on Ramakrishna's "fecal ecstasies" and to make the remarkable claim that "Ramakrishna not only experiences ecstasy while he defecates, *he defecates ecstasy*" (292; italics in text).

Ramakrishna's "Boys"

Many of the mistranslations found in *Kālī's Child* can be attributed to the book's basic thesis that Ramakrishna, having been the victim of sexual abuse, engaged in reenactment patterns with his own young male disciples. To this end, the prose throughout *Kālī's Child* is consistently manipulated in order to portray Ramakrishna in vaguely pedophilic terms. Ramakrishna, we read, was not a lover of women "or even of older men but of young, beautiful boys" (3). In order to strengthen this thesis, "boys," "young boys," "young male disciples" and variations on that theme are endlessly repeated throughout the text.

Kripal speculates about the nature of Ramakrishna's relationships not only with his teacher Tota Puri and the temple manager Mathur Babu, but also with Purna, Narendra, and other "boys." The ingenuity required to transform every available male associated with Ramakrishna into a "boy" is stunning. Among those who are called "boys" in *Kālī's Child* are the fifty-one-year old "boy Kedar" (KC, 66), the twenty-three-year-old "little Nityagopal" (274), the twenty-year-old "boy Rakhal" (66), and a thirty-five-year-old man from the Goswami family who in *Kālī's Child* becomes "a boy of fifteen" (67). In addition, all the young men who visited Ramakrishna, most of whom were studying in local colleges, are all "boys." Even when the source text refers to "devotees," Kripal changes the reference to "boy disciples" (70). With endless and needless repetition of the phrase "boy disciples" to sustain *Kālī's Child*'s muted pederastic pulse, the reader is lulled into thinking that somehow the "boy" in the phrase is very young indeed and somehow different and more significant than simply "disciple."

We have provided below several examples of how Ramakrishna's relationships have been described in ways that alter the context and depart from the tenor of the original source texts in Bengali:

> **KC, 67:** Again, when a boy of fifteen walks into a theater box to see Ramakrishna, M tells us that the saint stroked the young boy with his hand and asked him to sit down: "With you here, I get all excited."

This is what the *Kathāmṛta* says:

> **KA 2.121:** *Itimadhye Khordār Nityānanda Gosvāmi baṅśer ekṭi bābu āśiyāchen o Ṭhākurer ceyārer paścāte daṁḍāiyā āchen. Boyas 34/35 hoibe. Ṭhākur tāṁhāke dekhiyā ānande bhāsite lāglen. Tāṁhār hāt dhoriyā kato kathā koitechen. Mājhe mājhe tāṁhāke bolitechen, "Ekhāne bośo nā. Tumi ekhāne thākle khūb uddīpan hoy." Sosnehe tāṁhār hāt dhoriya jeno khelā koritechen. Sosnehe mukhe hāt diyā ādar koritechen.*
>
> *Gosvāmī coliyā gele Māṣṭārke bolitechen, "O boḍo ponḍit, bāp boḍo bhakto. Āmi Khordār Śyāmsundar dekhte gele, je bhog ekśo ṭākā dile pāvā jāy nā śei bhog ene āmāy khāvāy.*
>
> *"Er lakkhan boḍo bhālo; ekṭu neḍe ceḍe dile caitanya hoy. Oke dekhte dekhte boḍo uddīpan hoy. Ār ekṭu ho' le āmi dāṁḍiye poḍtum."*
>
> **Translation:** Meanwhile a person born in Nityānanda Gosvāmī's family from Khardah came and stood behind Thakur's chair. His age was 34 or 35. Thakur was filled with delight at the sight of him. He held his hand and talked with him. Every now and then he said, "Please sit down here. Your presence strongly enkindles in me [the thought of God]." He played tenderly with the young man's hands and lovingly stroked his face.
>
> When Goswami left, Thakur said to M, "He is a great scholar. His father is a great devotee. When I go to Khardah for darśan at the Śyāmsundar temple, he feeds me with the prasād that cannot be got even after paying a hundred rupees.
>
> "His traits are good. A little shaking will awaken his spiritual consciousness. Seeing him, there is great spiritual enkindling [in me]. If it had increased a little more, I would have stood up [in ecstasy]."

Besides shaving twenty years off the man's age in order to make him a "boy," *Kālī's Child* suppresses the fact—and eliminates the context—that the person belonged to the family of Nityānanda Gosvāmī. That leads to distorting the word *uddīpan* to mean "all excited" in order to strengthen the homoerotic subtext. The fact that the person belonged to a family closely associated with Caitanya, the fifteenth/sixteenth-century saint worshiped by many as an avatar, was the reason why Ramakrishna said that his presence enkindled (*uddīpan*) in him the thought of God.[18] Stroking a person's face with one's hand is a common way of expressing affection in Bengal. But the book distorts the text to: "stroked the young boy with his hand."

The next "boy" we meet is Purnachandra Ghosh (1871–1913), who was greatly respected by Ramakrishna's devotees for his spiritual attainments. In *Kālī's Child*'s Introduction we are introduced to "little boy Purna," who was one of Ramakrishna's "beloved boy disciples" (11). Beloved he certainly was, and young as well—but as a thirteen year old (the age when he first met Ramakrishna), Purna would not qualify as a "*little* boy." Purna would be married and working in a firm within three years. *Kālī's Child* nevertheless goes out of its way to belabor Ramakrishna's purported "homoerotic infatuation" with Purna (75). Should that charge not be sufficiently clear, Kripal continues: "Ramakrishna ... is in love with Purna. He wants to kiss and embrace Purna as if he were a woman and Purna a man." Purna, Kripal further asserts, was the "object of Ramakrishna's erotic desire," and this had been a "glaring scandal" (75). The reader is also informed that Ramakrishna "wanted to sexually engage Purna" (162).

Purna was a student in M's school when M brought him to meet Ramakrishna. M believed Purna to be spiritually gifted and had already begun to give Purna religious instructions. Ramakrishna agreed with M's assessment, declaring Purna to be an *īśvarakoṭi*, an ever-free soul. Ramakrishna often speaks of Purna in the *Kathāmṛta*, telling M, for example, that Purna has "great potential" (*khub ādhār*). "How else could he make me do japa for him? But he doesn't know any of this" (*Tā nā ho'le or jonyo jop koriye nile! O to e śob kothā jāne nā*) (KA 3.130). We are told that even at a young age Purna "commanded much respect from [Ramakrishna's] devotees for his spirituality" (Chetanananda 1989, 387). This respect was universal, both from Ramakrishna's lay devotees and monastic disciples.[19] Much against his will, Purna was forced to marry at a young age—a practice that was not uncommon for both young men and women at that time.

Giving Purna as an example, *Kālī's Child* bizarrely declares that "beloved boy disciples married and left the inner circle" of Ramakrishna's disciples (11). Yet Purna's marriage had nothing to do with his status as an *īśvarakoṭi* (Rakhal, another *īśvarakoṭi*, had married as well). *Kālī's Child* also asserts that Purna—because he married—"is never mentioned in the later accounts" (KC, 11). One wonders which "later accounts" Kripal is referring to, since Purna was deeply involved in the Ramakrishna Order until his death. Although this was a path he would not have voluntarily chosen, he married, had children, and held a job, yet remained close to Ramakrishna's disciples. In a rather touching turnabout, M sent his students to Purna for inspiration (Chetanananda 1989, 394).

While Vivekananda was in America, Purna saved all the newspaper clippings about him and read them aloud to gatherings at Balaram's house, where Ramakrishna's disciples often met. When Vivekananda returned to India from America, he visited Purna's home even before he reached the monastery. Purna was the first secretary of the Vivekananda Society, founded after Vivekananda's death, and when he had to move to Delhi and Simla because of his work, Ramakrishna's disciples would stay at Purna's home when they were in the area. When Ramakrishna's disciple, Swami Trigunatitananda, founded the first Hindu temple in America in San Francisco, it was Purna who sent him the pūjā vessels and other accoutrements necessary for Hindu ritualistic worship. Further, because Purna wrote well in English, he wrote many articles for *Brahmavadin*, the journal of the Ramakrishna Order, which later became the *Vedanta Kesari*.

As we can see, *Kālī's Child*'s charge that Purna is not "mentioned in the later accounts" is baseless. Neither do we have any indication anywhere that Purna was the recipient of Ramakrishna's sexual advances, nor is there any indication that there was any suspicion about Ramakrishna's behavior toward young men. Indeed, when Purna became quite ill in 1913, Purna's mother approached Sarada Devi, asking her to intervene to save his life—despite the fact that Purna's parents had strongly opposed his visiting Ramakrishna, fearing that Purna would lose interest in school and become a monk. Sarada replied, "What can I do, my dear? Ask the Master. He will make him well.'" Purna's mother said, "You can do it if you like, Mother." To this, Sarada replied, "No, I can only let him know." When Purna's mother left, Sarada remarked, "The Master told them [Purna's parents] that Purna would not live long if he were married, but she did not listen to him. She hurriedly arranged his marriage so that he could not be a monk" (Chetanananda 1989, 398). Purna died not long after this incident but remains to this day revered within the Ramakrishna tradition, as Chetanananda writes, "an ideal yogi and an ideal householder" (399).

Let us now examine how *Kālī's Child* presents Purna:

KC, 73–74: Now in his late forties, he [Ramakrishna] is talking to M about Purna, a boy of fifteen (KA 3.224) who figures prominently in the saint's secret talk: "If I see Purna one more time, then my anxious desire might lessen! How clever he is! He feels a very great attraction for me. He says, 'I also feel a strange sensation to see you.' (to M) They've taken him from your school. Will this cause you any trouble?" (KA 3.182).

Not surprisingly, a sexualized definition of *vyākulatā* as "anxious desire" is now offered instead of the more sedate but more accurate word, "longing." Later in the text, the phrase "strange sensation" is enclosed in quotation marks, again to raise doubt regarding the actual nature of that sensation. In spite of such manipulation, the book is unable to unravel the nature of Ramakrishna's "anxious desire" (KC, 74). A strategy, therefore, is invented to reveal the true nature of that desire. This is done by adding: "We are told that it has resulted in a situation that might cause M, the schoolteacher, trouble at school, but that is all" (74).

To what does this "it" in the previous sentence refer? Ramakrishna's "anxious desire" for Purna? The Bengali texts are clear: the "it" refers to Purna's visits to Dakshineswar, which had worried his parents (and indeed, many other parents as well, whose children used to visit Dakshineswar). Purna's parents were concerned that these visits would adversely affect his studies. But this fact is suppressed in *Kālī's Child* (KC, 73–74) and mentioned only in passing several pages later (79). M often took his students to Dakshineswar so they could get an opportunity to see Ramakrishna. We must remember that in India at this time, providing spiritual guidance to students was deemed praiseworthy. The "trouble at school" was the possibility of a complaint against M, who was Purna's teacher, for taking Purna to Dakshineswar against his parents' wishes.

The book then presents several events and excerpts from conversations in order to highlight Ramakrishna's alleged "anxious infatuation" (74) for the "boy" Purna.

KA 4.212: *Pūrner je abasthā, ete hoy śīghra dehanāś hobe—iśvarlābh holo, ār keno;—bā kichudiner madhye teḍe phum̐ḍe berube.*

Daibaśvabhāb—debatār prakṛti. Ete lokabhoy kom thāke. Jadi galāy mālā, gāye candan, dhūp dhunār gandha deoā hoy; tā ho'le samādhi hoye jāy!—ṭhīk bodh hoy je, antare Nārāyan āchen—Nārāyan deha dhāran kore esechen. Āmi ṭer peyechi.

Translation: Purna is in such an exalted state that either he will very soon give up his body—the body is useless after attaining God—or his inner nature will burst forth within a few days.

> He has a divine nature—the traits of a god. It makes a person less fearful of others. If a garland of flowers is put around the neck, the body is smeared with sandal-paste, and incense is burnt, the result will be samādhi. In that state one knows clearly that God (Nārāyaṇa) dwells in the body, that it is God who has assumed the body. I have understood this.

> **KC, 74:** In another passage, Ramakrishna explains that Purna possesses the "divine essence" of a god: "If you put a garland on his neck and sandalpaste on his body and then burn incense, he goes into *samādhi!*" (KA 4.212).

A few pages later in *Kālī's Child*, we see that Ramakrishna's words ("if a garland of flowers is put") have mysteriously evolved into his "habit" of garlanding Purna and "rubbing" sandal paste on his "'body'":

> **KC, 162:** In another passage, yet again in volume 4, we learn that Ramakrishna's habit of garlanding Purna with flowers and rubbing sandal-paste on his "body" would send the boy into *samādhi* (KA 4.212).

Why is the "body" placed in scare quotes? Because, the book suggests, the "body" really means the genitals. Let us look at three of the following passages from *Kālī's Child*:

> **KC, 160:** Just a few lines down, Ramakrishna reveals another secret. After telling his audience how he used to perform Tantric rituals with the Bhairavī, Ramakrishna becomes excited and turns to a disciple: "In that state I couldn't help but worship the little penises of boys with sandal-paste and flowers" (KA 4.232).

> **KC_2 352:** [Endnote] In one Tantric ritual, after the male partner has rubbed the *yoni* or "vagina" of his Śakti with sandal-paste, the Śakti then rubs her partner's *liṅgam* or "penis" with sandal-paste (YT 2.9). Ramakrishna may have been enacting the female role of this Tantric ritual.

> **KC, 160–61:** The vision has entered waking life: the boyish penis he played with in the dream-like vision of the other passage he now rubs with sandal-paste in the light of the day; and the laughter of the dream has been replaced by the seriousness and compulsion of the ritual act.

Approximately twenty years separate Ramakrishna's "dream-like vision" of the naked paramahaṁsa from his meeting with Purna. Connecting these two events, *Kālī's Child* claims that the "boyish penis" of the visionary paramahaṁsa that Ramakrishna "would fondle" (KC 1995, 160)—or according to the second edition, "would play with" (KC, 160)—now becomes Purna's penis that Ramakrishna "rubs" with sandalpaste. *Kālī's Child* provides an endnote (KC, 352) which offers the speculation that Ramakrishna "may have been" enacting a Tantric ritual. This speculation is deemed strong enough to transform it into an established fact. Although the *Kathāmṛta* clearly states: "if the body is smeared with sandalpaste" (KA 4.212), *Kālī's Child* renders this into "if you put ... sandalpaste on his body." Less than a hundred pages later, this phrase has evolved into "*rubbing* sandal-paste on his 'body'" (KC, 162; emphasis added), identifying the body as the penis. Kripal feels that it is now "reasonable to ask" if that is how Ramakrishna worshiped Purna (KC, 162).

Three more points: Ramakrishna describes in the *Kathāmṛta* his practices during his Tantric sadhana (KA 4.232). This was, as we have seen, long before Purna came to Dakshineswar. Secondly, in 4.212 the quote in question is in a separate paragraph. The Bengali original is quite neutral, and there is no indication that it is referring to Purna's case. Finally, *Kālī's Child* tells us that Ramakrishna told this to M "in secret" (KC, 344). This is not true. If we look up the passage in the *Kathāmṛta*, we find the room full of people and everyone heard what Ramakrishna said.

To add to this troubling atmosphere, thick with pederastic insinuations, we are told of "the seriousness and compulsion of the ritual act" (KC, 161). One certainly cannot accuse Kripal of subtlety here. But to any reader with knowledge of Bengali it is clear that texts have been distorted to create a scene fetid with sexual abuse, a scene which does not exist in any of the source texts on Ramakrishna, let alone the *Kathāmṛta* citation which is given in *Kālī's Child*.

Kālī's Child works hard to create the impression that Purna was the "object of Ramakrishna's erotic desire" (75). To that end, the book uses prejudicial language to strengthen that perception and conceals textual material which would work against this conjecture, as we can see below:

> **KC, 74:** In yet another passage, M tells us that Ramakrishna was so "anxious" to see Purna that he showed up at M's house late one night and asked M to fetch the boy, which M did (KA 3.224).

The reader is told that Ramakrishna "showed up" at M's house late one night and wanted to see Purna. We can note in passing the pejorative tone of that sentence: the reader is alerted that this is suspect behavior. Kripal tells us that M fetched Purna, but he does *not* tell us what happened afterward. Under this pederastic cloud of suspicion, Kripal leaves to the reader's imagination the queasy possibilities of what happened with Ramakrishna and "the boy" Purna. Interestingly, the *very next sentence* of this passage tells us: "The Master gave the boy many instructions about prayer and afterward returned to Dakshineswar." Such behavior does not lend itself to *Kālī's Child*'s portrait of Ramakrishna, so it is concealed.

Below we can see another example of how *Kālī's Child* takes any mention of Purna and turns it into a homoerotic selling point. Notice that there is no mention here of Ramlal, even though he is a central part of the sentence. We can also note the defining characteristic of Purna, yet again, as "the boy."

> **KA 4.286:** *"Śarīrer ei rog—kintu abidyā māyā rākhe nā. Ei dyākho, Rāmlāl, ki bāḍī, ki paribār, āmār mone nāi!—ke nā Pūrna kāyet tār janya bhābchi. Oder janya to bhābanā hoy nā."*
>
> **Translation:** "The body has this illness but *avidyā-māyā* cannot touch it. See this—there is no thought in the mind about Ramlal [Ramakrishna's nephew] or home or wife, but I am worrying about Purna, who is a kāyastha. I am not worrying about them!"
>
> **KC, 74:** Finally, Ramakrishna brags that even in his illness he is not deluded by *māyā*. To prove his point, he notes that his mind no longer dwells on his wife or his home. Now he thinks only of Purna, the boy (KA 4.286).

Apart from the blatantly prejudicial translation, it is clear that Ramakrishna is discussing *vidyāmāyā* and *avidyāmāyā*. He defines *avidyāmāyā* as identification with only one's own relatives and belongings; *vidyāmāyā*, in contrast, is identification with God and his devotees. Further, when the body is ill, it is often dragged into *avidyāmāyā*. It is in this context that Ramakrishna describes his own experience. His reference to Purna as a "kāyastha" is changed in *Kālī's Child* to "the boy" for obvious reasons—and that completely changes the context. Ramakrishna's reference to Purna as one who belongs to the kāyastha caste is important. In the fiercely caste-conscious Hindu society of that period, a brahmin showing concern for a kāyastha (which is below the brahmin in the caste hierarchy) showed that caste distinction was no barrier because Purna was a true devotee of God and caring for him was a sign of *vidyāmāyā*.

When Ramakrishna says that he has no thought in his mind about his wife (*paribār* can also refer to one's family), it does not mean that he did not care for her. The fact was that he cared for her *not simply* because she was his wife. That his love, concern, and respect for her were profound is amply documented by any number of incidents from their life together, material that is suppressed in *Kālī's Child.*

Below we can see an example of how even ontological principles are relentlessly sexualized to create a homoerotic scenario:

> **KA 4.271:** *Ṭhakur manir sohit pūrna sombandhe kothā koitechen. Śrīrāmakṛṣṇa—"Tomāy bolchi—e sob jīber śunte nāi—prakṛtibhābe puruṣke (īśvarke) āliṅgan cumban korte icchā hoy.*
>
> **Translation:** Thakur is talking to M about Purna.
>
> SRI RAMAKRISHNA: "Let me tell you—this should not be heard by all people—looking upon oneself as *prakṛti* one feels like embracing and kissing *puruṣa* (*īśvara*)."
>
> **KC, 74:** The Master is talking to M about Purna—
>
> Sri Ramakrishna—"What I'm telling you—this is not for every soul to hear—I want to kiss and embrace man (God) as a woman (KA 4.271)."

Here we can see that Kripal has inserted his own phrase "I want to" and has ascribed it to Ramakrishna in order to draw the conclusion that "he is in love with Purna. He wants to kiss and embrace Purna as if he were a woman and Purna a man" (KC, 75).[20] Again, let us recall that *puruṣa* and *prakṛti* are ontological categories with no sexual identity. In the text they are used in their philosophical sense, as is obvious from M's parenthetical reference to Īśvara, but in *Kālī's Child* these terms are translated as "man" and "woman."

> **KA 4.193:** *Tāṁr upar bhālobāsa jadi āse tār nām rāgabhakti. Baidhībhakti āsteo jato kkhan, jeteo tato kkhan. Rāgabhakti svayambhu liṅger mato. Tār joḍ khuṁje pāvā jāy nā. Svayambhu liṅger joḍ kāśī parjanta. Rāgabhakti, abatār ār tāṁr sāṅgopaṅger hoy.*
>
> **Translation:** If there is love for Him [God], then it is called rāga-bhakti. Vaidhī-bhakti can go away as fast as it comes. Rāga-bhakti is like a *svayambhu liṅga*: its roots cannot be traced. A *svayambhu liṅga*'s roots reach up to Kashi. The incarnation and his apostles have rāga-bhakti.
>
> **KC, 230:** In a strikingly translucent passage, Ramakrishna explains that it is this love, likened to a mystical phallus, that the incarnation shares with his disciples (KA 4.193).

The text is clear: rāga-bhakti means love for God and the incarnation and his disciples have this love. Rāga-bhakti is a form of devotion higher than vaidhī-bhakti (*rāga*, "love"; *vaidhī*, "ritualistic"). In *Kālī's*

Child the love for God is changed to the love "that the incarnation shares with his disciples." In keeping with the general tenor of the book, it is not surprising that *liṅga* is translated as "phallus" but how *svayambhu* (*svayam* + *bhu*, "self-become," i.e., the *liṅga* that is found in a natural state and not sculpted by hand) is rendered "mystical" is unclear.

For a slight change of pace, we can now take a look at how *Kālī's Child* depicts a section of the *Kathāmṛta* in which Ramakrishna describes the nature of a paramahaṁsa who can be like a child or a person overcome with divine madness:

> **KA 4.106:** *Paramahaṁser ābār unmāder avasthā hoy. Jakhon unmād holo, śibaliṅga bodhe nijer liṅga pūjā kortām. Jībanta-liṅgapuja. Ekṭā ābār muktā parāno hoto! Ekhon ār pāri nā.*
>
> **Translation:** "The Paramahaṁsa also gets into a state of madness. When I had the state of madness, I would worship my penis (*liṅga*) with the awareness that it was a Śivaliṅga. [It was the] worship of the living liṅga. A pearl used to be put on it! I cannot do that now.
>
> **KC, 161:** "The paramahaṁsa's state of madness also used to come [upon me]. I would become mad and worship my own penis with the awareness that it was Śiva's penis. This is called the worship of the living *liṅgam* [*jīvantaliṅgapūjā*]. And it became adorned with a pearl! Now I'm not able to do that (KA 4.106)."

In the first edition of *Kālī's Child*, the penultimate phrase was translated as: "And a little pearl would come out! Now I'm not able to do that (KA 4.106)" (KC 1995, 161). Regarding the "pearl," *Kālī's Child* is completely off the mark. It is remarkable that someone who is ostensibly a stickler for literal accuracy should write something so breathtakingly inaccurate. An endnote suggests that the "pearl" is "a ball of seminal fluid" (KC, 352).[21] The explanation is much simpler. It is customary in India to decorate the Śivaliṅga with garlands and ornaments such as jewels or necklaces. In order to make sense of the kind of "pearl" Kripal has in mind, he not only distorts the translation of the Bengali phrase, *ekṭā ābār muktā parāno hoto* ("A pearl used to be put on it") but also changes the active voice ("used to be put") to a passive voice ("became adorned").

It is important to keep in mind that in Bengali and other Indian languages, *liṅga* does not carry the weight which "penis" does in English. The Śivaliṅga as a religious icon represents Śiva, not "Śiva's penis." When Hindus worship a Śivaliṅga, they have in mind neither a "penis" nor "Śiva's penis," but the presence of the divine in the form of

Śiva. Thus the translation "Śiva's penis" is not only inaccurate but also culturally insensitive.

Purna is not the only recipient of *Kālī's Child*'s special attention. As we can see below, *Kālī's Child* distorts the text when it comes to Ramakrishna's relationships with Narendra and Nityagopal as well.

KA 1.204: *"Īśvarke joto lābh hobe, totoi bicār kombe. Tāṁke lābh hole ār śabda bicār thāke nā. Takhon nidrā—samādhi."*

Ei boliyā Narendrer gāy hāt bulāiyā mukhe hāt diyā ādar koritechen o bolitechen, "Hari Om, Hari Om, Hari Om."

Keno eirup koritechen o bolitechen? Śrī Rāmakṛṣṇa ki Narendrer madhye sākkhāt Nārāyan darśan koritechen? Er-i nām ki mānuṣe īśvar darśan? Ki āścarjja! Dekhite dekhite Ṭhakurer saṁjñā jāiteche. Oi dekho bahirjagater huṁsh coliyā jāiteche. Er-i nām bujhi ardha bāhjja-daśā—jāhā Śrī Gaurāṅger hoiyāchilo. Ekhon-o Narendrer pāyer upar hāt—jeno chal koriyā Nārāyaner pā ṭipitechen—ābār gāye hāt bulāitechen. Eto gā-ṭepā, pā-ṭepā keno? E ki Nārāyaner śebā korchen, nā śakti soñcār korchen?

Translation: "The nearer you approach God, the less you will reason and argue. Once he is attained, then all sounds—reasoning and arguing—come to an end. Then it is time for sleep—samādhi."

Saying this, he [Ramakrishna] affectionately stroked Narendra's body and touched his face, uttering "Hari Om, Hari Om, Hari Om."

Why is he doing and saying this? Is Sri Ramakrishna seeing Nārāyaṇa himself in Narendra? Is this what is meant by seeing God in human beings? What a wonder! Thakur is fast becoming unconscious. Look, he has lost consciousness of the outer world. This, I understand, is the state of semi-consciousness that Śrī Caitanya experienced. He still has his hand on Narendra's foot, as if he is massaging the feet of Nārāyaṇa. Again he strokes Narendra's body. Why so much of pressing of the body and feet? Is he serving Nārāyaṇa or perhaps he is infusing spiritual power?

KC, 228: In one such passage, Ramakrishna is caressing the body and mouth of Narendra. "Why?" M asks himself and his readers. "Is it because he sees Nārāyaṇa himself in Narendra? Is he having a vision of God in a man?" M's question is not answered as Ramakrishna rubs and presses Narendra's body and feet in an ecstatic state. M asks again, not at all sure of himself: "Is he transmitting his *śakti?*" (KA 1.204). M still receives no answer.

This is a fine example of both a stunning mistranslation as well as a misleading interpretation. Kripal renders the same Bengali phrase *gāye hāt bulāitechhen* [literally, "stroke the body"] in two different ways: "caressing the body" and "rubs and presses Narendra's body." In actuality what this phrase implies, given the context, is simply patting his back.

Second, Kripal writes: "M's question is not answered" and "M still receives no answer." The problem with this paraphrase is that M is not *asking* the question of anyone. These thoughts arise in his mind: the questions are purely rhetorical and their answer is obvious in the *Kathāmṛta*. Moreover, the statement that M was "not at all sure of himself"—although it is followed by a reference from the *Kathāmṛta*—is entirely Kripal's conjecture. It is neither a translation nor a paraphrase from the Bengali. Both M's uncertainty and the lack of "answer" are invented in *Kālī's Child* to plant doubt in the reader's mind regarding the reason for Ramakrishna's affectionate behavior toward Narendra.

Kālī's Child, continuing its pederastic subtext, introduces Nityagopal to its readers as "the little Nityagopal." At the age of twenty-three, the young man was hardly "little":

> **KA 5.129:** *Nityagopālke bhābābiṣta dekhiyā Ṭhākur tāhāke du'ek grās khāoāiyā dilen.*
>
> **Translation:** Seeing Nityagopal in an ecstatic state, Ramakrishna put a morsel or two into his mouth.
>
> **KC, 274:** But those who remained celibate won both Ramakrishna's favor and his food. Hence an ecstatic Ramakrishna feeds the little Nityagopal by grabbing both of his hands and intimately putting them to his mouth (KA 5.129).

Kālī's Child's distortions are clear: The reader is presented with an "ecstatic" Ramakrishna (which is incorrect—it was not Ramakrishna but Nityagopal who was in an ecstatic state), who feeds the "little Nityagopal" (who was little neither in age nor in stature) by "grabbing both of his hands" (the *Kathāmṛta* citation has neither a verb for "grabbing" nor a noun for "hand" and note the subtext inherent in "grabbing") and "intimately" (again the word is not in the citation, and again note the subtext) putting "little" Nityagopal's hands to his mouth. As appalling as this textual rendering is, what is omitted from the text is as significant as what is inserted: the book neglects to inform the reader that Ramakrishna fed only "a morsel or two" of food to Nityagopal. It is such manipulative insertions in the text, and careful omissions from it, followed by references to Bengali source books, which change the texts' context and meaning.

At this point we can examine a few examples of other "boys" who appear in *Kālī's Child.*

> **KC, 80:** Narayan was actually beat up by his family when he returned home from visiting Ramakrishna on more than one occasion.

Since the book claims that the beating took place "on more than one occasion," the author probably felt compelled to give "more than one" reference. Thus in an endnote (KC, 345) Kripal provides two references from the *Kathāmṛta* : KA 3.98 and 4.143. At KA 3.98 we see Narayan arrive at Dakshineswar and Ramakrishna referring to Narayan's having received a beating at home. But when we go to the second reference, KA 4.143, we find nothing at all about Narayan.

> **KC, 80:** In yet another passage, a piqued Ramakrishna scolds little Naren for abandoning his studies to visit him: "Your father will hurt you" (KA 3.196).

We can note in passing the use of "little Naren" for Narendra Nath Mitra, who as M's student was young, but certainly not "little." In the *Kathāmṛta* he is referred to as younger Naren (*Choṭo Naren*) to distinguish him from Narendra Nath Dutta, who was older than he. *Kālī's Child*'s "little Naren" seems less like a translation of *Choṭo Naren* than a strategy to create "little" boys around Ramakrishna. We are once again reminded of conjuring "little" Nityagopal (KC, 274), "little Naran" (318), and Sarat's "little brother" (80). More to the point, however, in the *Kathāmṛta* section quoted above (KA 3.196), we do not find Ramakrishna scolding the younger Naren and we do not see him saying: "Your father will hurt you." Both the situation as well as the context have been distorted here.

The context is this: Some days earlier, the younger Naren had said: "I cannot come often because of work, studying for the exams, etc." (*āmār kāj āche boliyā āsite pāri nā, parīkkhār jonnya poḍā—ityādi*). So when the younger Naren arrives after a few days, Ramakrishna reminds him that he had not sent for him. Naren smiles and says, "So what can be done?" Ramakrishna tells him, "[If you come] your work will suffer. Come when you have leisure" (*tā bāpu tomār aniṣṭa hobe, abasar hole āśbe*) (KA 3.196). Note particularly that nowhere is it said, as *Kālī's Child* would have us believe, "Your father will hurt you."

The author's motivation seems to be to invent a circumstance that would enable him to claim: "It was not an unreasonable fear: at one point, Naren stays three nights at Dakshineswar, apparently to escape his father's anger." No reference is provided, so it is unclear where this bit of information was unearthed. The author then continues:

> **KC, 80:** Ramakrishna was also afraid of Naren's father. In one passage he relates how he went to see Naren but then turned back in fear of Naren's father. Everyone laughs (KA 3.182).

In the *Kathāmṛta* reference cited above, we find something very different: Ramakrishna asks the younger Naren to take him to his house. Naren responds with a cheerful: "Please do come," but becomes nervous as they start moving toward the house, lest his father should know about it. It was *the younger Naren* who was afraid of his father, not Ramakrishna. And it is hearing about *Naren's* dilemma that makes everyone laugh, not any alleged fear on Ramakrishna's part.

> **KC, 80:** Paltu is also in trouble for seeing Ramakrishna (KA 3.129), as are Tarak (KA 3.124–25) and Dvija.

This sentence ends with an endnote reference (KC, 345), where we find two more references: KA 3.179 and KA 4.234. The reason why these two references, both dealing with Dvija, were pushed to endnotes instead of the usual parentheses is unclear until we check them and find that KA 4.234 mentions an incident when Dvija's father comes to meet Ramakrishna. Dvija's father is very respectful and quite impressed after meeting Ramakrishna and tells him: "I tell my children that studies are necessary. I don't forbid them to come to you, but I don't want them to waste their time fooling around with their friends."

The issue of neglected studies, in fact, was *the* reason why most parents objected to their sons' visits to Dakshineswar, but this information is carefully sidestepped in *Kālī's Child*. Amiya Sen notes in this connection that one of Ramakrishna's young disciples, Naran, visited Ramakrishna against his parents' wishes. Fearful that Naran's future success would be imperiled, "[Naran's] mother personally called on Ramakrishna so that she might persuade the saint to impress upon her son the importance of doing well in his course of study and getting settled early in life" (Amiya Sen 2001, 45; KA 2.109–110). Of course this is not mentioned in *Kālī's Child*. Instead, the reader is told that "Ramakrishna loves Naran, a boy of seventeen with beautiful fair skin" (KC, 65). In

Kālī's Child's two other references to Naran, he is predictably referred to as "little Naran" (KC, 235, 318).

> **KC, 80:** The families object to an unspecified crime. M fears for himself (KA 3.149).

In the *Kathāmṛta* reference above (KA 3.149) there is nothing at all about "families" or "unspecified crimes." Interestingly, this is the second time this particular passage is quoted in *Kālī's Child*. The first citation, which occurs six pages earlier (KC, 74), fails to report any hint of an "unspecified crime."

> **KC, 81:** Ramakrishna asks M if he could go to M's school to look for boys. M suggests that instead Ramakrishna wait at his house and that he bring the boys to him (KA 3.101).

In KA 3.101 we read that after talking about Narayan and Tejchandra, Ramakrishna expresses the wish to visit M's school. M assumes that Ramakrishna wants to meet Narayan; M therefore suggests that he can bring Narayan home himself and Ramakrishna can wait there. Ramakrishna then tells M that he wants to see if there are other boys in the school. M was teaching in a boys' school and, of course, besides Narayan and Tejchandra there *were* many other boys. Ramakrishna wanted to know whether there were other boys as spiritually inclined as Narayan and Tejchandra. M immediately agrees and invites Ramakrishna. The purpose of Ramakrishna's visits and his faith in M are apparent also from the instruction he gave M regarding another young devotee: "Bring Bankim here, otherwise you instruct him; your words will bring him illumination" (Prabhananda 1993, 220).

Kālī's Child's suggestion that Ramakrishna wanted to go to M's school "to look for boys" is both mischievous and misleading. Alleging that Ramakrishna's contemporaries were critical and suspicious of his relationship with his male disciples, *Kālī's Child* tells us that Ramakrishna developed his own philosophy to counter criticism regarding his love for "boys":

> **KC, 82:** Just as water is water, but only some water is appropriate for drinking and washing, so some people are more spiritually fit, more mystically "powerful" (*śakti*) than others—all men are *not* created equal (KA 3.181).

How did Thomas Jefferson get in here? If we look at the *Kathāmṛta* reference (KA 3.181), we find only the example regarding water meant for drinking and washing. Ramakrishna gives the example to show that although all are in essence divine, the manifestation of their divinity varies, just as all water, although essentially the same, can be differentiated on the basis of its fitness for drinking or washing. As one might suspect, the cited text does not say anything at all about all men being created equal or unequal.

Again belaboring the "boys" theme, *Kālī's Child* continues:

> **KC, 82:** Boys are particularly lucent bearers of God's light and power, for their breasts have not yet been covered over by the feces of worldly concerns and that most damaging of worldly realities—a job.

Breasts? The reader should be intrigued. The passage points to an endnote which provides the following (mistranslated) quote from the *Kathāmṛta*:

> "I said to Kedar, 'Nothing will happen if your mind dwells on lover-and-gold.' I wanted to pass my hand over his breast, but I could not. It was all knotted up inside. I couldn't enter a room that smelled of feces" (KA 4.230). (KC, 345)

But what does the careful reader find in the *Kathāmṛta*? Ramakrishna says that Kedar (who in 1885, the date of the citation, was fifty-three years old and yet, in the eyes of *Kālī's Child*, still a "boy" [KC, 66]) was all knotted up inside. Kedar's heart was like a room filled with feces, since his mind was preoccupied with materialistic pursuits powered by lust and greed. The Bengali word *buk* can mean chest, heart, breast, depending on the context. In the passage about Kedar, "chest" would have been the appropriate translation. But in a section that is subtitled "Pure Pots for the Milk of Love" (KC, 82), it helps to translate *buk* as "breast," just as it helps to transform an illustrative example into a distorted metaphor. In order to emphasize the primacy of purity in spiritual life, Ramakrishna gave the example of an unclean pot in which milk becomes quickly spoiled, whereas in a new pot, the milk remains fresh. Even so, one who is uncontaminated is able to retain the purity of the teaching and become enlightened faster than one who is not. This example becomes transformed in *Kālī's Child* into a metaphor where the "boys" become "pure pots" for "the milk of love." Interestingly, "of love" is *Kālī's Child*'s own contribution; the phrase is not in the *Kathāmṛta*. Nor, in fact, is the last phrase from the *Kālī's Child* citation above: "for their breasts have not yet been covered over by the feces of worldly concerns and that most damaging of worldly realities—a job." The words are Kripal's creation but the unsuspecting reader would not be aware of this fact.

Finally, in the *Kālī's Child* passage above: "Boys are particularly lucent bearers of God's light and power" (KC, 82), we find additional problems. When we read the referenced text (KA 4.230), it is unmistakable that Ramakrishna was referring to his own young disciples, not just generic "boys." We know, for example, that Ramakrishna did not care for some of the young friends that Naren and others brought along with them, because they were not spiritually inclined. But, as we have seen, *Kālī's Child* takes every opportunity to create the impression that Ramakrishna had a homoerotic attraction for "boys," whether the texts support such an allegation or not. For example:

> KC, 82: In another passage he [Ramakrishna] explains why he is so "excited" (*uddīpana*) in the presence of the boys: unlike the common man, they contain the sweet pudding of devotion (KA 2.50).

Here the author forces together two distant and completely unconnected passages from the *Kathāmṛta*, but the quote is deceptively referenced to make it appear as if he were citing one or two related phrases. In the *Kathāmṛta* citation given above (KA 2.50), we find Ramakrishna saying that he would be "enkindled by the thought of God" (*īśvarer uddīpan*) when he saw Rakhal doing japa. By omitting the word "God" from his translation, Kripal changes the context and the meaning of the quotation, his phrase insinuating that Ramakrishna became "excited in the presence of boys"—God somehow having gotten lost in translation.

Following Ramakrishna's statement regarding his being enkindled by the thought of God when he saw Rakhal doing japa, there is more discussion, after which Ramakrishna ate lunch and rested. *After* his rest, Ramakrishna said that though outwardly there may not be much difference in people, inwardly they might be quite different. In this context, Ramakrishna gives the example of a Bengali sweet preparation which looks the same from the outside, but is basically different depending on the kind of filling—whether custard or lentil—it has. It is the same with people, he said. Note again *Kālī's Child*'s use of "sweet pudding" with "boys," which brings us back to the book's basic thesis: that Ramakrishna was "a lover … of young, beautiful boys, those 'pure pots' … that could hold the 'milk' of his divine love" (KC, 3). There is nothing in the *Kathāmṛta* citation to warrant this "sweet pudding" and "boys" association, but *Kālī's Child* binds them together to maintain its sotto voce pederastic drumbeat.

> KC, 68: This radical passivity is evident in the way Ramakrishna is powerfully attracted to different boy disciples and the manner in

> which they in turn are attracted to him. "Their natures are very pure," Ramakrishna declares, "and so when they sing they attract me!"

Should the perspicacious reader hope to track down the origin of this supposed quotation from Ramakrishna, she or he will be disappointed. Unlike other citations which appear in *Kālī's Child*, this quote from the *Kathāmṛta* has the reference not in parentheses, but in an endnote (KC, 343). Yet when one turns to the endnote, all it says is: "Cf. KA 3.136." Should one persevere and read the *Kathāmṛta* 3.136, one will find absolutely nothing about these alleged words of Ramakrishna which Kripal "quotes." However, by the time Ramakrishna's "radical passivity" and "powerfully attracted" are combined with "boy disciples," the damage has been done—valid citation or not, valid translation or not.

We have below yet another example of Kripal's fixation on "boys," which is combined with inaccurate documentation. *Kālī's Child* uses Haramohan as an example of what happened when "one of those pure pots went bad." We read:

> Ramakrishna once "anxiously desired" to see Haramohan, but when the boy married, he quit coming as often, and when he did come, he brought his wife along, the two of them sitting together apart from Ramakrishna. Peeved at this new development, Ramakrishna told Haramohan to leave, explaining, "How can my body touch yours?" (KA. 4.109). (KC, 82–83)

Kālī's Child concludes with this final shot:

> The pot had gone bad, its pure milk wasted on a mere woman. (KC, 83)

What is the problem with Haramohan? When Ramakrishna first saw the young Haramohan, Ramakrishna said, he had many good tendencies. But later his life underwent a change and the young man developed worldly tendencies. Haramohan once came to meet Ramakrishna with his wife. Seeing those worldly tendencies, Ramakrishna told him to go away; he could not even touch him.

Was this change in Ramakrishna's attitude toward Haramohan due to his marriage, as *Kālī's Child* would have us believe? No. What, then, was the issue? Ramakrishna opens the subject of Haramohan with these words: "Attachment to lust and greed make a person small-minded (*hīnabuddhi*)." It was this *attachment* which Ramakrishna saw in Haramohan, and apparently it was this canker that Ramakrishna was aiming to cauterize by telling Haramohan to leave the room. Ramakrishna remarks in the *Kathāmṛta* that Haramohan did his wife's grocery shopping—the implication being that Haramohan was no longer a free man but followed the dictates of his wife. Furthermore, Ramakrishna mentions that Haramohan and his wife lived separately—i.e., they were no longer living with Haramohan's parents (as was the norm for Indian families of that time). This would be considered not only extremely selfish but also irreligious—neglecting one's duty to one's parents, who were to be served as embodiments of the divine, was against the dictates of dharma. We can remember that M also lived separately from his father and stepmother, which had distressed Ramakrishna.[22] Thus from Ramakrishna's perspective, and as we can see from the source texts, Haramohan's attachment to his wife (which is why he no longer lived with his parents) had put his life into a downward spiral and for this reason, Ramakrishna, disgusted, asked him to leave the room.

Nowhere in the cited *Kathāmṛta* text (4.109)—from which Kripal supposedly quotes—do we find Ramakrishna upset because of Haramohan's marriage per se. In fact, a year and a half later, on January 1, 1886, Ramakrishna *did* approach Haramohan and at that time he touched his chest (Chetanananda 1989, 331). Perhaps the cauterization technique worked, for later in life the source texts indicate that Haramohan had many spiritual experiences and was extremely close to Ramakrishna's disciples, monastic and lay. Haramohan became a staunch devotee—printing Suresh Dutta's *Śrī Śrī Rāmakṛṣṇa Deber Upadeś* ["Sayings of Sri Ramakrishna Deva"] as well as printing the pamphlets of Vivekananda—all at his own expense (332).

Thus, we can see that, contrary to the claim in *Kālī's Child*, Ramakrishna's reaction to Haramohan was not because the pot's "pure milk" had been wasted on "a mere woman." Nor was Ramakrishna's earlier response to Haramohan that of "anxiously desiring." An entirely different problem can be seen in the example below:

> **KC, 69:** In one scene, for example, a young boy comes to Ramakrishna and reveals to the Paramahaṁsa that he has seen him in his dreams, just sitting there saying nothing. An excited Ramakrishna breaks in: "That's very good! . . . You're attracted to me, isn't this so?" There is silence, followed by Ramakrishna's request that the boy come again. But he will make no promises, for his family objects (KA 4.149).

What is truly peculiar here is that Kripal does not mention in the reference above that the young boy referred to is Purna—even though the *Kathāmṛta* mentions it quite explicitly. By now the reader is well aware that Purna's parents objected to him visiting Ramakrishna because they feared his studies would suffer. Yet Kripal does not name "the young boy"—perhaps to give the reader the impression that this was yet *another* "young boy" whose parents objected to their son visiting Ramakrishna. The only reason this is advantageous to *Kālī's Child* is to again hammer upon the allegation that parents were worried about their sons being with Ramakrishna. To quote *Kālī's Child*: "He [Ramakrishna] 'ruins so many school boys.' The phrase carries both a sexual scandal and a social problem. . . . But even given the scandal of Ramakrishna's homosexual behavior, it was the social problem that was more basic, more troubling" (KC, 79).[23] Worse, *Kālī's Child* asserts:

> Ramakrishna's power over the boys and the disciples is mysterious, inexplicable, controversial. . . . It unites the human and the divine in the persons of Rādhā and Kṛṣṇa, it unites Ramakrishna and the disciples, it is discerned in a dream, and it is rejected by the social world as dangerous. (KC, 69)

To address the most obvious issues first: As we have repeatedly shown, there was nothing "controversial" about Ramakrishna's relationship with his young disciples. Every allegation which has been made in *Kālī's Child* has been investigated and found spurious. Throughout the course of this book, we have repeatedly shown that the only objection made concerning Ramakrishna and his young disciples was their parents' fear that by going off to Dakshineswar and spending time with Ramakrishna—a paramahaṁsa who most unhelpfully preached renunciation—the boys' studies would suffer. In an India where the middle-class job market was—and still is—intensely competitive and formidable effort was required to scale the heights of the increasingly rarified social strata of the middle class, this is not difficult to understand. Opportunities for educated Bengali males in colonial India were not easy to come by. For parents, an educated son with a good job was a mandatory investment in their old age. Similar objections are raised even today. A young son or daughter taking more than casual interest in religion raises the fear that their studies (and consequently, their futures) will suffer.

Given that, the only "mysterious" power which Kripal needs to address is how Purna's parents' objections to Purna visiting Ramakrishna became transubstantiated in *Kālī's Child* into "Ramakrishna's power over the boys ... is rejected by the social world as dangerous." *Dangerous?* Ramakrishna's influence over his disciples may well have been annoying to the boys' parents—who wants to hear about renunciation from one's teenage son?—but hardly dangerous. Further, and not surprisingly, there is no mention of Rādhā or Kṛṣṇa anywhere near this citation, though the *Kathāmṛta* reference would have the reader believe that at least some mention is there. What seems likely is that *Kālī's Child* pulled up their names in order to bring to mind its earlier comment on Rādhā and Kṛṣṇa's "erotic union" (KC, 68). If Rādhā and Kṛṣṇa have an "erotic union" then Ramakrishna and his (boy) disciples... One only need fill in the blanks. When "controversial" and "dangerous" are added to the mix, the reader can hardly be blamed for having an impression of a "troubled" Ramakrishna in the *Kathāmṛta* that is entirely unwarranted.

What is peculiar about this entire discussion of the "young boy" who visits Ramakrishna, is that the boy is Purna. Yet within a few pages, Kripal will again return to the same reference in the *Kathāmṛta* and this time Purna's name will be invoked.

> **KC, 74:** In yet another scene, M gets nervous when Purna scoots closer to Ramakrishna—will the boy's family hear about this visit too (KA 3.149)?

Yet this is *exactly* the same scene, the same date, time, page in the *Kathāmṛta* as the "young boy" above, who tells Ramakrishna that he dreamt of him. In fact, before he can tell Ramakrishna this, Ramakrishna asks him to come closer, since there is a roomful of people. As *Kālī's Child* makes much of this scene, let us look at it carefully:

First, the scene is in Balaram's drawing room in Calcutta and the room is filled with people. According to the *Kathāmṛta*, Ramakrishna is sitting with the devotees: M, Girish, Balaram, the younger Naren, Paltu, Dvija, Purna, Mahendra Mukherji, and "many devotees" (*anek bhakta*) are there. Many female devotees are also there, including M's wife, seated behind a screen. Trailokyanath Sannyal, Jaygopal Sen, and other members of the Brahmo Samaj arrive a little later. Those who have been in Balaram Bose's drawing room can attest that it is not spacious, so the room is fairly well crammed. Ramakrishna is talking with the devotees about his various sādhanas and his various spiritual realizations.

After a while Ramakrishna tells Purna: "Come here" (*ekhāne eśo*) so he can ask Purna questions about his spiritual life. *Kālī's Child* takes this exceedingly common phrase and refashions it into "scoot closer." What would be the point of such an idiosyncratic translation? Perhaps to bring to mind that portion of Purna's anatomy which is used to "scoot"? As the reader can see, there is nothing in *ekhāne eśo* (*ekhāne* means "here" and *eśo* means "[you] come") to warrant this description. Purna is merely sitting near Ramakrishna.

In an endnote the reader is informed that "'scoot closer' was a common request of Ramakrishna's" (KC, 344). To support this, two references from the *Kathāmṛta* are given: KA 3.99 and 3.209. In those citations we find nothing other than Ramakrishna saying, "Come and sit here." In the latter reference, there are so many people in the room that there is simply no place to sit. It is customary in India, as a mark of respect, not to sit close to a holy person unless one is invited to do so. Seeing that there was no place else for the musicians to sit, Ramakrishna invited them to sit near him so that the singing could begin.

Kālī's Child brings up yet again its spurious claim regarding Ramakrishna's "habit of garlanding Purna" and "rubbing sandal-paste on his 'body'" and proclaims that Purna's parents were "worried about such practices and suspected more than religion in this worship" (KC, 162) and cites KA 3.149 as a reference. Interestingly, Kripal has already mentioned this reference twice before (KC, 74 and 80). In the first reference, no mention is made of anything scandalous, just that M is "nervous." Six pages later, the same reference from the *Kathāmṛta* is given, and this time the reader is told: "The families object to an unspecified crime" (KC, 80). Now by page 162, when the same citation from the *Kathāmṛta* is brought up yet again, the reader is told that Purna's parents "suspected more than religion in this worship" (162). Yet there is nothing whatsoever in this increasingly familiar passage from *Kathāmṛta* 3.149 to warrant this claim, as we see in our discussion in this chapter.

In returning to the passage on KC, 74, we see a similar situation. Ramakrishna wants to ask Purna whether he has followed the instructions Ramakrishna has given him. Purna replies in the affirmative and then Ramakrishna asks him about his dreams, asking him in particular about dreams which are considered spiritually auspicious: "Do you dream of a flame? A lighted torch? A married woman? A cremation ground? It is good to dream of these things" (KA 3.149). Purna replies that he had dreamt of Ramakrishna sitting and instructing him (*bośe āchen—ki bolchen*). Ramakrishna then asks Purna to narrate an instruction (*upadeś*) he had received from him in the dream. Purna says that he cannot remember (*mone nāi*). Yet according to *Kālī's Child*'s rendition above, in Purna's dreams Ramakrishna is "just sitting there saying nothing" (KC, 69)—which is entirely different from what we have just read in the *Kathāmṛta* (KA 3.149). There is a profound difference between

Ramakrishna "just sitting there saying nothing" and Purna being unable to recollect the instructions he had received in his dream.

Ramakrishna continues by telling Purna that it does not matter; it—the dream—is very good (*khūb bhālo*). He tells Purna that he will make spiritual progress and asks, "You feel drawn to me, don't you?" (*āmār upar to ṭān āche?*). After a few minutes, Ramakrishna asks Purna whether he will be able to visit Dakshineswar; Purna says he cannot promise because it is not convenient. Both he and Ramakrishna—as well as some of the devotees in the room—are aware of Purna's parents' objections.

A couple of issues which *Kālī's Child* brings up require discussion here. First, let us look again at Kripal's translation: "M gets nervous when Purna scoots closer to Ramakrishna—will the boy's family hear about this visit too (KA 3.149)?" (KC, 74). This is misleading. It is quite clear from the text that M is *not* nervous because Purna is sitting near Ramakrishna, but because Girish inquires about the boy. The *Kathāmṛta* could not make it more evident if it tried:

> **KA 3.149:** GIRISH (*Māṣṭārer prati*): *Ke e cheleṭi?*
>
> MĀṢṬĀR (*birakta hoiyā*): *Chele ār ke?*
>
> GIRISH (*sahāsye*): It needs no ghost to tell me that.
>
> *Māṣṭārer bhoy hoiyāche pāche pāṁc jone jānite pārile cheler bāḍite goljog hoy ār tāṁhār nāme doṣ hoy. Cheleṭir soṅge Ṭhākur-o seijonya āste āste kothā koitechen.*
>
> **Translation:** GIRISH (*To M*): "Who is the boy?"
>
> M (*Annoyed, to Girish*): "Can't you see it's a boy?"
>
> GIRISH (*Smilingly to M, in English*): "It needs no ghost to tell me that."
>
> M is afraid that others will know who he is, which might create difficulties for Purna, and M himself might be blamed. This is also the reason that Thakur is speaking to the boy in a low voice.

As we can see, M is not nervous because Purna is sitting near Ramakrishna, but because Girish inquires about the boy. M is also irritated lest Girish's question about the boy bring attention to his presence. Since M was Purna's teacher, M knew he would be blamed for bringing the boy to Dakshineswar, should the word get out. Purna's family objected to his visits not because they were suspicious of Ramakrishna's character, but because such visits were considered a distraction from his studies. For this reason, Ramakrishna speaks to Purna in a low voice.

The last point which requires elaboration here is the Bengali word *ṭān*, which, according to Kripal, describes Ramakrishna's "dual desire for God and male disciples" (KC, 67). This is problematic, however, because of the associations with the English word "desire," which has sexual implications. *Ṭān* means a pull or tug, an attraction, or affection. While the English expression "he is attracted to" often carries sexual implications, the Bengali *ṭān* carries no such undercurrent. While perhaps it *could* be used as a word denoting sexual attraction, it would be a very odd usage. In general usage, *ṭān* has nothing to do with sex. One can have *ṭān* for, say, Hawaii. Or for Bach's cantatas. Or for lattes. Or for one's mother or dog or friends or garden. In colloquial Bengali, *ṭān* simply means "a pull."

What does Ramakrishna mean, then, when he asks Purna if he has *ṭān*—feels drawn—to Ramakrishna? Ramakrishna was Purna's spiritual teacher, and one expects that a disciple will feel drawn—and we are not talking about sexual attraction here—to one's guru. If one feels no such pull, it does not bode well for the student. As importantly, Ramakrishna believed Purna to be an *īśvarakoṭi*, a person born with exceptional spiritual qualities. There was a special "recognition" between Ramakrishna and Purna—Ramakrishna considered Purna an ever-free soul and Purna considered Ramakrishna to be an avatar. Like Narendra, Rakhal, M, and others belonging to Ramakrishna's "inner circle," there was a special concern on Ramakrishna's part not only about these disciples' individual spiritual lives but also about their particular roles in Ramakrishna's—for lack of a better word—*līlā*, his play on earth. The avatar and those belonging to his "inner circle" are considered deeply connected, the *īśvarakoti* also being a manifestation of the avatar. As Ramakrishna said to M (and it would equally apply to all in his inner circle):

> You are my own. The same substance (*sattā*), like father and son. Everyone coming here is like the kalmi creeper: when you pull one part of it, all the branches come toward you. You are all relatives—like brothers. . . . Until you came here, you didn't know who you were. Now you will know. God comes in the form of guru and teaches everyone. (KA 4.45)

If one feels queasy when reading *Kālī's Child*'s version of Ramakrishna and Purna—in which an "excited Ramakrishna" says to Purna, "You're attracted to me, isn't this so?" (KC, 69), we should remember the considerable background behind the comment. We should also keep in mind that Ramakrishna spoke of *ṭān* often (using the word sometimes as a noun, other times as a verb), to both male and female disciples, young and old, in various contexts. He says, for example, that his mind was still being pulled (*ṭene rekheche*) to a song (KA 5.136); that the young disciples had a pull toward God (*īśvarer dike ṭān*) from their very birth (4.230); that when God himself pulls (*ṭene lon*) a person, then the ego vanishes on its own (4.229)—the list goes on and on. Yes, Ramakrishna does have *ṭān* for his devotees—particularly those young male disciples who would for the most part renounce the world and become the first monastic members of the Ramakrishna Order—and they had *ṭān* for him. However we should also keep in mind that *all* of Ramakrishna's disciples—male and female, young and old—had *ṭān* for Ramakrishna, and from what we can gather from these male and female disciples, they felt this was reciprocated.

We can, for example, remember the famous incident concerning Gauri-Ma, a woman who would become Ramakrishna's disciple and to whom he gave the ochre cloth of sannyāsa. When Gauri-Ma was told by Ramakrishna's disciple Balaram that she should meet Ramakrishna, she replied, "I have seen many monks in my life, and I have no desire to see another. If your holy man has real power, then let him pull me" (Durga Puri, 69). The next day while doing pūjā, she had an overwhelming spiritual experience. That changed her mind, and she wanted to meet Ramakrishna. When Gauri-Ma arrived, she found Ramakrishna winding thread around a stick—indicating to her that she had indeed been "pulled" by him (70–73). *Ṭān* works for women as well.

Another documentation and translation issue found in *Kālī's Child* has its basis in the book's preoccupation with male nudity. We have already seen how *Kālī's Child* endlessly belabors Tota's nudity. Ramakrishna's occasional nudity gets the same response: "Often, Ramakrishna would dance naked, surrounded by his male disciples, or pace, or sit naked among them" (231–32). Sometimes, Kripal continues, "the boys would danced naked," to which he adds:

> Such practices did not always sit well with the locals. One scholar, after visiting the saint and witnessing such a show of dancing and singing, was supposed to have commented curtly: "Yes, a paramahaṁsa indeed."

Kripal's endnote (356) directs us to Sil's *Rāmakṛṣṇa Paramahaṁsa*, yet when we check the quoted text, we find Sil writing about Ramakrishna's increasing celebrity, not dancing naked with naked boys. Sil's text notes that the "distinguished intellectual and patriot from Bengal, Aśvinī Kumār Datta (1856–1923), who watched the devotees dance around Rāmakṛṣṇa in a circle with the master standing motionless and transfixed in *samādhi* for a long time, said to himself: 'Yes a paramahaṁsa indeed'" (Sil 1991, 108). We should note that the famed patriot-intellectual is referred to in *Kālī's Child* as "a scholar," and remains unnamed. Dutta was a life-long admirer of Ramakrishna, and his name appears often in Ramakrishna literature. In fact, Aswini Kumar Dutta appears prominently in the Appendix to the first volume of the *Kathāmṛta*. When we look at the text it becomes obvious that Dutta's words did not constitute what Kripal construes as a "curt comment." Dutta's comment was, in fact, highly appreciative since he says, regarding the dancing and singing that he witnessed: "What I saw then, I think I shall not forget in this or in the next life. Hearing and seeing that, I realized he was indeed a paramahaṁsa" (KA 1.262). Thus not only were there no problems "with the locals," there were no problems with Aswini Kumar Dutta either.

Kālī's Child informs the reader that Ramakrishna's visions were filled with naked boys: "It should also be noted that many of the personages that appeared in Ramakrishna's secret visions were naked. Many of them were boys" (KC, 232). Of all Ramakrishna's mystic visions which are found throughout five volumes of Bengali text, there are two visions which mention naked boys. The first vision is that of the naked paramahaṁsa boy who emerged from Ramakrishna's body; the second vision is with a boy thirteen or fourteen years old who looked like Purna. Scenes of boys or naked boys hardly constitute the majority of Ramakrishna's visions.

Those Pesky Five M's

We have already noted *Kālī's Child*'s preoccupation with the "Five M's" (*pañca makāra*) in earlier pages, and the text informs us that the only "M" that Ramakrishna "seems to have truly conquered was *matysa* or fish." But *Kālī's Child* also informs the reader that since fish was accepted as a legitimate food, "this victory ... was not much of a victory" (KC, 129). Victory over fish was not something which concerned Ramakrishna, it is true, nor did he feel compelled to complete all the Five M's. As is well known, Ramakrishna did not engage in *maithuna*, sexual intercourse, because he went into samādhi simply upon *seeing* it. The Bhairavi said that the goal of Tantra sādhana was to attain this state of divine union; therefore, it was unnecessary for Ramakrishna to physically undergo that M, or *makāra*. Ramakrishna relates this about his Tantra sādhana:

> I remember the day when, after observing the sexual bliss experienced by a pair of lovers in the act of intercourse, and knowing it to

> be the blissful sport (*līlābilās*) of Śiva and Śakti, I became transfixed (*mugdha*) and entered into samādhi. That day, after I regained external consciousness, the Brahmani said, "My child, you have attained the 'seat of bliss' (*ānandāsan*) and become established in the divine state (*dibyabhāb*). This is the last sādhana of the heroic state (*bīr-bhāb*) of worship." (LP 2.206)

Since Ramakrishna was already sitting on the roof, metaphysically speaking, there was no reason for him to climb up the stairs. We should keep in mind that Ramakrishna was a practical man. Whatever sādhana he engaged in, he wanted direct results. Therefore, the real question we have to ask about Ramakrishna and the Five M's is, *how were they religiously significant to Ramakrishna?* Their significance to Ramakrishna can be found in their practical result. For Ramakrishna, the purpose of the *makāras* was to attain God; the process was secondary.

Kālī's Child, on the other hand, views Ramakrishna as a "failed Tāntrika" because he did not engage in *maithuna*, sexual intercourse. "Ramakrishna," Kripal writes,

> could not consciously make it though the Five M's. . . . He simply could not bring himself to drink wine and could only fall into trances when presented with the challenge of the fifth and most important M, sexual intercourse. (KC, 129)

In other words, Ramakrishna "could only" fall into trances—i.e., escape from the "challenge" of sexual intercourse. Thus samādhi, considered the apex of spiritual achievement in the Hindu tradition, is something that one can simply "fall into" when trying to weasel out of a sexual encounter. It seems that here the cart has dragged away the horse. The point of all the *makāras* is to attain a higher state of spirituality, not just to have meat, fish, wine, parched grain, and sex. Many enjoy these pleasures—except for the parched grain—every day and, from all evidence so far, this has not led them to samādhi.

The purpose of *maithuna* is not sexual intercourse per se—anyone can have sex and most people do, but that does not constitute a part of one's sādhana unless it is practiced with rigorous discipline and self-control. We should recall that those who are too animalistic, that is, filled with *tamas*, are not allowed to practice *vīrabhāva*, the path of the hero. Those endowed with *sattva*—those who have a godlike temperament—also do not follow the *vīrabhāva*. It is not necessary. They are to follow the *daivībhāva*. For Kripal however, Tantra equals not only Vāmācāra but Vāmācāra with special emphasis on *maithuna*, "the most important M." Such a definitive stance is problematic because, as Amiya Sen points out, there are "no less than six different interpretations of *Vamachar* Tantra, each of these originating in the work of acknowledged authorities on the subject." Sen continues:

> Thus *Vamachar* is taken to be the collective name for those rites which predominantly use the left hand, that in which woman [*vama*] is included, that in which the position of the woman is to the left [*vama*] of the male practitioner, that which is characterized by *nivritti*, "return current," representing passivity and disengagement, that which is antinomian in character [*viruddha/viparita*] and that in which the male worships the Female Principle [*Parama Prakriti*] by ascribing femininity to oneself. This is baffling to say the least. (Amiya Sen 2001, 113)

Because *Kālī's Child* has such a narrow vision of Tantra, much mistranslation and misinterpretation follow in its wake. For example, we read:

> **KC, 127:** Granted, the fact that Ramakrishna was horrified at the thought of actual intercourse, indeed, that he seemed incapable of it (his penis was said to pull back up into its sheath, like the limbs of a tortoise, at the touch of a sexy woman [LP 4.APP])…

Why is it "granted" that Ramakrishna was "horrified at the thought of actual intercourse"? The source texts make it clear that Ramakrishna went into samādhi at the sight of a couple having intercourse. He also went into samādhi when he saw two dogs mating. He had no problem when he encountered Mathur Babu and his wife having sexual relations. Ramakrishna often joked with his disciples about sex and he was certainly no prude. What or whose horror are we discussing here?

Ramakrishna, Kripal writes, "cannot relate to woman as Lover," …

> all poor Ramakrishna can do is cry to his Mother and retreat into a state that looks as much like a defensive trance as a mystical state. For Ramakrishna, the goddess is a consoling Mother who protects her child from the adult dangers of sexuality and not … a Lover who grants the striving aspirant the bliss of union. (KC, 121)

Apart from the appalling tone of condescension ("all poor Ramakrishna can do is cry to his Mother"), this assumes that the only viable relationship in Tantra sādhana is *vīrabhāva*, the heroic state, and that *mātṛbhāva*, regarding God as one's Mother, is intrinsically immature. This assessment may have more to do with Western cultural norms than it does with Hindu religious practice. As we know, the Hindu tradition offers the sādhaka a variety of *bhāvas* from which to choose, depending on one's attitude and aptitude. Nor was Ramakrishna's religious preference unique: Ramprasad, Bengal's renowned poet-saint, was a Tāntrik who practiced *mātṛbhāva*, worshiping God as Mother, not *vīrabhāva*.

Strangely, Kripal writes that the "Bhairavī clearly tried to employ sexual intercourse as one of her means to teach Ramakrishna Tantric truths" and gives the example of the occasion when the Bhairavi brought a beautiful young woman to Ramakrishna (KC, 120). However, this example is bogus since the source texts which discuss the incident make it clear that the Bhairavi never expected nor wanted Ramakrishna to engage in *maithuna* with this young woman. The texts clearly state that the Bhairavi instructed Ramakrishna to worship this young naked woman as the Devī. When the worship was completed, the Bhairavi then instructed Ramakrishna to sit in the young woman's lap and do *japa*. Ramakrishna, seized with fear, fervently prayed to the Divine Mother to protect him during this sādhana: "O Mother, what is this command that you have given me who has taken complete refuge in you?" With that, Ramakrishna reports that his heart was filled with a divine power (*dibyabale hṛdoy pūrna hoilo*) and, uttering the appropriate mantras, he sat on the woman's lap and became absorbed in samādhi. Ramakrishna relates that when he returned to normal consciousness, the Bhairavi told him that he had successfully completed the most difficult aspect of the sādhana, in which most seekers stumble. Ramakrishna reported that the Bhairavi said:

> The rite is completed, my child; others restrain themselves with very great difficulty under such circumstances and then finish the rite with nominal japa only for a short time, but you lost body consciousness and became immersed in samādhi. (LP 2.205)

Ramakrishna concludes this incident by stating: "When I heard this, I became reassured and began to *praṇām* the Mother of the Universe (*jagadambā*) again and again with a grateful heart for enabling me to pass the examination successfully" (LP 2.205).

Kālī's Child conjectures that "the Bhairavī attempted to engage her disciple in the fifth M through a ritualized form of cunnilingus or through the oral consumption of sexual fluids." While Kripal admits that this is speculation, he nevertheless perseveres: "I think that there is good reason to take such a possibility seriously" (KC, 128). The reader may well wonder whether there *is* good reason to take this seriously, particularly when we examine the cited texts. Regarding what *Kālī's Child* refers to as Ramakrishna's "not ... particularly positive assessment of oral contact with the vagina," Kripal writes:

> **KC, 127:** Ramakrishna once compared men attached to lover-and-gold to the jackals and dogs who "wet their faces" in their mates' behinds. (KA 5.215)

Kripal's "translation" here is remarkable. Let us compare it with the *Kathāmṛta*:

> **KA 5.215:** *Sobbāi tyāg korbe keno? Ār tām̐r ki icchā je sakalei śiyāl kukurer mato kāminī-kāñcane mukh jubre thāke? Ār ki kichu icchā tām̐r noy? Konṭā tām̐r icchā, konṭā anicchā ki śob jenecho?*
>
> **Translation:** Why should everybody renounce? On the other hand, is it his [God's] wish that everyone should be immersed in *kāminī kañcaṇa* like jackals and dogs? Has he no other wish? Do you know what is his wish and what is not his wish?

Kripal has accused Nikhilananda of toning down his translation: "Can it be the will of God that all should revel in 'woman and gold' like dogs and jackals?" (GSR, 1013). Yet Kripal himself has clearly toned *up* his own translation/paraphrase ("wet their faces in their mates' behinds"). In fact, within one page, *Kālī's Child* has upped the ante to: "Ramakrishna's jackals wetting their faces in their mates' disgusting behinds" (KC, 128). While Nikhilananda's "revel in" is not literal, it nevertheless catches the spirit of the original fairly well. Having pondered the various possibilities, we feel that *mukh jubre thāke* (*mukh*, "face"; *jubre thāke*, "remain immersed/dipped") is actually best translated as "remain immersed in." If a person is "immersed" in something, that person's face is likely to be touched with whatever she or he may be immersed. Interestingly, the phrase *kāminī-kāñcan*, which *Kālī's Child* routinely translates as "lover and gold" is paraphrased here as "their mates' behinds," (cf. *kāminī-kāñcane mukh jubre thāke*) with the author's comment that this was "not a particularly positive assessment of oral contact with the vagina" (127). In the referenced Bengali text, there is no reference to anyone's behinds nor, as one might suspect, is there any assessment of oral sex.

We are not through with the topic yet, for *Kālī's Child* suggests that the evidence for the Bhairavi's attempt to engage her disciple in the fifth M through a ritualized form of cunnilingus or oral consumption of sexual fluids can be found in the texts. Let us examine this evidence:

KC, 128: The type and number of adjectives used in the texts to describe (or refuse to describe) Ramakrishna's Tantric practices suggest as much [i.e., cunnilingus or oral consumption of sexual fluids]: "horrific" (JV[5], 31), "filled with obscenities" (JV[5], 31), and "bizarre" (KA 3.24) all resonate quite well with Ramakrishna's jackals wetting their faces in their mates' disgusting behinds.

What do we find, however, in the cited portion of the *Jībanabṛttānta*? First and most importantly, Datta does not refer to "Ramakrishna's Tantric practices" here. What Ramchandra Datta is discussing, very briefly, is Tantra in general. In one particular sentence, Datta refers to Tantric practices as *bhayānak*, which can best be translated as "frightful" or "terrible"—*bhaya* meaning "fear": *Tantrer sādhan svabhāvataḥ ati bhayānak*, "Tantrik practices are by nature quite terrible" (JB, 31). This is only in one sentence, however; the following two sentences go on to say: "These practices test the strength of mind. In completing these practices, Paramahaṁsadeb benefited from the assistance of the Brahmani" (32).

In the *Kathāmṛta* citation which Kripal provides above (KA 3.24), Ramakrishna is discussing Śakti worship with a group of devotees. Ramakrishna says that the purpose of Śakti worship is to placate *avidyā*. In order to please the Divine Mother, one assumes a *bhāva* in which to worship her—that of a handmaid, the heroic attitude, or the attitude of a child. Ramakrishna goes on to say that with the heroic attitude (*vīra-bhāva*), one has intercourse (*ramaṇ*) with her to please her. Ramakrishna concludes by saying that Śakti sādhana is very difficult to practice (*sab bhārī utkaṭ*), that the Divine Mother cannot be cheated (*cālāki noy*). Kripal translates the word *utkaṭ* as "bizarre," but given the context, *utkaṭ* here simply means extreme or terrible. In the contemporary American idiom, perhaps the best way to translate the phrase is "it's no joke"—that is, Śakti sādhana is extremely difficult, not something to fool around with. Thus as we can see, there is nothing in any of the citations provided in *Kālī's Child*—and certainly none in the source texts—to indicate that Ramakrishna and the Bhairavi either engaged in oral sex or engaged in a ritualized consumption of sexual fluids.

Along the same lines as such presumed "oral sex," we move ahead to other problematic assertions: transcending purity with "disgusting substances":

KC, 165: In one of the visions (KA 3.46), Ramakrishna takes this lesson of the bearded Muslim to his usual Tantric extremes and tastes

> the disgusting substances of feces and pee with a flaming visionary tongue. Purity is transcended in a typically Tantric fashion. In the end, whether Ramakrishna saw Vedānta or Tantra in the "Muslim" teachings of Gobinda is difficult to say. The textual record is ambiguous at best.

The reader would find nothing "ambiguous" in the "textual record" if only the author had quoted the passage or at least paraphrased it without significant omissions. The vision Kripal quotes ends with these words of Ramakrishna: *dekhāle je sab ek*, "I was shown that everything is one." This vision was not about "transcending purity in a typical Tantric fashion" but rather the realization of the unity and oneness of existence. The vision of the bearded Muslim begins in the *Kathāmṛta* (KA 3.46) with these words of Ramakrishna: *āmi ek din dekhlām, ek caitanya—abhed*, "One day I saw that consciousness is one—undivided." There is no ambiguity about the nature of Ramakrishna's vision.

Tantra, *Kālī's Child* repeatedly drills the reader, was Ramakrishna's secret. Ramakrishna was also allegedly homoerotically inclined, and that too, is a secret. The Ramakrishna Order is hiding all this secret information, and that is yet another secret. There are a wearying number of secrets in *Kālī's Child*, none of which actually turn out to be secret when examined. Not only is nothing secret, the "secrets" which are purportedly hidden never existed in the first place—the Emperor's New Clothes in Bengali-to-English translations. But unlocking hidden secrets makes for good copy, so the reader is offered up more secrets as *Kālī's Child* progresses. We read for example:

> **KC, 220:** "Now I'm telling you something very secret—why I love Purna, Narendra, and all the others so much. I broke my arm while embracing Lord Jagannath in the erotic state. Then it was made known to me: 'You have taken a body. Now remain in the different states—the Friend, the Mother, and the rest—in relation to other forms of man'" (4.227–228). There is something secret, even scandalous, about this incident.

What does the *Kathāmṛta* actually say?

> **KA 4.227–28:** *Tomāder ati guhya kathā bolchi. Keno Pūrna, Narendra, eder sob eto bhālobāsi. Jagannāther soṅge madhur bhābe āliṅgan korte giye hāt bheṅge gelo. Jāniye dile, "Tumi śarīr dhāran korecho—ekhon nararūper soṅge sakkha, bātsalya eisob bhāb loye thāko."*

> **Translation:** I'm telling you a very secret thing—why I love Purna, Narendra and all the others so much. While going to embrace Jagannāth ["Lord of the Universe"] in a state of *madhura*-bhāva, my arm was broken. It was made known to me: "You have taken a body. Now live with the bhāva of *sakhya*, *vātsalya* etc. with human forms."

As one might expect by now, the Bengali text shows us nothing even remotely secretive and scandalous. Ramakrishna narrates an incident that had taught him that now, instead of approaching divine forms through *madhura* bhāva (the bhāva in which one regards one's *iṣṭa* as one's beloved), the time had come for him to live with human forms through other bhāvas.

According to *Kālī's Child*, the "erotic" is "a dimension of human experience that is simultaneously related both to the physical and emotional experience of sexuality and to the deepest ontological levels of religious experience" (KC, 23). Kripal translates *madhura* bhāva as "the erotic state" but that translation is misleading. In Hindu devotional tradition, *madhura* bhāva is characterized by the profound intimacy, trust and total selflessness that is present in the relationship with one's beloved. Further, *madhura* bhāva is seen as the apex of all bhāvas since it includes within it all the other bhāvas.

Having thus translated the text as "embracing Lord Jagannāth in the erotic state," Kripal raises a doubt: "What precisely *was* Ramakrishna doing in the vision?" Three pages later (KC, 223), "embracing" has mysteriously evolved into an "erotic encounter." Some sixty pages later (291), the "embracing" reference returns with: "he tried to embrace a *male* god in an erotic state" [emphasis added].

If only the author had known the tradition connected with Jagannāth, he would not have had to struggle so much to interpret the vision. "Embracing Jagannāth" is in practice nothing more than touching his image. Every year there is a Chariot Festival (*ratha-yātrā*) in Puri, where Jagannāth's ancient temple stands. During this festival, it is customary for devotees to "embrace" the deity. What this means in practice is an opportunity to *touch* the image that is taken out of the temple in a chariot, which is pulled by thousands of devotees. This act of "embracing" is a sacred ritual in which every devotee is free to participate. No practicing Hindu considers this as an act "to engage Lord Jagannāth in an erotic encounter" or to embrace "a male god in an erotic state." We know Hindus who have performed this rite over a hundred times. They would find the term "erotic encounter" either mystifying or hilarious.

More imagined erotic encounters will surely be found as the reader forges ahead. True to form, we find some lurking homoerotic dimensions where one would least expect them—looking at pictures, for example:

> **KC, 224:** For Vaishnavacharan, such a faith [in *naralīlā*, "God's play as man"] certainly carried homoerotic dimensions. Ramakrishna, for example, points out that Vaishnavacharan liked to look at a picture of a man (*mānuṣa*), for it aroused in him feelings of "tenderness" (*komala*) and "love" (*prema*) (KA 4.75).

Interestingly, *Kālī's Child*'s first edition declares that "Vaishnavacharan liked to look at pictures of *men*, for *they* aroused in him feelings of "tenderness" (*komala*) and "love" (*prema*)" (KC 1995, 224; emphasis added). We can note that the "homoerotic dimensions" of Vaishnavacharan's "faith" were planted through mistranslation. What does one actually find in the *Kathāmṛta*?

> **KA 4.75:** *Baiṣnavacaran mānuṣer chabi dekhe komal bhāb—premer bhāb—pachanda karto.*
>
> **Translation:** Vaishnavacharan liked pictures of people expressing tenderness and love.

The reader should note that *mānuṣer chabi*, "pictures of people," has been mistranslated as either "a picture of a man" or "pictures of men" to enhance the passage's homoerotic subtext. It is clear from the context that *mānuṣ* does not specifically refer to "men" but to people in general. Secondly, Vaishnavacharan was a follower of the Kartābhajā sect, which was overtly heterosexual. Finally, Vaishnavacharan's preference was for pictures expressing tenderness and love, but in *Kālī's Child*, this is twisted into Vaishnavacharan being "aroused" by tenderness and love. The reason for this mistranslation is to set the stage—in the very next sentence—for a "very similar practice" by Ramakrishna. Let us look at the following example:

> **KC, 224:** Ramakrishna, we might recall, sexually aroused himself with a very similar practice (KA 5.108).

What does the reader find in the *Kathāmṛta*? Again, nothing that she or he would be led to anticipate:

> **KA 5.108:** *"Āmār icchā je du'khāni chobi pāi. Ekṭi chobi, jogī dhuni jvele bośe ache; ār ekṭi chobi, jogi gāñjār kolke mukh diye ṭānche ār śeṭā dop kore jvole uṭche.*

> "*E śob chobite beś uddīpan hoy. Jemon solār ātā dekhle śottakār ātār uddīpan hoy.*"
>
> **Translation:** "My wish is to get two pictures. One picture, of a yogi sitting before a burning log; and another picture, of a yogi who is smoking hemp and the charcoal blazing up as he pulls.
>
> "Such pictures are good for enkindling spiritual consciousness. Just as an imitation fruit kindles the idea of a real one."

When the *Kathāmṛta* is examined to see whether Ramakrishna indeed "sexually aroused himself" by looking at "pictures of men," the flummoxed reader will wonder what could possibly be so arousing about a yogi sitting in front of a burning log or a yogi smoking hemp. What is the "very similar practice" to which *Kālī's Child* refers? It was simply Ramakrishna's wish to have two pictures. Moreover, it was only a wish—not "a practice"—and, even more importantly, it was obviously not meant for arousing himself sexually. As we have seen, the Bengali word *uddīpan*, "enkindling," is nearly always misused in *Kālī's Child*, which defines it in terms of sexual arousal. For example, "When I look at pictures of holy men I become aroused [*uddīpana*]" (KC, 67).

We have seen that Kripal goes out of his way to translate in such a way that "boys," "men," "man," etc. are employed in order give weight to his homoerotic thesis. We find the same thing again in the following example:

> **KC, 226:** "Now I only like God's play as man," the Paramahaṁsa noted calmly, as if it were now a self-evident truth instead of a detested Tantric practice (KA 4.75).

The *Kathāmṛta* reference, KA 4.75, refers only to the words within quotation marks, and the reference in parentheses should have been put immediately after "God's play as man," (*naralīlā*, "play as a human" would be an accurate translation, because the Bengali *nara* in this context does not refer specifically to "man"). The words appearing after the quote belong entirely to Kripal and have nothing to do with what can be located in the *Kathāmṛta*.

There is, of course, a particular reason why *Kālī's Child* persistently employs the word "man." In the following paragraph, the reader is informed how, when Ramakrishna's disciples began to arrive, he "finally had a man, indeed, young attractive boys, to desire" (KC, 226). Second, seeing God's play in human forms is neither a "detested practice" nor specifically a "Tantric practice." For instance, the *Śvetāśvatara Upaniṣad* (4.3) proclaims the presence of the Supreme Being in a woman, a man, a youth, a maiden, and an old person. Similar teachings can be found in virtually all sects of Hinduism. Finally, note the tone in "as if it were a self-evident truth" and the usage of "detested" with "Tantric practice"—this, again, to emphasize that Ramakrishna allegedly was a conflicted and unwilling homoerotic Tāntrik.

If Tantra was "Ramakrishna's secret," *Kālī's Child* can create another secret lurking around the corner in the form of Sarada, who—Kripal states—had a "Tantric past." We read:

> **KC, 225:** Sharada would later recall how she feared Ramakrishna's reaction but was relieved to discover that he did not become angry upon learning of her hidden Tantric past (LP 5.11.9).

Should diligent readers check *Līlāprasaṅga* 5.11.9, they will find no mention of Sarada's fearing Ramakrishna's reaction. What about her being a "Tāntrik" in the first place?

> **KC, 113:** Regardless of their traditional allegiances during the day, almost everyone, including Ramakrishna's own wife (LP 5.11.9), seems to have led secret midnight lives. Dakshineswar was a very secret place.

In LP 5.11.9 there is an incident where a woman who had received a mantra from the Kartābhajā tradition visits Ramakrishna. He knew about her initiation even though he had not been told about it. Later when the woman mentioned it to Sarada Devi, Sarada told her that she, too, had received that mantra before coming to Dakshineswar. Sarada had told Ramakrishna about it and he had advised her to offer the mantra at the feet of her *iṣṭa*, chosen ideal.

Some points need to be mentioned here: (1) Receiving a mantra from the Kartābhajā tradition does not necessarily imply actively participating in their way of life; (2) Sarada had received the mantra *before* she came to Dakshineswar and, having reached there, had offered it at the feet of her *iṣṭa*; (3) there is no textual evidence indicating any kind of "midnight lives" led by Sarada and others in Dakshineswar; (4) there was no "secret" about Sarada receiving the mantra: were it so, Saradananda would not have known about it and, if he wanted to keep it a secret, he would not have mentioned it in the *Līlāprasaṅga*.

In order to muddy the waters regarding the kind of relationship that existed between Ramakrishna and Sarada and the Bhairavi, *Kālī's Child* resorts to a by now familiar pattern of altering the context of the cited text:

> **KC, 166:** When challenged by the women of the village with the simple fact that Ramakrishna wished to be with his wife, the Bhairavī would snap back with the retort: "What can he say? It was *I* who opened his eyes!" (LP 2.17.10).

Yet when we turn to this *Līlāprasaṅga* citation (LP 2.17.10) we find that the Bhairavi's words were spoken in an entirely different context: "If anyone raised a question before her [Bhairavi] on any spiritual matter and said that he would ask Ramakrishna and have his opinion on it, she would flare up and say, 'What can he say? It is I who opened his eyes.'"

It would be easy for us to go on a great deal farther along this particular avenue, but we have given enough examples of stunning mistranslations, problematic documentation as well as speculations masked as "facts." As we have already stated, perhaps the most significant thing about these examples is that each of them, taken in isolation, may not seem serious enough to warrant questioning *Kālī's Child*'s theses. But taken together—not just the examples given in this chapter, for these are only a few samples of many more similar instances in the book—they *do* pose a problem, since many of them have been repeatedly invoked throughout the book, in nearly every chapter. Such has been the cumulative effect of this strategy that, by the end of *Kālī's Child*, the unwitting reader who is unfamiliar with the source texts is lulled into believing in every speculation as a well-reasoned argument based on textual evidence.

In the course of this book, we have reviewed a brief history of Ramakrishna scholarship over the last hundred years and examined the problematics of cross-cultural interpretation, especially as they manifested in *Kālī's Child*. Now it is time to step back and take a longer view of Ramakrishna studies in general. If *Kālī's Child* is an example of how Ramakrishna scholarship can go wrong, in what way can Ramakrishna studies go right? What do *Kālī's Child* and the ensuing controversy teach us about Ramakrishna and cross-cultural interpretation, and how do we, as Ramakrishna scholars, see the future of Ramakrishna scholarship? This will be the focus of the concluding chapter.

6

The Future of Ramakrishna Studies

> We must somehow take a wider view, look at the whole landscape, really see it, and describe what's going on here. Then we can at least wail the right question into the swaddling band of darkness, or, if it comes to that, choir the proper praise.
>
> — Annie Dillard, *Pilgrim at Tinker Creek*

During the years in which this book has come into being, we have endlessly revisited both the historical Ramakrishna—at least as much of the historical Ramakrishna we can access—and the evolving state of Ramakrishna studies as it has developed over the past century. What we have presented to our readers is the long and fascinating story of how interpreting Ramakrishna has been—and will remain—a work continually in progress.

Identity, Worldview, Motivation

There are a number of factors which profoundly affect the way any historical religious figure is interpreted. In this regard at least, interpreting Ramakrishna is no different from interpreting any other historical religious figure. When we sift these interpretive factors into a consistent pattern, we find three key elements: first, the interpreter's identity; second, the interpreter's worldview; and finally, the interpreter's motivation. These elements have shaped every interpretation of not only Ramakrishna but also other historical religious figures.

In assessing how interpreters' identities have influenced their views of Ramakrishna, we have seen that over the past century, Ramakrishna has been studied through disparate lenses—those of the insider or outsider; Hindu or non-Hindu; Indian or non-Indian; Western-educated or not; academic or religious practitioner or both; pre-modern, modern or post-modern. The combination and permutation of these identities have necessarily colored the approaches to Ramakrishna and the conclusions about him.

Next, just as every interpreter has seen Ramakrishna reflected through a prism of intertwined personal identities, so also the interpreter's worldview overlaps upon this core identity. Every interpreter's view of the world is first located in his/her individual identity, then reformatted through layers of diverse historical, political, cultural, social and religious backgrounds. To contextualize this within the framework of this book, it is apparent that Ramakrishna's interpreters' historical, political, cultural, social and religious backgrounds influenced their worldviews, and this was a crucial factor in their interpretations of Ramakrishna. We have seen in the opening chapter that every interpreter's worldview (and by implication, interpretation) was broadly shaped by history and culture. Every interpreter's worldview, from pre-modern to post-modern, has been influenced in one way or another by colonialism, Orientalism and the various boomeranging forces that were consequentially put into play.

The footprint of colonialism and Orientalism can be most clearly seen in Ramakrishna's earliest interpreters—M, Saradananda, and Ramchandra Datta. In altogether different ways, colonialism and Orientalism—viewed through the alternate universe of Western education, Western culture and Christianity—profoundly influenced how Max Müller interpreted Ramakrishna. Dhan Gopal Mukerji's version of Ramakrishna, on the other hand, demonstrates how Orientalism and colonialism combined to create social forces that would promote the creation of a fairy-tale Ramakrishna, a Ramakrishna drawn in the light of a romanticized Orientalist stereotype for Western export. Romain Rolland would recreate a romanticized Ramakrishna as well, making of Ramakrishna a Hindu deus ex machina who could extricate Western Europe from self-slaughter. Christopher Isherwood was deeply uncomfortable in Indian culture, yet saw Ramakrishna as an avatar—a radically free, radically truthful man, who knew neither bondage nor hypocrisy.

Crucially, Isherwood and other insider interpreters of Ramakrishna shared, to a large extent, a common worldview that the great majority of outsider interpreters did not share. Apart from the conviction that Ramakrishna was an avatar, insider interpreters also shared an acceptance of the basic underpinnings of Hindu religious thought: karma and reincarnation, for example, as well as the belief that the Reality which lies at the core of individual beings (Ātman) and the Reality which lies behind the universe (Brahman) are interrelated, even identical. Given this Hindu worldview, these insider interpreters would take as a given the concept that human beings possess the potential to overcome the limitations of the body/mind complex in order to realize their essentially divine nature. This worldview would set insider interpretations—no matter whether Indian or Western, contemporary or historical—apart from other interpreters. Not only would their understanding of Ramakrishna be different, their understanding of the nature of reality, external and internal, would be markedly different as well. Aside from this fundamental bifurcation regarding the nature of the human being and the nature of the external world, outsider interpreters would naturally view Ramakrishna as a human being like every other human being, interpreting him, his actions and teachings either through the lens of a fundamentally Christian worldview (Müller, et al.), or through modernity's default worldview, that of secular humanism refracted through the structures of psychoanalysis (Neevel, et al.).

We have seen that as psychoanalysis gained force throughout the twentieth century to become a powerful influence in Western thought, those who interpreted Ramakrishna through that worldview—beginning with Neevel and Masson and continuing through Jeffrey Kripal—would see a Ramakrishna who would be unrecognizable to both early interpreters and insider interpreters. A secular worldview would essentially be at odds with Hinduism's bedrock assumption of the innate divinity of the human being and the possibility of overcoming the demands of the body/mind complex. This basic disconnect between a secular worldview and a religious Hindu worldview necessarily impinges upon an interpreter's analysis of Ramakrishna. How does one, for example, interpret Ramakrishna's samādhi? As evidence of psychopathology—as an escape mechanism, for example? Or as absorption into a higher Reality through transformation of consciousness, having risen beyond the everyday body/mind identity? These fundamental differences in worldview necessarily affect one's interpretation.

Finally, behind the obvious factors that affect the interpretation of a historical religious figure are more subtle factors, such as the motivation(s) of the interpreter. All of us, for example, try to make sense of history, if only not to be condemned to repeat it. Incidents and personalities from the past provide useful templates for our understanding of the present. Differences in interpretations are due not only to the multiple identities and worldviews of the various interpreters but also, in many cases, to the *purpose* that powers their interpretations.

What makes us interested in one subject and not in another? Why are some of us religious scholars while others are engineers, why are some drawn to Greek and others to Sanskrit, why is Tantra fascinating to some and Nyāya to others? Our motives are influenced by our conscious or unconscious interests, agendas, personal priorities and biases. We have seen, for example, how Müller's interest in "reformed" Hinduism was a deeply personal issue for him and his interpretation of Ramakrishna was drawn along those lines. Every interpretation of Ramakrishna has followed a similar trajectory—the interpreter's interests, motives and drives are sometimes stated but often remain hidden from the reader. We have seen, for example, that *Kālī's Child* was not simply a Ph.D. dissertation, it was also a personal project of its author.

Obviously, all of these factors—identity, worldview and motivation—are present in the understanding and interpretation of Ramakrishna by the authors of this book as well. We are insiders, we are practitioner/scholars but not academics, and between the two of us, we span the Indian/non-Indian divide, though we both self-identify as Hindu. Our motivation in writing this book, first of all, was to go to the primary source texts on Ramakrishna and to recover—as much as possible—the Ramakrishna of history, who seemed to have receded into the background of a psychoanalytic reading powered by compromised translations, unsupported speculations, and questionable documentation. We also wished to have on record a critique of the theses presented in *Kālī's Child*, not only to highlight the problems in it but also to demonstrate that alternative readings of Ramakrishna, readings which are faithful to the primary sources, are possible. Yet another motivation behind this response was the sincere desire to encourage a healthier dialogue and exchange of ideas between the academic world and the community of practitioners.

Our reading of Ramakrishna is based upon our worldview. We believe that it is not only possible but *necessary* to transcend the physical and psychological limitations imposed by the body and mind, in order for a human being to become spiritually enlightened. We see Ramakrishna as one who had attained such a state. Such was the purity of his life that many of his followers have found it difficult to determine whether he was a human being who rose *up* to attain divine perfection or whether he was a divine being who came *down* to show the way to others. It is precisely at the meeting point of the human and the divine where the avatar resides. Whether Ramakrishna is labeled an avatar or a saint is not, in our opinion, particularly important. What *is* important are his teachings on personal integrity, the sanctity of all existence, and leading a God-centered life. The seemingly abstract principles of Vedānta, we believe, become tangible through Ramakrishna's life and teachings.

Thus we do not claim to be any more "objective" than any of those interpreters we have discussed. Like other interpreters of Ramakrishna, we ourselves have personal motives for writing this book. We are well aware that our identities and worldviews tilt this book in a particular direction, and it was this tilt that made the writing of this book possible. While "objectivity" has often been seen as the holy grail of good scholarship, we have also seen throughout the course of this book that objectivity cannot exist where personal interests, agendas, political and religious biases, and personal priorities intersect. Like all holy grails, true objectivity exists only in mythology. Human beings live in their minds and their minds create lenses through which they view themselves and the world around them.

It is through all these multitudinous lenses, external and internal, that Ramakrishna has been viewed. Like a kaleidoscope whose view changes with every click, the view of Ramakrishna has changed with every new prism, every new lens, every new mind. The historical Ramakrishna remains whoever he was; his interpreters have viewed him—and will continue to view him—through various historical, cultural, linguistic, religious, political, and often deeply personal lenses. It is this series of continually changing lenses that has given Ramakrishna studies its ever-changing focus and direction.

The changing lenses and the variety of interpretations they spawn provide us with a view or a facet of Ramakrishna's personality that may not have received adequate attention. These new interpretations may reveal to us a heretofore unexplored relevance of Ramakrishna to our own individual or collective situation. It would be absurd for anyone to claim that the last word on Ramakrishna has already been said or that nothing new remains to be known about him. In Ramakrishna's own words, "No limit can be placed on [the understanding of] God" (*bhagabāner iti korā jāy nā*). This holds good not only for God but also for all human beings, and particularly those like Ramakrishna, who are viewed by many as saints, prophets or avatars. The increasing number of studies and interpretations of Ramakrishna's life and teachings are a testimony to the vastness and depth of what he represented in his life, and what he continues to represent in the minds and hearts of people in succeeding generations.

Because of the complex interplay of identity, worldview and motivation, every interpretation of Ramakrishna will necessarily vary. The source texts themselves, however, will not. What we plumb from those texts is dependent upon a number of variables, external and internal. The texts remain just as they are, awaiting fresh interpretations as the years roll on.

The Ethics of Interpretation

Since interpretation is always a precarious adventure while texts remain the cliffs upon which all interpreters climb, translation and documentation are the tools upon which all interpreters rely. When the text in question is a particularly steep cliff—written, for example, in a foreign language and located in a foreign culture over a century ago—the methodology employed determines the quality and the value of the study. The challenge of interpretation in overcoming these inherent difficulties is enormous and this requires careful and accurate documentation and translation. The processes of translation and interpretation, although interrelated and thus inseparable, cannot be treated as identical. The lens of the interpreter, in addition to its own color, takes on the color of the translator's lens, when the two—interpreter and translator—are two distinct individuals.

To contextualize these issues with those presented in *Kālī's Child*, the interpretation in *Kālī's Child* was in itself not an issue. Every author should be free to present any interpretation of Ramakrishna which she or he believes to be valid. That interpretation, however, must be backed up with documentation that accurately cites what the source texts present. Further, the translation of those sources must be accurate as well. This, as we have seen throughout this book, is an exceedingly delicate and difficult task because of the inherent differences in language and culture, and it has to be undertaken with great care and sensitivity.

But, one may ask, does a presumed historical reality really matter in the long run? Do the "facts" of history and the "facts" of a historical personality have an independent knowable reality, which an interpreter should strive to uncover? Again, if a particular culture saw things differently a century ago, should the interpreter feel the need to take these factors into consideration? There is a view, currently propounded by postmodern textual critics, that what *really* happened in the past, which will always be unknowable to those in the present, is not as important as how relevant it is to the present. Those who hold this view are naturally less rigorous in their historical research than they are in making their study relevant to the immediate concerns of the present. *Kālī's Child*, for example, showed no evidence that advocacy of gay rights was a motive in its creation, but the gay liberation movement, as we have seen, would prove useful once *Kālī's Child* was published and the ensuing controversy broke loose. In this way, the issue of gay rights served to divert attention from the problems the book possessed regarding documentation, translation, and interpretation.

What, then, is the interpreter to do when contemporary agendas conflict with historical accuracy? Can Ramakrishna be used as a model for gay rights when there is no evidence for his homosexuality? We have argued throughout this book against appropriating a historical personality to promote a contemporary agenda, no matter how noble the agenda may be, no matter how much the injustice needs to be rectified. Even Isherwood, who stood in the forefront of gay rights long before others had the courage to do so, wrote that he "couldn't honestly claim him [Ramakrishna] as a homosexual, even a sublimated one, much as I would have liked to be able to do so" (Isherwood 1980, 249). Ashok Row Kavi, a contemporary gay rights leader in India, came to a similar conclusion, adding that he found *Kālī's Child* "culturally condescending and insensitive."[1]

Historical religious figures have often been used as political footballs to promote every possible noble and ignoble cause, and Ramakrishna has been no exception. On one hand, there has been an attempt to silence those who have critiqued *Kālī's Child* with charges of homophobia; on the other hand, in order to promote their own narrow political and social agendas, the forces of Hindutva have tried to silence the voice of Kripal and his supporters. Locating and examining a historical religious figure in the midst of these conflicting agendas is not unlike navigating a minefield.

Should this be seen as a deterrent, it is good to recognize that there is an even greater danger in not addressing these contentious and divisive issues at all. Even worse, the greatest danger that we can envision is a retreat from dialogue, circling our respective wagons and remaining in the safe confines of our own self-affirming and self-reifying groups, insider or outsider. It is better to hazard crossing a minefield than to inflict self-stagnation.

A Dialogic Model for the Future

We have mentioned that one motive behind the writing of this book was our deep interest in a healthy dialogue and exchange of ideas between the academic world and the world of the religious practitioner. During the long process of thinking through and writing this book, we have seen many changes in the way Ramakrishna has been perceived. We have also seen, with mounting dismay, the way in which insiders and outsiders have grown increasingly distrustful of one another and wary of mutual interaction. "Once burned, twice shy" seems to be the refrain from both camps. While academics have increasingly viewed the *Kālī's Child* controversy in terms of the rise of Hindutva—with all the trappings of hate mail, requested book banning, and the strictures of religious fundamentalism—the insider community has been tarred by association with a fundamentalist mindset that the vast majority do not share.

Just as the vast majority of Muslims do not subscribe to terrorism, so also the vast majority of Ramakrishna devotees, including those who strongly contest the theses presented in *Kālī's Child*, do not subscribe to Hindu fundamentalism. Simply because they contest the theses presented in *Kālī's Child* does not automatically align them with the forces of Hindutva, right-wing fundamentalism or religious orthodoxy. Indeed, more likely than not, those who are associated with the Ramakrishna movement, whether in India or in the West, tend to be politically and socially liberal and are generally disinclined to fundamentalism of any sort.

Yet despite all the commonalities we share, we in Ramakrishna studies, both insiders and outsiders, find ourselves at an impasse. The only way to break an impasse is to shatter it by moving through and beyond it. If this be the case, then where do we move from here, and how?

Long before this book was conceived, the issue of Ramakrishna studies and its future direction was addressed by Swami Tyagananda in a paper entitled "Reflections on Hindu Studies vis-à-vis Hindu Practice," which was written for the American Academy of Religion panel "Defamation/Anti-Defamation: Hindus in Dialogue with the Western Academy," organized by John S. Hawley in 2001. In this paper, Tyagananda spoke of the existing wall between the insider and outsider communities and suggested that an effort needed to be made to make the wall porous. This, he felt, would be a model for future Ramakrishna studies.

In a less specific and certainly unintentional way, Richard King has pointed out the direction of future Ramakrishna studies in his concluding chapter of *Indian Philosophy*. In addressing the problematics of philosophy in a post-colonial world, King suggested "constructing a cultural space based upon indigenous insights and orientations from the non-western world which is not easily assimilable by western culture, in either its modernist or postmodernist incarnations." King goes on to suggest that a "postwesternism" be developed, which not only allows for inter-cultural dialogue but also has the goal of ending the "philosophical hegemony of the western world." This post-westernism would be "motivated by a vision of the twenty-first century as an era which would be globally 'postwestern' rather than Eurocentrically 'postmodern.' Examining and engaging with Indian cultural traditions is one of the many important elements within such a process" (1999a, 233).

After reading this bracing suggestion, one wonders if some of these ideas of inter-cultural dialogue, which not so very long ago were undreamt of in the academy, could now be reaching some sort of slow critical mass. It was a lovely serendipity to discover J. C. Cleary's article "Buddhist Studies the Buddhist Way," which appeared in the *Harvard Divinity Bulletin* (Autumn 2005). Buddhist studies has contended with many of the same issues that Ramakrishna studies is now addressing. Running on a parallel track with our own concerns, Cleary writes: "To this day the scholarly study of religion revolves around various paradigms created by a small group of twentieth-century Western thinkers." As we have seen, Ramakrishna studies has been dominated by a variety of paradigms—all governed by the presuppositions of Western modernity—since its inception. "Naturally," Cleary continues, "these paradigms are strongly marked by their origins in the modern West, with the associated limitations and biases" (66).

As we have shown in detail throughout this book, the paradigms used for assessing Ramakrishna have been driven by the social and cultural biases, religious presuppositions and political and personal persuasions of his interpreters. To this date, indigenous paradigms—which carry within them those philosophical underpinnings and cultural worldviews that undergird every Ramakrishna source text—have scarcely been used. Indigenous interpreters have not, in general, been taken seriously by the academy. As we have seen, though *Kālī's Child* asserts that it uses indigenous categories, it does not. It is more accurate to say that it appropriates indigenous categories in order to make assessments based exclusively upon Western cultural and intellectual models, and occasionally upon Western appropriations of Eastern models.

The preceding chapters have shown in extensive detail that as recent Western cultural history has taken its bends and curves over the past century, Ramakrishna studies has been pulled along on a parallel journey, driven as it were, by changing intellectual paradigms which reflected Europe's and North America's changing values and cultural assumptions. Yet studies on Ramakrishna, at least those done in the West to this date, have not incorporated the enormous religious, philosophical or cultural background found in Ramakrishna's own tradition.

As Richard King recommends, Cleary also points to the need for employing indigenous paradigms in understanding non-Western texts. In this case, Cleary advocates using Buddhist paradigms for Buddhist studies:

> To ignore ... material from within the tradition only makes sense on the assumption that we (the modern scholars) can understand them (the Buddhist adepts) better than they understood themselves. It takes for granted that our own contemporary culture is aware of the full range of human possibilities. This is precisely the kind of false universalism, or pretended universalism, which we should be trying to move beyond. (66)

Not only *should* we try to move beyond, but, from what we have seen, we are convinced that the future integrity of Ramakrishna studies depends upon such a move. What we envision for the future of Ramakrishna studies is the expansion of the current paradigm in order to include indigenous insights from within the Hindu tradition.

What authentic indigenous insights should Ramakrishna studies take into account? First and most importantly, a respectful acceptance of the *possibility*, crucial to understanding Hindu religious figures, that the reality behind the universe and the reality behind an individual—known respectively as Brahman and Ātman—may be interrelated, even identical, and are essentially divine in nature. Secondly, Ramakrishna studies should include the *possibility* that the external reality as we experience it may not be the only, or even the most important, reality. Thirdly, this expanded paradigm would consider the limitations of human reason and the *possibility* of a different kind of knowledge that transcends (but does not contradict) reason. Finally, the expanded paradigm would include the *possibility* that human beings could fully realize and manifest their innate divinity by overcoming the identification with the body and mind to which gender and sexuality are tied. Ramakrishna studies needs to be at least open to all of these possibilities. It will be difficult to bridge the insider/outsider divide if these possibilities are summarily dismissed out of hand.

As the renowned Indian philosopher P. T. Raju has noted, Indian religious thought is both rational and supra-rational and consists of "a search for the ground of our being. . . . not through pure thought alone, but also through realization" (Raju, 8). He continues by stating that "the Supreme Being of the religious quest transcends reason, the quest was a quest for experience. . . . [which] must be capable of being discovered within man's conscious being. But this discovery is a matter of experience, not merely of logic" (8–9). We are already stepping well outside the confines of our usual Western interpretive paradigms, but let us continue with Raju's train of thought. He writes:

> The essence of religious experience is communion with the Divine. But communion is experience. . . . There is no *a priori* reason for limiting experience to sense experience, when there are other kinds of experience. The only question that can be and ought to be raised is about the truth-value of the different kinds of experience. . . . We ask ourselves, therefore, when and how an experience is true or false. To determine its truth or falsity, we have systems of philosophy with their branches like metaphysics, epistemology, ethics, etc. (9)

Incorporating some of these premises and incorporating some of these indigenous paradigms into Ramakrishna studies would provide an ideal environment for its future, for at the heart of future Ramakrishna studies lies the issue of the insider/outsider, practitioner/scholar divide. For the future of Ramakrishna studies to be fruitful, we would suggest that the divide, such that it is, be navigated in such a way that both groups can freely express their forms of knowledge and that each party be heard with respect. Neither the insider nor the outsider should consider their vantage to be solely valid and neither party should conceive their view to be, in contrast to the other, "objective."

In thinking through the future of Ramakrishna studies, we would like to suggest that it is possible for an insider to provide insight that is valuable in order for an outsider to gain knowledge. Conversely, we also suggest that it is possible for outsiders as well to provide insight that insiders may very well lack. Further, we would suggest that insiders and outsiders not be viewed as opposing camps, but rather as complementary groups offering complementary forms of knowledge that is valuable to all concerned. This being the case, it seems wise and, indeed, healthy to nourish more porous boundaries between the insider and outsider communities. Crossing these boundaries does not lead to weak scholarship any more than it leads to the creation of ambivalent practitioners. We are convinced that separating the knowledge of the academic from the knowledge of the practitioner serves neither the academic nor the practitioner, and it certainly does not serve the cause of knowledge in general.

We thus conclude this book on a note of hope. We strongly believe that Ramakrishna studies will be vastly strengthened if those who engage in it remain faithful to the source texts and attempt to view Ramakrishna through a variety of different perspectives in order to find a richer, fuller picture of a life that in many ways still remains a mystery to us all. We believe that this will happen. We also believe that a more sensitive, and nuanced treatment of Indian religious figures—Ramakrishna included—will lead to increased trust and respect from the insider community toward the academic community and vice versa.

Our journey into Ramakrishna studies has been a long and winding road, and an immensely gratifying one. While we both had long been familiar with insider literature, this book's unfolding introduced us to the world of outsider Religious studies scholars. We have been deeply impressed by their sincerity, dedication and intellectual rigor. We say this about those scholars whose work we critique as well as those scholars whose views tally more closely with our own. Our heartfelt admiration goes to those dedicated scholars, Eastern or Western, insider or outsider, whose quest for knowledge has enriched the world. And all of us remain gratefully in debt to the authors of the source texts, without whose work we would never have been able to catch a glimpse of that man who continues to intrigue us and inspire us, Ramakrishna.

Ph. No. : 350-1751

DIPAK GUPTA
Hd. of Econ. Dept.
Vidyasagar Ev. College
Calcutta

M'S THAKURBATI
(KATHAMRITA BHAVAN)
13/2, Guruprosad Chowdhury Lane.
Calcutta-700 006
[Near Thanthania Kali Temple]

October 24, 2002

Rev Swami Tyagananda Maharaj-ji,
Ramakrishna Vedanta Society,
58, Deerfield Street.
Boston, MA 02215, USA

Dear and Revered Swami Tyagananda Maharaji,

Conveying my respectful pronams unto you, I express my gladness to hear about your book project. It greatly distresses me that so much misinformation is being spread and I am surprised that it is being done by people who are considered scholars. I wish to put on record that my great-grandfather Sri Mahendra Nath Gupta's diaries (which provided the material for 'Sri Sri Ramakrishna Kathamrita') have always been with the family, living in M'S Thakurbati

Ph. No. : [illegible]

DIPAK GUPTA
Hd. of Econ. Dept.
Vidyasagar Ev. College
Calcutta

M'S THAKURBATI
(KATHAMRITA BHAVAN)
13/2, Guruprosad Chowdhury Lane.
Calcutta-700 006
[Near Thanthania Kali Temple]

(Kathamrita Bhavan), Calcutta, — and not with the Ramakrishna Order — and these diaries are being preserved with great care and love. Scholars with proper credentials who have approached us have always been provided access to this material. Any claim to the contrary is a willful distortion of facts.

With namaskar and best wishes once again,

Dipak Gupta. (M's great grandson).

Notes

Preface

1. While Nussbaum's book rings a much-needed alarm about India's increasing intolerance and violence, her assessment of the *Kālī's Child* controversy reveals a surprising lack of knowledge. Nussbaum links *Kālī's Child* to religiously inspired violence, since among the Indian readers who were outraged by *Kālī's Child* were members of the nationalist group RSS (Rashtriya Swayamsevak Sangh), who have taken a hard line against what they consider to be anti-Hindu sentiments. While this is not the place to thoroughly examine Nussbaum's book, it is important to address some of her more egregious errors. She writes, for example, that Kripal "drew on a diary of Ramakrishna that had previously been published only in part, in a version edited by Ramakrishna's own disciples, who, it emerges, had omitted many sexual and scatological references" (250). The "diary" in question (later published as the *Śrī-Śrī-Rāmakṛṣṇa-Kathāmṛta*) was not Ramakrishna's diary but M's. M published his diary himself, without one word changed. It was not edited or overseen by anyone apart from himself. Moreover, M's book was never "edited by Ramakrishna's own disciples"—the diary/book was entirely M's own project. M was, of course, Ramakrishna's disciple and M famously informs the reader that the *Kathāmṛta* only contains the words that he heard directly from Ramakrishna and the actions he personally observed.

It would appear that Nussbaum refers here to Swami Nikhilananda's much later English translation of M's Bengali *Kathāmṛta, The Gospel of Sri Ramakrishna*. Yet it is important to keep in mind that the *Kathāmṛta* is in Bengali, not English. The great majority of M's readers are not English readers, but Bengali readers who have read the text exactly as M wrote it. Even Nikhilananda's English translation retains nearly everything that M wrote in the original Bengali edition.

2. Again, this is not the place to deal with these parallel controversies, the only factor in common with the *Kālī's Child* controversy being the targeted academic and the enraged Hindu community. Paul Courtright's book *Gaṇeśa: Lord of Obstacles, Lord of Beginnings* (1985) and James Laine's *Shivaji: Hindu King in Islamic India* (2003) were both viewed as attacks on the Hindu tradition. The latter book was banned by the state of Maharashtra in 2004.

3. For example, we read in Mark Juergensmeyer's *Terror in the Mind of God: The Global Rise of Religious Violence*: "When an American scholar published a study of one of the RSS's spiritual heroes, Ramakrishna, revealing the homosexual aspects of his mysticism, the clamor of protest in India was enormous, especially among the right-wing supporters of the RSS and the political party they have spawned, the Bharatiya Janata Party (BJP)" (207). It would be much more accurate to say that those in India who were familiar with Ramakrishna

and Ramakrishna literature and who subsequently became aware of the *Kālī's Child* controversy were, by and large, outraged. This was universally true, no matter with which political party Ramakrishna devotees were aligned. There was outrage among Western Ramakrishna devotees as well, who know nothing of, or are indifferent to, the machinations of Indian politics.

4. Swami Tyagananda is currently the Hindu chaplain at both Harvard University and MIT and has been President of Harvard's United Ministry (now known as Harvard Chaplains).

5. See, for example, Parama Roy's *Indian Traffic*. Gwilym Beckerlegge's *The Ramakrishna Mission* takes several of Kripal's assertions at face value, and Peter Van der Veer's excellent *Imperial Encounters: Religion and Modernity in India and Britain* seems to accept Kripal's theses without question. Nicholas F. Gier's otherwise quite good *Spiritual Titanism* (SUNY Press, 2000) also accepts *Kālī's Child* as an authentic interpretation of Ramakrishna, and Malcolm McLean's *Devoted to the Goddess: The Life and Work of Ramprasad* recommends *Kālī's Child* for "a comprehensive study" on Ramakrishna (SUNY Press, 1998, 159). We have already noted Mark Juergensmeyer's reference to "the homosexual aspect of [Ramakrishna's] mysticism" (Juergensmeyer, 207).

Chapter 1

1. Part of the colonial enterprise was to essentialize the native population by ascribing to it fixed characteristics: Bengalis, for example, were effeminate, weak, dreamy, irresolute, irrational. By contrast, the British were rational, masculine, courageous, resolute. Those colonized often challenged the characteristics ascribed to them by radically inverting the pattern imposed upon them. Thus we encounter a reversed essentialism as a means of acquiring the power which lies behind the ability to control the stereotype. In this way the East was essentialized by a number of colonized Hindus as "spiritual" in contradistinction to an essentialized "materialistic" West. Vivekananda famously used this stereotype, along with his explicitly masculine Hinduism, as a native retort to the stereotype of the weak, effeminate Hindu. Throughout this book we employ overarching categories such as "East" and "West" to refer not so much to geographical locations as to general patterns of thinking and training.

2. For a larger discussion of this topic, see Sumit Sarkar's *An Exploration of the Ramakrishna Vivekananda Tradition* and Partha Chatterjee's *The Nation and Its Fragments*.

3. See Stephen Hay (ed.), *Sources of Indian Tradition*, vol 2. Second edition. (New York: Columbia University Press, 1988), 37.

4. For M's wish that the *Kathāmṛta* "should spread far and wide and its influence reach every corner of the land," see *Vivekananda in Indian Newspapers* 1893–1902, Sankari Prasad Basu and Sunil Bihari Ghosh, eds. (Calcutta: Basu Bhattacharyya & Co., 1969), 611. For reasons that prompted the writing of the *Līlāprasaṅga*, see Akshayachaitanya (95).

5. Taken from the Preface and Acknowledgements of *Sri Sri Ramakrishna Kathamrita Centenary Memorial*, D. P. Gupta and D. K. Sengupta, eds. No page number given.

6. According to Vivekananda scholar Sunil Bihari Ghosh, it is reasonable to assume that the "Part Three" of *Paramahaṁsadeber Ukti* was considered a sequel to the two booklets already published by the Brahmo Samaj—Part One referring to the book by Keshab Chandra Sen (1878) and Part Two to the book by Girish Chandra Sen (1887). Part Three of *Paramahaṁsadeber Ukti* was M's compilation (1892). Since Vivekananda expressed his appreciation for M's work in writing on February 9, 1889, it seems clear that either M read out his manuscript to Vivekananda while the latter was in Antpur or Vivekananda read the manuscript himself. Vivekananda conveyed his appreciation in writing rather than verbally as he was observing silence (*mauna*) during that time. An alternate theory about Parts One and Two of *Paramahaṁsadeber Ukti*, this one propounded by Vivekananda scholar Sankari Prasad Basu, was that M wrote all three parts of *Paramahaṁsadeber Ukti*, with the first two parts probably being published before 1889. Since neither the copies of these two parts are available nor is their existence confirmed by any evidence, the authors of this book are inclined to agree with Ghosh's theory.

7. See also CW 6.412–13 for more of Vivekananda's enthusiastic response to M's pamphlets.

8. See Nityatmananda, *Śrīma-Darśan*, 16 vols.

9. *Time*, "Religion" (November 2, 1942): 48–50.

10. *The New York Herald Tribune*, Book Review Section, Sept. 25, 1949.

11. "Master," a common term for a male schoolteacher in Bengal, was how M was occasionally referred to by Ramakrishna and others. In Nikhilananda's translation, "Thakur" was translated as "Master," as in spiritual master. The "Master" in the *Kathāmṛta* was replaced by "M."

12. According to Mahendranath Dutta, not only was Narendra unhappy with Ram's *Jībanabṛttānta*, but Balaram Bose and Suresh Mitra—both prominent householder disciples of Ramakrishna—were displeased as well. Besides mentioning these two specific names, Mahendra Dutta writes: "Narendra and others" (*Narendranath ityādi* ...) Who these "others" are remains unclear. (60–61)

13. See CW 6.207.

14. See, for instance, the text of the lecture Ram gave at the City Theater in Calcutta in 1893 in *Mahātmā Rāmacandrer Boktṛtābalī*, Part I, 3rd ed. (Calcutta: Sri Sri Ramakrishna Samadhi-Mahapith, 1938). Ram refers to Vivekananda as "a joyful presence free from the hold of lust and greed" (484) and affirms that whatever Vivekananda says is filled with truth and great power (486).

15. The *Jībanabṛttānta* was first published by the Order in 1945, with a foreword by Swami Madhavananda. In recent years there have been eight Bengali editions published since 1995.

16. See Aseshananda's *Glimpses of a Great Soul* and Prabuddhaprana's

Saint Sara: The Life of Sara Chapman Bull. Both Vrajaprana and Tyagananda have met several disciples of Swami Saradananda as well as North American children of parents who were disciples of Swami Saradananda. Those children, now aged, nevertheless retain the memory of their parents' warm reminiscences of Swami Saradananda, who was loved for his kindness and sweet disposition.

17. See also Saradeshananda's reminiscences in Purnatmananda, 38–39.

18. The word "bhāvamukha" is difficult to translate into English. A study of the Gauḍīya Vaiṣṇava texts is helpful in understanding *bhāva*, but a detailed analysis of "bhāvamukha" is beyond the scope of this book. Saradananda's elaborate explanation can be found in *Līlāprasaṅga* 3.1–121.

19. Apart from the unique material on Ramakrishna that was recorded by Ramakrishna's monastic disciples, also indispensable are Swami Nityatmananda's collected sixteen volumes of M's recorded reminiscences, which are available both in Bengali and English.

20. *Śrī-Śrī-Rāmakṛṣṇa-Deber Upadeś* [The Sayings of Sri Ramakrishna] was compiled by Suresh Chandra Dutta, one of Ramakrishna's close disciples. Many of the 595 sayings of the book were translated into English and published in the *Brahmavadin* from September 14, 1895–October 1, 1897 (Burke, 303).

21. While it is tempting to speculate that Saradananda's material would eventually form the core of what later became his *Līlāprasaṅga*, Saradananda had no idea at this point that he would ever write a biography of Ramakrishna. The material which Saradananda pulled together for Müller was based upon his own memory of whatever was known at the time. For this reason there is some incorrect information in Müller's book—for example, Müller writes that Ramakrishna's year of birth was 1833 instead of 1836. The lack of biographical sources and time was difficult enough, but Saradananda also had little idea of the type of information Müller wanted—that is, what material Müller would deem veridical and what would be dismissed as myth. In the end, the biographical material Müller received from Saradananda was written in a matter of weeks with few resources or guidelines to aid him.

22. It is fascinating to see how Mazumdar absorbed Western Victorian virtues and assimilated them thoroughly. As a born-and-bred Bengali, Mazumdar would have been well aware of the nuances in the Bengali language. Further, Mazumdar admits to being drawn by Ramakrishna's lack of sophistication, simplicity and candor. Describing Ramakrishna as a "poor, illiterate, shrunken, unpolished, diseased, half-dressed, half-idolatrous, friendless Hindu" and himself as a "Europeanized, civilized, self-centered, semi-skeptical, so-called educated reasoner," Mazumdar rhetorically asks: "Why should I sit long hours to attend to him, I who have listened to Disraeli and Fawcett, Stanley and Max Müller, and a whole host of European scholars and divines?" (Mazumdar, 3).

23. Prabuddhaprana 1990, 209. Taken from Romain Rolland's journal of May 14, 1927.

24. Mukerji studied at the University of California, Berkeley, transferred

to Stanford, and married fellow-student Pat Dugan in 1918. Mukerji lived for some years in the West, never succeeding in fitting into either the West or India. Suffering from depression, Mukerji committed suicide in New York in 1936.

25. Ernst van Alphen astutely notes that "the preference for the other in the case of exoticism is not produced by an interest in and subsequently knowledge of the other, but by a negative view of the observer's own identity or culture. The other is not a description, not even an interpretation of a reality, but the formulation of an ideal, desired identity" (2–3). This is precisely what we find in Mukerji's and Rolland's interpretations of Ramakrishna.

26. Published by Advaita Ashrama in Calcutta, the *Life* was written by Swami Nikhilananda and edited by Swami Madhavananda. The Foreword was written by Mahatma Gandhi.

27. Rolland describes Ramakrishna being anguished by not having attained the vision of Kālī. In desperation, Ramakrishna reached for Kālī's sword and was overwhelmed: "I saw an ocean of the Spirit, boundless, dazzling" (LR, 33). "Je perçus un océan d'esprit, sans limites, éblouissant" (Rolland 1947, 46).

28. Speaking of Ramakrishna's childhood ecstasies, for example, Rolland wrote that in Europe "the child would have been placed in a lunatic asylum and given a daily shower of psychotherapy" (*On mettrait le petit dans une maison de santé, sous la douche quotidienne de psychothérapie*) (1929, 25).

29. Swami Tripurananda, letter to Pravrajika Vrajaprana, February 6, 2004.

30. He was once asked what his name meant. "Gnaneswar," he explained, "is a common name, like Joe." "Ananda," he said, "means bliss. So you can call me Joe Bliss."

31. Tolstoy discovered Ramakrishna in 1903 by reading the German journal *Theosophischer Wegweiser*. He underlined Ramakrishna's aphorisms and wrote in his diary: "Much here is the same as my own understanding." In 1906, excerpts from Max Müller's *Sayings of Sri Ramakrishna Paramahamsa* were sent to Tolstoy. Referring to the book, Tolstoy told a friend that Müller's "selection of the 'sayings' is wonderful. Ramakrishna died 50 [sic] years ago. The most brilliant wise man!" (Vrajaprana 2006, 1100–101).

32. In 1945 Henry Miller returned to America from Paris, making a cross-country American journey while reading Romain Rolland. "Now that the trip is over," Miller later wrote in *The Air-Conditioned Nightmare*, "I must confess that the experience which stands out most strongly in my mind is the reading of Romain Rolland's two volumes on Ramakrishna and Vivekananda. . . . [and] the most masterful individual, the only person I met whom I could truly call 'a great soul,' was a quiet Hindu swami in Hollywood" (Miller, 18). The swami was Swami Prabhavananda.

33. Isherwood later decided to remove his own biographical material and publish it separately as *An Approach to Vedanta* (Hollywood: Vedanta Press, 1963).

34. According to the reminiscences of the late Swami Pramathananda, the secretary of Swami Madhavananda: "They had requested Swami Madhavanandaji

to proof-read the text and ensure its authenticity prior to its publication. Swami Madhavanandaji wavered at the outset and only reluctantly agreed to do so. Once he had agreed, however, his commitment ... his thoroughness, all at the cost of his own personal comfort and ease, at an age when most individuals would much rather take things easy, was very touching. . . . For the last chapter Swami Madhavanandaji had begun work at 7 a.m. and continued for almost eight hours without a break of any kind." A Devotee, "In Gratitude," *Vedanta* 319 (Sep-Oct 2004): 224.

35. Pravrajika Anandaprana, interview by Pravrajika Vrajaprana, March 27, 2003, Santa Barbara, California. Pravrajika Anandaprana copyedited the book and is thanked by Isherwood in the book's dedication.

36. Isherwood never did—Prabhavananda being virtually impossible to embarrass—yet Isherwood continually worried that he might. Also apparent in some of Isherwood's writings is his guilt that he never succeeded as a monk. For example, see *Diaries* 250, 261–62; *Lost Years*, 72, 81.

37. Don Bachardy, Isherwood's partner from 1953 until the latter's death in 1986, said in a phone conversation with Pravrajika Vrajaprana: "Chris believed that Ramakrishna was always acting freely. All later accounts of him restrict the freedom that he [Ramakrishna] exercised." Don Bachardy/Pravrajika Vrajaprana, June 7, 2004.

38. One of Isherwood's diary entries records, for example, that Prabhavananda says something apparently quite ordinary, the effect of which gave Isherwood goose pimples. "It is quite impossible to convey in words the effect made on you by things like this said by someone like Swami—because, of course, it is the man himself, present and speaking to you, and conveying in some otherwise banal sentence, a glimpse of what he is, that makes all the difference." (Isherwood 1997, 656)

39. See, for example, Nancy Wilson Ross, "Madman or Saint?" review of *Ramakrishna and His Disciples*, by Christopher Isherwood, *New York Times Book Review* (November 14, 1965), 22–24.

40. While one hesitates to generalize here, it is tempting to observe that in approaching a personality from the Hindu tradition, the lingering shadows of Orientalism would dictate that if God were to assume human form, the Euro-American world would know which ethnic group would be favored by his descent. If God's incarnation could be seriously considered, it could be considered only in terms of twentieth-century secularized Christianity—that which Europe and North America considered normative and "rational." That the idea of God incarnating as a Hindu would be automatically considered preposterous says a good deal about how entrenched Orientalist values were, and are. One may doubt that God exists or that a man born of a virgin could be an incarnation of God, but these beliefs can be discussed seriously and respectfully, without them automatically being deemed absurd. No such latitude could be given to Hindus and their avatars.

41. George Woodcock, review of *Ramakrishna and His Disciples*, by Christopher Isherwood, *Commonweal* (September 24, 1965): 703.

42. Don Bachardy said that writing under such constraints "took the mickey out of the book." Telephone interview of Don Bachardy by Pravrajika Vrajaprana, June 7, 2004.

43. See, for example, Francis X. Clooney's "Neither Here Nor There: Crossing Boundaries, Becoming Insiders, Remaining Catholic" in *Identity and the Politics of Scholarship in the Study of Religion* (New York and London: Routledge, 2004) as well as Jeffery D. Long's "Who Am I to Write a Book about Hindu Identity? Confessions of an Irish American Hindu," in his *A Vision for Hinduism: Beyond Hindu Nationalism* (London: I.B. Tauris & Co., 2007).

44. It needs to be mentioned that this depiction is not accurate in that it portrays Ramakrishna as a passive participant in the process. Ramakrishna's version of what happened is entirely different: "With a firm determination (*dṛḍhasaṁkalpa koriyā*) I sat for meditation again and, as soon as ... the Divine Mother appeared ... I looked upon knowledge as a sword (*gyān ke asi kolpanā koriyā*) and cut it mentally in two (*dvikhaṇḍa koriyā phellām*) with that sword of knowledge. There remained then no idea of differentiation (*vikalpa*) in the mind; it at once rose above the domain of all name and form, and I entered into samādhi (*samādhi-magna hoilām*)" (LP 2.295). Moreover, Neevel himself mentions in several places that Ramakrishna was strong-willed; no one could make him do what he did not want to do.

45. That Ramakrishna endorsed jñāna as well as bhakti is confirmed by no less a source than Sarada Devi. When the young Swami Vimalananda sought Sarada's support in pursuing some devotional practices at the Mayavati ashram (which was created exclusively for Advaita practice), Sarada famously replied in a letter dated August 31, 1902: "He who is our guru [Ramakrishna] was an Advaitin. You are all disciples of that guru, so you too are followers of Advaita. I can firmly say, you are all surely followers of Advaita." (*Āmāder guru jini, tini to advaita. Tomrā śei gurur śiṣya, takhon tomrā-o advaitabādī. Āmi jor koriyā bolte pāri, tomrā abaśya advaitabādī* [Lokeswarananda 1985, 785]).

46. Patricia Cohen, "Freud Is Widely Taught at Universities, Except in the Psychology Department," *New York Times*, November 25, 2007.

47. Ruth Vanita, co-author of *Same-Sex Love in India*, has written: "Gay activist Ashok Row Kavi recounts that when he was studying at the Ramakrishna Mission, a monk told him the Mission was not a place to run away from himself, and that he should live boldly, ignoring social prejudice. Row Kavi went on to found the Indian gay magazine *Bombay Dost*. (http://www.galva108.org/hinduism.html). See Row Kavi, 12–15; Vanita and Kidwai, 216. See also his interview, "India's Pioneer: Ashok Row Kavi" by Perry Brass: http://gaytoday.badpuppy.com/garchive/interview/050399in.htm, where he gratefully acknowledges the "sensible counseling" he received from Swami Harshananda of the Ramakrishna Order, who advised Row Kavi: "Accept it as natural."

48. Row Kavi writes: "It's not only the erroneous attitudes of Thakur's alleged sexuality that are wrong, what I found annoying was Kripal's derisive attitude towards Ramakrishna's various other qualities too. He is culturally condescending and hence insensitive, a quality that is a no-no in any anthropological work." E-mail correspondence with Swami Tyagananda, January 23, 2007. An earlier e-mail from Ashok Row Kavi to Pravrajika Vrajaprana and Swami Tyagananda states that Row Kavi has read *Kālī's Child* a number of times and has "very strong feelings about the book." He characterizes Kripal as "derisive and diabolic." E-mail correspondence: Ashok Row Kavi to Pravrajika Vrajaprana and Swami Tyagananda, May 15, 2006.

49. Śāktādvaita recognizes only the apparent, and not real, distinction between nirguṇa Brahman and its saguṇa Śakti. When Śakti dwells in Brahman in an unmanifested form, she is called nirguṇa. When she becomes manifest, she is called saguṇa. Thus: *Tvam eva sūkṣmā tvaṁ sthūlā vyaktāvyaktarūpiṇī / Nirākārāpi sākārā kastvāṁ veditum arhati*, "You are subtle, gross, manifest, unmanifest, with form and also without form. Who indeed can understand you?" (*Mahānirvāṇa Tantra*, 4.15). On the plane of relative existence, the power which helps manifest the real nature of Śakti is called vidyāśakti, and the power which makes a person forget the real nature of Śakti is called avidyāśakti (Dhireshananda 1962, 75).

50. Ramakrishna used to say, *Dayā jār nāi śe mānuṣ-i noy*, "A person without compassion is not really a human being." (KA 1.154)

51. It is important to keep in mind how profoundly different cultural roles and expectations are in India compared to the West. Alan Roland writes in *Cultural Pluralism and Psychoanalysis*: "For boys, the triangular relationship with mother and father is of another order from that of Westerners. *The boy never loses his mother*. Beginning with prolonged, early symbiotic mothering with intense gratification and physical affection … it is expected that he remain deeply attached to his mother and deeply involved with his original family throughout life. The young child, boy or girl, sleeps next to his mother until the next sibling is born, and then with another sibling, aunt, or uncle, but almost never alone. Strivings for separation, autonomy, initiative, and self-direction—the hallmark of current American child rearing—are discouraged in the Indian context for dependence and interdependence." (Roland 1996, 136–37)

52. E-mail from Narasingha Sil to Swami Tyagananda, July 26, 2007.

53. Kripal asserts that the Ramakrishna Order, which he characterizes as "the renouncer tradition," developed "a tortured reading of Ramakrishna's Tantric practices … [that] completely misses the whole point of Tantra" (KC, 124). It is more accurate to state that Kripal and the Ramakrishna Order disagree on what constitutes the "whole point of Tantra."

54. Bhajanananda quotes G. S. Ghurye's *Indian Sadhus* (Bombay: Popular Prakashan, 1966), 235.

55. Bhajanananda notes that "Sri Ramakrishna did not believe ... that all religions are one. He fully accepted the uniqueness of every religion as a separate path to the same ultimate Reality." (Bhajanananda 1980, 88)

56. For example, Bhajanananda's views on worship, taken from his May 1980 *Prabuddha Bharata* editorial, are discussed at some length in Usha Harding's *Kali: The Black Goddess of Dakshineswar* (York Beach, ME: Nicholas-Hayes, 1993). His writings have been reproduced widely on the internet and have appeared in the North America-based *Monastic Interreligious Dialogue* as well.

57. See also Sen 2001, 113–14.

58. For example, Ramakrishna says: "It is not harmful for one who follows the path of knowledge to have sex now and then with his own wife. The discharge of semen can be considered the same as the discharge of urine and feces. It is like defecation; once done, it is forgotten. You may enjoy a sweet made of homemade cheese (*chānā*) occasionally. (Mahimacharan laughs.) This is not so harmful for a householder. But it is extremely harmful for a sannyāsin." (KA 4.68)

59. For a fascinating background on the colonial construction of masculinity, see Mrinalini Sinha's *Colonial Masculinity: The "Manly Englishman" and the "Effeminate Bengali" in the Late Nineteenth Century* (New York: Manchester University Press, 1995) as well as Indira Chowdhuri's *The Frail Hero and Virile History: Gender and the Politics of Culture in Colonial Bengal* (New Delhi: Oxford University Press, 1998).

60. This information is provided in the opening pages of all the volumes of the *Kathāmṛta* and has been included in the single-volume Udbodhan edition as well.

61. See McLean 1989, 14–15.

62. See Kurtz, *All the Mothers are One*, 34–38; Roland 1996, 13–14.

63. For example, in *Ramakrishna Revisited* Sil cites and discusses *Kathāmṛta* 4.238 in which Ramakrishna relates his vision of the chakras. Sil's translation reads as follows: "I saw a twenty-two or twenty-three years old young man, just like myself, enter the *suṣumnā nāḍī* and engage in fellatio with the cunt-shaped lotuses: first with the anus, then the penis and the navel. The four-petalled, six-petalled, and ten-petalled lotuses, which had been drooping, now stood erect." Sil continues: "He also dreamt of the soul with a lolling tongue of fire touch dirt and taste shit—most probably a dream of anal intercourse." (1998, 77)

64. As Sumit Sarkar observed: "The remarkable thing about Ramakrishna's nature imagery is the unselfconscious ease with which he passes from similes conventionally 'beautiful,' to others that would seldom be mentioned in chaste late 19th century *bhadralok* [educated middle-class] writing. . . . Steadfastness in yogic devotion is conveyed by the image of a bird sitting with total concentration on its egg. But villagers defecating around a Kamarpukur pond can serve Ramakrishna's purpose as well, and as often, as sea or birds. . . . There is no 'dissociation of sensibility' [borrowing from T.S. Eliot] in Ramakrishna, no marking out of a distinct realm of subject or diction as proper or poetic." (Sarkar 1993, 15–16)

65. Jeffrey Kripal writes in "On Devotion, Debate and Dissent," his Foreword to Sil's later publication *Rāmakṛṣṇa Paramahaṁsa*, that he and Sil came up with similar findings concerning Ramakrishna, though they do not share each other's conclusions. (Sil 1998, xiii–xiv)

66. Sil writes: "Quite possibly he was … an 'unknown psychotic' in that he remained outwardly a normal individual, while 'forgetting' or 'repressing' his childhood experiences or traumas, and grew up to be a severely neurotic individual. . . . Thus his neurosis or psychosis accounts for his theosis." (1991, 38)

Chapter 2

1. Kripal writes that his textual study combined with his mystical/sexual experiences in Kolkata had profoundly changed and healed him: "I realized that … I had somehow, through dream and ecstasy and textual study, resolved the crisis of the crucified erection that had almost taken my life. . . . The incestuous connection between Mother and Lover had been severed, and both the Virgin Mother of my Catholic upbringing … and the Tantric goddess of Bengal … had been transformed into an imaginal Presence far closer to the Lover of my original myth-dream. . . . The Tantra, mediated through Freud, had helped to heal me" (2001a, 252–53).

2. About this aversion to chicken Kanchan Gupta writes: "Till as recently as the mid-20th century, Bengali *bhadralok* Hindus would not touch chicken or eggs—both were seen as 'Muslim food' or food meant for the *mlechchho*, both Muslim and Christian. Even Anglicized Bengalis who flaunted their disdain for conservative Hindu society by eating beef and cooking the prohibited meat at home, would not allow chicken to be served on their tables, leave alone consume it. If poultry had to be consumed to keep up with the Europeans, it was duck meat and duck eggs. The Brahmos were more liberal and chicken was served at some Brahmo homes … but it had to be cooked in a separate kitchen, most often in the courtyard. Later, this became the practice in most Bengali *bhadralok* Hindu households, although women rarely touched chicken or eggs; their bias against both did not, however, dampen their enthusiasm for *maachher jhol* and *mangshor jhol* [fish curry and mutton curry]." "A Chicken and Egg Story," *The Pioneer*, February 4, 2008.

3. For example, Kripal translates KA 2.67 as: "He grins again and again!" (KC, 232). Yet when we check KA 2.67 we find: *Mukhe ek ekbār hāsi jeno phāṭiyā poḍiteche*, which means, "Now and then a smile keeps appearing on his face." Again, where M describes Ramakrishna as "slightly smiling" (*īṣat hāsya koritechen*), *Kālī's Child* translates the words as "quipped with a grin" (KC, 132). On the same page of *Kālī's Child*, citing KA 2.141–42, Ramakrishna is reported to "growl" about those who "engage in sinful pleasures in the name of religion" (KC, 132). Yet on checking the citation, one finds instead: "he is saying" (*bolitechen*) (KA 2.142). There is nothing to suggest that Ramakrishna "growled".

4. Aditi Sen's e-mail states: "Jeff WAS my student for 8 months in Calcutta. He came from the University of Chicago with some Bengali. In his case it was fairly elementary. He did not have much knowledge of Indian culture or background. He was very serious & hardworking & a sweet person. My feeling for his book is he had a preconceived notion & worked on that. His Bengali definitely improved after 8 months but not beyond the intermediate stage." E-mail correspondence from Aditi Sen to Pravrajika Vrajaprana, October 25, 2000.

5. Since the Divine is all that exists and is the apparent source of everything, "creation" in the Hindu traditions represents the appearance of everything as a distinct entity, "preservation" is the state in which the distinction is sustained by the divine will, and "destruction" represents the return of everything to the divine source.

6. Another fascinating example is Hugh Urban's *The Economics of Ecstasy: Tantra, Secrecy and Power in Colonial Bengal*. In the book's Acknowledgments, he thanks both Rachel McDermott and Jeffrey Kripal, who have "helped to show me that it is possible to survive, transcend, and transform the debilitating neuroses that plague so many of us in the academic world" (2001, xii).

7. In *Roads of Excess* Kripal's journal entry of March 29, 1996, relates that a friend advises him to "see the pain of the [*Kālī's Child*] controversy as a beginning of a wonderful journey that will deepen and develop my and Ramakrishna's emotional lives. Astonishingly, he thus mirrored back to me … my own 'memorable fancy' about the work *for* the saint" (Kripal 2001a, 256; italics in text).

8. For example, the national anthem of Bangladesh, written by Tagore, contains the following line: *Takhon khelā dhulā sakal phele, O Mā, tomār kole chute āśi*: "Then setting aside all play, O Mother, I run back to your lap." One famous song to the Divine Mother says: *Kole tule nite āy Mā* "Come, O Mother, take me on your lap" and another: *O Mā tor kole lukiye thāki*: "O Mother, keep me hidden in your lap." In describing a mother holding a child, a person would normally say, *māyer kole śiśu jīśu*. A contemporary painting of Sarada Devi, depicting her holding a child on her lap, appears in many Indian homes today.

9. The other two citations KA 4.245 and KA 4.278 refer to two middle-aged visitors, Pandit Shyamapada Bhattacharya and Dr. Mahendralal Sarkar.

10. M writes in the *Kathāmṛta*: "*Kāche Nityagopāl chilen, tām̐hār kole pā chodāiyā dilen*" (KA 3.172). This was translated by Nikhilananda as: "He [Ramakrishna] placed his legs on the lap of Nityagopal, who was sitting near him" (GSR, 778). Dharm Pal Gupta translated the sentence as: "Nityagopal is close to him. Thakur stretches his legs out on Nityagopal's lap" (3.316). Malcolm McLean translates the phrase as: "He [Ramakrishna] put his feet in his [Nityagopal's] lap" (1983, 915). Finally, Sachindra Majumdar translates the sentence as: "He [Ramakrishna] spread his legs on his [Nityagopal's] lap" (3.165). It would appear that, at least in this instance, Bengalis have translated *pā* as "leg" whereas those unfamiliar with Bengali culture refer to *pā* as "foot."

Similarly with *on* the lap or *in* the lap. This variance in translation could be another instance of an outsider/insider divide.

11. Ramakrishna literally says here: *seikhānei tini*, "there one finds *tini*." *Tini* is a third-person pronoun in Bengali, which could mean either he or she (or even "it", when the reference is to Brahman). Ramakrishna often employed this pronoun to refer to the ultimate Reality, which he—at various times—identified with Brahman, the Divine Mother, Śiva or Viṣṇu, depending on the context. In this context of *neti neti*, it seems clear that *tini* refers to Brahman.

12. A Bengali equivalent would have been *śekhāne*.

13. The only indication a reader might have of this would be to read the second half of an endnote which states: "When the English translation (GM) paragraph numbers diverge from the Bengali text, I will note the English reference in parentheses" (KC, 337). What is not disclosed is that while Swami Jagadananda's English translation has paragraph numbers, the Bengali original does not have them. Thus providing paragraph numbers to locate the *Līlāprasaṅga* reference from the *Great Master* is completely useless and pointless.

14. The English "monomaniac" appears in parenthesis in the Bengali original (LP 5.66). This may or may not be due to the fact that Narendra reports that at this time he was reading "Abercrombie and other English philosophers."

15. We read, for example, in the *Caitanya Caritāmṛta*: "Vijuli Khān ... fell down at the lotus feet of Sri Caitanya Mahāprabhu, and the Lord placed his foot on his head" (Madhya Līlā, 18.209). A temple which Caitanya used to frequent in Narasiṁha Palli has an ancient statue of Narasiṁha which shows Prahlāda directly under Narasiṁha's foot. In the Śrīvaiṣṇava tradition, Nammālvār, whose parents left him at the feet of Viṣṇu's statue, is said to be the incarnation of the Lord's feet. Examples of the "infinite blessings" to be found at the Lord's (or the Divine Mother's) lotus feet are too copious to enumerate here.

16. It is difficult not to make a connection between Kripal's memories of his seminary dreams of "women bearing rich, milky food" and his seeming preoccupation with Ramakrishna's reference to his young disciples as "new pots"—that is, unspoiled by *kāminī kāñcana*. Ramakrishna often said that milk stored in a new pot will not turn sour, but should milk be stored in a pot where yogurt has been kept, it will turn sour. Perhaps predictably, Kripal sees "pure pots" as an illustration of Ramakrishna's homoerotic desires for his young male disciples.

17. See MK, 213. Amiya Sen also writes in this connection that in addition to the volumes M had already completed, he "was contemplating at least six to seven volumes after which he hoped to rearrange the entire material chronologically, possibly within a single volume" (2001, 47).

18. On the same note, Kripal's claim that "renouncer interpreters" have "sought to expel M from [Ramakrishna's] inner circle" (KC, 12) is simply breathtaking. Those with knowledge of the Ramakrishna tradition know how profoundly M is revered by monastics as well as by lay members.

19. The letter continues: "No doubt, Jeffrey J. Kripal one day appeared here, met several swamis, including myself, but what he has mentioned in his book is a fictional account. . . . I was amused to read in page 330 that Swami Prabhananda of the Ramakrishna Order is the only living person who had the opportunity to study the diaries in detail. Well, I do not think I have seen all the diaries, for, the diaries which are the possession of the descendants of M are their family property; they claim that all the diaries that were taken by interested persons for reading were not returned. One of the diaries seemed to have been lost. At my suggestion the late Anil Gupta, a grandson of M microfilmed the diaries, but I am sure all the diaries were not micro-filmed." Letter from Swami Prabhananda to Pravrajika Vrajaprana, March 5, 1997.

20. Elaine Pagels, "The Gospel Truth" in *The New York Times*. Op-ed, April 8, 2006.

21. Within the Hindu tradition, the imparting of spiritual teachings is governed by *adhikāribheda*. An *adhikārin* is a qualified spiritual aspirant, a fit student. *Adhikāribheda* addresses the fact that there is a difference in fitness between one student and another. Some have the ability to assimilate higher spiritual truths and some need to practice more sādhana (in this or future lives) before they will be able to do so. Therefore, when discussing Ramakrishna's *guhya kathā*, one needs to keep in mind that these talks were directed to those students whom he considered capable of understanding higher spiritual truths.

22. *Kālī's Child* also quotes G. M. Carstairs, Stanley N. Kurtz, Wendy Doniger, and others.

23. See Alan Roland's revealing *Cultural Pluralism and Psychoanalysis* as well as his *In Search of Self in India and Japan: Toward a Cross-Cultural Psychology*. Further, Sudhir Kakar makes it clear that the psychological makeup of Indians is significantly different from that of Westerners. Kakar's *The Analyst and the Mystic* reveals a culturally and psychologically nuanced approach to Ramakrishna. For approaches to Indian psychotherapy, see Girindrasekhar Bose, J. S. Neki, S. B. Verma, Ashis Nandy, Erna Hoch, et al.

24. In his Foreword to Adi Da Samraj's *Knee of Listening* (Middletown: Dawn Horse Press, 2004), Kripal enthuses that Adi Da relates "his Teaching to … earlier paradigmatic gurus, particularly Sri Ramakrishna, Swami Vivekananda [and others] … Adi Da manages to balance an obvious appreciation … to those who have come before him with a keen critical sense of where their teachings are inadequate or limited" (xiv).

25. The "Five M's" refer to the *pañca makāra*—the five transgressive elements whose Sanskrit names begin with the letter "M." The practice of the *vīra*, heroic devotee, entails the actual use of the five elements: wine (*madya*), meat (*māṁsa*), fish (*matsya*), parched grain (*mudrā*), and sexual intercourse (*maithuna*). The kind of Tantra practiced by an animalistic devotee (*paśu bhāva*) is identified with *tamas*, signifying that the person is not yet ready for the heroic practice of the *pañca makāras*. The heroic approach (*vīra bhāva*) is identified

with rajas—passion and dynamic activity. The divine approach (*divya bhāva*) is identified with sattva and the rituals entailed are purely internal and symbolic.

26. See Nivedita 1983, 168. Vivekananda himself mellowed, as far as his own attitude toward Vāmācāra is concerned. Swami Sadashivananda recalled that when Vivekananda was asked by a Buddhist monk whether he believed "all the religions of the world have produced *siddhas* (the perfected ones)," Vivekananda "not only replied in the affirmative but emphasized this with many illustrations. He added, 'Even in the condemned Vāmāchāra Tantra there have been great *siddhas*. But you know, our Guru Maharaj [Ramakrishna] used to say that that path is a dirty one'" (RSV, 400). Again, in a letter to the members of the Ramakrishna Order which provided some monastic rules, Vivekananda wrote: "None of you are fit for the Vāmāchāra form of practice. Therefore this should on no account be practised at the Math" (CW 7.494). Thus Vivekananda was not saying that it was not a spiritual path, but rather that the path was not suitable for monastics.

27. Nikhilananda translated a good deal of material which must have raised eyebrows in 1942. For example, "Gauri used to say that when a man attains ecstatic love of God all the pores of the skin, even the roots of the hair, become like so many sexual organs, and in every pore the aspirant enjoys the happiness of communion with the Ātman" (GSR, 346). Or again: "In the course of spiritual discipline, one gets a 'love body,' endowed with 'love eyes,' 'love ears,' and so on. . . . One even gets a sexual organ made of love" (115). Kripal himself acknowledged in a conversation with Vrajaprana that it took great courage for Nikhilananda—one of the few Hindus then living in the United States—to publish this in 1942.

28. KA 2.16 discusses *hṛt-padma*, "lotus of the heart"; KA 2.37 mentions the difference between a bee and a housefly, how the former drinks only the honey of the flowers, but the latter sometimes sits on the flowers and other times on garbage; KA 2.54 has a song in which Kālī's feet are compared to a blue lotus; KA 4.192 and KA 5.83 compare the relationship between God and the devotee as that between a flower and the bee, and KA 4.147 has no mention *whatsoever* of flowers.

29. Chetanananda's source is Swami Shantananda, "Svāmī Turiyānanda Mahārājer Sahit Kathopakathan," *Udbodhan*, 49 (1949), 530.

30. While "dressing Ramakrishna" could be construed to mean "providing Ramakrishna with clothes," the ambiguous way in which the sentence is constructed along with the highly sexualized context of the quote raises the question of whether Mathur literally dressed Ramakrishna himself.

31. It is not unlikely that Kripal picked this up from Sil's *Rāmakṛṣṇa Paramahaṁsa: A Psychological Profile*. About Tota, Sil writes: "Most probably the naked phallus of the big man made an abiding impression on Rāmakṛṣṇa" (1991, 67). Given the above, it is interesting that Sil has taken umbrage at Kripal's theory that Ramakrishna was homoerotically inclined.

32. The "proof" of Ramakrishna's purported "excitement" is that his "penis responds with a 'pearl' of lubricatory fluid, a physiological response that implies an actual erection" (161). But Kripal's "proof" is based on an incorrect translation combined with cultural ignorance: "it became adorned with a pearl!" (161, quoting KA 4.106) rather than the correct "A pearl would be put on it" (*muktā parāno hoto*). It is quite common during worship to decorate a Śiva liṅgam with jewels such as pearls.

33. Ramakrishna's disciples often referred to him as "Ṭhākur" or "Paramahaṁsadeva" or "Guru Mahārāj." Swami Vivekananda referred to him also as "Ātmarām"—one immersed in the Ātman.

34. Not only are not all secrets sexual, they are also not always associated with religion. Every country has intelligence services which work under a mandatory code of secrecy. Even Coca-Cola prosecuted a former employee for attempting to sell their secret formula. We tend to take any number of secrets for granted, unless they are associated with religion or sex.

Chapter 3

1. "Revealing and Concealing the Secret: A Textual History of Mahendranath Gupta's *Śrīśrīrāmakṛṣṇakathāmṛta*" was published in *Calcutta, Bangladesh and Bengal Studies* in 1992; "Ramakrishna's Foot: Mystical Homoeroticism in the *Kathāmṛta*" appeared in 1992 in *Religion, Homosexuality and Literature*, edited by Michael L. Stemmeler and José Cabezón; "Kālī's Tongue and Ramakrishna: 'Biting the Tongue' of the Tantric Tradition" was published in *History of Religions* in November, 1994.

2. Raab writes: "Psychological explanations alone are inadequate to account for [Ramakrishna's] later behavior and spiritual insights. . . . If Ramakrishna's visions had been solely the product of a sick psyche, it is doubtful that his teachings would have retained such a wide appeal among respected persons of both eastern and western traditions. Hence, an exploration of some alternative explanations of Ramakrishna's mystical visions is also needed." (326)

3. Conveyed to Vrajaprana in a conversation at his home in New York in 2002.

4. Even in India, where insider readership is highest, only 2,000 copies were printed. A second printing of another 2,000 copies was done in March 2003. E-mail to Pravrajika Vrajaprana from Swami Prabhananda, then head of the Ramakrishna Mission Institute of Culture, December 15, 2004.

5. As we have mentioned earlier, Nussbaum places the *Kālī's Child* imbroglio within the context of Hindu rightwing extremism and the threat this holds to India's history of democracy, tolerance, and religious pluralism.

6. Wendy Doniger writes in the book's Foreword, for example: "I found myself smiling often and laughing almost as often as I read it." So great was Doniger's delight that as she was reading the manuscript at the beach, Susan

Sontag and Norman Mailer offered to trade her their novels "so evident was my pleasure in [reading] it," Doniger attests. (KC, ix)

7. *The Statesman* is published in Kolkata but has a Delhi edition as well. According to *The Statesman* website (http://www.thestatesman.net), the paper's weekly circulation is approximately 180,000 with a Sunday circulation of 230,000. By contrast, *The Times of India*, one of the most widely read newspapers in India, has a daily circulation of 2.4 million.

8. While Sil's language should have been expected by those familiar with his scholarship, it is surprising that the staid, determinedly middle-class *Statesman* would print it. For example, Sil writes: "Indian Tantra with its secret sex, shit, piss, cock and cunt ..." Sil's conclusion was equally raw: "Kripal has ransacked Ramakrishna's *chora kuthuri* [lit., "back door," which Kripal believes to be the anus], unearthed its 'treasures' and served them on a rich platter—plain shit."

9. It should be noted, however, that for one living in India at that time, obtaining a copy of a book published by the University of Chicago, and extremely expensive by Indian standards, would be no easy task.

10. Apparently William Radice tried to defend *Kālī's Child* in a letter to *The Statesman*, but the letter was not published.

11. "Now Let It Rest," *The Statesman*, Vol CXXXI, No. 42, (February 18, 1997): 10.

12. To his credit, Kripal took it on the chin and apologized in *Kālī's Child*'s second edition for his error and for any wounded feelings his error may have caused.

13. This point was also corrected in *Kālī's Child*'s second edition.

14. There is no evidence of this, though it is clear that Narendra (later Swami Vivekananda) did not think highly of the book and did not want his name included in it. He was not, however, the only disciple of Ramakrishna to make this stipulation.

15. The scholar who was misquoted is Robert Ellwood. It should be mentioned that while Swami Tyagananda also never met Isherwood, Pravrajika Vrajaprana was acquainted with Isherwood and has known several of his friends for over forty years.

16. Sumit Sarkar, "Ramakrishna and the Calcutta of His Times" in *The Calcutta Psyche* ed. Geeti Sen. (Calcutta: Rupa & Co, 1991).

17. Telephone interview of Sumit Sarkar by Swami Tyagananda, February 8, 2005.

18. Sarkar's footnote states: "I feel now that my initial paper on Ramakrishna, entitled "*Kathamrita as Text: Towards an Understanding of Ramakrishna Paramahamsa*," despite its title, was insufficiently aware of these dimensions [the authorial strategy of M., for example]." (Sarkar 1993, 5)

19. Anita Katyal, "Book on Ramakrishna Kicks up a Controversy," *The Sunday Times of India*, April 6, 1997.

20. E-mail correspondence between Pravrajika Vrajaprana and D. P. Bagchi, June 5, 2005, and June 7, 2005.

21. In this connection Takayuki Yokota-Murakami has written: "When two cultures of considerably disproportionate political and economic forces meet, first, the alien conceptual framework of the culture of the greater power is imposed on the culture of the lesser power; second, what is important to be known in the former is grafted onto that of the latter, to the distortion and the deletion of aboriginal significations; third, the paradigms thus imposed become objectified and reified. The way of knowing is culturally specific, and deserves equal rights." (108)

22. Marshall was staying at the then-existent retreat house of Sarada Convent, where she was under the care of Gerda Zinn, a householder devotee. According to an interview with Zinn, Marshall had informed her that she was writing a book about Ramakrishna, and Zinn asked if she could read it. Zinn stated in a telephone interview with Vrajaprana on March 11, 2004, that she "remembered the incident *vividly*, as if it were yesterday." Zinn stated that Marshall was "influenced by Freud," and her manuscript suggested that Ramakrishna had a homosexual desire for Vivekananda. Zinn, who says she was "aghast," called Prabhavananda "to let him know." Prabhavananda asked Marshall to come to the convent to meet him. Apparently Prabhavananda, initially outraged, spoke extensively with Marshall and according to Zinn: "She changed her mind about Ramakrishna." According to the diary of Sarada Convent, Oct 6, 1962, their meeting and long lunch was friendly and enjoyable for all participants.

About this incident Isherwood writes in *My Guru and His Disciple*: "Swami was outraged. He met with the author, who was persuaded or intimidated into deleting this passage from the manuscript. I could understand Swami's indignation, although, as a homosexual, I couldn't altogether share it. Certainly, the author's statement about Ramakrishna and Vivekananda was irresponsible and unsupported by any convincing evidence. Still, it didn't shock me so much that I was unable to examine it, and my reactions to it, calmly." (247)

23. See, for example, Sarkar, 1992, and Sarkar, 1993. Sarkar reports that Ramakrishna is no longer the focus of his work.

24. The discussion occurred during a tea and conversation in 2001 at Boston College between Jeffrey Kripal and Swami Tyagananda, which was arranged and attended by Francis X. Clooney.

25. The monk in question is Robert Adjemian (also known as Brahmachari Nirvana Chaitanya). It also needs to be stated that this monk was never asked or expected to change his opinions.

26. Kripal writes that a "conspicuous feature of the controversies surrounding *Kālī's Child* … [is] the fact that my critics have been so strangely silent about any number of Indian intellectuals who have addressed the homoerotic dimensions of Ramakrishna's life both well before and after me" (Kripal 2004, 203). The Indian intellectuals Kripal cites are Sumit Sarkar, Parama Roy, and

Sudhir Kakar, whom we have discussed in earlier pages. Astonishingly, Kripal also includes in this list Ruth Vanita and Saleem Kidwai's book *Same-Sex Love in India*. One wonders whether Kripal actually opened the book, since there is nothing in Ruth Vanita's chapter, "Shri Ramakrishna Paramahansa," which supports any of Kripal's theses. Indeed, the chapter includes a long quotation from Ramakrishna's disciple Swami Vijnanananda on how Ramakrishna transmitted spiritual power to him as well as Vivekananda's familiar story of how Ramakrishna greeted him as an incarnation of Nārāyaṇa. The chapter's sources are *Ramakrishna and His Disciples*, Nikhilananda's *Gospel* and the *Great Master*.

Same-Sex Love in India does not define "love" via sexuality or eroticism. As Vanita and Kidwai point out in their Preface, their book "focuses on love, not sex." As importantly, they write that "ideas of what is sexual and what is not change with place and time" (xiii). Hence, Vanita notes in her essay on Ramakrishna that when Ramakrishna asked Narendra why he had continued to visit him, even when he was ignored, Narendra replied, "Do you think I come here just to have you speak to me? I love you. I want to see you. That is why I come." Vanita states that Ramakrishna's "most intense emotional relationships were with the young men who were drawn to him," but she also notes that "Ramakrishna had loving relationships with many devotees, married and unmarried, men and women." (231)

27. We can recall the famous apocryphal incident of Mīrābāi and Jīva Gosvāmī (Rūpa Gosvāmī according to another version): Jīva Gosvāmī was the head of the Vaiṣṇava community in Vrindaban. Mīrā wanted to meet him, but he refused to see her because he did not allow women in his presence. To this rebuff Mīrābāi replied: "Everybody in Vrindaban is a woman. Only Giridhar Gopāla is a man. Today I have discovered that there is another man besides Kṛṣṇa in Vrindaban." Deeply ashamed, Jīva immediately went to see Mīrā and paid his respects to her.

28. As Vivekananda told Nivedita: "I loved the man you see, and that held me. I thought him the purest man I had ever seen, and I knew that he loved me as my own father and mother had not the power to do" (Basu, 156). Or as Vivekananda said to M, seven months after Ramakrishna's death: "He tamed us by his love" (*tini bhālobeśe āmāder bośībhūto korechilen*) (KA 3.268).

29. While Narendra's arrival in Dakshineswar was generally a joyful occasion for Ramakrishna, suddenly Ramakrishna began treating Narendra with indifference. Ramakrishna did not acknowledge his presence, did not ask about him, and instead talked to others in the room. A week later when Narendra returned, the same thing happened. Narendra spent the day there, and Ramakrishna gave no sign of interest or even recognition. This continued for over a month and the entire time Narendra kept returning to see him. Noting that Narendra was continuing his visits despite the indifference he received, Ramakrishna said, "How is it that though I don't speak a word to you, you still continue to come here?"

Narendra replied, "Sir, it is not your words alone that draw me here. I love you and want to see you, therefore I come." (LSV, 289–90)

30. The scare quotes around "homosexuality" are Roy's own.

31. See http://www.ruf.rice.edu/~kalischi/secret.html. This was later reiterated in Kripal 2002, 199.

32. Most branches of the Ramakrishna Order perform the autumnal worship of Kālī, and many Ramakrishna devotees, including many monastics of the Order, have a personal devotion to her. It is not unusual for both lay and monastic members of the Ramakrishna Order to have in their personal shrines a small picture or image of Kālī, who is offered daily worship.

Chapter 4

1. *Kālī's Child* employs "two hermeneutical strategies" in its interpretation: psychoanalysis, which is "a product of [Kripal's] own cultural heritage" and the Hindu Tantra, which is "indigenous to Bengali culture" (KC, 6). But the Tantric categories manufactured for *Kālī's Child* have nothing to do with the philosophy that guides Tantra and everything to do with "magical power, strangeness, seediness, and sex," which is the book's reductionistic presentation of Tantra. According to Kripal, the philosophical expositions of Tantra are inauthentic because they are "designed to rid Tantra of everything that smacked of superstition, magic, or scandal" (KC, 28–29). Since this understanding of Tantra is neither supported by Tantra practitioners nor indigenous to Indian culture, the Tantric categories used in the book cannot be treated as indigenous.

2. Kripal was certainly addressing one "specific audience" when he warned his "devotional and Indian readers" that if they rejected him for his theses, they would find themselves rejecting "their own saint" Ramakrishna. He counseled them not to walk down that path (KC, xiv).

3. Ernst van Alphen writes in this regard: "When 'I' speak about the other, I remain in fact caught in the process of defining or demarcating my self-image. . . . 'We' cannot analyze alterity without at the same time analyzing 'our' identity." (Van Alphen, 15)

4. Kripal writes: "It is not my ideas that are the most troubling … it is my skin color and the accident of my birth. It is … the fact that these truths were spoken by an ethnic outsider that constitutes the deepest scandal" (Kripal 2004, 203). Yet as Kripal knows, two of his most vocal critics, Pravrajika Vrajaprana and Swami Atmajnanananda, are "ethnic outsiders" whose skin tone matches his own.

5. Kripal has responded to this criticism, disputing the "'one hundred million Hindus cannot be wrong' argument" by noting that this "works astonishingly like the 'one hundred million Christians cannot be wrong' thesis (remember evolution and the Scopes trial?) or the 'one hundred million Muslims cannot be wrong' position (*jihad* as a primarily internal or psychological category?). . . . In

any case, it turns out that they *can* all be wrong, and this for a very simple reason: ethnic or religious identity carries absolutely no necessary intellectual force and in many cases actually works against free radical inquiry and probable historical conclusion" (Kripal 2004, 203). However, linguistic incompetence and cultural ignorance cannot be classified in the same league as jihad and evolution. In the areas of Bengali language and Bengali culture, millions of Bengalis will surely have a deeper and more comprehensive knowledge than Kripal who lived in India for eight months and whose language skills, according to his Bengali tutor, never advanced "beyond the intermediate stage." (E-mail correspondence from Aditi Sen to Pravrajika Vrajaprana, October 25, 2000.)

6. For the danger of subjectivity in translating religious texts, see Nida, 154–55.

7. See KC, 325–28.

8. See KC, 4 ("mystico-erotic energies"); 6 ("mystico-erotic experiences"); 44 ("mystico-erotic union"); 45 ("mystico-erotic energy");196 ("mystico-erotic love"). The book abounds in such usages. For more examples, see KC, 24, 33, 44, 45, 50, 51, 89, 157, 188, 196, 199, 227, 236, 237, 240, 263, 266, 279, 291, 308, 313, 315, 316, 323, 325, 326. Instances of "erotic" used as simply "erotic" in the popular sense are too numerous to be mentioned here, but see KC, 5, 33, 67, 88, 96, 124.

9. See also White 2003, 13.

10. The Five M's consist of *madya*, wine; *māṁsa*, meat; *matsya*, fish; *mudrā*, parched grain, and *maithuna*, sexual union. These are used in the *Vāmācāra* (left hand) sect of Tantra. In the *Dakṣinācāra* (right hand) sect, the five forbidden substances are replaced with coconut juice, cheese, ginger, rice and honey. There are also sects which practice only the internal observances of the Five M's: steadying the mind, breathing in, breathing out, holding the breath, and meditation.

11. For a different view of what Tantra "feels like," see McDaniel 2000, 72–80.

12. Hugh Urban's criticism bears repeating here. According to Urban, Kripal's understanding of "Tantra" and his identification of Ramakrishna as a "Tantrika" is problematic because he ignores the fact that "the category of 'Tantra' as a singular, unified entity is itself an imaginary construction of 19th century British Orientalists. Ramakrishna and his disciples were themselves an important part of the way in which Tantra came to be defined in Western discourse. Second, Kripal lapses all too often into a very popular misconception of Tantra as something 'scandalous,' 'seedy,' 'sexy,' and 'dangerous,' which is defined primarily by the equation of eroticism and mysticism. . . . Sexuality is in fact but one, rather limited, and not necessarily the most important element of . . . Tantra." (Urban 1996)

13. See KC, 31: "In Ramakrishna's own words, this Tantric world is 'beyond form and the formless.'"

14. Kripal writes: "Everything depends upon one's hermeneutical stance" (KC, 45). While he recognizes this, he also displays remarkable impatience with the "hermeneutical stance" of those who disagree with him and summarily dismisses their views with allegations of censorship and denial.

15. While Kripal selectively quotes from Tantra books, his view of Tantra is primarily based on what he believes is "Tantric" in the *Kathāmṛta*, a book which does record some of Ramakrishna's Tantric practices and visions but is far from being a book *on* Tantra.

16. The non-academic translations of Nikhilananda, Majumdar and Dharm Pal Gupta skip *yonirūp* and translate *ramaṇ* as "commune" (GSR, 744, 830; Majumdar 4.242; Gupta 3.253). Gupta translates *ramaṇ* in the *Kathāmṛta*'s fourth volume as "play intimately" (4.448).

17. Kripal translates *yonirūp* as "vagina-like" (KC, 196, 324) or "vagina-shaped" (KC, 45, 127–29), and *ramaṇ* as "erotically playing" or "made love" (KC, 127). McLean translates the contested words as "intercourse with vagina-like lotuses" (McLean 1983, 4.1355). Sil translates them as "engaged in oral sex with the vagina-shaped lotuses" (Sil 1991, 64).

18. Nikhilananda's rendering of the vision appears on pages 744, 830, and 934 of the *Gospel of Sri Ramakrishna*. Page 934 significantly differs from the first two references. In contrast to the earlier references, Ramakrishna here speaks of the person in the vision who shook his *iḍā*, *piṅgalā* and *suṣumnā* nerves: "When I attained this state of God-Consciousness, a person exactly resembling myself thoroughly shook my Idā, Pingalā, and Sushumnā nerves. He licked with his tongue each of the lotuses of the six centers, and those drooping lotuses at once turned their faces upward. And at last the Sahasrāra lotus became full-blown."

19. We are indebted to Francis X. Clooney for this translation.

20. Patricia Leigh Brown, "Hey There, Couch Potatoes: Hot Enough for You?" *New York Times*, July 27, 2003.

21. Miller visited Swami Prabhavananda in Los Angeles in 1945 after returning to the United States from Paris. Depressed and anxious, Miller met with Prabhavananda and later wrote that he had "found the most masterful individual, the only person I met whom I could truly call 'a great soul,' [who] was a quiet Hindu swami in Hollywood" (Miller, 18). Miller met Prabhavananda only once but the meeting "left a great impression on my mind," as he wrote in a letter to Prabhavananda on August 2, 1956 (archives of the Vedanta Society of Southern California). On June 16, 1962, Miller wrote in a letter to the managing editor of Vedanta Press: "I shall remember [Prabhavananda] to the end of my days." In the same letter Miller wrote: "I can only say that Swami Vivekananda remains for me one of the great influences in my life—one of the great exemplars" (Letter of Henry Miller to Ursula Bond; archives of the Vedanta Society of Southern California).

22. An inquiry to the Ramakrishna-Vivekananda Center, the publisher of *The Gospel of Sri Ramakrishna*, elicited the following information: "I am sorry to

say that our records for the early years (beginning with the publication in 1942) are very scanty. But, taking our best guess, we would give you a total figure of approximately 60,000 copies sold to date." E-mail from Swami Vidananda to Pravrajika Vrajaprana, September 12, 2005. This number dims in comparison with the sale of the Bengali original, which has sold, literally, millions of copies. See the following note.

23. Swami Lokeswarananda has written: "After the first volume of the five-volume *Śrī Śrī Rāmakṛṣṇa Kathāmṛta* was published, seventeen more editions came out, and the seventeenth was reprinted twenty-two times. The second volume went through eleven editions, and the third volume had nine editions. The fourth volume also had nine editions, and the ninth was reprinted twenty-three times. The fifth volume had six editions, and the sixth edition was reprinted sixteen times." When the *Kathāmṛta*'s copyright with the Kathamrita Bhavan expired in 1983, "six publishing companies published various versions of the *Kathāmṛta*; within a few days, at least ten more companies also published the book. Yet the books from all these publishers—adding up to several hundred thousand copies—were completely sold out within a few days. . . . As a result of the tremendous competition, the price of the book was greatly reduced, thus allowing [it] to be read by more people. . . . In fact, in one Calcutta neighborhood there was such a rush to buy the book that the police had to be called in. . . . Articles in newspapers appeared bearing such captions as, 'The *Kathāmṛta* Sales Explosion.' One article published in Cochin's *The Week* bore the title, 'Ramakrishna Outsells Marx.'"(Lokeswarananda 1992, 15–16)

24. The quote comes from Kripal's "Textuality, Sexuality, and the Future of the Past: A Response to Swami Tyagananda" (http://www.hds.harvard.edu/dpa/news/news/kripal.html), which was written to counter Tyagananda's "*Kali's Child* Revisited: Or Didn't Anyone Check the Documentation?" Kripal characterizes Tyagananda's response as weak when addressing *Kālī's Child*'s homoerotic theses, "the subtleties of which Swami Tyagananda clearly does not understand, perhaps because he is not familiar with contemporary gender studies, queer theory, psychoanalysis, or feminism." A revised version of Kripal's article was later published in *Evam* (2002) and does not include this passage.

25. Personal correspondence from S. S. Sankaranarayanan to Swami Tyagananda, March 10, 2003.

26. See previous note. The quote is from Aurobindo's *Savitri: A Legend and a Symbol*, rev. ed. (Pondicherry: Sri Aurobindo Ashram, 1993), 528.

27. McLean translates the same passage in this way: "Krishna himself had to do much sadhana with Radha. She was the Brahmayoni, he had to worship it and meditate on it. From this Brahmayoni many universes were born. It's very mysterious! I used to see visions under the bel tree—flashing like fire!" (McLean 1983, 4.1348). Mazumdar translates it in a similar way: "Krishna himself went through intense spiritual practices with the emblem of Radha. The emblem is the birth sign [fn: symbol] of Brahman from which universes arise. Worship of that

emblem and meditation on it. Billions of universes are coming into being from this sign of Brahman (Brahma yoni). Very great secrets. I had visions of it under the bel tree. It scintillated." (Mazumdar, 4.237)

28. The richly diverse and often overlapping mythological accounts of these stories can be found in the *Mahābhārata* as well as many Purāṇas, especially *Śiva*, *Skanda*, *Kūrma*, *Vāmana*, *Liṅga*, and *Brahmāṇḍa*. For a good summary of the various versions, see Kramrisch, 153–61.

29. See Śvetāśvatara Upaniṣad, 6.9: *na tasya kaścit patir asti loke, na ceśitā naiva ca tasya liṅgam.*

30. Amiya Sen points out that the Vedānta/Tantra dialectic "reflects in many meaningful ways the far older contestations between the *Purva-Mimamsa* and *Uttara-Mimamsa* traditions. In its aversion for asceticism or speculation but the emphasis on *kriya* [action], Tantra may indeed have been a derivative of the *Mimamsa* traditions." Sen writes that Alex Sanderson's "Purity and Power among the Brahmins of Kashmir" in *Category of the Person: Anthropology, Philosophy and History* "broadly uphold[s] this claim" (2001, 127; 147). Significantly, Sen continues: "This suggests to me that the Vedanta-Tantra polemic is not so much a Brahminical–non-Brahminical, Great Tradition–Little Tradition polemic as inner differentiation within the polyvocal Brahminical tradition" (127).

31. For further reading along these lines, see Sugirtharajah 2003, 45–46. We are reminded here of Max Müller who was convinced that he alone had the hermeneutical key for understanding the Vedas. Hindus, were quite incapable of doing so. Müller urged: "Accept the *Veda* as an ancient *historical* [in contrast to religious] document, containing thoughts in accordance with the character of an ancient and simple-minded race of men. . . . Accept the past as a reality, study it and try to understand it, and you will then have less difficulty in finding the right way towards the future." (Müller 1902, 111)

32. McLean writes: "I think [Ramakrishna's] ambivalence tending on dislike of women, this fear of their presence and their power, stems from his homosexuality" (1983, lxxxv). Olson identifies Ramakrishna as a misogynist, yet adds: "Because Rāmakrishna was a product of his culture, he inherited and espoused many of the negative attitudes toward women in general gained from his cultural heritage" (1990, 38). Sil writes: "Ramakrishna's contempt for women was basically a misogynist attitude of an insecure male, who thought of himself as a woman in order to fight his innate fear of the female" (Sil 1998, 64). Sarkar wrote: "In conversations with male—and particularly young—disciples, Ramakrishna often struck a positively misogynist note" (Sarkar 1987, 27). Kripal's early writings on Ramakrishna show consistency on the subject: "[Ramakrishna's] relationship to Sharada was often marked by a flagrant misogyny" (1995b, 364).

33. Dharm Pal Gupta writes in his translation of the *Kathāmṛta*: "Sri Ramakrishna used the Bengali words *kamini kanchana* very frequently in the original five volumes of Sri Sri Ramakrishna Kathamrita. We believe he used this phrase to warn his disciples of lust and greed, which are the main obstacles

to spiritual progress. Moreover, Sri Ramakrishna looked upon all women as the very manifestations of the Divine Mother. Accordingly, we have used the term 'lust and greed,' or 'lust and gold,' instead of 'woman and gold' as a translation of *kamini kanchana*" (3. xiii).

34. See Atmajnanananda, 405–406.

35. One of the most famed and one which Ramakrishna sang often is: "*Rone eśeche kār kāminī?*" ("Who is that Woman yonder who lights the field of battle?") (KA 5.61). Other Bengali songs which use *kāminī* are easily found in songbooks such as *Saṅgīt-Saṅgraha* (Deoghar: Ramakrishna Mission Vidyapith), for instance: "*Kāminī jāmini-barone bāmā ke elo rone,*" "*Ke re kāminī naba daminī,*" "*Kakhono ki roṅge … kāla-kāminī.*"

36. See also Parama Roy, 96–97.

37. To this day, the Gauḍīya tradition does not shy away from these teachings. A quick survey of the internet shows several contemporary references to, for example, the "8 Aspects of Subtle Sex Life" (http://www.prabhupada.org/rama/?p=2748) or "Eight Aspects of Brahmacarya" (http://wiki.gaudiyakutir.com/Brahmacarya).

38. From the *Vairāgya Mārtaṇḍa*: *Smaraṇaṁ kīrtanaṁ keliḥ prekṣaṇaṁ guhya-bhāṣaṇam / saṇkalpo'dhyavasāyaś ca kriyā-nirvṛtir eva ca / etan-maithunam aṣṭāṇgaṁ pravandanti manīṣiṇaḥ / viparītaṁ brahmacaryam etad evāṣṭa-lakṣaṇam.* "Thinking of women, talking to them, playing with them, looking at them again and again, talking with them in secret, intending to have sex with them, making the effort to have sex, and indulging in sex—these, according to the wise, are the eight types of sexual intercourse, and it is these very eight aspects which are opposed to celibacy."

39. From Śaṅkarā's *Sarva-Vedānta-Siddhānta-Sāra-Saṁgraha*, 109–110: *Smaraṇaṁ darśanaṁ strīṇāṁ guṇakarmānukīrtanam / samīcīnatvadhīstāsu prītiḥ saṁbhāṣaṇaṁ mithaḥ / sahavāsaśca saṁsargo'ṣṭadhā maithunaṁ viduḥ.* "Thinking of women, looking at them, lavishly praising their qualities and deeds, imagining their proximity, loving them, talking to them in private, living with them, and having sex with them—are said to be the eight kinds of sexual intercourse."

40. We read Ramakrishna's words in another section of the *Kathāmṛta*: "He [Rakhal] lives with his family. He has a wife. And a son has been born to him. But he has realized that all these are illusory and impermanent. Rakhal and others will never be attached to the world" (KA 2.27). Rakhal's son died at a young age. Rakhal's wife, a sister of Ramakrishna's disciple Manomohan Mitra, was maintained by Rakhal after he left to become a monk, until her death at a fairly young age.

41. Sumit Sarkar writes a great deal on the hardships borne by Kolkata's ill-paid lowly clerical workers. Their work was demoralizing and culturally alienating, yet increasingly difficult to obtain. Sarkar quotes from the 1885 play *Kerani-Charit*: "We lose the day's salaries if we reach office a minute late …

half the salary goes on fines … there is not a single gap in our day's routine" (1990/91, 105. See also 1993, 28–31).

42. A few days before this conversation, Maku's baby son had died and another son had just been born to her.

43. Kripal presents as distorted a view of Sarada in "Perfecting the Mother's Silence" as we find in his distorted presentation of Ramakrishna in *Kālī's Child.* While we cannot address the many problems in that article here, it is enough to say that the number of errors—factual, linguistic and cultural—are simply stunning. To enumerate and address them all would require a lengthy essay. Apart from a large number of basic factual errors, however, the article's pervasive disparaging tone is as problematic as its gross inaccuracies. Throwaway remarks such as "perhaps she enjoyed the attention" (Kripal 2001b, 173) regarding Kripal's thesis that Sarada began to believe in her own divinity, are a case in point. Not only do they not provide more knowledge about Sarada, they only serve to make the article appear meanspirited.

44. Ramakrishna's disciples—Trigunatitananda, Abhedananda and M— were also given mantras by her.

45. We also read in *Māyer Kathā* what Sarada said about his concern for her: "Thakur, who was such a *tyāgi* (renunciant) nevertheless worried about me. One day he asked me: 'How much do you need for your expenses?' I replied, 'Five or six rupees will be enough.'" (MK, 348–49)

46. Rimli Bhattacharya writes: "One of the frequent charges against Girish Ghosh was that he 'ran his theatre with whores.'" (14)

47. Bhattacharya's endnote about this incident says: "Ramakrishna suffered from cancer of the throat. . . . In the course of his illness, he rested for a few months in a rented house in Shyampukur Street where entry to his chamber was strictly guarded by zealous disciples; Binodini, disguised as a saheb, succeeded in meeting him with the help of another devotee." (125)

48. Pravrajika Anandaprana, *A Historical Record: From Conversations with Swami Prabhavananda.* Unpublished reminiscences of Swami Prabhavananda. This excerpt is dated September 27, 1973.

49. For example, Kripal uses Bipinchandra Pal as a source on Ramakrishna, yet Bipinchandra never met Ramakrishna. Kripal uses the text to make a point (KC, 51), but admits in an endnote the unreliability of the source (KC, 341), and then uses the material again (KC, 77) to cement his thesis.

50. See also Chetanananda 1989, 155–71.

51. These reminiscences were originally written in English. Aseshananda (1899–1996) came to the United States in 1947 and never returned to India. All his writings were in English, hence the use of "Sri Ramakrishna" and "the Master" rather than "Thakur," etc.

52. Vrajaprana spent a good deal of time with Aseshananda, a disciple of Sarada Devi, who was in the United States from 1947 until his death in 1996 in Portland, Oregon.

53. According to Devamata's Introductory Note: "What I have told in these pages came to me from many sources—from the widowed wife [Sarada], from the immediate disciples and from householder devotees, with all of whom I was closely associated in India." (xv)

Chapter 5

1. See also Nida, 1–2.

2. *Chicago Manual of Style*, 15th edition (Chicago: The University of Chicago Press, 2003), 594.

3. See also Bhagavad Gītā 10.38, 18.63, 18.68, 18.75. Taittirīya Upaniṣad 2.1.1; Kaṭha Upaniṣad 1.3.17, 2.2.6; Śvetāśvatara Upaniṣad 2.10, 3.20; Muṇḍaka Upaniṣad 2.1.10, 3.1.7; Mahānārāyaṇa Upaniṣad 2.4. This is only an abbreviated list. One could produce, literally, pages of references for *guhya*.

4. It is tempting to wonder whether we are not harking back here to Kripal's earlier teenage fantasy of an ithyphallic Christ (Kripal 2001, 91) rather than the non-ithyphallic Śiva whom Ramakrishna worshiped in the Dakshineswar's Kālī temple.

5. Kripal is supposedly referring to a poem of Ramprasad here, as there is a citation from *Jivani o Samgraha* (Calcutta: Sahitya Samsad, 1971), no. 277. While *Kālī's Child* states: "Streams of blood ... let loose no doubt by her sword, flow ceaselessly down her round sexy thighs" (KC, 51), there is nothing even close to this in the cited text.

6. For other examples, see: KC, 4, 5, 32, 57, 65, 66, 68, 71, 75, 79, 86, 87, 91, 100, 108, 109, 130, 140, 142, 162, 163, 171, 209, 211, 220, 264, 269, 297. In this way, *Kālī's Child* can speak of Ramakrishna's transformation from a "troubled mystic" to a "confident god" by page 220.

7. See, for instance: KC, 78, 80, 81, 82, 100, 105, 108, 110, 115, 163, 173, 209, 220, 240, 300. In fact, there is an entire subheading entitled: "The Problem and the Scandal of Ramakrishna" (79).

8. The correct reference for this passage is: LP 4.73–74.

9. Here are a few examples of Ramakrishna's Vedānta teachings selected at random from the *Kathāmṛta*: *īśvara-i satya ār sob anitya*, "God alone is real, everything else is evanescent" (KA 4.65), highlighting an important Vedāntic insight that equates reality with eternality. See also KA 1.21, 1.94, 1.112, 1.114, 4.8, 4.88, 4.186, and 4.189. Ramakrishna also taught the real/unreal nature (*mithyā*) of māyā (KA 1.41); the identity of Self-realization and God-realization (4.9); the indivisible Saccidānanda being beyond the "play" (*līlā*) of God (2.192); śakti is the reflection, Brahman is the "real sun" (1.163); the personal God is a

wave in the ocean of consciousness (*cidānanda sāgar*) (1.94); and the individualized Self (*jīva*) is in reality none other than Brahman (5.143).

10. Kripal hedges his bets by an early disclaimer. The "historical record" of Ramakrishna's life, he points out, is "at best ambiguous and at worst impossibly distorting." He acknowledges that "the sequence or dating" of events in his account is "at best a tentative reconstruction and may well be revised with further historical research" (KC, 53–54). A "tentative reconstruction" would normally lead to a "tentative" conclusion. But the rest of the book displays the author's unflinching certainty in the truth of his own thesis and his summary dismissal of competing views.

11. *The Complete Works of Swami Vivekananda* are replete with references to Vivekananda's profound devotion to the Divine Mother. Apart from his well-known poems "Kali the Mother" (CW 4.384) and "And Let Shyama Dance There" (CW 4.506–10), there are, for example, enthusiastic affirmations of her in his letters such as "Jai Kali!" as well as more sober pronouncements: "Without the grace of Shakti, nothing is to be accomplished" (CW 7.484). One could add pages of citations on this subject because Vivekananda was an ardent devotee of Śakti and was deeply devoted to Sarada Devi.

12. *Śiva śaktyā yukto yadi bhavati śakta prabhavitum / Na ca devam devo na khalu kuśalaḥ spanditum api* (*Saundarya Laharī*, 1).

13. A close examination of the 86 songs Narendra sings in the *Kathāmṛta* demonstrates an extremely eclectic selection in vocal music. While some songs reflect Narendra's earlier Brahmo background, many more are distinctly and unapologetically devotional in character and come from Vaiṣṇava, Śākta (and occasionally Śaiva) traditions. None of these songs are in Sanskrit, none are "chants," and all are deeply imbued with bhakti. Reminiscences from his disciples indicate that he often sang devotional songs to Kālī.

14. For example, we see Swami Madhavananda, later the President of the Ramakrishna Order (and interestingly, the swami to whom Isherwood sent chapters of *Ramakrishna and His Disciples*) visiting M. Upon seeing M, Madhavananda does a complete *sāstaṅga* pranam (a full-body prostration) at his feet—an act which demonstrates Madhavananda's great reverence for M (Nityatmananda 6.98–105). Throughout the volumes of M's conversations, we see streams of both monastics and householders visiting M. He speaks incessantly of Ramakrishna and both monastics and householders seek his blessings and wisdom. Madhavananda, for example, asks him details about Ramakrishna's life. Far from a "divide," M constantly tells his nonmonastic visitors to spend time with the sādhus at Belur Math. Monks from Belur Math and surrounding areas go to M to learn from him. We repeatedly see M pressing the point that *sādhusaṅga*—association with the sādhus—is vital for spiritual life. M himself lived with the monks at the Baranagore Math for six months (Nityatmananda 6.iii–iv). M tells devotees to send their sons there in order to be inspired, adding: "Going there once is not enough. Repeated visits are needed" (Nityatmananda 6.45).

15. We should remember that very young village children in India do not wear diapers, only an upper garment, if that. Thus when they let loose, so to speak, it is obvious to all and it is not seen as particularly offensive.

16. One interesting instance: "When in Singapore Netaji [India's patriot Subhash Chandra Bose] would often commune with the monks of the Ramakrishna Mission and late at night he would drive to the Mission, change into priestly silk dhoti, shut himself up in the prayer room, rosary in hand and spend a couple of hours in meditation." Quoted in *The Springing Tiger* by Hugh Toye. In Lt. Col. N. C. Guha, "Swami Vivekananda's Influence on Netaji Subash Chandra Bose," *Vedanta Kesari* (August 2007): 308–12.

17. "Haripada has fallen into the clutches of a woman of the Ghoṣpārā sect. He cannot leave her. He says she takes him on her lap and feeds him, and it seems calls it Gopāla bhāva. I have alerted him many times. They call it maternal love! It is this kind of 'maternal love' that leads to danger." (KA 2.154)

18. The man's name was Yadavkishore Goswami and he belonged to the thirteenth generation of direct descendants of Nityānanda. Ramakrishna loved him dearly and had great regard for him not only for his august lineage but also for his character, learning and deep devotion. A man of renown among Gauḍīya Vaiṣṇavas, Yadavkishore was "the favorite student of 'Nyāya Ratna' Mahesh, the principal of the Sanskrit College, and in 1879 ... obtained the 'Vidyā Ratna' degree in literature" (Prabhananda 2001, 139).

19. Balaram, for example, asks Ramakrishna how it was possible for Purna to know all of a sudden that the world is illusory (*saṁsār mithyā gyān, Pūrṇer kemon kore holo*)? Ramakrishna's reply is significant: "The knowledge was acquired in earlier births. He has done a lot [of sādhana] in previous births. It is only the body that begins small and grows old, not the Ātman. You know how these [youngsters] are? They are like plants which grow fruit first and then flowers." (*Janmāntorīn. Pūrba pūrba janme śob korā āche. Śarīr-i choto hoy ābār bṛddha hoy—ātmā śeirūp noy. Oder kemon jāno,—phol āge tārpor phūl*) (KA 4.230–31).

20. In Bengali religious texts, *āliṅgan* is also used to denote the embrace of fellowship, generally between two men, less often between two women.

21. Kripal writes that he is "indebted to Narasingha Sil" for this interpretation. (KC, 352)

22. Ramakrishna was unhappy about M living apart from his father and stepmother, but as M maintained that it was his stepmother who broke up the family, perhaps Ramakrishna was more tolerant of M's separation.

23. Kripal quotes the *Līlāprasaṅga* here (LP 5.7.20), but the citation is nearly useless since it refers not to Saradananda's Bengali *Līlāprasaṅga* as it should, but to its English translation, *The Great Master*. What one finds when reading the *Līlāprasaṅga* (5.170–71) is the well-known boat incident in which Yogen (later Swami Yogananda), en route to Dakshineswar by boat, was asked by a fellow passenger where he was headed. When Yogen said that he was going to visit Ramakrishna, the passenger began to criticize Ramakrishna saying that

Ramakrishna was only posing as a holy man. Ramakrishna, the man said, "eats good food, sleeps on a mattress, and turns the head of school boys in the name of religion" (*bhālo khāccen, godite śuccen ār dharmer nām kore joto śob skūl cheleder māthā khāccen*). That is, while parents were trying hard to get their sons to study so that they could have successful careers and well-arranged marriages, Ramakrishna was teaching renunciation. No one accused Ramakrishna of sexual interest in, let alone sexual activity with, the boys. In fact, one of his young disciples suspected Ramakrishna of having sexual relations with Sarada Devi, and it was the same Yogen whom we see above in the boat. When Ramakrishna left his room in the middle of the night to relieve himself, Yogen decided to follow him—thinking that perhaps Ramakrishna was visiting Sarada in her quarters at night. When Ramakrishna discovered Yogen on his way back to his room, Ramakrishna congratulated him and approvingly said: "Observe a sadhu both by day and by night." That is, never be gullible about holy people. Their actions must be consonant with their words; they should be watched and tested.

Chapter 6

1. E-mail from Ashok Row Kavi to Swami Tyagananda, January 23, 2007.

Bibliography

Abjajananda, Swami. 2003. *Monastic Disciples of Swami Vivekananda*. Calcutta: Advaita Ashrama.

Akshayachaitanya, Brahmachari. 1977. Bengali. *Svāmī Sāradānander Jībanī*. Calcutta: Calcutta Book House.

Anandaprana, Pravrajika. *A Historical Record: From Conversations with Swami Prabhavananda*. Unpublished MS, courtesy of Pravrajika Anandaprana.

Aseshananda, Swami. 1954. "A Holy Woman of Modern India." *Vedanta and the West* 110 (Nov-Dec): 54–63.

———. 1982. *Glimpses of a Great Soul: A Portrait of Swami Saradananda*. Los Angeles: Vedanta Press.

Atmajnanananda, Swami. 1997. "Scandals, Cover-Ups, and Other Imagined Occurrences in the Life of Ramakrishna: An Examination of Jeffrey Kripal's *Kali's Child*." *International Journal of Hindu Studies* 1–2 (Aug): 401–20.

Basu, Shankari Prasad, ed. 1982. *Letters of Sister Nivedita*. Calcutta: Nababharat.

Beckerlegge, Gwilym. 2000. *The Ramakrishna Mission: The Making of a Modern Hindu Movement*. New Delhi: Oxford Univ. Press.

Bermann, Sandra and Michael Wood, eds. 2005. *Nation, Language, and the Ethics of Translation*. Princeton: Princeton Univ. Press.

Bhajanananda, Swami. 1980. "Sri Ramakrishna and the Vedic Ideal." *Prabuddha Bharata* (Mar): 83–90.

———. 1982a. "Three Aspects of the Ramakrishna Ideal–1." *Prabuddha Bharata* (Mar): 83–91.

———. 1982b. "Three Aspects of the Ramakrishna Ideal–2." *Prabuddha Bharata* (Apr): 166–74.

———. 1986. "What Ramakrishna Has Done for the World." *Prabuddha Bharata* (Dec): 492–505.

———. 1997. "Sri Ramakrishna the Unknown." *Prabuddha Bharata* (Mar): 86–92.

Bhattacharya, Rimli, ed. and tr. 1998. *Binodini Dasi: My Story and My Life as an Actress*. New Delhi: Kali for Women.

Bhattacharyya, N. N. 1999. *The Indian Mother Goddess*, 3rd ed. New Delhi: Manohar Publishers.

Breckenridge, Carol A., and Peter van der Veer, eds. 1993. *Orientalism and the Postcolonial Predicament*. Philadelphia: Univ. of Pennsylvania Press.

Bucknell, Katherine, ed. 1997. "Introduction." In *Christopher Isherwood Diaries Volume One: 1939–1960*: vii–xlix. London: Methuen.

Burke, Marie Louise. 1986. *Swami Vivekananda in the West, New Discoveries: The World Teacher, Part Two*. Calcutta: Advaita Ashrama.

Busch, Andrew and Brian Hatcher. 1998. "Do the People of Ramakrishna Mission in Calcutta Agree or Disagree with the View of Ramakrishna Proposed by Jeff Kripal in 'Kali's Child' (1995)?" ASIANetwork Freeman Foundation Student-Faculty Fellowship: Summary of Preliminary Report, Summer 1998 Projects. http://www.asianetwork.org/programs/freeman/1998sff/abstracts.html

Chatterjee, Partha. 1993. *The Nation and Its Fragments: Colonial and Postcolonial Histories*. Princeton: Princeton Univ. Press.

Chattopadhyay, Nalini Ranjan. 1978. Bengali. *Śrī Rāmakṛṣṇa o Baṅga Raṅgamañca*. Calcutta: Mandal Book House.

Chetanananda, Swami. 1989. *They Lived With God: Life Stories of Some Devotees of Sri Ramakrishna*. St. Louis: Vedanta Society of St. Louis.

———. 1990. *Ramakrishna as We Saw Him*. St. Louis: Vedanta Society of St. Louis.

Chowdhuri, Indira. 2001. *"The Frail Hero and Virile History" : Gender and the Politics of Culture in Colonial Bengal*. Oxford Univ. Press.

Clarke, J. J. 1997. *Oriental Enlightenment: The Encounter between Asian and Western Thought*. London and New York: Routledge.

Cleary, J. C. 2005. "Buddhist Studies the Buddhist Way." *Harvard Divinity Bulletin* (Autumn): 66–74.

Clément, Catherine, and Sudhir Kakar. 1993. French. *La Folle et le saint*. Paris: Éditions du Seuil.

Datta, Ramchandra. 1934. Bengali. *Śrī Śrī Rāmakṛṣṇa Paramahaṁsadeber Jībanabṛttānta*. 5th ed. Kolkata: Sri Yogodyan.

Deshpande, G. T. 1971. *Indological Papers*, vol. 1. Nagpur: Vidarbha Samshodhana Mandal.

Devamata, Sister (Laura Glenn). 2005. *Sri Ramakrishna and His Disciples*. 2nd ed. Cohasset: Vedanta Centre.

Dey, B. 1982. "The Story of the Kathamrita." In *Sri Sri Ramakrishna Kathamrita Centenary Memorial*, edited by D. P. Gupta and D. K. Sengupta. Chandigarh: Sri Ma Trust.

Dhireshananda, Swami. 1962. Bengali. "Svāmī Vivekānanda O Advaitavād." *Udbodhan* 65, no. 2–3 (Feb-Mar): 73–81, 137–44.

———. 1980. Bengali. "Nānā Dṛṣṭite Rāmakṛṣṇa," *Udbodhan* 82, no. 5 (May): 219–26.

Durga Puri. 1955. *Gauri Ma*. Calcutta: Saradeswari Asrama.

Dutta, Aswini Kumar. 1976. "Reminiscences of Sri Ramakrishna." In *Sri Ramakrishna in the Eyes of Brahma and Christian Admirers*. Calcutta: Firma KLM Ltd.

Dutta, Mahendra. 2000. Bengali. *Guruprān Rāmacandrer Anudhyān*. 2nd ed. Calcutta: Mahendra Publishing Committee.

Eastern and Western Admirers. 2004. *Reminiscences of Swami Vivekananda*. 4th ed. Calcutta: Advaita Ashrama.

Eastern and Western Disciples. 1979. *Life of Swami Vivekananda*. Two vols, rev. ed. Calcutta: Advaita Ashrama.

Farquhar, J. N. 1967. *Modern Religious Movements in India*. Reprint (1st Indian ed.), Delhi: Munshiram Manoharlal. (Orig. pub. New York: Macmillan & Co., 1919.)

Freud, Ernst L., ed. 1960. *Letters of Sigmund Freud*. Translated by Tania & James Stern. New York: Basic Books.

Gambhirananda, Swami. 2005. Bengali. *Śrī Mā Sāradā Devī*. 9th ed. Kolkata: Udbodhan Kāryālay.

Gargi, Sister [Burke, Marie Louise]. 2003. *A Heart Poured Out: A Story of Swami Ashokananda*. New York: Kalpa Tree Press.

Ghanananda, Swami. 1970. *Sri Ramakrishna and His Unique Message*. 3rd rev. ed. London: Ramakrishna Vedanta Centre.

Ghosh, Pranab Ranjan. 1982. "Sri Ramakrishna Kathamrita: Sri M.'s Unique Contribution to Bengali Literature." In *Sri Sri Ramakrishna Kathamrita Centenary Memorial*, edited by D. P. Gupta and D. K. Sengupta. Chandigarh: Sri Ma Trust.

Ghosh, Sunil Bihari. 1983. Bengali. "Kathāmṛta Prakāśan (Granthapañjī)." In *Śrī Rāmakṛṣṇa O Tam̐r Kathāmṛta*. Howrah: Ramakrishna Vivekananda Ashrama.

Guharoy, Malati. 1992. Bengali. *Gaurī-Mā*. Kolkata: Sri Prakashani.

Gupta, Dharm Pal, trans. 2001–2005. *Sri Sri Ramakrishna Kathamrita*. 4 volumes. Chandigarh: Sri Ma Trust.

Gupta, Ishwari Devi. 1982. "Preface and Acknowledgements." In *Sri Sri Ramakrishna Kathamrita Centenary Memorial*. D. P. Gupta and D. K. Sengupta, eds. Chandigarh: Sri Ma Trust.

Gupta, Mahendranath [M]. 1912. *The Gospel of Sri Ramakrishna According to M (Mahendra), a Son of the Lord and Disciple, Or the Ideal Man for India and for the World*, Part 1. San Francisco: San Francisco Vedanta Society. (Reprint of 1907 Madras edition.)

———. *Śrī-Śrī-Rāmakṛṣṇa-Kathāmṛta*. Bengali. Vol. 1 (19th reprint, 1985), vol. 2 (17th reprint, 1983), vol. 3 (16th reprint, 1985), vol. 4 (19th reprint, 1985), vol. 5 (15th reprint, 1985). Kolkata: Sri M's Thakurbati.

Haberman, David L. 1994. *Journey through the Twelve Forests: An Encounter with Krishna*. New York: Oxford Univ. Press.

———. 1997. Review of *Kali's Child* by Jeffrey Kripal. *The Journal of Asian Studies* 56, no. 2 (May): 531–32.

———. 2001. Acting as a Way of Salvation: *A Study of Rāgānugā Bhakti Sādhana*. Delhi: Motilal Banarsidass.

Hansbrough, Alice. 2007. "Reminiscences of Swami Vivekananda." *Prabuddha Bharata* (Jun): 385–89.

Hatcher, Brian A. 1999. "Kālī's Problem Child: Another Look at Jeffrey Kripal's Study of Śrī Rāmakṛṣṇa." *International Journal of Hindu Studies* 3, no. 2 (Aug): 165–82.

Hawley, John Stratton. 1998. Review of *Kali's Child* by Jeffrey Kripal. *History of Religions* 37, no. 4 (May): 401–404.

———. 2004. "The Damage of Separation: Krishna's Loves and Kali's Child." *Journal of the American Academy of Religion* 72, no. 2 (Jun): 369–93.

Hayes, Glen Alexander. 1997. Review of *Kali's Child: The Mystical and the Erotic in the Life and Teachings of Ramakrishna*, by Jeffrey J. Kripal. Religious Studies Review 23, no. 1 (Jan): 95–96.

Isherwood, Christopher. 1946. "The Problem of the Religious Novel." *Vedanta and the West* 9 (Mar-Apr): 61–64.

———. 1965. *Ramakrishna and His Disciples*. New York: Simon and Schuster.

———. 1980. *My Guru and His Disciple*. New York: Farrar, Straus, Giroux.

———. 1997. *Christopher Isherwood Diaries: Volume One: 1939–1960*, edited by Katherine Bucknell. New York: HarperCollins.

———. 2000. *Lost Years: A Memoir 1945–1951*, edited by Katherine Bucknell. New York: HarperCollins.

Jackson, Carl T. 1994. *Vedanta for the West: The Ramakrishna Movement in the United States*. Bloomington: Indiana Univ. Press.

Jhingran, Saral, 1989. *Aspects of Hindu Morality*. Delhi: Motilal Banarsidass.

Juergensmeyer, Mark. 2003. *Terror in the Mind of God: The Global Rise of Religious Violence*. 3rd ed. Berkeley: Univ. of California Press.

Kakar, Sudhir. 1991. *The Analyst and the Mystic: Psychoanalytic Reflections on Religion and Mysticism*. Chicago: Univ. of Chicago Press.

———. 2001. *Ecstasy*. New Delhi: Viking.

Kermode, Frank. 1965a. "The Old Amalaki." *New York Review of Books* (Jun 17): 18–20.

———. 1965b. Response to Gavin Lambert's "One Man's Vedanta." *New York Review of Books* (Sep 16): 26–27.

King, Richard. 1999a. *Indian Philosophy: An Introduction to Hindu and Buddhist Thought*. Washington, DC: Georgetown Univ. Press.

———. 1999b. *Orientalism and Religion: Postcolonial Theory, India and 'The Mystic East.'* London and New York: Routledge.

Kopf, David. 1969. *British Orientalism and the Bengal Renaissance: The Dynamics of Indian Modernization 1773–1835*. Berkeley and Los Angeles: Univ. of California Press.

Kramrisch, Stella. 1992. *The Presence of Śiva*. Princeton: Princeton Univ. Press.

Kripal, Jeffrey J. 1991. "Revealing and Concealing the Secret: A Textual History of Mahendranath Gupta's *Śrīśrīrāmakṛṣṇakathāmṛta*." In *Calcutta, Bangladesh and Bengal Studies*, edited by Clinton B. Seely. Lansing: Michigan State Univ..

———. 1994. "Kali's Tongue and Ramakrishna: 'Biting the Tongue' of the Tantric Tradition." *History of Religions* 34, no. 2 (Nov): 152–89.

———. 1995a. *Kālī's Child: The Mystical and the Erotic in the Life and Teachings of Ramakrishna*. Chicago: Univ. of Chicago Press.

———. 1995b. Review of *Sri Ramakrishna: A Prophet for the New Age*, by Richard Schiffman. *Journal of the American Academy of Religion* 63, no. 2 (Summer): 363–65.

———. 1998a. *Kālī's Child: The Mystical and the Erotic in the Life and Teachings of Ramakrishna*. 2nd edition. Chicago: Univ. of Chicago Press.

———. 1998b. "Mystical Homoeroticism, Reductionism, and the Reality of Censorship: A Response to Gerald James Larson." *Journal of the American Academy of Religion* 66, no. 3: 627–35.

———. 2000. "A Garland of Talking Heads for the Goddess." In *Is the Goddess a Feminist?*, edited by Alf Hiltebeitel and Kathleen M. Erndl. New York: New York Univ. Press.

———. 2000/2001a. "Secret Talk: Sexual Identity and the Politics of Scholarship in the Study of Hindu Tantrism." *Harvard Divinity Bulletin* 29, no. 4 (Winter): 14–17.

———. 2000/2001b. "Textuality, Sexuality, and the Future of the Past: A Response to Swami Tyagananda." Website of Harvard Divinity Bulletin: http://www.hds.harvard.edu/dpa/news/news/kripal.html. No longer available.

———. 2001a. *Roads of Excess, Palaces of Wisdom: Eroticism and Reflexivity in the Study of Mysticism*. Chicago: Univ. of Chicago Press.

———. 2001b. "Perfecting the Mother's Silence: Dream Devotion and Family in the Deification of Sharada Devi." In *Seeking Mahādevī: Constructing the Identities of the Hindu Great Goddess*, edited by Tracy Pintchman. Albany: State Univ. of New York Press.

———. 2002. "Textuality, Sexuality, and the Future of the Past: A Response to Swami Tyagananda." *Evam: Forum on Indian Representations* 1: 1 & 2: 191–205.

———. 2004. "Being John Woodroffe." In *Identity and the Politics of Scholarship in the Study of Religion*. New York and London: Routledge.

Kurtz, Stanley N. 1992. *All the Mothers Are One: Hindu India and the Cultural Reshaping of Psychoanalysis*. New York: Columbia Univ. Press.

Larson, Gerald James. 1997. "Polymorphic Sexuality, Homoeroticism, and the Study of Religion." *Journal of the American Academy of Religion* 65, no. 3: 655–65.

———. 1998. "Polymorphic Sexuality, Homoeroticism, and the Study of Religion Revisited: A Rejoinder." *Journal of the American Academy of Religion* 66, no. 3: 637–39.

Lokeswarananda, Swami. ed. 1985. Bengali. *Śatarūpe Sāradā*. Kolkata: Ramakrishna Mission Institute of Culture.

———, 1992. *The Way to God as Taught by Sri Ramakrishna*. Calcutta: Ramakrishna Mission Institute of Culture.

M. [See Gupta, Mahendranath.]

Majumdar, Sachindra Kumar. 2001. *Conversations with Sri Ramakrishna: An Exact and Complete Translation of M's Gospel*. CD format. Greenville: SRV Retreat Center.

Masson, J. Moussaieff. 1974. "Sex and Yoga: Psychoanalysis and the Indian Religious Experience." *Journal of Indian Philosophy* 2: 309–320.

———. 1979. "Indian Psychotherapy?" *Journal of Indian Philosophy* 7: 327–33.

———. 1980. *The Oceanic Feeling: The Origins of Religious Sentiment in Ancient India*. Dordrecht, Holland and Boston: D. Reidel Publishing Co.

Mazumdar, P. C. [Mazoomdar P. C.]. 1976. "The Hindu Saint." In *Sri Ramakrishna in the Eyes of Brahma and Christian Admirers*, edited by Nanda Mookerjee. Calcutta: Firma KLM Ltd. Originally titled "Sri Ramakrishna Paramahamsa." (Reprinted from *Theistic Quarterly Review*, Oct–Dec 1879.)

McDaniel, June. 1989. *The Madness of the Saints: Ecstatic Religion in Bengal*. Chicago: Univ. of Chicago Press.

———. 2000. "Interviews with a Tantric Priest: Feeding Skulls in the Town of Sacrifice." In *Tantra in Practice*, edited by David Gordon White. Princeton: Princeton Univ. Press.

McDermott, Rachel. 2000. "Raising Snakes in Bengal: The Use of Tantric Imagery in Śākta Poetry Contests." In *Tantra in Practice*. Edited by David Gordon White. Princeton: Princeton Univ. Press.

McLean, Malcolm. 1983. "A Translation of the *Śrī-Śrī-Rāmakṛṣṇa-Kathāmṛta* with Explanatory Notes and Critical Introduction." PhD diss., Otago Univ.

———. 1989. "Women as Aspects of the Mother Goddess in India: A Case Study of Ramakrishna." *Religion* 19: 13–25.

———. 1996. Review of *Kali's Child*. *South Asia: Journal of South Asian Studies*. New Series 19 no. 1 (Jun): 116–17.

Miller, Henry. 1945. *The Air-Conditioned Nightmare*. New York: New Directions.

Mookerjee, Nanda. ed. 1976. *Sri Ramakrishna in the Eyes of Brahma and Christian Admirers*. Calcutta: Firma KLM Ltd.

Mukerji, Dhan Gopal. 1926. *The Face of Silence*. New York: E. P. Dutton.

Müller, F. Max. 1899. *Auld Lang Syne (Second Series): My Indian Friends* (New York: Charles Scribner's Sons.

———. 1901. *Last Essays (Second Series): Essays on the Science of Religion*. London: Longmans, Green and Co.

———. 1902. *The Life and Letters of the Right Honourable Friederich Max Müller, Edited by His Wife*. Vol. 2. London: Longmans, Green, & Co.

———, trans. 1962. *The Upaniṣads* in two volumes. Part 1. Oxford: Clarendon, *Sacred Books of the East*, Vol. 15. Reprint, New York: Dover. (Orig. pub. 1879.)

———. 1975. *Ramakrishna: His Life and Sayings*. New York: Charles Scribner's Sons. Reprint. New York: AMS Press. (Orig. pub. 1899.)

———. 1976. "A Real Mahatman (With Precepts of Ramakrishna Paramahamsa)." In *Sri Ramakrishna in the Eyes of Brahma and Christian Admirers*, edited by Nanda Mookerjee, 43–65. Calcutta: Firma KLM Ltd., 1976. (Orig. pub. 1896.)

———. 1985. *Chips from a German Workshop*, Vol. 1. *Essays on the Science of Religion*. New York: Charles Scribner and Company. Reprint, Chico: Scholars Press. (Orig. pub. 1869.)

Nandy, Ashis. 1980. *At the Edge of Psychology: Essays in Politics and Culture*. Delhi: Oxford Univ. Press.

———. 1983. *The Intimate Enemy: Loss and Recovery of Self under Colonialism*. Delhi: Oxford Univ. Press.

Neevel, Walter G. Jr. 1976. "The Transformation of Ramakrishna." In *Hinduism: New Essays in the History of Religions*, edited by Bardwell L. Smith. Leiden: E. J. Brill.

———. 1997. "Śri Rāmakrishna: At Play in His Mother's Mansion." In *Hindu Spirituality: Postclassical and Modern*, edited by K. R. Sundararajan and Bithika Mukerji. New York: Crossroad Pub. Co.

Nida, Eugene A. 1964. *Toward a Science of Translating*. Leiden: E. J. Brill.

Nikhilananda, Swami. 1942. *The Gospel of Sri Ramakrishna*. New York: Ramakrishna-Vivekananda Center.

———. 1962. *Holy Mother*. New York: Ramakrishna-Vivekananda Center.

[Nikhilananda, Swami, and Swami Madhavananda.] 1971. *Life of Sri Ramakrishna*. Calcutta: Advaita Ashrama.

Nirvedananda, Swami. 1940. *Sri Ramakrishna and Spiritual Renaissance*. Calcutta: Ramakrishna Mission Institute of Culture.

Nityatmananda, Swami. 1982–97. Bengali. *Śrī Ma Darśan*. 16 vols. Calcutta: General Printers and Publishers.

Nivedita, Sister. (Margaret Noble). 1948. *Notes of Some Wanderings with the Swami Vivekananda*, 3rd ed. Calcutta: Udbodhan Office.

———. (Margaret Noble). 1983. *The Master as I Saw Him*. 13th ed. Calcutta: Udbodhan Office.

Nussbaum, Martha C. 2007. *The Clash Within: Democracy, Religious Violence, and India's Future*. Cambridge: Harvard Univ. Press, Belknap Press.

Olson, Carl. 1990. *The Mysterious Play of Kālī: An Interpretive Study of Rāmakrishna*. Atlanta: Scholars Press.

———. 1997. Review of *Kali's Child* by Jeffrey Kripal. *International Journal of Hindu Studies* 1, no. 1 (Apr): 201–202.

———. 1998. "Vivekānanda and Rāmakṛṣṇa Face to Face: An Essay on the Alterity of a Saint." *International Journal of Hindu Studies* 2, no. 1 (Apr), 43–66.

Omkareshwarananda, Swami. 1946. Bengali. *Premananda* Part II. Deoghar: Sri Ramakrishna Sadhan Mandir.

Openshaw, Jeanne. 1995. Review of *Kali's Child* by Jeffrey Kripal. *Times Higher Educational Supplement*, no. 1206 (Dec 15): 22.

Padoux, André. 1996. French. Review of *Kali's Child* by Jeffrey Kripal. *Archives de Sciences Sociales des Religions* 94 (Avril-Juin): 85–86.

———. 2002. "What Do We Mean by Tantrism?" In *The Roots of Tantra*, edited by Katherine Anne Harper and Robert L. Brown. Albany: SUNY Press.

Parsons, William B. 1997. "Psychoanalysis and Mysticism: The Case of Ramakrishna." *Religious Studies Review* 23, no. 4 (Oct): 355–60.

Patton, Laurie L. 1996. Review of *Kali's Child* by Jeffrey Kripal. *Journal of the History of Sexuality* 7, no. 2 (Oct): 287–89.

Pollock, Sheldon. 1993. "Deep Orientalism? Notes on Sanskrit and Power Beyond the Raj." In *Orientalism and the Post-Colonial Predicament*, edited by Carol Breckenridge and Peter van der Veer. Philadelphia: Univ. of Pennsylvania Press.

Prabhananda, Swami. 1987. *First Meetings with Sri Ramakrishna*. Madras: Sri Ramakrishna Math.

———. 1993. *More About Ramakrishna*. Calcutta: Advaita Ashrama.

———. 1997. Bengali. *Sāradananda Carit*. Kolkata: Udbodhan Kāryālay.

———. 1999. Bengali. "Śakti Sādhanā o Śrī Rāmakṛṣṇa." *Udbodhan*, vol. 101, no. 9 (Sep): 549–54.

———. 2001. *Journeys with Ramakrishna*. Chennai: Sri Ramakrishna Math.

———. 2004a. "Holy Mother: The Guardian Angel of the *Kathamrita*–I." *Vedanta Kesari* (Aug): 302–307.

———. 2004b. "Holy Mother: The Guardian Angel of the *Kathamrita*–II." *Vedanta Kesari* (Sep): 346–51.

———. 2004c. "Holy Mother: The Guardian Angel of the *Kathamrita*–III." *Vedanta Kesari* (Oct): 378–82.

Prabuddhaprana, Pravrajika. 2002. *Saint Sara: The Life of Sara Chapman Bull the American Mother of Swami Vivekananda*. Calcutta: Sri Sarada Math.

———. 1990. *Tantine: The Life of Josephine MacLeod*. Calcutta: Sri Sarada Math.

Prabhavananda, Swami. 1968. *Swami Premananda: Teachings and Reminiscences*. Hollywood: Vedanta Press.

Purnatmananda, Swami, ed. 2004. *Reminiscences of Sri Sarada Devi by Monastics, Devotees, and Others*. Translated by Maloti Sen Gupta. Kolkata: Advaita Ashrama.

Raab, Kelley Ann. 1995. "Is There Anything Transcendent About Transcendence?" *Journal of the American Academy of Religion* 63, no. 2, (Summer): 321–41.

Radice, William. 1998. Review of *Kali's Child* by Jeffrey J. Kripal. *Bulletin of the School of Oriental and African Studies* 61, no. 1: 160–61.

Raju, P. T. 1985. *Structural Depths of Indian Thought*. New York: State Univ. of New York Press.

Ray, Rajat K. 1997. Review of *Kali's Child* by Jeffrey Kripal. *Indian Economic and Social History Review* 34, no 1: 101–104.

Richards, David. 1995. *Masks of Difference: Cultural Representations in Literature, Anthropology and Art*. Cambridge: Cambridge Univ. Press.

Roland, Alan. 1988. *In Search of Self in India and Japan: Toward a Cross-Cultural Psychology*. Princeton: Princeton Univ. Press.

———. 1996. *Cultural Pluralism and Psychoanalysis*. New York: Routledge.

———. 1997. "The Spiritual Self and Psychopathology: Theoretical Reflections and Clinical Observations." Paper presented for "Dharma: The Categorical Imperative" at the National Institute for Advanced Studies, Simla, Jul 18, 1997; Bangalore, Jul 29, 1997.

———. 2002. "The Uses (and Misuses) of Psychoanalysis in South Asian Studies: Mysticism and Child Development." Paper presented at the South Asia Conference, Univ. of Wisconsin, Madison, Oct 11, 2002. Reproduced on the *Sulekha* website: http://alan-roland.sulekha.com/blog/post/2002/11/the-uses-and-misuses-of-psychoanalysis-in-south.htm.

Rolland, Romain. 1947. French. *La Vie de Ramakrishna: Essai sur la Mystique et l'Action de l'Inde Vivante*. Paris: Éditions Stock.

———. 1965. *Life of Ramakrishna*. Translated by E. F. Malcolm-Smith. 7th ed. Calcutta: Advaita Ashrama. (Orig. pub. 1929.)

———. 1990. *Selected Letters of Romain Rolland*, edited by Doré, Francis and Marie-Laure Prévost, Delhi: Oxford Univ. Press.

Row Kavi, Ashok. 1999. "The Contract of Silence." In *Yaraana: Gay Writing from India*, edited by Hoshang Merchant. New Delhi: Penguin Books India.

Roy, Parama. 1998. *Indian Traffic: Identities in Question in Colonial and Postcolonial India*. Berkeley and Los Angeles: Univ. of California Press.

Said, Edward W. 1978. *Orientalism*. New York: Random House.

———. 2005. "Representing the Colonized: Anthropology's Interlocutors." In *Jean François Lyotard: Critical Evaluations in Cultural Theory*, edited by Victor E. Taylor and Gregg Lambert. London: Routledge.

Saradananda, Swami. 1952. *Sri Ramakrishna: The Great Master*. Translated by Swami Jagadanananda. 4th ed. Madras: Sri Ramakrishna Math.

———. 1991. Bengali. *Śrī-Śrī-Rāmakṛṣṇa-Līlāprasaṅga*. 2 vols. Kolkata: Udbodhan Kāryālay.

Saradeshananda, Swami. 1982. *The Mother as I Saw Her: Being Reminiscences of Holy Mother Sri Sarada Devi*, translated by J. N. Dey. Madras: Sri Ramakrishna Math.

———. 1981. Bengali. *Śrī-Śrī-Māyer Smṛtikathā*. Kolkata: Udbodhan Kāryālay.

Sarkar, Sumit. 1985. "The Kathamrita as Text: Towards an Understanding of Ramakrishna Paramahamsa." *Occasional Papers on History and Society* 22. New Delhi: Nehru Memorial Museum and Library.

———. 1990/91. "Ramakrishna and the Calcutta of His Times." In *The Calcutta Psyche*, edited by Geeti Sen. Delhi: India International Centre.

———. 1992. "'Kaliyuga,' 'Chakri' and 'Bhakti': Ramakrishna and His Times." *Economic and Political Weekly*, Jul 18, 1992: 1543–66.

———. 1993. *An Exploration of the Ramakrishna Vivekananda Tradition*. Shimla: Indian Institute of Advanced Study.

Schneiderman, Leo. 1969. "Ramakrishna: Personality and Social Factors in the Growth of a Religious Movement." *Journal for the Scientific Study of Religion* 8 (Spring): 60–71.

Sen, Akshaykumar. 2000. Bengali. *Śrī-Śrī-Rāmakṛṣṇa Puṁthi*. 6th ed., 13th reprint. Kolkata: Udbodhan Kāryālay.

Sen, Amiya P. 1993. *Hindu Revivalism in Bengal*. Delhi: Oxford Univ. Press.

———. 2001. *Three Essays on Sri Ramakrishna and His Times*. Shimla: Indian Institute of Advanced Study.

Sen, Keshab Chandra. 1976. "A Hindu Saint." In *Sri Ramakrishna in the Eyes of Brahma and Christian Admirers*, edited by Nanda Mookerjee. Calcutta: Firma KLM Ltd.

Sharma, Arvind. 2004. "Hindus and Scholars." In *Religion in the News* (Spring): 7/1. http://www.trincoll.edu/depts/csrpl/RINVol7No1/Hindus%20and%20Scholars.htm

Sharma, Renuka. 2001. "The Foot in the Lap or Kripal's Discontent": A Review of *The Mystical and the Erotic in the Life and Teachings of Ramakrishna* by Jeffrey Kripal. *Sophia* 40, no 2 (Dec): 77–82.

Sil, Narasingha P. 1991. *Rāmakṛṣṇa Paramahaṁsa: A Psychological Profile*. Leiden: E. J. Brill.

———. 1997. "The Question of Ramakrishna's Homosexuality." *The Statesman*, Jan 31.

———. 1998. *Ramakrishna Revisited: A New Biography*. Lanham: Univ. Press of America.

Sinha, Mrinalini. 1995. *Colonial Masculinity: The "Manly Englishman" and the "Effeminate Bengali" in the Late Nineteenth Century*. Manchester Univ. Press.

Spivak, Gayatri Chakravarty. 2005. "Translating into English." In *Nation, Language and the Ethics of Translation*, edited by Sandra Bermann and Michael Wood. Princeton: Princeton Univ. Press.

Smith, Huston. 2000. "Methodology, Comparisons, and Truth." In *A Magic Still Dwells: Comparative Religions in the Postmodern Age*, edited by Kimberley C. Patton and Benjamin C. Ray. Berkeley: Univ. of California Press. 172–81.

Śrī-Śrī-Māyer Kathā. 1995. Bengali. Kolkata: Udbodhan Kāryālay.

Subrahmanian, Kamala. 1981. *Srimad Bhagavatam*. Bombay: Bharatiya Vidya Bhavan.

Sugirtharajah, Sharada. 1998. "Women in Hinduism." In *Themes and Issues in Hinduism*, edited by Paul Bowen. London: Cassell.

———. 2003. *Imagining Hinduism: A Postcolonial Perspective*. London and New York: Routledge.

Tapasyananda, Swami. 1982. "Mahendranath Gupta: The Recorder of the *Gospel of Sri Ramakrishna*." In *Sri Sri Ramakrishna Kathamrita Centenary Memorial*, edited by D. P. Gupta and D. K. Sengupta. Chandigarh: Sri Ma Trust.

Torgovnick, Marianna. 1998. *Primitive Passions: Men, Women, and the Quest for Ecstasy*. Chicago: Univ. of Chicago Press.

Tyagananda, Swami. 2000. "*Kali's Child* Revisited or Didn't Anyone Check the Documentation?" (photocopied manuscript).

Urban, Hugh B. 1996. Review of *Kali's Child* by Jeffrey Kripal. *Chicago South Asia Newsletter* 20, no. 1 (Winter).

———. 1998. Review of *Kali's Child* by Jeffrey Kripal. *Journal of Religion* 78, no 2, (Apr): 318–20.

———. 2001. *The Economics of Ecstasy: Tantra, Secrecy, and Power in Colonial Bengal*. New York: Oxford Univ. Press.

Vaidyanathan, T. G. 1997. "Kripal and *Kali's Child*" Review of Jeffrey Kripal's *Kali's Child*. *The Hindu*, May 4.

Vaidyanathan, T. G., and Jeffrey J. Kripal. 2002. *Vishnu on Freud's Desk: A Reader in Psychoanalysis and Religion*. Oxford: Oxford Univ. Press.

Van Alphen, Ernst. 1991. "The Other Within." In *Alterity, Identity, Image: Selves and Others in Society and Scholarship*, edited by R. Corbey and J. Th. Leerssen. New York: Editions Rodopi.

Van der Veer, Peter. 2001. *Imperial Encounters: Religion and Modernity in India and Britain*. Princeton and Oxford: Princeton Univ. Press.

Vanita, Ruth. 2000. "Shri Ramakrishna Paramahansa." In *Same-Sex Love in India: Readings from Literature and History*, edited by Ruth Vanita and Saleem Kidwai. London: Macmillan Press.

Vanita, Ruth and Saleem Kidwai, eds. 2000. *Same-Sex Love in India: Readings from Literature and History*. London: Macmillan Press.

Vivekananda, Swami. 1972. *The Complete Works of Swami Vivekananda*, in 8 volumes. Calcutta: Advaita Ashrama.

———. 1997. *The Complete Works of Swami Vivekananda*, volume 9. Calcutta: Advaita Ashrama.

Vrajaprana, Pravrajika. 1997. Review of *Kali's Child* by Jeffrey Kripal. *Bulletin of Hindu-Christian Studies*, 10: 59–60.

———. 2006. "World Thinkers on the Ramakrishna Movement." In *The Story of the Ramakrishna Mission: Swami Vivekananda's Vision and Fulfillment*, edited by Swami Lokeswarananda, Swami Prabhananda, Swami Bhajanananda, et al. Kolkata: Advaita Ashrama.

Walker, Steven F. 1998. Review of *Kali's Child* by Jeffrey Kripal. *Religion* 28, no. 2, (Apr): 209–211.

White, David Gordon. 2000. *Tantra in Practice*. Princeton: Princeton Univ. Press.

———. 2003. *Kiss of the Yogini: "Tantric Sex" in Its South Asian Contexts.* Chicago: Univ. of Chicago Press.

Yokota-Murakami, Takayuki. 1998. *Don Juan East/West: On the Problematics of Comparative Literature*. Albany: SUNY Press.

INDEX

The index below is admittedly rudimentary. We did not include entries such as "Ramakrishna," "*Kālī's Child*," "Jeffrey Kripal," "mysticism" and a number of other topics, as the great majority of this book's pages are devoted to addressing these subjects.